C#

Tips & Techniques

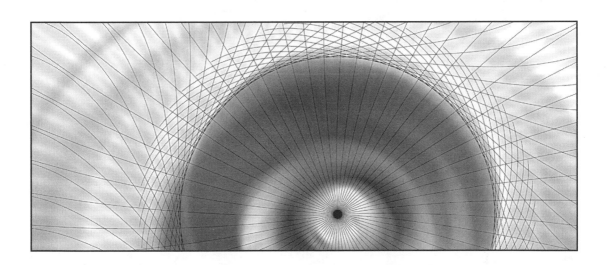

About the Author

Charles Wright is systems editor for *The Denver Post*. He has coauthored a personal computer column at a major California newspaper, served as technical coordinator for the Minneapolis Star Tribune Online Project, and was part of the team that helped launch AT&T's Interchange service in 1995. He has been in the newspaper business for more than 30 years, and is the author of numerous books on C++ and C# programming.

C#

Tips & Techniques

Charles Wright

Edited by Kris Jamsa

McGraw-Hill/Osborne

New York Chicago San Francisco
Lisbon London Madrid Mexico City Milan
New Delhi San Juan Seoul Singapore Sydney Toronto

McGraw-Hill/Osborne
2600 Tenth Street
Berkeley, California 94710
U.S.A.

To arrange bulk purchase discounts for sales promotions, premiums, or fund-raisers, please contact **McGraw-Hill**/Osborne at the above address. For information on translations or book distributors outside the U.S.A., please see the International Contact Information page immediately following the index of this book.

C# Tips & Techniques

1234567890 CUS CUS 0198765432

ISBN 0-07-219379-4

Publisher	Brandon A. Nordin
Vice President & Associate Publisher	Scott Rogers
Acquisitions Editor	Jim Schachterle
Project Editors	Janet Walden & Elizabeth Seymour
Acquisitions Coordinator	Tim Madrid
Technical Editor	Bill Burris
Copy Editor	Lisa Theobald
Proofreader	John Schindel
Indexer	David Heiret
Illustrators	Michael Mueller & Lyssa Wald
Computer Designers	Carie Abrew, Jean Butterfield & George Toma Charbak
Series Design	Roberta Steele
Cover Series Design	Greg Scott

This book was composed with Corel VENTURA™ Publisher.

To Tammy Ray, my wife, who has put up with me rising at 3 A.M. and working well into the night for the last several months, and who has given me endless encouragement to continue writing. And to The Bear and The Angel, my Pomeranian friends, who have kept me company during the lonely hours of writing. Finally, to Star, our 21-year-old blue point Siamese who served as a beacon of light with a sense of humor. Sadly, he was killed during the last week this book was being produced. His light now shines in Heaven.

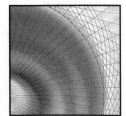

Contents at a Glance

Contents

Acknowledgments

After five programming books, one thing that I have learned is that an author does not write a book in isolation. The author is only one member of a much larger team that makes the book a reality.

In this case, that team is the folks at McGraw-Hill/Osborne who are responsible for the new Tips & Techniques series. The result of their efforts is a power set of books that help the reader to solve problems. Specifically, I would like to thank Jim Schachterle, Janet Walden, and Elizabeth Seymour, the acquisitions editor and project editors, respectively, on this book, as well as Bill Burris, the technical editor. Bill was particularly helpful in reviewing the programs presented in this book and for helping me to avoid some serious programming errors. His critique only helped to make the programs better.

For the last few years, I also have benefited from the wisdom and knowledge of Kris Jamsa of Jamsa Media Group. Kris has more than 90 computer books to his credit, and he has been more than willing to share with me the experience of bringing a book from idea to reality.

There are many more people on these teams that I do not know by name, but I know they are there because of their dedication to producing a quality book. To those people as well, a sincere "thank you."

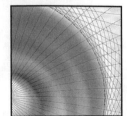

Introduction

For several years, Microsoft has been working on a new development platform called .NET. This new platform is designed to give developers the power to write component-based programs that take advantage of networked environments. Microsoft's new programming language, C# (pronounced "C-sharp"), is a derivative of the C, C++, and Visual Basic languages designed to run under the .NET environment.

Despite many of the claims I have seen floating around the Internet, C# is not a revolutionary language. Microsoft has blended recent technologies, such as Java, with old technologies, such as Smalltalk, to produce a hybrid language, giving it a syntax that is very similar to C++.

Is C# a language whose time has come? That remains to be seen. Certainly C#—or the .NET environment for that matter—could not have happened ten or even five years ago. Microsoft is betting that advances in technology, such as faster computers and cheaper memory, over the last few years, will make languages that exploit intermediate language output more viable than they have been in the past.

The biggest advantage of C# will be to developers. The language is designed to reduce programming errors and to speed up the development cycle. If you already are familiar with C++, learning C# will be easy. The result will be a shorter cycle from program idea to finished product.

What This Book Covers

Any single book on Windows programming with the C family of languages likely is not complete. There is just too much material to cover in a single volume. This book does not even attempt to cover all aspects of programming in C#. Instead, it shows you some techniques for using the C# language. Along the way, it covers the syntax and grammar of the C# language and gives you the basics on building programs in C#.

This book contains 18 chapters. You will start out learning about the .NET Framework and the C# language, then continue on to object-oriented programming and how to use many of the advanced programming concepts in C#.

Chapter 1: Introduction to C# and .NET   The opening chapter gives you an overview of the .NET Framework and an introduction to the C# language. You also will meet many of the command-line tools that you will use as you develop C# programs.

Chapter 2: Developing C# Applications Within Visual Studio .NET   You will look at the new Visual Studio .NET integrated development environment. You will cover the steps for creating a C# program using Visual Studio, and look at the wizards and tool windows available in the development environment.

Chapter 3: Getting Started with C#   There's only one way to learn a new programming language, and that is by programming using the language. This chapter presents the parts of C# and compares them with different languages. You'll start building Windows and command-line programs using C#—a project that displays the date and time in a Windows form in both Visual C# and in Visual Basic.

Chapter 4: Laying a C# Foundation   This chapter presents the syntax of C# and the operators and symbols used in the language. You'll examine *safe* and *unsafe* code, and will learn how to use the language to test the range of value in a variable. Then you will look at program control statements and loops, and get an introduction into scope.

Chapter 5: Data Types in C#   C# is a type-safe language, and a well-founded understanding of how C# handles data types is important. This chapter discusses objects, references, and value-type variables. You'll use read-only variables and constants, and get an introduction to string handling in C#.

Chapter 6: Structures in C#   The structure is one of the oldest objects, and was used even before the concept of object-oriented programming became a reality. It still has a place in C#. In this chapter, you'll learn how to declare and use structures, and how to use methods and properties in a structure.

Chapter 7: Understanding C# Classes   Along with the structure, the class is the basic programming unit in C#. You will examine how to define classes, and how to use instance and static members. You'll look at constructors and destructors, and how to include member methods in a class.

Chapter 8: Object-Oriented Programming and C#   Programmers usually consider a language object-oriented if it demonstrates three characteristics: encapsulation, inheritance, and polymorphism. You will examine how C# implements these concepts using its various object types. You also will look at *abstract* classes and learn about the Object Browser.

Chapter 9: Handling Exceptions   Exceptions occur when unexpected events and errors occur in a program. If you do not handle them in your code, they will make your program abort. C# is very keen on exceptions, and tends to throw exceptions where other languages would simply return an error code from a method. You will look at the underlying support for exception handling and how to use it.

Chapter 10: Advanced C# Concepts   Because it is a modern language, C# implements some advanced and modern programming techniques. You'll look at namespaces, assemblies, references, and interfaces. You also will take a look at reflection, a concept that gives your programs the ability to probe objects and discover information about them.

Chapter 11: Using Arrays   C# brings Visual Basic array techniques to the C family of programming languages. You will look at how C# manages arrays and how to declare and create single- and multi-dimensional arrays. You also will examine jagged arrays, which basically are arrays of arrays.

Chapter 12: File Operations   If you do any significant programming, eventually you will want to read from and write to files. C# implements file operations using streams. You will see how C# streams can be used to manipulate data in a file, in memory, or over a network. You also will examine some of the built-in classes and how to use them to manipulate files.

Chapter 13: Writing Windows Forms Applications   Windows programming using Visual C# involves forms. A form is roughly the equivalent of a dialog box, but Visual C# gives forms extended capability. If you have programmed in Visual C++ and are used to the *view* classes, you won't find them in C#.

Chapter 14: Debugging C# Programs   Like it or not, most substantial programs that you write in C# are going to have problems. Part of the development phase for any program is the debugging cycle. You will learn about the tools available to debug programs, and examine some built-in classes that are designed solely to help you to find and fix errors in a program.

Chapter 15: Building the User Interface   How you present and accept information from a user will determine whether your program is easy to use or is a cumbersome operation that users resent. You will look at how to add menus—including context menus—and toolbars to a program. You'll also learn how to use an image list to place icons on toolbars, and how to make controls respond to changes in the form's size. You will begin construction of an editor project that will perform most of the tasks that you can do using Notepad.

Chapter 16: Using Windows Controls   Forms are convenient containers for Windows controls. A control is an object that presents information to a user, and accepts information and actions from a user. You will look at a couple of common *view* controls, ListView and TreeView, and how to use them on a form.

Chapter 17: Using the Common Dialogs   The Windows Common Dialog library gives programs a common "look and feel," shortening the time it takes users to learn how to use a new program. In this chapter, you will examine the common dialog objects that are available in C#, and add printing capabilities to the editor project you began in Chapter 15.

Chapter 18: Using Events and Delegates   Controls and forms communicate with one another using *events*. This is analogous to the Windows messages used in programming with Visual C++. To handle an event, you assign a *delegate* to the event. However, events and delegates have uses far beyond simple control messages. You will look at these uses, and how to implement and use events and delegates.

How to Read This Book

This book was created to help the average Visual C++ or Visual Basic programmer make the transition to C#. Occasionally, and for convenience, the text will point out similarities to and differences between C# and these other languages.

This book is by no means an exhaustive compilation of information on C#. No book on any of the C programming languages could hope to be complete. Even the expansive Microsoft Developers Network help file provided with Visual Studio has many vacant spots in its information. Programming is an ever-changing field, and most programming languages are dynamic.

C# is not a language that lends itself to compartmentalization. To present one concept, you often have to draw from other concepts that have not been presented yet. Although the chapters in this book build on the previous chapters, occasionally the text will have to point you to a future chapter to cover a given topic.

While there is an occasional snippet of code, most of the code is presented in this book in the form of complete programs. Sometimes the program may be trivial and used to demonstrate just one point, but it will compile and run, and thus should be considered the starting point for you to experiment with the topic. I always have been a proponent of presenting complete programs as examples. Many times in my 25 years of programming, I have entered some sample code from a book only to find that it will not compile because a component not mentioned in the text is missing. With a complete program, if you try something that doesn't work, you always can return to the original code and try something else. The idea for the employee sorting program in Chapter 18 came from a sample program that dismissed the sorting problem with a comment, "just a sample—does not do any actual sorting." Duh. That's three-fourths of the code, and the whole aim of the project. In this sample, I show how to create and use the delegate methods to sort records. The program is complete, it will compile with the current version of C#, and it will sort the records.

The code in this book is intended to be a guide to show you how to implement features and constructs in the C# language. You should use it in that sense and not assume that a particular use for an object means that it always should be used that way. I maintain that programming is more of an art than a science, and you should feel free to "step outside the box" and try something different. Your imagination is more important than any simple how-to example.

In this regard, I have never been a stickler for "proper code." Taking a program from initial concept to working reality often involves considerable imagination, and usually those who chant the "proper code" mantra are unimaginative sorts that simply manipulate code. Just because you know how to code does not mean that you know how to produce a well-designed, efficient program. That comes from experience, which usually means trying new techniques and making mistakes.

Using This Book's Companion Web Site

USE IT   Throughout this book's chapters, we will present several sample C# programs. In many cases, you can simply cut-and-paste into your own programs the solutions— or portions of the code—that we present. All of this book's code is readily available from the McGraw-Hill/Osborne Web site at www.Osborne.com.

PART I

The .NET Environment and C#

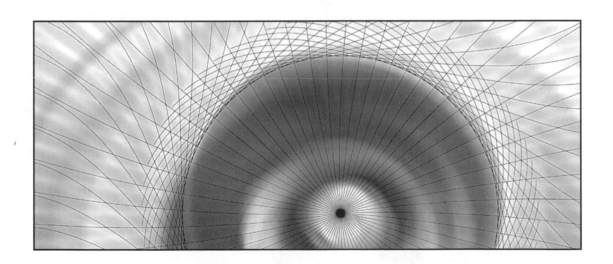

CHAPTER 1

Introduction to C# and .NET

TIPS IN THIS CHAPTER

The primary language for developing applications for small computer systems over the past 20 or so years has been the C programming language, developed by Dennis Ritchie for the UNIX operating system in the 1970s. C offered programmers much of the control over the physical computer that they had in Assembly, but it also offered the ease of programming afforded by a high-level language such as FORTRAN.

In the last decade, much of the development has been done in the C++ language developed by Bjarne Stroustrup. C++ turned the C language into a modern, object-oriented language while retaining the basic, low-level qualities of the C language. Today, when most people mention programming in C, they actually mean C++.

C and C++ have many similarities. One of these is that both languages have a long learning curve. Despite intensive study, it can take years to learn the features and nuances of C++ and to use the power of the language to write large applications.

Over the last few years, Microsoft introduced and developed Visual Basic, which rapidly became a favorite among programmers who wanted to develop programs quickly for specific purposes. Visual Basic is based loosely on the syntax and statements of BASIC, and offers a compiled language with a shorter learning curve than C++. Visual Basic for Applications is commonly used with many applications to provide a means for the user to write *macros*.

From its beginning, the developers of C# (pronounced "C Sharp") wanted to create a language that combines "the high productivity of Visual Basic and the raw power of C++." This sounds slightly oxymoronic. With such a claim come tradeoffs, and usually "high productivity" comes at the cost of "raw power." This is also true of C#. You will experience the "high productivity" but at the cost of power. To get at the "raw power of C++," you will have to revert to features in C# that let you write C++ code from within C# and call library modules written in C++. If you do much of this, though, your application probably is more suited to C++ than C#.

The developers also used the word "modern" to describe the language, but in many ways C# is a throwback to earlier days of programming for small computer systems. It is an object-oriented and "type-safe" language loosely derived from C++. While much of the syntax and keywords will be familiar to C++ programmers, C# is *not* a refinement of the C++ language.

C# is one of the languages supported by Microsoft's Visual Studio 7.0 development environment, which also supports Visual Basic, Visual C++, VBScript, and JScript. C#—along with the current version of Visual Basic and "managed" C++—is based on the Next Generation Windows Services (NGWS) platform, now called the .NET software development environment.

The "services" part of NGWS should give you a clue as to the focus of the language. C# is "component-oriented." The .NET environment itself is component-oriented, and thus the underlying design of C# is to make it easier to write components. Over the last few years we have had access to a number of component-oriented tools such as the Component Object Model (COM) and ActiveX. C# and the .NET framework simplifies component writing. You do not have to use an IDL (interface definition language) file to create a component, and you do not have to create type libraries to use the components in a program. When you create a component with C#, the component contains all of the information—the *metadata*—it needs to describe itself.

Along the way, you will see many of the terms usually used with components to describe C# concepts. You will see *methods* instead of *functions* and *properties* and *fields* instead of *variables*.

The .NET framework defines a Common Language Specification (you may sometimes see this as Common Language Subset) and provides a Common Language Runtime (CLR) module. Programs that support the .NET framework are compiled to intermediate code modules, and the CLR provides the translation to the native language for the computer.

Unlike the pseudocode (or P-code that most of us have learned to hate), the intermediate language (IL) in the .NET environment provides more than an interpreter. When you run a program that has been compiled into IL, the .NET framework recompiles the intermediate code into native code.

Looking at C#

One of the biggest advantages to C# is that programmers who have invested a lot of time and work in learning the C++ language do not have to discard that knowledge to begin developing programs in a new language. There are some new concepts and techniques, and some new function names to learn, but generally the syntax is similar to C++.

In addition, programmers do not need to discard code they have already written. C# contains mechanisms to call library functions in existing code and in system libraries. You still may call the same Windows functions that you used in C++, and in many cases you may choose between the Windows function and the .NET framework. The following short program, *MsgBox.cs*, for example, displays two message boxes, one right after the other. The first message box results from a call the Windows API *MessageBox()* function, and the second results by a call to the CLR's *MessageBox* class *Show()* method. You will have difficulty distinguishing between the two. (In the final analysis, both message boxes are generated by the Windows function.)

```
//
//  MsgBox.cs -- demonstrate using the Windows API message box and the
//               .NET framework message box.
//
//               Compile this program with the following command line:
//                     C:>csc msgbox.cs
//
namespace nsMsgBox
{
    using System.Windows.Forms;
    using System.Runtime.InteropServices;
    class clsMain
    {
//  Import the dll and prototype the MessageBox function.
        [DllImport("User32.dll")]
        public static extern int MessageBox (int hwnd, string Message,
                                             string Caption, int Flags);
        static public void Main ()
        {
```

```
//  Call the Windows API function
        MessageBox (0, "Hello C# World", "Howdy",
                    (int) MessageBoxButtons.OK
                | (int) MessageBoxIcon.Exclamation);
//  Call the CLR method
        System.Windows.Forms.MessageBox.Show ("Hello, C# World!",
                    "Howdy",
                    MessageBoxButtons.OK, MessageBoxIcon.Exclamation);
        }
    }
}
```

Although C# is a new language, it is difficult to find any new concepts in the language. It is largely patterned after Java, a technology developed by Sun Microsystems, and is based on the Visual Basic programming model. Along the way, it borrows heavily from the syntax and keywords of C and C++, and you will find many of the concepts of the Smalltalk programming language in C#. That is not surprising, however, because C++ has a lot of similarities with Smalltalk.

The Java language attempts to provide developers with a platform-independent language. Through the Java Virtual Machine (JVM) intermediate language interpreter, Java's goal was to provide a "write-once, run-anywhere" language that would free developers from having to write a different program for every computer platform and every operating system. The developer would use the same code, and the JVM would provide the interface between the program and the platform and operating system.

Through C# and the .NET framework, Microsoft is attempting to achieve the same goal. Rather than compile programs into native code for computers running Windows on the Intel processor platform, languages such as C# that use the .NET platform compile into an IL. The CLR then dynamically transforms this IL code into the native code for a computer platform. Theoretically, at least, an operating system need only implement the CLR to give developers the ability to run their programs.

That is amazingly similar to the Java concept and has led many in the programming industry to make statement such as "C# is simply Java by another name." Whether C# is a Sun in Microsoft disguise is not important. What is important is the .NET platform. The technology offered in the .NET program goes beyond the JVM.

While C# appears based on the Visual Basic programming model, it does not yield completely to that model. Instead, C# draws the concepts of the C-family of languages and Visual Basic to meet somewhere in the middle. The development probably is better for Visual Basic than it is for the C languages. Visual Basic cedes several statements and keywords, such as the *Option Base* keyword and the *Variant* data types, to work with .NET.

Figure 1-1 illustrates how the C# developers built the language around key features available in various operating systems, programming languages, components, and distributed environments.

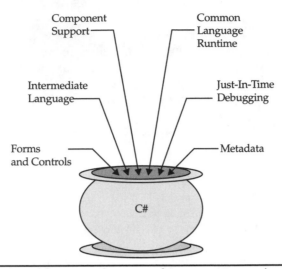

Figure 1.1   C# was developed from a melting pot of programming techniques

Using C# Instead of C++

If you are new to programming, it might be of some comfort to know that C# is much easier to learn than C++ as a first language. The C and C++ languages are powerful languages, but they do let you perform operations that you should not.

C# is a *type-safe* language, and it hides much of the underlying problems that a newcomer to programming might have with C or C++. For example, C# uses pointers, but the programmer does not have to deal with them directly. Instead, the language hides pointers under the name *reference-type* variables.

C# uses much of the same syntax used in C++, and the learning probably will be shorter if you later migrate to C++ after learning C#. Programmers already familiar with C++ will have to surmount their bias toward the language. (C++ programmers have a tendency to look with disdain on Visual Basic programs, and C# seems more like Visual Basic than like C++.) It may be difficult to get used to some of the restrictions C# places on various operators and statements, but these restrictions are intended to reduce bugs and to promote rapid development.

In this book, I will occasionally refer to the way you'd do something in C++ and compare it with the C# method. Generally, changes from the C++ method will produce a slight reduction in the "power" of statements and operations but will be geared toward simplicity and ease of operation. For example, after a long day of programming in C++, you might write something like the following:

```
#include <stdio.h>

void Function (double *);

void main (void)
```

```
{
    int arr [10];
    Function ((double *) arr);
}
void Function (double *arr)
{
    for (int x = 0; x < 10, ++x)
        arr[x] = x * 3.14159;
}
```

Syntactically, this program is 100 percent correct, and the compiler will not so much as issue a warning. However, it also is guaranteed to produce a crash. Writing 10 double values into an array of 10 integers is going to overwrite something on the stack. That is part of the power of programming in C++, but also one of its dangers.

In such an instance, the C# compiler takes the helm. It simply will not let you do something like this. The equivalent code in C# would appear like the following:

```
class clsMain
{
    static public void Main ()
    {
        int [] arr = new int [10];
        Function ((double []) arr);
    }
    static public void Function (double [] arr)
    {
        for (int x = 0; x < 10; ++x)
            arr[x] = x * 3.14159;
    }
}
```

No matter how you cast the variables, you cannot coax the C# compiler into letting you get away with this operation. This is part of the type-safety of C#. The language guarantees that a variable of a certain data type will always contain a value of that data type before you can use the variable.

This does not mean that you will not have bugs in a program that compiles correctly. You still will find yourself dropping into infinite loops or such, but the probability of that happening is greatly reduced. And the fact that C# allow access to most objects only through pointers (the reference-type variable) leads to its own set of bugs.

All of this leads to a shorter debugging cycle, which in turn means shorter development times. In-house developers and those working at software houses should find a higher level of productivity when using C#. Recreational programmers or hobbyists will appreciate seeing results faster.

C# code is also compatible with other languages that support the .NET framework. For example, you will find it much easier to interface with programs and controls written in the .NET version of Visual Basic and other programming languages.

When to Use C# and C++

Back in the 1970s, before most colleges had computer science departments, I was studying programming as part of the Mathematics Department at the local university. A common amusement on the computer (a rather large and lumbering beast compared with the personal computer today) was to toss random points into a square that measured 1 unit per side. We then calculated the distance of a point from the lower left corner of the square (the square'e origin). The distance across a 1×1 square from corner to corner is the square root of 2, so a point could have a distance greater than or less than 1 unit.

Theoretically, if you tossed enough points into the square, the ratio of the number of points with a distance less than 1 unit to the total number of random points you tossed would approximate *pi/4*. Now, we're talking a lot of points to come up with just this reasonable approximation—in fact, millions of points. But then, computers in the 1970s didn't have a lot better to do than entertain math students. The exercise also proved a good test for our random-number generating routines. The closer we could approximate *pi* with the fewest number of points meant that the random-number generator was working better. Most languages today have random-number routines as part of their library code.

USE IT   To compare execution times, I wrote a program to throw 10 million such points using both C# and C++. The C# program was a little easier to write and had a few less lines than the C++ program. Then I ran each program 10 times to get a good approximation of the times it took to execute the programs. The programs use several floating-point operations.

These programs, shown next, are both Visual Studio projects, so you do not have to worry about command-line compiling yet. After you copy the projects to your computer, start the Visual Studio, and then select File | Open Solution. Maneuver to the directory where you copied the files and look for the *CalcPi.sln* file in the C# or CPP subdirectory. Double-click this file to open the project.

The listing for both programs follows if you want to compare your times. The computer I used was an 866 MHz dual Pentium III-processor with 512 MB of RAM running Windows 2000 Server. First, the C# program, *CalcPi.cs*:

```
using System;

namespace CalcPi
{
    /// <summary>
    /// Summary description for Class1.
    /// </summary>
    class Class1
    {
        static void Main(string[] args)
        {
            const int throws = 10000000;
            DateTime now = DateTime.Now;
            Random rand = new Random ((int) now.Millisecond);
            int Inside = 0;
            for (int i = 0; i < throws; ++i)
```

```
        {
            double cx = rand.NextDouble();
            double cy = rand.NextDouble();
            double distance = Math.Sqrt ((cx * cx) + (cy * cy));
            if (distance < 1.0)
                ++Inside;
        }
        double pi = 4 * (double) Inside / (double) throws;
        DateTime End = DateTime.Now;
        TimeSpan Diff = End - now;
        Console.WriteLine ("pi = " + pi);
        Console.WriteLine ("Elapsed time = {0} milliseconds" ,
                          Diff.TotalMilliseconds);
    }
  }
}
```

The C++ program required a few extra lines of code, but most of those were the *#include* statements at the beginning of the file. You don't need those with C#. The C++ listing for *CalcPi.cpp* follows:

```
// CalcPi.cpp : Defines the entry point for the console application.
//

#include <stdio.h>
#include <windows.h>
#include <time.h>
#include <stdlib.h>
#include <math.h>

int main(int argc, char* argv[])
{
    const int throws = 10000000;
    SYSTEMTIME now;
    SYSTEMTIME end;
    GetSystemTime (&now);
    srand ((unsigned) time (NULL));
    int Inside = 0;
    for (int i = 0; i < throws; ++i)
    {
        double cx = (double) rand() / (double) RAND_MAX;
        double cy = (double) rand() / (double) RAND_MAX;
        double distance = sqrt ((cx * cx) + (cy * cy));
        if (distance < 1.0)
            ++Inside;
```

```
    }
    double pi = 4 * (double) Inside / (double) throws;
    GetSystemTime (&end);
// Note: the following interval calculation will give an incorrect
// result if the program is run exactly on the hour.
    int msStart = 1000 * 60 * now.wMinute + 1000 * now.wSecond
                  + now.wMilliseconds;
    int msEnd = 1000 * 60 * end.wMinute + 1000 * end.wSecond
                  + end.wMilliseconds;
    int milliseconds = msEnd - msStart;
    printf ("pi = %6f\n", pi);
    printf ("Elapsed time = %d milliseconds\n", milliseconds);
    return 0;
}
```

Both programs were tested in the release version. (The release version is compiled without any debugging information. To compile it, select Build | Configuration Manger and then select Release from the Active Solution Configuration box of the Configuration Manager dialog box.) The relative times were not surprising, and both programs came up with a reasonable approximation of *pi* to four decimal places. The closest the C++ program came was 3.14158, and the closest the C# program came was 3.14157—essentially the same number.

The C# program ranged from 3185 to 3285 milliseconds to toss the 10 million points, with an average time of 3222 milliseconds. The longest time differed from the shortest time by 100 milliseconds, or about 3.1 percent of the average time.

The C++ program, on the other had, ranged in time from 1573 to 1592 milliseconds, with an average time of 1583 milliseconds. The difference between the longest and shortest times was only 19 milliseconds, about 1.2 percent of the average time.

Outside the Visual Studio integrated development environment (IDE), the C# program did considerably better, turning in an average time of about 1998 milliseconds. The C++ program times did not change much outside the IDE, but they did turn in times as short as 1542 milliseconds.

In addition, if you do not *optimize* the C++ code when you compile the program, it will turn in considerably worse times than the C# program. Visual Studio normally applies optimization when it compiles the release version of a program. It is reasonable to assume that the CLR code is optimized and would have an edge over the C++ program in this case. However, optimization is part of the power of C++.

Just so there is no argument, these are code execution times. Each program gets the start time at the beginning of the program and the end time just after it calculates the value of *pi*. The times do not include the time it takes the .NET framework to compile the IL code into machine code for the computer, or the time it takes the operating system to load the C++ program.

Even outside the IDE, the C++ program turned in times that were nearly 30 percent faster. Of course, a case could be made that you could design a program that would show that C# is faster. To be sure, this program was not designed specifically for either language. It is a common mathematical exercise, originally written in FORTRAN, that I simply translated into C# and C++. In addition, a personal computer is not the best device to use when you want to resolve a time interval down to the millisecond. These programs assume both time methods will exhibit the same inaccuracies on the same computer, and repeated executions should average out any errors.

No programming language is suitable for every type of application, and C# is no exception. If your program is processor intensive, you might want to consider writing it in C++. That is a decision you, as the programmer, will have to make. Remember that a graphics program or other mathematics-intensive program may perform *billions* of floating-point operations during the course of its run.

On the other hand, C# certainly is easier if you are writing a program that will run over the Internet, or if you want to write small components that perform specific tasks. Many large applications will benefit from C# as well. In a word processing application, for example, you are not going to type any faster if the application is written in C# or C++. Most programs will fall somewhere between the two extremes.

Despite the self-appointed "keepers of the languages" who would impose a rigorous scientific dogma upon us, programming is an art. You select the language in much the same way a painter selects the medium for a painting—oil, watercolor, charcoal, for example—or the poet selects the meter for the verse. Your selection criteria might include such things as your familiarity and comfort with a language, its efficiency, and its underlying support for the fundamental purpose of the program.

Distinguishing .NET from Other Environments

C# is only one part of a programming architecture designed around a network distributed platform. The platform may be a single machine, a local intranet, or even other networks located across the Internet. That *platform* is what Microsoft calls the *.NET Framework*, which is designed to support a managed code environment in which programs may safely and securely operate on a single computer or across a distributed network.

The .NET environment is also designed to allow programs to operate across different operating systems. The .NET framework comprises two major components:

- The CLR provides core services such as memory and thread management. It manages code written for the .NET environment and enforces type-safety.

- For developing programs that run under the CLR, the .NET Framework offers a library of reusable, object-oriented classes that simplify programming tasks and speed up development time. The library of classes supports development programs that run as command-line programs and as Windows applications.

The CLR is the latest development in COM, which it is designed to replace. The CLR is designed to alleviate many of the problems that plagued COM while retaining COM's better features. Some of the advantages of the new CLR over the old COM are better interoperability between languages, easier deployment of components, and improved versioning.

Language interoperability is provided by having C# and Visual Basic—along with a managed-code version of C++ and other languages that support .NET—use a common IL. With COM, it was not uncommon to write a C++ component that was totally useless to Visual Basic programs. In addition, interfacing C++ programs to modules such as ActiveX controls written in Visual Basic often required considerable programming gymnastics.

Code management is at the core of the CLR, and the CLR is at the core of the .NET environment. Any programming language that targets the CLR is subject to code management. Programmers are free to create objects in the heap memory without having to worry about freeing the memory before the program exits. In older code, programs that allocated heap memory and failed to free it left behind memory leaks that persisted even after the program ended. Repeated instances of running the program might make the computer run low on memory.

Managed code modules also have varying degrees of security applied to them, depending on whether they originated on the local computer, a local network, or over the Internet. Modules that do not have a high degree of trust, such as those originating on the Internet, might not be able to perform some operations, such as opening and writing to files.

The security and programming model used by the .NET Framework means that many applications that had to be installed on a computer now may be deployed over the Internet. A program may run components from different vendors and from various Internet sites, and each component would have its own security and permissions on the local computer. That could mean that, in many cases, you would not have to wait endless months for a vendor to provide a service pack or program upgrade to fix or improve software. Components on the Internet sites could be updated more quickly, and deployment would be greatly simplified.

The .NET environment supports development of a number of program types such as *console applications*. Such programs have the advantage of being utility command-line programs that have access to the Windows graphical user interface (GUI). In this book, you will explore many of the features of C# using console applications. In fact, the environment provides a set of reusable GUI objects in the Windows forms classes. For projects involving the Web, a similar set of objects are included in the Windows Web forms classes.

You will see references to a "Portable Executable" (PE) format file throughout the course of using the Visual Studio and the .NET Framework Software Development Kit (SDK). A PE file contains a block of information for the program's metadata. The metadata contains information about the object types in your program, security information, and custom attributes you use in your program.

The primary tool used to develop C# applications for the Windows platform is Visual Studio .NET. This integrated development environment includes compilers and debuggers for C#, Visual Basic, and Visual C++, and it supports JScript.

USE IT   Visual Studio and the .NET SDK include a number of tools to help in writing programs and migrating existing code to the .NET environment. Among them are the following tools:

- **DbgCLR.exe**   The Microsoft CLR Debugger, a Visual Studio–like debugger with a GUI.

- **Cordbg.exe**   A command-line based runtime debugger that uses the CLR debugging application programming interface (API).

- **Ilasm.exe**   The Microsoft Intermediate Language Assembler, which generates files in the Portable Executable format from an intermediate language file. You can run the code generated by this utility to test whether the intermediate code performs as expected.

- **Ildasm.exe**   A disassembler that converts a Portable Executable format file into a text file that can be used by *Ilasm.exe*.

- **Aximp.exe**   An ActiveX control importing tool. This program converts the type definitions in a COM type library for an ActiveX control into a Windows Forms control. This tool is handy for converting existing components to the .NET Framework.

- **Sn.exe**, **Al.exe**, and **GacUtil.exe**   These three programs provide utilities to create a security key, add the key to an assembly, and then add the assembly to the assembly cache.

You do not need to run Visual Studio to use these tools. You may choose to write many of your programs without the overhead that comes with an integrated development environment. A number of new editors are showing up on the Internet that support the C# syntax, which you can use without the IDE. You can find a particularly good one, written in C#, at **http://www.icsharpcode.net/ opensource/sd**.

An update to Windows Explorer also provides a panel for viewing the global assembly cache, which is a hidden directory in the Windows or WinNT directory.

The .NET framework SDK is a part of the Visual Studio .NET installation, but it is available on a separate CD and may be installed on your computer without having to install the complete integrated development environment.

When you install the .NET SDK, you can install code samples, tutorials, and QuickStarts to help acquaint you with the framework and programming mode.

Using the Common Language Runtime

Programmers in the past have linked their code with various libraries and made use of external components for their applications. In addition to the runtime library, a number of specialized code libraries are available. Dynamic link libraries (DLLs) have provided another source of code at runtime. The code for the Windows Application Programming Interface, for example, resides in several DLLs that a program can call as needed.

For C#, the .NET environment defines more than 1000 classes that a programmer may access directly or use as a base for deriving new classes to extend their functionality. The .NET Framework is a library of components along with the supporting classes and structures.

The CLR is the environment used by the .NET environment. The CLR manages code at runtime and provides services that make program development easier. The code that you write for the CLR is called *managed code*.

Microsoft describes the process of running code under the CLR as running with a "contract of cooperation" with the runtime environment. Managed code undergoes a process of "verification" before the CLR will let it run on the computer. The CLR provides a type-safe environment in which no application will cause a memory fault, an attempt to access memory that it does not own. This is a common problem among C++ programmers who forget to initialize a pointer before attempting to access memory. Such bugs can go unnoticed through the debugging process, and they might only show up when the code is released to users.

Usually problems such as unitialized pointers will never get beyond the C# compiler. C# does use pointers, per se—it hides them from the programmer in the form of reference-type variables. The compiler simply will not allow your code to use a pointer variable—or any variable for that matter—until you have assigned it a value. There are some exceptions, such as an *out* parameter for a method, but these generally result in type-safe assignments to the variables.

The C# coding process is not perfect, though. It is still possible for the compiler to let a variable past an initialization test, and you wind up with a null value in a reference-type variable. For example, if a font or brush initialization fails at runtime and you attempt to use the variable, you are going to get a program fault.

The CLR watches the code and catches these situations. When this happens, the program, through the CLR, throws an exception. The programmer may include code in the program to watch for exceptions and handle them in the program. If not handled, the exception will cause the program to end. The CLR, however, is designed so that the demise of a single program will not affect other programs running on the computer.

Programmers will find the CLR much more flexible when it comes to language interoperability. It used to take considerable programming gymnastics to make C++ and Visual Basic programs and modules work together, for example. Sometimes it was virtually impossible.

Another feature of the CLR is "garbage collection." Most C++ programmers are familiar with the concept of a *memory leak*: You create an object in the heap memory but forget to free up the memory before your program ends. The result is memory that has been assigned but is unusable. *Garbage collection* watches for unused objects in the heap and automatically frees them when it determines that the object no longer can be referenced by any code in a program. In fact, C# does not provide any statements through which you can directly free objects. You cannot control when garbage collection occurs. However, C# does provide ways, such as the *System.GC* class, by which you can nudge the garbage collection or keep an object in memory past its normal lifetime.

USE IT The following short C# program, *gc.cs*, shows how you can force garbage collection using methods from the *System.*GC class. The program first gets the amount of memory that has been allocated, creates 10,000 instances of a nonsense class, and then asks the garbage collector to fix it up:

```
//
// gc.cs -- Demonstrates forced garbage collection
//
//          Compile this program with the following command line:
//                  C:>csc gc.cs
//
namespace nsGarbage
{
    using System;
    class clsMain
    {
        static public void Main ()
        {
            long Mem = GC.GetTotalMemory (false);
            Console.WriteLine ("Beginning allocated memory is " + Mem);
            for (int x = 0; x < 10000; ++x)
```

```
        {
            clsClass howdy = new clsClass ();
        }
        Mem = GC.GetTotalMemory (false);
        Console.WriteLine ("Allocated memory before " +
                            "garbage collection is " + Mem);
        GC.Collect ();
        Mem = GC.GetTotalMemory (true);
        Console.WriteLine ("Allocated memory after " +
                            "garbage collection is " + Mem);
    }
}
class clsClass
{
    public clsClass () { }
    public int x = 42;
    public float f = 2E10f;
    public double d = 3.14159;
    public string str = "This here's a string";
}
}
```

The *GetTotalMemory()* method returns the CLR's estimate of how much memory has been allocated for your program. You will probably see larger numbers at the beginning than at the end because of the number of objects that are needed for startup.

Visual Studio–supported languages that use the CLR include C#, Visual Basic, and Managed C++. Programs written in these languages will share a common runtime environment, and modules written in one language are supposed to appear transparent to a program written in another language.

Visual Basic programmers will have to give up some niceties to code in .NET. For example, the Option Base statement is gone in Visual Basic .NET, and you will no longer be able to use a variable without declaring it. This is necessary, of course, in the interest of type-safety. The CLR guarantees that a variable of a given data type will always contain a value of that data type. Undeclared variables in Visual Basic assumed the *Variant* data type, which could hold values of virtually any type. In Visual Basic .NET, you will have to declare all variables before you use them.

Language interoperability is made possible through the Common Language Specification (CLS) and the Common Type System (CTS). Supported languages adhere to the CLS, which defines how programs and modules may expose objects to other programs. If your program adheres to the CLS, it is "guaranteed" to be accessible from a program or module written in any other language that supports the CLS. The Common Type System determines how data types are declared, used, and managed in the CLR, and it is a key element in language interoperability.

The .NET framework allows developers and computer users (or administrators in the case of a business environment) to configure how programs and modules may access and use local resources. Developers can put the configuration information into a file (hark! remember the old .INI file) and thus not need to recompile the program when a setting changes. The configuration file is an XML (eXtensible Markup Language) format file, and the .NET framework provides classes in the *System .Configuration* namespace to manipulate the information in these files.

The .NET environment also supports the concept of *rich data*. At one time, it was fairly easy to break down the data that a program used into things like strings, numbers, dates, and currency values. Now that data may include e-mail, hypertext links, sound files, video, and the like. The Web tools in C# allow you to include and manipulate these new data types.

Viewing Intermediate Language Code

The C# compiler converts source code files to an IL, which theoretically may be used to run the same program on different operating systems and computer platforms. When you run a program, the runtime sends this IL (Microsoft Intermediate Language, or MSIL) to a *just-in-time* (JIT) compiler, which converts the code into native code for the computer on which the program is running. Microsoft uses the term *just-in-time* to indicate an action that is taken only when it is necessary.

USE IT   You can view the MSIL code by using the IL Disassembler, too, *ildasm.exe*:

1. Run a Visual Studio .NET command line, and then type **ildasm** at the command prompt.

2. When the Disassembler window appears, choose File | Open.

3. Maneuver to a directory in which a program compiled from a C# program is located. The *CalcPi.exe* program will serve well—the program is short enough that there isn't a lot of intermediate code.

4. When you display the program in the Disassembler, you should see three lines. The first is a line containing the full path to the program file. Below that is the Manifest, and directly below that is a line that should read *CalcPi*. This last line is the namespace you used in the program. If you did not use a namespace, it will contain the name of the first class in the program. Double click the plus sign (+) symbol next to the *CalcPi* item. This will reveal the classes in the namespace.

5. Click on the plus sign (+) symbol next to the *Class1* item—which is the only class in the namespace to display the members of the class. The first line shows the class declaration as seen by the IL compiler. The *ctor* item is the class constructor. The *CalcPi.cs* program does not have a constructor, so the C# compiler provided it with a default.

6. The last line shows the *Main()* method, the only method in *Class1*. Double-click this item to display the IL code for the method. The Disassembler with the IL code should look like Figure 1-2.

7. To write the program code to a text file, return to the Disassembler window and press CTRL-D, or choose File | Dump.

8. Save the intermediate code in a file with an extension *.il*, such as *dump.il*. Examine the files in the directory where you wrote the file. The Disassembler should have written a resource file, *dump.res*, as well.

Now that you have disassembled the code, you can assemble it again to provide debug information. Type the following command:

```
C:>ilasm /debug /resource=dump.res dump.il
```

This command re-creates the original program as *dump.exe*, but with debugging information, and is ready to run through one of the .NET debuggers.

```
Class1::Main : void(string[])                                    _ □ ×
            int32 V_2,
            int32 V_3,
            float64 V_4,
            float64 V_5,
            float64 V_6,
            float64 V_7,
            valuetype [mscorlib]System.DateTime V_8,
            valuetype [mscorlib]System.TimeSpan V_9)
IL_0000:  call        valuetype [mscorlib]System.DateTime [mscorlib]System.D
IL_0005:  stloc.0
IL_0006:  ldloca.s    V_8
IL_0008:  call        instance int32 [mscorlib]System.DateTime::get_Millisec
IL_000d:  newobj      instance void [mscorlib]System.Random::.ctor(int32)
IL_0012:  stloc.1
IL_0013:  ldc.i4.0
IL_0014:  stloc.2
IL_0015:  ldc.i4.0
IL_0016:  stloc.3
IL_0017:  br.s        IL_0050
IL_0019:  ldloc.1
IL_001a:  callvirt    instance float64 [mscorlib]System.Random::NextDouble()
IL_001f:  stloc.s     V_4
IL_0021:  ldloc.1
```

Figure 1.2   The Intermediate Language Disassembler gives you a platform to view the intermediate code used for C# programs

Taking Advantage of Just-In-Time Debugging

One of the better features of an integrated development environment such as Visual Studio is JIT debugging. Whether your program is a Windows application or a command-line program, even the best of planning will not guarantee that your program will not throw an exception at some time. In the case of a Windows application that you develop in Visual Studio, eventually you are going to have to test it outside the IDE.

If your program *does* throw an exception and you do not handle it, your program is going to exit. On a computer with Visual Studio .NET or the .NET framework SDK installed, the exception pops up a dialog box that gives you the option of entering one of the debugging programs to find and fix the error.

USE IT   To demonstrate exception throwing, the following program, *Throw.cs*, intentionally causes an exception that it does not handle. Use a text editor such as Notepad to enter the program, and then compile and run it outside the IDE. Remember that to compile C# from the command line, you need to run the Visual Studio .NET command line.

After you install the IDE, choose Start | Programs | Visual Studio .NET 7.0 | Visual Studio .NET Tools | Visual Studio .NET Command Line. You will see a window that looks much like a Windows command window, but the environment variables will be set to compile and test .NET programs.

```
//   Throw.cs -- Intentionally throws an exception to demonstrate
//               Just-In-Time debugging.
//
//               Compile this program with the following command line:
//                    C:>csc /debug:full Throw.cs
//
namespace nsThrow
{
    using System;
    class clsMain
    {
        static public void Main ()
        {
            Console.WriteLine ("This program intentionally causes an error.");
            int x = 42;
            int y = 0;
            int z = x / y;
        }
    }
}
```

Compiling the program will create two new files. The *Throw.pdb* is the "program database" file that contains line and symbol information for the debuggers. The other file is the executable file, *Throw.exe*, which is the program you will run. When you run this program, you will get an exception almost immediately. The error will cause the Just-In-Time Debugging dialog box to appear, as shown in Figure 1-3.

Assuming you have Visual Studio. NET installed, the Just-In-Time Debugging dialog box will offer two choices. The first option is to run the CLR debugger, the graphical debugger supplied with the .NET framework. The second option is to run the Microsoft Development Environment, which is Visual Studio itself. Figure 1-4 shows the program file open in the Microsoft Development Environment.

With either debugger, the source code for the program will open automatically, and the line that caused the exception will be highlighted in yellow.

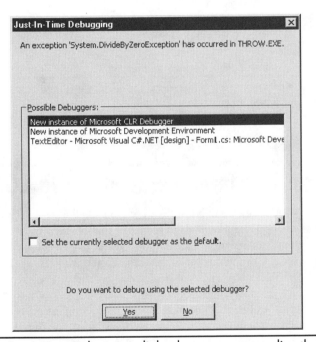

Figure 1.3   Using the Just-InTime Debugging dialog box, you can go directly from running a .NET program to debugging it

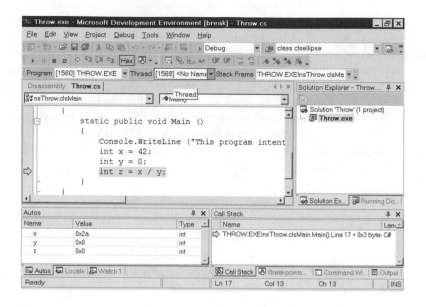

Figure 1.4   Opening the program in the Microsoft Development Environment highlights the line where the exception occurred

Exploiting the .NET Interoperability with COM

Microsoft has put a lot of thought into the design of components that will be used with the .NET framework. The goal is to eliminate many of the problems that plagued the systems that we used in the past to create components for programs. Over the years, as programs got more complex and exceeded the memory capacity of the machines on which they were to run, it became convenient to break them into smaller blocks that could be loaded on demand. The early form of this was the *overlay* file, which, when loaded into memory, actually overlaid part of the code for the program.

When dynamic link libraries (the DLL on Windows) came along, they brought the possibility of programs sharing code. This saved considerable memory, especially with multitasking or multi-user operating systems such as UNIX, and later Windows.

Next came COM, which uses the DLL. COM has two advantages. First, it is language independent. A COM component can be shared between programs written in different languages as long as those languages are aware of the COM specification. COM also brings the possibility of being able to run the components across machine boundaries.

The .NET environment is meant to operate with existing COM components. A .NET utility, *tlbimp.exe*, is provided to read the type library used with the COM object and to create a *proxy* library. Once you create the proxy library, you can use the COM component just as you would use any other .NET class.

USE IT   The .NET provides tools to help you perform these tasks. Once a COM component, such as a custom Windows control, has been registered, you may view it with the OLE/COM Object Viewer and examine the interface with the TypeLib Viewer.

To use the TypeLib Viewer:

1. Start Visual Studio .NET, and then select Tools | OLE/COM Object Viewer. The viewer window should appear, as shown in Figure 1-5.

2. To view the type library for a COM object, click on the plus (+) sign next to the Type Libraries item.

3. Locate the name of the COM object in the list and double-click it to display the TypeLib Viewer, as shown in Figure 1-6.

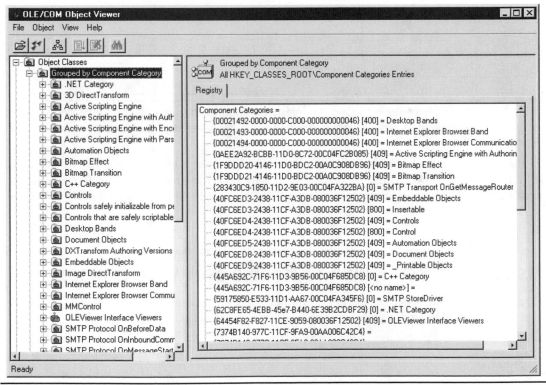

Figure 1.5   The OLE/COM Object View is the starting point for examining COM modules

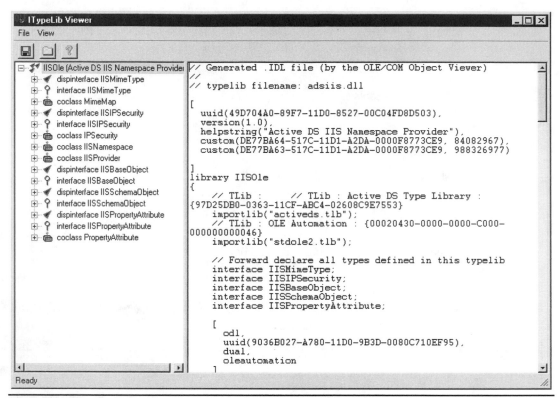

Figure 1.6 The TypeLib Viewer shows the interface listing for a COM object; COM and ActiveX programmers will recognize this as the IDL file generated by Visual Studio

But COM is another topic, and this book is about C#. However, at times you will have to interrogate the interface for a COM module. If you have done some COM programming, you will recognize the text in the viewer as the interface definition file (IDF) generated when you create a COM project in Visual Studio.

Using .NET Versioning to Handle Software Updates

C# and .NET provide better versioning capabilities than the resource files permitted with C++. When you place an assembly in the global assembly cache, its name is made up of the assembly name and its version number. It is possible, then, for several different versions of an assembly to be stored in the assembly cache. A version of an assembly consists of the four parts that are familiar to C++ programmers: First are the major and minor numbers, followed by the build number and the revision number. The version of an assembly is written with periods between the parts in the form *Major .Minor.Build.Revision.*

The major and minor numbers are intended to indicate new releases of an assembly, but assemblies with different major and minor numbers may be compatible with one another. The build and revision numbers are intended to indicate bug fixes and Quick Fix Engineering changes.

The ability to have different versions in the assembly cache overcomes a major problem with COM objects and DLLs. If you have only one program using the DLL files, installing a new version is no problem. You simply update the component files at the same time. However, if the files are shared between programs, updating the files for one may *break* the other applications. A program should be compatible with the assembly if the major and minor revision numbers are the same as in the application's manifest.

The CLR performs version checking only on shared assemblies. Private assemblies—those that you place in the same directory as your executable file—do not get checked before they are linked or loaded to run with your program. This is so you can have control over the contents of the directory in which you install your files.

Assemblies in the global assembly cache are intended to be shared among applications. For these assemblies, the CLR will compare the version number for a shared assembly with the one that was recorded when the application was compiled. Assemblies in the cache must be prepared for the cache and given a security key. An assembly contains two keys, one private and the other public. Only programs that "know" the private key will be able to use a shared assembly.

In Chapter 10, you will create the security keys that a shared assembly needs, add them to the assembly, set the version number, and place the assembly in the global assembly cache.

USE IT   When you compile your program and add a reference, the compiler imbeds the version of the shared assembly into the application's manifest. To view a manifest:

1. Return to the IL Disassember program, *ildasm.exe*. Change to the directory where you have stored a program such as the *gc.cs* program earlier in this chapter.

2. Open the executable file in the disassembler using the following command line:

   ```
   C:> ildasm gc.exe
   ```

3. Double-click the line that reads *MANIFEST* to open the MANIFEST window, as shown in Figure 1-7.

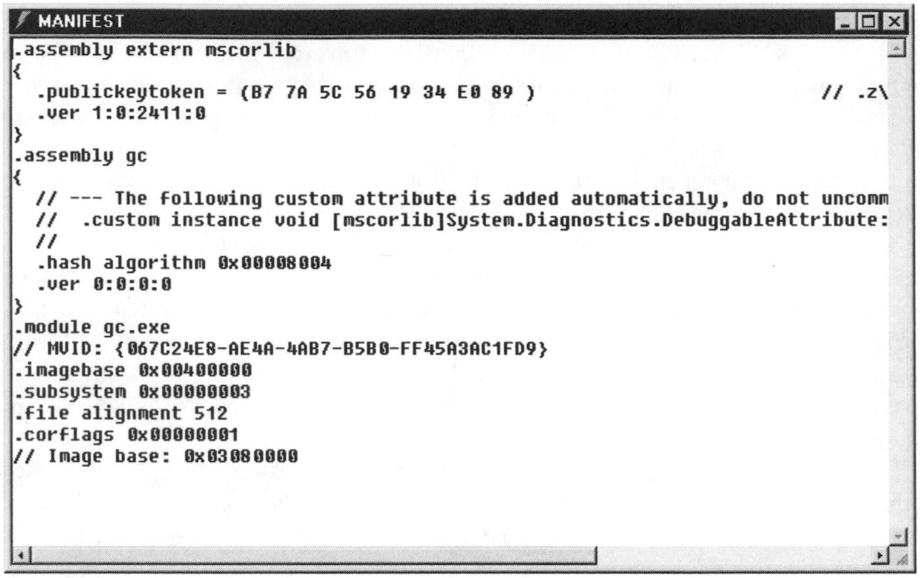

```
 / MANIFEST                                                      _ □ ✕
.assembly extern mscorlib
{
    .publickeytoken = (B7 7A 5C 56 19 34 E0 89 )                // .z\
    .ver 1:0:2411:0
}
.assembly gc
{
    // --- The following custom attribute is added automatically, do not uncomm
    //   .custom instance void [mscorlib]System.Diagnostics.DebuggableAttribute:
    //
    .hash algorithm 0x00008004
    .ver 0:0:0:0
}
.module gc.exe
// MVID: {067C24E8-AE4A-4AB7-B5B0-FF45A3AC1FD9}
.imagebase 0x00400000
.subsystem 0x00000003
.file alignment 512
.corflags 0x00000001
// Image base: 0x03080000
```

Figure 1.7   The fourth line of the manifest for *gc.exe* shows that it needs Version 1.0 of the *mscorlib* assembly. The third number in the version is the build, and the fourth is the revision number.

The first item in the manifest shown here is the *mscorlib* assembly. This is akin to linking a C++ application with the runtime library when you compile the program. The C# compiler automatically includes *mscorlib* when you compile the program, regardless of whether you use any of the .NET code in your program.

Querying Class Capabilities Through .NET Reflection

The assembly's manifest contains a collection of information about the assembly called *metadata*. The metadata tells about the external assemblies it needs to execute and security information. Your program can use the information in the metadata through *reflection*, the ability to determine information about an object's members at runtime. Java programmers probably will be familiar with reflection, and reflection in C# is similar.

USE IT   A common use for reflection is to discover information about the members of an object. In C#, all classes inherit from the *object* class. To see what members a class you define inherits from *object*, run the following program, *Reflect.cs*:

```
// Reflect.cs -- Uses reflection to show the inherited members of a class
//
//                  Compile this program with the following command line:
//                          C:>csc Reflect.cs
//
using System;
using System.Reflection;

namespace nsReflect
{
    class clsReflection
    {
    }
    class clsMain
    {
        static public void Main ()
        {
            clsReflection refl = new clsReflection ();
            Type t = refl.GetType ();
            Console.WriteLine ("The type of t is " + t.ToString());
            MemberInfo [] members = t.GetMembers ();
            Console.WriteLine ("The members of t are:");
            foreach (MemberInfo m in members)
                Console.WriteLine ("    " + m);
        }
    }
}
```

The *clsReflection* class is empty, but when you run the program you see that it contains five member methods, four of which are inherited from *object* (the *.ctor* item is the default constructor for the class):

```
The type of t is nsReflect.clsReflection
The members of t are:
   Int32 GetHashCode ()
   Boolean Equals (System.Object)
   System.String ToString ()
   System.Type GetType ()
   Void .ctor ()
```

Add a field, a property, and a method to the *clsReflection* class, as shown in the following listing:

```
class clsReflection
{
```

```
      private double pi = 3.14159;
      public double Pi
      {
          get {return (pi);}
      }
      public string ShowPi ()
      {
          return ("Pi = " + pi);
      }
}
```

Recompile and run the program, and you will see the members you just added to the list:

```
The type of t is nsReflect.clsReflection
The members of t are:
  Int32 GetHashCode()
  Boolean Equals(System.Object)
  System.String ToString()
  Double get_Pi()
  System.String ShowPi()
  System.Type GetType()
  Void .ctor()
  Double Pi
```

You can use reflection to execute a class member directly. The following program, *Reflect2.cs*, uses reflection to get the *ShowPi()* method and then executes it using the *Invoke()* method:

```
// Reflect2.cs -- Uses reflection to execute a class method indirectly
//
//                Compile this program with the following command line:
//                      C:>csc Reflect2.cs
//
using System;
using System.Reflection;

namespace nsReflect
{
    class clsReflection
    {
        private double pi = 3.14159;
        public double Pi
        {
            get {return (pi);}
        }
        public string ShowPi ()
```

```
        {
            return ("Pi = " + pi);
        }
    }
    class clsMain
    {
        static public void Main ()
        {
            clsReflection refl = new clsReflection ();
            Type t = refl.GetType();
            MethodInfo GetPi = t.GetMethod ("ShowPi");
            Console.WriteLine (GetPi.Invoke (refl, null));
        }
    }
}
```

Reflection is similar to the C++ Run Time Type Information (RTTI), which allows a programmer to obtain information about a class at runtime. Once the type of an object is obtained, an object can be cast to that type. However, C# carries this much further than the C++ RTTI, and you can discover details about a class, such as its member, at runtime.

CHAPTER 2

Developing C# Applications
Within Visual Studio .NET

TIPS IN THIS CHAPTER

If you are migrating from an earlier version of Visual Studio and you used Visual C++, you may find that Visual Studio .NET takes a little getting used to. The integrated development environment has been completely redesigned.

A number of tools that you may have used, such as the ClassWizard, are gone, and they have been replaced by a number of new tools. The redesigned Class View, for example, performs the function of the old ClassView pane of the Workspace window and incorporates many of the features of the ClassWizard.

If, on the other hand, you are moving to the .NET environment from an earlier version of Visual Basic, you might find some familiar elements in the Visual Studio .NET environment, but many of the tool windows have been changed.

Whether you are writing a Visual C++, Visual Basic, or Visual C# project, you now will use the same development environment. In previous versions, the Visual C++ development environment was considerably different from the Visual Basic environment.

In addition to providing the new C# language and a new development environment, Visual Studio .NET also gives Visual Basic some much desired updates, such as support for multi-threaded programs. Many of these updates make Visual Basic, Visual C#, and Visual C++ more compatible, leading to interoperability among programs written in the different languages. In previous editions of these programming environments, it often took considerable programming tricks to make a Visual C++ program work with one written in Visual Basic, for example.

Installing Visual Studio .NET

The current version of Visual Studio .NET comes on four CDs or a single DVD disc. The CDs include the Visual Studio environment, the MSDN help files, and Windows component updates. The component updates disc includes any service packs you need for your operating system and the .NET Software Development Kit (SDK). By comparison, the Enterprise Edition of Visual Studio version 6.0 came on four CDs, plus another two for the MSDN help system, so the current version is considerably more compact.

Visual Studio .NET is an advanced development environment that works best on an advanced computer running an advanced version of Windows. It will not install on a Windows 95 computer, but it will install on Windows 98 and Windows NT 4.0.

Microsoft recommends that Visual Studio .NET be installed on a computer that has at least a Pentium II class processor running at 400 MHz, and with at least 256MB of memory. That may be more wishful thinking than it is practical, however.

On such a test machine, the performance was not really strong, but if you have a lot of patience, it will work. Moving to a similar machine with dual Pentium II 400 MHz processors and 512MB of memory helped a little, but it was still not up to the performance of Visual C++ 6.0. On the other hand, an 866 MHz machine with two Pentium III processors and 512MB of memory yielded more than acceptable performance.

When you insert the CD (or the DVD), the setup program should run automatically after a few seconds. If it does not, open the drive's directory and run *Setup.exe*. If you are installing on a Windows server machine, you should have Internet Information Services (IIS) and FrontPage Server Extensions installed. The installation program will warn you if these services are not installed. You do not need these components to install the Setup program, but without them you will not be able to develop Web server applications using these components. To install these components, you must use your original Windows installation CD.

Beyond the server extensions, the setup program gives you three options, which you must perform in sequence:

1. *Windows Component Update*   The setup program will check the revision levels of the components on your system. Likely, you will have to update several components before installing Visual Studio .NET. These include any operating system service packs, Internet Explorer 6.0, and the .NET Framework SDK. You must perform this step before continuing.

2. *Install Visual Studio .NET*   This step will install the integrated development environment (IDE), tools, and links to the MSDN help files to the hard disk.

3. *Check Service Releases*   This step is optional and will check the Web for updates and service releases for Visual Studio and tools.

The entire installation process may take up to an hour, depending on the speed of your computer. During the component update step, your computer will have to reboot after any operating system service packs are installed and after Internet Explorer 6.0 is installed. The setup program will give you the opportunity to enter a user password so it can log on automatically between reboots. The automatic reboot feature will not work if you do not use a password. Do not remove the Windows Component Update disk until all the items have been installed.

When the component update is finished, you will see a "Congratulations" screen. Click Done to continue installing Visual Studio. Step 2 on the setup screen should now be enabled. Re-insert the first CD and click the Visual Studio .NET item.

After accepting the usual Microsoft agreement, click Continue to display the Options window, as shown in Figure 2-1.

To install the entire package, you will need about 1.2GB of disk space. Clicking an item in the tree on the left side of the Options window will make a brief description of the features appear in the Feature Description window on the middle right. In addition, if you let the mouse hover over an item, a brief description will appear in a tool tip.

After you have selected the options you want to install, click Install Now at the lower right. This step will take some time, depending on the speed of your computer and the number of items selected. On a computer with the minimum configuration recommended by Microsoft, the installation can take well over an hour. During this time, you will be asked to insert the second and third CDs.

When the installation is complete, you will return to the Setup window, where service releases will be checked. Click Service Releases and you will have the option of installing any service releases from disk or CD, or, if you have an Internet connection, installing any updates over the Internet.

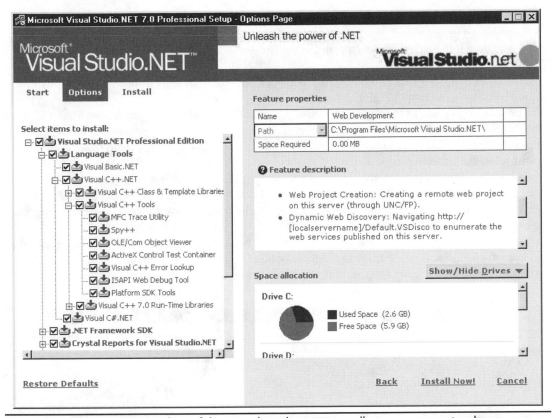

Figure 2.1   The Options window of the Visual Studio .NET installation program is where you select components to install

Running Visual Studio

By default, the setup program creates a program group on the Start menu under Programs. You may find it easier to create one or more shortcuts on your desktop to launch various programs. To create a shortcut, follow these steps:

1. Open the folder in which you installed Visual Studio. The default location is *Program File\ Microsoft Visual Studio .Net*.

2. Open the *Common7* subdirectory, and then open the *IDE* folder.

3. Locate the *DevEnv.exe* program. Hold down the right mouse button and drag the icon out of the folder window, and then drop it onto the desktop.

4. From the popup window, select Create Shortcut Here.

5. For convenience, you might want to create a desktop shortcut for the Visual Studio command prompt. The command prompt is the *vsvars32.bat* file in the *Common7\Tools* folder. Right-click and drag this item to the desktop and select Create Shortcut Here.

When you first run Visual Studio .NET, it will open with the Start page displayed and the My Profile option selected, as shown in Figure 2-2.

The Start page contains the beginning steps for personalizing and configuring Visual Studio for your needs and likes. The IDE contains six preset profiles from which you may select, or you can create a custom profile. (Yes, if you counted the profiles, you'll see seven, but if you select VS Macro Developer, it will select the Custom profile.)

The Visual Studio Developer is a general purpose profile. You will not go wrong leaving this selection as is, which is set up for C# programming. However, if you are migrating from an earlier version of Visual Studio, selecting one of the other profiles might make the tool window arrangement on the IDE a little more familiar.

The Keyboard Layout item will let you select a keyboard setup that matches that of an earlier version of Visual Studio. Selecting one of these options will make the shortcut keys *roughly* similar to earlier versions. (Pressing CTRL-W still will not summon the ClassWizard, however.)

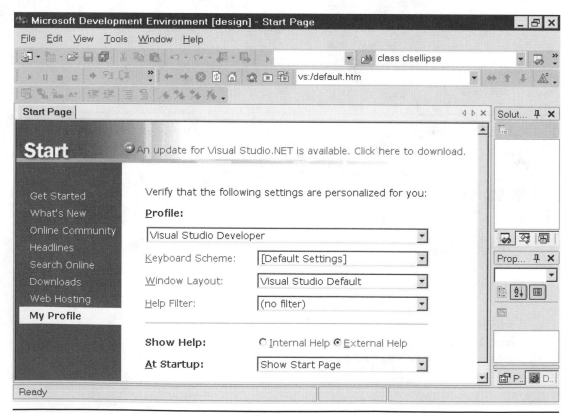

Figure 2.2   You start configuring the Visual Studio with the My Profile option on the Start page

The same is true for the Window Layout item. Selecting an earlier version of Visual Studio will rearrange the tool windows so they are roughly the same as the earlier IDE. For example, selecting Visual Basic 6 will display the Toolbox automatically. Selecting Visual C++ 6.0 will position the Class View and Resource View windows on the left side of the screen, approximately where the Workspace Window appeared in Visual C++ 6.0 (the Solution Explorer also will appear here).

The Help Filter is an abbreviated list of the filters that you will find on the MSDN help system. You can select the startup filter for the help file using this item. For working with code in this book, you should set the filter to Visual C# or Visual C# And Related.

If you select the Internal Help radio button in the Show Help area, the MSDN help file will display as a window within Visual Studio. and you will be able to select the help file from a tab in the client area (the client area is the portion of Visual Studio form where the Start page is now displayed). If you select External Help, MSDN help will open as a separate application window, similar to the MSDN display in Visual Studio 6.0.

By default, Visual Studio will display the Start page every time you start the IDE. You can select another option for display in the At Startup area. If you choose another startup option, you can always display the Start page later by choosing Help | Show Start Page.

Visual Studio will use your options each time you start the IDE. If you choose to display the Start page (a good idea), the Get Started item will be selected each time you run Visual Studio, as shown in Figure 2-3.

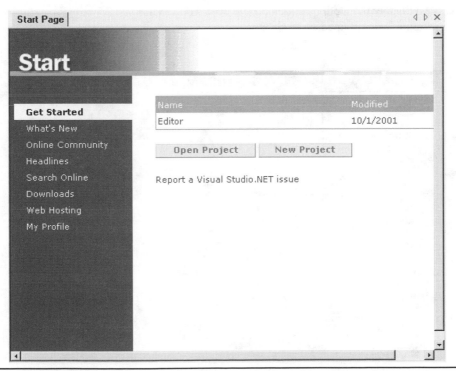

Figure 2.3   The Get Started item on the Start page is the launching point when you run Visual Studio. Use the tab at the top to select the Start page

The Get Started page will display a list of projects that you last worked on (the number of projects displayed is configurable), along with buttons to open and create projects.

After you have started Visual Studio and opened a project, you are ready to get to work. At this point, you may not need the Start page displayed. You can hide and display the Start page as needed to keep your work area clear. To hide the Start page, select the Start Page tab at the top left of the Visual Studio form, and then click the X symbol in the upper right of the form. To display the Start page again, choose Help | Show Start Page.

Using the Visual Studio Options Dialog Box

As in past versions, Visual Studio is a highly customizable program. The options you selected on the Start page present only general settings for the programming environment, such as the screen and keyboard layouts. You may override these settings and select more specific settings using the Visual Studio Options dialog box.

For example, from the Start page, you may have selected the Visual C++ 6 keyboard scheme, which selects a collection of keyboard shortcuts. In the Options dialog box, however, you may override and modify any of the individual shortcut keys.

USE IT To display the Options dialog box, choose Tools | Options. A dialog box similar to Figure 2-4 will appear.

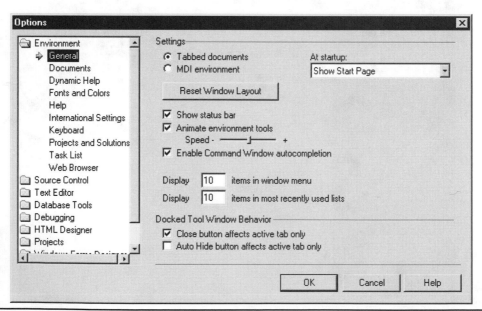

Figure 2.4 The Options dialog box is where you set individual preferences in Visual Studio

The Options dialog box is divided into two sections. The Navigation panel on the left selects the general categories. It is arranged in a tree format and displays as folders. Clicking a folder displays a list of pages inside the folder, which contain settings for Visual Studio. For example, if you click the Environment folder on the Navigation panel and then select the General page, the dialog box should appear as shown in Figure 2-4.

The right side of the Options dialog is the Page panel. When you select a page in the Navigation panel, the settings for the page will display here.

By default, when you are developing a program, Visual Studio will display source code files and other editing windows using tabs at the top of the client area. To switch between windows, you need only select the appropriate window's tab. Earlier versions of Visual Studio, however, displayed these windows in multiple-document interface (MDI) mode; to open a window, you had to click the window's title bar or select the window from the Window menu. If you are migrating from an earlier version of Visual Studio, you may initially prefer the MDI environment, which you may select from the General page's Settings area of the Options dialog.

From the General page's Settings area, you may set the number of projects displayed on the Start Page and in the recently used Projects list on the File menu. The default is four, but if you work on many projects simultaneously, you may want to increase this value. Enter the number in the Display ___ Items In Most Recently Used Lists text box.

A great many options can be customized from the Options dialog box. You may find that the help information for each page is complete and descriptive. Select the page you want to modify and click the Help button. A help window paragraph describing the page and each item on it will appear.

If you're new to Visual Studio .NET, you'll probably want to use the default settings for most of these options. With experience, however, you may decide to tweak the options to reflect your habits and the way you use the Visual Studio tools. At that point, you can experiment with the various options in this dialog box.

Customizing Toolbars and Menus

Visual Studio .NET contains a number of toolbars—27 in all—that you may display or hide on command. Some toolbars contain only a single toolbar button, but others can have a number of buttons. In addition, the various Visual Studio menus contain a number of commands not represented on the toolbars.

With so many menus, toolbars, and buttons available, it would seem that a command is available for every need. But no matter how carefully a menu or toolbar system is designed, it cannot cover the needs of all users. To accommodate your need for custom toolbars and menus, Visual Studio has provisions for adding or removing buttons from the various toolbars, and you can even create new toolbars from existing commands. You can also add or remove commands from the menus.

USE IT   Here's how you access and modify the menus and toolbars in Visual Studio .NET.

1. Choose Tools | Customize to display the Customize dialog box shown in Figure 2-5. Opening this dialog box puts the Visual Studio menus and toolbars into editing mode. The dialog box contains three tabs for displaying and modifying toolbars and for setting toolbar options.

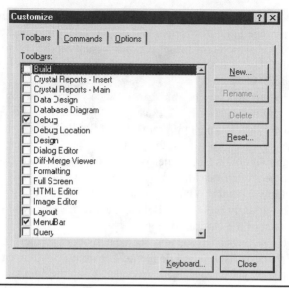

Figure 2.5 Use the Customize dialog box to modify existing toolbars and to create your own

2. The Toolbars tab contains a list of toolbars available in Visual Studio. Click to place a check mark in the box next to the toolbar name to make it visible. A toolbar must be visible before you can modify it.

3. For this example, you'll add Redo and Undo commands to the Text Editor toolbar. Place the checkmark next to Text Editor to make its toolbar visible. The unmodified toolbar is shown here:

4. Open the Commands tab, and select Edit from the Categories box. A list of editing command buttons will appear in the Commands box.

5. Click and hold the left mouse button on the Undo icon in the Commands box. Drag the Undo icon to the Text Editor toolbar. As you move across the toolbar, notice that a heavy bar appears between the buttons when your cursor passes over. The bar identifies the location where the new button will be inserted when you release the mouse.

6. Move to the end of the toolbar and release the mouse button. The new toolbar button should appear on the toolbar.

7. Repeat the process for the Redo button. If you drop a button in the wrong spot, just grab it again with the left mouse button and drag it where you want it to appear. You also can rearrange any existing toolbar buttons this way. When you finish, the toolbar should look like this:

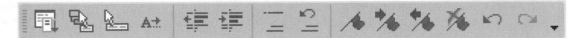

QUICK TIP

If you cannot locate a toolbar on the Visual Studio frame, try checking and unchecking the toolbar selection on the Toolbars tab while watching the frame window to see where the toolbar appears and disappears.

Removing a button from the toolbar is even easier than adding one. You simply left-click and drag it to an empty part of the Visual Studio frame. When you release the mouse, the button will disappear. Be careful not to drop it on another toolbar, however, or the button will move to that toolbar instead of disappearing.

▶ NOTE

To restore a toolbar to its original state, select the Toolbars tab, select the toolbar in the list, and click the Reset button. Any changes you made to the toolbar will be undone.

You can even create your own toolbars:

1. Select the Toolbars tab, and click the New button.

2. Name the new toolbar in the New Toolbar dialog box that appears.

3. Click Close to close the New Toolbar dialog box. Your toolbar will appear in the Toolbars tab list, and a small floating toolbar with no buttons will appear to the left or right side of the Customize dialog box.

   At this point, notice that the Rename and Delete buttons have become active. You can rename or delete custom toolbars, but you cannot rename or delete toolbars that are built into Visual Studio.

4. Now move to the Commands tab and drag and drop command buttons to this new toolbar until it contains all the commands you want.

5. Close the Customize dialog box. You now can move your custom toolbar and dock it on the frame with the other Visual Studio toolbars.

You also can open the Options dialog box from within the Customize dialog box. Click the Keyboard button and the Options dialog box will appear with the Keyboard page of the Environment folder on the Navigation panel selected. From this page's Settings panel, you can modify and add keyboard shortcut keys. You can also make changes to other pages within the Options dialog box.

Here's how you can modify menus.

1. Select the Commands tab on the Customize dialog box.
2. Click the top level menu that you want to modify. For this example, you'll add the Full Screen command to the Edit menu.
3. Select the View item in the Categories list and then click the Edit menu on the Visual Studio frame.
4. Scroll through the Commands list until you find the Full Screen item. Click and drag this item to the Edit menu. Drop the item where you want it to appear.

You can rearrange, remove, and add other items to the menus using the same techniques you used for the toolbars.

Adding Items to the Tools Menu

In addition to numerous built-in tools, you can add your own programs to the Visual Studio Tools menu. Eventually, you may develop custom programs that can help in your programming efforts. Rather than running these programs from a command line, you can place them in the Visual Studio Tools menu for easy access.

In the Chapter02 folder on the Web site for this book is a project named *MessageBoxBuilder*. The program created by this project displays a form from which you can build a message box visually and then save the generated code in the system clipboard. After closing the form, you can retrieve the message box code by pasting it into your program. The Message Box Builder form is shown in Figure 2-6.

The source code for the Message Box Builder is too long to show here. However, it is included on the book's Web site, so you can modify it to meet your particular needs. It will generate the code needed for message boxes in Visual C#, Visual C++, and Visual Basic. The program was originally written in C++, but this version is written in C#. As your programming skills in C# develop, you can experiment with the code.

 USE IT Here's how you add this tool to the Tools menu:

1. Copy the Release version of the compiled code to your hard disk, and note the directory to which you copied it. For this example, assume the program was placed in the *C:\bin* directory.

2. From the Visual Studio Tools menu, select External Tools to display the External Tools dialog box shown in Figure 2-7. Click the Add button to add a new external tool.

3. In the Title box, enter the name of the tool as you want it to appear on the menu.

4. In the Command box, enter the full path where you placed the program file.

5. If your tool needs any startup arguments, you can add them in the Arguments box. Alternatively, you can check the Prompt For Arguments box, and Visual Studio will display a prompt into which you can type arguments when you use the tool.

6. Add a startup directory by typing it in the Initial Directory box. The Message Box Builder does not require any arguments or an initial directory.

7. Click OK to close the External Tools dialog box. Examine the Tools menu and you should see your new item listed just above the External Tools item. Choose the item to start the Message Box Builder.

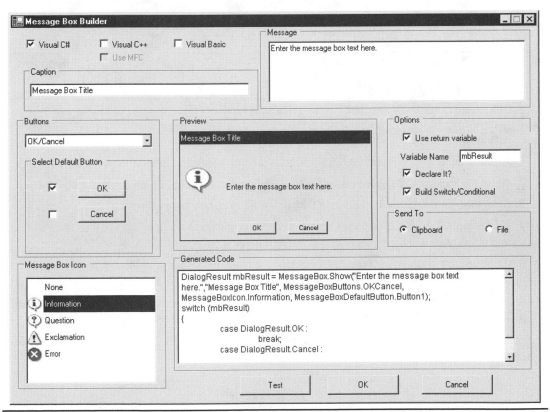

Figure 2.6   The Message Box Builder tool builds message boxes visually and generates the code for Visual C#, Visual C++, and Visual Basic

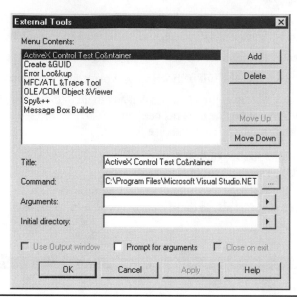

Figure 2.7   Customize your Tools menu by adding commands in the External Tools dialog box

Now we'll use the Message Box Builder.

1. Select a language at the upper left of the Message Box Builder dialog box (it defaults to C#).

2. Enter the message box title and text in the Caption and Message fields.

3. Select the button sequence and icon that you want to appear on the message box.

4. On the right side of the dialog box, you can select options to declare and use a return variable, and to build a *switch* statement to test the return value.

5. As you select options, the program will build a sample message box in the center of your screen. This is only an approximation of the message box. To see how the message box will actually appear, click the Test button.

6. Click OK in the Message Box Builder dialog to copy the generated code to the clipboard.

7. Move to the position in the source code where you want the message box code to appear, and paste the code at that location.

Test Driving Visual Studio .NET

To examine the tool windows in Visual Studio, you need to open a project in the IDE. Many of the tool windows are inactive or empty without an active project. At this stage, do not try to remember the steps you use for creating a project. For this chapter and the next, when you need to create a project, the text will outline these steps again.

Now let's open a project to make the tool windows visible.

1. With Visual Studio displaying the Start page, make sure the Get Started page is displayed and click the New Project button to display the New Project dialog box shown in Figure 2-8.

2. The New Project dialog box is split into three sections. On the left is the Project Types panel. Here, select the language you want to use. For this project, select Visual C# Projects.

3. On the right is the Templates panel. Select Windows Application. Visual Studio will use your selection in this panel to create the basic code and objects for your program.

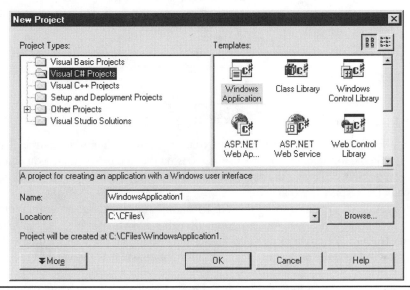

Figure 2.8   Use the New Project dialog box to create a new application in Visual Studio

4. At the bottom of the dialog box are two boxes for entering project name and location information. The default project name is *WindowsApplication1*. Although that name is not very descriptive, it's fine for this project because you are concerned with accessing tool windows rather than creating a real project. You can leave the name as is or change it to something else.

5. In the Location box, you can override the default directory to place it in another location, or click the Browse button to the right of the Location box to select a directory.

6. Click OK to create the project. Visual Studio will create a form as part of the project and fill the various tool windows with information about the project.

USE IT   At this point, the first stop is the Solution Explorer tool window at the upper right of the Visual Studio frame, shown here. (If the Solution Explorer does not appear, press CTRL-ALT-L to display it.)

The Solution Explorer lists the components of your program in a hierarchical tree display. The solution name is on the top line, and the project name is on the line below that. You can expand items under the project name by clicking the plus (+) symbol or collapse the display by clicking the minus (−) symbol when the display is expanded.

The References item contains a list of the .NET Runtime files that your program will use. You can think of these as "library" files that your program will call when you run it.

The *AssemblyInfo.cs* file contains *attributes* describing how your program will be put together. Eventually, you will use these attributes to embed information, such as the version number, in your program file.

The last item in the Solution Explorer is the *Form1.cs* file. This is the starting point for your programming efforts. It contains the initial class, *Form1*, for your project. The Visual Studio Wizard names it *Form1.cs* by default, but you may rename it by right-clicking the item and selecting Rename from the popup menu. (You also can rename the file from the Properties tool window, which is described later in "Using the Properties Tool Window.")

Information about the classes is contained in the Class View tool window. To display this window, press CTRL-SHIFT-C. Notice that it occupies the same area of the Visual Studio frame as the Solution Explorer, and you can move between the Class View and the Solution Explorer by clicking the appropriate tab along the bottom of the window. Expand the tree in the Class View tool window by clicking the plus symbols until it looks like this:

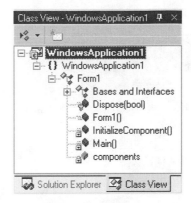

C# requires that you include at least one class in your project. A *class* is the basic building block for a C# program, and it contains the variables and code that the program will use. For a Windows application, Visual Studio creates a default class called *Form1*. The *Form1* item in the Class View is the entry for this default class.

You may change the class name, but doing so is not as simple as changing the file name in the Solution Explorer. The default code prepared by Visual Studio contains references to the *Form1* class, so you will need to change the name using the Properties tool window to make sure all of these references are changed as well. You will do this in the next tip.

Under the *Form1* class name are the methods and variables Visual Studio created as part of the project. A *method* is the object-oriented term for a *function*, a basic unit of code in a program using C#. A *variable*—often called a *field* in a C# class—represents a memory location for storing information.

Notice that one of the methods is named *InitializeComponent()*.Visual Studio uses this method to set the start properties for objects in your code. You may examine this method in the source code file, but you should not modify it. Any changes you make in this method will be lost because Visual Studio will rewrite the method when you change properties in the Properties tool window.

Press CTRL-ALT-X to display the Toolbox shown in Figure 2-9. By default, the Toolbox will appear on the left side of the Visual Studio frame. The Toolbox contains objects that you can add to Visual Studio projects, and its contents will change according to the project type and the task you are currently performing. With the Windows form displayed, for example, the Toolbox displays a Windows Forms list containing the various controls you may place on a form. If the Toolbox does not appear as shown in Figure 2-9, click the Windows Forms bar labeled "Windows Forms" on the Toolbox.

You will use the Toolbox throughout this book when you prepare Windows applications using C#. In later chapters, you will use the Toolbox to place control objects on the form.

To place an object on the form, you click the object name in the Toolbox and move the mouse cursor over the form. Notice that the mouse cursor changes to an icon representing the object you selected. When the mouse cursor appears over the form where you want the object to appear, click the mouse again and the object will drop on the form.

Now you can practice placing objects on the form.

1. Click the Button object in the Toolbox and drag the button near the bottom of the form.

2. Click the CheckBox item and drag the check box somewhere near the middle of the form.

Figure 2.9 The Toolbox contains objects that you can add to a Visual Studio project

At this point, the Visual Studio frame should look something like that shown in Figure 2-10. For this exercise, it doesn't matter where the controls are placed on the form.

> ## QUICK TIP
>
> *If you accidentally draw the wrong object on the form, you can delete the object by selecting it on the form and pressing the* DELETE *key.*

Not all the objects in the Toolbox will be visible on the form when you draw them. From the Toolbox, drag the ColorDialog item on the form. Instead of appearing on the form, a panel opens below the form and the object appears in the panel. This is an example of a *hidden control*. It is a part of your project,

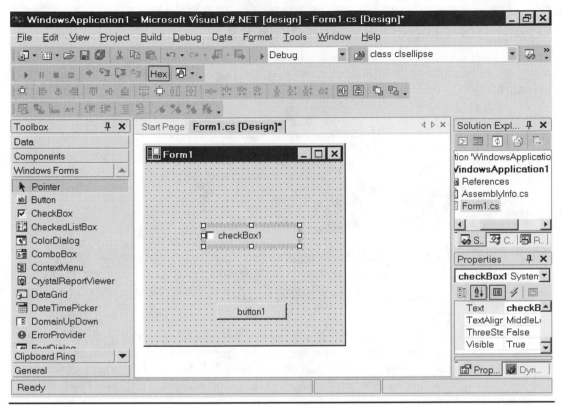

Figure 2.10   Visual Studio after you have placed a couple of controls on the form

but it does not automatically appear on the form. The ColorDialog item is an example of a *common dialog*, which is covered in Chapter 17.

Notice that the Toolbox title bar contains a pushpin icon. This is the Autohide button. When the pushpin icon is laying on its side, the Toolbox will slide off the screen each time you move the mouse cursor away after selecting and drawing a control. Also, notice that when the Toolbox is visible in Autohide mode, part of the form is covered by the Toolbox. If you click the pushpin to disable autohide and "pin" the Toolbox to the screen, the window containing the form display adjusts so that the entire form is visible. When you are designing a form and adding several controls, it often is more convenient to disable autohide so you can see the entire form and the Toolbox at the same time. Most of the tool windows in Visual Studio have autohide buttons on their title bars.

Using the Properties Tool Window

Now that you have placed a couple of objects on the form, select the Button object. Press the F4 key to display the Properties tool window, as shown next. The Properties tool window will appear in the lower-right corner of the Visual Studio frame, sharing window space with the Dynamic Help tool window.

The Properties tool window is a key player in the Visual Studio scheme. You probably will use this tool window more than any other. The contents of the Properties tool window will change to reflect the object you currently have selected, either on the form or in one of the other tool windows. The left column of the tool window lists the names of the properties, and the right column contains the values of the properties.

USE IT   Notice the small toolbar across the top of the Properties tool window. The buttons on this toolbar will help you navigate through the properties of an object. Some objects have only a few properties, while others have a lengthy list. The first button on the toolbar causes the properties to be listed by category. Click this button, and then select the check box that you added to the form earlier. Scroll through the properties, and you'll see subsections with labels such as Appearance, Layout, Design, and Behavior.

Now click the second button on the Properties toolbar—the Alphabetic button. Scroll through the properties again and you will find that the categories have been removed and all the properties have been arranged in alphabetic order.

The third and fourth buttons switch the list between properties and events. An *event* is an action that you can respond to in your code, and which may be generated by an action on the part of the program's user, such as clicking a button, or by the operating system. (You also can trigger events in your code. Events are covered in Chapter 18.)

The fifth button displays the property pages for your project. Normally, this button will be enabled only when you have your project name selected in the Solution Explorer or Class View. You use these property pages to modify program parameters such as the assembly name, the project type, and the output path.

The Properties tool window will display a brief description of a property. With an object on the form selected, you can right-click any item in the Properties tool window and a short menu containing Reset and Description items will appear. If you select the Description item, a short description of each property, as you select it, will appear below the Properties tool window. Selecting the Reset item with a property selected will change the value of the property to its original or default value.

In the last tip, you were cautioned that you should change the name of a class using the Properties tool window. Here's how you do this.

1. Display the source code file by pressing the F7 key. Visual Studio will respond by adding another tab in the client area and displaying the source code file. Notice the line at the top that starts the class definition:

```
public class Form1 : System.Windows.Forms.Form
```

2. Move to the Class View tool window and then select the name of the class, *Form1*. If you expand this item, you will notice a method also named *Form1*. This is the class *constructor* method, which must have the same name as the class. (Constructors are covered in Chapter 5.)

3. Return to the Properties tool window and click the Properties button from the toolbar.

4. Locate the line containing "Name," and change the name of the class to **MainForm**.

5. Press the ENTER key, and you can examine the Class View tool window again. You'll see that the class name and the name of the constructor method both have changed from *Form1* to *MainForm*. In fact, all references to *Form1* in the source code have been changed to *MainForm*.

You should remember that these changes will be made to objects that were prepared and maintained by Visual Studio tools. If you added references to *Form1* in the above example, or if you manually edit the code, the changes may not be made. To be safe, you should always search through your code for any remaining references to the old name when you make changes manually.

Using IntelliSense

IntelliSense is Microsoft's term for a code completion technique that makes it possible to view class member information and method parameter details without leaving the keyboard. It is not new to Visual Studio .NET; IntelliSense is available in earlier Visual Studio versions as well. You can invoke IntelliSense at any time in a source code file by pressing CTRL-SPACEBAR.

 Here's how to use IntelliSense to insert an object into your source code.

1. Make sure the source code file is visible by pressing F7. Scroll through the source code until you find the constructor function shown in the following listing. Note that if you did *not* change

the class name in the last tip, the constructor will be named *Form1()* instead of *MainForm()*. The body of the method is enclosed in a set of curly braces.

```
public MainForm()
{
    //
    // Required for Windows Form Designer support
    //
    InitializeComponent();
    //
    // TODO: Add any constructor code after InitializeComponent call
    //
}
```

2. Start a blank line at the bottom of the method (after the last //). In the blank line, begin typing the name of the button object that you added to the form earlier. If you did not change the *Name* property, the name of the button is *button1*. After you type the letter *b*, press CTRL-SPACEBAR to invoke IntelliSense. A window will pop up with a list of objects and properties for the *MainForm* class with Visual Studio's best guess highlighted, as shown in Figure 2-11.

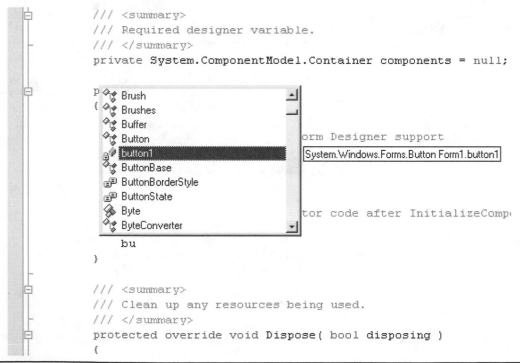

Figure 2.11   Using IntelliSense, Visual Studio will help you identify the name of a variable or object

3. Use the up and down arrow keys to scroll through the list until you find the name of the variable or object you are typing, and then press ENTER. Visual Studio will insert the selected name into your source file.

4. IntelliSense automatically activates to display the properties and methods available for an object. After you have typed the word *button1* in the source file, type a period immediately after the name. This is the *member of* operator. IntelliSense will pop up another window showing all of the available members of the *Button* class.

5. Using the arrow keys, move to the property or method you want to use and press ENTER. IntelliSense will insert the name into your source code.

Getting Help

With more than 1000 classes in the .NET Runtime code, it is virtually impossible for you to remember all the methods and properties available to each of them, or how to enter the code to create an instance of a class.

When you installed Visual Studio and C#, you also installed the Microsoft Developer's Network (MSDN), which serves as the help file for Visual Studio. The obvious advantage to using MSDN is that it is constantly evolving and can be supported over the Web. You can look up a topic from the version that you installed with Visual Studio, or you can visit the MSDN Web site and get the same information, along with any corrections or updates that have been made. Some of the topics in the installed MSDN refer you to the Web site.

The help file's appearance is determined by whether you selected internal or external help on the Start page or in the Options dialog box. Regardless of which option you selected, though, a Dynamic Help tool window is always available on the Visual Studio frame.

USE IT   To display the Dynamic Help tool window, choose Help | Dynamic Help. The window shares space with the Properties tool window at the bottom right of the Visual Studio frame, and you can also open it by clicking its tab at the bottom. The Dynamic Help tool window is shown here:

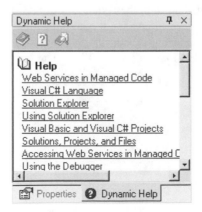

Dynamic help gives you almost instant access to the help topics related to your current task. The contents of the Dynamic Help tool window will track the current selection and update to show the help topics. The following example shows you how to use this window.

1. Select the Solution Explorer tab just above Dynamic Help. The first topic in the Dynamic Help tool window will then be Solution Explorer.

2. Select the Class View tab, and the first topic will change to Class View.

3. Select a button object on a form and the topic will change to reflect the help available for buttons.

4. Assuming you selected internal help from the Start page or the Options dialog box, you can click a topic to open a window in the client area and display the help topic. If you selected external help, you can click a topic to display a topic window separate from Visual Studio. In either case, you can navigate from the help window to other topics.

5. Just below the Dynamic Help item on the Help menu are selections for Contents, Index, and Search. These three menu items correspond to the three buttons on the Dynamic Help window's toolbar. Select one of these three items, again using internal help, and you'll see a tool window on the right side of the Visual Studio frame. All three of these items share the same window space as the Solution Explorer and the Class View.

6. The Contents item displays the help system in a hierarchical tree. Expand the tree until you find the topic you want. When you select it in the tree, the help system will display the topic in a window in the client area, placing a tab for it at the top.

7. The Search item will search through the text and titles in the help system for the search word or phrase that you enter. Instead of displaying a topic directly, the search will display a Search Results tool window at the bottom of the Visual Studio frame. When you select an item in the Search Results, the help system will open a tab panel in the client area and display the page. The search components are shown in Figure 2-12.

8. Use the check boxes on the Search tool window to restrict the search to help page titles only or to broaden the search by looking for related words. After you get a set of search results, you can check the Search In Previous Results box to restrict any further searches to the results already displayed.

9. The Index item (the middle button in the Dynamic Help toolbar) is the most direct route to a help topic, but you must have some idea of where the information may be indexed. However, it does provide almost instantaneous feedback. Select this item and a tab will be added in the same area as the Solution Explorer and Class View. The Index tab is shown here:

10. As you search using the name of the topic you are looking for, the list in the Index tab changes to reflect the current search. You can backspace and correct for any dead ends in the search process until you find the topic you are looking for.

11. If only one topic was found based on your search, it will be displayed in the client area when you press the ENTER key. Many times, however, the Index search will return more than one item. In this case, a list of items found will appear in the Index Results tool window, which will be added to the Visual Studio frame in the same area where you saw the Search Results tool window. You can select an item from the list to display it in the client area.

12. You can also filter the help topics using any of the Contents, Search, or Index methods by choosing a filter in the Filtered By box. The default filter is the one you selected on the Start page. Because the help system is CD-bound (there is no option to install it on hard disk as there was in Visual Studio 6), changing filters may take several seconds.

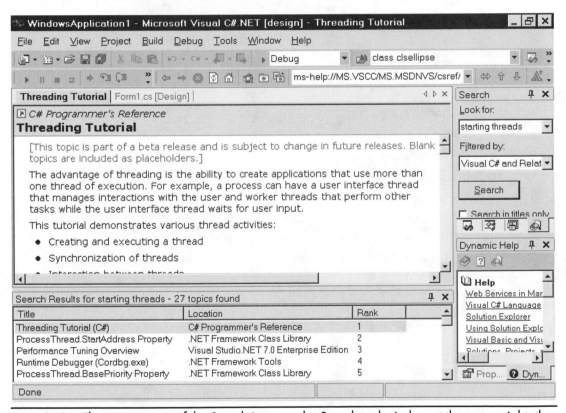

Figure 2.12   The components of the Search item are the Search tool window at the upper right; the Search Results tool window at the bottom and the help page display in the client area

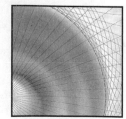

PART II
The C# Language

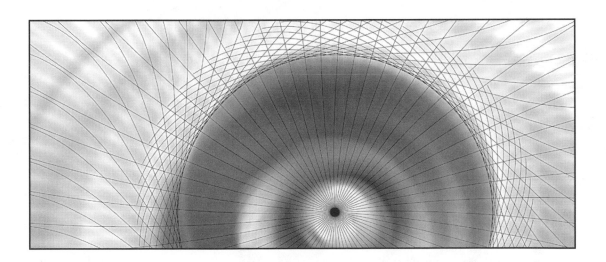

CHAPTER 3

Getting Started with C#

TIPS IN THIS CHAPTER

If you are a typical programmer interested in learning a new language, you're probably anxious to get started writing C# programs. Even if you are familiar with other languages that might be similar to C#—such as C++, Visual Basic, and Java—you still can learn a lot of new information about using C#.

In this chapter, you start writing C# programs. First, you will write the traditional "Hello, World!" program using both C# and C++ to see the difference—and the similarities—between the two languages. Then you will write the not-nearly-as-traditional Visual Basic clock program in C# and Visual Basic, again to see the similarities and difference between the two languages. Later chapters will introduce you to writing programs for the World Wide Web and how to use Web forms.

Introducing a New Language

More than 2000 computer programming languages are in use throughout the world. That's only about a third the 6800 spoken languages, but it's certainly enough to qualify as a cybernetic Tower of Babel. Some of these are specialized languages that accomplish limited tasks, others are experimental. One, called the *W language, exists "solely to irritate the programmer," according to one review.

Now one more language is on the scene: C#.

When you finish this chapter, you should realize that C# is not just C++ in a new wrapper, nor is it a new Visual Basic. Rather, it borrows from concepts of both and then folds and rolls them together to produce a new language. As you have seen in the first two chapters, C# is not the answer to every programming project or problem. Instead, it is another language you may add to your repertoire and toolkit.

In a "training" language such as BASIC or Pascal, you can study concepts in virtual isolation. For example, you can learn how to write statements and expressions in BASIC without having to know about subroutines. C# is not a training language, and the elements of C# cannot easily be pigeonholed. To understand statements and expressions, you must understand how to write functions. For that, however, you need a basic understanding of the C# class, because C# does not allow you to write functions outside of a class. But, then, it is difficult to understand how a class operates without understanding functions. While learning C#, you occasionally get some exposure to new concepts. This book will use notes to resolve these "forward" references.

If C# is your first programming language, you will find numerous references in the Microsoft Developers Network (MSDN) documentation pointing out how a C# construct is applied in C++ or Visual Basic. This book will present the C# concepts without assuming that you already know C++ or Visual Basic, but occasionally it will point out how a construct is similar to, or different from, a construct in another language. You may find it convenient to study Visual C++ or Visual Basic concurrently, but it should not be necessary for understanding the concepts presented here.

Using C# Code Modules

You can write C# programs and then compile and run them from the command line. The .NET framework and the Visual Studio provide a number of tools to help you to write and test programs from the command line.

Despite the fact that Microsoft has released the specifications for C# and the Common Language Runtime (CLR) in the hopes that other platforms will eventually support C#, much of the C# library code is designed to support Windows programming. Ultimately, of course, the intent of the Visual Studio tools and Visual C# is to help you write programs for Windows.

C# is a *component-oriented* language. As such, it is much easier for you to write programs in separate components using C# than it is using the constrictions of C++. Such modular programming helps you build upon existing code, and you can even use stand-alone executable programs as modules in another executable program.

What makes C# components possible is the C# assembly. An *assembly* is a self-defining module and may be an *.exe* or *.dll* file type. Within the assembly's compiled code, a *manifest* contains all the information another module might need to access the assembly. The assembly is the major building block of the .NET concept and gives your program the ability to use code contained in other modules, even if those modules are written in Visual Basic or any other language that supports the .NET programming model.

▶ *NOTE*

Often in the MSDN help files and other places, you may see the manifest referred to as metadata. The metadata is roughly equivalent to the type library in Component Object Model (COM) programming. Metadata contains at least three key pieces of information about the object: the name of the object, the names of all the fields and properties (the variables) in the object and their types, and the names of all the functions in the object and the types and names of each function. The metadata, or manifest, also contains information about the version number of the object, the security permissions needed to access its internal components and the processor and operating system, and other information. The metadata makes it possible for your code to call functions and use classes in code that has already been compiled, and makes it possible for you to write modules that you may call from other programs.

In this chapter, you will get a quick introduction to assemblies and how to use them; in Chapter 10 you will create shared and private assemblies, and learn how to use the global assembly cache.

Using the class Keyword

C# is an *object-oriented* programming language: you cannot write a C# program without defining at least one object, called a *class*, that will hold the code that your program will execute. The class is the basic object mechanism in C# (but it is not the only object). Except for a few notable exceptions, all the variables that you use in a program and all the functions that you write must be members of a class.

Although you create objects using variable names, you should know the important differences between an object and an ordinary variable in object-oriented programming (OOP). An ordinary variable contains only value information. An object may have methods that define the operations that the object may perform and the operations that functions may perform on the object. In addition, an object may contain fields, which are ordinary variables that contain values.

To define a class, you use the *class* keyword followed by the *identifier* that you want to use for the class name. Follow the class name with an open brace, and then define the variables and functions that you want to be *members* of the class:

```
class clsName
{
    // Member variables and functions will go here
}
```

If you are a C++ programmer, you may note with some interest that the definition does not include a semicolon at the end of the class definition. C++ requires the semicolon, but the C# language specification states that the semicolon is optional, which makes it less likely that those moving to C# from C++ or Visual Basic (or even other languages such as Pascal) will make repeated errors by adding or omitting the semicolon. C++ programmers likely will include the semicolon out of habit; Visual Basic programmers likely will omit it. The C# compiler will accept the definition either way.

Because C# is a new language, no clear conventions have emerged to define how you write a class name. In Visual C++, you generally prefix the class name with a capital *C*, as *CMyClass*. In Visual Basic, the convention is to prefix the name with *cls*, as in *clsMyClass*. You may adopt either or neither method. The C# library classes do not use prefixes, which makes it easier to remember and use them. For example, to use the *Write()* function in the *Console* class, you would write simply *Console.Write()* rather than *CConsole.Write()* or *clsConsole.Write()*.

Using the Main( ) Function in its Various Forms

After you have defined a class, you may define the functions and variables that your program will use. C# does not permit you to declare functions and variables in *global* space—that is, you cannot declare them outside a class definition (or a similar construct called a *structure*, which you will encounter in Chapter 6).

Your program must define at least one function, and it must be called *Main()*, which is the *entry point* for your program. C++ programmers should be careful to note that the function name begins with a capital *M*, whereas a C++ program must contain a *main()* function with a lowercase *m*. If you write the C# function using *main()*, the compiler will tell you that you have not defined an entry point for your program. When you run your program, Windows will transfer control to *Main()* and your program will begin executing.

The fact that *Main()* must be a member of a class, of course, presents a quandary. You cannot declare a function outside a class, but you cannot create a class object until you define a function in which to declare the object. To avoid this dilemma, you declare *Main()* as a *static* function, which allows you to execute the function before declaring a class object.

▶ *NOTE*

The static keyword means the same as it does in C++ and imparts special properties and limits on the function that you declare as static. In Visual Basic, the shared keyword is the equivalent of the static keyword. When you declare a function static, you may call the function before you declare an instance of the class. When you declare a variable static, you may set or retrieve the value of the variable without declaring an instance of the class. In addition, without declaring an instance of a class, static functions may access only other static functions and static variables in the class. The non-static members simply do not exist until you declare a class instance.

To define a function, you must write its *return type*. A function does not have to return a value, in which case its return type is *void*. If a function does return a value, the return value may be any of the fundamental data types that will be covered in Chapter 5, or it may be a user-defined data type such as a class or structure data type. The *Main()* function must either be void or it must return a type *int*.

Following the return type, you write the function name, which must begin with an underscore or an upper or lowercase letter. After the first character, a function name may contain letters or numbers. The function name may not contain any of the C# operators, such as the "+" for addition or the "*" for multiplication.

The definition of a function must include a *parameter list*, which you write inside a set of parentheses immediately following the function name. The parameter list must include the data type and names of the parameters, and you separate the parameters with a comma. You must include the parameter list even if the function does not use parameters (in which case, the function has an empty parameter list).

Following the parameter list, you begin the body of the function with an open brace, the same as you use for the class definition. After the open brace, you write any *statements* that the function will execute.

In its minimum form, then, a program will include at least one class definition and one function definition:

```
class clsName
{
    static void Main ()
    {
    }
}
```

As written, this program will not do any useful work, but it will compile without error and you can run it from the Windows command line. It is the minimum code that a C# program may contain.

Your program will execute the statements in *Main()* one after another, and when it executes the last statement, the program will exit and return control to the operating system. If you provide *Main()* with a return type of *int*, the last line of the function must be a *return* statement, and it must pass an integer value back to the operating system:

```
class clsName
{
    static int Main ()
    {
        // Program statements here
        return (0);
    }
}
```

By convention, C and C++ programs return *0* to the operating system when the program executes without any errors, and they return a non-zero value if an error occurs. If your *Main()* function returns a value, you should observe this convention. This makes it possible for scripts that run a program to determine whether the program ran successfully.

The *Main()* function also may contain a parameter list. If it does, you use a single parameter, an *array* of type *string*, as follows:

```
class clsName
{
    static int Main (string [] args)
    {
        // Program statements here
        return (0);
    }
}
```

In the preceding program are two points of note, one for C++ programmers and another for Visual Basic programmers. C++ programmers should note that the array declaration in the parameter list contains brackets ([])between the data type and the parameter name. In C++ you are used to writing *main()* with the brackets *after* the parameter name, as follows:

```
int main (int argc, char *args[])
```

This definition declares *args* as an array of *char pointers*. The compiler will thrash you soundly if you write *Main()*—or any other function for that matter—in this way. In C#, adding the brackets between the data type and the variable name means that the identifier following is to be taken as an *array* of the data type preceding. (An array actually is an instance of the *Array* class.) In Chapter 11, you will learn that to declare an array in your code, you must use *two* sets of brackets—an empty set after the data type to identify the variable as an array, and another set after the variable name to declare the size of the array.

Visual Basic programmers should note that the *return* statement ends with a semicolon. The semicolon is part of the C# *syntax*, and all statements must end with a semicolon regardless of whether you write them on one line or over several lines. You must pay attention to where and when you use the semicolon; Chapter 4 contains a more thorough discussion of statements.

▶ *NOTE*

Visual Basic programmers may be more familiar with the C# string type than C++ programmers. In C++, a string is an array of type char. In C#, the string type is an object, an instance of the String class. In C++, the arguments to main( ) are an integer value that contains the number of arguments and a string array containing those arguments. In C#, the Array object that contains the strings maintains its own count, and thus the count is not needed as a parameter to Main( ).

Accessing C# Library Classes

The C# assemblies contain more than 1000 classes (some sources claim as many as 2,500, but I've never counted them). By comparison, the Microsoft Foundation Class (MFC), a popular library for C++ Windows programming, contains about 200 classes. With such a large number of classes in the C# library, plus those that you create for your program, there is a great chance of name duplication. To avoid colliding with a system assembly class name, for example, you might have to be creative in your naming, which might lead to some long or confusing names.

To avoid name duplication, the C# assemblies protect the class names through a set of *namespaces*. C# borrows the namespace concept from C++. Namespaces define logical spaces for naming identifiers. While identifiers—class names or the names of subordinate namespaces—must be unique within the same namespace, they may duplicate the names of identifiers in other namespaces without interfering with one another. A namespace is like a surname; if two people are named Isaac, as long as they have different surnames, there will be no problem distinguishing between the two.

USE IT The majority of C# library classes are in the *System* namespace. To access an object in a namespace, you may write the *fully qualified name* of the object. For example, the *Console* class is in the *System* namespace, so you will access the class using the syntax *System.Console*. The following short program contains a call to the *WriteLine( )* function in the *Console* class:

```
class clsMain
{
    static public void Main()
    {
        System.Console.WriteLine ("Hello, World");
    }
}
```

You may shorten the syntax by telling the compiler that you want to access items in a particular namespace with the *using* keyword. After you declare that you are using a particular namespace, the compiler will search the namespace to resolve identifiers. In the following short program, you declare that you are using the *System* namespace:

```
using System;
class clsMain
{
    static public void Main()
    {
        Console.WriteLine ("Hello, World");
    }
}
```

Notice that the *using* statement is outside the class definition. If you write the declaration inside a class definition, the compiler will issue an error. After the *using* statement, you no longer need to use the fully qualified name for the *Console* class.

Namespaces may be nested as well. For example, the *MessageBox* class is nested in the *Windows.Forms* namespace, which itself is nested in the *System* namespace. To access the *MessageBox* class, you may use the fully qualified name, as shown in the following code:

```
System.Windows.Forms.MessageBox.Show ("Hello, World", "Hello",
                        System.Windows.Forms.MessageBoxButtons.OK,
                        System.Windows.Forms.MessageBoxIcon.Information);
```

That is a lot of typing for a single statement. You must use the fully qualified name to access the *Show()* function and the flag definitions in the *MessageBox* class. The more typing you do, the greater the chances that you will make an error. It is much easier to use the *using* statement and let the compiler resolve the identifiers, as shown in the following snippet:

```
using System.Windows.Forms;
. . .
MessageBox.Show ("Hello, World", "Hello",
                MessageBoxButtons.OK, MessageBoxIcon.Information);
```

You will use these techniques in the next few tips when you write console and Windows programs. In "Writing and Using Your Own Namespaces" later in this chapter, you will also learn how to create and use your own namespaces.

Creating a Command Line Program

The simplest form of a C# program simply writes to the console. To create a program, you will need to create a *source code* file using a plain text editor such as Notepad. The C# compiler does not really care what file name you use, or what the extension is, so long as it is a valid Windows file name. By convention, Microsoft recommends that C# source code files have an extension of *.cs*.

USE IT Visual Studio .NET uses its own command prompt. Here's how you compile a program from the command line:

1. Choose Start | Programs | Microsoft Visual Studio .NET 7.0 | Visual Studio .NET Tools | Visual Studio .NET Command Prompt.

2. The command window that appears includes all the environment variables you need to use Visual Studio compilers and tools. Just running a Windows command prompt will not work.

3. Start Visual Studio .NET command prompt and change to the directory where you want to save your program files.

4. Start the text editor and enter the following code. In this sample, you will use a namespace. You might as well get used to namespaces; when you create a project using Visual Studio wizards, the generated source file always will have a namespace.

```
namespace nsFirst
{
    using System;
    class clsMain
    {
        static public void Main()
        {
            Console.WriteLine ("Hello World from C#!");
        }
    }
}
```

5. Save the program file as *First.cs*. Exit the text editor, and compile the program using the following command line:

```
C:>csc first.cs  <Enter>
```

The compiler will respond by telling you a bit about itself, including the compiler version and the version of the CLR that it is using. Then it will display a copyright notice. When the command prompt returns, run the program and you should see the following output:

```
C:>first  <Enter>
Hello World from C#!

C:>
```

6. The *Console.WriteLine()* function adds a *newline* character to the text. A newline character in Windows is a combination of two characters—a carriage return and a line feed. You can build a single output line using multiple output statements by using the *Write()* function instead. When you use *Write()*, you must insert the newline characters yourself. For the preceding program, change the *WriteLine()* statement to the following two statements:

```
Console.Write ("Hello World ");
Console.Write ("from C#!\r\n");
```

▶ **NOTE**

The Console.Write() function is the nearest equivalent to the C++ printf() function. By default, printf() outputs a carriage return/line feed combination using the single escape character, \n. The Console.Write() function, however, outputs only a line feed. To get the two-character sequence, you must write a carriage return using the \r character followed by \n.

The backslash (\) in front of a character signals the C# compiler to treat the character that follows as a special character, called an *escape* character. C# implements the same escape sequences used in C++ programming, as shown in Table 3-1.

If you attempt to use any other character preceded by a backslash, the compiler will issue an error that you have used an "unrecognized escape sequence."

Escape Sequence	Meaning
\a	Bell character. Beeps the computer speaker.
\b	Backspace character. Moves the caret one position to the left.
\f	Form Feed character. Moves the caret to the top of the next page on a printer. For screen output, prints the control character.
\n	Newline. Moves the caret to the next line. For screen output, moves the character to the beginning of the next line.
\r	Carriage return. Moves the caret to the beginning of the current line. For screen output, further text will overstrike and replace text on the current line.
\t	Horizontal tab. Outputs a tab character.
\v	Vertical tab. Moves the character down a predetermined number of lines. For screen output, prints the control character.
\"	Double quote character. Prints a double quotation mark. Normally, a double quotation mark ends the output string. When used with a backslash, the compiler interprets the double quotation mark as an ordinary character.
\\	Backslash character. Prints the backslash character itself.

Table 3.1   The C# Escape Sequences

Adding References to a Command Line Program

The C# assemblies are contained in a group of *dynamic link library* files with an extension of *.dll*. To use these assembly files, you must tell the compiler what files you want to access by adding a *reference* to your program. When you compile a program from the command line, the compiler automatically adds a reference to the *System.dll* library file.

Among the *System* namespace and assembly are classes and operations that you will need to write basic programs, access the console devices, create arrays, and handle exceptions.

If you do nothing but use the *System* assembly, however, you will limit the ability of your programs. To add functionality, you will need to add references to other assemblies. In the tip "Creating a Windows Program" later in this chapter you will find that the Visual Studio wizards add most of the references you will need. Adding your own in Visual Studio is an easy task.

USE IT From the command line, however, you must specifically list the references you want to add at the time you compile your program. You list the reference using the */r* compile flag.

1. First, modify the preceding code so it looks like the code shown next. The changes will make the text display in a message box rather than write to the screen. The *MessageBox* class is in the *System.Windows.Forms* namespace, so you will need to declare that you are "using System.Windows.Forms."

```
namespace nsFirst
{
    using System;
    using System.Windows.Forms;
    class clsMain
    {
        static public void Main()
        {
            MessageBox.Show ("Hello, C# World!", "Howdy",
                    MessageBoxButtons.OK, MessageBoxIcon.Exclamation);
        }
    }
}
```

2. Save the program under a different file name, such as *Msg.cs*. Compile the source code with the following command line:

```
C:>csc /r:system.windows.forms.dll msg.cs   <Enter>
```

3. Run the program, and instead of printing to the screen, you should see a Windows message box similar to the one shown next. The Windows message box is generated by a function that you can access in the *System.Windows.Forms.dll* assembly.

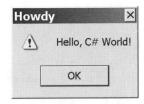

You can add multiple assemblies during the compilation by separating them with commas on the command line, but you must include the full file name for each assembly. Suppose you want to use both the Windows forms and Web services assemblies. You would use the following command line:

```
C:>csc /r:System.Windows.Forms.dll,System.Web.Services.dll msg.cs   <Enter>
```

The MSDN help file contains information about what assembly to use for a particular class. If you display the help page for the "*MessageBox* class," you see the following at the bottom of the page:

```
Requirements
Namespace: System.Windows.Forms
Platforms: Windows 97, Windows NT 4.0, Windows Millennium Edition,
          Windows 200, Windows XP
Assembly: System.Windows.Forms.dll (in System.Windows.Forms.dll)
```

The assemblies themselves are located in a subdirectory of the Windows directory. For example, if you are using Windows NT or 2000, you will find the assembly files in the Winnt\Microsoft.Net\ Framework\v1.0.2914 directory. The last directory in the path will depend upon the version you have installed.

Comparing the Results with C++

C++ programmers will see some notable differences—and some similarities—between the C# code and what they would write in a C++ program. The next tip will show a comparison for Visual Basic programmers.

For one, in C++ you normally begin a program by including either the *stdio.h* or *iostream.h* header file for a console-based program, or the *windows.h* header file for a program that uses the Windows application programming interface (API).

C#, however, does not use header files and does not have a *#include* preprocessor directive as does C++. In fact, although you will read in the MSDN documentation and other places about the C# "preprocessor," the C# compiler does not actually have a preprocessor.

USE IT To produce the console output, a C++ program would look like the following:

```
#include   <stdio.h>

void main (void)
```

```
{
    printf ("Hello, C++ World!");
}
```

Creating a Windows Program

The "Hello, World" program has been a classic example for console output since Brian Kernighan and Dennis Ritchie wrote *The C Programming Language* in 1988. It has been used to demonstrate console output in many different languages.

Command line programs using console output are useful for exploring the syntax and structure of a new language and for writing those "quick hit" programs that perform a single task that you need to use only once. As mentioned earlier in this chapter, the ultimate purpose of Visual Studio is to provide you with tools for writing Windows programs.

No equivalent "classic" program is available to demonstrate the creation of a simple Windows program—particularly a Windows program written in C#. In the last couple of tips, you improvised by accessing Windows functions from a command line program.

In this tip, you will use Visual Studio tools to create a simple Windows program that will contain a text box in which you may enter text and a couple of buttons, one to display a message box containing the text you entered and another to end the program.

1. From Visual Studio, create a new project by choosing File | New | New Project to display the New Project dialog box. You also may press CTRL-SHIFT-N to display the dialog box.

2. In the Project Type box, select Visual C# Projects, and in the Template box select Windows Application.

3. In the name field, provide a name for your project. The default provided by Visual Studio is WindowsApplication followed by a sequence number. Call this project **Form**. Make sure the Location field contains the name of the directory you want to use, and then click OK.

4. The Visual Studio Form Wizard will create the Form project and display a blank form. Depending upon how you have configured Visual Studio, your screen should look similar to Figure 3-1.

5. If the Toolbox window is not visible (by default, it should appear on the left side next to the blank form), choose View | Toolbox. (You can also display the Toolbox window by pressing CTRL-ALT-X.) Choose the Windows Forms bar in the Toolbox to display a list of the controls you can place on the form.

6. Turn off AutoHide. When designing a form, it is easier to turn off AutoHide. If you leave it on, the Toolbox window will cover part of your form when it appears, making it difficult to position your controls. When you become more experienced, you can leave AutoHide turned on and double-click the controls to add them all at once, arranging them after hiding the Toolbox window. Right click the Toolbox window title bar (the blue bar at the top of the Toolbox) and make sure the AutoHide item is not checked. You should have the "Dockable" item checked.

7. Click the TextBox item on the Toolbox to select an edit box control. Move the cursor over the form and the cursor will change to a crosshair with the icon for a text box attached.

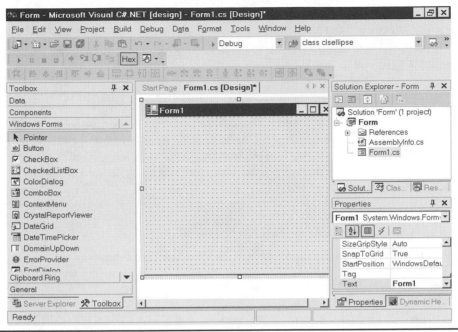

Figure 3.1   The blank Form project before you add any controls or code to the blank form. Notice the highlighted label, "Form1.cs (Design) ." This is the Design tab for the form.

8. Move the cursor to the position where you want the upper-left corner of the text box to appear (refer to the next illustration). Click and hold the left mouse button and move to the lower-right position to complete the text box. Release the mouse button and the text box will appear.

9. Use the same method to draw two buttons on the form. Select the Button item on the Toolbox and draw the buttons as shown in the following illustration. (Chapter 13 covers Windows forms projects more thoroughly. The purpose here is to get you to the point at which you can create Windows forms project in Visual Studio, so you will not need to change the button labels.)

10. Double-click the first button (the one labeled "button1") and Visual Studio will open the *Form1.cs* source code file and add a function to hold the code you will write for the button.

11. Click the Design tab for the form and double-click the second button (the one labeled "button2") to add a function for this button.

▶ **NOTE**

The default when you double-click a button is to add an event handler for the button's click event. When you want to add default event handlers for more than one control, you can select multiple controls by holding down the CTRL key and clicking each control. When you select the last control, double-click it instead of single clicking. Visual Studio will add the default event handlers for each of the controls you have selected.

12. Now add one line to the code for each function, as follows:

```
protected void button2_Click (object sender, System.EventArgs e)
{
    Application.Exit();
}


protected void button1_Click (object sender, System.EventArgs e)
{
    MessageBox.Show (this, textBox1.Text, "TextBox",
                     MessageBoxButtons.OKCancel, MessageBoxIcon.Exclamation);
}
```

13. Build and run your program. To build—or compile—the program, choose Build | Build, or press CTRL-SHIFT-B. To run the program, select Debug | Start, click the Debug toolbar button, or press the F5 key.

14. Enter some text in the text box and click the button labeled "button1." A message box containing the text you typed in the text box will appear. The message box should also have OK and Cancel buttons. Click one or the other to close the message box and repeat the process after typing some different text.

15. Click the button labeled "button2" to end the program. The event handler for this button calls the *Application* class *Exit()* method. The *Exit()* method does not actually close the application, but closes the application's message loops and forces the call to *Run()* in *Main()* to return, effectively ending the program.

Comparing the Results with Visual Basic

A simple project that Visual Basic instructors often use to demonstrate forms and controls is one that displays a digital clock on the form, ticking away the seconds while the form is displayed on the screen.

There isn't much difference between a clock program created in Visual Basic and one created in C#. You use the same methods to build the form, and the code to generate the clock display is similar.

1. Create the project using Visual C#. In the New Projects dialog box, select Visual C# Projects in the Project Types box and Windows Application in the Templates box. Name the project **Clock** and place it in the directory where you keep your C# projects.

2. Using the same techniques you used in the previous tip, add a two Label controls to Form1. Draw the labels fairly large so that they span nearly the entire form, one right above the other. The depth should be about a third of the width, but do not be too concerned about the actual size.

3. In the Properties window, select the Font property and click the button that appears in the Property field.

4. In the Font dialog box that appears, set the point size to 24 for both Label controls. The larger type size will make the text more readable.

5. Now add a Timer control to the form by double-clicking the Timer item on the Toolbox. In Visual Basic 6, the icon for the timer appeared on the form itself. In Visual Studio .NET, the Toolbar does not clutter the form with invisible controls. Instead, it places the icon for the timer in a box just below the form. It will appear this way when you prepare this same project using Visual Basic.

6. Double-click the timer icon you just added and Visual Studio will add a function, *timer1_Tick()*, to handle the timer ticks. Add a function named *SetClock()* right after *timer1_Tick()* and make the code read as follows:

```
protected void timer1_Tick (object sender, System.EventArgs e)
{
    SetClock ();
}
protected void SetClock()
{
    string str = DateTime.Now.ToString();
    int index = str.IndexOf (" ");
    label1.Text = str.Substring (index + 1);
    label2.Text = str.Substring (0, index);
}
```

7. Near the top of the *Form1.cs* file, locate the *public Form1()* function. Add the following code to this function after the call to *InitializeComponent()*.This will initialize the controls and start the timer.

```
public Form1()
{
    //
    // Required for Windows Form Designer support
    //
    InitializeComponent();
    //
    // TODO: Add any constructor code after InitializeComponent call
```

```
        //
        label1.TextAlign = ContentAlignment.MiddleCenter;
        label2.TextAlign = ContentAlignment.MiddleCenter;
        timer1.Interval = 1000;
        timer1.Start ();
        SetClock();
    }
```

8. Build the project and run the program. You should see a dialog box with a digital clock ticking off the seconds, as shown in the left image of Figure 3-2.

9. Next, close the C# project and create the same project in Visual Basic. In the New Project dialog box, select Visual Basic in the Project Types box and Windows Application in the Templates box. Again, name the project **Clock** and place it in the directory where you keep your Visual Basic projects.

10. Perform the *same* steps that you performed to create the C# project to add the Label and Timer controls to the form. Use the Properties tool window to set the *TextAlign* property to *MiddleCenter* and the font point size to 24 for both Label controls.

11. After you double-click the *timer1* control to add the function to handle the ticks, add a *SetClock()* subroutine (you called it a function in Visual C#) so the code looks like the following:

```
Protected Sub Timer1_Tick(ByVal sender As Object, ByVal e As System.EventArgs)
    SetClock()
End Sub
```

The code should be changed to this:

```
Protected Sub SetClock()
        Dim str As String
        Dim Index As Short
        str = Now.ToString()
        Index = str.IndexOf(" ")
        Label1.Text = str.Substring(Index + 1)
        label2.Text = str.Substring(0, Index)
End Sub
```

After coding the C# program, this should be almost *déjà vu* to you. The method of getting the current time is slightly different here, but the methods of extracting the time and setting the text for the Label control are identical.

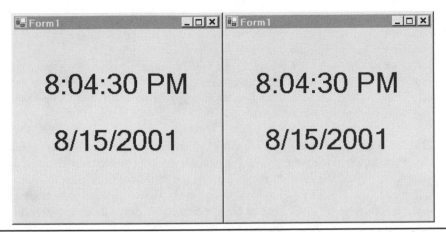

Figure 3.2   The form on the right is from a C# program, and the one on the left is from a
Visual Basic project

12. Now, near the top of the file, find the *Public Sub New()* function. Add the same code after
the *InitializeComponent()* that you added to the C# program. However, remember to remove
the semicolons at the end of each line:

```
label1.TextAlign = ContentAlignment.MiddleCenter
label2.TextAlign = ContentAlignment.MiddleCenter
timer1.Interval = 1000
timer1.Start ()
SetClock()
```

13. Build and run the project. Even experienced programmers will not be able to tell the difference
between the two forms shown in Figure 3-2.

Understanding White Space and Tokens

When you write a C# program, you use an alternating sequence of *white space* and *tokens*. White space
is any character that does not display on the screen and results only in caret movement. A token is any
of the C# operators, punctuation, or keywords, or any identifiers you use for classes, namespaces,
variables, or functions. Basically, a token is anything that is not white space.

▶ *NOTE*

*In Windows terminology, the caret is the marker on the screen that indicates the position where the
next character you type will appear. In most text editors, the caret may be a blinking vertical bar;
on the command line it is a blinking underscore character. A program may draw the caret in any
shape it needs, and may use an icon-type image to represent the caret. By contrast, the word cursor
is reserved for the symbol that marks the position of the mouse on the screen. It always is formed
using a bitmapped image.*

The basic example of white space is the space character. When you press the spacebar on your keyboard, the caret moves one space to the right, but does not display anything on the screen. Other white space characters include the tab, the carriage return, and the line feed.

C# uses white space only to separate tokens, and you can have as many white space characters—including combinations of different white space characters—as you need between tokens to make your program more readable. (A quoted string is a single token, however, and white space characters that appear within the string are part of the token.)

USE IT   The C# compiler ignores extra white space between tokens. Because the compiler looks for a semicolon to mark the end of a statement, you may write statements that extend over more than one line. In Visual Basic, for example, you use the underscore character to indicate a single statement continues to the next line. In C#, you do not need to write any such continuation character, and if you do the compiler usually will issue an error. Being able to write a single statement over more than one line helps you to keep your code neat and more readable.

As mentioned, anything that is not white space is a token. A token may be a single character such as a plus (+) sign, a word operator such as *new,* or the name of a variable or a class that you have defined in your code. Except for within a quoted string, a token cannot contain white space. If you are a C++ programmer, you know about operators that have more than one character, such as the increment operator (++). (If you do not program in C++, the increment operator and other operators will be covered in the next chapter.) You must write these characters together with no space in between. If you include a space between these characters, the compiler will interpret these particular symbols as two unary plus signs. You will not get an error, but the code will not do what you expect.

Commenting Your Code

Keeping your code neat and readable at all times is a goal in itself—like keeping your desktop and work area neat. Unless you are an inmate of the W.C. Fields School of Filing, you will spend more time looking for an item on a messy desk than you will using the item.

Keeping neat code is not always enough, however. Unless you do not plan to use your program code any longer than today, you will need to *comment* your code as well. You may have a good memory, and you may remember from day-to-day what code you wrote and what tasks that code performed. At some point, though, you will need to put your code aside and work on another project. Comments will help you, and other programmers, decipher the code and understand what function you intended the code to perform.

C# allows three methods of commenting code, including one method that marks the text so you may later extract the comments into an XML (eXtensible Markup Language) file. The XML method is discussed in the next tip, "Documenting Your Code with XML Comments."

You may use the old C style of comments, which uses the slash-asterisk sequence (/*) to mark the beginning of a comment block and asterisk-slash (*/) to mark the end of the comment block. The C compiler ignores any text or code between these markers. When you use the /* to mark the beginning of a comment, you must provide the ending marker, even if the comments extend to the end of the file. If you do not include the ending marker, the compiler will tell you that it found the end of the file without a matching */.

USE IT This C style of commenting is handy when you need to add a long comment. Typically, programmers use C-style comments to add descriptive text at the top of a source code file or at the beginning of a class or function to describe the intended purpose of the class or function, like so:

```
/*
    test.cs - This file contains test code
              Created May 19, 2001
              Last Modified June 21, 2001
              Programmer: Ada Lovelace
 */
namespace nsTest
{
/*
    class clsMain defines the entry point for the program
 */
    class clsMain
    {
/*
    Main() is the program entry point
        Parameters: none
        Returns: void
 */
        static void Main()
        {
        }
    }
}
```

C-style comments also are handy when you need to "comment out" a large block of code to prevent it from being compiled—for example, for testing purpose.

You may use the C commenting method to comment a single line or a partial line, as shown in the following:

```
int iCelsius = 5 * (iFahr - 32) / 9;   /* Calculate Celsius temperature */
```

Inside a quoted string, the C# compiler will not look for or recognize comment markers. Markers inside a string become a part of the string:

```
Console.WriteLine ("Hello, C# /* This is a comment */ World!");
```

If you included this snippet in your code, the comment would print as part of the output string:

```
Hello, C# /* This is a comment */ World!
```

You also may use the C-style comment markers inside a statement to exclude a part of the statement from the program. The following two statements are identical to the compiler because it strips the comments out when it compiles the code:

```
C /*Celsius temp */ = 5 * (F /* Fahrenheit temp */ - 32) / 9;
C = 5 * (F - 32) / 9;
```

This example is not a *good* method of commenting your code, but it often is handy for isolating portions of a statement for debugging purposes.

The second method of commenting C# code is the more modern C++ comment marker, a set of two slash marks (//). When you use the double slashes, you do not have to provide an end of comment marker. The compiler ignores the text or code from the comment marker to the end of the line. The newline character becomes the end of comment marker:

```
//  This line is a comment
This line is not a comment
```

For short comments or for comments at the end of the line, the C++ method is easier to use. You must remember to add the comment marker to each line of the comment, however.

```
//
//    test.cs - This file contains test code
//             Created May 19, 2001
//             Last Modified June 21, 2001
//             Programmer: Charles Babbage
//

int iCelsius = 5 * (iFahr - 32) / 9;   // Calculate Celsius temperature
```

Not every line needs a comment. Newcomers to programming tend to add too many or too few comments. A simple assignment statement, shown here, is self explanatory and does not need a comment:

```
iFahr = 68;       // Set the Fahrenheit temperature to 68
```

However, sometimes such comments will be useful, as in the following:

```
int nPos = 20;    // Position in the line begins at column 20
```

There are no hard-and-fast rules for determining when you need to add a comment to your code. At least in the early stages of programming, you should tend toward the "too many" end of the extreme. Six months later, when you return to work on your program or to fix a bug, it is far easier to ignore or remove a comment than it is to determine why you wrote a block of code in a certain way.

Documenting Your Code with XML Comments

Visual Studio provides a handy feature that allows you to document your C# code using XML. XML is a machine independent, standardized method of describing structured information such as the fields in a database table. It uses "tags" similar to those used in HTML, which are used for marking up Web pages.

In C#, the XML comments begin with three slash marks (///). The slash marks are not part of the XML specification, but the compiler uses them to extract the text to create a document containing the XML text. You can use XML comments to document classes and structures; members of classes such as fields, events, properties, and methods; and namespaces. You cannot use it to document individual statements in a function.

1. Open the C# Clock project that you created earlier in this chapter.

2. Move to the *SetClock()* function that you added toward the bottom of the file and open a blank line above the function definition. In the blank line, type three slash marks with no spaces between them. When you type the third slash mark, Visual Studio adds the following to the file:

```
/// <summary>
///
/// </summary>
```

3. It is your job to write the summary that describes the function. While you are typing between the *summary* tags, each time you press the ENTER key, Visual Studio will start the next line with three slash marks.

4. The XML feature also recognizes parameters to functions and will add the tags to document the types and uses of the parameters. Move to the *timer1_Tick()* function, open a blank line, and type three slashes. The following text will appear in the file:

```
/// <summary>
///
/// </summary>
/// <param name="sender"> </param>
/// <param name="e"> </param>
```

5. Once again, it is your job to add the actual documentation, but Visual Studio takes care of the mundane stuff, such as remembering and creating the proper XML tags.

Using the C# Debugger

Apart from the text editor, probably the most commonly used tool in Visual Studio is the debugger. Unless you are very good or, more likely, lucky, errors are going to creep into your program, even if they are just typing errors.

Using the debugger, you can run your program in a protected environment. You can stop and restart the program, make changes to the code, and inspect variables, memory, and CPU registers. The debugger will do almost anything except write your program for you.

The C# debugger includes menus, dialog boxes, tool windows, and toolbars. You will get to know the tool windows in a tip later in this chapter. In this tip, you will take a close look at the Debug toolbar and the Debug Location toolbar. Visual Studio .NET includes a number of changes from previous editions of Visual Studio, and the MSDN help file does not contain descriptions about these toolbars.

USE IT The Debug toolbar is shown in Figure 3-3. Some buttons may seem advanced at this point, but at some point during your debugging experience you will probably use all of them.

Originally, the Debug toolbar was huge, containing 34 buttons and some other tools. Many of those buttons simply toggled on and off the various tool windows. Microsoft has moved the buttons to toggle the tool windows into a single button at the far right of the toolbar, thus reducing the toolbar to 10 tools. Pressing the last button reveals a menu of tool windows. Table 3-2 summarizes the toolbar buttons in the order they appear on the toolbar.

The Debug Location toolbar contains only three tools, each of which displays a drop down box when you pause your program in the debugger.

The Program box displays the current program that contains the code your program is executing. A program running in the .NET Framework can execute code in more than one program, and this box is handy for determining the source of bugs.

The Thread box shows the ID for the currently executing thread. A thread is an execution point in a program, and every program has at least one thread. In a multi-threaded application, each thread essentially is a separate process running in the same program space. Each has its own stack and set of variables. The thread that was executing when you paused the program displays in this box, and you may view other threads by selecting one from the drop-down box.

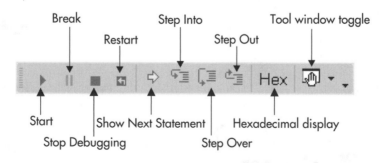

Figure 3.3   The Debug toolbar at the top contains handy tools to start and manipulate your program in the debugger. The Debug Location toolbar at the bottom comes into play when you pause your program during a debugging session.

Toolbar Button	Description
Start	Runs the program in the debugger. The program will stop at breakpoints. When a program is paused, this becomes the Continue button.
Break	Pauses the program at the current execution point. While paused, you may examine program variables, memory and CPU registers, and other environment information.
Stop Debugging	Ends the debugging session. Program variables, memory, and CPU register contents are lost.
Restart	Stops the program and restarts the debugging session in single-step mode. Use the F10 and F11 keys to execute statement, or click the Start button to put the debugger in run mode.
Show Next Statement	Moves the caret to the current statement (the current statement is the next statement that will be executed).
Step Into	Steps into a function call in the current statement, the same as pressing F11.
Step Over	Executes function calls in the current statement and returns to the current function. If you have set a breakpoint in a function, execution will pause at the breakpoint.
Step Out	Completes execution of all of the statements in the current function and displays the next statement to execute in the calling function.
Hexadecimal Display	When a program is paused, toggles the display of values in the Watch, Locals, This, and Autos tool windows between decimal and hexadecimal.
Tool window toggle	A two-part tool button. When you press the down arrow to the right of this button, Visual Studio displays a list of tool windows that you can toggle on and off. When you select a tool window, Visual Studio "remembers" the last selection and pressing the button on the left toggles on and off the remembered selection.

Table 3.2   The Debug Toolbar Buttons and Their Uses

The Stack Frame box displays the name of the method currently executing. The sequence of calls that led to the current execution point are listed in order in the drop-down box. In a program that executes other modules and assemblies, you can navigate to the calling point by selecting it in the drop-down box. System assemblies include no debugging information, but you may view an assembly listing by selecting an item in this box.

To start the debugger, open or create the project that you want to debug. Make sure you have selected the debug version of your program (select Debug from the combo box on the Standard toolbar).

Display the Debug toolbar and click the Start button. (The Standard toolbar also contains a Start button next to the combo box you used to select the Debug version of your program.) Visual Studio will compile any files that you have updated since your last compile and start the program in the debugger.

In addition to running your program in the debugger, you may attach the debugger to a process that you are running outside Visual Studio. Attaching to a process is particularly handy for programs that you did not write in Visual Studio, such as those you compiled from the command line. For command line programs, you can insert debugging information when you compile your program by specifying */debug:full* on the command line, as shown here:

```
c:>csc /debug:full MyProg.cs  <Enter>
```

To attach to a process, choose Debug | Processes to display the Processes dialog box.

From the Available Processes box, select the process you want to debug, and then click Attach. This will display another dialog box listing the program type and the name of the process you selected.

For C# and Visual Basic programs, select the Common Language Runtime and Native types (they already should be selected by default).

Click OK and then click the Close button in the Available Processes dialog box.

▶ *NOTE*

In computer jargon, a process is a program that has been loaded into the computer's memory and is running. A program refers to the source or object files that the operating system uses to create the process.

The Solution Explorer will show that you are attached to the process but do not have a solution loaded. Click Pause on the Debug toolbar and Visual Studio will display an Assembly code listing of the program at the execution point.

If you have compiled the program with debug information, you also will see the source code lines in the Assembly code listing and the name of the source code file will display in the Solution Explorer. Click the Solution Explorer entry to display the source code file.

Using the Output and Task List Windows

While you are developing and writing your programs, you will want to compile your program from time to time to catch any programming errors. When using Visual Studio, the Output and Task List windows will help you to locate and correct any errors in your code.

The Output and Task List windows normally are at the bottom of Visual Studio, just below the text editing windows. The windows may not be visible when you first open a project, but when you compile the project the windows will appear. You also may display the windows by selecting the View menu, then the Other Windows item. On the submenu, select either the Output or Task List item.

If your compile is successful, the Output window will appear and report that the build was successful. If errors occur, however, the Task List window will appear, listing the errors found during the compilation.

To demonstrate an error, open the *Clock* program you created earlier in this chapter and follow these steps.

1. Open the *Form1.cs* source code file and change the first line in the *SetClock()* function to introduce an error. The line should look like the following, omitting the *T* in *DateTime*:

   ```
   string str = Dateime.Now.ToString();
   ```

2. Build the program, and the Task List will appear as shown here. The Task List window will list the errors the compiler finds when you build a project.

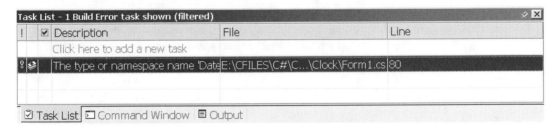

3. The error message will appear in the Description column, which probably will not be wide enough to display the entire message. Move your mouse over the line and in about a half second the entire error message will display in a pop-up window. You could adjust the width of the column, but typically the error message will be too long to display conveniently in the Task List.

4. Double-click the error message and Visual Studio will display the source line containing the error. If the error is an identifier or keyword, the item will be highlighted.

5. To get help on the error, select the line and press F1. The MSDN help file will display the page describing the error. More often than not, you will be able to figure out the error from the description without consulting the help file.

Deciphering the Task List Window

The Task List window is part of Visual Studio's project management system. In addition to displaying the build error list, the task list automatically lists sections of code that you mark with special tokens, tasks that you specifically add to the list, and shortcuts you place in a source code file.

Visual Studio editor will scan your source code looking for tokens in commented lines that indicate tasks to be entered in the list. To show the list, right-click any place on the Task List window except the title bar. Select Show Tasks from the popup menu, and then select Comment. If your program code contains any "TODO" lines, the text will appear in the task list. Typically, Visual Studio wizards add the TODO lines when you create a project. You can add to this list by adding your own TODO comments in the source code file.

You can add your own tokens to display in the list as well.

1. Choose Tools | Options.

2. In the Options dialog box, expand the Environment item and click Task List to display a list of the tokens Visual Studio editor looks for in the source code. To the right side of the dialog box is a Name field, where you may add your own tokens. Type **HACK** in the Name field, then click Add. The new token will appear in the Token List.

3. Close the Options dialog box and return to the source code file. Someplace in the file, type the following line:

```
// HACK: Need to bum the code to speed up this function
```

4. Open the Comments section of the task list as described previously. You should see the item in the list. Double-click the item and Visual Studio will move the comment into the source code file.

User tasks are not associated with any particular token. You can add a user task with any message you want. To do so, simply click the line that reads Click Here To Add A New Task, add the text you want for the task, and press ENTER. If you need to display the tasks, right-click on the Task List and select Show Tasks | User from the popup menu, or choose All to display all the tasks.

Notice the check boxes next to the user tasks in the task list. You can check off the items as you take care of the tasks without removing the item from the list. When you check the box, Visual Studio displays the associated text in strikethrough format.

Shortcuts are special bookmarks that Visual Studio adds to the task list.

1. To add a shortcut, place the caret on the line that you want to bookmark.

2. Press CTRL-K followed immediately with a CTRL-H. Or, choose Edit | Bookmarks | Add/Remove Task List Shortcut. Visual Studio adds an icon in the selection bar on the left side of the editing window.

Shortcuts also have check boxes and are displayed with strikethrough text when you check the box. You can double-click the task list item to open the source code file and move the caret to the line containing the shortcut.

Writing and Using Your Own Namespaces

Every C# program contains at least one namespace, the *global* or *unnamed* namespace (this is true of C++ programs as well). All classes that you define outside of a named namespace are in the global namespace. Class names must be unique within a namespace, including the global namespace, but classes in different namespaces may use the same name without interfering with one another.

USE IT   Creating a namespace is the same as creating a class, except you use the *namespace* keyword instead of a class name. After typing the keyword, type the name of the namespace. The namespace block begins with an open brace and ends with a closing brace:

```
//  Declare a class in global namespace
class clsClass
{
    // Methods, fields and properties go here
}


//  Declare a namespace
namespace nsName1
{
    class clsClass
    {
        // Method, field and properties go here
    }
}
```

By now, you should be aware that Visual Studio wizards that deal with C# projects are keen on namespaces. Every time you create a project using the wizards, the wizard-generated code contains at least one namespace. Namespaces help isolate your code to make sure you do not duplicate the names of classes in the system assemblies.

This book will prefix namespace names with *ns* to distinguish them from class names, which will further help to avoid duplicating names.

Using the Console Class

The C# *Console* class provides access to the console (the display and keyboard) and provides the functionality of the C and C++ standard devices *stdin*, *stdout*, and *stderr* streams. A *stream* is a sequence of data flowing from one part of your computer to another, such as from a program to the display.

The *Console* class contains mostly static members, so you never actually have to declare an instance of the class to access the methods and fields. The methods allow you to manipulate the streams so that you can redirect the input and output to other devices, such as a file. These methods will be covered in Chapter 12. For now, it is the keyboard input and screen output methods that are of interest.

Two methods write to the screen: *Write()* and *WriteLine()*. The two methods are virtually identical, except that *WriteLine()* ends the output with a carriage return/linefeed combination.

Normally you will use a string parameter to *Write()* and *WriteLine()*, as you did earlier in this chapter. The functions are "overloaded" so you may pass any of the fundamental data types as a parameter. For example, in the following snippet, *Write()* outputs the characters *4* and *2* to the screen:

```
int x = 42;
Console.Write(x);
```

For reading from the console, the *Read()* method returns one character at a time, but it does not return until the user presses the ENTER key. *Read()* stores any extra characters, including the carriage return, for successive calls to the method. *ReadLine()* returns a string to the calling function but strips the line ender from the input.

The fact that C# buffers input text leads to some curious and confusing results at times. If you want to read only the first character the user types, for example, you should call *Read()* followed by a call to *ReadLine()*, and then discard the string returned by *ReadLine()*.This will clear any remaining characters out of the input buffer and prepare for the next call to *Read()*. The following short program shows how this works:

```
/*
    read.cs. A simple command line program that reads from
    the console using Console.Read() and Console.ReadLine().

    Compile this program using the following line:
        C:>csc read.cs
 */

using System;
class clsSimple
{
    static void Main()
    {
        Console.WriteLine ("Reading just one character using the Read()" +
                            "function without clearing the buffer");
        int arg;
        Console.Write("Type one or more characters: ");
        while ((arg = Console.Read()) > 10)
        {
            if (arg == 13)
                Console.WriteLine (" <EOL>");
            else
                Console.Write (Convert.ToChar(arg));
        }
        Console.WriteLine();
        Console.WriteLine ("Now, using the Read() function and " +
                            "clearing the buffer");
        Console.Write("Type one or more characters: ");
        arg = Console.Read ();
        string str = Console.ReadLine();
        Console.WriteLine ("The character is " + Convert.ToChar(arg));
    }
}
```

The *Read()* method always leaves at least one character in the buffer, even if it is just the ENTER key—a carriage return. Following the call to *Read()* with a call to *ReadLine()* effectively clears out the buffer and prepares for the next read.

Formatting Output and Strings

Outputting text and values one at a time could lead to some long and repetitious code. Fortunately, C# provides a method for formatting output. The same formatting sequences also work for the *string* data type.

▶ *NOTE*

Although string appears to be a fundamental data type, C# actually implements the string type as a class named String. When you declare a variable of type string, you are creating an instance of the String class. Chapter 5 covers the use of the String class. You may use the same formatting for String that you use for console output by calling the Format() method.

This statement would output the word *Item* followed by a tab and then the word *Stuff*.

```
Console.WriteLine ("Item\tStuff");
```

In C and C++, you learned to format arguments as part of the string using the percent (%) character, followed by a sequence that indicates the data type, the field width, and the precision to be used in the output. C# formatting achieves the same result, but the form is considerably different.

 USE IT   To encode an argument in a C# string, type an open brace followed by the parameter number. You may provide optional formatting and width information, but you must end the sequence with a closing brace:

```
Console.WriteLine ("The answer is {0}", 42);
```

Here, the *WriteLine()* function replaces the *{0}* with the number *42* and outputs the following line:

```
The answer is 42
```

Notice that you do not need to provide the data type as you did with C and C++ formatting. The parameters—including numeric constants—are derived from the *object* class, which contains methods to convert the value to characters.

You may follow the argument number with an optional field width and formatting string in the form *{N,W:F}*, where *N* is the argument number, *W* is the field width, and *F* is the format string. You may provide an optional precision value as part of the format string.

The field width may be positive or negative. If the width is positive, the argument will display to the right of the field with preceding blanks. If the width is negative, the argument will display to the left of the field with trailing blanks.

The format character—the format *flag*—is not case sensitive. As in C and C++, the character determines how the value will be printed. Table 3-3 summarizes the format characters.

Following the format flag, you may enter an optional precision, which specifies the minimum number of digits to output. In the case of a floating value, the precision determines how many digits will print after the decimal point.

The following program, *Format.cs*, shows some of the possible combinations of the widths, flags, and precisions:

```
/*
    Format.cs. Demonstrates some of the formatting flags for writing text
               to the console.

               Compile this program with the following command line:
                   C:>csc format.cs
*/
namespace nsFormat
{
    using System;
    class clsFormat
    {
        static readonly double e = 2.71828;
        static void Main()
        {
            Console.WriteLine ("Integer dollar amount: {0,0:C}", 3);
            Console.WriteLine ("Floating dollar amount: {0,0:C}", 3.29);
            Console.WriteLine ("Integer value: {0,0:D5}", 1024);
            Console.WriteLine ("Integer value: {0,0:N5}", 1024742);

            Console.WriteLine ("Integer value: {0,0:N}", 1024742);
            Console.WriteLine ("Integer value: {0,0:N5}", 1024742);
            Console.WriteLine ("Integer value: {0,0:X}", 1024742);
            Console.WriteLine ("Floating point e: {0,0:F3}", e);
            Console.WriteLine ("Floating point e: {0,-8:F5}", e);
            Console.WriteLine ("Floating point e: {0,-8:E2}", e);
            Console.WriteLine ("Floating point e: {0,-8:E}", e);
        }
    }
}
```

Character	Description	Format
C or c	Local currency format	Writes the value using the local currency character and format.
D or d	Integer	If you supply a precision, the field will be padded with leading 0's.
E or e	Scientific	The precision sets the number of decimal places (the default is 6). At least one digit follows the decimal point.
F or f	Fixed point	The precision specifies the number of decimal places; may be 0.
G or g	General	Uses E or F formatting, whichever is more compact.
N or n	Number	Formats the number with embedded commas if the value exceeds 999. A number following this flag specifies the number of decimal places to print.
X or x	Hexadecimal	Formats a hexadecimal (base 16) number using the precision specifier.

Table 3.3   C# Output and String Formatting Flags

The output from *Format.cs* is shown here:

```
Integer dollar amount: $3.00
Floating dollar amount: $3.29
Integer value: 01024
Integer value: 1,024,742.00000
Integer value: 1,024,742.00
Integer value: 1,024,742.00000
Integer value: FA2E6
Floating point e: 2.718
Floating point e: 2.71828
Floating point e: 2.72E+000
Floating point e: 2.718280E+000
```

The format string also may be in the *##.##*, notation, similar to the PRINT USING format used in BASIC. You may combine dollar signs, commas, and periods in the string to produce a formatted output picture, as shown in the following program:

```
/*
    Picture.cs.  Uses the #, 0 and comma characters to format output
*/
using System;
```

```
class clsFormat
{
    static void Main()
    {
        Console.WriteLine ("Using the # character");
        Console.WriteLine ("\tInteger dollar amount: {0,0:$###.##}", 3);
        Console.WriteLine ("\tFloating dollar amount: {0,0:$###.##}", 3.29);
        Console.WriteLine ("\tInteger value: {0,0:###,###}",1428);
        Console.WriteLine ("\tFloating point value: {0,0:#,###.#####}",
                           1428.571);

        Console.WriteLine ("Using the $ character");
        Console.WriteLine ("\tInteger dollar amount: {0,0:$000.00}", 3);
        Console.WriteLine ("\tFloating dollar amount: {0,0:$000.00}", 3.29);
        Console.WriteLine ("Using the comma alone");
        Console.WriteLine ("\tInteger value: {0,0:000,000}", 1428);
        Console.WriteLine ("\tFloating point value: {0,0:0,000.000}",
                           1428.571);
    }
}
```

Compiling and running *Picture.cs* shows the following output:

```
Using the # character
    Integer dollar amount: $3
    Floating dollar amount: $3.29
    Integer value: 1,428
    Floating point value: 1,428.571
Using the $ character
    Integer dollar amount: $003.00
    Floating dollar amount: $003.29
Using the comma alone
    Integer value: 001,428
    Floating point value: 1,428.571
```

In the preceding formats, you may substitute *String.Format* for *Console.WriteLine* to format the text in a string. The *String.Format()* method is a static member and you may use it either when you declare the string or when you assign the string a value, as shown in the following snippet:

```
string str;
str = String.Format ("The value is {0,0:#:###.#####}", 1428.571);
// or the following declaration assignment
string str = String.Format ("The value is {0,0:#:###.#####}", 1428.571);
```

Using Preprocessor Directives

The C# language does not have a preprocessor in the sense that the C and C++ preprocessors read the source files and provide replacements before passing the code on to the compiler. The C# preprocessor uses some of the same preprocessor directives as C and C++ preprocessors, but their use is much more limited. For example, the *#define* command cannot contain a value. The following line would be valid in C and C++ but will cause a compiler error in C#:

```
#define    PI      3.14159
```

In C#, you can only define *PI*, but you cannot give it a value. You then can use the definition in a *#if* directive to determine whether the symbol has been defined, but you cannot use it to substitute text in the code. Thus, you cannot use *#define* to write macros in the C++ sense. You may use symbols in a *#define* directive only to provide for conditional compilation, similar to the *#ifdef* directive command in C++.

Table 3-4 summarizes the C# preprocessor commands.

You can pass the compiler definitions through the command line using the */define:* or */d:* flag:

```
C:>csc /define:SYMBOL program.cs   <Enter>
```

The following program, *PreProc.cs*, does not do anything, but it shows how you can use most of the preprocessor commands:

```
namespace nsPreProc
{
    using System;
    class clsMain
    {
        static public void Main()
        {
#if ALTMAIN
#warning Compiling alternate statement
            Console.WriteLine ("Using alternate Main()");
#elif OTHERMAIN
#warning Compiling other statement
            Console.WriteLine ("Using other Main()");
#else
#warning Compiling main
            Console.WriteLine ("Using Main()");
#endif
        }

#line 200
#if SHOWERROR
        int iVar;
#error This is line 23 but the error report should show line 202
#endif

    }
}
```

Preprocessor Directive	Meaning
#if, #else, #elif, #endif	Provide for conditional compilation.
#define, #undef	Define and undefine identifiers. No definition may be given to the identifer.
#warning	Issues a warning when the code is compiled.
#error	Generates an error when the code is compiled.
#line	Modifies the compiler's internal line counter.
#region, #endregion	Provides a region that may be collapsed.

Table 3.4   The C# Preprocessor Directives and Their Meanings

Compile this program from the command line several times using the following commands (notice in the last example that you may shorten */define* to */d*):

```
C:>csc PreProc.cs  <Enter>
C:>csc /define:ALTMAIN PreProc.cs  <Enter>
C:>csc /define:OTHERMAIN PreProc.cs  <Enter>
C:>csc /define:SHOWERROR PreProc.cs  <Enter>
C:>csc /d:OTHERMAIN,SYMBOL PreProc.cs  <Enter>
```

You may use the NOT operator (*!*) to reverse the sense of the *#if* test. Writing *#if !SYMBOL* would be true if *SYMBOL* is not defined. In addition, you may test for multiple symbols by combining the test in a set of parentheses using the logical operators AND (*&&*) and OR (*||*). The following test is true if *SYMBOL1* is defined and *SYMBOL2* is not defined:

```
#if (SYMBOL1 && !SYMBOL2)
```

The *#region* and *#endregion* are not preprocessor directives. Rather, Visual Studio editor uses these directives to define a portion of text that you may "collapse," thus hiding the lines of code. These directives are useful only when developing programs using Visual Studio.

USE IT   Here's how you can show how collapsing text works.

1. Start Visual Studio and open the C# *Clock* project.
2. Add *#region* in front of the *Form1()* constructor function as shown in the following:

```
#region Form1 constructor
        public Form1()
        {
            //
            // Required for Windows Form Designer support
            //
            InitializeComponent();
```

```
              //
              // TODO: Add any constructor code after InitializeComponent call
              //
              label1.TextAlign = ContentAlignment.MiddleCenter;
              timer1.Interval = 1000;
              timer1.Start ();
              SetClock();
          }
      #endregion
```

3. When you define the region, notice that the editor places a minus (−) symbol in a small box in the left margin next to the *#region* directive. You can click this symbol and the region will collapse into one line, with a box displaying the text "Form1 constructor". The minus symbol changes to a plus (+) symbol, indicating the text is collapsed. If you let the mouse hover over this line, the text of the constructor will appear in a tool tip.

Visual Studio uses the *#region* directive to hide the *InitializeComponent( )* function when it creates a Windows application project. Visual Studio and its wizards maintain *InitializeComponent( ),* and you should not add any code to this function, so usually it makes no difference if the function is hidden. Should you need to examine the code in *InitializeComponent( ),* just expand the region, or let the mouse hover over the collapsed region.

You need to remember a couple of rules when using the *#region* directive. First, you must end a region with the *#endregion* directive. Second, you cannot overlap regions and code within *#if* and *#endif* directives. If you have a *#if* directive inside a region, the *#endif* directive must be within the region. Similarly, if you have a *#region* directive within a *#if* block, the *#endregion* must be within the block.

CHAPTER 4

Laying a C# Foundation

TIPS IN THIS CHAPTER

earning any new language always involves understanding the fundamentals of the language. Whether you are new to programming or have experience in one or more other languages, you need to understand how the new language uses variables and how to put together the lines of code—the statements—that make a program work.

As a language, C# has been described variously as "easy to learn" and "simple" compared with other languages. Comments such as these, however, generally come from programmers. The truth is, if C# is your first programming language, it is not any easier to learn than C, C++, or Visual Basic. You still need to figure out how to use basic data types, how to apply operators, and how to put together basic programming elements. It's kind of like learning to drive a car—you need to learn the basics, such as how to apply the brakes, how to steer the car, and how to make turns, whether the car has an automatic or a manual transmission, and no matter what model of car you are learning to drive.

If you already program in C++ or Visual Basic, the learning curve becomes shorter, of course. Many of the concepts and structures of C++ and Visual Basic are included in C#. But C# is a good first language, and in many ways, C# is better as a first language because C# is less flexible than C++. That means that once you learn how to use object-oriented programming techniques in C#, how to define classes, and how to write functions or subroutines, you'll find it easier to apply those concepts to C++ than it would be the other way around.

In Chapter 3, you learned how to put together basic programs in C#, and you compared them with similar programs in C++ and Visual Basic. In this chapter, you will learn about the fundamental data types, and how to write expressions and statements and apply the C# operators. You will use this knowledge to build loops and program control statements.

Fundamental Data Types

A *variable* is a name, or identifier, that you use to label a memory location where your program stores a value. C# is a *strongly typed* language, which means that you must declare a data type for every variable that you use in your program. The compiler uses the data type to determine how much storage to set aside for each variable.

The C# language defines three types of variables: value types, reference types, and pointer types. Visual C# stores the values for each variable type differently and performs operations on the variable types very differently.

The C# value types include the simple data types—the integral, floating point, and decimal types summarized in Table 4-1—along with the structure type (*struct*) and the enumerated type (*enum*).

Value Type	Size in Bytes	Meaning
byte	1	Unsigned byte. May be zero (0) or any positive value up to 255. Use this data type to hold character values in the ASCII character set.
sbyte	1	Signed byte. May be any value from −128 to 127.
bool	1	Used to hold the Boolean values *true* (1) and *false* (0).

Table 4.1   The Simple Value Types Defined by C#

Value Type	Size in Bytes	Meaning
char	2	Unicode character. By default, C# uses 16-bit Unicode encoding for individual characters and strings.
short	2	Signed short value. May hold any number from –32,768 to 32,767.
ushort	2	Unsigned short value. May be zero or any positive value to 65,537.
int	4	The basic *integral* data type. Used to hold positive or negative whole numbers (numbers without a decimal point). Values range from –2,147,483,648 to 2,147,483,647.
uint	4	Unsigned integer. May be zero or any positive value to 4,294,967,295.
float	4	Floating point number (a number that contains a decimal point).
long	8	Signed large integer.
ulong	8	Unsigned large integer.
double	8	Double-precision floating point number.
decimal	16	Fixed-precision floating point value typically used for calculations involving money.

Table 4.1   The Simple Value Types Defined by C# *(continued)*

C#'s data-typing mechanism is basically the same as that used in C, C++, and Visual Basic, except that C# is much more restrictive than these other languages. Visual Basic programmers, however, may object to this generalization by saying that you can use a variable without declaring a data type. When you use a variable in Visual Basic without declaring it, the compiler actually casts the variable to a *Variant* data type. The *Variant* type uses 16 bytes, and thus it is large enough to hold a value of any of the simple data types. In addition, C# is a *type-safe* language, which means that the compiler guarantees that a variable of a particular data type will always hold a value of that data type. For example, you cannot assign a floating point value to an integral variable without specifically *casting* the value to the integral data type. To assign a floating point value to an integral variable, you run the risk of losing *precision*, and the compiler will issue an error. By specifically casting a value of one type to another type, you tell the compiler that you intend to perform the assignment. In such an assignment, the cast is *explicit*, as shown in the following snippet:

```
int x;
float y = 8.3;
x = (int) y;
```

Here, *y* is a floating point type and contains a higher precision than the integral type. When you make such an explicit cast, the program will strip off the part of the number that follows the decimal point and assign just the whole number part to the integral variable. The cast tells the compiler that you want to do this, so it allows the operation.

You can, however, go the other way in most instances. For example, you can assign an integral data type to a floating point variable so long as the assignment will not cause a loss of precision. For example, you can assign an *int* value to a *float* variable and the compiler will perform the cast automatically. The cast in this case is *implicit*. Notice in Table 4-1 that C# stores a *long* value in 8 bytes and a *float* type in 4 bytes. If you attempt to assign a *long* value to a *float* variable, you will lose precision and the compiler will issue an error message.

The reference types include those variables that you declare to hold *objects*—instances of a class, an array, or a delegate. Simply declaring a reference type variable does not allocate storage for the object. Rather, the declaration sets aside memory to hold a *reference* to an object. The value stored in the reference variable essentially is the address of the location of the actual object. In C and C++, that is a *pointer*, but C# makes this fact invisible to the programmer.

When you create objects using reference-type variables, the Common Language Runtime (CLR) manages the objects. You cannot access the object directly; you must use the reference variable to access or modify object values or to execute object functions. When the CLR determines that your program no longer can access the referenced object, it will delete the object from memory. You cannot delete the object directly, but you can write a destructor function to free any resources the object used.

The C# pointer types are the same as the C and C++ pointers, and C# makes no attempt to mask them as reference types. Nor does the CLR manage these types. Pointer types allow you to violate the type-safety of C#, so you may use pointer types only in code that you mark as *unsafe*.

Variable Categories

Not all variables are created equal. A variable will have a specific lifetime and access, depending upon how, where, and with which keywords you declare it. The lifetime and access determine what the *C# Language Reference* calls the variable *category*. In C and C++ terms, the category is roughly equivalent to the storage class.

In addition to the three variable types, C# defines seven variable categories that are summarized in Table 4-2. In the table, the category determines the *scope* of a variable and how you may use the variable.

Category	Example	Usage
static variables	*ClassName.VariableName*	All instances of an object containing a static variable share the same value. Changing the value of one changes the value for all instances of the object. To access a static variable in another class, you must specify the class name.
instance variables	*InstanceName.VariableName*	Your program creates instance variables when you create an object from the definition using the *new* operator. To access an instance variable, you must specify the instance name (the name of the variable you declared to identify the object).

Table 4.2   Categories of Variables Defined in C#

Category	Example	Usage
array elements	*ArrayName*[index]	You create array elements by creating the array and specifying the number of elements. You must use the zero-based index inside square brackets to access array elements.

reference parameters	*FuncName* (ref Type *VarName*)
	{
	}
		You create a reference parameter using the *ref* keyword in a function parameter list. Modifying a reference parameter modifies the original value. Note that this is *not* the same as a reference-type variable. Reference parameters exist only in the function in which they are used as parameters.

output parameters	*FuncName* (type out *VarName*)
	{
	}
		Create output parameter by using the *out* keyword in the parameter list. Similar to reference parameters, except the definite assignment rules are different.

value parameters	FuncName (type *VarName*)
	{
	}
		Any variables in a parameter list that do not contain the *out* or *ref* keyword are value parameters. Value parameters exist only in the function in which you declare them as parameters.

local variables	*FuncName* ()
	{
	   type *VarName*;
	}
		You declare these variables in a function or in a block, in a *for* statement or a *switch* statement. Local variables exist only in the block or statement in which you declare them.

Table 4.2   Categories of Variables Defined in C# *(continued)*

The category of a variable defines how and when the variable gets created and destroyed when you run a C# program, and it defines the range of the statements in a program that may access the variable.

Examining C# Operators

Even in the simplest programs that use variables, you will use *operators* to perform actions on the values the variables contain. The word "operator" is used in the same way in programming as it is in mathematics: it is a symbol or word that indicates an action to perform on one or more values. The values are the *operands* for the operator.

The simple act of assigning a value to a variable involves an operator—the *assignment* operator, or equals sign. The operand on the left side of the equals sign must be a variable and is called the *lvalue* of the assignment operation (*lvalue* gets its name from the fact that it is on the *l*eft side of the equals sign). On the right side of the assignment operator, you must have a value or an expression that equates to a single value. This may be a number, another variable, or a complex equation. A C# program fully evaluates the right side of the assignment operation before performing the operation. Although you will not see the word often, the value on the right side of the equals sign is the *rvalue*.

All operators require at least one operand. Operators that require only one operand are called *unary* operators (sometimes called *monadic* operators). Those that require two operands are *binary* or *dyadic* operators. C# contains only one *ternary* operator, the *conditional* operator, which requires three operands.

Operators also have precedence to insure that a program will evaluate an expression in a consistent and orderly fashion. For example, a program must resolve a member field before it can apply any other operators. Thus, the *member of* operator has a very high precedence. Many operators have equal precedence, in which case the compiler will apply them from left to right. Assignment operators are applied from right to left, however, which is logical, because a program must evaluate the *rvalue* in an assignment before applying it to the *lvalue*.

Table 4-3 summarizes the C# operators according to precedence.

Operator	Precedence	Category	Meaning	Example
.	1	Primary	Member of	*object.member_name*
[]	1	Primary	Subscript	*array[element]*
()	1	Primary	Function call	*FunctionName (arguments)*
()	1	Primary	Subexpression	*(Expression)*
new	1	Primary	Allocate memory	*new type*
++	1	Primary	Postfix increment	*variable++*
--	1	Primary	Postfix decrement	*variable--*
typeof	1	Primary	Type retrieval	*typeof(object type)*
sizeof	1	Primary	Size of type	*sizeof(object type)*
checked	1	Primary	Range checking	*checked (expression)*
unchecked	1	Primary	Range checking	*unchecked (expression)*
!	2	Unary	Logical not	*!variable*
++	2	Unary	Prefix increment	*++variable*
--	2	Unary	Prefix decrement	*--variable*
~	2	Unary	Ones complement	*~variable*
+	2	Unary	Unary plus	*+42 or +variable*
−	2	Unary	Unary minus	*−42 or −variable*
()	2	Unary	Cast	*(type) variable*

Table 4.3　The C# Operators Listed in Order of Precedence

Operator	Precedence	Category	Meaning	Example
*	3	Multiplicative	Multiply	*expression * expression*
/	3	Multiplicative	Divide	*expression / expression*
%	3	Multiplicative	Modulo	*expression % expression*
+	4	Additive	Addition	*expression + expression*
−	4	Additive	Subtraction	*expression−expression*
<<	5	Shift	Shift left	*a << b*
>>	5	Shift	Shift right	*a >> b*
<	6	Relational	Less than	*a < b*
>	6	Relational	Greater than	*a > b*
<=	6	Relational	Less than or equal to	*a <= b*
>=	6	Relational	Greater than or equal to	*a >= b*
is	6	Relational	Compatibility	*expression is object type*
==	7	Equality	Equality	*a == b*
!=	7	Equality	Inequality	*a != b*
&	8	Logical	Bitwise AND	*a & b*
|	9	Logical	Bitwise OR	*a | b*
^	10	Logical	Bitwise XOR	*a ^ b*
&&	11	Conditional	Conditional AND	*expression && expression*
||	12	Conditional	Conditional OR	*expression || expression*
? :	13	Conditional	Conditional	*x = a ? b : c*

Table 4.3   The C# Operators Listed in Order of Precedence *(continued)*

Operator	Precedence	Category	Meaning	Example

=
 *=
 /=
 %=
 +=
 −=
 <<=
 >>=
 &=
 ^=
 |=
	14	Assignment	Assignment	x = expression;
				 x += expression;
				 x |= expression;
				 x &= expression;

Table 4.3   The C# Operators Listed in Order of Precedence *(continued)*

The C# compiler normally ignores extra white space. However, you need to remember that for an operator that is made up from more than one symbol—such as the increment, decrement, and the shift operators—you must write the symbols with no space in between the symbols. If you put a space between the symbols, the compiler will assume two operators instead of one. In most cases, the compiler will issue an error; in some cases, however, such a mistake will not cause an error, but the result will not be what you expect.

In the following statement, for example, the increment operator steps up the value of *var* by one before assigning its value to *y*, but a space has been added between the two plus symbols:

```
int var = 0;
// Statements;
int y = + +var;
```

This is a perfectly valid statement in C#, and the compiler will not so much as issue a warning. It will apply the unary plus operator to *var* twice, resulting in no change to the variable's value. The same applies the prefix decrement operator. If the space appears between the symbols in C#, the compiler will apply the unary minus operator twice, resulting in no change to the variable's value.

Written as postfix operators (after the operand), the increment and decrement operators will cause an error if you put a space between the symbols. This is because the unary plus and minus operators require an operand on the right.

C++ programmers probably have run across this at some time, but Visual Basic programmers should be wary until they get used to working with operators formed with multiple symbols. Errors such as this are insidious and difficult to find. You want to use extra white space to make your code more readable, sometimes doing so can be dangerous in C#.

Understanding Value Types

If there is any such thing as an "ordinary" type variable, the C# value-type variable would be it. A value-type variable stores its value directly in the memory location identified by the variable name.

When you declare a value-type variable and assign it a data type, the variable can hold only a value of the data type. So, for example, a variable of type *int* can contain only an *int* type value. In addition, when you assign a value to a value-type variable, C# makes a copy of that value and places it in the memory location identified by the variable.

USE IT The following snippet assigns a value to one variable, and then assigns that variable to another:

```
int x;
int y = 42;
x = y;
```

In this case, when you assign *y* to *x*, you make a copy of the value of *y*, 42, and place it in *x*. If you later change the value of *y*, you do not affect the value of *x*. This may seem obvious, especially to programmers, but it is not necessarily the case with reference-type variables.

In C#'s unified type system, every type—even the simple types—is derived directly or indirectly from the *object* class, and you may treat simple data types and value-type variables as objects. You may use methods in the *object* class as instance members of the value. In the following statements, you first assign the string *42* to *str* and then the value *65* to *x*:

```
object o = 42;
string str = o.ToString();
o = 65;
int x = (int) o;
```

These are examples of *boxing*, which allows a program to treat any value or value-type variable as an object. You may create an instance of *object* and assign it a value of one of the simple data types. A reverse process, *unboxing*, retrieves the simple data type from the *object* instance. Boxing and unboxing will be covered later in this chapter in "Boxing and Unboxing."

Understanding References

The word *reference* has a dual meaning in C#, and it is easy to get confused. For example, the reference parameter *category* back in Table 4-2 is not the same as a reference-*type* variable. References indicate that you are using an *address* for a variable or object rather than the variable or object itself. That is, you *refer* to the variable or object indirectly. The difference is in how your program uses the reference.

When you declare a reference-type variable, you set aside enough memory to hold an address. To create the object and assign the address to the variable, you use the *new* operator, as shown in the following snippet:

```
// Declare a reference-type variable
clsClassName var;
// Create the object itself and assign the address to the reference variable
var = new clsClassName ();
```

In the second statement, when you use the *new* operator to create the object, C# sets aside enough memory in the heap to hold an instance of *clsClassName*, and then it assigns the address in the heap to the reference-type variable. Reference-type variables, then, refer to objects that you create on the heap.

A reference parameter, on the other hand, has nothing to do with the heap. When you pass a value as a reference parameter, you are passing the address of an object, regardless of where your program stores the object. If you pass a reference-type variable as a reference parameter, your program makes a *copy* of the address, just as it makes a copy of any value-type variable, and you may change the contents of the parameter without changing or destroying the original object.

USE IT The following program, *Refs.cs*, shows that a reference-type variable really is nothing more than a value-type variable that contains a reference. You first pass a reference-type variable to a parameter normally. Then you pass the reference-type variable as a reference parameter.

```
/*

    Refs.cs -- demonstrates that reference-type variable actually is a
               value-type variable that contains a reference. Shows the
               difference between a reference-type variable and a
               reference parameter.


            Compile this program with the following command line:
                    csc refs.cs
 */


namespace nsReferences
{
    using System;
    class clsMain
    {

        static void Main ()
          {
// Create an instance of clsFirst
            clsFirst first = new clsFirst (21);
// Show the value for first.Variable before doing anything
                Console.WriteLine ("Before function call, first.Variable = "
                                   + first.Variable);
// Pass first to the function that does use a reference value as a parameter
                ShowValue (first);
```

```
            Console.WriteLine ("After function call, first.Variable = "
                        + first.Variable);
// The original value of first.Variable should not change, although
// you created a new instance of clsFirst in the function. Changing the
// value of a reference-type variable did not affect the original object.

// Now do the same thing except pass it to a function that uses a
// reference parameter.
            Console.WriteLine ("\n\nBefore function call, first.Variable = "
                        + first.Variable);
            ShowReference (ref first);
            Console.WriteLine ("After function call, first.Variable = "
                        + first.Variable);
// The original variable should change because you stored a new reference
// value in the original variable.
        }

        static public void ShowValue (clsFirst var)
        {
            Console.WriteLine ("In function, var.Variable = " + var.Variable);
            var = new clsFirst (42);
            Console.WriteLine ("New value for var.Variable = "
                        + var.Variable);
        }
        static public void ShowReference (ref clsFirst var)
        {
            Console.WriteLine ("In function, var.Variable = " + var.Variable);
            var = new clsFirst (42);
            Console.WriteLine ("New value for var.Variable = "
                        + var.Variable);
        }
    }

    class clsFirst
    {
        public clsFirst (int var)
        {
            m_Var = var;
        }
        public int Variable
        {
            get
            {
```

```
            return (m_Var);
        }
        set
        {
            m_Var = value;
        }
    }
    private int m_Var;
}
}
```

The output from *Refs.cs* shows that although you change the contents of the value-type parameter, the contents of the original variable remain unchanged. When you pass a reference-type variable, changing the contents also changes the contents of the original variable:

```
Before function call, first.Variable = 21
In function, var.Variable = 21
The new value for var.Variable = 42
After function call, first.Variable = 21

Before function call, first.Variable = 21
In function, var.Variable = 21
The new value for var.Variable = 42
After function call, first.Variable = 42
```

Unlike value-type variables, for which each variable holds a copy of a value, reference-type variables can reference the same object. Each reference-type variable holds a copy of the *reference*, but that reference may be the same for more than one variable. The following program, *Refs1.cs*, uses two references for the same object. When you change the object for one, you also change the object for the other:

```
/*
    Refs1.cs - Shows that two reference-type variables may refer (or point)
               to the same object. Changing the object using one variable
               changes the object for the other variable.

           Compile this program with the following command line:
               csc refs1.cs
 */
namespace nsReference
{
    using System;
    class clsMain
```

```
    {
        static public void Main ()
        {
            clsClass first = new clsClass (42);
            clsClass second = first;
            second.m_Var /= 2;
            Console.WriteLine ("first.m_Var = " + first.m_Var);
        }
    }
    class clsClass
    {
        public clsClass (int var)
        {
            m_Var = var;
        }
        public int m_Var;
    }
}
```

In this code, both *first* and *second* reference the same object: an instance of class *clsClass*. When you modify the field *m_Var* in *second*, you also change *m_Var* in *first*.

Writing Expressions

In C#, an *expression* is any combination of identifiers, values, and operators that your program can evaluate to produce a result. An expression may be as simple as a single number or a string, or it may be a complex mathematical equation.

To write an expression, you must use at least one variable or a constant value. If you use more than one value or variable, you must combine them with an operator to tell the compiler what action to perform on the values or variables.

C# uses the same syntax that you learned in math classes for writing expressions. Generally, when using binary operators you write the first operand, the operator, and then the second operand. There are no *implied* operations in programming; you must include the operator. In math class, you learned that you could multiply variable *a* times variable *b* by writing *ab*, which uses an implied operator. In programming, you must write the multiplication operator between the operands, like so: *a* * *b*.

A C# program evaluates an expression using the *precedence* of the operators. The multiplication and division operators, for example, are applied first, and then any addition or subtraction are accomplished.

The left-to-right order of evaluating expressions means that the order in which you write the operands may make a difference in the result, particularly when using integers. For example, to convert a Fahrenheit temperature to Celsius, you first apply a constant, nine-fifths, to the temperature, and then add 32. Mathematically, the following two statements are the same:

```
int Fahr = 9 / 5 * Celsius + 32;
int Fahr = 9 * Celsius / 5 + 32;
```

In programming, however, multiplication and division have the same precedence, so in the first statement your program first evaluates *9/5*, giving an integer value of *1*. Then it multiplies that value by *Celsius* and finally adds 32 to the result. For a Celsius temperature of 20, this would yield a result of 52, quite different from the correct value of 68.

In the second statement, your program first multiplies *9* by *Celsius*, giving an integer value of *180*. Then the program divides that value by *5* and adds *32*, giving the correct value of 68. Particularly when using integer arithmetic, you need to be aware that the order of the expression and how you write the expression will affect the result.

USE IT   You may change the order of the expression by writing a subexpression enclosed in parentheses. Referring back to Table 4-3, you can see that parentheses used to group a subexpression has the highest precedence, so any operations in parentheses will be evaluated first.

Using the temperature example, to convert back from Fahrenheit to Celsius, you need to subtract 32 from the Fahrenheit temperature before applying the constant five-ninths. To properly evaluate the expression, you must write the subtraction operation inside a set of parentheses:

```
int Celsius = 5 * (Fahr - 32) / 9;
```

You may write expressions as arguments to a function call. For example, if you had a temperature in Fahrenheit and you wanted to call a function that needs a Celsius temperature, you could write the conversion equation as an argument, as in the following:

```
int Fahr = 68
Func (5 * (Fahr - 32) / 9);
```

Your program would evaluate the expression fully and pass the function a single value, the Celsius equivalent of the Fahrenheit temperature.

Writing Statements

A *statement* is the smallest unit of execution in a programming language. Expressions may be evaluated, passed as arguments, and used in larger expressions, but they do not execute. Execution requires a statement.

Unlike C and C++, C# does not let you ignore the result obtained from an expression. Instead, you must use the result in some way in a statement, such as an assignment or a function call. C and C++, on the other hand, allow you to ignore the result of an expression because, in the past, programs often were used with Assembly code, and programmers used expressions to set the flags in the central processor before calling an Assembly routine. C#, of course, is not designed to be used with Assembly code, and the compiler assumes that you should do something with an expression.

Statements in C# may be *simple* or *compound*. A simple statement in C# always ends with a semicolon (;). A compound statement encloses zero or more simple statements inside a set of curly braces: {and}. Compound statements often are used with loop and conditional expressions. For the purposes of discussion, a *statement* is a simple statement.

When you write a statement in C#, it continues until you end it with a semicolon, even if the statement extends over several lines. You do not need to use a "continuation" symbol, such as the underscore character in Visual Basic, at the end of each line of a single statement over several lines.

USE IT   The C# compiler ignores line ending characters, and the fact that a statement ends with a semicolon lets you write more than one statement on a single line. C and C++ programmers need to be aware that C# does not contain a comma operator that they might have used to write multiple statements on one line. For example, when incrementing a couple of variables, a line such as the following is common in C and C++:

```
++x, ++y;
```

This line, however, will cause a syntax error in C#. To write the line in C#, you would use a semicolon in place of the comma:

```
++x; ++y;
```

This makes the two increment operations distinct statements, and is what the C# compiler is expecting.

In C and C++, the comma may be an operator, as in the preceding snippet, or simply a separator used to separate parameters in a function declaration, a function call, or in parameter declarations. C and C++ guarantee that the statements on either side of a comma operator will be evaluated left to right. In C#, the comma is only a separator, with no guarantee of the order of evaluation.

Using Managed Code

The C# compiler creates programs using *managed code*. It does not generate code that is native to a particular computer and can run, for example, only on computers that use Intel processors. Instead, the compiler generates code using an *intermediate* language.

When you run a program compiled using the C# compiler, you load the intermediate code into memory. The CLR takes care of translating the code to the proper instructions for the computer. The combination of .NET Frameworks and .NET Runtime is not unlike the Java Frameworks and Java Runtime.

If you think this is similar to the pseudocode (P-code) or interpreted languages from days of yore, you are correct. Microsoft is betting that modern computers are fast enough to overcome the disadvantages that plagued such systems in the past. Java has proven that, for some applications at least, the concept of intermediate code is sound if the computer is fast enough or speed is not a major consideration, such as over an Internet connection. The downside is that the runtime environment robs you of some of the advantages that you paid for when you bought a faster computer.

Using the intermediate language approach does have some advantages, however. One of them is that you can write and compile a program that, theoretically, will run on computers using processors other than

Intel, or on other operating systems that support the .NET environment. Using an intermediate language, C# is able to provide type-safe code and code that may be used by programs written in languages other than C#.

Unlike C and C++, C# does not let you tinker with the heap memory. Instead, the CLR manages the heap memory. When you create an object using the *new* keyword, the request gets passed on to the CLR.

Using managed code, you do not need to clean up the heap memory as you do in C and C++. When the CLR determines that the code in a program no longer can access an object on the heap, it will destroy the object, thus freeing the memory. This can take some time, however, and objects may persist for some time between the point where they go out of scope and the time the CLR destroys them. C# does implement *destructors*, special functions that execute automatically when the runtime code destroys an object. Traditionally, programmers have written their cleanup code as destructors. However, you still must wait until the CLR destroys an object before the destructor executes.

USE IT   Having an object languish beyond its intended lifetime is not always a good thing, especially if the object uses system resources or devices that might be needed by other parts of your code or by other programs.

For example, from the beginning of Windows programming, it has been common practice to destroy graphics device interface (GDI) objects such as pens, fonts, and brushes when you no longer need them. Originally, the resources for these objects were limited, and if you failed to delete the objects, they would persist even after your program ended. Since Windows 95, however, the operating system removed these objects when your program ended. Still, a running program that does not clean up after itself can consume a lot of resources, and it still is common practice to free up resources when you are through using them.

In C#, most of the classes that implement and use system resources also implement the CLR *IDisposable* interface and provide a *Dispose()* method that you may call to free the resources when you are finished using them. The following code snippet, for example, creates an owner-draw list box that displays a list of fonts, including some text in the list box, as shown in Figure 4-1.

A default Windows installation may have only a few fonts installed, and letting the resources linger would not be a serious problem. However, the list box creates a new font each time it needs

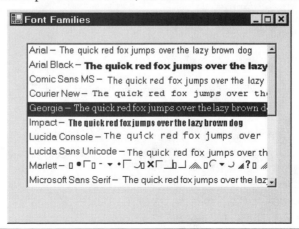

Figure 4.1   The Font Families form project creates a new font object each time it draws an item in the list box

to redraw a line, and scrolling through the list several times could leave a number of unused *Font* objects in memory. Also, a typical Windows installation probably has a word processing program or other application that adds to the system's font list, further compounding the problem.

```csharp
FontFamily [] fonts;
public Form1()
{
    //
    // Required for Windows Form Designer support
    //
    InitializeComponent();
    //
    // TODO: Add any constructor code after InitializeComponent call
    //
    fonts = FontFamily.Families;
    foreach (FontFamily font in fonts)
        listBox1.Items.Add ("");
}
private void listBox1_OnDrawItem(object sender,
                                 System.Windows.Forms.DrawItemEventArgs e)
{
    Rectangle rc = e.Bounds;
    Font fntSample = new Font (fonts[e.Index], 8, GraphicsUnit.Point);
    Brush brush;
    string str = fonts[e.Index].Name + " -- ";
    if (listBox1.GetSelected (e.Index))
    {
        e.Graphics.FillRectangle (Brushes.DarkBlue, rc);
        e.DrawFocusRectangle ();
        brush = Brushes.White;
    }
    else
    {
        e.Graphics.FillRectangle (Brushes.White, rc);
        brush = Brushes.Black;
    }
    e.Graphics.DrawString (str, listBox1.Font, brush, rc);
    StringFormat format = new StringFormat (StringFormatFlags.LineLimit);
    SizeF size = e.Graphics.MeasureString (str, listBox1.Font);
    str = "The quick red fox jumps over the lazy brown dog";
    rc = new Rectangle (rc.Left + (int) (size.Width + .5),
        rc.Top, rc.Width, rc.Height);
    e.Graphics.DrawString (str, fntSample, brush, rc, format);
    fntSample.Dispose();
}
```

After the list box drawing code displays the font name and the sample text, it no longer needs the font, so it calls the *Font* object's *Dispose()* method.

By default, forms that you use in Windows applications implement *IDisposable*, and if your form uses any system resources that you do not implement through the Properties tool window, you should remove them in the form's *Dispose()* method.

You may implement the *IDisposable* interface in classes that you declare. An *interface* in C# is similar to a class that contains only abstract methods. An interface defines methods but does not implement any code. *IDisposable* defines only a single method, *Dispose()*, and any class that derives from *IDisposable* must implement a method override for *Dispose()*, as shown in the following snippet:

```
class clsClass : IDisposable
{
    public void Dispose()
    {
        // Free up any system resources here.
    }
    // Add other methods, fields and properties.
}
```

Unlike a class, all members of an interface are *public* by default, and the compiler will issue an error if you specify any other access keyword for an interface member. To implement the *Dispose()* method, you must specify the *public* keyword.

To use another access level, you may implement your own *Dispose()* method without deriving a class from *IDisposable*. The advantage of using an interface, however, is that a program can use the *is* operator to determine whether a class supports a method implemented through an interface.

Using Logical Operators

The C# logical operators combine the bits in one operand with the corresponding bits in the second operand and then return the result. The operators are the same as the C and C++ *bitwise* operators, and they perform in the same way as the Visual Basic *And*, *Or*, and *Xor* operators.

The operators combine bit 0 in one operand with bit 0 in the other operand, then bits 1, and then other bits until all of the bits have been combined according to the logical operation. Both operands must be an integral data type, such as a *byte*, *char*, *short*, *int*, or *long*. You cannot use *float*, *double*, or *decimal* operands with the bitwise operators. In addition, the bitwise operators promote their operands to type *int* and always return an *int* value regardless of the actual data type of the operands. To assign the result of a bitwise operation to a variable with a precision less than *int*, you will need to cast the result, as in the following snippet:

```
char lower = 'a';
char upper = (char) (lower ^ 0x20);
```

Table 4-4 is a truth table showing the results of the operations on individual bits in the two operands.

Bit 1	Bit2	Bit1 & Bit2	Bit1 | Bit2	Bit1 ^ Bit2
1	1	1	1	0
1	0	0	1	1
0	1	0	1	1
0	0	0	0	0

Table 4.4   Truth Table for the C# Bitwise Operators

USE IT   In an *AND* operation, the resulting bit is 1 only if the corresponding bit in both operands
is 1. In an *OR* operation, the result is 1 if one or both corresponding bits is 1. In an *XOR*
operation, the result is 1 if one, and only one, of the corresponding bits is 1.

The following program listing, *Bitwise.cs*, shows the result of each operation on two values:

```
//
//  Bitwise.cs -Shows the effect of bitwise operators.
//
//  Compile this program with the /unsafe compiler flag:
//          C:>csc /unsafe Bitwise.cs
//
namespace nsBitwise
{
    using System;
    class clsMain
    {
        static public void Main ()
        {
            ushort x = 15542;
            ushort y = 21845;
            Console.Write ("x = {0} = ", x);
            ShowBits (x);
            Console.Write ("\ny = {0} = ", y);
            ShowBits (y);
            ushort result = (ushort) (x & y);
            Console.Write ("\nx & y    = ");
            ShowBits (result);
            Console.WriteLine (" = " + result);

            Console.Write ("\nx = {0} = ", x);
            ShowBits (x);
            Console.Write ("\ny = {0} = ", y);
            ShowBits (y);
```

```
        result = (ushort) (x | y);
        Console.Write ("\nx | y     = ");
        ShowBits (result);
        Console.WriteLine (" = " + result);

        Console.Write ("\nx = {0} = ", x);
        ShowBits (x);
        Console.Write ("\ny = {0} = ", y);
        ShowBits (y);
        result = (ushort) (x ^ y);
        Console.Write ("\nx ^ y     = ");
        ShowBits (result);
        Console.WriteLine (" = " + result);
    }

    static void ShowBits (ushort x)
    {
        int size;
        unsafe
        {
            size = sizeof (short) * 8;
        }
        for (int i = size - 1; i >= 0; --i)
        {
            Console.Write ((x >> i) & 1);
            if ((i % 4) == 0)
                Console.Write (' ');
        }
    }
}
}
```

When you compile and run *Bitwise.cs*, you should see the following output. Compare the results of the operation on individual bits with the truth table:

```
x = 15542 = 0011 1100 1011 0110
y = 21845 = 0101 0101 0101 0101
x & y     = 0001 0100 0001 0100   = 5140

x = 15542 = 0011 1100 1011 0110
y = 21845 = 0101 0101 0101 0101
x | y     = 0111 1101 1111 0111   = 32247

x = 15542 = 0011 1100 1011 0110
```

```
y = 21845 = 0101 0101 0101 0101
x ^ y     = 0110 1001 1110 0011  = 27107
```

The *XOR* operator often is called the "toggle" operator because you can use it to turn an individual bit on and off repeatedly. If you *XOR* a bit with 1, the result always will be the opposite of the original bit. In the following program, *Toggle.cs*, you set a character to the letter *a* and then repeatedly toggle it with the value *32*. Notice that in each successive iteration of the loop, the character switches between uppercase and lowercase:

```
//
//  Toggle.cs -Uses XOR operator to toggle the case of a character.
//
//  Compile this program with the following command line:
//          C:>csc Toggle.cs
//
namespace nsToggle
{
    using System;
    class clsMain
    {
        static public void Main ()
        {
            char ch = 'a';
            char toggle = (char) 0x20;
            for (int x = 0; x < 4; ++x)
            {
                Console.WriteLine ("In iteration {0}, ch = {1}",
                                    x + 1, (char) ch);
                ch = (char) (ch ^ toggle);
            }
        }
    }
}
```

The *for* loop steps through the bitwise operation four times, and with each iteration the case of the letter changes. To make a character always lowercase, you can *OR* the character with *0x20*, and to make the character always uppercase, you can *AND* the character with *0xFFDF*.

Using Relational, Equality, and Conditional Operators

You use the relational operators to compare the relative values of two operands to determine whether the values are equal or one value is less than or greater than the other. The relational operators return a Boolean value, either *true* or *false*.

The equality operators set contains two operators, the *equality* operator (==) and the *inequality* operator (!=), which are the same as the C and C++ operators. Visual Basic, however, uses = as the equality operator and <> to test for inequality.

You use conditional operators to compare two Boolean values and to perform a conditional assignment. Comparisons involving the conditional *AND* and the conditional *OR* operators return a Boolean *true* or *false*. C++ programmers need to be aware that these operators behave differently in C#. There are no equivalent operators in Visual Basic.

Generally, you will use the relational, equality, and conditional operators in conditional statements and as loop control statements. Conditional statements are covered in "Using Program Control Statements," and loop controls statements in "Writing Loops," later in this chapter. Because of the way these operators perform, you often may have to combine several of them in a single statement.

USE IT   In C++, you can use the conditional operators to test simply for zero or non-zero values. In C#, you may use the conditional operators *only* to compare two Boolean values. This severely limits their usefulness, of course, and means more typing on your part because you must reduce the operands to Boolean values. For example, the following C++ statement tests whether both of two variables is non-zero:

```
if (a && b)
    Statement;
```

The C# compiler will reject this construction and issue an error if the operands are not Boolean type variables. In C#, the two operands for a conditional operator must equate to Boolean values, so you would have to write something similar to the following:

```
if ((a != 0) && (b != 0))
    Statement;
```

This is similar to the test you must perform in Visual Basic, but the underlying math is different. The Visual Basic *And* and *Or* operators are bitwise operators, and they combine the bits of the two operands. You first must boil them down to Boolean values so that the proper bits are being combined to get the same test results:

```
' Visual Basic equivalent
if (a <> 0) And (b <> 0) then _
    Statement
```

The C# *conditional* operator allows you to assign one of two values to a variable depending on the result of a test condition. The conditional operator itself is the only ternary operator in C# and is the same as the C and C++ conditional operator. Visual Basic has no conditional operator. To use the C# conditional operator, you write the test condition followed by a question mark (?). Then you write the expression that will be used if the test is *true*, a colon (:), and finally you include the expression to use if the test is false:

```
var = test ? : expr1 : expr2;
```

Here, your program will perform *test*, which must equate to a Boolean value. If *test* is *true*, the result of *expr1* will be assigned to *var*. If *test* is *false*, the result of *expr2* will be assigned to *var*. The data type of *expr1* and *expr2* must be the same data type as *var*.

The following simple program, *Compare.cs*, assigns one of two strings to a variable depending upon whether the command line argument is greater than 10:

```
//
//   Compare.cs - Demonstrates using the conditional operator to assign one of
//               two values to a variable.
//
//   Compile this program with the following command line:
//           C:>csc Compare.cs
//
namespace nsCompare
{
    using System;
    class clsMain
    {
        static public void Main (string [] args)
        {
            int TestArg;
            try
            {
                TestArg = int.Parse (args[0]);
            }
            catch (FormatException)
            {
                Console.WriteLine ("Please enter a number value.");
                return;
            }
            catch (IndexOutOfRangeException)
            {
                Console.WriteLine ("Please enter an argument");
                return;
            }
            string str;
            str = TestArg > 10 ? "The test is true" : "The test is false";
            Console.WriteLine (str);
        }
    }
}
```

To run this program, enter the program name followed by a number argument. If you do not enter an argument, the program will throw an *IndexOutOfRange* exception, which is caught by the second exception handler. If you enter anything other than a number as a parameter, the *int.Parse()* method will fail and throw a *FormatException* and the program will prompt you to enter a number.

Using Assignment Operators

While most languages provide only a single assignment operator—the equals sign or equivalent—C# has no fewer than 11 assignment operators. In addition to the basic equals sign, which assigns the result of an expression to a variable, the other 10 assignment operators combine arithmetic or logical operations with the assignment.

In programming, it is common to use a variable in an arithmetic expression and then assign the result of the expression to the variable itself, such as in the following:

```
var = var op expr;
```

You still can write assignment expressions this way in C#, but the rich set of assignment operators lets you combine the arithmetic operation with the assignment operation. The assignment operators are the same as those used in C and C++, but there are no equivalent operators in Visual Basic. The 10 assignment operators in Table 4-5 are the *compound assignment* operators.

Operator	Example	Operation
+=	var += expr	Adds the result of *expr* to the value of *var*.
−=	var −= *expr*	Subtracts the result of *expr* from the value of *var*.
*=	var *= expr	Multiples the result of *expr* with the value of *var*.
/=	var /= expr	Divides the value of *var* with the result of *expr*.
%=	var %= expr	Modulo divides the value of *var* with the result of *expr*. The operands must be integer data types.
&=	var &= expr	Performs a bitwise *AND* of the value of *var* with the result of *expr*. The operands must be integer data types.
|=	var |= expr	Performs a bitwise *OR* of the value of *var* with the result of *expr*. The operands must be integer data types.
^=	var ^= expr	Performs a bitwise *XOR* of the value of *var* with the result of *expr*. The operands must be integer data types.
>>=	var >> expr	Shifts the bit in *var* to the right the number of times specified by the result of *expr*. The operands must be integer data types.
<<=	var <<= expr	Shifts the bit in *var* to the left the number of times specified by the result of *expr*. The operands must be integer data types.

Table 4.5   The C# Compound Assignment Operators and Examples

C# evaluates a compound assignment as though you had written the expression using the operator in the right expression and a simple assignment. For example, if you need to add 12 to a variable's value, you could write either of the following statements in C#:

```
var = var + 12;
var += 12;
```

Although C# evaluates the two statements similarly, they are not materially equivalent, and the difference is important. In the first statement, a program would evaluate *var* twice, once when the expression on the right is evaluated and again before the actual assignment is made. The second statement evaluates *var* only once.

C# first evaluates *var* and makes a temporary copy of the result. It then performs the addition operation using the copy and, finally, assigns the result to *var*. The difference may sound trivial, but consider something like the following:

```
int x = 0;
int [] arr = new int [10};
while (x < 10)
{
    arr[x++] += 42;
}
```

If C# simply substituted the long method, the equivalent statement inside the loop would appear like the following, which would increment *x* twice:

```
arr[x++] = arr[x++] + 42;
```

C# avoids this problem by evaluating the expression on the left only once and storing a temporary copy of the value. Sequentially, C# first evaluates the expression using the plus sign (+) operator before performing the assignment.

USE IT   The following short command line program shows some of the possible operations using compound assignments. Notice that the value on the right may be an expression.

```
//
//  Assign.cs - Demonstrates compound assignment operators
//
//  Compile this program with the following command line:
//          C:>csc Assign.cs
//
namespace nsAssignment
{
    using System;
    class clsMain
    {
```

```
        static public void Main ()
        {
//
//   Start with an integer variable
        int Var = 2;
//
//   Show the starting value
        Console.WriteLine ("At the beginning, Var = {0}", Var);
//
//   Multiply the variable by something
        Var *= 12;
        Console.WriteLine ("After Var *= 12, Var = {0}", Var);
//
//   Add something to the variable
        Var += 42;
        Console.WriteLine ("After Var += 42, Var = {0}", Var);
//
//   Divide the variable by something
        Var /= 6;
        Console.WriteLine ("After Var /= 6, Var = {0}", Var);
//
//   Shift the bits in the variable four spaces to the left
//   This is the same as multiplying by 16 (2 to the fourth power)
        Var <<= 4;
        Console.WriteLine ("After Var <<= 4, Var = {0}", Var);
//
//   Shift the bits in the variable four spaces to the right using
//   an expression on the right. This is the same as dividing
//   by 16.
        int Shift = 3;
        Var >>= Shift + 1;
        Console.WriteLine ("After Var >>= Shift + 1, Var = {0}", Var);
//
//   Modulo divide the variable by something
        Var %= 6;
        Console.WriteLine ("After Var %= 6, Var = {0}", Var);
    }
  }
}
```

When you compile and run *Assign.cs*, you will see the following output:

```
At the beginning, Var = 2
After Var *= 12, Var = 24
```

```
After Var += 42, Var = 66
After Var /= 6, Var = 11
After Var <<= 4, Var = 176
After Var >>= Shift + 1, Var = 11
After Var %= 6, Var = 5
```

A compound assignment is valid if the operation on the two values is valid and the compiler permits the assignment. For example, you cannot perform a compound shift assignment if either of the values is a floating type such as a *double*, because the compiler does not allow the operation.

Understanding C# Type Operators

For the most part, your programs will deal with values of variables, or values that objects might contain. Because C# is a type-safe language, at times you'll need to deal with objects as *types* rather than as values. C# provides a class, *System.Type*, and two operators, *typeof* and *is*, to make these operations easier.

C# uses *reflection* to determine type information at runtime. Reflection objects encapsulate assemblies and modules, and you can use such an object to create an instance of a particular class and determine the methods, properties, and fields available. The *System.Type* class and the *typeof* operator are at the core of such operations.

USE IT   The *typeof* operator returns the type of an object as a variable of the *System.Type* class. Once you have a variable of *System.Type*, you can inquire about object members without having to create an instance of the object. The following short program, *TypeInfo.cs*, lists all of the available methods in the *System.IO.FileStream* class:

```
//
//   TypeInfo.cs -- uses the typeof operator to retrieve the methods
//                  available in a class.
//
//   Compile this program with the following command line:
//          C:>csc TypeInfo.cs
//
namespace nsTypeInfo
{
    using System;
    using System.IO;
    using System.Reflection;
    class clsMain
    {
        static public void Main ()
        {
            Type t = typeof (FileStream);
```

```
        MethodInfo [] methods = t.GetMethods ();
        foreach (MethodInfo temp in methods)
            Console.WriteLine (temp.ToString ());
    }
  }
}
```

You use the *is* operator to determine whether it is safe to cast an instance object to a particular type. This is particularly handy in *event handlers,* such as those used with Windows controls, where the sender usually is of type *object.*

For example, if a group of four radio buttons control the *View* property of a *ListView* control, you could capture all the button presses in a single event handler, checking that the sender type is from a *RadioButton* object. Then you could safely cast the object that caused the event to a *RadioButton* object, as shown in the following snippet:

```
private void ViewChanged(object sender, System.EventArgs e)
{
    if (!(sender is RadioButton))
        return;
    RadioButton button = (RadioButton) sender;
    if (button.Equals (radioButton1))
        listView1.View = View.LargeIcon;
    else if (button.Equals (radioButton2))
        listView1.View = View.SmallIcon;
    else if (button.Equals (radioButton3))
        listView1.View = View.List;
    else if (button.Equals (radioButton4))
        listView1.View = View.Details;
}
```

This is an efficient method of handling events generated by radio buttons. You must assign the event handler to each of the radio buttons, but by assigning the same event handler to related buttons you minimize the amount of code that you have to maintain.

Using *unsafe* Code

Reference variables contain the memory address of an object or other variable. Essentially, a reference variable contains a *pointer* to the object or variable, but you use the variable as though it contained the object or value directly. A reference variable in C# is similar to the C++ concept of a reference variable.

Normally, you will not need to use pointers directly in C#, but at times you will need to call a function in a library written in C++ that requires a parameter that is a pointer to a variable. In addition, using pointers can sometimes improve the efficiency of your code even in C#, such as while copying one array to another.

C# provides the mechanism for using pointers with the *unsafe* keyword. You may declare an entire function as *unsafe* or just a block of statements in a function. In addition to pointers, other uses for *unsafe* code include the *sizeof* operator, which is used only in *unsafe* statements or blocks.

To use *unsafe* code, you must compile your program using the */unsafe* compiler flag:

```
C:>csc /unsafe progfile.cs
```

The Microsoft Developers Network documentation strongly discourages the use of unsafe code in most cases, such as when you simply want to write "C++ code in C#." Such programming would defeat the intent of a type-safe language and would be better suited to a C++ program.

USE IT *Arrays* are particular targets for pointers in C#. An array is a managed object, so any array variable is a reference type variable. The following snippet declares two arrays, initializes one of them, and uses the assignment operator to set the second array equal to the first:

```
int [] arr1 = new int [] {1, 4, 2, 8, 5, 7};
int [] arr2 = new int [arr1.Length];
arr2 = arr1;
```

This looks like perfectly good code that should set the values in the second array equal to the values in the first array. Actually, you are discarding the second array and setting the reference variable *arr2* equal to the first array reference, *arr1*. If you subsequently change one of the values in *arr1*, the corresponding value in *arr2* also will change. The two variables point to the same array object.

To copy the members of one array to another, you can declare an *unsafe* function to perform the copy, as in the following *IntCopy.cs* program:

```
//
//  IntCopy.cs - Demonstrates use of pointers to copy an array.
//
//  Compile this program with the /unsafe compiler flag:
//          C:>csc /unsafe IntCopy.cs
//
namespace nsType
{
    using System;
    class clsMain
    {
        public static void Main ()
        {
            int [] arr1 = new int[] {1, 4, 2, 8, 5, 7};
            int [] arr2 = new int[arr1.Length];
            IntCpy (arr2, arr1, arr1.Length);
            arr1[0] = 142857;
            for (int x = 0; x < arr1.Length; ++x)
            {
```

```
            Console.Write ("arr1[{0}] = {1}    ", x, arr1[x]);
            Console.Write ("arr2[{0}] = {1}\n", x, arr2[x]);
        }
    }

    static unsafe public void IntCpy (int [] dst, int [] src, int size)
    {
        if ((size > dst.Length) || (size > src.Length))
        {
            ArgumentException e = new ArgumentException
                        ("The size argument is too large for one " +
                         "of the array arguments");
            throw (e);
        }
        fixed (int* Src = src, Dst = dst)
        {
            int* pSrc = Src;
            int* pDst = Dst;
            for (int n = 0; n < size; ++n)
            {
                *pDst++ = *pSrc++;
            }
        }
    }
}
}
```

This code creates two identical but independent arrays. If you make a change to a value in one of the arrays, the other array is not affected.

You should note with interest the *fixed* statement in the *IntCpy()* function for a couple of reasons. First, an array is a managed object, and the CLR is free to move the object in memory. If you have programmed for Windows, you may recognize that this is similar to the *handle* used for global memory objects. When you declare a *fixed* block of code, the CLR locks into memory the variables you declare in the following set of parentheses. The memory lock is effective for the next statement or block of statements. You may use a *fixed* statement only within an *unsafe* function or block of code.

Variables declared in a *fixed* statement are read only, so you may not modify their contents. If you need to modify the value of a *fixed* variable, such as to step through a loop, you must declare another variable and assign it the value of the *fixed* variable.

Second, C++ programmers may find the declarations within the *fixed* statement curious. In C++, this type of declaration would declare *Src* to be a pointer-to-integer variable and *Dst* an ordinary integer variable. In C++, to make both variables pointer variables, you would have to declare them like so:

```
int *Src, *Dst;
```

In C#, the pointer-type declaration applies to the entire set. The difference between the C++ and C# syntax is just enough to be irritating. Until you get used to the differences, the compiler will let you know if you confuse the two languages.

Using the *sizeof* Operator

The *sizeof* operator is borrowed from C and C++ returns the size of a data type in bytes. In C#, you may use the *sizeof* operator only to the get the size of a value-type data type. The return value is the amount of storage that you need to hold a variable of the data type.

You cannot use *sizeof* to get the size of a reference-type data type, such as a class or an array. Although the MSDN documentation does not mention it, you may not use the *sizeof* operator on a variable, a function parameter, or an expression. This is in sharp contrast to C and C++ and severely limits the use of the operator.

In addition, you may use the *sizeof* operator only in a function or block of code that you have marked as *unsafe*.

You also may use the *sizeof* operator on a structure, because the *struct* data type is a value-type. However, if the structure contains any reference-type members such as a *string* or an array, the compiler will reject the *sizeof* operation. The operator will return the size of a structure, including any padding that the compiler might add, to make sure the size of the structure fits within convenient byte boundaries.

On a 32-bit Windows operating system, the compiler usually adds padding to make sure the size of a structure is divisible by either the size of a word or 4. The sizes of all of the members in the following snippet total 14, but the *sizeof* operator returns a value of 16:

```
struct TestStruct
{
    int     x;
    double  y;
    char    ch;
};
```

USE IT The following short program, *Sizes.cs*, prints the sizes of several C# data types. Notice the *Main()* function itself is declared *unsafe*:

```
//
//  Sizes.cs -- returns the sizes of C# data types.
//              Compile with the following command line:
//                  csc /unsafe Sizes.cs
```

```
//
namespace nsSizes
{
    using System;
    struct TestStruct
    {
        int     x;
        double  y;
        char    ch;
    };

    class clsMain
  {
        static public unsafe void Main ()
        {
            Console.WriteLine ("The size of a bool is " + sizeof (bool));
            Console.WriteLine ("The size of a char is " + sizeof (char));
            Console.WriteLine ("The size of an int is " + sizeof (int));
            Console.WriteLine ("The size of a long is " + sizeof (long));
            Console.WriteLine ("The size of an double is " + sizeof
(double));
            Console.WriteLine ("The size of TestStruct is "
                               + sizeof (TestStruct));
        }
    }
}
```

These are only a few of the data types available in C#. Try changing the source lines to use other data types such as *decimal*, *float*, or a *byte*. Since the beginning of C#, the *decimal* type variously has reported sizes of 10, 12, and 16 bytes as the language has evolved.

Boxing and Unboxing

Ultimately, C# treats all variables and values as objects. C# contains a special data type named *object* that will accept values of any data type, whether they are value-type or reference-type. Sometimes you will find it convenient to treat value-type variables as objects.

When you declare an instance of *object*, you allocate space on the heap for an instance of the variable's class and the object becomes a managed object. For example, if you assign a variable of type *int* to an instance of *object*, your program creates an instance of the *int* class in the heap and assigns a reference to the instance to the *object* variable, as shown in Figure 4-2.

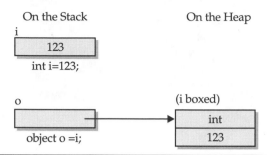

Figure 4.2 Boxing involves creating a reference-type variable to hold a value-type value

The process of assigning a value-type variable or value to an instance of *object* is called *boxing*. You can convert an object back to a value-type through *unboxing*. Boxing is an *implicit* conversion because the *object* data type will accept any value. Unboxing requires an *explicit* conversion, however. The following snippet boxes an integer value and then unboxes the value and assigns it to another *int* variable:

```
object o = 4096;        // Box a number
int val = (int) o;      // Unbox and assign to a variable
```

You should be careful that the value you unbox is the same data type as the value you boxed.

If you attempt to unbox a *long* value and cast it to an *int*, as in the following snippet, the compiler will not issue a warning error:

```
long LongVal = 4096;
object o = LongVal;     // Box the long variable
int val = (int) o;      // Unbox as a long
```

This code would compile without error, but when you run your program, it will throw an *InvalidCastException*. Even if an implicit conversion were allowed, such as assigning an *int* value to a *long* variable, the program still will throw an exception.

The reason an exception is thrown is that the *object* instance contains type information. If the unboxing operation does not use the same data type as the box operation, the *object* instance code throws the exception.

You can see that the *object* instance contains type information by using the *is* operator to test for the data type.

USE IT   The following program, *Boxing.cs*, boxes *int*, *long*, and *struct* value types and an instance of a class, which is a reference-type variable:

```
//
//  Boxing.cs - Demonstrates boxing and unboxing value-type variables.
//
```

```csharp
//  Compile this program with the following command line:
//          C:>csc Boxing.cs
//
namespace nsBox
{
    using System;

    struct Point
    {
        public Point (int x, int y)
        {
            cx = x;
            cy = y;
        }
        public override string ToString ()
        {
            return ("(" + cx + ", " + cy + ")");
        }
        public int cx;
        public int cy;
    }

    class clsMain
    {
        static public void Main ()
        {
            long LongVal = 9600;
            object o = LongVal;
            ShowObject (o);
            o = 4096;
            ShowObject (o);
            Point point = new Point (42, 96);
            ShowObject (point);
            clsBox test = new clsBox();
            ShowObject (test);
        }
        static public void ShowObject (object o)
        {
            if (o is int)
                Console.WriteLine ("The object is an integer");
            if (o is long)
                Console.WriteLine ("The object is a long");
            else if (o is Point)
                Console.WriteLine ("The object is a Point structure");
```

```
            else if (o is clsBox)
                Console.WriteLine ("The object is a clsBox class object");
            Console.WriteLine ("The value of object is " + o + "\r\n");
        }
    }
    class clsBox
    {
        public override string ToString()
        {
            return ("\"-- clsBox --\"");
        }
    }
}
```

Notice that the last line in the *ShowObject()* function does not even bother to test for the data type. To write the output, the *Console.WriteLine()* function calls the *ToString()* method in *object* to write the string associated with the object.

For your classes and structures, you may override the *ToString()* method to provide your own string output. When you compile and run *Boxing.cs*, you should see the following output:

```
The object is a long
The value of object is 9600

The object is an integer
The value of object is 4096

The object is a Point structure
The value of object is (42, 96)

The object is a clsBox class object
The value of object is "-- clsBox --"
```

The *Point* structure and the *clsBox* class definitions contain overrides for the *ToString()* method. Try commenting out these functions, and then recompile and run the program. The *Console.WriteLine()* function will print the fully qualified names of the structure and the class.

Using *checked* and *unchecked* Statements

Variables represent memory locations in which your program stores a value. When you set aside memory for a variable, the location has a limited number of bits in which to store the value. Even in the central processing chip, the registers that hold values temporarily have a limited number of bits.

Variables, then, may hold a limited range of values. If the value you attempt to store in a memory location exceeds that range, an *overflow* occurs, which means that the value is too large for the data type. In the case of floating point values, the value can become so small that the data type no longer can represent it adequately, and once again an overflow occurs.

Under normal conditions, a program cannot detect an overflow condition. The value simply gets truncated, and any expression that uses the value in calculations is likely to produce an incorrect result. In the case of a signed integer, the largest value a variable can hold is 2,147,483,647.

USE IT   In the following program, *OverFlow.cs*, you assign that maximum value for a signed integer to two variables, and then increment one of the variables and print the result:

```
//
//  OverFlow.cs -- Demonstrates using checked keyword to detect an overflow.
//
//          Compile this program with the following command line:
//              C:>csc OverFlow.cs
//
namespace nsOverflow
{
    using System;
    class clsMain
    {
        static public void Main ()
        {
            int large = 2147483647;
            int larger = large;
            ++larger;
            Console.WriteLine ("large = " + large);
            Console.WriteLine ("larger = " + larger);
        }
    }
}
```

When you compile and run this program, you see the following output:

```
large = 2147483647
larger = -2147483648
```

Even though you incremented the variable, its value became negative. Incrementing it caused the most significant bit (the sign bit) to become 1, and the value suddenly became the most negative value that the variable could hold. Now add a line to multiply the incremented value by 2:

```
++larger;
larger *= 2;
```

The situation has gone from bad to worse. The value now is 0, and if you attempt to divide another value by *larger*, which you know should not be zero, you will get a divide-by-zero error. Without additional code to test questionable values, your program cannot detect overflow until the problem becomes serious enough to cause an exception.

C# provides a mechanism by which your program can detect and recover from such overflow problems. By default, the C# compiler builds a program without range checking on variables. You can protect potential problem statements by marking them as *checked*. Replace the increment statement in *OverFlow.cs* with the following statement:

```
larger = checked (++larger);
```

Recompile and run the program again. When you run the program, the statement will cause your program to throw an *OverflowException*. You still need to handle the exception, but the original problem will not continue to compound itself.

Change the code in *OverFlow.cs* so that it looks like the following (the code is on the Web site for this book as *OvrFlow1.cs*):

```
//
// OvrFlow1.cs -- Demonstrates using checked keyword to detect an overflow.
//
//          Compile this program with the following command line:
//               C:>csc OvrFlow1.cs
//
namespace nsOverflow
{
    using System;
    class clsMain
    {
        static public void Main ()
        {
            int large = 2147483647;
            int larger = large;
            try
            {
                larger = checked (++larger);
            }
            catch (OverflowException e)
            {
                Console.WriteLine ("The operation caused an overflow");
                Console.WriteLine (e.Message);
            }
            Console.WriteLine ("large = " + large);
            Console.WriteLine ("larger = " + larger);
        }
```

```
        }
}
```

This program differs from the *OverFlow.cs* program because the *checked* keyword is used inside a *try* block. Your program now prints a couple of error messages when the overflow occurs, and the value of *larger* remains unchanged. Use the code in the *catch* block to recover from the error or gracefully exit the program.

In addition to a single statement, you can mark a block of statements as *checked* by placing them inside a set of braces:

```
checked
{
    ++larger;
    larger *= 2;
}
```

If either of the statements causes an overflow, the program will throw an *OverflowException*.

C# also provides an *unchecked* keyword to counter the effects of the *checked* keyword. By default, the compiler builds a program as *unchecked*, but you may specify the */checked* compiler option. The following command line would enable overflow checking for all statements in *OverFlow.cs*:

```
C:>csc /checked OverFlow.cs
```

When you use the */checked* flag, you may exclude a statement or block of statements from overflow checking by using the *unchecked* keyword.

Finally, change the code in *OverFlow.cs* so that it looks like the following:

```
//
//  OvrFlow2.cs -- Demonstrates using checked keyword to detect an overflow.
//
//          Compile this program with the following command line:
//              C:>csc /checked OvrFlow2.cs
//
namespace nsOverflow
{
    using System;
    class clsMain
    {
        static public void Main ()
        {
            int large, = 2147483647;
            int larger = large;
            unchecked
            {
                ++larger;
```

```
                larger *= 2;
            }
            Console.WriteLine ("large = " + large);
            Console.WriteLine ("larger = " + larger);
        }
    }
}
```

Compile the program using the */checked* compiler flag. When you run the program, the statements again produce the incorrect result, and the program does not throw an exception.

Writing Loops

Looping is a fundamental concept in programming. Looping allows a program to repeat a statement or block of statements repeatedly until a certain condition is satisfied. C# borrows from both C and Visual Basic for its loop constructs.

C# provides four different loop statements. Each loop type has its own use, as summarized in Table 4-6.

Each loop statement has its own advantages and limitations. For example, the *while* loop may not execute if the test expression is false initially. If you need to execute the block of code at least once, the *do ... while* loop would be a better choice.

Each loop statement requires a *test expression*, which you write inside a set a parentheses immediately after the loop statement. More properly, this expression is a *control* expression, because it determines whether the loop will execute. Except for the *foreach* loop, the expression must evaluate to a Boolean value (it must equate to *true* or *false*). The loop will continue to repeat until the test expression evaluates to false. The *foreach* loop repeats once for each array element or object collection in the test expression.

The *while* loop is the basic loop statement. It will continue to execute the statement or block of statements until the conditional expression is false, so you must initialize any control variable before entering the *while* loop, and your loop code must provide some method of modifying the control

Statement	Uses
while	Executes the statement or block of statements following until the test expression is false. If the expression is false initially, the loop statements will not execute.
do ... while	Similar to the *while* loop except the test is performed after the loop block executes. The block of statements will execute at least once.
for	Useful for looping a specific number of times. The loop control statement provides for an initialization and increment as well as a test condition.
foreach	Loops once for each element in an array. Similar to the Visual Basic *For ... Each ... Next* statement. There is no C or C++ equivalent.

Table 4.6   *C# Loop Statements*

variable or otherwise exiting the loop. The basic form of the *while* loop is shown in the following snippet:

```
while (expr == true)
{
    // statements
}
```

In this case, you do not include a semicolon after the test expression. If you end the test expression with a semicolon, the compiler will interpret the object statement to be an *empty* statement. The compiler will not issue an error, but the loop will not execute properly.

If the test expression—*expr*—is false initially, the *while* loop will not execute. If you need to insure that the loop will execute at least once, you can use the *do ... while* form:

```
do
{
    //statements;
} while (expr == true);
```

The *do ... while* loop will execute the statements in the loop body before evaluating the control expression. Notice that unlike the *while* loop, you must include a semicolon after the control expression. In addition, the braces for a *while* loop are optional (you do not need them for a single statement), but the braces are *required* for the *do ... while* loop, even if only one statement is included in the loop.

The *for* loop is useful for executing a block of code a specific number of times. The control expression is a compound statement consisting of three parts, as shown in the following code:

```
for (initializing statement; test expression; increment expression)
{
    // statements;
}
```

The first statement is the *initializing* statement, in which you may set the initial value for a control variable. You may declare and initialize a variable in this statement. The second statement is the test expression itself. Your program will evaluate this expression *before* each iteration of the loop. The third statement is the *increment* statement. Despite its name, you may perform any operation in the increment statement, but usually the operation will involve modifying any control variables.

You use the *foreach* loop to step through the elements in an array. You *must* declare a unique variable in the control expression, and its data type must match the data type of the array. Each time through the loop, C# assigns the variable the value of the array element, starting with the first and continuing to the last:

```
foreach (type var in array)
{
    // statements
}
```

The variable that you declare in the control expression is read-only, so you may not use it to assign values to the array elements. This limits the utility of the *foreach* loop, but it is handy when you need only to retrieve the values of array elements.

The following snippet initializes an array, and then reads the elements and prints them using a *foreach* loop:

```
int [] arr = new int [5] {1, 2, 3, 4, 5};
foreach (int var in arr)
{
    Console.Write (var + " ");
}
```

You may use two special statements within a loop. The *continue* statement ends the loop immediately and transfers control back to the beginning of the loop. Statements in the loop after the *continue* statement executes will be ignored. If the test expression is still true, the loop will execute again. The *break* statement aborts the loop and transfers control to the first statement following the loop.

USE IT   The following program, *Loops.cs*, uses three different loop types to accept integer values from the console, store the values in an array, and print them back to the console:

```
namespace nsLoops
{
    using System;
    class clsMain
    {
        static public void Main ()
        {
            int [] arr = new int [5];
            for (int x = 0; x < arr.Length; ++x)
            {
                bool done = false;
                while (!done)
                {
                    Console.Write ("Enter a value for element {0}: ", x);
                    string str = Console.ReadLine ();
                    int val;
                    try
                    {
                        val = int.Parse (str);
                    }
                    catch (FormatException)
                    {
                        Console.WriteLine ("Please enter an " +
                                           "integer value\r\n");
                        continue;
```

```
                }
                arr[x] = val;
                done = true;
            }
        }
        int index = 0;
        foreach (int val in arr)
        {
            Console.WriteLine ("arr[{0}] = {1}", index, val);
            ++index;
        }
    }
  }
}
```

Notice the *continue* statement in the *while* loop. If the conversion from the input string to an integer fails, the program control will transfer to the *catch* block. You do not want to execute the statements that follow the *catch* block because the value you obtained is invalid. The *continue* statement restarts the *while* loop without changing any values, and the program once again asks the user to enter a value. If the conversion succeeds, the converted value is assigned to the array element, the *done* variable is set to true, and the loop exits. Control then returns to the *for* loop.

▶ **NOTE**

Loops.cs uses an exception handler to make sure the user entered a proper value. An exception is an unexpected error that prevents the program from continuing normally. When handling an exception, the code after the try statement is the guarded block. In this case, if the conversion fails, the program control will transfer to the first statement in the catch block. If the conversion succeeds, the program will ignore the catch block entirely. C# uses exceptions extensively, and they will be covered in Chapter 9.

Several alternatives to the while loop can be used. For one, you could omit the test variable altogether and use the constant *true*. If the conversion succeeds, you'll want to exit the loop anyway, so you could rewrite the code simply using a *break* statement, as shown here:

```
while (true)
{
    Console.Write ("Enter a value for element {0}: ", x);
    string str = Console.ReadLine ();
    int val;
    try
    {
        val = int.Parse (str);
    }
```

```
    catch (FormatException)
    {
        Console.WriteLine ("Please enter an integer value\r\n");
        continue;
    }
    arr[x] = val;
    break;
}
```

Using Program Control Statements

Computers are electrical machines, but they have one characteristic that differentiates them from other machines. Computers can make decisions. Normally, a program flows from one statement to the next, but most languages provide some method that allows a program to test a condition and provide alternative code depending upon the results of that test.

C# provides the same conditional statements that you find in C and C++. The basic conditional statement is the *if* statement. In C and C++, the *if* statement tests for a zero or non-zero value. If the test is zero, it is deemed to be *false*; if it is non-zero, the test is *true*.

The following snippet will execute *statement* because the target of the conditional statement—the variable *x*—is non-zero:

```
int x = 5;
if (x)
    statement;
```

The same statement in C#, however, would result in a compiler error. The *if* statement in C# can only test Boolean values. To make the above snippet work in C#, you would have to rewrite it as follows:

```
int x = 5;
if (x != 0)
    statement;
```

The snippet is acceptable to the C# compiler because *x != 0* results in a Boolean value—it is either *true* or *false*. The C# method is more verbose and requires more typing, but it does have one beneficial side benefit. A common error in C and C++, particularly among newcomers and those switching over from Visual Basic, is to write something like *if (x = 5)* when they really mean to write *if (x == 5)* using the equality operator. To the C and C++ compilers, this is a perfectly valid statement. The result is that the program always assigns 5 to the variable, and the test always is *true*. In C#, this type of error would result in a compiler error because the expression inside the parentheses does not evaluate to a Boolean value.

You must enclose the conditional expression within parentheses, but it does not end with a semicolon. The statement that follows the conditional may be a compound statement enclosed within a set of braces. In this case, if the conditional expression is *true*, the entire block of statements will execute; if the expression is *false*, the entire block will be ignored:

```
if (conditional expression)
{
    statement1;
    statement2;
    // More statements if needed
}
```

You may provide an alternative statement or block of statements to perform if the test is false by using the *else* keyword:

```
int x = 5;
if (x != 0)
    // statement if true;
else
    // statement if false
```

The alternative statement may be a single statement or a compound statement enclosed in braces. To avoid confusion, many programmers prefer to enclose the conditional statements within braces even if only one statement is used, as in the following snippet:

```
if (x != 0)
{
    // statement if true;
}
else
{
    // statement if false
}
```

You may test multiple conditions by using the *else if* syntax. You may chain as many *else if* statements as you need:

```
if (condition1)
    // statement;
else if (condition2)
    // statement
else if (condition3)
    // statement
else
    // statement
```

Notice that the last element in the chain is an *else* without an *if*. You do not have to provide this element, but if you do, it must be the last element in the chain.

In C#, each condition must evaluate to a Boolean value, *true* or *false*. When your program executes this snippet, it will test each condition until one evaluates to *true* and then execute the statement or block of statements following. The program then will ignore the rest of the chain, even if more than one condition is *true*. If none of the conditions is *true*, the statement following the *else* will execute. *One and only one* statement or block of statements in the chain will execute; your program will ignore all other statements in the chain.

If your conditional chain involves testing for integer values, you can use the C# *switch* statement. The statement is similar to the C and C++ *switch* statement, with some differences.

The *switch* statement evaluates an expression and then transfers control to a block of statements (a *case*) that matches the result of the expression:

```
switch (expression)
{
    case 1:
        statements;
        break
    case 42:
        statements;
        break;
    default:
        statements;
        break:
}
```

Here are some rules to follow when using a *switch* statement:

- The test expression *must* be an expression (or a variable) that results in an integer value such as *bool*, *int*, *long*, or *short int*. You cannot use a *float* or *double* value for the test value. You may, however, use a *string* variable.

- You mark the alternate blocks of code that your program may execute by using the *case* statement. The value following the *case* keyword must be an integer constant value or a string constant (the same data type as the test expression). You cannot use a variable after *case*, nor can you use a floating point value. If the value matches the result of the test expression, the block of statements following the *case* statement will execute.

- The *case* statements must be enclosed in a set of braces. Even if you provide only one *case*, you must enclose it within braces.

- You must end each *case* statement with a "jump" statement, a statement that transfers program control to another statement (there is an exception, as shown in the next paragraph). This may be a *break*, a *goto*, a *continue*, or a *return* statement. The *continue* statement may be used only if the *switch* statement is inside the body of a loop.

Normally in C#, you cannot simply let one *case* "fall through" to the next, as is possible in C and C++. However, if you do not provide any statements in a *case*, you do not have to provide a jump statement. This makes it possible to use the same code for multiple *case*s, as in the following code:

```
switch (expr)
{
    default:
        // Default statements
        break;
    case 0:
    case 42:
    case 1:
        // Statements for case 0, 1 and 42
        break;
    case 22:
        // Statements for case 22
        break;
    case 86:
        // Statements for case 86
        goto case 22;   // Transfer control to case 22
}
```

Here, cases 0, 1, and 42 will execute the same block of code. The *break* statement terminates the *switch* and transfers control to the first statement following the closing brace. If you use a *goto*, you may specify another *case* to execute, as in case 86. C and C++ programmers should note that this is different from the C *switch* statement, in which the *break* is optional.

The *case* statements do not need to be in numerical order, nor do you need to provide a case for every possible value for the test expression. A special case, *default*, will execute if none of the *case* statement constants matches the test result. The *default* case is optional.

USE IT The following program, *switch.cs*, shows how you might use a switch statement to select a string to output after parsing input from a user:

```
//
//  Switch.cs - Demonstrates use of the switch statement for selecting
//              an input value.
//
//              Compile this program with the following command line:
//                  C:>csc Switch.cs
//
namespace nsSwitch
{
    using System;
    class clsMain
    {
        static void Main ()
        {
            bool done = false;
```

```
do
{
    clsAnimal dog = new clsAnimal (1);
    clsAnimal cat = new clsAnimal (2);
    clsAnimal goldfish = new clsAnimal (3);
    clsAnimal aardvark = new clsAnimal (4);
    Console.WriteLine ("Select one of the following:");
    Console.WriteLine ("\t1 -- For dogs");
    Console.WriteLine ("\t2 -- For cats");
    Console.WriteLine ("\t3 -- For goldfish");
    Console.WriteLine ("\t4 -- For aardvarks");
    Console.Write ("Enter Your selection (0 to exit): ");
    string strSelection = Console.ReadLine ();
    int iSel;
    try
    {
        iSel = int.Parse(strSelection);
    }
    catch (FormatException)
    {
        Console.WriteLine ("\r\nWhat?\r\n");
        continue;
    }
    Console.WriteLine ("You selected  " + iSel);
    switch (iSel)
    {
        case 0:
            done = true;
            break;
        case 1:
            Console.WriteLine (dog);
            break;
        case 2:
            Console.WriteLine (cat);
            break;
        case 3:
            Console.WriteLine (goldfish);
            break;
        case 4:
            Console.WriteLine (aardvark);
```

```
                                break;
                    default:
                        Console.WriteLine ("You selected an invalid " +
                                            "number: {0}\r\n", iSel);
                        continue;
                }
                Console.WriteLine ();
            } while (!done);

            Console.WriteLine ("\nGoodbye!");
        }
    }
    class clsAnimal
    {
        public clsAnimal (int Type)
        {
            PetType = Type;
        }
        private int Type;
        public int PetType
        {
            get {return (Type);}
            set {Type = value;}
        }
        public override string ToString()
        {
            switch (PetType)
            {
                default:
                    return ("Unknown pet");
                case 1:
                    return ("Your pet type is a dog");
                case 2:
                    return ("Your pet type is a cat");
                case 3:
                    return ("Your pet type is a goldfish");
                case 4:
                    return ("Your pet type is an aardvark");
            }
        }
```

```
        }
}
```

When you compile and run *Switch.cs*, the program will prompt you to enter a selection and then pause for you to enter a number:

```
Select one of the following:
    1 -- For dogs
    2 -- For cats
    3 -- For goldfish
    4 -- For aardvarks
Enter Your selection (0 to exit):
```

The *switch* statement selects which of the instances for *clsAnimal* to print to the screen, and the class instance prints the proper string. If you enter a non-integer value, the program will ask "what?" and continue.

Understanding Scope in C#

Depending on how and where you declare a variable, only a limited number of statements may access it. For example, if you declare a variable in a function, only statements within that function may access the variable. This range of statements is called the *scope* of a variable. Within the scope of a variable, the variable name must be unique. Uniqueness, however, is a relative thing in an object-oriented language. In C#, the name you give a variable that you declare in a function is simply the identifier that you assign to it. Within a function, you cannot declare two variables of the same name.

If you are a C++ programmer, you should re-read the previous paragraph. C# does not allow you to "hide" a variable within a function by declaring another variable of the same name in a smaller scope. You should note some changes between Visual C++ 6.0 and Visual C++ 7.0 as well. The following snippet would be acceptable in C++:

```
void Function ()
{
    int x = 5
    int y = 42;;      // y has "function" scope
    while (x-- > 0)
    {
        int y = 23;  // y has "block" scope
    }
}
```

The variable *y* inside the *while* loop has smaller scope, and thus hides the variable declared in the function. In C#, however, the compiler will not allow this type of declaration. The variable inside the *while* loop has "child" scope, and it redefines the variable declared in function scope. The C# compiler would reject the new declaration and issue an error.

For a loop or conditional statement, the child scope begins at the opening parenthesis in the statement and ends after the last statement in the loop or conditional block. You may declare variables with the same name in different child scopes so long as one scope is not a child of the other. The following, for example, is acceptable to the C# compiler:

```
for (int x = 0; x < 10; ++x)
{
    // Loop statements
}
for (int x = 5; x < 15; ++x)
{
    // Loop statements
}
```

▶ *NOTE*

Visual C++ programmers should note that this would not be acceptable in Version 6.0, but it is acceptable in Visual C++ 7.0. This syntax has been acceptable for the Borland C++ compiler for some time.

You also may declare a variable in a function that has the same name as a variable in the class containing the function. In this case, the compiler can uniquely identify the variables, as in the following snippet:

```
namespace nsScope
{
    using System;
    class clsMain
    {
        int Var = 42;
        static public void Main ()
        {
            clsMain cls = new clsMain();
        }
        public void ShowVar()
        {
```

```
        int Var = 23;
        Console.WriteLine ("Class variable = " + this.Var);
        Console.WriteLine ("Function variable = " + Var);
    }
  }
}
```

The variable *var* that you declare as a member of a class may be identified by using the *this* qualifier. The *this* variable, which will be covered in Chapter 7, is an intrinsic variable that uniquely identifies an instance of a class or structure.

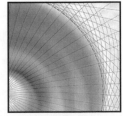

CHAPTER 5
Data Types in C#

TIPS IN THIS CHAPTER

V ariables represent memory locations your program uses to store values. In C#, variable types are divided into two broad categories: value-types and reference-types. A value-type variable directly contains its value—that is, the memory location contains the value you assign to the variable. A reference-type variable holds the memory address of another value or object and thus *refers* to the actual value. (There is also a pointer-type that you can use in unsafe code.)

You create value-types when you declare a variable using one of the simple, or fundamental, data types. Value-type variables are the closest you will find to "ordinary" variables in C#.

You may declare value-type variables in a function, or you may declare them as members of a class or structure. When you declare a value-type variable in a function, the process is essentially the same as that in C++. The program sets aside space on the stack to hold the variable's value. The variable is called a *local variable* because it exists only within the scope of the function. You assign a value to the variable and use the variable as though it were the value itself. When the function ends and control returns to the calling function, the variable goes out of scope and the program adjusts the stack. The variable—and its value—is lost.

When you declare a value-type variable within a class, it is called a *field*. A field is an *instance variable* and persists as long as the class object is in scope. In all other respects, C# treats a field as an ordinary variable. When you use it as an argument in a function call, the program makes a copy of the value, and the called function may not modify the contents of the field through the argument variable.

In either case, C# does not initialize a value-type variable when you declare the variable. After you declare a variable, you must initialize it, and C# enforces initialization through assignment rules. In C and C++, you can use a variable without initializing it. The compiler might issue a warning, but it will not prevent you from using an unassigned variable in an expression or a function call.

The C# compiler keeps track of the variable during the compilation process and will issue an error if you attempt to use a variable before you assign it a value. This *definite assignment rule* keeps you from introducing random and probably incorrect values into your program.

The value-types also include the *structure* and the *enumerated* data types. Structures are the topic for Chapter 6, and the *enum* type is the topic of a tip later in this chapter.

A Quick Look at Objects

The simple data types such as *int*, *double*, or *char* represent the "dumb" side of variables in an object-oriented programming language. When you declare a variable using one of the simple types, the focus is on the *value*, hence the C# appellation "value-type."

On the other side are the *objects*, which focus on the state of the variable rather than just the value. An object may contain one or more values, but it also may contain information about how the values were set and how they can be retrieved.

In the traditional task- or procedure-oriented approach to programming, the flow proceeds from one statement to the next. A variable simply represents a memory location in which the computer stores a value. You can trace the program flow simply by stepping through the statements. Procedure-oriented programming deals with one value at a time.

In object-oriented programming, declaring an object may create any number of values, invoke additional code that manipulates the values, and provide methods to maintain and retrieve the values.

C# creates and maintains objects in the program *heap*. The heap, sometimes called the *free store*, is an area of memory your program sets aside for temporary storage of data whose size or existence cannot be determined until the program is executing. When a C# program creates an object in the heap, it then refers to the object indirectly through the memory address. The variable that holds the address in C# is a *reference-type* variable.

Declaring an object in C# is a two-step process. First, you must declare a reference-type variable to hold the memory address. The variable essentially is a special case of a value-type and is subject to the same scope rules in C# as value-type variables. If you declare the variable in a function, the variable goes out of scope when the function returns, and the value—the address of the object to which it refers—is lost, the same as for a value-type variable.

Unlike value-type variables for the simple data types, a C# program initializes reference-type variables to 0. In C++, this is called a *NULL* pointer value, and in Visual Basic it is the same as setting the value to *Nothing*.

In the second step, you actually create the object using the *new* operator. The new operator sets aside enough memory in the heap to hold the object and establishes a memory address for the object. The *new* operator returns the address, which you then assign to the reference-type variable.

The following code shows that simply declaring a reference-type variable does not create the object:

```
namespace nsTest
{
    using System;
    class clsMain
    {
        public clsMain()
        {
            Console.WriteLine ("Object created");
        }
        static public void Main ()
        {
            clsMain obj;
        }
    }
}
```

In C#, the *class* represents the basic object. When you declare and create a class object, you are creating an *instance* of the class. When you place the preceding code in a program and run it, the "Object created" message never appears. Add the following line to the *Main()* function and try the code again:

```
obj = new clsMain();
```

When you run the code with this line, the "Object created" message will appear. Declaring a reference-type variable only reserves storage for an object's address. The object is created when you use the *new* operator.

The class is not the only reference-type variable you will encounter in C#. Other types are the *string*, *delegate*, *interface*, and *object*.

In C#, Everything Is an Object

Simple data types present problems for object-oriented languages. As convenient as it might be, representing fundamental types as objects is not very efficient in terms of execution time. Thus, most object-oriented languages have a dual type system, one to represent the fundamental data types and another to represent objects.

C# is no exception. The original Beta 1 version of Visual C# attempted to represent all data types as objects, but the language framers backed away from the concept by the time the second revision was released.

Instead, C# now lets you treat values as object whenever it is convenient by providing an *object* keyword. The *object* keyword declares an instance of the *Object* class from the .NET Common Language Runtime (CLR). An *object* is a universal data type and may be familiar to Visual Basic programmers through the *Object* data type. In Visual Basic 7.0, the *Object* data type is compatible with the C# *object* type.

Every value in C# inherits from the *Object* class, and you may use methods within *Object* or any value or variable, whether it is a value-type or a reference-type. For example, *Object* contains a *ToString()* method that converts the value to a string. You may apply *ToString()* even to constant values, as shown in the following statement:

```
string str = 42.ToString();
```

This statement would assign the string *42* to the variable *str*. The *Object* class *ToString()* provides default conversions for every object type. Derived objects may override this function.

> ► **QUICK TIP**
>
> *Visual Basic programmers should be aware that Microsoft has dropped the Variant data type with the introduction of Visual Studio 7.0. In Visual Basic, when you used a variable without declaring it as a particular data type, the Visual Basic compiler automatically gave it a Variant data type. Variant essentially was a universal data type that could hold a value of any type. You no longer may use an undeclared variable in Visual Basic 7.0. For example, simply writing the statement x = 42, where x is an undeclared variable, no longer works. To use a universal data type, you first must declare the variable as type Object, as in the following snippet:*
>
> ```
> Public Class clsClass
>     Private Function Func()
>         Dim x as Object
>         x = 42
>     End Function
> End Class
> ```

To make it easier to extract the value assigned to an *object* variable, *Object* also contains a *GetType()* method. If you attempt to retrieve any data type other than that assigned to the variable, your program will throw an *InvalidCastException*.

Declaring and Initializing Variables in C#

When you declare a value-type variable in a C# function, or a field in a C# class, the compiler does not initialize the variable. You cannot use a variable until you have given it an initial value.

One of the reasons for this restriction is that the C# language is type safe and guarantees that a variable of a given data type will contain a value of that data type. The easiest way to initialize a variable is when you declare it. A statement in which you both declare and initialize a variable is called a *declaration assignment* statement:

```
int var = 42;
```

This statement declares *var* to be a variable of type *int*, and then assigns *42* as the initial value.

The compiler does initialize reference-type variables to *null* when you declare them. However, the compiler still will not let you use a reference-type variable until you assign it a value. In the following snippet, the compiler will display an error that you are attempting to use an unassigned local variable:

```
public void Func ()
{
    clsMain main;
    object o = main;
}
```

This does not mean that you cannot run into trouble using an unassigned reference-type variable. Although the compiler assigns a default value of *null* to a reference-type variable, you can use the variable even if you assign it a *null* value yourself. The following code demonstrates a common operation and is virtually guaranteed to throw a *NullReferenceException*:

```
public void Func ()
{
    clsMain main = null;
//  Some statements in between to make you forget about the null
    object o = main;
    Console.WriteLine ("main = " + o.ToString());
}
```

The point here is that, while you may make it a practice to initialize value-type variables when you declare them, it is better to let the compiler handle any default assignment for reference-type variables. When you assign *null* to a reference-type value, the assignment satisfies the compiler's *definite assignment rules*, and it will not test the value to make sure it is valid.

The value *null* is a C# *literal* value and is a null reference that does not point to any object. C# contains only two other literal values, *true* and *false*.

Definite Assignment Rules

To assure type safety, the compiler examines your code to make sure that you have assigned a value to a variable before you use it. In an assignment, the compiler tests the assignment to make sure you are assigning a value of the proper data type to the variable.

In some cases, such as when assigning an *int* value to a *long* variable, the compiler will perform an implicit cast to make the data types the same if the intrinsic cast will not result in a loss of precision. An *int* is smaller than a *long*, and it is safe to cast a value with less precision to one with a higher precision:

```
int x = 4096;
long y = x;          // Implicit cast to a higher precision type
```

The reverse is not necessarily true, however. The compiler will not permit you to assign a value with a higher precision to a variable with a lower precision using an implicit cast. To do this, you must perform an *explicit* cast by writing the data type inside a set of parentheses before the value:

```
long y = 4096;
int x = (int) y;           // Requires an explicit cast
```

The compiler applies assignment rules to variables to make sure they have been *definitely assigned*. A variable that you declare in a declaration assignment statement is considered definitely assigned. Beyond that, the compiler tests to make sure that all paths that lead to the statement where you use a variable contains an assignment expression for the variable. The following snippet will compile because all possible paths to the *Console.WriteLine()* statement in which you use the variable contains an assignment:

```
long x;
if (true)
    long x = 42;
Console.WriteLine ("x = " + x);
```

The conditional statement always is true, and the compiler can detect that fact. However, if you use a variable within the test, the compiler will not test the variable. The following snippet will cause the compiler to complain that you are attempting to use an unassigned variable:

```
long x
bool b = true
if (b)
    long x = 42;
Console.WriteLine ("x = " + x);
```

The definite assignment rule also is satisfied if you use a variable as an argument to a function that uses it as an *out* parameter. In the following short program, *Area.cs*, the compiler allows you to print the value of *Area* because it appears as an *out* parameter to *GetArea( )*:

```
namespace nsArea
{
    using System;
    class clsMain
    {
        static public void Main ()
        {
            double Area;
            int Radius = 42;
            GetArea (Radius, out Area);
            Console.WriteLine ("The area of a circle with radius {0} is {1}",
                               Radius, Area);
        }
        static void GetArea (int radius, out double area)
        {
            const double pi = 3.14159;
            area = pi * radius * radius;
        }
    }
}
```

In this code, the compiler does not actually track the variable to make sure you give it a value in *GetArea( )*. It simply assumes the assignment was made. When it compiles the *GetArea( )* function, it then will issue an error if you do not assign an *out* parameter a value.

Using Value-Types

The value-types include the simple data types, structures, and the enumerated types. Although structures are the topic for a separate chapter, you should have a basic understanding of structures. C# actually implements the simple data types using structures built into the .NET Framework.

A structure is fundamentally the same as a class, with some restrictions. A structure, for example, cannot inherit from an ancestor structure or class, and it may not be used as a base to derive new structures or classes. A structure may contain constructors and other functions, but it may not contain a destructor function.

Defining Structures Within C#

You define a structure using much the same syntax that you use to define a class. You use the *struct* keyword followed by the name that will become the data type for the structure. Within a set of braces, you declare the fields and other members of the structure:

```
struct Sample
{
    int   x;
    long y;
    static double z;
};      // Semicolon here is optional
```

Once you have defined a structure, you may declare instances of the structure using the name as the data type for the variable:

```
Sample samp;
```

A structure is a value-type, so simply declaring the variable creates an instance of the structure. You do not need to use the *new* operator to create the instance and assign the address to the variable. You may use the *new* operator, but it has no effect when declaring an instance of a structure. An instance of a structure is created on the stack, and using the *new* operator does not force C# to create the instance in the heap.

USE IT   Just declaring an instance of a structure does not initialize the member fields, however. You first must assign values to *all* of the members before you can use the variable that contains the instance of the structure. If you fail to assign a value to even one member, the compiler will issue an error that you are attempting to use an unassigned structure variable, but it will not tell you which member you did not initialize. The following program, *Struct.cs*, does not use the member *var* in structure *POINT*, but the compiler still generates an error:

```
//
//  Struct.cs - Issue an error message if you do not initialize all of
//              the fields in  a structure
//
//              Compile this program with the following command line:
//                  C:>csc Struct.cs
//
using System;

namespace nsStruct
{
    struct POINT
    {
        public int cx;
        public int cy;
        public int var;
        public override string ToString ()
        {
            return ("(" + cx + ", " + cy + ")");
        }
```

```
    }
    class clsMain
    {
        static public void Main ()
        {
            POINT pt;
            pt.cx = 24;
            pt.cy = 42;
            Console.WriteLine (pt);
        }
    }
}
```

When you compile this program, the compiler issues the following error:

```
struct.cs(22,32): error CS0165: Use of unassigned local variable 'pt'
```

The error message does not tell you that you did not initialize *var*, but instead complains that you did not initialize *pt*, the instance of the *POINT* instance. To compile the program, you must assign a value to *pt.var* even if you do not use it.

You can, however, use individual members of the structure in this case. Change the *Console.WriteLine()* statement as follows and recompile the program:

```
Console.WriteLine ("(" + pt.cx + ", " + pt.cy + ")");
```

The compiler now simply issues a warning that you did not initialize *var*, but the program still compiles.

Declaring and Using Simple Data Types

With these basic facts about structures in mind, it is time to examine how C# implements the simple data types.

Within the *System* namespace is a set of predefined structures that define the simple data types. The keyword you use to declare a value-type variable using one of the simple data types actually is an alias for its associated structure definition. For example, the keyword *int* is an alias for *System.Int32*, and *double* is an alias for *System.Double*. Simple data types and their structures are shown in the following table.

Simple Data Type	Aliased Structure	Simple Data Type	Aliased Structure
Sbyte	System.SByte	Uint	System.UInt32
Byte	System.Byte	Long	System.Int64
Char	System.Char	Ulong	System.UInt64
Bool	System.Boolean	Float	System.Single
Short	System.Int16	Double	System.Double

Simple Data Type	Aliased Structure	Simple Data Type	Aliased Structure
Ushort	System.UInt16	Decimal	System.Decimal
Int	System.Int32		

USE IT The structure name is indistinguishable from the data type. To declare an *int*, for example, you could create an instance of the *System.Int32* structure, and then use the instance in every way that you would use the *int* variable:

```
//
//  TestInt.cs -- shows that using an instance of the System.Int32 structure
//                is the same as using the int keyword.
//
//                Compile this program with the following command line:
//                    C:>csc TestInt.cs
//
namespace nsTestInt
{
    using System;
    class clsMain
    {
        static public void Main ()
        {
            System.Int32 x;
            OutInt (out x);
            Console.WriteLine ("The integer is " + x);
            x = 42;
            ShowInt (x);
            ChangeInt (ref x);
            Console.WriteLine ("The integer is " + x);
        }
        static void OutInt (out int val)
        {
            val = 42;
        }
        static void ShowInt (int val)
        {
            Console.WriteLine ("The value passed is " + val.ToString());
        }
        static void ChangeInt (ref System.Int32 val)
        {
            val *= 2;
        }
    }
}
```

When you compile and run *TestInt.cs*, you should see the following output:

```
The integer is 42
The value passed is 42
The integer is 84
```

The compiler does not really care whether you use *int* or *System.Int32*. It cannot tell the difference, because *int* is simply an alias for *System.Int32*. (Actually, because you have declared that you are using the *System* namespace, you may shorten the declaration simply to *Int32*).

Each structure contains fields and methods used to define and manipulate the value. Each structure has *MinValue* and *MaxValue* fields that hold the lower and upper limits for the data types. Your program uses these values when you use the *checked* keyword to prevent data overflow and underflow. You can read these values from your program code, as in the following snippet:

```
Console.WriteLine ("The maximum value for Int32 is " + Int32.MaxValue);
Console.WriteLine ("The minimum value for Int32 is " + Int32.MinValue);
```

The structures also contain methods to manipulate the values, including *Parse()* to convert a *string* to the data type represented by the structure and *ToString()* to convert the data type to a *string*. When you write *42.ToString()*, for example, the code actually invokes the method for the structure's instance for *42*.

Creating Enumerated Lists

Enumerated values are the last of the value-types. An enumerated value is a convenient alias for a value or a set of values. Once you establish the enumerated list, you can refer to a value by name rather than having to remember a value. An enumerated value is read-only, and once established, you cannot change its value.

An enumerated type may be any of the integer data types except *char* or *bool*. It may be *sbyte*, *short*, *int*, or *long*, or the unsigned equivalent of these four data types. If you do not specify a data type for the enumeration (the *underlying* data type), the default is type *int*.

To declare an enumerated value, you use the keyword *enum* followed by the identifier you want to use for the enumerated list. Next comes an optional colon and data type. You must write the enumerated identifiers inside a set of braces and separate them with commas:

```
enum Numbers : long
{
    Zero, One, Two, Three
}
```

This declaration defines an enumerated list starting with *Numbers.Zero*, which represents a long value of 0, through *Numbers.Three*, which represents a long value of 3. The enumerated values by default begin at 0 and increase by a value of 1 as you step through the list. You may, however, assign any member any value, and the sequence will resume with the new value:

```
enum IntNumbers
{
    Zero, Three = 3, FortyTwo = 42, FortyThree, FortyFour
}
```

You need to understand that although the enumerated list has an underlying data type, the list itself essentially is a new data type. To use a value from the list, you must cast it back to the data type:

```
int x = (int) IntNumber.FortyTwo;  // The cast is required
```

Declaring an *enum* type does not create a variable, so you may define an enumeration outside of a class. When declared in this way, the enumeration becomes *public*, and it may be used by any class that can access its namespace.

USE IT If you declare an *enum* as a member of a class, you may declare it as *private*, *protected* or *public*. A *private* enumeration may be used only by members of the class, and a *protected* enumeration can be used by members of the class and any classes that you derived from it. A *public* enumeration may be used by any class that has access to the namespace containing the class, but you must access the enumeration from outside the class by using its qualified name. In the following program, *Enum.cs*, you declare an *enum* for the days of the week in one class, and then access it from another class using the class name, the member operator, the identifier for the *enum*, another member operator, and finally the enumeration member:

```
//
//  Enum.cs - Demonstrates using a public enum in one class from
//              another class
//
//              Compile this program with the following command line:
//                  C:>csc enum.cs
//
namespace nsEnum
{
    using System;
    class clsMain
    {
//  Define the enum type
        public enum Weekdays
        {
                Sun, Mon, Tues, Wed, Thurs, Fri, Sat, Count
        }
        static public void Main ()
        {
            clsSecond second = new clsSecond();
            second.ShowEnum ();
        }
```

```
    }
    class clsSecond
    {
        public void ShowEnum()
        {
// Use the class name with the enum name
            Console.WriteLine ("Tuesday is day {0} in the week",
                                    (int) clsMain.Weekdays.Tues);
        }
    }
}
```

Notice the *public* modifier on the definition of *Weekdays*. Enumerations are subject to the same access levels as member variables and functions. Without the *public* modifier, the *ShowEnum()* function in *clsSecond* would not be able to access *Weekdays*.

If a base class contains an enumerated type, classes that you derive from the base class will inherit the enumeration. Derived classes may override and modify an enumeration by using the *new* keyword. In the following example, *BaseEnum.cs*, the base class uses the *Weekday* enumeration with Sunday equal to 0. The derived class, for whatever reason, needs to start the week with Sunday equal to 1, so it overrides the enumeration using the *new* keyword:

```
//
//  BaseEnum.cs - Demonstrates how a derived class may override an existing
//                enumeration in a base class
//
//           Compile this program with the following command line:
//                C:>csc baseenum.cs
//
namespace nsEnum
{
    using System;
    class clsBaseClass
    {
// Define the enum type
        public enum Weekdays
        {
            Sun, Mon, Tues, Wed, Thurs, Fri, Sat
        }
        static public void Main ()
        {
            Console.WriteLine ("In base class, Sunday = " +
                                (int) Weekdays.Sun);
            clsNewClass second = new clsNewClass();
            second.ShowEnum ();
        }
```

```
    }
    class clsNewClass : clsBaseClass
    {
        public new enum Weekdays
        {
                Sun = 1, Mon, Tues, Wed, Thurs, Fri, Sat
        }
        public void ShowEnum()
        {
//  Use the class name with the enum name
            Console.WriteLine ("In derived class, Sunday = " +
                                (int) Weekdays.Sun);
        }
    }
}
```

When you compile and run *BaseEnum.cs*, you should see the following output:

```
In base class, Sunday = 0
In derived class, Sunday = 1
```

The override does not affect the base class enumeration and thus will not affect the base class code or any other classes that are derived from the base class.

Using Reference Types

References provide an indirect access to an object. You should be careful that you don't confuse the C# reference-type variable with the C++ reference variable. In C++, a reference is often called an *alias* because it is always coupled with an existing object. You must initialize a C++ reference at the time you declare it, and once initialized, you cannot change the object to which it refers. A C++ reference variable contains a pointer—the memory address—of another variable, but you use it as though it were the referenced variable itself.

The C# reference-type variable is more like the C++ *pointer* variable. It contains a pointer just like a reference. You may assign a reference-type variable a value when you declare it, but this isn't necessary. Later, you may change the value to point to another object.

Microsoft has designed C# so that, syntactically, you use the reference-type variable in much the same way that you use a C++ reference variable, using the member operator—a period—to address members of an object instance. In fact, C# does away will all the C++ resolution operators other than the period.

In C#, the reference-type variables are those that hold references to classes, arrays, delegates, and interfaces. Classes are covered in Chapter 7, arrays are the topic for Chapter 11, and delegates and events are discussed in Chapter 18. But objects in C# are intertwined, and you should have some understanding of the basic types when they come up in discussions, so they'll be discussed briefly here.

USE IT   The following short program first declares a reference type variable, and then creates the object that the variable will reference:

```
// RefType.cs -- Demonstrate declaring a reference type variable
//               and creating an object the variable will reference.
//
//               Compile this program with the following command line:
//                    C:>csc RefType.cs
using System;
using System.IO;


namespace nsRefType
{
    class clsMain
    {
        static public void Main ()
        {
// Declare the reference type variable
            FileStream strm;
// Create the object the variable will reference
            strm = new FileStream ("./File.txt",
                                    FileMode.OpenOrCreate,
                                    FileAccess.Write);
        }
    }
}
```

You could combine the two lines to declare the variable and create the object in a single statement:

```
// Declare the reference type variable and create the object
    FileStream strm = new FileStream ("./File.txt",
                                    FileMode.OpenOrCreate,
                                    FileAccess.Write);
```

Basics of C# Classes

The class is the primary data structure in C#. Without a class, there is no C# program. The C# class serves as a container for data members such as fields and constants and for functions. Any C# program must contain at least one class to hold the *Main()* function, although you may write individual modules for a program that do not contain the *Main()* function.

You declare and define a basic class using the *class* keyword followed by a set of braces. Within the braces, you declare the member fields, fields, and properties that your class will use. A class definition also may have *attributes* and modifiers, which will be covered in Chapter 7.

C# does not make a distinction between the declaration and definition. In C++, it is common to define a class in one file and then write the code for the member methods in another file. In C#, you must provide the code when you define the class. In C++, when you write the code for methods within the class definition, the methods are called *inline*. Although the C# members methods may look like C++ inline code and it may be convenient for you to think of them that way, the C# compiler does not actually treat them as inline.

USE IT The following snippet declares a class that includes and implements a couple of member methods:

```
class clsCircle
{
    const double pi = 3.14159;
    public double Area (double radius)
    {
        double area = pi * radius * radius;
        return (area);
    }
    public double Circumference (double radius)
    {
        double circumference = 2 * pi * radius;
        return (circumference);
    }
}
```

C# classes support *inheritance*, and you may use a class as a base to define a new class. The new class inherits all the fields, properties, and methods of the base class. A class may be *abstract*, in which case you *must* use it as a base class. You may not declare an instance of an abstract class directly. Abstract classes are the basis of an *interface*, which also is a reference-type object.

Declaring Arrays in C#

An array in C# is a group of variables of the same data type that you access using an index number. In most programming languages, the elements of an array are "contiguous" in memory—all the elements of the array occupy consecutive addresses. There is no such requirement in the C# language definition, which leads to some interesting constructions.

Declaring and creating an array in C# actually creates an instance of the *System.Array* class. The class instance handles the details of allocating memory to deal with the array elements. The *Array* class constructor is *protected*, so you may not create an instance of the class directly. Instead, to create an array you must follow some definite rules that establish the data type and the size of the array at the time that you declare and create it.

USE IT To declare an array, you write its data type followed by a set of square brackets. The brackets may not contain a value or variable. Then you write the identifier for the array, as shown in the following code:

```
int [] IntArray;      // Declares an array variable IntArray of type int
```

Just declaring an array does not create the array, nor does it create an instance of the *Array* class. To create an instance of the *Array* class, you must use the *new* operator, followed by the data type again and then a set of square brackets containing the array size:

```
IntArray = new int [10];   // Create an array of type int with 10 elements
```

As with the class, you may declare and create the array in a single statement:

```
int [] IntArray = new int [10];  // Declare and create a 10-element array
```

Array indexing always begins with a *0*. The first element in the array has an index of 0 and the last has an index of one less than the size of the array (so, for example, the last element of a 10-element array has an index of *9*). There is no *Option Base* statement to start indexing at 1 as there is in Visual Basic. In fact, Visual Basic 7.0 no longer supports the *Option Base* statement, making arrays in C# and Visual Basic compatible.

C# performs the same array bounds checking as Visual Basic. If you try to access a non-existent array element, your program will throw an *IndexOutOfRange* exception.

Understanding Interfaces

A C# *interface* is similar to a class, except its purpose is to declare a set of methods but not implement the methods. In an interface, you provide only function declarations; you do not provide any code for the member functions. Thus, all of the member functions are *abstract* functions, and you cannot declare an instance of an interface directly. In C++ terms, it is convenient to think of an interface as an abstract class that contains only pure virtual functions. To implement an interface, you must derive a class from it and provide code for the functions.

An interface also may not contain fields. The default access for members is *public*, and the compiler will issue an error if you try to give a member any other access.

The primary purpose of an interface is to describe a behavior but not define that behavior. Defining the actual behavior is up to the class that inherits from the interface. The interface becomes an ancestor class for the class that inherits from the interface. Although you may not declare an instance of an interface directly, you may cast an object to an interface type. This makes the interface useful for querying whether a class supports a particular method that is defined in an interface.

USE IT You met an example of using an interface in Chapter 4 with the C# *IDisposable* interface. (The convention in COM programming is to begin the name of an interface with a capital *I*; C# inherits that convention.) By using the *is* operator, you were able to determine whether a class implemented a particular method, and thus whether it was safe to call that method. The following program, *ISample.cs*, performs such a test:

```
//
//  ISample.cs - Demonstrates a safe method of determining whether a class
//                implements a particular interface
//                Compile this program with the following command line:
//                      C:>csc isample.cs
//
namespace nsInterfaceSample
{
    using System;
    class clsMain
    {
        static public void Main ()
        {
// Declare an instance of the clsSample class
            clsSample samp = new clsSample();
//  Test whether clsSample supports the IDisposable interface
            if (samp is IDisposable)
            {
//  If true, it is safe to call the Dispose() method
                IDisposable obj = (IDisposable) samp;
                obj.Dispose ();
            }
        }
    }
    class clsSample : IDisposable
    {
//  Implement the IDispose() function
        public void Dispose ()
        {
            Console.WriteLine ("Called Dispose() in clsSample");
        }
    }
}
```

If the test *samp is IDisposable* is true, you know that it is safe to call the *Dispose()* member because *clsSample* inherits from *IDisposable* and must implement the method. Notice that you cast the *clsSample* instance to *IDisposable* before calling the method. If you tried to call the following instance method and *clsSample* did not contain a *Dispose()* method, the compiler would generate an error:

```
if (samp is IDisposable)
{
//  If true, it is safe to call the Dispose() method
    samp.Dispose ();
}
```

In this case, the test result would be false and the conditional code would not execute anyway. However, if *clsSample* did not have a *Dispose()* method, the compiler would generate an error. By casting to an *IDisposable* type, you avoid the compiler error and determine whether you may safely call the *Dispose()* method.

Using Delegates to Create a Callback Function

A *delegate* is similar to an interface except that it declares a *single* method without implementing it, while an interface declares a *group* of methods. You will use delegates extensively in Windows programming to provide methods to respond to *events*, such as the messages sent from the controls on a dialog box.

A delegate is similar to the C and C++ *function pointer*. A function pointer, however, may contain only the address of a *static* method. A delegate, on the other hand, may refer to instance methods in classes. This is because a delegate, like many other mechanisms in C#, is implemented through a class, the *System.Delegate* class, which can store the address of a class instance as well as a pointer to a method.

Delegates come in two flavors, *single-cast* and *multi-cast*. A single-cast delegate provides for a single method when the delegate is invoked. A single-cast delegate may return a value, such as the result of an arithmetic operation or an object pointer. A multi-cast delegate allows you to assign more than one method to the delegate. Each method is called in order each time you invoke the delegate. A multi-cast delegate may not return a value.

▶ *NOTE*

Although multi-cast delegates are not allowed to return values, the current implementation of Visual C# does permit you to define multi-cast delegates that do return values. This sometimes can lead to confusing and erroneous results.

USE IT   Normally, you will use delegates with *events*, but you are not required to use delegates in this way. The following program, *Delegate.cs*, shows a minimum implementation of a delegate. It performs two different arithmetic operations depending upon which function, *Square()* or *SquareRoot()*, has been assigned to the delegate.

```
//  Delegate.cs - Demonstrates the minimum implementation of a delegate
//               Compile this program with the following command line:
//                    C:>csc Delegate.cs
//
namespace nsDelegate
{
    using System;

    class clsMain
```

```
        {
//  Declare the delegate type
        public delegate double MathHandler (double val);
//  Declare the variable that will hold the delegate
        public MathHandler DoMath;

        static public void Main ()
        {
            double val = 31.2;
            double result;
            clsMain main = new clsMain ();
//  Create the first delegate
            main.DoMath = new clsMain.MathHandler (main.Square);
//  Call the function through the delegate
            result = main.DoMath (val);
            Console.WriteLine ("The square of {0,0:F1} is {1,0:F3}",
                               val,  result);
//  Create the second delegate
            main.DoMath = new clsMain.MathHandler (main.SquareRoot);
//  Call the function through the delegate
            result = main.DoMath (val);
            Console.WriteLine ("The square root of {0,0:F1} is {1,0:F3}",
                               val, result);
        }
        public double Square (double val)
        {
            return (val * val);
        }
        public double SquareRoot (double val)
        {
            return (Math.Sqrt (val));
        }
    }
}
```

The call to *DoMath( )* either squares the value or finds the square root of the value, depending on which function has been assigned to the delegate. When you run the program, you see the following output:

```
The square of 31.2 is 973.440
The square root of 31.2 is 5.586
```

A common technique in C++ to select from a group of functions is to set up an array of function pointers, and then compute the index of the array to determine what function to call. This way, you can perform in just a few of lines of code what otherwise would require a lengthy *switch* statement. You can't do that in C#, but you may declare an array of delegates, as in the following declaration:

```
public delegate void CommandHandler();
public CommandHandler [] DoCommand;
```

In your code, you would then create the array of function pointers (or delegates) and assign the functions to the delegate array elements:

```
clsMain main = new clsMain();
main.DoCommand = new CommandHandler []
{
    new clsMain.CommandHandler(main.FunctionOne),
    new clsMain.CommandHandler(main.FunctionTwo),
    new clsMain.CommandHandler(main.FunctionThree),
    new clsMain.CommandHandler(main.FunctionFour),
    new clsMain.CommandHandler(main.FunctionFive),
    new clsMain.CommandHandler(main.FunctionSix)
};
```

Using the *object* Data Type

Classes may inherit the properties, fields, and methods of a *base* class. In C#, all classes ultimately derive from a single super-class, called the *Object* class. Although it is the ultimate base class for all classes that you define and use in C#, the *Object* class contains no fields or properties and only a few methods.

The *object* data type is an alias for the *Object* class. You may declare an instance of *object* directly, but it has limited use. The ultimate purpose of *object* is to define and implement the methods that derived classes will need.

As with the structures used as the base for the simple data types, the *Object* class is indistinguishable from the *object* data type. Any time you need to use an *Object* instance, you may use the *object* type instead. The following two declarations are identical to the compiler:

```
Object obj = new Object();
object obj = new object();
object obj = new Object();
```

Because it is the ultimate base class, you may cast any data type—whether value-type or reference-type—to an *Object* type. This makes it the ultimate universal data type, and it's the data type used to box and unbox value-types.

USE IT You may use the *object* type as a universal parameter to a function to which you may need to pass more than one data type. You also may use *object* as the return type for a function, in which case you may return any data type. When you use *object* in the latter way, as in the following short program, *Obj.cs*, the boxing is automatic, and your function must take care not to try to unbox any data type other than the type you pass it:

```
//  Obj.cs - Demonstrates automatic boxing and unboxing to pass an
//           undetermined data type to a function.
//           Compile this program with the following command line:
//               C:>csc Obj.cs
//
namespace nsObject
{
    using System;
    class clsMain
    {
        static public void Main ()
        {
            double d = 3.14159;
//  Pass a double to Square ()
            object o = Square (d);
            ShowSquare (o);
//  Pass an int to Square ()
            o = Square (42);
            ShowSquare (o);
//  Pass a float to Square ()
            o = Square (2.71828F);
            ShowSquare (o);
        }
//  Square() returns the boxed square of a value if the data type is
//  int or double. Otherwise, Square() returns a null reference
        static object Square (object o)
        {
            if (o is double)
                return ((double) o * (double) o);
            if (o is int)
                return ((int) o * (int) o);
            return (null);
        }
        static public void ShowSquare (object o)
        {
            if (Object.Equals (o, null))
                Console.WriteLine ("The object is null");
            else
                Console.WriteLine ("The square is " + o);
        }
    }
}
```

The *Square()* function contains code to square an *int* and a *double* data type, but not a *float*. When you pass the function a *float* data type (the value 2.71828 has an *F* suffix), it returns a *null* reference.

Passing Variables to Functions

Programming languages normally use one of two systems to pass variables in function calls: *call by reference* and *call by value*.

In call by reference, the program passes the address—a reference—of a variable, and any changes the function or subroutine makes to the variable will be reflected in the original variable. This is the system used by FORTRAN and other early computer languages.

In the call-by-value system, the program makes a copy of the variable's value and passes the copy to the function or subroutine. The function is free to modify and apply operators to the variable, but changes will not be made to the original variable.

C# uses call by value regardless of whether the variable is a value-type or a reference-type. (As demonstrated in Chapter 4, a reference-type variable actually is a value-type variable that contains a reference.)

C# provides a mechanism through the *ref* keyword that you may pass a value-type argument by reference to a function. When you use the *ref* keyword in a method's parameter list, a call to the method actually passes the address of a variable as the value for the parameter, but you use the value as though it were the variable itself. This is useful when you need to get more than one value from a function.

USE IT   The following example, *Point.cs*, uses two reference variables in a function that computes the x and y coordinates of a point on a circle. The *Circle()* method returns the points in the reference variables and the area of the section of the circle as the return value:

```
//
//  Point.cs -- demonstrate returning values through reference parameters.
//
//              Compile this program with the following command line:
//                   C:>csc Point.cs
namespace nsPoint
{
    using System;
    class clsMain
    {
        static public int Main (string [] args)
        {
            int angle;
            int radius = 100;
            try
            {
                angle = int.Parse (args[0]);
            }
```

```
            catch (IndexOutOfRangeException)
            {
                Console.WriteLine ("usage: point [angle in degrees]");
                return (-1);
            }
            catch (FormatException)
            {
                Console.WriteLine ("Please use a number value for " +
                                "the angle in degrees");
                return (-1);
            }
            int cx = 0;
            int cy = 0;
            double Area = Circle (angle, radius, ref cx, ref cy);
            Console.WriteLine ("The point on the circle is at ({0}, {1})",
                            cx, cy);
            Console.WriteLine ("The area of the circle is {0,0:F3}", Area);
            return (0);
        }
        static public double Circle (int angle, int radius,
                                    ref int cx, ref int cy)
        {
            const double radian = 57.29578;
// Convert the angle to radians
            double fAngle = (double) angle / radian;
// Compute the x position of the point
            cx = (int)((double) radius * Math.Cos (fAngle) + 0.5);
// Compute the y position of the point
            cy = (int)((double) radius * Math.Sin (fAngle) + 0.5);
//  Compute the area of the pie section
            return ((double) radius * (double) radius * fAngle / 2.0);
        }
    }
}
```

The *Circle()* method returns three values, and x and y coordinates of the point on the circle (assuming the center of the circle is at 0,0 and there may be some round-off error) in the reference values, and the area of the section of the circle.

You should notice three points in this code. First, notice that you must use the *ref* keyword both on the call to the argument list when you call the *Circle()* method and in the parameter list when you define the method. C# does not automatically convert the arguments to reference variables as C++ does.

Second, the *cx* and *cy* values are initialized when they are declared. Even though you initialize the variables in the *Circle()* method, the compiler will not let you pass them as arguments unless you initialize them first. The compiler has no way of knowing whether the method—which may be in another module, for example—will attempt to use the uninitialized values, so it issues the error.

You may call a function using a variable that has not been initialized if you use the *out* keyword instead of *ref*. The *out* specification is the same as a *ref*, but by using it you tell the compiler that you intend to give the variable a value in the *Circle()* method. You could rewrite the variable declaration and function call as shown in the following:

```
int cx, cy;
 double Area = Circle (angle, radius, out cx, out cy);
```

Then you would define the *Circle()* method to use the *out* parameters as well:

```
static public double Circle (int angle, int radius,
                        out int cx, out int cy)
```

Even though *out* and *ref* are both references, you cannot mix *out* and *ref* keywords. If you use *out* in the method declaration, the matching variable in the argument list when you call the method must also be *out*.

Finally, in the *Circle()* method, the variable *radian* is declared using the *const* modifier. This establishes the variable as a read-only or constant value. When you declare a *const* parameter, you must initialize the variable at the same time you declare it. After that, you may not change the value of the variable. In this case, *radian* represents a trigonometric constant, and you would not want to modify it, even accidentally.

Using Fields and Properties

A variable that you declare as a member of a class may be either a *field* or a *property*. A field is an ordinary variable, one for which the value is the focus. A property is a more object-oriented variable that includes methods to store and retrieve a value. A property usually stores a value in a field, but that is not required.

You declare a field in a class definition the same way you declare a variable in a function, except you may include an access level—*public*, *protected*, or *private*. If you do not include an access keyword, it will default to *private*. You also may initialize a field at the same time you declare it:

```
public int var = 0;
```

From within Visual Studio, you may add fields to a class directly or you may use the Field Wizard, shown in Figure 5-1.

1. To display the Field Wizard, you need to display the Class View tool box, which shares space in Visual Studio with the Solution Explorer. If the Class Wizard is not visible, type CTRL-SHIFT-C, or choose View | Class View.

2. Open the tree in Class View until the class in which you want to add a field is visible. Right-click the class name.

3. From the context menu, select the Add item. Then select the Add Field item from the popup submenu. The Field Wizard should display.

4. In the Field Wizard, you may select only one of the Field Access values in the drop-down box. In the Field Type box, you may select one of the predefined values in the drop-down box or enter another data type such as a class name. The Field Name that you enter will be the identifier that you will use for the field. The Field Wizard will check the identifiers already used in the class, such as methods, properties, or other fields, to make sure you do not duplicate a name.

5. You can use the Field Modifiers button group to make the new field *static* or *const*. If you click the Constant button, you must enter the initial value in the Field Value box. If you click None or Static, the Field Wizard will not let you enter anything in the Field Value box.

6. The Comment field is a convenient point to enter a description of the new field. The Field Wizard will include any text you enter here in XML comment format using three slash marks. Although the label hints that typing the comment marker, "//", is optional, do not type them unless you want them included in the XML comment along with the three automatically included.

7. Finally, click the Finish button and the Field Wizard will check the class to make sure the field identifier is unique. If it is, the Field Wizard will add the new field to your class. If it is not unique, you will get a message to that effect and have a chance to change the field name.

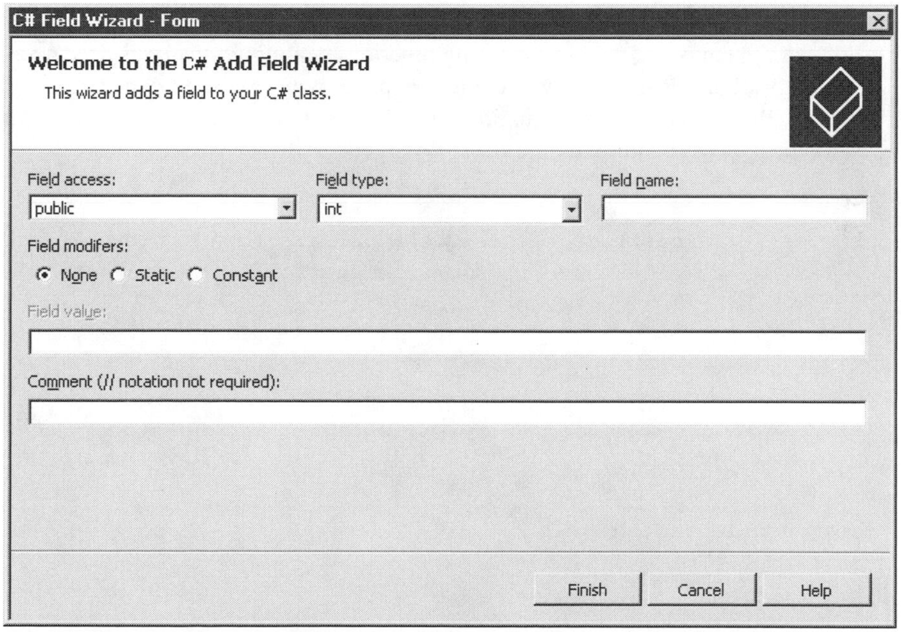

Figure 5.1   The Field Wizard contains selection boxes you use to enter all the information needed to declare a field

A property is a "smart" field. You declare a property the same way you declare a field, except you include *accessor* functions to store and retrieve the values. You may include a *get* accessor to retrieve the value or a *set* accessor to store a value, or you may include both *get* and *set* accessors:

```
public int Var
{
    get
    {
        // Statements to retrieve a value
    }
    set
    {
        // Statements to store a value
    }
}
```

A property's data type may be any of the simple data types, or it may be a user-defined type such as a class object or a structure. You may *override* a property in a derived class.

Simply declaring a property does not set aside any memory to store a value. To store a value, you need to set aside a field. You commonly will use *private* fields to store values and *public* or *protected* properties to access the fields. This gives you an opportunity to include code to make sure the field contains a valid value or to convert the value from one data type to another.

USE IT   For example, most of the programming functions dealing with angles need a value in *radians*, but it is more convenient for people to work with angles in degrees. The following program, *Property.cs*, stores an angle in radians in a *double* field but uses a property with an *int* data type to access and set the field:

```
//
//  Property.cs -- Demonstrates access to a private field through a property.
//                 Compile this program with the following command line:
//                      C:>csc Property.cs
//
namespace nsProperty
{
    using System;
    class clsMain
    {
        const double radian = 57.29578;
        const double pi = 3.14159;
        int Angle
        {
            get
            {
                int angle = (int) (fAngle * radian + 0.5);
                angle = angle == 360 ? 0 : angle;
                return (angle);
```

```
        }
        set
        {
            double angle = (double) value / radian;
            if (angle < (2 * pi))
            {
                fAngle = angle;
                Console.WriteLine ("fAngle set to {0,0:F5}", fAngle);
            }
            else
            {
                Console.WriteLine ("fAngle not modified");
            }
        }
    }
    double fAngle = 0.0;    //  Angle in radians
    static public int Main (string [] args)
    {
        int angle;
        try
        {
            angle = int.Parse (args[0]);
        }
        catch (IndexOutOfRangeException)
        {
            Console.WriteLine ("usage: circle [angle in degrees]");
            return (-1);
        }
        catch (FormatException)
        {
            Console.WriteLine ("Use a number for the angle in degrees");
            return (-1);
        }
        clsMain main = new clsMain();
        main.Angle = angle;
        Console.WriteLine ("The angle is {0} degrees", main.Angle);
        return (0);
    }
  }
}
```

Syntactically, you use a property the same way you use a field, but your program accesses the value through the *get* and *set* accessors. In this example, notice the use of the *value* variable. You do not need to declare *value* because it is an *intrinsic* variable that a program passes to the *set* accessor. The data type for *value* will be the same as the property's data type, in this example an *int* type.

In this example, the *set* accessor first converts the integer angle value in degrees to a *double* value in radians. If the value is less than two times *pi* (a full circle), it stores the result in the *private* field. Otherwise, the accessor simply prints a message that the field value was not changed. The accessor is both converting the data type and assuring that the field contains a primary angle value.

When you retrieve the value, the *get* accessor first converts the value of the field variable to an integer. If the value is 360 (which may happen due to round-off error), it returns a 0. Otherwise, it returns the angle in degrees.

Using a property is the same as using a field. You simply use the property identifier in an expression or assignment operation. If the property does not contain a *get* accessor, using the property in an expression will cause the compiler to generate an error. Similarly, if the property does not contain a *set* accessor, attempting to assign a value to the property will cause a compiler error.

The Visual Studio Property Wizard shown in Figure 5-2 is a convenient method for adding a property to a class. The Property Wizard will create the *get* and *set* accessors as needed.

You summon the Property Wizard the same way you displayed the Field Wizard except you select Add Property from the popup submenu. The access, type, name, and comment boxes are the same as for the Field Wizard. For the Accessors, you may select either *get*, *set*, or both. Normally, a property will use both *get* and *set* accessors, so the default is to add both to the property.

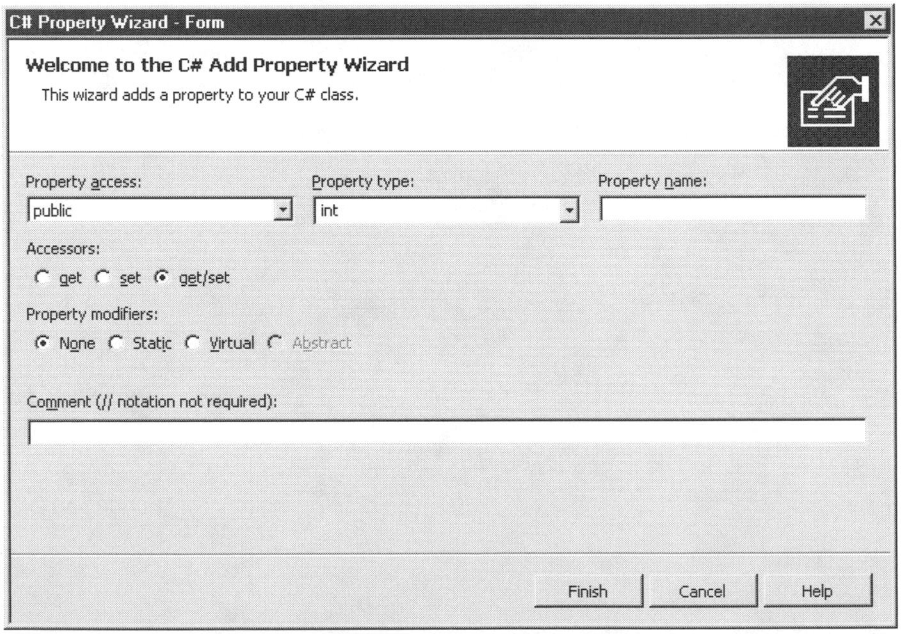

Figure 5.2   The Property Wizard dialog box contains controls that let you set the elements for a property and to add the property to a class

In the Property Modifiers button group, notice the Virtual and Abstract selection, which did not appear in the Field Wizard. You may declare a property as *virtual*, in which case you may override the property in a derived class.

The Abstract button is enabled only if you are adding the property to an Abstract class. If you select this button, the property itself will be declared as *abstract*, and you may not provide code for the *get* and *set* accessors. Instead, you must override the property and provide the code in a derived class.

Using String Interning to Reduce Memory Consumption

C# implements the *string* data type through the *System.String* class. When you declare a *string* variable and give it a value, you are actually creating an instance of the *String* class. The class contains a number of powerful methods for formatting and manipulating strings, and C# also provides other classes that provide methods to format a string for display and to treat a string as a *stream* object.

Because it is an instance of a class, a string variable is a reference-type variable. String handling always has been a problem area for newcomers to C and C++, but the *String* class handles most of the details of string handling and makes it almost as easy as BASIC string handling.

When you use a string literal in a program, the compiler must store the string in program code so that it may retrieve the string when you run the program. If you use the same string literals repeatedly, keeping a copy of each use in the program could use up a lot of memory very quickly.

In Visual C++ you can get around this by defining a string constant using the preprocessor *#define* directive and then setting a compiler option (*/Gf* in Visual C++) to reference this constant each time you use the constant identifier.

C#, however, does not use the *#define* directive in this way, but it still provides a method for conserving memory when using string constants. The CLR maintains an internal table of string literals that you can use in your program. This table, the *intern pool*, stores a copy of each unique string literal you use in your program. When you use a string literal in your program, C# checks the table to see whether another literal matches the one you are using. If it finds a match, the reference is set to point to the internal table entry. If no match of an existing literal is found, a new table entry is created. This process saves memory, especially for programs that use strings heavily.

USE IT You can retrieve the reference to an entry in the intern pool by using the *Intern()* method in the *String* class. If you define a string literal in one part of your code and later want to retrieve the reference, you would use code similar to the following:

```
string str1 = "This string is interned";
//  Additional program code;
string str2 = String.Intern (str1);
```

This is really the same as simply assigning *str2* the reference in *str1*.

Encoding Strings in C#

The *char* data type in C# is a 16-bit value based on the C++ wide character type. By default, it uses the Unicode encoding scheme, The *String* class implements a C# string in an array of characters. The *String* class is immutable, so once you declare and initialize a *string* variable, you cannot change its value.

However, you may assign a new string to a *string* variable at any time. In this case, C# discards the old string and creates a new instance of *String* to hold the new value. If you need a string that you can modify, C# provides a separate class, the *StringBuilder* class. (If your program makes many changes to a string, you could leave many unreferenced string objects in the heap memory. These objects will persist until the CLR removes them.)

You may use the same formatting that you use for the *Console.Write()* and *Console.WriteLine()* methods to format the contents of a string. However, this is not the most efficient method because each operation on the string creates a new copy. The *StringBuilder* class provides methods to build a string more efficiently.

For example, while you may read the value of an individual character in a *String* object using an index, you cannot set a character in the same way. In the following code, the compiler will allow the second statement but will issue an error on the third:

```
string str = "ABCDEf";
char ch = str[5];        // ch is now equal to f
str[5] = 'F';            // Error. Cannot set the indexer value
```

The *StringBuilder* class, however, has no such restriction. Unfortunately, the *StringBuilder* class has other restrictions. While you may create a *String* object using the string data type, you must build a *StringBuilder* object using the *new* operator. In addition, the *StringBuilder* class is in the *System.Text* namespace, so you must include a *using System.Text;* statement in your code.

The *StringBuilder* class includes methods for building and modifying text and to insert, remove, and replace characters in the string. Once you have built the string using *StringBuilder*, you can assign it to a *string* variable using the *ToString()* member.

USE IT The following program, *Builder.cs*, opens a text file and reads it line by line. It then splits the line into words to count the number of words, and then builds an output string with the *StringBuilder* object showing the line number in the file, the number of words in the line, and the number of characters:

```
//
//  Builder.cs -- Demonstrates manipulating a string read as a line from a file
//                Compile this program with the following command line:
//                     C:>csc Builder.cs
//
namespace nsBuilder
{
    using System;
    using System.Text;
```

```csharp
    using System.IO;
    class clsMain
    {
        static public int Main ()
        {
// Create a stream object and open the input file
            FileStream istream;
            try
            {
                istream = new FileStream ("sample.txt", FileMode.Open,
                                                FileAccess.Read);
            }
            catch (Exception)
            {
                Console.WriteLine ("Could not open sample.txt for reading");
                return (-1);
            }
// Associate a reader with the stream
            StreamReader reader = new StreamReader (istream);
// Declare a new StringBuilder
            StringBuilder strb = new StringBuilder ();
// Counter for the lines
            int Lines = 0;
            while (reader.Peek() > 0)
            {
                ++Lines;
// Clear out the string builder
                strb.Length = 0;
// Read a line from the file
                string str = reader.ReadLine();
// Split the line into words
                string [] Data = str.Split (new char [] {' '});
// Build the output line to show line, word and character count
                strb.AppendFormat ("Line {0} contains {1} words and {2} " +
                    "characters:\r\n{3}",
                    Lines, Data.Length, str.Length, str);
// Write the string to the console
                Console.WriteLine (strb.ToString ());
            }
            istream.Close ();
            return (0);
        }
    }
}
```

When you compile and run *Builder.cs*, the program will read each line in the file and then insert line, word, and character count information. It will then print the information and the line itself to the console. With each iteration of the loop, you clear the contents of the *StringBuilder* object by setting its length to 0.

Now create a text file named sample.txt and add several lines to it. You should see output similar to the following:

```
Line 1 contains 10 words and 48 characters:
The quick red fox jumps over the lazy brown dog.
Line 2 contains 16 words and 70 characters:
Now is the time for all good men to come to the aid of their Teletype.
Line 3 contains 8 words and 45 characters:
Peter Piper picked a peck of peppered pickles.
```

Characters come in different sets and encoding systems, so strings must be able to handle and contain these different character systems. There is ASCII, which represents characters in 7 bits; extended ASCII, which uses 8 bits; and Unicode, which uses 16 bits. At times you will need to convert from one to the other.

The *System.Text* namespace contains a class, *Encoding*, that allows you to convert among the various encoding schemes. The *Encoding* class is an abstract class, so you cannot create an instance of it directly. You can use it to build your own custom conversion, or you can use one of the derived C# classes shown in the following table:

Encoding Class	Use
ASCIIEncoding	Encodes Unicode characters as single 7-bit ASCII characters.
UnicodeEncoding	Encodes each Unicode character as two consecutive bytes.
UTF7Encoding	Encodes Unicode characters using the UTF-7 (UCS Transformation Format, 7-bit form) encoding. Supports all Unicode character values.
UTF8Encoding	Encodes Unicode characters using the UTF-8 (UCS Transformation Format, 8-bit form) encoding. Supports all Unicode character values.

USE IT The following program, *Convert.cs*, reads a file called *Sample.asc* in ASCII format and rewrites the text to another file called *Sample.wcs* in wide (16-bit) character format:

```
//  Convert.cs -- Reads an ASCII encoded file and writes the text
//                to another file in wide character format.
//                Compile this program with the following command line:
//                    C:>csc Convert.cs
//
namespace nsConvert
{
    using System;          // For Console class
    using System.Text;     // For encoding classes
    using System.IO;       // For FileStream class
```

```
    class clsMain
    {
        static public int Main ()
        {
// First, make sure both the input and output files can be opened
            FileStream ostream;
            FileStream istream;
            try
            {
                istream = new FileStream ("Sample.asc", FileMode.Open,
                                                FileAccess.Read);
            }
            catch (Exception)
            {
                Console.WriteLine ("Cannot open Sample.asc for reading");
                return (-1);
            }
            try
            {
                ostream = new FileStream ("Sample.wcs", FileMode.Create,
                                                FileAccess.ReadWrite);
            }
            catch (Exception)
            {
                Console.WriteLine ("Cannot open Sample.wcs for writing");
                istream.Close ();
                return (-1);
            }
// Create a stream reader and attach the input stream with ASCII encoding
            StreamReader reader = new StreamReader (istream,
                                            new ASCIIEncoding());
            string str = reader.ReadToEnd ();
// Create a stream writer and attach the output stream using Unicode encoding
            StreamWriter writer = new StreamWriter (ostream,
                                            new UnicodeEncoding());
// Write the text to the file.
            writer.Write (str);
// Flush the output stream
            writer.Flush ();
// Close the streams
            ostream.Close ();
            istream.Close ();
            return (0);
        }
    }
}
```

To see the results in the output file, you will need a viewer that will let you look at the contents in byte format, such as in hexadecimal. (As it happens, you can use a project called *HexView* in the Chapter05 directory of the book's Web site. Although it isn't a hex editor, it is simple enough that you can understand it with limited knowledge of C#, and it uses *StringBuilder* to show how to create a custom view by building the text line by line.)

Data Conversion in C#

In a perfect world of programming, every value that you try to assign to a variable would have the same data type as the variable itself. Some programming languages use only a single data type, and might achieve this ideal. In C#, however, you eventually are going to have to convert one data type to another.

The compiler allows some *implicit* conversions automatically when it can determine the nature of the conversion and when the conversion would not cause a loss of precision. You could, for example, assign the integer value *42* to a variable with a *long* data type and the compiler would allow it implicitly. However, you could not assign the string "42" to a *long* because the compiler would not be able to determine the nature of the conversion.

 In some cases, you may perform an *explicit* conversion by using the *cast* operator, writing the new data type inside a set of parentheses. You could assign a *long* value to an *int* data type using an explicit cast, as in the following snippet:

```
long lVal = 42;            // Implicit conversion;
int iVal = (long) lVal;    // Explicit conversion
```

The compiler needs the cast operator because a *long* value uses more memory, 8 bytes, to store a value and the *int* type requires only 4 bytes. Thus, the conversion *might* cause a loss of precision, and you must tell the compiler that you really want to perform this conversion.

C# also contains some shorthand symbols and data conversion classes that permit some conversions, and most of the simple data type structures include a *Parse()* method to convert a string to their data types.

For example, you can suffix a number with *L* to indicate that it is a *long* value when the data type may not be evident, such as a value used in an expression. Therefore, writing *42L* is the same as writing *(long) 42*. To convert the same number to a *double*, you could write *42.0* or *42D*, and the compiler would interpret these as an explicit cast *(double) 42*. You also could add the *F* suffix to convert the value to a *float* data type, as in *42F* (in C#, a *float* is a single-precision floating type and requires 4 bytes, while a *double* is a double-precision floating type and requires 8 bytes).

Money values usually require an explicit conversion. If you wanted to assign $2.35 to a *decimal* variable, for example, you cannot simply write *decimal dVar = 2.35*. The compiler would reject the cast because it would not allow an implicit conversion from a floating type to a decimal type. To do this, you could use *(decimal)* cast, or you could use the *M* suffix (think of *M* for **M**oney), as in *decimal dVar = 2.35M*.

Writing numbers with exponents can sometimes be a problem. For example, for Avogadro's number, 6.022045×10^{23}, you could write something like the following:

```
double Avogadro = 6.022045 * 100000000000000000000000D
```

Counting out that many zeros, though, is likely to lead to errors, and if you leave off the *D* suffix, the compiler will reject the value as being too large for an integer value. C# allows a much easier method by letting you write *E* to indicate an exponent value. The *E* must be preceded by a number constant, and the number that follows would be the exponent of the number 10. Writing Avogadro's number reduces to simply *6.022045E23*. Notice that you write the *E* without including leading or trailing spaces. To the compiler, inserting spaces here would indicate separate values. You can, however, use a plus sign (+) between the *E* and the exponent to indicate a positive exponent and a minus sign (–) to indicate a negative exponent.

Converting a string to a number is a fairly common practice in programming. Command-line arguments are passed to a C# program as strings rather than numbers. Most of the numeric simple data types contain a *Parse()* method to convert a string to a number.

For example, to convert the string "42" to the integer value *42*, you could write the following code:

```
string str = "42";
int iVal = int.Parse (str);
```

Alternatively, you could use one of the static methods in the *Convert* class:

```
string str = "42";
int iVal = Convert.ToInt32 (str);
```

With both of these methods, you must be careful that the string contains a convertible value. If, for example, *str* is a command-line argument and the user types "42.0" instead of simply "42", your program is going to throw a *FormatException*. Handling user errors such as this is the topic of Chapter 9.

CHAPTER 6

Structures in C#

TIPS IN THIS CHAPTER

The *structure* is one of the oldest and best known data mechanisms in modern programming. The structure and its predecessors have been known by other names, such as a *record* and a *block*, and most modern programming languages support it in some form.

At minimum, a structure is a collection of data fields that may be of different types. A programmer may access the fields in a structure individually or collectively as a single unit. You can use a structure to save a block of data to a file in a single write, or you can pass a structure as an argument in a function call.

It is not surprising, then, that the authors of C# incorporated the structure into the new language. In C#, a structure is similar to a class, but it has some unique properties and some important restrictions that set it apart from the class.

For one, a variable that implements a C# structure is a *value-type* variable, whereas a class variable is a *reference-type* variable. You can pass a structure as an argument in a function call the same way you can pass any of the simple data types. When you use a structure as an argument, the program makes a copy of all the fields and passes the copy to the function. Or, you may pass a structure as a reference argument by using the *ref* keyword.

A C# structure inherits many of its characteristics from the C++ structure, which in turn is built on the structure as it existed in C. A structure may have fields—individual data units—of different data types. It also may contain functions—or methods—including constructor functions.

The Evolution of the Structure

The structure's history began when programmers realized a need to group together related information, often with different data types, as a single item. A structure fits the bill, for example, when a programmer needs to group together personnel information such as name, address, salary, and other information for an employee, treating the collection of information as a single unit and writing it to a storage medium as a block.

The original structure in C was little more than a convenient mechanism to hold variables that contained related information. A C structure may contain only data elements, such as the simple data types in C#. A C structure cannot contain functions or methods, but it can contain a pointer to a function (called a *delegate* in C#).

The structure, then, is one of the earliest programming objects and predates the development of object-oriented languages. The concept of a structured block of data elements was behind the class concept of the Smalltalk programming language.

When Bjarne Stroustrup was developing the C++ language, he brought the structure over and borrowed heavily from C to build the C++ class. In fact, a C++ structure is barely distinguishable from a class. In C++, the structure elements are *public* by default, while class members are *private* by default. Both the structure and the class in C++ may contain functions, including constructors and destructors, and both may be used as bases for deriving new classes and structures. In fact, in C++ you may derive a class using an existing structure as a base, or you may derive a new structure using an existing class as a base.

Despite the publicity and hype about the power of C#, the structure as implemented in C# is actually less powerful and versatile than it is in C++. For example, you cannot define your own default constructor (one with no parameters) or give a structure a destructor. Still, the structure is a useful mechanism.

Although the C# structure is derived from the *Object* class, you cannot use it as a base to derive a new structure or class. If you do, as in the following snippet, the compiler will issue an error that you "cannot inherit from a sealed class":

```
struct stPoint
{
    int cx;
    int cy;
}
class clsCircle : stPoint
{
}
```

This tells you something about the internal makeup of the structure. In C#, a *sealed class* cannot be used as a base class from which to derive a new class. In fact, the compiler will issue exactly the same error message if you define *stPoint* in the preceding code as a sealed class:

```
sealed class stPoint
{
    int cx;
    int cy;
}
class clsCircle : stPoint
{
}
```

Internally, then, the definition of a structure must be the same as or close to that of a sealed class. The compiler and a C# program, however, treat the class and the structure as very different object types, and some restrictions apply as to what you may include in a structure.

A structure may not inherit from another structure or from a class definition. However, it may inherit from an interface definition, and if it does, the structure must implement the methods declared in the interface.

A C# structure may contain a constructor function, but it may not contain a destructor function (actually, the structure *inherits* a destructor function, and you may not override it). If the structure does implement a constructor function, the parameter list for the constructor must not be empty— that is, you must pass one or more arguments to a structure's constructor function.

In a structure, you cannot initialize the member fields when you declare them. In addition, you cannot initialize the fields when you declare an instance of a structure. You can, however, pass initial values through a constructor. This makes the constructor more important in C# than it is in C++.

An instance of a structure is always a value-type variable, which means that a C# program creates the structure instance on the program's stack. This is true whether or not you declare the instance using the *new* operator. Assuming that you have defined a structure *stPoint*, both of the following lines of code result in the same declaration:

```
stPoint point;
stPoint point = new stPoint;
```

The *new* operator is not without value when used with a structure, however. You will need to use *new* if you want to initialize the fields in a structure when you declare a structure instance.

A structure is a *user-defined* value-type data type. In most respects, a C# program treats a structure instance the same way it treats an instance of a simple data type. You can use the *sizeof* operator on a structure definition, but if the structure contains any reference-type members, the compiler will not allow you to use the *sizeof* operator on the structure.

Because the structure is a value-type object, it is a particularly convenient alternative to the class when the object contains mostly data fields. You may use the assignment operator directly to copy the fields in a structure. By contrast, when you use the assignment operator on class objects, you deal with the reference rather than the contents of the class. The following program, *CmpStCls.cs*, shows this difference:

```
//
//  CmpStCls.cs -- Demonstrates assignment operator on structures and classes.
//                 Compile this program with the following command line:
//                     C:>csc CmpStCls.cs
//
namespace nsCompare
{
    using System;
//
// Define a structure containing the x and y coordinates of a point
    struct stPoint
    {
        public int cx;
        public int cy;
    }
//
// Define a class containing the x and y coordinates of a point
    class clsPoint
    {
        public int cx;
        public int cy;
    }
    class clsMain
    {
        static public void Main ()
        {
// Declare two structure variables
            stPoint spt1, spt2;
// Initialize the members of only one structure
```

```
            spt1.cx = 42;
            spt1.cy = 24;
// Assign the first structure to the second
            spt2 = spt1;
// Now modify the first structure
            spt1.cx = 12;
            spt1.cy = 18;
// Show the results
            Console.WriteLine ("For structures:");
            Console.WriteLine ("\tThe point for spt1 is ({0}, {1})",
                            spt1.cx, spt1.cy);
            Console.WriteLine ("\tThe point for spt2 is ({0}, {1})",
                            spt2.cx, spt2.cy);

// Now do the same thing with instances of the class
            clsPoint cpt1, cpt2;
            cpt1 = new clsPoint();
// Initialize the members of only one class instance
            cpt1.cx = 42;
            cpt1.cy = 24;
// Assign the first class instance to the second
            cpt2 = cpt1;
// Modify the first class
            cpt1.cx = 12;
            cpt2.cy = 18;
// Show the results
            Console.WriteLine ("\r\nFor classes:");
            Console.WriteLine ("\tThe point for cpt1 is ({0}, {1})",
                             cpt1.cx, cpt1.cy);
            Console.WriteLine ("\tThe point for cpt2 is ({0}, {1})",
                            cpt2.cx, cpt2.cy);
        }
    }
}
```

For the structure, assigning one variable to the other *copies* the values from one structure to the other. The contents are then independent. When you change the contents of one structure, you do not affect the contents of the other structure.

When you compile and run *CmpStCls.cs*, you should see the following output:

```
For structures:
        The point for spt1 is (12, 18)
        The point for spt2 is (42, 24)
```

```
For classes:
        The point for cpt1 is (12, 18)
        The point for cpt2 is (12, 18)
```

When you perform the same operation on the class variables, C# simply copies the reference value from one variable to the other. The two variables then reference the same object; so when you change the values for one variable, you also change the values for the other.

The class is more code-, or state-, oriented than the structure, and for methods, the fact that the two variables refer to the same object does not make much difference.

However, if your object is primarily a collection of data fields, you might consider using a structure instead of a class.

Defining Structures

The definition of a structure begins with the *struct* keyword. You can precede the keyword with the *internal* access keyword to limit access to the structure definition to the current code module. If the structure is defined within a class definition, you can precede the *struct* keyword with any access keywords.

After the *struct* keyword, you type the name that you want to use to identify the structure. No conventions exist for a structure name. In C++, however, programmers often use all capital letters to identify structures and to distinguish their names from class names:

```
struct POINT
```

If you intend to implement an interface with the structure, you may add the inheritance operator after the identifier and then name the interface that you want to inherit from. If you inherit from more than one interface, separate the names with commas. This sequence forms the structure's *interface list*. If you do inherit from one or more interfaces, your structure must implement the methods declared in the interfaces:

```
struct stSTRUCT : ICloneable, IDisposable
{
    // Data fields and methods
// Implement the ICloneable interface
    public object Clone ()
    {
        return (this);
    }
// Implement the IDisposable interface
    public void Dispose()
    {
    }
}
```

After the structure name (or the interface list, if you included one), you begin the body of the structure with an open brace, which is usually typed on a line by itself. After declaring the members of the structure, you end the definition with a closing brace. C# does not require a semicolon after the closing brace as do C and C++, but the compiler will not consider it an error if you include the semicolon. Omitting the semicolon makes the syntax more consistent, but including the semicolon makes it easier for programmers who also work in C and C++.

USE IT Because a structure is a user-defined data type, you can declare a function using a structure as a return type. C# must permit this because returning a simple data type essentially involves returning the contents of the structure from which the simple type was derived. When the function returns, the contents of the structure are copied into the variable in the calling function. (Using a structure as a return type also is permitted in C and C++.) This makes the structure especially useful for returning several values from a single function.

The C runtime library contains a structure named *tm* that has a number of members dealing with time. You can pass a time value to the *localtime()* function to get a pointer to a *tm* structure with the components of the time value stored in the structure. You then can pass the structure pointer to several other functions to get a string formatted with time information. The string has a well-known format, and a lot of code has been written to parse such strings, especially on the UNIX operating system.

C# does not have a similar function, nor does it use pointers directly, but it is easy to duplicate the process. The following program *Tm.cs*, declares a *tm* structure and a function called *LocalTime()* to assign the contents based on a C# time value. Another function, *AscTime()*, then formats and returns a string based on the UNIX string format:

```
//  tm.cs - demonstrates using a structure to return a group of variables
//          from a function
//
//          Compile this program using the following command line:
//              D:>csc tm.cs
//
using System;
using System.Globalization;

namespace nsStructure
{
    struct tm
    {
        public int tm_sec;      // Seconds after the minute
        public int tm_min;      // Minutes after the hour
        public int tm_hour;     // Hours since midnight
        public int tm_mday;     // The day of the month
        public int tm_mon;      // The month (January = 0)
        public int tm_year;     // The year (00 = 1900)
        public int tm_wday;     // The day of the week (Sunday = 0)
        public int tm_yday;     // The day of the year (Jan. 1 = 1)
```

```csharp
        public int tm_isdst;      // Flag to indicate if DST is in effect
    }
    class clsMain
    {
        static public void Main()
        {
            DateTime timeVal = DateTime.Now;
            tm tmNow = LocalTime (timeVal);
            string strTime = AscTime (tmNow);
            Console.WriteLine (strTime);
        }
        static public tm LocalTime(DateTime tmVal)
        {
            tm time;
            time.tm_sec = tmVal.Second;
            time.tm_min = tmVal.Minute;
            time.tm_hour = tmVal.Hour;
            time.tm_mday = tmVal.Day;
            time.tm_mon = tmVal.Month - 1;
            time.tm_year = tmVal.Year - 1900;
            time.tm_wday = (int) tmVal.DayOfWeek;
            time.tm_yday = tmVal.DayOfYear;
            TimeZone tz = TimeZone.CurrentTimeZone;
            time.tm_isdst = tz.IsDaylightSavingTime (tmVal) == true ? 1 : 0;
            return (time);
        }
//
//  Returns a string representing a time using UNIX format
        static public string AscTime (tm time)
        {
            const string wDays = "SunMonTueWedThuFriSat";
            const string months = "JanFebMarAprMayJunJulAugSepOctNovDec";
            string strTime = String.Format ("{0} {1} {2,2:00} " +
                         "{3,2:00}:{4,2:00}:{5,2:00} {6}\n",
                         wDays.Substring (3 * time.tm_wday, 3),
                         months.Substring (3 * time.tm_mon, 3),
                         time.tm_mday, time.tm_hour,
                         time.tm_min, time.tm_sec, time.tm_year +
                         1900);
            return (strTime);
        }
    }
}
```

When you compile and run *Tm.cs*, you should see the program print a string formatted exactly like the UNIX string, similar to the following:

```
Wed Aug 29 03:36:39 2001
```

A number of C runtime functions return strings in this format. The C string contains 26 characters. The twenty-fifth is a linefeed character, and the twenty-sixth is a null terminator. In C#, of course, you do not need the null terminator, so the string is 25 characters long.

Notice that because a structure is a user-defined type, you do not need to include the *struct* keyword when declaring an instance of a structure, as you must do in C.

Structures may contain instances of other structures or even of classes. However, a structure cannot contain an instance of itself because that would cause an endless definition. For example, the following structure includes an instance of itself:

```
struct POINT
{
    int cx;
    int cy;
    POINT pt;
}
```

If you attempt to declare an instance of this structure, the *POINT* member would attempt to create another instance of *POINT*, which would attempt to create another instance of *POINT*. Even if your computer had all of the memory in the universe, eventually it would run out without completing the instance. The C# compiler cuts this short by issuing an error telling you that the definition would cause a "cycle in the structure layout."

You could, however, include an instance of another structure within a structure definition so long as the definition does not cause a cycle. The following code defines a *POINT* structure and then uses the definition in a *RECT* structure:

```
struct POINT
{
    int cx;
    int cy;
}
struct RECT
{
    POINT UpperLeft;
    POINT LowerRight;
}
```

In this definition, the *POINT* structure becomes a convenient method of describing the position of opposite corners of a rectangle, which is all you need to define a rectangle.

Using Structures as Value-Type Objects

A structure is a value-type object, and as such, C# treats it the same that it treats any other value-type variable, such as variables you declare using the simple data types. When you pass a structure as an argument to a function, the program makes a copy of all the structure members on the stack.

The call-by-value system used by the C family of programming languages does have the advantage of protecting the original variable from accidental modification. A programmer must take some purposeful steps to enable the code to modify the original variable.

USE IT Regardless of how you declare a structure instance, the variable containing the instance is always a value-type variable. The following program, *ValType.cs*, demonstrates this by declaring an instance of a *POINT* structure normally and attempting to modify it in a function call, and then by creating an instance using the *new* operator and attempting to modify it in the same way:

```
//
//  ValType.cs -- Demonstrates that C# always creates a structure instance as
//                a value-type variable even using the new operator.
//                Compile this program using the following command line:
//                     C:>csc ValType.cs
//
namespace nsValType
{
    using System;
// Define a POINT structure
    struct POINT
    {
        public int  cx;
        public int  cy;
    }
    class clsMain
    {
        static public void Main()
        {
// Declare an instance without the new operator
            POINT point1;
            point1.cx = 42;
            point1.cy = 56;
// Attempt to modify the contents in a function call
            ModifyPoint (point1);
// Show the contents
            Console.WriteLine ("In Main() point2 = ({0}, {1})",
                                point1.cx, point1.cy);
// Declare an instance using the new operator
```

```
            POINT point2 = new POINT ();
            point2.cx = 42;
            point2.cy = 56;
// Attempt to modify the contents in a function call
            ModifyPoint (point2);
// Show the contents
            Console.WriteLine ();
            Console.WriteLine ("In Main() point2 = ({0}, {1})",
                                point2.cx, point2.cy);
        }
        static public void ModifyPoint (POINT pt)
        {
            pt.cx *= 2;
            pt.cy *= 2;
            Console.WriteLine ("In ModifyPoint() pt = ({0}, {1})",
                                pt.cx, pt.cy);
        }
    }
}
```

Even by declaring an instance using the *new* operator, the program still is unable to modify the structure in a function call. When you compile and run *ValType.cs*, you should see the following output:

```
In ModifyPoint() pt = (84, 112)
In Main() point2 = (42, 56)

In ModifyPoint() pt = (84, 112)
In Main() point2 = (42, 56)
```

Using Structures as References

The structure is a convenient device when you need several data elements in an object. It is efficient in that it does not require your program to allocate a block in the heap memory. However, because it is a value-type object, it is less efficient if you often pass a large structure as an argument to functions. Your program has to set aside stack space for the structure when it performs the function call and then copy all the members of the structure into this stack space.

At other times, you may want to make it possible for a called function to modify the contents of a structure that you pass as an argument. In other ways, you may want the structure to be—or act like—a reference-type object.

Earlier in this chapter you used a structure as the return type for a function. Once again, this is not particularly efficient for large structures. When your function returns, the program must copy the contents on the structure in the called function into the structure in the calling program.

Reference-type variables avoid these problems because the program must deal with only one value, the address of the reference-type object. Reference-type variables have some advantages over value-type variables. The compiler will assume a reference-type variable is initialized when you create the instance. Even if you do not provide a constructor function, C# will initialize the members of a reference-type object to 0.

However, C# does not automatically initialize value-type objects such as the simple data types or structures when you declare variables. You must assign them values before you can use them, even when you use them with the *ref* keyword in a function call.

USE IT   The following program, *RefType.cs*, shows this. It first defines a class and a structure. In *Main()*, it creates an instance of both the class and the structure and attempts to use them in function calls without initializing member fields:

```
namespace nsRefType
{
    using System;
    struct POINT
    {
        public int cx;
        public int cy;
    }
    class clsPoint
    {
        public int cx;
        public int cy;
    }
    class clsMain
    {
        static public void Main ()
        {
            clsPoint pt1 = new clsPoint();
            POINT pt2;
            UseClass (pt1);
            UseStruct (ref pt2);
        }
        static public void UseClass (clsPoint pt)
        {
            pt.cx = 24;
            pt.cy = 42;
        }
        static public void UseStruct (ref POINT pt)
        {
            pt.cx = 24;
            pt.cy = 42;
        }
```

```
    }
}
```

When you compile this program, the compiler issues an error that you are attempting to use an unassigned variable, *pt2*. The idea behind the program is to pass a large structure to a function that will initialize the structure. However, you cannot pass the structure until you initialize it. This isn't a problem for the small *POINT* structure in the example program; a couple of lines of code will initialize the structure members so that you can use it in a function call. However, if you used the *tm* structure from earlier in this chapter, "pre-initializing" the structure might involve a dozen lines of code.

Fortunately, C# provides a default constructor function for value-type variables that will initialize all the members to 0. If you *declare* the structure instance using the *new* operator, your program will call this default constructor. In *RefType.cs*, change the declaration for *pt2* to the following line and recompile the program:

```
POINT pt2 = new POINT ();
```

The compiler accepts the declaration and now considers the variable initialized. Using the *new* operator simply forces a call to the default constructor. It does not change the structure instance from a value-type to a reference-type.

The default constructor is always available for all value-type objects, and you cannot override it when you declare a structure. However, you may add other constructors to a structure.

▶ *NOTE*

Overriding a function is the process of providing a function with the same name and parameter list as a function in a base object. To override a function, you use the override keyword in your object definition. The function in the base object should be declared a virtual to make it overridable.

You could use this same technique to declare and initialize any of the simple data types. The following two statements declare *x* as an *int* and initialize the variable to 0:

```
int x = new int ();
int x = 0;
```

For a simple data type, you don't save any typing, but for the structure, where you may have to initialize many fields, it is a useful technique.

Adding Functions to Structures

The structure has characteristics of both a value-type object and a reference-type object. As a value-type object, the structure focuses on the contents of the members. However, like a class object, a structure may contain methods.

A structure cannot be used as a base for deriving new structures, and it may not inherit from other structures. Ultimately, however, the structure is derived from the *Object* class, and thus it does inherit the methods available to the *Object* class. In the process, the structure inherits default constructor and destructor functions. You can provide other constructors, but you cannot override the default constructor and destructor. However, you can override other methods in the *Object* class.

For example, the *Object* class contains a *ToString()* method that simply prints the fully qualified name of the object. However, you can override *ToString()* to customize the output when you use the object in a call to *Console.Write* or *Console.WriteLine*, which will call the *ToString()* method to print the object as a string:

```
int x = 42;
Console.WriteLine (x);
```

This statement would print the text *42* on the console screen.

USE IT You can take advantage of this in the *Tm.cs* program from earlier in this chapter to provide the UNIX string output in the structure itself. Then you can completely eliminate the *AscTime()* function:

```
//  tm1.cs - demonstrates overriding the ToString() method to provide a custom
//           string output.
//
//           Compile this program using the following command line:
//                 D:>csc tm1.cs
//
namespace nsStructure
{
    using System;
    using System.Globalization;
    struct tm
    {
        public int tm_sec;        // Seconds after the minute
        public int tm_min;        // Minutes after the hour
        public int tm_hour;       // Hours since midnight
        public int tm_mday;       // The day of the month
        public int tm_mon;        // The month (January = 0)
        public int tm_year;       // The year (00 = 1900)
        public int tm_wday;       // The day of the week (Sunday = 0)
        public int tm_yday;       // The day of the year (Jan. 1 = 1)
        public int tm_isdst;      // Flag to indicate if DST is in effect
        public override string ToString()
        {
            const string wDays = "SunMonTueWedThuFriSat";
            const string months = "JanFebMarAprMayJunJulAugSepOctNovDec";
```

```
            return (String.Format ("{0} {1} {2,2:00} " +
                            "{3,2:00}:{4,2:00}:{5,2:00} {6}\n",
                            wDays.Substring (3 * tm_wday, 3),
                            months.Substring (3 * tm_mon, 3),
                            tm_mday, tm_hour, tm_min,
                            tm_sec, tm_year + 1900));
        }
    }
    class clsMain
    {
        static public void Main()
        {
            DateTime timeVal = DateTime.Now;
            tm tmNow = LocalTime (timeVal);
            Console.WriteLine (tmNow);
        }
        static public tm LocalTime(DateTime tmVal)
        {
            tm time;
            time.tm_sec = tmVal.Second;
            time.tm_min = tmVal.Minute;
            time.tm_hour = tmVal.Hour;
            time.tm_mday = tmVal.Day;
            time.tm_mon = tmVal.Month - 1;
            time.tm_year = tmVal.Year - 1900;
            time.tm_wday = (int) tmVal.DayOfWeek;
            time.tm_yday = tmVal.DayOfYear;
            TimeZone tz = TimeZone.CurrentTimeZone;
            time.tm_isdst = tz.IsDaylightSavingTime (tmVal)==true ? 1 : 0;
            return (time);
        }
    }
}
```

The program is more compact without the *AscTime* function, but it is not as compact or as efficient as it could be. You could improve the program by making the *tm* structure initialize itself when you declare an instance and pass a time value.

You cannot override the default constructor or destructor, but you can *overload* the constructor. Overloading a function is similar to overriding a function, except the new function and the overloaded function coexist. You *must* provide a parameter list that differs in the number or data type of the function you are overloading. Overloading is a topic for Chapter 7, but if you have programmed in C++ you may be familiar with the process.

A constructor cannot have a function return type, nor may it return a value. You may give a constructor an access keyword, but for the structure anything other than *public* is useless. A *private* constructor could be called only by a member of the class, which would be inefficient because of C#'s type-safety rules. A *protected* constructor also could be called by a derived object, but you cannot use a structure as a base object.

If you do provide a custom constructor for a structure, the constructor *must* assign a value to all the member fields in the structure. This is because C# is a *type-safe* language that guarantees that every variable and field contains a legitimate value for its data type. When you initialize an instance of a structure through a constructor function, the compiler marks the variable as initialized. If you fail to initialize one or more members, you would violate the type-safety rules of C#.

The compiler enforces the type-safety rules by checking that the constructor assigns every member of the structure a legal value. It is this requirement (along with access rules) that makes a *private* constructor useless. Even a *private* constructor would have to initialize all the fields to meet the compiler's requirements.

You may provide as many constructor overloads as you need, but each must have a different parameter list. In the case of the *tm* structure, you may compact it even more by providing a constructor that accepts a time value:

```
//  tm2.cs - demonstrates a custom constructor function for a structure
//          Compile this program using the following command line:
//              D:>csc tm2.cs
//
namespace nsStructure
{
    using System;
    using System.Globalization;
    struct tm
    {
        public tm (DateTime tmVal)
        {
            tm_sec = tmVal.Second;
            tm_min = tmVal.Minute;
            tm_hour = tmVal.Hour;
            tm_mday = tmVal.Day;
            tm_mon = tmVal.Month - 1;
            tm_year = tmVal.Year - 1900;
            tm_wday = (int) tmVal.DayOfWeek;
            tm_yday = tmVal.DayOfYear;
            TimeZone tz = TimeZone.CurrentTimeZone;
            tm_isdst = tz.IsDaylightSavingTime (tmVal) == true ? 1 : 0;
        }
        public int tm_sec;      // Seconds after the minute
        public int tm_min;      // Minutes after the hour
        public int tm_hour;     // Hours since midnight
        public int tm_mday;     // The day of the month
        public int tm_mon;      // The month (January = 0)
```

```
    public int tm_year;       // The year (00 = 1900)
    public int tm_wday;       // The day of the week (Sunday = 0)
    public int tm_yday;       // The day of the year (Jan. 1 = 1)
    public int tm_isdst;      // Flag to indicate if DST is in effect
    public override string ToString()
    {
        const string wDays = "SunMonTueWedThuFriSat";
        const string months = "JanFebMarAprMayJunJulAugSepOctNovDec";
        return (String.Format ("{0} {1} {2,2:00} " +
                    "{3,2:00}:{4,2:00}:{5,2:00} {6}\n",
                    wDays.Substring (3 * tm_wday, 3),
                    months.Substring (3 * tm_mon, 3),
                    tm_mday, tm_hour, tm_min,
                    tm_sec, tm_year + 1900));
    }
}
class clsMain
{
    static public void Main()
    {
        DateTime timeVal = DateTime.Now;
        tm tmNow = new tm (timeVal);
        Console.WriteLine (tmNow);
    }
}
}
```

The structure definition is now longer, but the structure is mostly self contained. For convenience, you could place the definition in another file or in an assembly to make it easier to use in other programs. You have reduced your primary code, the *Main()* function in the *clsMain* class, to only three lines of code. The structure itself handles most of the implementation details, which is one of the goals of object-oriented programming.

Adding Properties to a Structure

Normally, to access the fields you declare in a structure definition, you will need to mark them as *public*. The default access for structures is *private*, which means that only member methods can access them.

As with any object, at times you will want to provide some protection for certain fields to make sure they contain legal values. In addition, you may want to provide one or more operations on a field value when your program reads it.

In such cases, you can include a *property* in the structure. For the programmer, a property acts like a field, but it uses member functions—accessors—to manipulate the values. You read a value through a *get* accessor and assign a value through a *set* accessor.

Properties do not set aside storage for variables. They provide you with accessor functions with which you can return, set, or compute values. Normally, you will use a public property to allow safe access to a private field.

USE IT In describing a rectangle using two points (the upper-left and lower-right corners, for example), it is possible to define the rectangle as not "normal"—that is, the x value of the left side might be greater than the x value of the right side, or the y value of the top might be greater than the y value of the bottom. Using the *System.Drawing.Rectangle* class, you can define a rectangle that has a negative width, or depth, or both.

Many times, you will want to make sure a rectangle is normal, with only a positive width and height values. The following program, *Rect.cs*, uses properties to assign values to the upper-left and lower-right points that describe the rectangle. A read-only property called *Rectangle* returns a *System.Drawing.Rectangle* object that always will have positive width and height values. Another read-only property, *Normal*, returns a normalized copy of the rectangle without altering the original rectangle.

```
//   Rect.cs - Demonstrates the use of properties to control how values are
//            saved in fields
//
//            This is a Visual Studio project. To compile outside of Visual
//            Studio, use the following command line:
//                 C:>csc rect.cs
//
using System;
using System.Drawing;

namespace nsRect
{
    struct POINT
    {
        public POINT (int x, int y)
        {
            this.cx = x;
            this.cy = y;
        }
        public int cx;
        public int cy;
        public override string ToString ()
        {
            return (String.Format ("({0}, {1})", cx, cy));
        }
    }
```

```csharp
struct RECT
{
    public RECT (Rectangle rc)
    {
        m_UpperLeft.cx = rc.X;
        m_UpperLeft.cy = rc.Y;
        m_LowerRight.cx = rc.X + rc.Width;
        m_LowerRight.cy = rc.Y + rc.Height;
    }
    // Define constructors
    public RECT (POINT pt1, POINT pt2)
    {
        m_UpperLeft = pt1;
        m_LowerRight = pt2;
    }
    public RECT (int x1, int y1, int x2, int y2)
    {
        m_UpperLeft.cx = x1;
        m_UpperLeft.cy = y1;
        m_LowerRight.cx = x2;
        m_LowerRight.cy = y2;
    }
    public RECT (POINT pt1, int Width, int Height)
    {
        m_UpperLeft.cx = pt1.cx;
        m_UpperLeft.cy = pt1.cy;
        m_LowerRight.cx = pt1.cx + Width;
        m_LowerRight.cy = pt1.cy + Height;
    }
    // Property to get and set the upper left point
    public POINT UpperLeft
    {
        get {return (m_UpperLeft);}
        set {m_UpperLeft = value;}
    }
    // Property to get and set the lower right point
    public POINT LowerRight
    {
        get {return (m_LowerRight);}
        set {m_LowerRight = value;}
    }
// Property to return a normalized rectangle
    public System.Drawing.Rectangle Rectangle
    {
```

```csharp
            get
            {
                RECT rc = Normal;
                return (new Rectangle (rc.UpperLeft.cx, rc.UpperLeft.cy,
                    rc.LowerRight.cx - rc.UpperLeft.cx,
                    rc.LowerRight.cy - rc.UpperLeft.cy));
            }
        }
// Property to return a normalized copy of this rectangle
        public RECT Normal
        {
            get
            {
                return (new RECT (
                    Math.Min (m_LowerRight.cx, m_UpperLeft.cx),
                    Math.Min (m_LowerRight.cy, m_UpperLeft.cy),
                    Math.Max (m_LowerRight.cx, m_UpperLeft.cx),
                    Math.Max (m_LowerRight.cy, m_UpperLeft.cy))
                    );
            }
        }
        private POINT m_UpperLeft;
        private POINT m_LowerRight;
        public override string ToString()
        {
            return (String.Format ("Upper left = {0}; Lower right = {1}",
                m_UpperLeft, m_LowerRight));
        }
    }
    class clsMain
    {
        static public void Main ()
        {
            // Define a "normal" rectangle
            POINT pt1 = new POINT (-10,30);
            POINT pt2 = new POINT (100, 100);
            RECT rc = new RECT (pt1, pt2);
            Console.WriteLine ("RECT: " + rc);
            Console.WriteLine ("Normal: " + rc.Normal);
            Console.WriteLine ("Rectangle: " + rc.Rectangle + "\n");
            // Define a rectangle with normal x but not y
            pt1.cx = 100;
            pt1.cy = 50;
            pt2.cx = 200;
```

```
          pt2.cy = 20;
          rc.UpperLeft = pt1;
          rc.LowerRight = pt2;
          Console.WriteLine ("RECT: " + rc);
          Console.WriteLine ("Normal: " + rc.Normal);
          Console.WriteLine ("Rectangle: " + rc.Rectangle + "\n");
          // Define a rectangle with normal y but not x
          pt1.cx = 200;
          pt1.cy = 50;
          pt2.cx = 100;
          pt2.cy = 80;
          rc.UpperLeft = pt1;
          rc.LowerRight = pt2;
          Console.WriteLine ("RECT: " + rc);
          Console.WriteLine ("Normal: " + rc.Normal);
          Console.WriteLine ("Rectangle: " + rc.Rectangle + "\n");
// Define a rectangle with both values of upper left greater
// than the lower y
          pt1.cx = 225;
          pt1.cy = 180;
          pt2.cx = 25;
          pt2.cy = 35;
          rc.UpperLeft = pt1;
          rc.LowerRight = pt2;
          Console.WriteLine ("RECT: " + rc);
          Console.WriteLine ("Normal: " + rc.Normal);
          Console.WriteLine ("Rectangle: " + rc.Rectangle + "\n");
          // Define a rectangle with points equal
          pt1.cx = 75;
          pt1.cy = 150;
          pt2.cx = 75;
          pt2.cy = 150;
          rc.UpperLeft = pt1;
          rc.LowerRight = pt2;
          Console.WriteLine ("RECT: " + rc);
          Console.WriteLine ("Normal: " + rc.Normal);
          Console.WriteLine ("Rectangle: " + rc.Rectangle + "\n");
      }
    }
}
```

Compiling and running *Rect.cs* should result in the following output. The *Rectangle* property always has positive width and height values regardless of how you define the rectangle.

```
RECT: Upper left = (-10, 30); Lower right = (100, 100)
Normal: Upper left = (-10, 30); Lower right = (100, 100)
Rectangle: {X=-10,Y=30,Width=110,Height=70}

RECT: Upper left = (100, 50); Lower right = (200, 20)
Normal: Upper left = (100, 20); Lower right = (200, 50)
Rectangle: {X=100,Y=20,Width=100,Height=30}

RECT: Upper left = (200, 50); Lower right = (100, 80)
Normal: Upper left = (100, 50); Lower right = (200, 80)
Rectangle: {X=100,Y=50,Width=100,Height=30}

RECT: Upper left = (225, 180); Lower right = (25, 35)
Normal: Upper left = (25, 35); Lower right = (225, 180)
Rectangle: {X=25,Y=35,Width=200,Height=145}

RECT: Upper left = (75, 150); Lower right = (75, 150)
Normal: Upper left = (75, 150); Lower right = (75, 150)
Rectangle: {X=75,Y=150,Width=0,Height=0}
```

You can use the *Rectangle* property in any method where a normalized *System.Drawing.Rectangle* object is required.

CHAPTER 7
Understanding C# Classes

TIPS IN THIS CHAPTER

I n object-oriented programming, an *object* often is considered an element that emphasizes behavior rather than content. It is largely self-describing and often controls access to its data members.

The C# structure is capable of satisfying most of the requirements of an object, but C# places artificial barriers on the structure so that it cannot achieve all the principles of an object. For example, a structure exhibits encapsulation, but you cannot derive new objects from a structure in C#, and therefore it cannot exhibit inheritance or polymorphism.

The primary mechanism through which C# achieves the principles of object-oriented programming is the *class*. Most programmers who have dealt with object-oriented languages are familiar with the class concept. In fact, many programmers shun the structure in favor of the class because they are more familiar with the class.

The C++ class was patterned after the structure. In fact, in most cases in C++, the class and structure are interchangeable. Although there are some important differences between the two, such as the default access for members, structures often can serve the same role as classes. In C#, the class apparently came first and the structure was patterned after it, with some important restrictions that were not placed on classes. As pointed out in Chapter 6, a structure acts very much like a *sealed* class. (For Visual Basic programmers, the *sealed* keyword is the C# equivalent of the *NonInheritable* keyword.)

The class is all important in C#. Without a class to contain at least the *Main()* function, you simply do not have a C# program. (You can place the *Main()* function in a structure and write a complete C# program without defining a single class.)

Defining a class is the same as defining a structure, except you use the *class* keyword. You follow the *class* keyword with the identifier, the name you will use for the class. You follow that with a set of braces. Within the braces, you declare any fields that your class will use and define any properties or methods. The following snippet declares a simple class that contains one field, one property, and one method:

```
class clsSample
{
    private int iVal;
    public int iProp
    {
        get
        {
            return (iVal);
        }
        set
        {
            iVal = value;
        }
    }
    public override string ToString ()
    {
        return ("This is a simple class");
    }
}
```

You may add a semicolon after the closing brace as you would in C++, but the C# compiler does not consider it an error if you omit the semicolon.

No convention for naming classes exists, except that the name should describe the purpose of the class. In Visual C++, programmers often prefix the class name with a capital *C*. In Borland C++, a capital *T* (for *turbo*, heralding back to the days of Turbo C++) is used. Visual Basic programmers often use a lowercase *cls*.

When defining a class, you may prefix the *class* keyword with a modifier such as *abstract*, *sealed*, or *new*. You also may use one of the access specifiers: *public*, *protected*, *internal*, or *private*. You cannot use just any of these modifiers for any class, however. Depending on where you define a class, some of the modifiers may not be available. For example, you can use the *new*, *protected*, and *private* modifiers only on a class that you define within another class (a *nested* class).

You may also include *attributes* before the *class* keyword and any other modifiers. An attribute is a C# method of associating declarative information with code elements such as a class, field, property, or method. You may create your own attributes, or you may use an existing C# attribute. And if you no longer need a particular class but you need to keep it in your program to support existing code, you could use the *obsolete* attribute:

```
[obsolete] class clsOldClass
{
    // class members
}
```

When you write your program and try to create an instance of *clsOldClass*, the compiler will issue a warning and tell you that the class is obsolete. Using a class marked *obsolete* is not an error, but every time you access a member of the class, the compiler will issue a warning. If you keep using an obsolete class, you eventually will have so many warning messages that it will be difficult to pick out the real errors.

After the class name, you may include a list of items from which you want to inherit by typing a colon followed by a base list. A C# class may inherit from only one other class, but it may inherit from multiple interfaces at the same time. When you inherit from more than one item, you separate the items in the base list with commas:

```
// Derive a class from the C# TextReader class and from
// the IDisposable interface

class clsDerivedClass : TextReader, IDisposable
{
    // Class members
}
```

If you do inherit from an interface, your class is responsible for implementing any methods or properties defined but not implemented by the interface.

In C++, you may inherit from one of any number of classes through *multiple inheritance*, but it's possible that a class could inherit multiple copies of an ancestor class. Multiple inheritance can be tricky even for experienced programmers, and unless your class hierarchy is written to support multiple inheritance, writing code in this way can introduce problems. Still, multiple inheritance occasionally can be a powerful and useful tool for C++ programmers. The C# designers decided that multiple inheritance is rarely used and avoided the problem by eliminating it from C#.

You may not use an access specifier for the inheritance. A class inherits the members of a base class using the same access levels declared in the base class. In addition, you may not use the *virtual* keyword on the base class name when deriving a new class. For inheritance purposes, the *virtual* keyword has meaning only in a multiple inheritance hierarchy, which C# does not permit.

The default access for class members is *private*, the same as for the C# structure. Each member has its own access keyword, and if you do not include an access, it will default to *private*:

```
class clsClass
{
    public int Var1;      // The public keyword does not associate
                          // with members that follow
    int Var1;             // No access keyword, so defaults to
                          // private access
}
```

Defining a class simply establishes a template for the compiler. Except for *static* members, which have special properties and restrictions, the class definition does not create an instance of the class. When you declare an instance of a class, the compiler reserves memory for the fields and initializes all the field members to 0. In C#, a class instance is a reference-type object, so you must create it using the *new* operator.

To create an instance of a class, you first declare a variable to hold the reference. When you do this in a function, your program reserves memory on the stack to hold the reference value. Then you use the *new* operator to create the object in the heap. The *new* operator returns the address—the reference— of the newly created object, which you then store in the stack memory. Normally, you will perform these two steps in a single statement:

```
clsClass ClassVar = new clsClass();
```

A class may contain *static* fields, properties, or methods. In addition, it may contain a *static* constructor function. When you define a class using a *static* field, your program sets aside memory for the field when the program first runs. Regardless of how many instances of a class you create, only one copy of a *static* field is available, and it will contain the same value for all class instances. The *static* keyword is the C# equivalent of the Visual Basic *Shared* keyword.

For efficiency, C# also creates a *static* variable when you use the *const* keyword on a field. In fact, the compiler will issue an error if you do use both the *static* and *const* keywords when you declare a field. This is only reasonable, and it does conserve memory. A *const* must be initialized at the time you declare it and you cannot assign it a different value later. The value will be the same for all instances of the class, so it makes little sense to create a new *const* field for every class instance.

You may declare fields, properties, and methods as *static*. C# does not specifically prohibit *const* methods and properties, but for all practical purposes, only fields may be marked *const*.

How you access a class member depends on whether you have declared the member using the *static* or *const* modifier. A class member without the *static* or *const* keyword is considered an *instance member,* and you access it using the instance variable identifier. A *static* or *const* member is a *class member,* and you must use the class name rather than the instance identifier to access the member. In either case, you use the "member of " operator, a period (.), between the class or instance name and the member name.

The following short program, *Members.cs*, shows access to both *static* and non-*static* members of a class:

```
//
//   Members.cs -- Demonstrates access to static and non-static members
//
//                 Compile this program using the following command line:
//                       C:>csc Members.cs
//
namespace nsMembers
{
    using System;
    class clsMain
    {
        static public void Main ()
        {
//
// Access a static member using the class name. You may access
// a static member without creating an instance of the class.
            Console.WriteLine ("The static member is pi: "
                               + clsClass.pi);
//
// To access a non-static member, you must create an instance
// of the class.
            clsClass instance = new clsClass();
//
// Access a static member using the name of the variable containing
// the instance reference.
            Console.WriteLine ("The instance member is e: "
                               + instance.e);
        }
    }
    class clsClass
    {
//
// Declare a static field. You also could use the const keyword
// to create a static field.
        static public double pi = 3.14159;
//
```

```
// Declare a normal member, which will be created when you
// declare an instance of the class.
        public double e = 2.71828;
    }
}
```

In *clsClass*, you could have used the *const* keyword to create a *static* field as well. The *const* modifier has the added advantage that you cannot later change the value of the field. This makes it especially useful for mathematical constants or standing text strings.

Taking Advantage of Built-In Classes

Most C++ programmers are familiar with class libraries, such as the Microsoft Foundation Class (MFC) or Borland's excellent Object Windows Library (OWL). A class library provides the basic classes that you will need to implement a programming model. MFC and OWL are designed primarily for Windows programming, but other class libraries might be built on other foundations.

C# does not use a class library in the same sense, but the .NET Framework provides many predefined, or built-in, classes that you may use to begin your programming. Many of these classes, such as the *Console* class, are *sealed,* and others, such as the *Delegate* class, have a special attribute so that you may not derive custom classes from them. Others are *abstract*, meaning you must derive your own classes from these classes to use them.

It is convenient to think of the built-in classes as class libraries. Functionally, the collection operates in the same way as a class library. More than 1000 classes (some sources say more than 2,000) are defined in this "library," many of them directly usable.

Most of these classes are in the *System* namespace or in one of the namespaces defined within the *System* namespace. The *Console* class, which defines the standard input and output operations, is in the *System* namespace, and the Windows common dialogs are in the *System.Window.Forms* namespace. You have used the *Console* class often in command line programs in earlier chapters.

Microsoft has packaged the code for these classes into various assemblies. For example, the *System.Windows.Forms* code is in the *System.Windows.Forms.dll* assembly. The C# compiler automatically adds references to the assemblies when you build your program. To demonstrate this, enter the following short command line program, *Assembly.cs*:

```
namespace nsAssemblies
{
    using System;
    using System.Windows.Forms;
    class clsMain
    {
        static public void Main ()
        {
            MessageBox.Show ("Using System.Windows.Forms", "Assemblies",
                        MessageBoxButtons.OK,
```

```
                              MessageBoxIcon.Exclamation);
        }
    }
}
```

The program does nothing but display a simple message box. However, you compile it using either of the following command lines:

```
C:>csc assembly.cs
C:>csc /r:System.Windows.Forms.dll assembly.cs
```

If you were lucky enough to experience the original beta release of Visual Studio .NET, you may remember that the compiler added a reference only to the basic *System* assembly classes. Others, such as forms classes, were packaged in other assemblies, requiring you to include references to them on your command line.

For this program, neither of the command lines gives an error. The first command line shows that the compiler adds the reference for you. The second command line shows that the assembly for the forms classes is still a separate assembly.

The *System* namespace is not the only root namespace used by C#. A lesser known *Microsoft* namespace contains a number of utility classes and classes used by the .NET environment. The *Microsoft* namespace has three nested namespaces:

- The *Microsoft.CSharp* namespace contains classes that support compilation and code generation using the C# language.

- The *Microsoft.VisualBasic* namespace contains the Visual Basic .NET Runtime.

- The *Microsoft.Win32* namespace contains classes to handle events raised by the operating system and to access the system registry.

USE IT   You will probably have little use for classes in the first two namespaces, but the third, *Microsoft.Win32*, contains some interesting and useful classes. The MSDN documentation is sparse on the events classes, but you can use the registry classes to read and write to the system registry. The following program, *RegKey.cs*, reads system information from the registry and prints the type and speed of each processor in your computer:

```
namespace nsRegKey
{
    using System;
    using Microsoft.Win32;
    class clsMain
    {
        static public void Main ()
        {
            int x;
            string RegID =
```

```
                    "HARDWARE\\DESCRIPTION\\System\\CentralProcessor\\";

        for (x = 0; x < 4; ++x)
        {
            string ValueID = RegID + x;
            RegistryKey key = Registry.LocalMachine;
            Object cpuType;
            object cpuSpeed;
            key = key.OpenSubKey(ValueID);
            if (key == null)
                break;
            cpuType = key.GetValue("VendorIdentifier");
            cpuSpeed = key.GetValue("~MHz");
            Console.WriteLine ("Processor {0} is {1} {2}",
                        x,
                        cpuSpeed == null ? "speed unknown"
                            : cpuSpeed.ToString() + " MHz",
                        cpuType == null ? "type unknown"
                            : cpuType.ToString());
            key.Close ();
        }
        Console.WriteLine ("\r\nThis computer has {0} {1}",
                        x, x == 1 ? "processor" : "processors");
    }
  }
}
```

When you run this program, you should see output similar to the following, depending upon how your computer is configured:

```
Processor 0 is 864 MHz GenuineIntel
Processor 1 is 864 MHz GenuineIntel

This computer has 2 processors
```

▶ **CAUTION**

In most cases, it is safe to read from the system registry. However, you should not write to the registry unless you are familiar with registry operations and you understand what you are doing. On Windows NT class machines, you can write only to certain parts of the registry unless you have Administrator privileges. Windows 98 machines have no such restriction. With both operating systems, you can do serious damage to the operating system or installed programs by writing the wrong information in the wrong place.

Using the *SystemEvents* class requires an understanding of events delegates, a topic for Chapter 18. However, the following code will show you how to intercept events generated by the system.

```
//
// Event.cs -- Demonstrates using the Microsoft.SystemEvents class
//              to intercept an event generated by the system.
//
//              Compile this program with the following command line:
//                  C:>csc Event.cs
//
namespace nsEvent
{
    using System;
    using System.Windows.Forms;
    using Microsoft.Win32;
    class clsMain
    {
//
// Define the delegate
        public delegate void UserEventHandler (object obj,
                                    UserPreferenceChangedEventArgs args);
//
// Declare a variable that will hold the delegate
        static public event UserEventHandler ShowEvent;
        static public void Main ()
        {
//
// Create the delegate using the event handler (below)
            ShowEvent = new UserEventHandler (EvHandler);
//
// Create the event handler using the new operator
            UserPreferenceChangedEventHandler handler =
                        new UserPreferenceChangedEventHandler(ShowEvent);
//
// Add the delegate to the system delegate list. This is a multi-cast
// delegate and you must use the += operator to add the delegate. Use
// the -= operator to remove the delegate
            SystemEvents.UserPreferenceChanged += handler;
//
// Show a message box to keep the program alive while you cause an event
            MessageBox.Show ("Hey! C Sharp", "System Events");
//
// Remove the delegate from the system delegate list
            SystemEvents.UserPreferenceChanged -= handler;
        }
```

```
//
// Declare and define the method that will be used as the
// event handler function
        static void EvHandler (object obj,
                               UserPreferenceChangedEventArgs args)
        {
//
// Retrieve the category of the change
           UserPreferenceCategory cat = args.Category;
//
// Build a string for the message box
           string str = "User changed the " + cat.ToString() +
                        " category";
//
// Show the change event
           MessageBox.Show (str, " event category");
        }
    }
}
```

The *SystemEvents* constructor is not *public*, so you cannot create an instance of the class. However, all its members are *static*, so you may access them directly without creating an instance.

The class exposes a number of system events that you may intercept. In addition, the *InvokeOnEventsThread()* method may be used for events that the class does not expose. The events exposed by *System.Events* are shown in the following table:

Event	Description
DisplaySettingsChanged	Occurs when the user changes the display settings.
EventsThreadShutdown	Occurs before the thread that listens for system events is terminated. Delegates will be invoked on the events thread.
InstalledFontsChanged	Occurs when the user adds or removes fonts.
LowMemory	Occurs when the system is running out of available memory.
PaletteChanged	Occurs when the user switches to an application that uses a different palette.
PowerModeChanged	Occurs when the user suspends or resumes the system operation.
SessionEnded	Occurs when the user is logging off or shutting down the system.
SessionEnding	Occurs when the user is trying to log off or shutdown the system.
TimeChanged	Occurs when the user changes the time on the system clock.
TimerElapsed	Occurs when a windows timer interval has expired.
UserPreferenceChanged	Occurs when a user preference has changed.

The methods used to create and set the delegate, and to handle the event, are essentially the same for each of the events. You write the code for the event handler. Within your class or function, you define a delegate that matches the signature of the event handler and declare a variable or field to hold the delegate. You then create the delegate and assign it to the event handler variable. Then you add the delegate to the *SystemEvents* delegate list.

The code example uses the *UserPreferenceChanged* event. You can cause an event simply by summoning the display properties window and changing one of the pages. Or you can open the Control Panel and change one of the system properties shown in the following table. Changing the display or system property will cause the system to fire an event.

Property	Description
Accessibility	Specifies user preferences associated with accessibility of the system.
Color	Specifies user preferences associated with system colors.
Desktop	Specifies user preferences associated with the system desktop. This may be a change in the desktop background images or the desktop layout.
General	Specifies user preferences not associated with any other category.
Icon	Specifies user preferences for icon settings, including icon height and spacing.
Keyboard	Specifies user preferences for keyboard settings, such as the typematic rate.
Locale	[To be supplied.]
Menu	Specifies user preferences for menu settings.
Mouse	Specifies user preferences for mouse settings, such as double-click time, speed, or mouse sensitivity.
Policy	Specifies user preferences for policy settings, such as user rights and access levels.
Power	Specifies user preferences for system power settings.
Screensaver	Specifies user preferences associated with the screensaver.
Window	Specifies user preferences associated with the size and characteristics of windows.

You could use these values in a *switch* statement to filter out the change you want your program to handle. An example of the *switch* appears after the following listing for *Event.cs*.

After creating and assigning the event handler as a delegate, you display a message box. This message box keeps the program alive while you make a modification to the display properties (or other property). Your program just as easily may perform another task. The system delivers the event message through a thread that is separate from your main program thread.

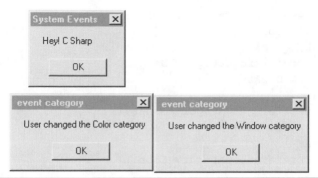

Figure 7.1 Changing the Scheme setting altered the system color and window characteristics, generating two events

Compile and run the program. When the silly message box appears, right-click somewhere on the desktop and select Properties from the context menu to show the Display Properties dialog. Make a change—such as selecting a new screen saver or changing the color scheme for the desktop. Then click Apply, and the system will generate an event that your program will capture. Be aware that one change—for example, the Scheme on the Appearance page—may generate more than one event. Changing from one color scheme to another on a test machine generates two events, one for the system colors and another for the window characteristics, as shown in Figure 7-1.

For multiple events, the message boxes showing the events will display one right after the other. You will have to close the topmost message box before closing the others.

You can enclose the event categories in a *switch* statement, as shown in the following variation on *EvHandler( )*:

```csharp
//
// Declare and define the method that will be used as the event
// handler function
static void EvHandler (object obj, UserPreferenceChangedEventArgs args)
{
//
// Retrieve the category of the change
    UserPreferenceCategory cat = args.Category;
//
// Build a string for the message box
    string str = "User changed the ";
    switch (cat)
    {
        case UserPreferenceCategory.Accessibility:
            str += "Accessibility";
            break;
```

```
          case UserPreferenceCategory.Color:
              str += "Color";
              break;
          case UserPreferenceCategory.Desktop:
              str += "Desktop";
              break;
          case UserPreferenceCategory.General:
              str += "General";
              break;
          case UserPreferenceCategory.Icon:
              str += "Icon";
              break;
          case UserPreferenceCategory.Keyboard:
              str += "Keyboard";
              break;
          case UserPreferenceCategory.Menu:
              str += "Menu";
              break;
          case UserPreferenceCategory.Mouse:
              str += "Mouse";
              break;
          case UserPreferenceCategory.Screensaver:
              str += "Screensaver";
              break;
          case UserPreferenceCategory.Window:
              str += "Window";
              break;
//
// Don't care about these categories, so just return
          case UserPreferenceCategory.Power:
          case UserPreferenceCategory.Policy:
          case UserPreferenceCategory.Locale:
          default:
              return;
      }
      str += " category";
//
// Show the change event
      MessageBox.Show (str, " event category");
}
```

You could use the *case* statement to call specific methods to handle the category. You do not need to provide case statements for every category (this code shows all of them for reference only), just those that you want to handle. Use the *default* case to catch any categories that you do not want to handle and simply be returned from the event handler.

In addition, the event handler does not have to be a *static* method. The *delegate* object is capable of storing a class instance along with the event handler method. In the preceding code, it was easier to declare the handler as *static* so that it wasn't necessary to create an instance of *clsMain*.

The user event change is one of the more involved events to catch and process. It has its own event handler class and includes many categories, but it is useful. For example, if a program displays a graphic from a file, when the user changes the screen resolution, you may want to enable another graphic to display the window. Not all event handling is that involved, though.

Referring to the Current Object Using the *this* Keyword

The concept of the class as an object that contains both data and code was pioneered by the Xerox Palo Alto Research Center. When the center introduced its Smalltalk programming language in 1980, the class had a rather strange property called *self*.

The Smalltalk *self* variable was an intrinsic property of a Smalltalk class. It was inherited by each instance of a class when the instance was created, and it referred to the instance itself. The property made the class object "self-aware," so that the class code could call functions outside the class and let the other functions know where the particular instance was located in memory. These functions then could access specific code and variables in a specific class instance.

When the C++ class was introduced, it too had a similar intrinsic variable, but it was named *this*. The variable functioned the same as the Smalltalk *self* variable. The *this* variable contains a pointer to the class instance. The name made for some interesting conversational high jinks. Phrases like "the *this*" and "this *this*" sounded strange to non-programmers and made them wonder whether the programmers were speaking in some sort of code.

C# does not overtly use pointers, but classes in C# still use the *this* intrinsic variable. In C#, *this* is a reference-type variable that refers to the class instance. You can use *this* only within methods that are members of the class instance; outside the instance, the variable has no meaning. In its simplest use, *this* can help resolve ambiguities:

```
class POINT
{
    public POINT (int cx, int cy)
    {
        this.cx = cx;
        this.cy = cy;
    }
    public int cx;
    public int cy;
}
```

In this code, the variables *cx* and *cy* in the parameter list for the constructor function are, well, just *cx* and *cy*. There is no further way to qualify them. If you simply assigned *cx* to *cx* in the constructor, you would be assigning the parameter value to itself. The *cx* and *cy* that you declare as members of the class, however, are *instance fields*, and you may uniquely identify them by prefixing them with *this*. Even with a dozen instances of *POINT*, the code always will point to the proper field in the instance.

Methods that you declare as *static* are class members, and you cannot use *this* in the code for these methods. It is possible to call a *static* method without creating an instance of a class, so the *this* pointer is meaningless. A *static* method, however, may access *static* fields and properties.

USE IT The *this* intrinsic variable is most useful for identifying the class instance to functions outside the class, as shown in a roundabout way in the following short program, *This.cs*:

```
//
// This.cs -- Demonstrates using the this intrinsic variable, which
//            allows a class instance to identify itself
//
//            Compile this program with the following command line:
//                  C:>csc this.cs
//
namespace nsThis
{
    using System;
    class clsMain
    {
        static public void Main ()
        {
//
// Declare an array of classes
            clsThis [] arr = new clsThis[]
                            {
                            new clsThis(), new clsThis(), new clsThis(),
                            new clsThis(), new clsThis(), new clsThis()
                            };
//
// Ask each instance in the array to identify itself
            foreach (clsThis inst in arr)
            {
                Console.WriteLine ("This is instance Number " +
                                    inst.Identify().Instance);
            }
        }
    }
    class clsThis
    {
```

```
        public clsThis ()
        {
            m_Instance = ++Count;
        }
        private static int Count = 0;
        public int Instance
        {
            get
            {
                return (m_Instance);
            }
        }
        private int m_Instance;
        public clsThis Identify ()
        {
//
// Return this instance of the class
            return (this);
        }
    }
}
```

The *Main()* function first creates an array of class instances. Using the static field *Count*, each instance of *clsThis* saves a unique sequence number for itself. *Main()* then asks each instance to identify itself. The *Identify()* method simply returns an instance of itself, resulting in the following output:

```
This is instance Number 1
This is instance Number 2
This is instance Number 3
This is instance Number 4
This is instance Number 5
This is instance Number 6
```

After getting a reference to the instance, the *ShowInstance()* method uses the reference to access the *Instance* property and write it to the screen.

Protecting Class Members Using Access Keywords

One of the underlying concepts of the object-oriented principle of *encapsulation* is that an object may control access to its own members. A class may include fields or methods that it needs to maintain information used internally, but these fields or methods may have no practical use outside the class itself. If external functions were allowed to modify this data, they could corrupt the data needed by the class instance.

In C++, you set the *protection* or *access* level of class members using one of the three access keywords: *public*, *protected*, or *private*. C# provides two additional access keywords, as shown in the following table:

Keyword	Description
public	The member is accessible to any external or internal function. The field or method is completely exposed.
protected	The member is accessible only to member methods in the class and to member methods of derived classes.
private	Only member methods may access the field or method. This is the highest level of protection.
internal	The member is *public* to classes in the assembly but *private* to other classes. The member is exposed only to the current code unit. This is the equivalent of the Visual Basic *Friend* keyword (but very different from the C++ *friend* keyword).
protected internal	Only members of the class or derived classes in the assembly may access the member. The member is *protected* within the assembly but *private* to classes in other assemblies.

There is no need to provide a *private internal* access level. Access to class members that you declare *private* inherently are limited to the class itself, and therefore no functions outside the assembly can access *private* members.

In both the class and the structure, access to members defaults to *private*. You must assign each member its own access keyword. If you do not, it automatically reverts to *private*. Unlike C++, access keywords are not *associative*: they do not remain in effect until you declare another access keyword.

USE IT In the following snippet, the second declaration is *private* and does not inherit the *public* declaration of the preceding variable:

```
class clsMain
{
    public int PublicVar;      // specifically declared public
    int InternalVar;           // Defaults to private
    protected ProtectedVar;    // specifically declared protected
```

When you assign a member an access level of *public* or *protected*, you "expose" the member to the world outside the class. An access of *public* completely exposes the member, and assigning a level of *protected* exposes the member to derived classes.

Ordinarily, you will make data fields of your class *private* and provide *public* or *protected* properties to give access to the fields.

Using Class Member Methods and Properties

The class satisfies the object-oriented criterion that an object focus on behavior rather than content. The original C structure, from which the C# class ultimately evolved, could focus only on content. The structure could have only data elements as members. It could not contain functions, although it could contain function pointers.

The function—the "method" in object-oriented programming—gives the class the ability to maintain and control its own data members. A method is a *named block* of code. In the C family of programming languages, the method (and its non–object-oriented cousin, the function) is the only element that contains code. In C#, this extends to the property, which provides the functionality of a method but still appears like a field. Every method in C# must be a member of a class or a structure. Within the class, a method has an access level that determines the extent to which it is exposed to the outside world. You may apply any of the C# access levels to a function.

Every method must have a return type. If a method does not return a value, you must give it a return type of *void*. A method may return one value, and if you give a method a return type, you must return a value of that data type. The return type may be any of the C# simple data types, or it may be a user-defined data type such as a class reference or a structure. The declaration and definition of a method must match the following pattern:

```
[attribute] [modifier_list] <return_type> MethodName ([parameter_list])
{
    // Body of method
}
```

The items between brackets are optional. The parentheses following the method name are required even if the method does not take any parameters. Note that you do not write a semicolon after the declaration. C# does not differentiate between a method declaration and its definition. C# does not require or permit the function *prototype* that you use in C and C++ programming. After the parameter list, you must write the *body* of the method, which can consist of zero or more statements within a set of curly braces.

You execute the code in a method by *calling* the method. The call consists of writing the method name followed by an *argument list* enclosed in parentheses. The number and data types of the argument must match exactly the number and data types in the method's parameter list. If the argument list does not match the method's parameter list, the C# compiler will assume that you are calling an undefined method.

Ordinarily, in a method call you will save the return value in another variable. However, unlike other expressions, C# does permit you to ignore a method's return value in a function call:

```
class clsSomeClass
{
    static public void Main()
    {
```

```
// Saving the return value in the following statement is optional
      int x = SomeMethod (42, 3.14159);
    }
    static int SomeMethod (int x, double y)
    {
//
      int var = (int) (x * y);
// The method must return a value that is the same data type as
// the method's return type.
      return (var);
    }
}
```

The C# compiler does not require you to use any of the parameters in the body of the function and will not issue an error or a warning if you do not use one or more of the parameters. (As you saw in Chapter 6 in the section "Passing Variables to Functions," if you use the *out* specification on a parameter, you must assign it a value.)

The modifier list is optional and may include any of the five access levels that you use for any class member. If you do not specify an access keyword, the method defaults to *private*, and only other member methods may execute the code in the method.

In addition to an access level, you may specify several other modifiers, as shown in the following table. Some of the modifiers are mutually exclusive and you cannot use them together. For example, you cannot use the *new* and *override* modifiers on the same method. The *override* modifier implements an *abstract* or a *virtual* method declared in a base class. The *new* modifier hides a "normal" method in a base class. Other modifiers may conflict with access keywords. You cannot, for example, use the *abstract* or *virtual* keywords on a method that you declare as *private*. The *abstract* and *virtual* methods are inheritance mechanisms, and *private* methods are not visible to derived classes. Thus, no inheritance scheme could support a combination of these modifiers.

Modifier	Description
abstract	Declares a method without providing a body of code for it. To use this modifier, the class in which it is a member also must be declared *abstract*. You must override an *abstract* method in a derived class. You cannot use *abstract* to modify a *private* method.
extern	The method is implemented elsewhere. This is useful for calling Windows API functions. You cannot use this modifier with the *abstract* modifier.
new	The method's name and parameter list are the same as a method in a base class. Used to hide, but not override, a method in a base class. You cannot use this modifier with the *override* modifier.
override	Used to override a *virtual* or *abstract* method in a base class. When you override a *virtual* method, the *override* method replaces the *virtual* method. When you override an *abstract* method, you provide code to implement the method.

Modifier	Description
static	Declares the method to be a class member rather than an instance member. You may call *static* methods without declaring an instance of the class.
unsafe	Uses code such as pointers or the *sizeof* operator that the C# compiler may consider a violation of the type-safety rules of C#.
virtual	Used in a base class to declare and define a method that you expect to override in a derived class. You must provide a body of code for the method, but if you override the method in a derived class, the method in the derived class will be used instead.

The *virtual* method is the primary mechanism by which C# supports the object-oriented principle of polymorphism. When a derived class overrides a *virtual* method, the derived class method replaces the method in the base class, permitting a derived class to modify the behavior of a base class. Polymorphism is a topic for Chapter 8.

USE IT   The *extern* declaration is useful for calling native code in dynamic link libraries (DLLs) that were not written in C#. Often, you may need to use more than one modifier on a method. The following program, *GetUser.cs*, imports two Windows libraries to call the *GetUserName( )* functions and then to display the user name in a message box using the Windows function rather than the C# *MessageBox* class. It also uses the *[DllImport]* attribute to identify the external libraries where the program will find the functions:

```
//
//  GetUser.cs -- demonstrates compound modifiers and calls
//                to external API
//
//                Compile this program with the following command line:
//                      C:>csc /unsafe GetUser.cs
//
namespace nsUser
{
    using System;
    using System.Runtime.InteropServices;
    class clsMain
    {
        [DllImport ("user32.dll")]
        static public extern int MessageBox(int hWnd, string msg,
                                            string title, int type);
        [DllImport ("advapi32.dll")]
        static unsafe extern public bool GetUserName(byte [] str,
                                            long *size);
```

```
        static public void Main ()
        {
            clsMain main = new clsMain();
            byte [] user = new byte[256];
            long size = (long) user.Length;
            unsafe
            {
                if (main.GetUserName (user, &size) == false)
                    Console.WriteLine ("Error getting user name");
            }
            string strUser = "";
            foreach (byte ch in user)
            {
                if (ch < 32)
                    break;
                strUser += (char) ch;
            }
            main.MessageBox (0, "The current user is " + strUser, "Howdy", 0);
        }
    }
}
```

Notice that you do not need to declare that you are using the *System.Windows.Forms* namespace as you do when you use the C# *MessageBox* class. However, you do have to reference the *System.Runtime.InteropServices* namespace.

You should also notice the modifiers on both *MessageBox()* and *GetUserName()*. Typically, you use the *extern* modifier with the *[DllImport]* attribute to call a method in a library that was not written in C#. If the library was written in C#, you do not need the *extern* modifier. Instead, you simply include a reference to the C# assembly when you compile the program.

The *static* modifier is required when you use the *[DllImport]* attribute. The function becomes a member of the class in which you declare it, but its address must be fixed at runtime rather than when you declare an instance of the class. The *[DllImport]* attribute also requires the *extern* modifier to notify the compiler that the function code is implemented elsewhere. You may not provide a body for an imported function.

In addition, you need to pass a pointer to the *GetUserName()* for a variable that contains the length of the string, so you must use the *unsafe* modifier. Passing a pointer means that you may use the function only in an *unsafe* block of code even though you have marked the function itself as *unsafe*.

GetUserName() also writes the user name in 8-bit characters, so you may not pass a string for the first parameter. Instead, you need to pass it an array of type *byte* and then convert the array into a string. Most Windows API functions also have a wide-character counterpart using the same name but suffixed with a capital *W*. The following declaration would reference the wide-character version of *GetUserName()*:

```
[DllImport ("advapi32.dll")]
static unsafe extern public bool GetUserNameW(char [] str,
                                           long *size);
```

To use the wide-character function, you need to pass it a *char* array rather than a *byte* array. In C#, a *char* type is a 16-bit character. You still need to convert the *char* array to a string, however.

When you compile and run *GetUser.cs* you should see a message box similar to that shown in Figure 7-2. This message box is created by the *MessageBox()* function in *User32.dll* rather than the C# *MessageBox* class.

Properties may use the same modifiers as methods except for the *extern* modifier. A property is a mechanism that provides the functionality of a method, yet retains the appearance of a field to the programmer. Because of this dichotomy, properties are subject to the rules of both fields and methods. You cannot mark a field as *extern*; likewise, you cannot declare a property as *extern*.

To mark a property as *abstract*, you must provide a *get* or *set* accessor, or both, but you cannot provide a body for the accessors. An abstract property must be either *public* or *protected* because it must be visible at least to the derived class. The syntax for an abstract property is shown in the following snippet:

```
abstract public int Prop
{
    get;
    set;
}
```

You can declare an abstract property only in an abstract class. When you derive a new class from the abstract class, you must override the property and provide a body for the accessors. The override property in the derived class must match the abstract property in access level, data type, and accessors. For example, if you do not provide a *set* accessor in your abstract property, the property in the derived class may not include a *set* accessor.

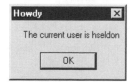

Figure 7.2   The message box was generated by a call to the Windows API from a C# program. Eventually, even the C# *MessageBox* class calls this function

USE IT   Use the following short program, *Abstract.cs*, to experiment with abstract properties. Try commenting out one of the accessors, first in the base class and then in the derived class.

```
//
// Abstract.cs -- Demonstrates the use of an abstract property.
//
//                 Compile this program with the following command line:
//                      C:>csc Abstract.cs
//
namespace nsAbstract
{
    using System;
    using System.Runtime.InteropServices;
    class clsMain
    {
        static public void Main ()
        {
            Console.WriteLine (clsAbstract.StaticMethod());
        }
    }
//
// To use the abstract modifier on a method, the class also must
// be declared as abstract.
    abstract class clsAbstract
    {
//
// To declare an abstract method, end the declaration with a semicolon.
// Do not provide a body for the method.
        abstract public int AbstractMethod();
//
// An abstract class may contain a static method. You do not have
// to declare an instance of the class to access a static method.
        static public double StaticMethod()
        {
            return (3.14159 * 3.14159);
        }
        abstract public long Prop
        {
            get;
            set;
        }
    }
//
// Inherit from the abstract class. The following class implements
// the AbstractMethod().
```

```
// The access level of the derived class method must be the same
// as the access level of the base class abstract method.
   class clsDerivedFromAbstract : clsAbstract
   {
       override public int AbstractMethod()
       {
           return (0);
       }
       override public long Prop
       {
           get
           {
               return (val);
           }
           set
           {
               val = value;
           }
       }
       private long val;
   }
}
```

The *Abstract.cs* program does not produce any output. Notice that the base class *abstract* property does not have a body for either the *get* or *set* accessors, and it therefore cannot reference a member field to store a value. You must provide the field in the derived class.

Using the *static* Modifier with Class Members

When you use the *static* modifier on a method, property, or field, you give the member some special properties but impose some additional restrictions as well. The *static* modifier declares the identifier to be a member of the class rather than an instance member.

A C# program creates *static* fields when the program first runs. In addition, it determines and stores the address of *static* functions and properties. This allows you to access *static* members even before you declare an instance of the class.

USE IT   When you declare a *static* field, your program creates only one copy of the field, which is shared by all instances of the class. (The C# *static* modifier is the same as the Visual Basic *Shared* modifier.) In the following short program, *Static.cs*, the constructor for the *clsStatic* class increments a *static* member field. Each time you create an instance of the class, the field is incremented and becomes a counter of how many times you used the class:

```
//
// Static.cs -- Demonstrates how a static field is shared by
//              multiple instances of a class.
```

```
//
//                   Compile this program with the following command line:
//                        C:>csc Static.cs
//
namespace nsStatic
{
    using System;
    class clsMain
    {
        static public void Main ()
        {
            for (int i = 0; i < 20; ++i)
            {
                clsStatic inst = new clsStatic();
            }
            Console.WriteLine ("Created {0} instance of clsStatic",
                              clsStatic.Count);
        }
    }
    class clsStatic
    {
        static public int Count
        {
            get {return (m_Count);}
        }
        static private int m_Count = 0;
        public clsStatic ()
        {
            ++m_Count;
        }
    }
}
```

Methods and properties that you declare as *static* may not access non-*static* class members, nor may they use the *this* variable. Non-*static* members are created when you declare an instance of a class. Because you may use *static* members without declaring a class instance, the non-*static* members may not exist at the time you use a *static* method or property.

You see this in the *Main()* method, which must be declared as *static*. If you add non-*static* fields, properties, and methods to the class containing the *Main()* function, you have seen that you cannot access them without declaring an instance of the class:

```
class clsMain
{
    private int count = 0;
    public int TestFunc()
```

```
    {
        return (42);
    }
    static public void Main ()
    {
// The following will generate two errors because both count and
// TestFunc() are non-static members of the class
        count = TestFunc();
    }
}
```

This also means that if you declare a *static* property and you need to associate it with a field, the field also must be declared as *static*. The *Static.cs* program in the preceding example uses a *static* property to return the value of the *static* field holding the count. Although the field is *static*, it is *private*, so without a *set* accessor in the *Count* property, methods outside the class may not modify the value.

The *static* modifier is more restricted in C# than it is in C++. For example, you cannot declare a *static* variable within a method even if the method itself is *static*. Commonly, *static* variables are used in C++ functions to provide a counter or another value that will not change between function calls. If you need such a variable in C#, you must declare it as a member of the class.

In addition, some uses of the *static* modifier do not have any meaning in C#. In C++, you may use the *static* keyword on a global variable to restrict access to the current code module. In C#, though, there are no global variables, so this use of *static* does not apply. Instead, C# uses the *internal* keyword when you need to prevent external code modules from accessing a member.

Declaring Constructors and Destructors

Like the structure, a class may contain constructor functions to initialize class members when you declare an instance of the class. Unlike the structure, a class may declare a default constructor—one that has an empty parameter list. A class also may declare a single destructor function, which is not permitted in a structure definition.

A constructor function executes automatically when you declare an instance of a class. If you do not declare a constructor function for a class, C# provides the class with a default constructor. You may provide more than one constructor to extend the ways in which you may declare an instance of your class.

QUICK TIP

You should realize that if you do write constructors functions for a class, C# will not automatically provide a default, parameterless constructor. If you want to continue using a constructor without parameters, you will need to declare it as well.

A constructor may have an access keyword. To declare an instance of the class directly, however, you must provide at least one *public* constructor. Constructors declared as *protected* and *private* do have their uses, however. In addition, a constructor may not have a return type, and the compiler will issue an error if you attempt to return a value from a constructor.

When you define multiple constructors, you must provide each with a parameter list that differs in the number or data type of the parameters. The C# compiler identifies a constructor by its signature, a combination of the function name and parameter list. All constructors must use the same name as the class, so the only way to differentiate between them is to provide different parameter lists.

USE IT The following short program, *Constrct.cs*, declares three different constructors for a class, including one with no parameters to replace the default constructor:

```
// Constrct.cs - Demonstrates the use of multiple constructors
//               in a class definition.
//
//               Compile this program with the following command line:
//                    C:>csc Constrct.cs
//
namespace nsConstructor
{
    using System;
    struct POINT
    {
        public POINT (int cx, int cy)
        {
            this.cx = cx;
            this.cy = cy;
        }
        public int cx;
        public int cy;
    }
    class clsMain
    {
        static public void Main ()
        {
            clsRect rc1 = new clsRect();
            clsRect rc2 = new clsRect (10, 12, 84, 96);
            POINT pt1 = new POINT (10, 12);
            POINT pt2 = new POINT (84, 96);
            clsRect rc3 = new clsRect (pt1, pt2);
        }
    }
    class clsRect
    {
// The following constructor replaces the default constructor
```

```
    public clsRect ()
    {
        Console.WriteLine ("Default constructor called");
        m_Left = m_Top = m_Right = m_Bottom  = 0;
    }
    public clsRect (int cx1, int cy1, int cx2, int cy2)
    {
        Console.WriteLine ("Constructor 1 called");
        m_Left = cx1;
        m_Top = cy1;
        m_Right = cx2;
        m_Bottom = cy2;
    }
    public clsRect (POINT pt1, POINT pt2)
    {
        Console.WriteLine ("Constructor 2 called");
        m_Left = pt1.cx;
        m_Top = pt1.cy;
        m_Right = pt2.cx;
        m_Bottom = pt2.cy;
    }
    public POINT UpperLeft
    {
        get {return(new POINT(m_Left, m_Top));}
        set {m_Left = value.cx; m_Top = value.cy;}
    }
    public POINT LowerRight
    {
        get {return(new POINT(m_Right, m_Bottom));}
        set {m_Right = value.cx; m_Bottom = value.cy;}
    }
    private int m_Left;
    private int m_Top;
    private int m_Right;
    private int m_Bottom;
    }
}
```

The compiler decides which constructor to call based on the signatures of the various constructors. If it cannot find a matching constructor, the compiler will issue an error that none of the "overloaded" methods takes the type of arguments you are trying to pass. It will then list the line numbers of the class constructors. For example, try adding the following line to the *Main()* function in *Constrct.cs* and recompile the program:

```
clsRect rc4 = new clsRect (pt1);
```

The compiler will print the following error message:

```
Constrct.cs(29,27): error CS1501: No overload for method 'clsRect' takes '1'
arguments
Constrct.cs(35,16): (Location of symbol related to previous error)
Constrct.cs(40,16): (Location of symbol related to previous error)
Constrct.cs(48,16): (Location of symbol related to previous error)
```

A class may contain one *static* constructor. The constructor is for use by the runtime code only, and it may not have an access modifier. Other than *static*, you may not use any other modifiers when you declare the constructor. In addition, a *static* constructor may not take any parameters, although it does not replace the default parameterless constructor.

You cannot call a *static* constructor, nor do you have any control over when it gets called. The C# language specification guarantees that the runtime code will call the *static* constructor before you create any instances of the class or reference any other *static* members.

USE IT Because it is *static*, the constructor may access only other *static* class members. The primary purpose of a *static* constructor is to initialize any static variables with values that may not be known when the program is compiled. Thus, you may pass values to your program and store them in other *static* variables, or you may examine the environment for information you need for the *static* constructor.

The following program, *SysInfo.cs*, uses a *static* constructor to collect information about the runtime environment such as the current time zone and the program name for the command interpreter:

```
// SysInfo.cs -- Demonstrates use of static constructor
//
//              Compile this program with the following command line:
//                    C:>csc SysInfo.cs
//
namespace nsSysInfo
{
    using System;
    using System.Runtime.InteropServices;
    using System.Windows.Forms;
    class clsMain
    {
        static public void Main()
        {
            Console.WriteLine ("Current user is " +
                                clsSystemInfo.User);
            Console.WriteLine ("Current Time Zone is " +
                                clsSystemInfo.TZ);
            Console.WriteLine ("Current domain is " +
                                clsSystemInfo.Domain);
            Console.WriteLine ("Current host is " +
```

```
                                clsSystemInfo.Host);
            Console.WriteLine ("Command interpreter is " +
                                clsSystemInfo.ComSpec);
    }
}
class clsSystemInfo
{
    [DllImport ("kernel32.dll")]
    static extern public long GetEnvironmentVariable (string name,
                                            byte [] value, long size);
    static clsSystemInfo ()
    {
        m_User = SystemInformation.UserName;
        m_Host = SystemInformation.ComputerName;
        DateTime now = DateTime.Now;
        TimeZone tz = TimeZone.CurrentTimeZone;
        m_TimeZone = tz.IsDaylightSavingTime(now)
                    ? tz.DaylightName : tz.StandardName;
        m_Domain = SystemInformation.UserDomainName;
        byte [] comspec = new byte [256];
        if (GetEnvironmentVariable ("COMSPEC", comspec, 256) > 0)
        {
            foreach (byte ch in comspec)
            {
                if (ch == 0)
                    break;
                m_ComSpec += (char) ch;
            }
        }
    }
    static public string User
    {
        get
        {
            return (m_User);
        }
    }
    static public string TZ
    {
        get
        {
            return (m_TimeZone);
        }
    }
```

```
        static public string Domain
        {
            get
            {
                return (m_Domain);
            }
        }
        static public string Host
        {
            get
            {
                return (m_Host);
            }
        }
        static public string ComSpec
        {
            get
            {
                return (m_ComSpec);
            }
        }
        private static string m_User;
        private static string m_TimeZone;
        private static string m_Domain;
        private static string m_Host;
        private static string m_ComSpec;
    }
}
```

Obviously, all of this information is available through various other classes or methods, but it is convenient to have it in one place. By simply defining the class and giving it a *static* constructor, the information is ready by the time you try to access any of the members.

When you run the program, you should see output similar to the following. The values on your computer will be different, of course, but you do not have to modify the program, or store it in a data file, to get the current information.

```
Current user is hseldon
Current Time Zone is Mountain Daylight Time
Current domain is RCICH
Current host is JUBALHARSHAW
Command interpreter is C:\WINNT\system32\cmd.exe
```

The *clsSystemInfo* class in the preceding example contains nothing but *static* members. It makes little sense to declare an instance of the class because there are no instance members. Such a declaration would only waste memory. Still, there is nothing to prevent you from declaring an instance.

You can prevent accidentally creating an instance by defining a *protected* or *private* constructor. A *protected* constructor would prevent you from declaring an instance of the class directly, but you (or another programmer) could derive another class from *clsSystemInfo* and still declare an instance of it directly. You use a *protected* constructor for a class that you *must* use as a base class without declaring it *abstract* or adding any *abstract* members to the class.

The solution is to provide a *private* constructor. The constructor does not need to take any parameters because you will not be able to call it anyway. Simply declare the constructor as follows:

```
private clsSystemInfo () { }
```

With this simple declaration, you prevent any possible instance of the class being created.

In addition to constructors, a class may contain a single destructor function. The runtime code will call the destructor when the Common Language Runtime (CLR) performs garbage collection and decides that no more references to the class exist.

A destructor may not have an access level, nor may it have parameters. You may declare a destructor as *unsafe* in case you need to reference any code outside the module, but you may not specify any other modifiers for a destructor. To declare a destructor, you use the name of the class as the function name but precede it with a tilde character (~):

```
~clsSystemInfo()
{
    // Include any cleanup code here
}
```

Creating Constants and *readonly* Fields

In C++, it often is convenient to provide a *preprocessor directive* to create a *literal constant*. This saves you a lot of typing, and the C++ preprocessor will replace all occurrences of a string with the value associated with it. For example, you could define a literal named *PI* using the following preprocessor directive:

```
#define PI     3.14159
```

Then, every time the preprocessor encounters *PI*, it will replace it with the value 3.14159. This is an example of a *macro* in C and C++.

In his book, *The C++ Programming Language*, Bjarne Stroustrup pans the use of such macros as unnecessary. Stroustrup prefers that you declare and use a *constant* instead; so you would use something like the following in global memory to define a value:

```
const double pi = 3.14159;
```

C# does not use preprocessor macros, nor does it allow you to declare variables in global memory. However, it does allow you to declare constants as members of a class or in a function. To do this, you use the *const* keyword as in the preceding snippet.

You must initialize a *const* variable when you declare it. Once initialized, you cannot change the value of a *const*. If you attempt to modify it, the compiler will issue an error and will not compile your program.

Although you may declare *const* variables in a function, in practice it is better to make a *const* a class member rather than a local variable in a function. This is because in the C# implementation, you may pass a *const* as an argument to another function, but in the called function it will be an ordinary variable:

```
static public void Main ()
{
    const double pi = 3.14159;
    Func (pi);
}
static public Func (double pi)
{
// pi at this point is not a constant. You may modify it in the function,
// but the original constant will not be modified
    pi = 0.57721;
}
```

However, if you declare a *const* as a member of the class, the called function will have access to the value and will not be able to modify it:

```
class clsMain
{
    const double pi = 3.14159;
    static public void Main ()
    {
        Func ();
    }
    static public Func ()
    {
// pi is a constant member of the class. Func() may use it but not
// modify its value. The following line will generate an error:
        pi = 0.57721;
    }
}
```

At times you may need to use a constant value, but you will not know the value when you compile the program. In such a case, you will need to assign the constant a value based upon current conditions or upon a computed value.

For this case, you can use the *readonly* modifier on a field. You may assign a *readonly* field a value when you declare it, or you may assign the value in the constructor function for the class. Any attempt to assign the field a value at any other time will cause a compile error. If you do not assign the field a value when you declare the field or in the constructor, the field will default to 0 and you will not be able to modify it. You may assign the field a value when you declare it, however, and later modify the value in a constructor.

USE IT   As an example, you can measure angles using several different systems. The most common are degrees, radians, and mils. All the functions in the *System.Math* class that deal with angles use radians.

The following program, *ReadOnly.cs*, declares a class named *clsArea* that may be used to calculate the area of a pie slice by passing it a conversion factor and then setting the angle and radius of the circle. The default is radians so the default value of the *readonly* field *m_Factor* defaults to 1. However, this program will use the more human-friendly degree as a base and let the class do the conversion. You can pass it another value in the constructor, and the code will modify the *m_Factor* field:

```
//
// ReadOnly.cs -- demonstrates the use of readonly variables
//
//                Compile this program with the following command line
//                     C:>csc ReadOnly.cs
//
namespace nsReadOnly
{
    using System;
    class clsMain
    {
        static double DegreeFactor = 1;
        static double MilFactor = 0.05625;
        static public void Main ()
        {
            double degrees = 42;
// 1 degree = 17.77778 mils
            double mils = degrees * 17.77778;
// 1 degree = 0.017453 radians
            double radians = degrees * 0.017453;
            clsArea InDegrees = new clsArea (DegreeFactor);
            InDegrees.Angle = degrees;
            InDegrees.Radius = 50;
            Console.WriteLine ("Area of circle is {0,0:F1}", InDegrees.Area);

// Radians are the default, so you can use the parameterless constructor
            clsArea InRadians = new clsArea ();
            InRadians.Angle = radians;
            InRadians.Radius = 50;
            Console.WriteLine ("Area of circle is {0,0:F1}", InRadians.Area);

            clsArea InMils = new clsArea (MilFactor);
```

```csharp
            InMils.Angle = mils;
            InMils.Radius = 50;
            Console.WriteLine ("Area of circle is {0,0:F1}", InMils.Area);
        }
    }
    class clsArea
    {
        public clsArea ()
        {
        }
        public clsArea (double factor)
        {
            m_Factor = factor / 57.29578;
        }
        private const double pi = 3.14159;
        private const double radian = 57.29578;
        private readonly double m_Factor = 1;
        public double Angle
        {
            get {return (m_Angle);}
            set {m_Angle = value;}
        }
        public double Radius
        {
            get {return (m_Radius);}
            set {m_Radius = value;}
        }
        private double m_Angle;
        private double m_Radius;
        public double Area
        {
            get
            {
                return (m_Radius * m_Radius * pi * m_Angle
                        * m_Factor /  (2 * pi));
            }
        }
    }
}
```

Just for testing, all three instances of the *clsArea* class use the same angle, 42 degrees, converted to degrees, radians, and mils, and a radius of 50 for the circle. Within the limits of floating-point error, all three instances of the class should return the same value, 916.3, for the area of the slice.

Nesting One Class Within Another

A class definition itself may contain the definition for another class. This is particularly handy when you must pass a number of values to the constructor, and the values do not vary much over successive instances of the class. You simply define a *nested* class—a class within a class—and then pass an instance of the nested class in the constructor for the outer class.

In Visual C++, for example, this is a common practice when passing a dialog box class the information it needs to initialize the fields on the form.

You can define a nested class using any of the five access levels. More often than not, however, you will need to declare the nested class as *public* so other classes may declare instances as needed. The following snippet shows an example of a nested class:

```
class clsOuter
{
    public class clsNested
    {
        // Nested class member declarations
    }
    public clsOuter (clsNested data)
    {
        m_Data = data;
    }
    clsNested m_Data;
    // Outer class member declarations
}
```

This works well in C++, where assigning one class object to another copies all the values in from one instance to the other. In C#, however, classes are always reference-type objects, and assigning one class object to another simply copies the reference. In this case, you run the risk of corrupting the values for other instances.

You can overcome this by implementing the *ICloneable* interface for the nested class, and then using the *Clone()* method to create a copy of the nested class in the outer class:

```
class clsOuter
{
    public class clsNested : ICloneable
    {
        // Nested class member declarations
        public object Clone ()
        {
            return (new clsNested ());
        }
    }
```

```
    public clsOuter (clsNested data)
    {
// Make a copy of the data object
       m_Data = data.Clone();
    }
    clsNested m_Data;
    // Outer class member declarations
}
```

USE IT   Using the *ReadOnly.cs* example from earlier in this chapter, the following program, *Nested.cs*, uses a nested data class to pass the data to an instance of *clsArea*. After you create the instance for one measurement system, you then change the values in the data object for the next measurement system. The constructor for *clsArea* clones the object to obtain its own copy:

```
//
// Nested.cs -- demonstrates the use of a nested class to contain data
//
//            Compile this program with the following command line
//                    C:>csc Nested.cs
//
namespace nsReadOnly
{
    using System;
    class clsMain
    {
        static double DegreeFactor = 1;
        static double MilFactor = 0.05625;
        static double RadianFactor = 57.29578;
        static public void Main ()
        {
            double angle = 90;
            double radius = 50;
//
// Declare an instance of the nested class
            clsArea.clsData data = new clsArea.clsData (angle, radius,
                                                        DegreeFactor);
            clsArea InDegrees = new clsArea (data);

//
// Change the values to mils
            data.Factor = MilFactor;
            data.Angle = angle * 17.77778;
            clsArea InMils = new clsArea (data);

//
```

```
        // Change the values to radians
            data.Angle = angle / 57.29578;
            data.Factor = RadianFactor;
            clsArea InRadians = new clsArea (data);

            Console.WriteLine ("Area of pie of {0,0:F3} degrees is {1,0:F1}",
                                InDegrees.Data.Angle, InDegrees.Area);
            Console.WriteLine ("Area of pie of {0,0:F3} radians is {1,0:F1}",
                                InRadians.Data.Angle, InRadians.Area);
            Console.WriteLine ("Area of pie of {0,0:F3} mils is {1,0:F1}",
                                InMils.Data.Angle, InMils.Area);

        }
    }
    class clsArea
    {
        public class clsData : ICloneable
        {
            public clsData (double angle, double radius, double factor)
            {
                m_Angle = angle;
                m_Radius = radius;
                m_Factor = factor / 57.29578;
            }
            public double Angle
            {
                get {return(m_Angle);}
                set {m_Angle = value;}
            }

            public double Radius
            {
                get {return(m_Radius);}
                set {m_Radius = value;}
            }
            public double Factor
            {
                get {return(m_Factor);}
                set {m_Factor = value / 57.29578;}
            }
            private double m_Angle = 0;
            private double m_Radius = 0;
            private double m_Factor = 1;
            public object Clone ()
            {
                clsData clone = new clsData (m_Angle, m_Radius,
```

```
                                                m_Factor * 57.29578);
                return (clone);
            }
        }
// Provide a constructor to clone a clsData object
        public clsArea (clsData data)
        {
// Clone the data object to get a copy for ourselves
            m_Data = (clsData) data.Clone();
        }

        public clsData Data
        {
            get {return (m_Data);}
        }

        private clsData m_Data;
        private const double pi = 3.14159;
        private const double radian = 57.29578;

        public double Area
        {
            get
            {
                return (m_Data.Radius * m_Data.Radius * pi
                       * m_Data.Angle * m_Data.Factor /  (2 * pi));
            }
        }
    }
}
```

The *clsData* class is now controlling access to the values, and the *clsArea* class concentrates on manipulating the data. As the number of data fields increases, the nested data class becomes more useful, especially if only a few values change between class instances.

Overloading and Name Hiding

Within a class definition, methods must be unique enough that the compiler can identify the definition in a call to one of the methods. To identify a method, the compiler builds a *signature* of each method in a class. The signature consists of the method name and the number and data type of the parameters.

The compiler considers the signature of a method as unique if the method name differs from the name of any other method in the class, or if the number or data type of the parameters in the parameter list is different from that of other methods with the same name. In preparing the signature of a method, the compiler looks only at the method name and the data types of the parameter list. It does not consider the names of the parameters or the return type as part of the signature.

Because the compiler uses a signature for methods rather than just the method name, you may write methods using the same name so long as you provide a different parameter list. The process of writing methods with the same name but with a different parameter list is called *overloading* the method.

A classic example of overloading is to provide methods that return the square of a number. You first write a method that returns the square of an *int,* as in the following snippet:

```
int SquareInt (int x)
{
    return (x * x);
}
```

Later, you might find that you also need a method that returns the square of a *long* value, so you write another function, *SquareLong( )*:

```
long SquareLong (long x)
{
    return (x * x);
}
```

Now you have two method names to remember. If you want to square an *int* value, you must remember to call the *SquareInt( )* method. Similarly, you must remember to call the *SquareLong( )* method to get the square of a *long.*

A simpler way is to write the two methods with the same name, but with different parameters:

```
int Square (int x)
{
    return (x * x);
}
long Square (long x)
{
    return (x * x);
}
```

Now you have only one method name to remember. The compiler can identify the methods because their signatures are different. If you pass an *int* to *Square( )*, the compiler knows that you want to call the first method. If you pass a *long* value, the compiler will call the second method. The following simple program, *Overload.cs,* will compile and run properly even though the *clsMain* class contains two methods named *Square( )*:

```
//
// Overload.cs -- Provides a simple example of function overloading
//
```

```
//              Compile this program with the following command line:
//                    C:>csc Overload.cs
//
namespace nsOverload
{
    using System;
    class clsMain
    {
        static public void Main ()
        {
            int iVal = 16;
            long lVal = 24;
            Console.WriteLine ("The square of {0} is {1}\r\n",
                                iVal, Square(iVal));
            Console.WriteLine ("The square of {0} is {1}",
                                lVal, Square(lVal));
        }
        static int Square (int var)
        {
            Console.WriteLine ("int Square (int var) method called");
            return (var * var);
        }
        static long Square (long var)
        {
            Console.WriteLine ("long Square (long var) method called");
            return (var * var);
        }
    }
}
```

When you compile and run *Overload.cs*, you will see from the console output that the program calls the proper method.

Another common use for overloading is to provide multiple constructor functions for a class, as you saw earlier in this chapter. Constructors *must* have the same name as the class name, so the only way to identify the constructors is through the parameter list.

Constructors are also one reason the compiler does not consider the return type as part of the signature. A constructor cannot have a return type, and attempting to return a value from a constructor results in an error. In addition, C# allows you to discard the return value from a method, so it cannot always determine from the return type which method you want to call. In *Overload.cs*, for example, you are not discarding the result; you're simply using it as a parameter to *Console.WriteLine()*. Here, too, the compiler could not determine from the return type which method you want to call.

Another use for overloading is to redefine how the C# operators perform on an object. When you redefine an operator, it is called *operator overloading*. When you overload an operator, you are simply giving the operator a different meaning when it is used with a particular object type. The original meaning of the operator remains the same for other object types.

Operator overloading in C# is considerably more restricted than it is in C++. Only a few C++ operators cannot be overloaded. In C#, however, you can overload only the unary, binary, and comparison operators. You cannot overload any of the 11 assignment operators.

A convenient use for operator overloading is to extend the use of the operators for class objects. If, for example, you attempt to add one class object to another, you would confuse the compiler. However, you can overload the addition operator and provide code for the compiler to add one class to another.

The syntax for overloading an operator begins with the *static* keyword. All user-defined operator overloads must be declared *static*. Then you add the access keyword, which must be *public*. These two keywords will begin all operator overloads that you write for class objects.

Next, you write the return type, which should be the same type as the object for which you are writing the overload. For example, if you are writing an overload to add two objects of type *clsClass*, the return type should be *clsClass*. Then you use the keyword *operator* to indicate to the compiler that the code will overload an operator. The operator you want to overload comes next, followed by the parameter list. An overloaded operator method must have the same number of parameters that the original operator would need as operands. For example, the addition operator requires two operands, so an overloaded addition operator would require two parameters. Finally, you provide the code that the compiler will use to implement the overloaded operator.

The following snippet shows the declaration for an overloaded addition operator for a class named *clsClass*:

```
public clsClass operator +(clsClass obj1, clsClass obj2)
{
    // Statements to implement the overload
}
```

The parameters do not have to be the same data type so long as you provide code to add different data types. Typically, however, you will use the same data type for both parameters.

USE IT   The following program, *Plus.cs*, defines a *clsPoint* class and then overloads the addition operator so you may add two *clsPoint* objects:

```
//
// Plus.cs -- demonstrates overloading the addition operator for two
//            class objects.
//
//            Compile this program with the following command line:
//                  C:>csc Plus.cs
//
namespace nsOverload
{
    using System;
    class clsMain
    {
        static public void Main ()
```

```csharp
        {
            clsPoint point1 = new clsPoint (12, 28, "This is part");
            clsPoint point2 = new clsPoint (42, 64, " of a string");
            clsPoint point3 = point1 + point2;
            Console.WriteLine ("Results for point3:");
            Console.WriteLine ("\tPoint is at " + point3);
            Console.WriteLine ("\tstr = " + point3.str);
        }
    }
    class clsPoint
    {
        public clsPoint () { }
        public clsPoint (int x, int y, string str)
        {
            m_cx = x;
            m_cy = y;
            this.str = str;
        }
        private int m_cx = 0;
        private int m_cy = 0;
        public int cx
        {
            get {return (m_cx);}
            set {m_cx = value;}
        }
        public int cy
        {
            get {return (m_cy);}
            set {m_cy = value;}
        }
        public string str = "";

        static public clsPoint operator +(clsPoint pt1, clsPoint pt2)
        {
            clsPoint point = new clsPoint();
            point.cx = pt1.cx + pt2.cx;
            point.cy = pt1.cy + pt2.cy;
            point.str = pt1.str + pt2.str;
            return (point);
        }

        public override string ToString()
        {
            return ("(" + m_cx + "," + m_cy + ")");
```

```
            }
        }
}
```

The two points at (12, 28) and (42, 64) are then added together to get a new point at (54, 92), as shown in the following output:

```
Results for point3:
        Point is at (54,92)
        str = This is part of a string
```

If you comment out the operator overload, recompile, and run *Plus.cs*, the compiler will tell you that you cannot apply the addition operator to the class objects. The operator overload tells the compiler what to do when you add the objects.

Name hiding involves providing identical methods, properties, or fields, one in a base class and the other in a derived class. Unlike the *override* modifier, which you will encounter in Chapter 8, the hidden member does not replace the base class member.

You use name hiding when the base class member is not declared as *abstract* or *virtual*. For example, you may want a derived class method to perform a different operation but not replace the operation in the base class.

Name hiding lets you completely redefine a member in the derived class. Unlike the *virtual* and *abstract* keywords, you may hide a field as well as properties and methods. The data types for fields and properties do not have to be the same in both classes. Methods may have the same or different parameter lists and return types.

USE IT   To hide a member of a base class, declare a member in the derived class using the *new* keyword and the same identifier as the base class. The data types for fields and properties do not have to be the same as those used in the base class.

The following program, *Hide.cs*, is basically senseless because the derived class hides all the members of the base class, so the inheritance is meaningless. However, it does show examples of hiding fields, properties, and methods:

```
//
// Hide.cs -- Shows name hiding in a derived class
//
//            Compile this program with the following command line:
//                  C:>csc Hide.cs
//
namespace nsHide
{
    using System;
    using System.Reflection;
    class clsMain
    {
        static public void Main ()
```

```csharp
        {
            clsBase Base = new clsBase();
            clsDerived Derived = new clsDerived ();
            Base.x = 42;
            Derived.x = 42;
            Console.WriteLine ("For the base class:");
            Console.WriteLine ("\tThe type stored in clsBase is "
                                + Base.TypeOf());
            Console.WriteLine ("\tMathOp () returns {0,0:F3} for {1}",
                                Base.MathOp(42), 42);
            Console.WriteLine ("For the derived class:");
            Console.WriteLine ("\tThe type stored in clsDerived is "
                                + Derived.TypeOf());
            Console.WriteLine ("\tMathOp () returns {0,0:F3} for {1}",
                                Derived.MathOp(42), 42);
        }
    }
    class clsBase
    {
        protected int m_x;
        public int x
        {
          get {return (x);}
          set {m_x = value;}
        }
        public double MathOp (int val)
        {
            return (Math.Sqrt ((double) val));
        }
        public string TypeOf ()
        {
            return ("integer");
        }
    }
    class clsDerived : clsBase
    {
// Hide the variable m_x in the base class
        new protected double m_x;
// Hide the property x in the base class
        new public double x
        {
          get {return (x);}
          set {m_x = value;}
        }
```

```
// Hide the method MathOp in the base class
      new public double MathOp (int val)
      {
           return ((double) (val * val));
      }
// Return a different string for the derived class
      new public string TypeOf ()
      {
           return ("long");
      }
   }
}
```

The output shows that the members of the base class are still present and active, even though the base class implements the members differently:

```
For the base class:
      The type stored in clsBase is integer
      MathOp () returns 6.481 for 42

For the derived class:
      The type stored in clsDerived is long
      MathOp () returns 1764.000 for 42
```

You use name hiding only on members that are declared as *public* or *protected* in the base class. Members declared as *private* are not visible to the derived class and thus cannot be hidden. The compiler will issue an error if you attempt to hide a *private* member.

CHAPTER 8

Object-Oriented Programming and C#

TIPS IN THIS CHAPTER

You are on a hillside looking across a broad, green valley with mountains on the other side. Beneath you is a road that floats slightly above the surface and winds down the hill and across the valley, disappearing through a gap in the mountains on the far side of the valley. You look closer and find that the road is made of interlocking tiles made of pages of programs.

The scene is from the mind of Robert Tinney, the artist who used to draw those great covers for the old *Byte* magazine. Along with the model railroad cover, this scene depicting the programming road was one of my favorites.

You can look at Tinney's tiled road as your personal path through programming or one that our collective culture and technology are following through a valley of code. The point is that you must follow this road one tile at a time, as each page on the programming road builds upon the previous one. One of the tiles on this road is labeled *object-oriented programming*. We are now squarely on this OOP section of the road, and what lies ahead fades from readability.

Our world is a collection of objects. For example, a number of houses probably line the street on which you live. Each house is an object; you don't know what is inside, but each house functions as a distinct unit. Entering one, you can break the house down into other objects—rooms—each of which has its own set of objects. One room may contain a file cabinet, a desk, and a computer. You think of these objects as distinct items rather than a collection of parts.

Even where no natural markers delimit objects, we make them up. We divide our world into nations, states, and further into counties and cities. No black line marks the location where western Colorado becomes eastern Utah, but everybody knows the border is there.

In object-oriented programming, you treat your code in a similar way. You take all the collective parts that make up something—the methods, fields, and properties that describe and object and determine its behavior—and wrap them into a single definition.

In the C family of programming languages, we began our walk through the object-oriented part of the road when we encountered the *structure*, the device that allowed us to put all the identifiers that describe something into a single variable. A program could then pass the structure to other functions as a single object. Although the structure could not directly contain functions, it could have a function pointer as a member and you could call the function using this pointer.

Then came C++. Probably the single most important concept C++ brought with it was that the structure could implement functions rather than just contain function pointers. Then C++ applied security to the structure by giving it access keywords. With C++, the structure could describe an object, manipulate the parts inside, and control access to the structure members. This led us to the C++ class, which changed our thinking from that of procedure-oriented code to object-oriented programming.

C# further refines the concept and the power of the class by requiring that all functions and data be members of a class. In C# terminology, the functions in a class become *methods* and the data members become *fields*. A third element, the *property,* is a hybrid of the method and field. It acts and performs like a method, but to the programmer it appears for all purposes like a field. You won't find properties, as implemented by C#, in the C++ language. The C# property comes indirectly from Visual Basic.

Basics of Object-Oriented Programming

Object-oriented programming does not actually require that you use a special language such as C++ or C#. You can write object-oriented programs in most languages, such as COBOL, FORTRAN, or, if you really work at it, ordinary BASIC. Generally, though, programmers consider a language "object-oriented" if it implements three basic concepts:

- **Encapsulation**   The language must provide a mechanism that allows an object to contain all of the information about itself and to control and manipulate that information. C# provides encapsulation through the structure and the class.

- **Inheritance**   The language must provide some means of allowing the programmer to use the definition of an object to define a new object that incorporates the elements of the original object. In C#, the class provides the mechanism for inheritance, but the structure does not.

- **Polymorphism**   When an object inherits from another object, some method to modify the original object's behavior must be included so that it describes the new object. The class in C# exhibits polymorphism through the *virtual* keyword.

Object-oriented programming has numerous advantages. Among them are object reuse and ease of design and coding. As you write more and more class definitions, you will start to notice a similarity between objects that you have already written and those that you need for a new project. These will form the basis for your own library of objects, called a class library.

Objects also offer increased reliability. As you reuse objects, you will continue to refine them until they become very stable, and your confidence in your own class library will improve. Creating a library speeds up your development time because you do not have to reinvent the classes you already have written.

For example, once you develop a *TextLine* class to help you display a line of text on the screen in a word processing program, you will find that you can use that same class in other programs, even projects not involving word processing.

As your class library develops, you'll notice some classes becoming more *abstract*. Abstraction allows the programmer to ignore the details of a class implementation and concentrate on the project at hand.

Determining exactly what an object is sometimes takes experience. In its essence, an object is simply a "thing" that contains identifiable components. Once you identify the components, you can add them as member fields in a class and then write the methods and properties you need to access and modify them.

The original structure in C fell short of the goal of object-oriented programming. While it did encapsulate the information needed to describe an object, it did not provide any method for the structure to use to control access to the information or to manipulate the structure members. Still, it was a useful device that gave programmers something to identify with when they made the transition to C++.

The structure got new life when it moved into C++. In C++, the structure keeps many of the properties of the C structure and also gains the ability to contain functions and control access to members using access keywords. It can also inherit from a class or another structure, and you can derive new structures or classes from an existing structure. In addition, a structure may contain *virtual* functions, so it could exhibit polymorphism. Thus, in C++, the structure meets all the criteria for a fully qualified object.

This is not true in C#, however. While the C# structure *does* meet the criteria for encapsulation, it is a dead end on the evolutionary chain. A class or another structure cannot inherit from it, and it cannot inherit from a class or other structure. It also may not contain *virtual* functions, so it cannot meet the criteria for polymorphism. The C# structure, then, is not a true object, but is merely a device for encapsulation.

C# enforces encapsulation through the class. You cannot declare any data objects or methods outside of a class. You can *define* a structure outside of a class, but the definition itself does not set aside any memory. (It should be noted that a structure may contain a *static* field and thus the definition does set aside storage in "global" memory in the same way that a *static* class member reserves memory outside of an instance of the class.)

Encapsulation also controls the *visibility* or *exposure* of a class member. A class may conceal a sensitive member by marking it *private*, in which case it is not visible to other classes or even derived classes. It then may control access to the member through a *public* property. A class may have a *protected* member, exposing it to derived classes only. This type of control could not be enforced if C# allowed you to declare variables and functions outside of a class or structure.

Encapsulating Your Data

Encapsulation allows you to collect all the information about an object and place that information into a single, distinct unit, which you then may refer to using a single identifier. You can pass the entire object to functions using a single variable name.

USE IT   For example, if you wanted to set up a group of classes to hold the database records for your books and movies, you would first identify what books and movies have in common. Both books and movies have a title. Then they have a copyright date. Armed with that, you have enough information to set up a class that describes the objects in your book and movie libraries.

Next, you identify what is different between your books and movies. Books have an author and they have a page count. Movies, on the other hand, do not necessarily have authors, but they have a running time and a medium, such as VHS or DVD.

You can now *derive* two new classes from the library object class, one for books and another for movies. Your class structure might look something like the following:

```
namespace nsLibrary
{
    public class clsLibrary
    {
        protected clsLibrary () { }
        protected string m_Title = null;
        public string Title
        {
            get {return(m_Title);}
        }
        protected int m_Copyright;
        public int Copyright
        {
```

```csharp
            get {return(m_Copyright);}
        }
    }
public class clsBook : clsLibrary
{
    public clsBook (string title, string author, int copyright)
    {
        m_Title = title;
        m_Author = author;
        m_Copyright = copyright;
    }
    private string m_Author = null;
    public string Author
    {
        get {return(m_Author);}
    }
    private int m_Pages;
    public int Pages
    {
        get {return (m_Pages);}
        set {m_Pages = value;}
    }
    override public string ToString ()
    {
        return (string.Format ("Book {0} ({1}) by {2} has {3} pages",
                               Title, Copyright, Author, Pages));
    }
}
public enum MovieMedium {VHS, DVD, Laser};
public class clsMovie : clsLibrary
{
    public clsMovie (string title, int copyright,
                     MovieMedium medium)
    {
        m_Title = title;
        m_Copyright = copyright;
        m_Medium = medium;
    }
    private int m_RunTime;
    public int RunTime
    {
        get {return (m_RunTime);}
        set {m_RunTime = value;}
    }
    private MovieMedium m_Medium;
    public string Medium
```

```
    {
        get
        {
            return (m_Medium.ToString ());
        }
    }
    override public string ToString ()
    {
        return (string.Format ("Movie {0} ({1}) is in {2} " +
                               "format and runs {3} minutes",
                               Title, Copyright, Medium, RunTime));
    }
    }
}
```

The *clsLibrary* class used here is pretty simple. You might identify other common properties and later add them to the class. For example, you might want to add a movie rating or a string that contains a brief description.

The important idea is that you have identified common elements and *encapsulated* them into a single definition. Then you identified dissimilar properties and created new classes to hold these different properties through *inheritance*.

By adding the *ToString()* method, you also used *polymorphism. ToString()* is a member of the *Object* class, from which all classes in C# are derived. Adding the method to your class changes the behavior.

Inheriting from a Base Class

The OOP principle of inheritance allows you to draw upon code that you have already written in other object definitions. You may use an existing object to build a new object by *deriving* from the existing object. When you derive one object from another in C#, the new object inherits all of the methods, properties, and fields of the existing object.

C# supports inheritance through the class. When you inherit one class from another, the new class is called the *derived* class and the class from which it inherits is the *base* class.

Inheritance does not mean that the new class will automatically have access to all the members in the base class. A base class may still control access to its members and prevent derived classes from accessing them by using the *private* access keyword.

To derive a new class from an existing class, you first write the class name using any of the modifiers from Chapter 7. You then add a colon after the new class name and follow with the name of the base class:

```
class clsBase
{
    // Base class member methods, properties and fields
```

```
}
class clsDerived : clsBase
{
    // Derived class member methods, properties and fields
}
```

Although the definition of the base class may include modifiers such as *abstract* or *unsafe*, you cannot *add* modifiers to it when you derive the new class. You must include the name of the base class by itself following the colon.

A derived class inherits the members of a base class with the same access levels declared in the base class. In C++, you may "upgrade" the protection level of base class members by inheriting a base class as *protected* or *private*. C#, however, does not support any modifiers before a base class name, including protection levels.

A class may inherit from one class only, although the base class itself might be derived from another class. C# does not support the C++ system of multiple inheritance, in which you may specify more than one class as a base. Multiple inheritance leads to the possibility that a class may eventually inherit multiple copies of an ancestor class. Designing such a scheme requires care to avoid this condition, but you don't have to worry about this in C#.

A base class in C# exposes members to derived classes by making the members *public* or *protected*. A derived class may not access *private* members of a base class.

USE IT When you derive a class from a base class, the derived class becomes forever linked to the base class. There is no way to programmatically "un-inherit" a class. To do that, you would have to remove the inheritance and recompile your program. When you declare an instance of a derived class, you automatically declare an instance of the base class.

The following program, *Inherit.cs*, shows that creating an instance of a derived class also instantiates a base class. The function in which you declare the instance has access to the *public* members of the base class:

```
namespace nsInherit
{
    using System;
    class clsMain
    {
        static public void Main ()
        {
            clsDerived derived = new clsDerived();
            derived.Property = 42;
            derived.ShowField();
        }
    }
//
// Define a base class with a private field and a public Property
    class clsBase
    {
```

```
        private int m_Field;
        public int Property
        {
            get {return (m_Field);}
            set {m_Field = value;}
        }
        public void ShowField ()
        {
            Console.WriteLine ("The value of m_Field is " + m_Field);
        }
    }
//
// Define a derived class that inherits from the clsBase
    class clsDerived : clsBase
    {
//  For now, the derived class needs no members
    }
}
```

Although you declared only an instance of the derived class, the *Main()* method has access to the members in *clsBase*. You do not need to declare a separate instance of the base class.

You may derive a class from a base class in another assembly as long as you mark the base class *public*. By default, classes in a single assembly are *internal*, meaning they are private to the assembly. You do not need the source code for an assembly to derive a new class from one of its member classes.

The following program, *Access.cs*, defines a *public* class named *clsBase* that you intend to use as a base class in another assembly. You then compile the program to produce an assembly, the executable file. By itself, this program does nothing, although it contains a *Main()* method (this example will also show how you may inadvertently create a security hole):

```
//
//  Access.cs - demonstrates deriving a new class from a base class in
//              another assembly. Also demonstrates how a derived class
//              may provide a public property to expose a protected member
//              of a base class.
//
//              Compile this program with the following command line:
//                  C:>csc Access.cs
//
namespace nsAccess
{
    using System;
    class clsMain
    {
        static public void Main ()
        {
```

```
            }
        }
//
// Declare a base class with a private field, then declare
// a protected property to access the field
    public class clsBase
    {
        private int m_Private;
        protected int Private
        {
            get {return (m_Private);}
            set {m_Private = value;}
        }
        public void ShowField ()
        {
            Console.WriteLine ("The value of private field m_Private is "
                              + m_Private);
        }
    }
}
```

Compile *Access.cs* to create the assembly. In the same directory, add the following program, *Access1.cs*, which derives a new class from the *clsBase* class in *Access.cs*:

```
//
//  Access1.cs - demonstrates deriving a new class from a base class in
//               another assembly. Also demonstrates how a derived class
//               may provide a public property to expose a protected member
//               of a base class.
//
//               Compile this program with the following command line:
//                   C:>csc /r:access.exe Access1.cs
//
namespace nsAccess
{
    using System;
    class clsMain
    {
        static public void Main ()
        {
            clsDerived derived = new clsDerived ();
            derived.AccessIt = 42;
            derived.ShowField ();
        }
    }
```

```
//
// Derive a class from the base class and give it a public
// property to access the private field in the base class
    class clsDerived : clsBase
    {
        public int AccessIt
        {
            get {return (Private);}
            set {Private = value;}
        }
    }
}
```

Compile *Access1.cs* by providing a reference to the *Access.exe* assembly using the following command line:

```
C:>csc /r:access.exe Access1.cs
```

Run the program *Access1.exe* to see the output. When you use another .NET program as a reference in this way, it is a *private assembly* and must be located in the same directory as your program file.

Any inheritance chain inevitably leads to security holes when you use the *protected* keyword to secure members, yet still make them available to derived classes. For example, a base class may provide a *private* field and then establish a *protected* property to permit derived classes to access the field indirectly. Later, another programmer studies the class structure and decides to expose the method though a *public* property. The *Access.cs* and *Access1.cs* programs show an example of this. There is nothing you can do about this, but you should be aware that it can happen.

Designing a Base Class

In the preceding examples, it is possible for you to declare an instance of the base class directly, but this is not always desirable. Sometimes a base class is incomplete and expects a derived class to implement certain methods.

You can prevent an instance of the base class from being declared in two ways. First, you can give the base class a *protected* constructor. Only a derived class can create an instance of a base class with a *protected* constructor.

USE IT   The following code shows a class derived from a base class with a *protected* constructor. You cannot create an instance of the base class directly, but when you create an instance of the derived class, it will create an instance of the base class and call the constructor for you:

```
class clsBase
{
    protected clsBase() {}
```

```
}
class clsDerived : clsBase
{
    // Derived class members
}
```

When you use a protected constructor, there is no guarantee that a derived class will implement any other code the base class needs. A program could declare an empty derived class to implement the base class.

A second, better method is to declare your base class as an *abstract* class, particularly if your base class needs to assure that any derived class will provide additional code. An abstract class may contain abstract methods and properties.

To define an abstract class, use the *abstract* keyword when you declare the name of your class:

```
abstract class clsAbsClass
{
    // Class members here
}
```

When you attempt to create an instance of an abstract class, the compiler will issue an error and will not compile your program.

An abstract method or property in an abstract class is inherently *virtual*. The concept of virtual functions and the abstract class is important in the OOP principle of polymorphism. In the tip, "Polymorphism: Changing Class Behavior Using Virtual Methods" later in this chapter, you will override virtual methods in a derived class.

Hiding Base Class Members

When you inherit from a base class, your derived class may access all the *public* and *protected* members of the base class as though they were members of the derived class. You do not need to qualify the names of the base class members.

You do not have to use the base class members. When you design a base class, you may provide for a number of inheritance possibilities. If you do not need a base class member and you want to use the identifier in your derived class, you may *hide* the base class name by using the *new* keyword. When used this way, *new* is a modifier rather than an operator because it creates a new class member and not a new object.

The *new* modifier does not replace or override the base class member. It simply creates a new member in the derived class with the same name as a member of the base class. The base class will still be able to use its member, but the derived class will access the *new* member. You cannot use it to hide base class members that are *private* because those members are not exposed to the derived class and there is no need to hide them.

The derived class member does not have to be the same data type or have the same access level as the base class member, nor does it have to be the same type. A method, property, or field in a derived class may hide a method, property, or field in the base class. When you do this, your derived class will be able to access the hidden member by qualifying the name with the keyword *base*, but functions outside the base and derived classes may not access the base class member.

USE IT   The following snippet shows an example of name hiding in a derived class.

```
//
// Declare a base class with a protected method, a public method and
// a public field.
    public class clsBase
    {
        protected void Method()
        {
        }
        public void ShowField ()
        {
            Console.WriteLine ("The value of public field AnInt is " + AnInt);
        }
        public int AnInt;
    }
//
// Derive a class from the base class and hide members of
// the base class
    class clsDerived : clsBase
    {
// Hide the protected base class Method() with a private field
        new private int Method;
// Hide the public int base class member with a double field
        new public double AnInt;
// Provide an alternate property for external functions to access
// the base class public int field
        public int BaseMember
        {
// Note the use of the keyword base to qualify the base class
// member name.
            get {return (base.AnInt);}
            set {base.AnInt = value;}
        }
    }
```

In this snippet, the base class field *AnInt* no longer is exposed through the derived class even though it is declared as *public*. Only methods and properties in the base and derived classes may access it.

Calling Constructors and Destructors in Order

When you create an instance of a class, the runtime code will call the constructor for the class automatically. Then, when the Common Language Runtime (CLR) destroys the instance, it will call any destructor function that you have declared.

If the instance is for a class that inherits from one or more base classes, the program will call the base class constructors before calling the constructor for the class instance. The calling sequence starts with the most distant ancestor first.

When the CLR destroys the object, it calls the destructors in the reverse order. First, the derived class constructor executes, and then the first base class up the chain is executed. This continues until the most distant ancestor destructor is called.

USE IT   You can see this sequence by making the constructors and destructors write messages to the console when they execute. The following program, *Order.cs*, declares a sequence of base classes and then creates an instance of the last derived class:

```
// Order.cs - shows the order in which constructors and destructors
//            are called in a C# program.
//
//            Compile this program with the following command line:
//                 C:>csc Order.cs
//
namespace nsOrder
{
    using System;
    class clsMain
    {
        static public void Main ()
        {
            clsLastChild child = new clsLastChild ();
            Console.WriteLine ();
        }
    }
//
// Declare a base class and have its constructor and destructor
// print messages.
    class clsBase
    {
        public clsBase ()
        {
            Console.WriteLine ("Base class constructor called");
        }
        ~clsBase ()
        {
            Console.WriteLine ("Base class destructor called");
```

```
        }
    }
// Derive a class from clsBase. Have the constructor and destructor
// print messages.
    class clsFirstChild : clsBase
    {
        public clsFirstChild ()
        {
            Console.WriteLine ("First Child constructor called");
        }
        ~clsFirstChild ()
        {
            Console.WriteLine ("First Child destructor called");
        }
    }
// Derive a class from clsFirstChile. Have the constructor and destructor
// print messages as well.
    class clsLastChild  : clsFirstChild
    {
        public clsLastChild ()
        {
            Console.WriteLine ("Last Child constructor called");
        }
        ~clsLastChild ()
        {
            Console.WriteLine ("Last Child destructor called");
        }
    }
}
```

The output from *Order.cs* is shown in the following:

```
Base class constructor called
First Child constructor called
Last Child constructor called

Last Child destructor called
First Child destructor called
Base class destructor called
```

By establishing this calling sequence, C# is able to guarantee that any resources needed by derived classes will be created before the derived class constructor is called. Any fields in the base classes are initialized and ready for the derived class when its constructor executes. The destructor sequence assures that any base class resources in use by the derived class will be available until the derived class is destroyed.

Preventing Inheritance — The Sealed Modifier

You can prevent an instance of a base class by defining it as *abstract* or by giving it a *protected* constructor. Sometimes, however, you might want to make it impossible to derive a class from another.

You could accomplish this by giving the class a *private* constructor. However, doing that would also keep you from declaring *any* instance of the class. The *private* constructor does have its uses, but it is not particularly useful in ending an inheritance chain.

In C++, there is no way to prevent inheritance other than by providing a *private* constructor. If you define a class, you may inherit from it. C# does provide such a mechanism in the *sealed* keyword. To seal a class, simply use the *sealed* keyword when you define the class:

```
sealed class clsClass
{
    // Class members
}
```

Once you use the *sealed* modifier on a class definition, no further inheritance is possible. Many of the .NET Framework classes are *sealed*. You should be careful using the *sealed* keyword when building a library of classes and be certain that you will not need to derive further classes from a class that you have sealed.

USE IT   Sometimes it might be necessary to seal a class for security reasons, or because there is nothing to be gained by using it as a base class. The *System.Console* class is an example of such a class. It contains only *static* methods and properties. In addition, the class is designed so that it will not throw an exception if you attempt to write to the console in a program where the console does not exist, such as in a Windows forms application. Allowing you to derive a new class from it might compromise this protection, so the class has been sealed.

The following code attempts to derive a new class from the *System.Console* class to provide a method to write to the standard error device:

```
class clsMyConsole : Console
{
    static public WriteError (string str, params object[])
    {
        // Code here to implement method
    }
}
```

The compiler will reject this definition. If you need to write to the standard error device, you can invoke the *Error* property, which is a *TextWriter* object:

```
Console.Error.WriteLine (<params>);
```

Polymorphism: Changing Class Behavior Using Virtual Methods

In a class hierarchy such as that presented by the .NET Framework, you start with a very general class that describes the basic nature of the chain of classes. Then you derive successively more specific classes until you get to the final descendent class, the one that you will create in your program.

A hierarchy may have several branches. In each branch, many of the classes may have common methods, and each class in the branch can build upon its ancestor classes. Many times, however, a method might have the same purpose but a different implementation.

Using the OOP principle of polymorphism, you can provide the specific code needed for a method for each class and have your program call the proper method. The primary concept by which C# supports polymorphism is the *virtual* method.

When you write a virtual method, you are telling the compiler that a derived class may provide a different implementation for the method. The derived class does not have to provide a different implementation, however, in which case it would use the base class method.

USE IT The following short program, *Virtual.cs*, declares a base class and then derives two classes from the base class. One derived class overrides the *virtual* method in the base class and the second does not:

```
//
// Virtual.cs -- Demonstrates the use of a virtual method to override
//               a base class method.
//
//               Compile this program with the following command line:
//                   C:>csc Virtual.cs
namespace nsVirtual
{
    using System;
    class clsMain
    {
        static public void Main ()
        {
            clsBase Base = new clsBase();
            clsFirst First = new clsFirst();
            clsSecond Second = new clsSecond();
            Base.Show();
            First.Show();
            Second.Show ();
        }
    }
    class clsBase
    {
```

```
        public void Show ()
        {
            Describe ();
        }
        virtual protected void Describe ()
        {
            Console.WriteLine ("Called the base class Describe() method");
        }
    }
    class clsFirst : clsBase
    {
        override protected void Describe ()
        {
            Console.WriteLine ("Called the derived class Describe() method");
        }
    }
    class clsSecond : clsBase
    {
    }
}
```

Compiling and running *Virtual.cs* shows the following output:

```
Called the base class Describe() method
Called the derived class Describe() method
Called the base class Describe() method
```

When the base class instance calls *Show()*, the *Describe()* method in the base class executes. However, the first derived class overrides the virtual method *Describe()*, and calling the *Show()* method results in the first derived class printing its own description. The second derived class, however, does not override the *virtual* method, and thus the call to *Show()* executes the base class method.

When you use the *virtual* keyword on a method or property, any derived class is still able to access the base class member by prefixing its name with the *base* keyword:

```
class clsBase
{
    virtual VirtFunc ()
    {
    }
}
class clsDerived : clsBase
{
    override VirtFunc ()
    {
    }
    public void OtherFunc ()
```

```
    {
        base.VirtFunc ();       // Calls the base class method
        VirtFunc ();            // Calls the derived class method
    }
}
```

You can use this technique when you want to execute both the base class and the derived class methods.

USE IT   The following program, *Poly.cs*, defines a base class to contain the fields and properties that you will need to draw lines on a window. It then serves as the base for a *clsPoint* class, which draws a small cross inside a box to mark the point. Although a *Point* structure is included in the .NET library, you cannot derive a new class from a structure, so you need to provide code to draw the point symbol.

The base class also serves as the basis for a *clsLine* class, which draws a line using just a starting point, a length, and an angle. This is much easier to use than computing the two end points for a line, which the Windows drawing methods require.

In turn, the *clsPoint* class is the base for a *clsCircle* class. This is a not a particularly exciting class, except that it allows you to draw a circle using only the center point and the radius. However, *clsCircle* serves as the base class for a *clsEllipse* class, which draws an ellipse at any angle. After drawing the ellipse, the *clsEllipse* class then calls the base method to draw the center point, which in turn calls the *clsPoint.Draw()* method to show the center point. The Windows drawing methods will draw an ellipse only vertically or horizontally, but ellipses in real life appear at many different angles. The *clsEllipse* class uses *Bezier* points to draw the ellipse. Now, you cannot exactly draw an ellipse using *Bezier* points, but the code in *Poly.cs* comes extremely close:

When you run *Poly.cs*, your window should look like the one shown here. Experiment with the lines and ellipses and you will see how much easier it is to use the classes compared with the graphics device interface (GDI) methods.

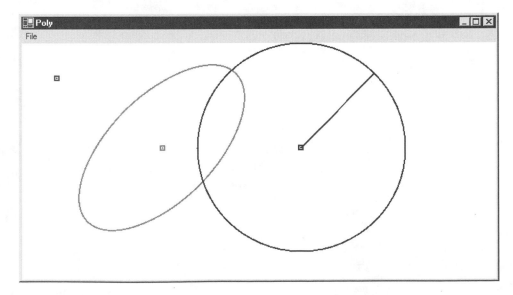

The listing for *Poly.cs* is shown here:

```csharp
using System;
using System.Drawing;
using System.Collections;
using System.ComponentModel;
using System.Windows.Forms;
using System.Data;

namespace Poly
{
    /// <summary>
    /// Summary description for Form1.
    /// </summary>
    public class clsMain : System.Windows.Forms.Form
    {
        private System.Windows.Forms.MainMenu mainMenu1;
        private System.Windows.Forms.MenuItem menuItem1;
        private System.Windows.Forms.MenuItem mnuFileExit;
        private System.Windows.Forms.Label label1;
        /// <summary>
        /// Required designer variable.
        /// </summary>
        private System.ComponentModel.Container components = null;

        public clsMain()
        {
            //
            // Required for Windows Form Designer support
            //
            InitializeComponent();
            InitForm ();

            //
            // TODO: Add any constructor code after InitializeComponent call
            //
        }
        clsPoint pt = new clsPoint (50, 50);
        clsEllipse ellipse = new clsEllipse (200, 150, 150, 75, 450);
        clsCircle circle = new clsCircle (400, 150, 150);
        clsLine line = new clsLine (400, 150, 150, 450);
        private void InitForm ()
        {
            pt.color = Color.Red;
            this.MaximumSize = new Size (this.Bounds.Width,
```

```
                                      this.Bounds.Height);
    this.MinimumSize = this.MaximumSize;
    ellipse.color = Color.DarkOrange;
    line.color = Color.Blue;
}
/// <summary>
/// Clean up any resources being used.
/// </summary>
protected override void Dispose( bool disposing )
{
    if( disposing )
    {
        if (components != null)
        {
            components.Dispose();
        }
    }
    base.Dispose( disposing );
}


#region Windows Form Designer generated code
/// <summary>
/// Required method for Designer support - do not modify
/// the contents of this method with the code editor.
/// </summary>
private void InitializeComponent()
{
    this.label1 = new System.Windows.Forms.Label();
    this.mnuFileExit = new System.Windows.Forms.MenuItem();
    this.menuItem1 = new System.Windows.Forms.MenuItem();
    this.mainMenu1 = new System.Windows.Forms.MainMenu();
    this.SuspendLayout();
    //
    // label1
    //
    this.label1.BackColor = System.Drawing.SystemColors.Window;
    this.label1.Dock = System.Windows.Forms.DockStyle.Fill;
    this.label1.Name = "label1";
    this.label1.Size = new System.Drawing.Size(680, 341);
    this.label1.TabIndex = 0;
    this.label1.Paint +=
                    new System.Windows.Forms.PaintEventHandler
                    (this.label1_Paint);
    //
```

```csharp
// mnuFileExit
//
this.mnuFileExit.Index = 0;
this.mnuFileExit.Text = "Exit";
this.mnuFileExit.Click += new
                    System.EventHandler(this.mnuFileExit_Click);
//
// menuItem1
//
this.menuItem1.Index = 0;
this.menuItem1.MenuItems.AddRange
                    (new System.Windows.Forms.MenuItem[] {
                    this.mnuFileExit});
this.menuItem1.Text = "File";
//
// mainMenu1
//
this.mainMenu1.MenuItems.AddRange
                        (new System.Windows.Forms.MenuItem[] {
                            this.menuItem1});
//
// clsMain
//
this.AutoScaleBaseSize = new System.Drawing.Size(5, 13);
this.ClientSize = new System.Drawing.Size(680, 341);
this.Controls.AddRange(new System.Windows.Forms.Control[] {
                        this.label1});
this.Menu = this.mainMenu1;
this.MinimizeBox = false;
this.Name = "clsMain";
this.Text = "Poly";
this.ResumeLayout(false);

}
#endregion

/// <summary>
/// The main entry point for the application.
/// </summary>
[STAThread]
static void Main()
{
    Application.Run(new clsMain());
}
```

```
    private void mnuFileExit_Click(object sender, System.EventArgs e)
    {
        this.Close ();
    }

    int m_cx = 100;
    int m_cy = 50;

    private void label1_Paint(object sender,
                        System.Windows.Forms.PaintEventArgs e)
    {
        pt.Show(e);
        ellipse.Show (e);
        circle.Show (e);
        line.Show (e);
    }
}
abstract public class clsShape
{
    protected clsShape() { }
    ~clsShape ()
    {
        if (m_Pen != null)
            m_Pen.Dispose ();
        if (m_Brush != null)
            m_Brush.Dispose ();
    }
    protected Pen m_Pen = null;
    protected SolidBrush m_Brush = null;
    public Color color
    {
        get
        {
            if (m_Brush == null)
                m_Brush = new SolidBrush (Color.Black);
            return (m_Brush.Color);
        }
        set
        {
            if (m_Brush != null)
                m_Brush.Dispose ();
            m_Brush = new SolidBrush (value);
        }
    }
```

```
            protected virtual SolidBrush brush
            {
                get
                {
                    if (m_Brush == null)
                        m_Brush = new SolidBrush (Color.Black);
                    return (m_Brush);
                }
            }
            protected virtual Pen pen
            {
                get
                {
                    if (m_Pen == null)
                        SetPen ();
                    return (m_Pen);
                }
                set {SetPen ();}
            }
            private void SetPen ()
            {
                if (m_Brush == null)
                    m_Brush = new SolidBrush (Color.Black);
                if (m_Pen != null)
                    m_Pen.Dispose ();
                m_Pen = new Pen (m_Brush, 2);
            }
            public void Show (PaintEventArgs e)
            {
                Draw (e);
            }
            virtual protected void Draw (PaintEventArgs e)
            {
            }
            protected void Rotate (int angle, Point ptCenter, Point [] ptControl)
            {
//
// If the angle is 0, there's nothing to do
                if (angle == 0)
                    return;
// The angle is in tenths of a degree. Convert to radians
                double fAngle = (angle / 10.0) / 57.29578;
// Calculate the sine of the angle
                double fSine = Math.Sin (fAngle);
```

```csharp
// Calculate the cosine of the angle
        double fCosine = Math.Cos (fAngle);
// Translate the center point so it can be the center of rotation
        double fRotateX = ptCenter.X - ptCenter.X
                            * fCosine - ptCenter.Y * fSine;
        double fRotateY = ptCenter.Y + ptCenter.X
                            * fSine - ptCenter.Y * fCosine;
        for (int x = 0; x <  ptControl.Length; ++x)
        {
//
// Rotate the control point and add the translated center point
            double fNewX = ptControl[x].X * fCosine
                            + ptControl[x].Y *fSine + fRotateX;
            double fNewY = -ptControl[x].X * fSine
                            + ptControl[x].Y *fCosine + fRotateY;
// Put the new values in the control point
            ptControl[x].X = (int) fNewX;
            ptControl[x].Y = (int) fNewY;
        }
    }
}
public class clsPoint : clsShape
{
    protected clsPoint () { }
    public clsPoint (int cx, int cy)
    {
        m_cx = cx;
        m_cy = cy;
    }
    public int cx
    {
        get {return(m_cx);}
        set {m_cx = value;}
    }
    public int cy
    {
        get {return(m_cy);}
        set {m_cy = value;}
    }
    protected int m_cx;
    protected int m_cy;
    override protected void Draw (PaintEventArgs e)
    {
        Point pt1 = new Point (m_cx, m_cy - 1);
```

```
            Point pt2 = new Point (m_cx, m_cy + 1);
            e.Graphics.DrawLine (pen, pt1, pt2);
            pt1.X = m_cx - 1;
            pt2.X = m_cx + 1;
            pt1.Y = pt2.Y = m_cy;
            e.Graphics.DrawLine (pen, pt1, pt2);
            e.Graphics.DrawRectangle (pen, m_cx - 3, m_cy - 3, 6, 6);
        }
    }
    public class clsLine : clsShape
    {
        protected clsLine () { }
        public clsLine (int cx, int cy, int length, int angle)
        {
            m_Start = new Point (cx, cy);
            m_End = new Point (cx + length, cy);
            m_Angle = angle;
        }
        protected Point m_End;
        protected Point m_Start;
        protected int m_Angle;
        override protected void Draw (PaintEventArgs e)
        {
            Point ptStart = new Point (m_Start.X, m_Start.Y);
            Point [] ptEnd = new Point[1] {new Point (m_End.X, m_End.Y)};
            Rotate (m_Angle, ptStart, ptEnd);
            e.Graphics.DrawLine (pen, ptStart, ptEnd[0]);
        }
    }
    public class clsCircle : clsPoint
    {
        protected clsCircle () { }
        public clsCircle (int cx, int cy, int radius)
        {
            m_cx = cx;
            m_cy = cy;
            m_Radius = radius;
        }
        protected int m_Radius;
        override protected void Draw (PaintEventArgs e)
        {
            e.Graphics.DrawEllipse (pen, m_cx - m_Radius, m_cy
                             - m_Radius, 2 * m_Radius, 2 * m_Radius);
            DrawCenter (e);
```

```
        }
        public void DrawCenter (PaintEventArgs e)
        {
            base.Draw (e);
        }
    }
    /// <summary>
    /// Draws an ellipse using Bezier points
    /// </summary>
    public class clsEllipse : clsCircle, IDisposable
    {
        protected clsEllipse () { }
        public void Dispose ()
        {
        }
        public clsEllipse (int cx, int cy, int horiz, int vert, int rotate)
        {
            m_cx = cx;
            m_cy = cy;
            m_Radius = horiz;
            m_Vert = vert;
            m_Rotate = rotate;
        }
        protected double m_Eccentric;
        protected int m_Vert;
        protected int m_Rotate;
    /// <summary>
    /// Overridden from the clsCircle class
    /// </summary>
    /// <param name="e"></param>
        override protected void Draw (PaintEventArgs e)
        {
            int OffsetX = (int) (2 * m_Radius
                        * (2 * (Math.Sqrt(2) - 1) / 3) + 0.5);
            int OffsetY = (int) (2 * m_Vert
                        * (2 * (Math.Sqrt(2) - 1) / 3) + 0.5);
            Point [] ptEllipse = new Point [13]
                    {
                    new Point (m_cx + m_Radius, m_cy),
                    new Point (m_cx + m_Radius, m_cy - OffsetY),
                    new Point (m_cx + OffsetX,  m_cy - m_Vert),
                    new Point (m_cx,            m_cy - m_Vert),
                    new Point (m_cx - OffsetX,  m_cy - m_Vert),
                    new Point (m_cx - m_Radius, m_cy - OffsetY),
```

```
                        new Point (m_cx - m_Radius, m_cy),
                        new Point (m_cx - m_Radius, m_cy + OffsetY),
                        new Point (m_cx - OffsetX,  m_cy + m_Vert),
                        new Point (m_cx,            m_cy + m_Vert),
                        new Point (m_cx + OffsetX,  m_cy + m_Vert),
                        new Point (m_cx + m_Radius, m_cy + OffsetY),
                        new Point (m_cx + m_Radius, m_cy)
                        };
            Point ptCenter = new Point (m_cx, m_cy);
            Rotate (m_Rotate, ptCenter, ptEllipse);
            e.Graphics.DrawBeziers (pen, ptEllipse);
            base.DrawCenter (e);
        }
    }
}
```

Notice that it takes 13 points to draw an ellipse using *Bezier* points. You actually draw the ellipse in four arcs, and you need four points to describe each arc—two end points and two control points. The end point for one arc is the starting point for the next arc.

As further proof that the base class *Show()* method actually calls the derived class *Draw()* methods, try calling the base class methods directly. Create an array of type *clsShape* to hold the objects, and then initialize the array in the *InitForm()* method. The following code shows how you would do this (the C# compiler will cast the objects to the base class automatically):

```
clsPoint pt = new clsPoint (50, 50);
clsEllipse ellipse = new clsEllipse (200, 150, 150, 75, 450);
clsCircle circle = new clsCircle (400, 150, 150);
clsLine line = new clsLine (400, 150, 150, 450);
// Add the following array.
clsShape [] Shapes;
private void InitForm ()
{
// Initialize the new array to contain the shape objects.
    Shapes = new clsShape [] {pt, ellipse, circle, line};
    pt.color = Color.Red;
    this.MaximumSize = new Size (this.Bounds.Width, this.Bounds.Height);
    this.MinimumSize = this.MaximumSize;
    ellipse.color = Color.DarkOrange;
    line.color = Color.Blue;
}
```

Now modify the *label1_Paint()* event handler to call the base class *Show()* methods in a *foreach* loop, as shown in the following:

```
private void label1_Paint (object sender,
                       System.Windows.Forms.PaintEventArgs e)
```

```
{
    foreach (clsShape shape in Shapes)
    {
        shape.Show (e);
    }
}
```

In this code, the *foreach* loop is oblivious to the actual object. It contains only references to *clsShape* objects, and the loop code calls the base class methods.

Using Virtual Properties

You can declare *virtual* properties as well as methods with the same result. In this case, you should remember that if the base property uses a *private* field member for storage, the derived class property still does not have access to the base class field. In such a case, the derived class property must provide its own field.

> **USE IT** The program that follows, *VProp.cs*, defines a *virtual* property in the base class, which is then overridden in the derived class. The properties are *protected*, so the only way a method outside the classes may access the properties is through the *public* member functions in the base class. The derived class provides no code to access the properties:

```
//
// VProp.cs -- Demonstrates the use of a virtual property to override
//             a base class property.
//
//             Compile this program with the following command line:
//                  C:>csc VProp.cs
namespace nsVirtual
{
    using System;
    class clsMain
    {
        static public void Main ()
        {
            clsBase Base = new clsBase();
            clsFirst First = new clsFirst();
            Base.SetString ("This should set the base class property");
            First.SetString ("This should set the derived class property");
            Console.WriteLine ();
            Console.WriteLine (Base.GetString());
            Console.WriteLine (First.GetString());
        }
    }
```

```csharp
class clsBase
{
    public void SetString (string str)
    {
        StrProp = str;
    }
    public string GetString ()
    {
        return (StrProp);
    }
    virtual protected string StrProp
    {
        get
        {
            Console.WriteLine ("Getting Base string");
            return (m_BaseString);
        }
        set
        {
            Console.WriteLine ("Setting Base string");
            m_BaseString = value;
        }
    }
    private string m_BaseString = "";
}
class clsFirst : clsBase
{
    override protected string StrProp
    {
        get
        {
            Console.WriteLine ("Getting derived string");
            return (m_DerivedString);
        }
        set
        {
            Console.WriteLine ("Setting derived string");
            m_DerivedString = value;
        }
    }
    private string m_DerivedString = "";
}
}
```

The output from *VProp.exe* shows that the methods in the base class did access the overridden property in the derived class:

```
Setting Base string
Setting derived string

Getting Base string
This should set the base class property
Getting derived string
This should set the derived class property
```

Defining an Abstract Class

In the preceding examples, you were not required to derive new classes from the base class or even override the method or property in any derived class. Using *virtual* methods declares only that you *may* derive a new class from the base class, and the derived class *may* provide its own implementation for the *virtual* methods and properties.

In C# you may declare a class *abstract* to signal to the compiler that the class cannot be used directly. To use the members of the class, the programmer must derive a new class using the *abstract* class as a base.

C++ has no equivalent keyword. To create an abstract class in C++, you must include at least one *pure virtual function* as a class member. A pure virtual function is a function that you declare as a class member, but you set its address to 0. C# also uses the *abstract* keyword to indicate a pure virtual function, which you will meet shortly.

When used on a class definition, the C# *abstract* keyword is the equivalent of the Visual Basic *MustInherit* keyword.

 To declare an *abstract* class, use the keyword before the *class* keyword and the class name:

```
abstract class clsAbstract
{
    // Class members
}
```

You cannot use the *sealed* modifier with the *abstract* modifier. The *sealed* declaration specifies that you cannot derive a class from the definition, and the *abstract* modifier declares that you must derive a class from it. The two modifiers are mutually exclusive, and the C# compiler will issue an error if you use both.

An *abstract* class does not have to contain *abstract* members. Simply declaring a class *abstract* is enough to prevent you from declaring an instance of the class. It may contain *virtual* members, or members that are neither *virtual* or *abstract*. When you provide a *virtual* member, you may override it in the derived class.

Declaring an Abstract Function

When you declare a class using the *abstract* keyword, you may include *abstract* methods or properties. You do not need to provide a body of code for *abstract* class members; you simply declare them and follow the declarations with a semicolon. Then, when you derive a class from the abstract class, it must implement the *abstract* members.

 USE IT   Many of the .NET library classes are defined as *abstract*. An *abstract* class is not intended to be used directly, either by external functions or by derived classes. The *System.IO.TextReader* class is an example. It provides the basic methods to examine and read from a stream or string, but it does not know whether a stream or string is being examined. The exact source for the read is determined by derived classes, the *StreamReader* and *StringReader* classes. The *TextReader* class contains two *abstract* methods, *Peek( )* and *Read( )*, which the derived classes must implement.

To declare a class abstract, use the *abstract* modifier when you define your class. Declare any methods or properties that a derived class must provide by declaring them *abstract* as well, but do not write a body for them.

In the following program, *Abstract.cs*, the base class contains a method that calls an abstract method and reads and writes abstract properties. Notice that in the derived class, you replace the *abstract* keyword with *override* and then provide a body for the method and property accessors:

```
//
// Abstract.cs -- Demonstrates the use of an abstract class, including
//                an abstract method and abstract properties.
//
//                Compile this program with the following command line:
//                     C:>csc Abstract.cs
//
namespace nsAbstract
{
    using System;
    class clsMain
    {
        static public void Main ()
        {
// Create an instance of the derived class.
            clsDerived derived = new clsDerived (3.14159);
// Calling GetAbstract() actually calls the public method in the
// base class. There is no GetAbstract() in the derived class.
            derived.GetAbstract();
        }
    }
//
// Declare an abstract class

    abstract class clsBase
```

```
        {
// Declare an abstract method. Note the semicolon to end the declaration
        abstract public void Describe();
//
// Declare an abstract property that has only a get accessor. Note that you
// do not provide the braces for the accessor
        abstract public double DoubleProp
        {
            get;
        }
//
// Declare an abstract property that has only a set accessor.
        abstract public int IntProp
        {
            set;
        }
// Declare an abstract property that has both get and set accessors. Note
// that neither the get or set accessor may have a body.
        abstract public string StringProp
        {
            get;
            set;
        }
//
// Declare a method that will access the abstract members.
        public void GetAbstract ()
        {
// Get the DoubleProp, which will be in the derived class.
            Console.WriteLine ("DoubleProp = " + DoubleProp);
// You can only set the IntProp value. The storage is in the
// derived class.
            IntProp = 42;
// Set the StringProp value
            StringProp = "StringProperty actually is stored in " +
                        "the derived class.";
// Now show StringProp
            Console.WriteLine (StringProp);
// Finally, call the abstract method
            Describe ();
        }
    }
//
// Derive a class from clsBase. You must implement the abstract members
    class clsDerived : clsBase
    {
```

```
// Declare a constructor to set the DoubleProp member
        public clsDerived (double val)
        {
            m_Double = val;
        }
// When you implement an abstract member in a derived class, you may not
// change the type or access level.
        override public void Describe()
        {
            Console.WriteLine ("You called Describe() from the base " +
                              "class but the code body is in the \r\n" +
                              "derived class");
            Console.WriteLine ("m_Int = " + m_Int);
        }
//
// Implement the DoubleProp property. This is where you provide a body
// for the accessors.
        override public double DoubleProp
        {
            get {return (m_Double);}
        }
//
// Implement the set accessor for IntProp.
        override public int IntProp
        {
            set {m_Int = value;}
        }
// Implement StringProp, providing a body for both the get
// and set accessors.
        override public string StringProp
        {
            get {return (m_String);}
            set {m_String = value;}
        }
// Declare fields to support the properties.
        private double m_Double;
        private int m_Int;
        private string m_String;
    }
}
```

When you compile and run *Abstract.cs*, you should see the following output. Notice that the derived class does not provide any storage for the *abstract* members.

```
DoubleProp = 3.14159
StringProperty actually is stored in the derived class
You called Describe() from the base class but the code body is in the
derived class.
m_Int = 42
```

An *abstract* member may not be declared using the *static*, *const*, *readonly*, or *virtual* modifiers. The *abstract* member must be visible to the derived class, so you cannot declare an *abstract* member as *private*. If an abstract property does not declare an accessor, the code in the derived class may not provide a body for that accessor. The *DoubleProp* property, for example, does not declare a *set* accessor, so the *override* code in the derived class may not implement the *set* accessor.

Members that you declare as *abstract* are inherently *virtual* members, so the base class method *GetAbstract()* looks for the implementation in a derived class. This is an important part of the principle of polymorphism.

Using the Object Browser

The Visual Studio Object Browser allows you to examine objects—assemblies and modules, for example—and determine what they contain even if you do not have the source code. The browser gets the information from the object *manifest*, which is an integral part of a .NET component.

USE IT   With the *Poly.cs* program open in Visual Studio, press CTRL-ALT-J to start the Object Browser, which is shown here. The Object Browser can help you to explore a project or solution, and to find objects used by your program.

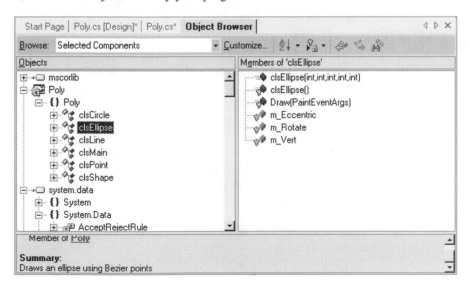

The Object Browser contains three panes. At the left is the objects pane, which shows the components in the current browsing scope, such as the namespaces, classes, and structures. This is a tree control, so you can click the plus (+) symbol to the left of an entry to show items within that object. This is amazingly much faster than looking up a method in the MSDN just to find out what parameters the method needs.

On the right side of the window is the members pane. Initially, this pane will be empty. It will display the members of a class or another object after you select it in the objects pane. To display the *clsEllipse* class members here, click the + symbol next to the Poly item on the object pane (this is the Poly code module). Next, click the + symbol next to the { } Poly item (this is the *Poly* namespace). Now *select* the clsEllipse item (in this case, click the item rather than the + symbol). All the methods, properties, and fields in the *clsEllipse* class will appear in the members pane on the right.

The third pane is the description pane, located across the bottom of the window below the objects and members panes. This pane displays information about the item you have selected in either the objects or members pane, including any XML comments that you have placed on the object.

Examine the description for the *clsEllipse* class, as shown in the illustration. Now go back to the source code and locate the *clsEllipse* class. Add the following XML comment just before the class definition (note the three slash marks instead of two; if you type three slash marks, Visual Studio will add the first and third lines for you):

```
/// <summary>
/// Draws an ellipse using Bezier points
/// </summary>
```

Return to the Object Browser and again look at the description pane. The description you just typed (less the slash marks) should appear in the description pane.

Setting the Browsing Scope

You may browse an entire project or select a limited collection of components to browse. At the top of the Object Browser is a Browse combo box, and to the right of this combo box is a Customize button that will be disabled if you have selected Active Project in the combo box.

The Active Project selection will display all the objects your program uses, including those in the .NET assemblies.

USE IT Choosing Selected Components in the combo box will enable the Customize button, which you can click to display the Selected Components dialog box shown here. The Selected Components dialog box offers options to limit the Object Browser's display.

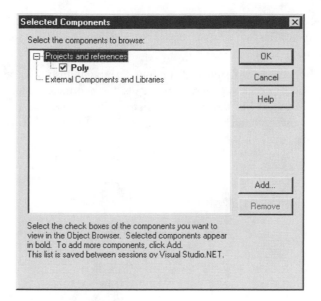

If you have included several projects in one solution, each project will be listed in the Selected Components dialog box. Checking the box next to a project name will include it in the component list that you want to browse.

Using the Objects Pane

You use the object pane to discover classes in a namespace and to determine the hierarchy of classes. Eventually, of course, everything derives from the *Object* class, but many more ancestor classes may exist in between.

 Again using the *Poly* project, the following steps show how to discover information about ancestor classes and interfaces using the Object Browser:

1. Return to the source code and locate the *clsEllipse* class. Add the *IDisposable* interface to the inheritance list so the class declaration appears like the following line:

   ```
   public class clsEllipse : clsCircle, IDisposable
   ```

2. Return to the Object Browser and open the Poly item in the tree. Navigate through the hierarchy until you find the *clsEllipse* class.

3. Click the + symbol and you should see an entry labeled "Bases and Interfaces." Open this item, and you will see the first ancestor class, *clsCircle*, and the *IDisposable* interface that you just added.

4. Click the + symbol next to *clsCircle* and continue opening items until you come to the end. Eventually, you should come to *Object*, which ends the inheritance chain. The objects panel at this point should appear like the one shown in this illustration. The tree control listing in the objects pane shows you the hierarchy of classes leading to the class you have selected.

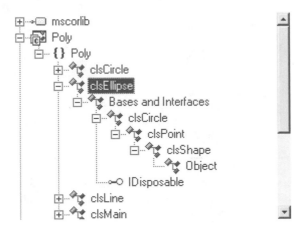

5. The base list includes the *clsPoint* and *clsShape* classes, eventually ending with the *Object* listing. You can select each base class to display the members in the members panel.

6. Finally, select the *IDisposable* entry to display a list of its members. In an interface, you will need to override each of the methods in the interface.

Using the Members Pane

You use the members pane to discover the exact implementation of a member method, property, or field.

The icon next to the object name indicates its type. A magenta block indicates a method, a cyan (blue) block is a field, and the hand holding what appears to be a card is a property. Superimposed on the bottom left of the icon you may see a key that indicates the member is *protected* or a lock that indicates the member is *private*. The lack of a key or lock means the member is *public*.

 Using the *Poly* project, locate the *clsEllipse* class as in the previous tip. Click on it to select the class. The members will appear in a list in the members pane.

If you let the mouse cursor hover briefly above an icon in the members pane, a tool window will pop up showing available information on the item, including any modifiers and access level. For a method, it also will show the return type and the names and data types of any parameters.

If the Properties tool window is not displayed on the lower right of the Visual Studio screen, press the F4 key to display it. As you select an object, some of its properties will display in the Properties window. You may modify those properties that display in bold type from the Object Browser.

Navigating the Object Browser

The Object Browser is also a convenient navigation point for your project or solution. You can sort objects and members alphabetically or by object type or access level.

The next illustration shows the Object Browser toolbar that appears across the top of the Object Browser dialog box.

USE IT To experiment with these buttons, use the *Poly* project and open the Object Browser. Then open the tree and select either the *clsMain* or the *clsShape* objects. These two objects contain enough members that changes in the sorting will be apparent quickly.

To the right of the Customize buttons are several buttons that can help you limit the object display and arrange the appearance of the panes. The first button is the sort button for the objects pane, and the second is the sort button for the members pane. Click on the arrow next to each button to display a list of the sort options.

The next two buttons allow you to step backward through your selections or to step forward after you have used the Step Back button. As you search for a particular object, you may select a number of items and eventually not remember where you were in the objects or members panes hierarchy. These buttons help you to find your way. The final button is the Find button, described in the next tip.

You can move directly to an object by double-clicking the item in the objects or members pane. For example, double-click the *clsEllipse* item, and Visual Studio will open the source code file and move the caret directly to the definition for the *clsEllipse* class.

Searching for Symbols

The final button on the Object Browser toolbar summons the Find Symbol dialog box, shown here. The Find Symbol dialog box contains the usual controls you would expect on a search dialog box. When you search for an object, the Object Browser will open a pane just below the description pane showing you the results of the search.

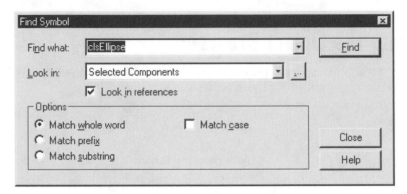

USE IT If you are not sure where in the hierarchy a particular class or object is located, you can search for the name using the Find Symbol dialog box. For example, the following procedure shows you how to determine in which namespace you would find the *ListBox* class.

1. Click the Find button in the Object Browser to display the Find Symbol dialog box.

2. Type **ListBox** in the Find What box, and then click the Find button. A panel will open below the description pane listing all the locations where the search found the *ListBox* class. First, you see that there is a *ListBox* class in the *System.Windows.Forms* namespace. Also in this namespace is a method named *ListBox()*, which would be the constructor for the *ListBox* class.

   The dialog box contains other controls that you would expect to find on a search dialog box, such as the Search dialog box in Notepad.

3. Click the Close button to hide the Find Symbol dialog box.

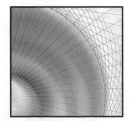

CHAPTER 9

Handling Exceptions

TIPS IN THIS CHAPTER

E ven the best programs can run into problems. No matter how carefully and thoroughly you design and write your program, every program can run into unforeseen errors. Good developers know that the *real* bugs in a program are found after it's turned over to users.

The problems might not be the result of any shortcoming in your code. Instead, for example, the program may need to use a serial port that the user has not installed on the computer, or a disk may be full and a file that the program needs may not be able to be opened or created.

The traditional method for detecting errors—the one used by the C language—is to have the library functions by which your code performs operations return an "error code" when an operation fails. The problem with this approach, however, is that the programmer is still able to ignore the error, either on purpose or by oversight. If the problem is so severe that the program cannot continue, the program is eventually going to crash, probably unexpectedly and with results that are not very user friendly.

The following C program, for example, will crash even though it does not ignore the return value. The syntax is proper, but because you cannot open a file without a name, the call to *fopen* is going to fail. Still, the program does not test for an error indicated by the return value and attempts to read from a file using a NULL pointer to it:

```c
#include    <stdio.h>

void main (void)
{
    FILE *fp = fopen ("", "r");
    char str[256];
    fread (str, 1, 256, fp);
    fclose (fp);
}
```

This program points out that not testing for an error is a dangerous practice. In this case, you may pass the *fp* variable to one or more functions before a problem actually occurs. Properly coded, you should abort the program if the *fopen()* function returns an error, as in the following snippet:

```c
FILE *fp = fopen ("","r");
if (fp == NULL)
{
    fprintf (stderr, "Cannot open file");
    return;
}
```

C++ brought with it the concept of *exceptions* and *exception handling*. An exception is an abnormal or unexpected event that makes it impossible for a program to continue. It may be caused by a program error undetected by the compiler, such as an empty file name, or by a hardware fault.

Exception handling is a graceful way for a language to respond to errors. Rather than simply allow the program to crash, the runtime code signals back to the program that an error has occurred. The program may handle the exception and use it to correct any faults or to exit gracefully. A program cannot ignore an exception. If the program does not handle the exception, the runtime code will cause the program to end.

The programmer does not have write specific error-checking code, however. Instead, he or she may rely on handling and processing the exception passed back to it by the runtime code.

In C++, exceptions are often the only way in which a method can signal an error. A class constructor method, for example, cannot return a value in C++, and the compiler considers it an error to attempt to return a value. If the constructor detects an error in initializing class members, it may signal the calling method by throwing an exception.

C# is based almost entirely on the class concept, and many of the .NET classes use constructors that perform operations that may generate errors. The *FileStream* class, for example, attempts to open a file when you create an instance of the class. If the open fails, it will cause an exception.

Handling Exceptions

Exceptions and exception handling are built into C++ and are a primary mechanism for error detection in C#. In fact, C# makes extensive use of exceptions. Many of the .NET library classes detect illegal values such as an empty file name or failed operations and use the exception mechanism to signal the error.

In the preceding C program, for example, the error occurs when you attempt to open a file using an empty file name. However, the error does not cause a problem until you attempt to use the NULL value returned by the *fopen()* function. Until you attempt to use the return value, you will not notice the problem.

C# will detect the error when you attempt to open the file, and it will use the exception mechanism to signal the program. The following code will result in an exception when you try to open a file using an empty file name:

```
namespace nsException
{
    using System;
    using System.IO;
    class clsMain
    {
        static public void Main ()
        {
            FileStream strm = new FileStream ("", FileMode.Open,
                                              FileAccess.Read);
        }
    }
}
```

The *FileStream* constructor attempts to open the file. Because it is a constructor, it cannot return an error code. Instead, it throws an exception when it detects the error. The only way your program can detect and respond to a failure is by catching the exception thrown by the constructor.

When the Common Language Runtime (CLR) detects an error, it will *throw* an exception. When this happens, you have the option to *catch* the exception and *handle* the error. If you do not catch the exception, your program is going to end—rather abruptly. The CLR is not going to let your program damage its memory or that of any other program running on the computer.

To catch an exception, you must execute the suspect statement within a *guarded* block of code, which you create using the *try* keyword followed by a set of braces:

```
try
{
    // Statements to execute within the guarded block
}
```

The braces are *not* optional. You must use them even if you have only one statement in the guarded block. You can have an empty guarded block, but you still must use the open and close braces.

To catch an exception, you must provide an alternate block of code using the *catch* keyword followed by another set of braces. If you use a guarded block, you must provide an alternate block of code. The alternate block also may be a *finally* block, which you will encounter in this chapter. The exception process passes an object derived from the C# *Exception* class, and you must provide a parameter type for the object:

```
catch (Exception e)
{
    // Alternate statements following the guarded block
}
```

The alternate code block must follow the guarded block immediately. No statements may appear between the ending brace for the guarded block and the *catch* keyword. You may include comments between the two blocks, but nothing that would generate code:

```
try
{
    // Statements to execute within the guarded block
}
// No code statements are allowed here but comments
// are permitted.
catch (Exception e)
{
    // Alternate statements following the guarded block
}
```

Programmers usually refer to this collective block of statement as a *try ... catch* block because you cannot have one without the other. (As with anything, there is an exception to this rule. You may use a *finally* block after a *try* statement.)

To detect and handle the situation in the file open error in the C program shown earlier, your C# program would implement code such as the following:

```
namespace nsException
{
    using System;
    using System.Windows.Forms;
```

```
using System.IO;
class clsMain
{
    static public void Main ()
    {
        FileStream strm;
        try
        {
            strm = new FileStream ("", FileMode.Open,
                                        FileAccess.Read);
        }
        catch (Exception e)
        {
            MessageBox.Show (e.Message, "File Error");
        }
    }
}
```

In this example, the CLR is going to notice that the file name is empty and thus is an illegal value, and it will throw an argument exception that is not related to the file operation: The program should display a message box telling you that an "Empty path name is not legal."

Using Exception Handling in the CLR

The .NET Framework and the C# languages are component-oriented, so the exception mechanism was deliberately designed to make sure that an exception that is thrown while the program is executing code in a component is not overlooked or missed by a client program.

If an exception is thrown while component code is executing, the component may handle the exception, in which case the client may not be aware the exception was thrown. However, if the component does not handle the exception, it is passed back to the client program.

USE IT   The following program uses a component that attempts to open a file rather than perform the operation in the main, or client, program. First, enter the following program, *fopen.cs*, and compile it with the command line option shown at the top of the listing to create a library, or *.dll*, file:

```
// Fopen.cs -- program to show exception handling in a component
//
//          Compile this program with the following command line:
//              C:>csc /t:library Fopen.cs
//
namespace nsFileOpen
{
```

```
using System;
using System.IO;
public class clsFile
{
    FileStream strm;
    public clsFile (string FileName)
    {
        strm = new FileStream (FileName, FileMode.Open,
                                         FileAccess.Read);
    }
}
}
```

Add the following program, *FileOpen.cs*, in the same directory as the preceding program. When you compile this program, include a reference to the *fopen.dll* library file you just created using the */r* compiler option:

```
// FileOpen.cs -- Catches an exception that was thrown in a component
//
//                Compile this program with the following command line:
//                     C:>csc /r:fopen.dll FileOpen.cs
//
namespace nsFileOpen
{
    using System;
    using System.IO;
    class clsMain
    {
        static public void Main ()
        {
            clsFile file;
            try
            {
                file = new clsFile ("");
            }
            catch (Exception e)
            {
                Console.WriteLine (e.Message);
                Console.WriteLine ("Exception handled in client");
            }
        }
    }
}
```

In these programs, the exception occurred in the component, which did not handle the exception. The CLR then passes the exception back to the client program.

Often, this model will be the best design for components, but it relies on you writing specific exception code each time you try to create an instance of the class. The samples so far have used the *Exception* class, which is a general-purpose exception class. The CLR, however, may throw many types of exceptions, and you might want to provide specific code to handle each type of exception.

Exception handling requires considerable support from the runtime code. If, for example, your program calls a method, the compiler knows ahead of time the address of the method. However, it cannot know what block will execute when an exception is thrown. That decision is made when the program runs, based upon the exception thrown and the *catch* blocks available.

Using *try* and *catch* Blocks

The method by which you intercept and process exceptions is the *try ... catch* block. Although they are separate statements and you use separate blocks of code for each, the *try* and *catch* statements are inseparably linked. You cannot use one without the other.

The code that you write inside the *try* block is *guarded* or *protected*. When your program throws an exception, the runtime code uses the *call stack* to find a *try* block. The stack is a reserved portion of memory where a program stores function call information. As a program calls successive functions, the program saves the address of the next statement to execute on the stack along with information about parameters and local variables, and then the program transfers control to the function being called.

When an exception occurs, the program first creates an exception object containing information about the exception. It then begins stepping back through the stack, successively returning to each calling function. As the program returns through the stack, it checks to see whether each function call was executed in a guarded block. If it finds such a block, it looks for a *catch* block that expects an object matching the exception object.

For example, if your program throws a *FileNotFoundException*, the exception code will look for a *catch* block that expects a *FileNotFoundException* object:

```
try
{
    // Guarded code
}
catch (FileNotFoundException e)
{
    // Exception handling code
}
```

If the program finds such a block, it transfers control to the first statement within the *catch* block. Otherwise, it continues searching back through the stack until it eventually gets to the *Main()* method. If it still cannot find a matching *catch* block, the program will exit. The process of stepping back through the stack is called *unwinding* the stack.

The stack unwinding is like a function return, except no value is returned to the calling function. Like a return, however, any variables or objects created in the method are destroyed and their values are lost. No further statements in a calling method are executed. This is why it is important that you handle the exception as close to the point where it is thrown as possible, particularly if the program is in the middle of a critical operation.

USE IT   In C++, the language guarantees that any destructors of local class objects will be called even though their lifetime ends because of the stack unwinding. That apparently does not happen in C#. In the following program, *Unwind.cs*, the program is five function calls deep before it throws an exception. In each function, a new class object is created using local variables. By the time the exception is thrown, three local class objects will be lost during the stack unwind:

```
// Unwind.cs -- Shows that stack unwinding in C# does not necessarily call
//              destructors.
//              Compile this program with the following command line:
//                  C:>csc Unwind.cs
//
namespace nsStack
{
    using System;
    using System.IO;
    class clsMain
    {
        static public void Main ()
        {
            clsMain main = new clsMain();
// Set up the try ... catch block
            try
            {
                main.TestStack ();
            }
            catch (FileNotFoundException e)
            {
// Show the contents of the Message string in each class object
                if (clsFirst.Message == null)
                    Console.WriteLine ("First message is null");
                else
                    Console.WriteLine (clsFirst.Message);
                if (clsFirst.Message == null)
                    Console.WriteLine ("Second message is null");
                else
                    Console.WriteLine (clsSecond.Message);
                if (clsFirst.Message == null)
                    Console.WriteLine ("Third message is null");
```

```csharp
                else
                    Console.WriteLine (clsThird.Message);
// Show the exception object message
                Console.WriteLine (e.Message);
            }
        }
        void TestStack ()
        {
// Create a new clsFirst object and call a method in it
            clsFirst first = new clsFirst ();
            first.FirstFunc();
        }
    }
    class clsFirst
    {
        ~clsFirst ()
        {
            Message = "clsFirst destructor called";
        }
        static public string Message = null;
        public void FirstFunc()
        {
// Create a new clsSecond object and call a method in it
            clsSecond second = new clsSecond();
            second.SecondFunc ();
        }
    }
    class clsSecond
    {
        ~clsSecond ()
        {
            Message = "clsSecond destructor called";
        }
        static public string Message = null;
        public void SecondFunc()
        {
// Create a new clsThird object and call a method in it
            clsThird third = new clsThird();
            third.ThirdFunc ();
        }
    }
    class clsThird
    {
        ~clsThird ()
```

```
    {
        Message = "clsThird destructor called";
    }
    static public string Message = null;
    public void ThirdFunc()
    {
        ThrowException ();
    }
// By the time the program gets here, it is five method calls deep.
// Throw an exception to force a stack unwind.
    private void ThrowException ()
    {
        throw (new FileNotFoundException ());
    }
  }
}
```

When the stack unwinds to the *catch* block, the output shows that the static strings in each class are still *null*, indicating that the destructors were not called. Unfortunately, nothing in the MSDN documentation or in the *C# Language Reference* describes what happens to local class objects when the stack unwinds.

A similar program on the book's Web site, named *cppUnwnd.cpp*, uses the same sequence of method calls in C++. As the stack unwinds, the C++ class destructors set the *static* string to show that the destructors were called.

Calling destructors during a stack unwind is more important in C++ than it is in C#. A C++ class may allocate heap memory for member variables, and the destructor is the last chance the class has to free the memory. In C#, the CLR frees the memory.

The results of this experimental code indicate that you should not rely on code in a destructor method to execute when an exception is thrown.

Catching an Exception

As the stack unwinds, the runtime code looks for a *catch* block that expects an object matching the exception that was thrown. The base class for all exception objects in C# is the *Exception* class.

Your program may throw many different types of exceptions, such as a *NullReferenceException.* when you attempt to use an object that does not contain a valid reference, or an *ObjectDisposedException* if you attempt to read from or write to a file that you already have closed.

In C#, it is legal to cast an object to an ancestor class, so a *catch* block that expects an *Exception* object always will catch an exception. Unfortunately, it will not provide you with much information about the exception that was thrown.

Not all statements need to be protected with a guarded block of code. The process of assigning a value to one of the simple data types such as *int x = 0*, for example, is not going to cause an exception. However, some arithmetic operations such as division by a variable might lead to a *DivisionByZeroException*.

Exception handling is specific. When the CLR encounters a problem and throws an exception, it creates an object of a specific type. In addition to *Exception*, there are 84 specific exception classes. Obviously, testing for all of them in a *catch* block would make every program monumental.

USE IT   Rather than test for every exception type, then, you probably will want to use a specific exception object in your *catch* statement and provide code to recover from it. The following program, *FormExcp.cs*, is missing a closing brace in the format string for the *Console.WriteLine()* method and will throw a *FormatException*. The code looks specifically for this exception:

```
// FormExcp.cs -- demonstrates catching a specific exception
//
//                Compile this program with the following command line:
//                    C:>csc FormExcp.cs
//
namespace nsExceptions
{
    using System;
    class clsMain
    {
        static public void Main ()
        {
            const double pi = 3.14159;
            try
            {
                Console.WriteLine ("pi = {0,0:F5", pi);
            }
            catch (FormatException e)
            {
                Console.WriteLine (e.Message);
            }
        }
    }
}
```

At times it seems that C# *should* throw an exception but does not, apparently for reasons of type-safety. Instead, it uses a built-in exception handler. One of these types of exceptions is the *DivideByZeroException* using non-integer data types. If you attempt to divide an integer value by zero, the CLR will throw a *DivideByZeroException*. However, if you use a *double* type, the operation will return an "Infinity" value, as shown in the following program, *DivZero.cs*:

```
// DivZero.cs -- Demonstrates division by zero using int and double
//
//                Compile this program with the following command line:
//                    C:>csc DivZero.cs
//
```

```
// DivZero
namespace nsDivZero
{
    using System;
    class clsMain
    {
        static public void Main ()
        {
// Set an integer equal to 0
            int IntVal1 = 0;
// and another not equal to 0
            int IntVal2 = 57;
            try
            {
                Console.WriteLine ("{0} / {1} = {2}",
                        IntVal2, IntVal1, IntResult (IntVal2, IntVal1));
            }
            catch (DivideByZeroException e)
            {
                Console.WriteLine (e.Message);
            }
// Set a double equal to 0
            double dVal1 = 0.0;
            double dVal2 = 57.3;
            try
            {
                Console.WriteLine ("{0} / {1} = {2}",
                        dVal2, dVal1, DoubleResult (dVal2, dVal1));
            }
            catch (DivideByZeroException e)
            {
                Console.WriteLine (e.Message);
            }
        }
        static public int IntResult (int num, int denom)
        {
            return (num / denom);
        }
        static public double DoubleResult (double num, double denom)
        {
            return (num / denom);
        }
    }
}
```

When you compile and run this program, you get the following curious output:

```
Attempted to divide by zero.
57.3 / 0 = Infinity
```

The integer division throws a *DivideByZeroException*, but the floating point division returns a *tokenized* result indicating it is "Infinity." Mathematically, of course, this is incorrect, not to mention dangerous. In some applications, such as a scientific analysis program, you might want this result to show that as a variable approaches zero, the result approaches infinity. In other applications, such as an accounting program, the fact that the operation does not throw an exception means that you could perform a number of incorrect calculations before the problem shows up.

Using Multiple *catch* Blocks

Not uncommonly, you might need to provide alternate blocks of code for different exception types. For example, if you are attempting to open a file, you might want to handle the *ArgumentException* in one block in case the file name is empty or contains an invalid character, the *FileNotFoundException* if the file cannot be located, and the *DirectoryNotFoundException* if the path is invalid.

At other times, you will want to provide specific code for one or more specific exceptions and then process the more general *Exception* object in its own block of code.

C# allows you to "stack" exception handlers. You may provide one exception block after another:

```
try
{
    // Guarded code
}
catch (First Exception Type)
{
}
catch (Second Exception Type)
{
}
```

You can continue stacking *catch* blocks until you run out of exception types. You cannot, however, duplicate blocks using the same exception type. In addition, the order is important. The runtime code will stop looking for an exception when it finds a block that expects the exception type thrown.

USE IT   The following program, *Except.cs*, attempts to open a file in a guarded block, and then it provides catch blocks if the file name is invalid, the file is not found, or the directory is not found. After that, it provides a block to catch all other exceptions:

```
// Except.cs -- Demonstrates stacking catch blocks to provide alternate
// code for more than one exception type.
//
```

```
// Compile this program with the following command line:
//    C:>csc Except.cs
//
namespace nsExcept
{
    using System;
    using System.IO;
    class clsMain
    {
        static public void Main (string [] args)
        {
            if (args.Length == 0)
            {
                Console.WriteLine ("Please enter a file name");
                return;
            }
            try
            {
                ReadFile (args[0]);
            }
            catch (ArgumentException)
            {
                Console.WriteLine ("The file name " + args [0] +
                        " is empty or contains an invalid character");
            }
            catch (FileNotFoundException)
            {
                Console.WriteLine ("The file name " + args [0] +
                            " cannot be found");
            }
            catch (DirectoryNotFoundException)
            {
                Console.WriteLine ("The path for " + args [0] +
                            " is invalid");
            }
            catch (Exception e)
            {
                Console.WriteLine (e);
            }
        }
        static public void ReadFile (string FileName)
        {
            FileStream strm = new FileStream (FileName, FileMode.Open,
                                                FileAccess.Read);
```

```
        StreamReader reader = new StreamReader (strm);
        string str = reader.ReadToEnd ();
        Console.WriteLine (str);
    }
  }
}
```

In this code, notice that the block for the general *Exception* class is the last *catch* block in the chain. If you attempt to place it anywhere but at the end, the compiler will generate an error.

Run the program with a file name as an argument, using several different command lines. First try it with just " " (two double quotation marks) as the parameter, and then give it the name of a file you know does not exist.

Using the Exception Classes

The examples so far have used the *Exception* class to catch exceptions thrown in a program or component. While this will catch all exceptions, sometimes it is too general. In the case of an attempt to open a file, did the open attempt fail because of an illegal file name? Or was it because the file name was empty? Or was it simply because the file could not be found?

In addition to the *Exception* class, the .NET Framework derives at least 84 classes using *Exception* as a base class. Each provides specific information about the error that caused the exception, as shown in the following table.

Exception Class	Explanation
ApplicationException	Base class for exception classes in the *System.Application* namespace; four derived classes; thrown when a non-fatal application error occurs.
CodeDomSerializerException	Thrown when a serialization error occurs and line number information is available.
InvalidPrinterException	Thrown when trying to access a printer using invalid printer settings.
IOException	Base class for exception classes in the *System.IO* namespace; four derived classes; thrown when an I/O error occurs.
IsolatedStorageException	Thrown when isolated storage fails.
PathTooLongException	Thrown when a path name or file name is too long.
CookieException	MSDN does not indicate when this exception is thrown.
ProtocolViolationException	Thrown when an error occurs while using a network protocol.
WebException	Thrown when an error occurs while accessing the network through a plugable protocol.
MissingManifestResourceException	Thrown when the main assembly does not contain the resources for the neutral culture, and they are required.

Exception Class	Explanation
SUDSGeneratorException	MSDN does not indicate when this exception is thrown.
SUDSParserException	MSDN does not indicate when this exception is thrown.
SystemException	Base class for exception classes in the System namespace; 51 derived classes.
UriFormatException	Thrown when an invalid Uniform Resource Identifier (URI) is detected.
SoapException	Thrown when a Web Service method is called over Simple Object Access Protocol (SOAP) and an exception occurs.

Three of these classes serve as base classes for yet more detailed exception classes. The *IOException* and *ApplicationException* each have four derived exception classes. *SystemException* has no fewer than 51 derived classes.

The abundance of exception objects probably is an extreme case of overkill, especially in the *SystemException* class. You cannot use the *same* code block to catch multiple exceptions, so the large number of possibilities tends to complicate code by stacking exceptions that you might expect. There is some overhead as the stack unwinds and the runtime code looks for matching exceptions.

USE IT   An alternative when you need to catch one of the exceptions derived from other exception classes is to catch the base class itself and then provide *if* statements to sort out the exact exception. The following program, *IOExcept.cs*, does this with the *IOException* class:

```
// IOExcept.cs -- Demonstrates using if statements to sort out an IOException
//
//              Compile this program with the following command line:
//                   C:>csc IOExcept.cs
//
namespace nsExcept
{
    using System;
    using System.IO;
    class clsMain
    {
        static public void Main (string [] args)
        {
            if (args.Length == 0)
            {
                Console.WriteLine ("Please enter a file name");
                return;
            }
            ReadFile (args[0]);
        }
```

```csharp
static public void ReadFile (string FileName)
{
    FileStream strm = null;
    StreamReader reader = null;
    try
    {
        strm = new FileStream (FileName, FileMode.Open,
                                        FileAccess.Read);
        reader = new StreamReader (strm);
        while (reader.Peek() > 0)
        {
            string str = reader.ReadLine();
            Console.WriteLine (str);
        }
    }
    catch (IOException e)
    {
        if (e is EndOfStreamException)
        {
            Console.WriteLine
                    ("Attempted to read beyond end of file");
        }
        else if (e is FileNotFoundException)
        {
            Console.WriteLine ("The file name " + FileName +
                            " cannot be found");
            return;
        }
        else if (e is DirectoryNotFoundException)
        {
            Console.WriteLine ("The path for name " + FileName +
                            " cannot be found");
            return;
        }
        else if (e is FileLoadException)
        {
            Console.WriteLine ("Cannot read from " + FileName);
        }
        reader.Close();
        strm.Close ();
    }
    catch (Exception e)
    {
        Console.WriteLine (e.Message);
```

```
            }
         }
      }
}
```

With this code, you are handling all the exception objects derived from *IOException* in one block, and all other exceptions are handled in a second block. The runtime code needs only test two blocks for a match.

Throwing an Exception

In addition to the exceptions the CLR might throw, your program can throw exceptions as well. In at least a couple of cases, you might want to throw an exception.

First, your code might handle an exception and decide that the program cannot handle the error directly. You can rethrow the same exception or throw another exception and leave the error handling to another function further up the stack.

Second, your program might throw an exception as a means of aborting a failed operation that is several method calls deep. The methods that were called to get to the code leading up to the error will not have to test for error code and make decisions based on them.

In writing code to throw an exception, you may use one of the existing .NET exception classes. The information you may pass back through an exception in these classes is limited, however, so you can derive your own classes from *Exception* and provide custom information.

USE IT   In the following program, *Rethrow.cs*, the code to get the file name from a user is in the *Main()* method. Once a file name has been obtained, the program calls another method to open and read the file and then print the contents to the screen.

The *ReadFile()* method catches and processes any *IOException* the file operations might throw. The code to get the file name is in *Main()*, so if the exception type is *FileNotFoundException*, it simply rethrows the exception object. Then you have the option of processing any other *IOException* object. This code simply prints the error to the screen and throws another *IOException*.

```
//  Rethrow.cs -- Demonstrates rethrowing an exception from a method.
//
//                Compile this program with the following command line:
//                     C:>csc Rethrow.cs
//
namespace nsRethrow
{
    using System;
    using System.IO;
    class clsMain
    {
        static public void Main ()
```

```csharp
    {
        while (true)
        {
            Console.Write ("Please enter a file name (return to exit): ");
            string FileName = Console.ReadLine ();
            if (FileName.Length == 0)
                break;
            try
            {
                ReadFile (FileName);
                break;
            }
            catch (IOException e)
            {
                if (e is FileNotFoundException)
                    Console.WriteLine ("The file " + FileName +
                                        " was not found");
            }
            catch (Exception e)
            {
                Console.WriteLine (e.Message + "\n");
                break;
            }
        }
    }
    static public void ReadFile (string FileName)
    {
        FileStream strm;
        StreamReader reader;
        try
        {
            strm = new FileStream (FileName, FileMode.Open);
            reader = new StreamReader (strm);
            string str = reader.ReadToEnd ();
            Console.WriteLine (str);
        }
        catch (IOException e)
        {
// If file not found, go back and get another name
            if (e is FileNotFoundException)
                throw (e);
// Code here to handle other IOException classes
            Console.WriteLine (e.Message);
            throw (new IOException ());
```

```
            }
        }
    }
}
```

Once back in *Main()*, if the *IOException* indicates that the file was not found, the exception handler simply informs the user and loops to get another file name. Any other I/O exceptions would have been processed in *ReadFile()*, and the program loops to get another file name. Any other non-I/O exceptions cause the program to print the error message and exit.

You can use the technique of throwing an exception to overcome the *divide by zero* exception problem. If you throw the *DivideByZeroException*, it behaves normally:

```
static public double GetResult (double num, double denom)
{
    double result = Math.Sqrt (num / denom);
    if (Double.IsInfinity(result))
        throw (new DivideByZeroException());
    return (result);
}
```

You then may catch the *DivideByZeroException* normally in the calling method.

C# and the CLR use the .NET exception classes, but when you throw the exception, you may create your own exception object to provide custom information. To create your own exception object, you must derive a new class from *Exception* or from one of the .NET classes:

```
public class CustomException : Exception
{
    // Your exception members
}
```

USE IT   The following program, *CustExcp.cs*, uses a class derived from *Exception* and contains members to return line, column, and text from a method. It searches a file line by line for a given string. If it finds the string, it closes the file and throws an exception using the derived class to pass the information back to the calling method:

```
//
// CustExcp.cs -- Demonstrates defining and using a custom exception class
//
//              Compile this program with the following command line:
//                      C:>csc CustExcp.cs
//
namespace nsCustomException
{
    using System;
    using System.IO;
```

```csharp
    class clsMain
    {
        static public void Main (string [] args)
        {
            if (args.Length < 2)
            {
                Console.WriteLine ("usage: CustExcp FileName String");
                return;
            }
            try
            {
                ReadFile (args[0], args[1]);
                Console.WriteLine (args[1] + " was not found in " +
                                    args[0]);
            }
// Custom exception thrown. Display the information.
            catch (clsException e)
            {
                Console.WriteLine ("string {0} first occurs in {1} " +
                                    "at Line {2}, Column {3}",
                                    args[1], args[0], e.Line, e.Column);
                Console.WriteLine (e.Found);
                return;
            }
// Check for other possible exceptions.
            catch (ArgumentException)
            {
                Console.WriteLine ("The file name " + args [0] +
                        " is empty or contains an invalid character");
            }
            catch (FileNotFoundException)
            {
                Console.WriteLine ("The file name " + args [0] +
                                " cannot be found");
            }
            catch (DirectoryNotFoundException)
            {
                Console.WriteLine ("The path for " + args [0] +
                                " is invalid");
            }
            catch (Exception e)
            {
                Console.WriteLine (e);
            }
```

```
        }
    static public void ReadFile (string FileName, string Find)
    {
        FileStream strm;
        StreamReader reader;
        try
        {
            strm = new FileStream (FileName, FileMode.Open);
            reader = new StreamReader (strm);
            int Line = 0;
            while (reader.Peek () >= 0)
            {
                ++Line;
                string str = reader.ReadLine ();
                int index = str.IndexOf (Find);
                if (index >= 0)
                {
                    reader.Close ();
                    strm.Close ();
                    clsException ex = new clsException ();
                    ex.Line = Line;
                    ex.Column = index + 1;
                    ex.Found = str;
                    throw (ex);
                }
            }
            reader.Close ();
            strm.Close ();
            return;
        }
        catch (IOException e)
        {
// If file not found, go back and get another name
            if (e is FileNotFoundException)
                throw (e);
// Code here to handle other IOException classes
            Console.WriteLine (e.Message);
            throw (new IOException ());
        }
    }
}
// Define a class derived from Exception
class clsException : Exception
{
```

```
        public int Line = 0;
        public int Column = 0;
        public string Found = null;
    }
}
```

In *CustExcp.cs*, the exception does not indicate an error. Instead, you are using the *clsObject* to return a collection of information from the *ReadFile()* method, namely the line number, column number, and the text of the line where the string was found.

It isn't a good idea to use exceptions routinely to return information from a method. This program simply demonstrates the use of a custom exception. However, for constructors and other methods that cannot return information, a custom exception class may be the only way to return error data.

Scope in Exception Blocks

All variables have *scope*, a limit on the range of program statements that may access the variables. This is true even for the variables that you declare or use in a block of code connected with exception handling.

In the previous examples, you might have noticed that the variables to hold the *FileStream* and *TextReader* objects were declared outside the *try* block, but the object actually was created inside the block, like so:

```
FileStream strm;
StreamReader reader;
try
{
    strm = new FileStream (FileName, FileMode.Open);
    reader = new StreamReader (strm);
    // Other statements . . .
}
```

It is usually more convenient to declare and create the object in a single assignment declaration, but the block of code following the *try* statement and code within the block is subject to the block scope rules of C#. If you declare the *strm* variable inside the *try* block, the variable will have block scope and will not be available outside the *try* block.

You will find this type of declaration common in C# (as well as C++). The only way a constructor may return an error is by throwing an exception. The only constructors for the *FileStream* class open the stream at the same time. If you want to use the variable outside the *try* block yet still catch the exception, you must use separate statements for the declaration and the assignment.

USE IT   The *catch* block creates a different scope from the *try* block. It, too, is subject to the C# block scope rules. If you declare a variable inside the *try* block, it will not be available in the *catch* block. If you need to make a variable available to both the *try* and *catch* blocks, you must declare it outside of either block.

```
try
{
// The following objects are in scope only in the try block
    FileStream strm = new FileStream (FileName, FileMode.Open);
    StreamReader reader = new StreamReader (strm);
}
catch (Exception)
{
    // The strm and reader objects are out of scope in the catch block
}
// The strm and reader objects are out of scope here
```

In addition, you may not use the *goto* statement to jump to a label inside a *try* or *catch* block. The only path to the block of statements after a *try* statement is through the *try* statement itself. The only path to the *catch* block statements is by throwing an exception. In this sense, the *catch* statement and block look and act like a function within a function.

Using Exceptions with *checked* Variables

C# and the CLR provide options to check the ranges of values that may result from certain operations. You may apply range checking to an entire assembly or module, or you may apply it to single statements.

When you use range checking, the CLR will throw an *OverflowException* if the value of a statement exceeds the maximum value that the data type can hold. For example, the maximum value that an unsigned integer may hold is 4,294,967,295. That is considerably less than the size of many hard drives used by personal computers. If you assign that value to a variable, as in the following snippet, and then increment the variable, the result of the operation will be 0:

```
uint BigVal = 4294967295;
++BigVal;
Console.WriteLine ("The new value of BigVal is " + BigVal);
```

The result is an *overflow* condition, wherein the value has reached its maximum value and rolled over to its minimum value. The program has no way of knowing that the overflow has occurred other than to check constantly after performing such operations on a suspected value.

USE IT Using the *checked* keyword gives you a vehicle for detecting such errors without having to write interminable error-checking code. To apply range checking to an operation, use the *checked* keyword followed by a set of braces. Inside the braces, include the statements you want to check:

```
uint BigVal = 4294967295;
checked
```

```
{
    ++BigVal;
}
```

If the statement within the *checked* block overflows, the program will throw an *OverflowException*. In the case of a floating-type value such as a *double* or *float*, the program also will throw an *OverflowException* if the operation attempts to store a value that is too small. You may detect this error in a *try ... catch* block:

```
uint BigVal = 4294967295;
try
{
    checked
    {
        ++BigVal;
    }
}
catch (OverflowException e)
{
    // Code to handle the overflow
}
```

You need to remember a couple of things about the *checked* keyword. First, although the MSDN documentation says that you may use a set of parentheses to enclose a *checked* expression, the compiler invariably will tell you that a brace ({) is expected. You must enclose any *checked* expressions inside a set of braces.

Second, this set of braces delimits a code block in C#, and variables declared within the block cannot be used outside the block, including the *catch* block if you attempt to catch the exception.

```
checked
{
    uint BigVal = 4294967295;
    ++BigVal;
}
CallFunction (BigVal);    // Error -- BigVal is undeclared here.
```

To avoid having to write a *checked* block every time you want to guard against an overflow, you may apply range checking to an entire assembly or module by using the */checked* compiler option, as shown in the following command line:

```
C:>csc /checked ProgFile.cs
```

With this option, all statements in the module will undergo range checking, and an *OverflowException* will be thrown whenever such a condition happens. Obviously, range checking involves some overhead, so you should apply the flag only to modules that need extensive range checks. Otherwise, it is more efficient to use the *checked* keyword in your code to guard against suspect operations.

You do not need to apply the */checked* flag to all components in a program. If one component requires extensive range checking and the others do not, you may compile just the single component with the flag.

If you do compile a module with the */checked* flag, you may exempt individual statements using an *unchecked* block:

```
uint BigVal = 4294967295;
unchecked
{
    ++BigVal;
}
```

In a component compiled with the */checked* flag, this snippet will not cause an *OverflowException*.

Terminating a Program in an Exception Block

Even with exception checking, the errors a program encounters during the course of its run may make it impossible for it to continue. If your program specifically communicates over a serial line, for example, and no serial ports have been installed in the computer, it makes little sense for the program to continue running.

If something unexpected happens that throws an exception and your program must exit, you may need to catch the exception and provide code to exit gracefully. For example, you might want to restore some data files back to their original content.

If you catch the exception in the *Main()* method, you can take whatever action is necessary to end the program and then execute the *return* statement. Returning from *Main()* automatically terminates a program.

Errors and exceptions, however, usually do not happen so conveniently. If problems were that predictable, they would be more inconveniences than problems. Often, your code may be several method calls deep and have a number of class objects created when a problem occurs.

C# provides two methods to exit an application in such cases. Both of these methods are *static* methods in their respective classes, so you do not have to create an instance of the class to call them:

- **Environment.Exit(ReturnVal)**   Terminates the program and delivers the return value to the operating system as an exit code.

- **Application.Exit()**   Notifies all message loops that they must terminate, closes any windows the application has open, and ends the program.

USE IT The *Environment* class is defined in the *System* namespace. This is the method you normally would use to terminate command line programs. The following program, *EnvExit.cs*, is three method calls deep before it throws an exception and calls *Environment.Exit()*:

```
// EnvExit.cs -- Demonstrates the use of Environment.Exit() in
//               a command line program.
//
//               Compile this program with the following command line:
//                    C:>csc EnvExit.cs
namespace nsEnvExit
{
    using System;
    class clsMain
    {
        static public void Main ()
        {
            FirstFunction ();
            Console.WriteLine ("Application ends");
        }
        static public void FirstFunction()
        {
            SecondFunction ();
            Console.WriteLine ("First Function ends");
        }
        static public void SecondFunction()
        {
            ThirdFunction ();
            Console.WriteLine ("First Function ends");
        }
        static public void ThirdFunction()
        {
            try
            {
                Exception e = new Exception ();
                throw (e);
            }
            catch (Exception)
            {
                Console.WriteLine ("No other lines should print " +
                                    "to the console");
                Environment.Exit (-1);
            }
        }
    }
}
```

Other than in the *catch* block, none of the *Console.WriteLine( )* methods executes. The application simply exits without returning from the method calls.

The *Application* class is defined in the *Systems.Windows.Forms* namespace and normally is the method you would use to exit from a Windows forms application. It first notifies all message pumps in the application to stop, then closes any forms the program has created, and then exits the application. Other than the fact that it does not return an exit code to the operating system, the exit is similar to the *Environment.Exit( )* method.

Understanding the *finally* Block

When an exception occurs inside a guarded block of code, C# provides a mechanism for providing a block of code that will execute regardless of the result of the exception. This is the *finally* block.

A *finally* block following a *try* block will execute regardless of whether your program throws an exception. It will execute regardless of whether you catch and process the exception. Even if your program exits in a *catch* block, the statements in the *finally* block will execute. In short, when used with an exception try, the *finally* block will execute. Period.

A *finally* block must follow a *try* statement. If you use one or more *catch* blocks following the *try* block, the *finally* block must follow any *catch* blocks. The *finally* block is like an end run for the exception catching process. It takes no parameter list, and it has no exception handler object that you may use in the block. A *finally* block is written like a *catch* block:

```
try
{
    // Guarded block
}
finally
{
    // Statements to execute
}
```

You may use a *finally* block with *catch* blocks. If you do this and your program throws an exception, the code in the *catch* blocks will execute before the *finally* block code executes.

USE IT   The following program, *Finally.cs*, shows some possible combinations of the 2*finally* block:

```
// Finally.cs -- Demonstrates the possible uses of a finally block
//
//              Compile this program with the following command line:
//                   C:>csc Finally.cs
//
namespace nsFinally
{
```

```csharp
    using System;
    class clsMain
    {
        static public void Main ()
        {
            try
            {
                NoProblem ();
            }
// No exception possible here. Use finally without a catch
            finally
            {
                Console.WriteLine ("No problem at all\r\n");
            }
            try
            {
                SmallProblem ();
            }
            catch (clsException e)
            {
                Console.WriteLine (e.Message);
            }
            finally
            {
                Console.WriteLine ("But not big enough to exit\r\n");
            }
            try
            {
                BigProblem ();
            }
            catch (DivideByZeroException e)
            {
                Console.WriteLine (e.Message);
                Environment.Exit (-1);
            }
            finally
            {
                Console.WriteLine ("But the finally block still executes.");
            }
        }
        static public void NoProblem()
        {
        }
```

```
        static public void SmallProblem ()
        {
            clsException ex = new clsException();
            ex.Message = "Small problem encountered";
            throw (ex);
        }
        static public void BigProblem ()
        {
            clsException ex = new clsException();
            ex.Message = "Big trouble. Applicaion must end.";
            throw (ex);
        }
    }
// Define a custom exception class just for a personalized message
    public class clsException : Exception
    {
        new public string Message = null;
    }
}
```

Regardless of whether the program throws an exception, and regardless of whether the exception was caught and whether the exception caused the program to exit, the *finally* block executes.

Running this program will cause the Just-In-Time Debugging dialog box to appear, because the *catch* block expects a *DivideByZeroException* object rather than the custom exception object. Click No in the dialog box to close it, and the message from the *finally* block should print.

CHAPTER 10
Advanced C# Concepts

TIPS IN THIS CHAPTER

In the last few chapters, you have learned the basics of programming in C#—how to declare and use classes, data types, and structures—and the principles of object-oriented programming. You should now be at a point at which you can create useful programs using C#.

In the next few chapters, you will start using files, streams, arrays, and Windows forms. You will create more projects in the Visual Studio environment and add controls such as text boxes, buttons, view objects, and toolbars to forms and dialog boxes.

C# and the .NET Framework provide a number of advanced programming features that allow you to examine and create objects at runtime without knowing their types, to invoke methods indirectly, and to allow a program to process multiple statements at the same time.

In this chapter, you will look at such advanced concepts as running multiple threads in a program, examining the capabilities of a class using interfaces, and creating classes using reflection, which lets your code query an object about its methods, members, properties, and other attributes.

Examining a Class Through Interfaces

Although you may not need to use the C# language's advanced features for most of your programming, you probably will need to use them from time to time. For example, when you use a ListView control on a Windows form, you may want to be able to sort the columns in the ListView object. The easiest way to do this is to implement an *interface*.

An interface definition is similar to a class definition, but it contains only abstract methods and/or properties. It provides a means by which your code can determine whether a class or structure implements a method or property defined by an interface. A class can inherit from an interface just as it can inherit from any class, but the derived class must implement all of the members defined in the interface. A class may inherit from only one base class, regardless of whether that class is abstract, but it may inherit from more than one interface.

You can use interfaces with reflection to find out whether a certain method is available, and then invoke the method indirectly. For example, the *ICloneable* interface defines only a single method, *Clone()*, which you normally would use to create a copy of the current instance of a class. Using the *is* operator, you can query whether the class implements the *ICloneable* interface. If it does, then you know that the class provides a *Clone()* method.

The following short program, for example, will not compile. Although you are testing whether the class implements the *ICloneable* interface, the compiler still will reject the program because the class does not actually contain a *Clone()* method:

```
using System;
using System.Reflection;

namespace nsReflection
{
    class clsMain
    {
        static public void Main ()
        {
```

318 C# Tips & Techniques

```
            clsCloneTest first = new clsCloneTest();
            clsCloneTest clone = null;
            if (first is ICloneable)
            {
                clone = (clsCloneTest) first.Clone ();
            }
            else
            {
                Console.WriteLine = ("Cannot clone object");
            }
        }
    }
    class clsCloneTest
    {
    }
}
```

Reflection is the .NET mechanism that allows you to discover information about an object at runtime rather than when you compile a program. By using reflection, you can change the code in the preceding program to invoke the process indirectly if the class implements the *ICloneable* interface:

```
if (first is ICloneable)
{
    Type t = first.GetType();
    MethodInfo m = t.GetMethod ("Clone");
    clone = (clsCloneTest) m.Invoke (first, null);
}
else
{
    Console.WriteLine ("Cannot clone object");
}
```

Now the program is acceptable to the compiler. Because the class does not implement the *ICloneable* interface, the *Clone()* method will not be called. To test this, modify the *clsCloneTest* class so that it implements the *ICloneable* interface, as shown in the following code:

```
class clsCloneTest : ICloneable
{
    public object Clone ()
    {
    Console.WriteLine ("Cloned myself, eh");
    return (this);
    }
}
```

Recompile and run the program again and you will see that the *Clone()* method is invoked.

In this chapter, you will take a close look at reflection, and you'll learn how to use interfaces. You'll also learn how to load a .NET module at runtime and create instances of a class indirectly.

Using Multiple Execution Paths

You might want to assign a portion of your program to perform tasks in the background while letting the main portion of the program continue interacting with the user. You can do this by starting a *thread* in your program.

A thread is a discrete execution path in a program. It has its own stack space, and it can execute methods and create objects simultaneously with the main execution path (the main thread) in a program. C# makes creating new threads an easy task, and with Visual Studio .NET, threads are being introduced into Visual Basic.

You create a thread object using the *System.Threading.Thread* class, giving it a method to call when it starts. This method then becomes the thread equivalent of the *Main()* method for a program. The following short program implements a thread that does nothing but tell you that it has started:

```
using System;
using System.Threading;

namespace nsThreads
{
    class clsMain
    {
        static public void Main ()
        {
// Create the thread object
            Thread thrd = new Thread (new ThreadStart (Run));
// Start the thread.
            thrd.Start ();
// Wait for the thread to terminate.
            thrd.Join ();
        }
        static void Run ()
        {
            Console.WriteLine ("Hello, thread world!");
        }
    }
}
```

When you invoke the thread's *Start()* method, it begins executing the method you defined as its start method. When it exits that method, the thread terminates. It does not return to the method in which it was invoked.

In this chapter, you will use threads to create a multi-user Web proxy server that waits for a browser program to request Web access. When it gets a request, the server starts a thread to handle the request and then waits for another request while the first thread is running.

Separating Code in Namespaces

In many C++ textbooks, the namespace is treated as an advanced topic. You can actually write many powerful and effective programs in C++ without having to venture into namespaces.

You also can write C# programs without namespaces, but the program will not be able to do much. As soon as you need to display a window or read or write to a file or to the console, you need at least a preliminary knowledge of namespaces. For the examples in earlier chapters in this book, you have dealt with namespaces to use the classes in the .NET Framework.

Essentially, a namespace declares a *scope*. It adds another element to the name of an object and helps you organize code. By separating the names of objects into namespaces, you can virtually guarantee a unique name for each of your objects.

You declare a namespace by entering the *namespace* keyword followed by the name of the namespace. After that, you include the members of the namespace between a set of open and close braces:

```
namespace MyNamespace
{
    // Namespace definitions.
}
```

Namespace names must be unique, but you may declare blocks containing namespace elements at any point:

```
namespace MyNameSpace
{
    class clsMain
    {
        // Class member declarations
    }
}
namespace MyNameSpace
{
    class clsMyClass
    {
        // Class member declarations
    }
}
```

Using two namespace blocks is the same as enclosing both class definitions inside one namespace block, as shown in the following:

```
namespace MyNameSpace
{
    class clsMain
    {
        // Class member declarations
    }
    class clsMyClass
    {
        // Class member declarations
    }
}
```

This may sound trivial, but, within a file, a namespace block must be complete. The file in which you declare a namespace must contain both the opening and closing braces. By being able to join namespace blocks using the same name, you can use the same namespace in more than one file. When the compiler puts the files together, it will create a single namespace block.

Within a namespace, you can define and declare classes, interfaces, delegates, enumerations, and structures. In C#, a namespace may not directly contain a field, property, or method; you must place those as members of structures or classes. When you declare a member of a class or structure that is within a namespace, the namespace name becomes part of the *fully qualified name* for the member.

Within a program, each fully qualified name must be unique. Two classes or structures, or a structure and a class, may have the same name as long as they are in different namespaces. The namespace becomes a part of the class type definition name.

Namespaces may be user-defined—those that you define in your program code—or system-defined—those that are part of the runtime code. The .NET code that ships with Visual C# includes two "root" namespaces: the *System* namespace that defines the fundamental classes and services, and the *Microsoft* namespace that contains compilation and code generation in the languages supported by .NET along with classes relating to system events and registry use.

Nesting Namespaces

Namespaces may contain other namespaces. When you *nest* namespaces and define classes or other objects as part of the nested namespace, each namespace becomes a part of the fully qualified name. When you write the fully qualified name of an object, you separate the namespace names with periods.

The outer namespace is called the *root,* or first-level, namespace. The nested namespace is called the second-level namespace. You may nest namespaces as deeply as necessary to separate the elements of your code, but you will usually never need to go beyond a second-level namespace.

USE IT   The following program, *Names.cs*, defines three namespaces. One is nested inside the other, and the nested namespace contains a *public* enumeration. It shows that to access the enumeration from within the *nsFirst* namespace, you must preface the name with the *nsNested* namespace only. The *nsNested* namespace is within the scope of *nsFirst*. From the *nsSecond* namespace, however, you must use the fully qualified name for the enumeration.

```csharp
using System;

namespace nsFirst
{
    class clsMain
    {
        static public void Main ()
        {
            nsSecond.clsClass cls = new nsSecond.clsClass ();
            for (nsNested.WeekDays x = nsNested.WeekDays.Sunday;
                            x < nsNested.WeekDays.DaysInWeek;
                            ++x)
                cls.ShowDay (x);
        }
    }
    namespace nsNested
    {
        public enum WeekDays
            {
                Sunday, Monday, Tuesday, Wednesday,
                Thursday, Friday, Saturday, DaysInWeek
            };
    }
}

namespace nsSecond
{
    class clsClass
    {
        public void ShowDay (nsFirst.nsNested.WeekDays day)
        {
            Console.WriteLine (day);
        }
    }
}
```

Running the program lists the days of the week on separate lines. There are, of course, easier ways to achieve the same result, but the intent here is to cross namespace boundaries and use fully qualified names.

> ▶ **QUICK TIP**
>
> ───
>
> *A single namespace name can include a period, but this does not mean that the fully qualified name contains more than one namespace name. A namespace name may contain periods even without nesting namespaces.*

Specifying Namespaces with the *using* Directive

To avoid having to use the fully qualified name of every class in your program, you may declare that you want to reference objects in a namespace with the *using* keyword. You already have seen examples of the *using* keyword in programs. For example, you can access members of the *System.Console* class by using the fully qualified name:

```
System.Console.WriteLine ("Text");
```

Alternatively, you may declare that you are *using* the *System* namespace, so that you can use only the name of the *Console* class:

```
using System;
class clsMain
{
    static public void Main()
    {
        Console.WriteLine ("Text");
    }
}
```

When used in this way, the *using* keyword is a *directive*. Notice that when you include the *using* keyword in this syntax, it must reside outside any class definition. This is the most common way to include the *using* keyword. The *using* keyword does have some other purposes, however.

First, you can create an alias to a class or a namespace with the *using* keyword. In this sense, the *using* keyword is also a directive, and it instructs the compiler to replace your alias with the name of the class or namespace that the alias represents.

To create an alias, type in the *using* keyword followed by the alias name. Then include the equals sign and the name of the class or namespace that you want to alias:

```
using MyForms = System.Windows.Forms.Form;
```

This directive will let you use *MyForms* any time you need to reference the *System. Windows. Forms .Form* class. After issuing the directive, you can then create a form using the following snippet:

```
public Form1 : MyForms
{
    // Class member declarations
}
```

Creating an alias is useful when classes with the same name appear in different namespaces. To reference class names uniquely, you would have to use their fully qualified names each time; otherwise the C# compiler would gripe that the references are "ambiguous." After awhile, this can become tedious.

There are, in fact, some ambiguous references in the *System* namespace. For example, the .NET Runtime includes three different *Timer* classes. One class is in the *System. Windows. Forms* namespace and is optimized for use with a Windows form. Another is in the *System. Timers* namespace and includes general purpose timers that do not require a message loop as does the *Timer* class in *System. Windows. Forms*.

Assuming you want to use a message box and a general-purpose timer, you will need to declare that you are using both the *System. Windows. Forms* namespace and the *System. Timers* namespace. If you enter the following code (a complete program example will follow shortly), for example, the compiler will tell you that the reference to the *Timer* class is ambiguous:

```
using System;
using System.Windows.Forms;
using System.Timers;

namespace nsNamespaces
{
    class clsMain
    {
        static Timer timer;
        static public void Main ()
        {
            timer = new Timer (2000);
            timer.AutoReset = false;
            timer.Start ();
            MessageBox.Show ("Waiting for timer to expire", "Text");
        }
    }
}
```

The alternative is to leave out one *using* directive and to type the fully qualified name of the member you want to access. If you do this, you will have to refer to the class by its fully qualified name each time. So if you left out the *using System. Windows. Forms* directive, you would have to refer to the message box as *System. Window. Forms. MessageBox*.

USE IT Alternatively, you can create an alias for the *MessageBox* class, as shown in the following program, *Alias.cs*:

```
// Alias.cs -- demonstrates using an alias to resolve ambiguity
//
//            Compile this program with the following command line:
//                 C:>csc Alias.cs
using System;
using MsgBox = System.Windows.Forms.MessageBox;
using System.Timers;

namespace nsNamespaces
{
    class clsMain
    {
        static Timer timer;
        static public void Main ()
        {
// Create the timer object.
            timer = new Timer (2000);
// This is a one-shot timer. Set auto reset to false
            timer.AutoReset = false;
// Assign the event handler method.
            timer.Elapsed += new ElapsedEventHandler(ProcessTimerEvent);
// Start the timer.
            timer.Start ();
// Wait for the timeout to occur.
            MsgBox.Show ("Waiting for timer to expire", "Text");
        }


// Timer event handler.
        private static void ProcessTimerEvent (Object obj, ElapsedEventArgs e)
        {
            MsgBox.Show ("The timer has expired. Press \"OK\" " +
                    " to terminate the program",
                    "Timer Expired");
            timer.Close ();
            Environment.Exit (0);
        }
    }
}
```

In this sample, you are using only the *MessageBox* class from the *System.Windows.Forms* namespace. After you create the alias, the compiler will reference the *MessageBox* class any time you use *MsgBox*.

Taking a Closer Look at the *using* Statement

C# adds another dimension to the *using* keyword that is not available in C++. In addition to a directive, the *using* keyword can also be a statement. When used as a statement, the *using* keyword can be passed one or more objects that you will use in the statement and the runtime code will dispose of the objects when the statement completes.

A *using* statement must be a compound statement, so you must include a set of open and close braces after the statement. In addition, you must pass it one or more objects that implement the *IDisposable* interface. You may declare the object within the *using* statement or pass it the identifier of an existing object:

```
using (<IDisposable object>)
{
    // statements that use object
}
// Alternatively, declare the object first
IDisposableObject obj = new IDisposableObject ();
using (obj)
{
    // Statements that use obj
}
```

At the end of the block of statements, the runtime code will automatically call the object's *Dispose()* method. You must be careful not to use the disposable object after the closing brace in the *using* statement. If you do, your program will throw an exception because the object no longer is valid.

USE IT This form of the *using* keyword is useful when you need to employ one or more objects temporarily and assure that the objects are disposed of when you are finished using them. The following program, *Using.cs*, draws three concentric circles on a form, declaring the drawing pen in a *using* statement:

```
// Using.cs -- Demonstrates using as a statement
//
//          Compile this program with the following command line:
//                C:>csc Using.cs
using System;
using System.Windows.Forms;
using System.Drawing;
using Pen = System.Drawing.Pen;
using PaintHandler = System.Windows.Forms.PaintEventHandler;

namespace nsForm
{
    class clsMain : Form
    {
```

```
public clsMain ()
{
    this.Text = "Using Statement";
    this.Paint += new PaintHandler(this.OnPaint);
}
static public void Main ()
{
    Application.Run(new clsMain());
}
private Color [] clr = new Color []
            {
                    Color.Red,
                    Color.Green,
                    Color.Blue
            };

private void OnPaint (object obj, PaintEventArgs e)
{
    Rectangle client = this.ClientRectangle;
    int side = (client.Right - client.Left) / 3;
    for (int x = 0; x < 3; ++x)
    {
        using (Pen pen = new Pen(clr[x], (float) 2.0))
        {
            client = Rectangle.Inflate (client, -10, -10);
            e.Graphics.DrawEllipse (pen, client);
        }
    }
}
    }
}
```

In this example, as each circle is drawn, the runtime code disposes of the old pen so you do not have to worry about it in your code.

Adding References

C# is a component-oriented language. The code that implements the classes and other objects in the various namespaces in the .NET Framework are contained in components called *assemblies*. When you use the namespaces in the .NET Framework, the C# compiler includes in your compiled program a *reference* to the assembly that contains the code.

In turn, when you run your program, the .NET Framework loads the required assemblies into memory. By loading assemblies on demand, the size of the compiled program can be kept small.

For example, a program that simply prints a message to the console may be only about 3000 bytes when compiled.

This is sharply different from C++, where the basic library code is included as a part of the compiled program. As a result, compiled C++ programs tend to be large. A simple C++ program that writes only a line of text to the console usually will be larger than 30,000 bytes.

The smaller code size translates into shorter load times when you run your program. Initially, it may take extra time to load the system assemblies into memory, but it is likely that Windows already will have cached the code.

In the .NET Framework, an assembly is a self-describing block of code. An assembly may be a single executable file, or it may be a dynamic link library. The advantage of an assembly is that you may *reference* it from another program and use or build upon the classes defined in the assembly without having the source code.

Assemblies may be private or shared. To use a private assembly, it must be in the same directory as the main executable program file. A shared assembly, however, is placed in the *global assembly cache*, and it may be used by adding a reference to it to your program. Using a shared assembly is actually not that easy, because it must have a security key and you must know the key to use the assembly.

USE IT   In this example, you first will create a dynamic link library for use as a private assembly. Then in the next tip you will create and use a *module* file rather than a dynamic link library from the same source code file. After that, you will use the module file to create a shared assembly, which you will place in the global assembly cache.

First, create a file named *Circle.cs,* as shown in the following listing. Notice that this file does not have a *Main()* method. You may include *Main()* if you want the assembly to be self-executing, but for a library module you do not need to include the method.

```
//  Circle.cs -- File to be used as a library assembly
//
//              Compile this file with the following command line:
//                  C:>csc /t:library Circle.cs
using System;

namespace nsCircle
{
// A structure to define a Cartesian point.
    public struct POINT
    {
        public POINT (int x, int y)
        {
            cx = x;
            cy = y;
        }
        public int  cx;
        public int  cy;
```

```csharp
        public override string ToString()
        {
            return (String.Format ("(" + cx + ", " + cy + ")"));
        }
    }
    public class clsCircle
    {
// Two constructors to define the circle.
        public clsCircle (double radius, POINT center)
        {
            m_Center = center;
            m_Radius = radius;
        }
        public clsCircle (double radius, int cx, int cy)
        {
            m_Center.cx = cx;
            m_Center.cy = cy;
            m_Radius = radius;
        }
        public clsCircle ()
        {
            m_Center.cx = 0;
            m_Center.cy = 0;
            m_Radius = 0;
        }
        public double Radius
        {
            get {return (m_Radius);}
            set {m_Radius = value;}
        }
        public POINT Center
        {
            get {return (m_Center);}
            set {m_Center = value;}
        }
// Fields to contain circle data.
        POINT m_Center;
        private double m_Radius;

// Constants to make life easier
        private const double pi = 3.14159;
        private const double radian = 57.29578;
// Return the area of the circle
        public double Area
```

```
        {
            get {return (m_Radius * m_Radius * pi);}
        }
// Return the diameter of the circle
        public double Diameter
        {
            get {return (2 * m_Radius);}
        }
// Return the coordinates of a point on the circle at a given angle.
        public POINT PointOnCircle (double degrees)
        {
            POINT pt;
            double fAngle = degrees / radian;
// Compute the x position of the point
            pt.cx = (int)((double) m_Radius * Math.Cos (fAngle) + 0.5);
// Compute the y position of the point
            pt.cy = (int)((double) m_Radius * Math.Sin (fAngle) + 0.5);
            return (pt);
        }
// Return the area of a slice determined by a given angle.
        public double AreaOfSlice (double degrees)
        {
            double fAngle = degrees / 57.29578;
            return (Area * fAngle / (2 * pi));
        }
    }
}
```

Compile this file as a library using the */target* parameter (a shortened form is */t*) using the following command line:

```
C:>csc /t:library Circle.cs
```

Now create a program that will use the assembly. The following program, *Geom.cs*, uses a different namespace, so at the top you include a line indicating that you are using the namespace *nsCircle* that you declared in the *Circle.cs* source file:

```
// Geom.cs -- Demonstrates using an assembly.
//
//          Compile this program with the following command line:
//              C:>csc /r:circle.dll Geom.cs
using System;
using nsCircle;
```

```
namespace nsGeometry
{
    class clsMain
    {
        static public void Main ()
        {
            double angle = 32.6;
// Create an instance of the circle class.
            clsCircle circle = new clsCircle (420, 0, 0);
// Get the point on the circle at the angle.
            POINT pt = circle.PointOnCircle (angle);
// Show the total area of the circle.
            Console.WriteLine ("The area of the circle is " + circle.Area);
// Show the point.
            Console.WriteLine ("The point on the circle is at " + pt);
// Show the area of the slice between 0 degrees and the angle.
            Console.WriteLine ("The area of the slice is " +
                                    circle.AreaOfSlice (angle));
        }
    }
}
```

Compile this program using the */reference* compiler flag to add a reference to the *Circle.dll* assembly (the short form is simply */r*). Follow the flag with a colon and then the name of the assembly you want to reference:

```
C:>csc /r:circle.dll Geom.cs
```

If you copy the executable file to another directory, don't forget to copy the *.dll* file along with it. If the files are not in the same directory, your program will throw an exception because the runtime code will not be able to find the *Circle.dll* assembly.

Building a Module File

You can also compile the assembly as a .NET module and add it to your program with the */addmodule* compiler switch. This step produces an intermediate file with an extension of *.netmodule* rather than a dynamic link library. You then can add the module to your program code by using the */addmodule* compiler switch.

Preparing the .NET module file is the first step toward creating a shared assembly. A *module* is a loadable code unit that contains enough type information for the runtime code to locate the object information when the module is loaded into memory. It usually is smaller than a dynamic link library file, and it too must be located in the same directory as the executable file.

USE IT First, copy the *Circle.cs* and *Geom.cs* files to another directory. On the book's Web site, these have been copied to the Chapter10\Module directory. Compile the *Circle.cs* file as a .NET module using the following command line:

```
C:>csc /t:module Circle.cs
```

The file that results from the compile will be *Circle.NetModule*. If you compare the dynamic link library file from the last tip with the *.NetModule* file using the Intermediate Language Disassembler (IldAsm.exe), you will see that the *.NetModule* file contains no *.assembly* section. Thus, to add the module to your program, you cannot use the */r* compiler switch. Instead, you must use the */addmodule* compiler switch.

Compile the *Geom.cs* file and add the *Circle.NetModule* file to it by using the following command line:

```
C:>csc /addmodule:Circle.NetModule Geom.cs
```

When you run the *Geom.exe* program, you should see the same output displayed for the program in the previous tip.

If you examine the manifest in the *Geom.exe* file using *Ildasm.exe*, you will see that it contains information about the *Circle.NetModule* file and the classes it contains, whereas the executable in the previous tip did not. By using a module, you are creating a multiple-file assembly. The executable and all the modules that you add to it represent a single assembly.

Creating a Shared Assembly

By using a *shared assembly*, you can freely move the executable file around without having to worry about copying a dynamic link library or *.NetModule* file with it. The assembly lives in the global assembly cache, and the runtime code knows where to find it.

Creating a shared assembly requires several steps:

1. Compile the source file to produce a .NET module file with an extension of *.netmodule*.

2. Create a public and private encryption key pair using the Strong Name utility, *Sn.exe*.

3. Create the assembly, adding the encryption key pair to it. You do this with the Assembly Generation tool, *Al.exe*.

4. Add the shared assembly to the global assembly cache using the Global Assembly Cache tool, *GacUtil.exe*.

The first step is the same one you used to create a *.NetModule* file in the preceding tip. Copy the *Circle.cs* and *Geom.cs* files to another directory (the Chapter10\SharAssy directory on the book's Web site). Compile the *Circle.cs* source file with the following command line:

```
C:>csc /t:module Circle.cs
```

Next, generate the encryption key pair using *Sn.exe*. When you create the assembly in step 3, the *Al.exe* utility will add these keys to the assembly. Only programs that "know" the assembly's private encryption key will be able to use the assembly members. A program "learns" this key when you compile the program and add a reference with the assembly file in the same directory as the program's source file.

Create the encryption key pair with the following command line. By convention, the file containing the keys has an extension of *.snk*.

```
C:>sn -k Circle.snk
```

The file can have any name you want to give it, but to keep your code from becoming too confusing, you will probably want to give it the same name as your assembly file, but using the *.snk* extension.

Next, create the assembly file itself. This will be a *.dll* file, but it will contain the encryption keys for the assembly. When you compile a program that uses the assembly, this *.dll* file must be present in the same directory as the source file. (For assemblies that you develop in the Visual Studio IDE, you handle this a little differently. Those steps will be detailed later in this tip.)

Create the assembly using the *Al.exe* utility with the command line shown next. At this point, you should add a version to the assembly. The version will become a part of the assembly name in the cache. For private assemblies, you did not have to worry about a version number because the compiler simply ignored it. Use the following command line, replacing the version number with whatever version you want for the assembly:

```
C:>al /keyfile:Circle.snk /version:1.0.0.0 /out:Circle.dll Circle.NetModule
```

► **QUICK TIP**

You need to be aware that for a program to use the shared assembly, the first two numbers of the version must match the assembly against which you compiled your program. You can have multiple shared assemblies with the same name so long as their versions are different. The last two numbers in the version are the build number and the revision number, respectively.

You now have a complete assembly in the *Circle.dll* file. If you examine the manifest using *IlDasm.exe*, as shown in Figure 10-1, you will see that the public encryption key has been added as part of the assembly section.

To add the assembly to the global assembly cache, use the *GacUtil.exe* utility, specifying the */i* flag, to install it. The command line should be as follows:

```
C:>gacutil /i Circle.dll
```

Alternatively, you can open the global assembly cache using Windows Explorer, and then drag the assembly from a folder and drop it into the cache.

On a Windows NT or Windows 2000 system, you will need administrator privileges to add or remove assemblies from the global assembly cache. This prevents unauthorized users from tinkering with the cache.

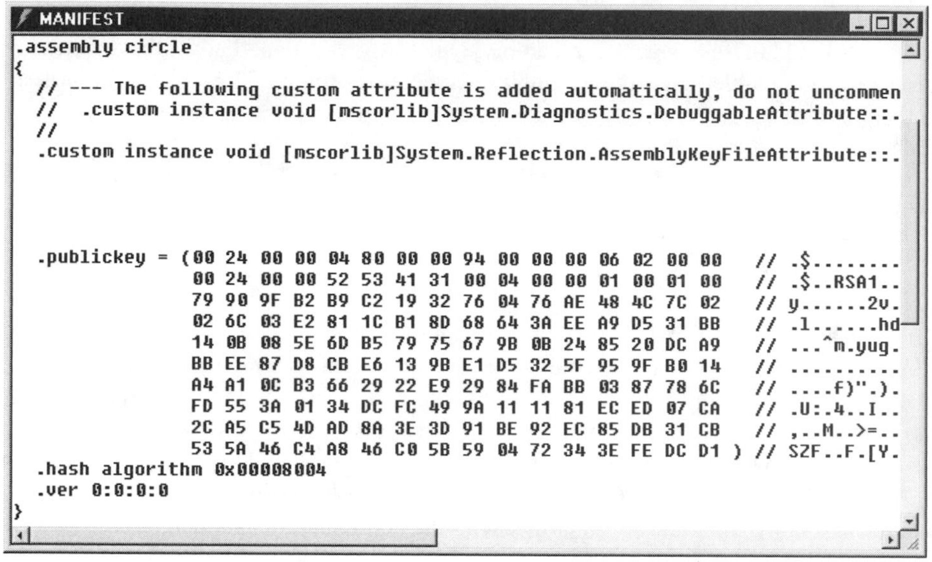

Figure 10.1   Examining the assembly manifest shows the *al.exe* utility has added the encryption key to the newly created assembly

If you examine the global assembly cache, you should see the *Circle* assembly in the listing, with the version number 1.0.0.0, as shown in Figure 10-2.

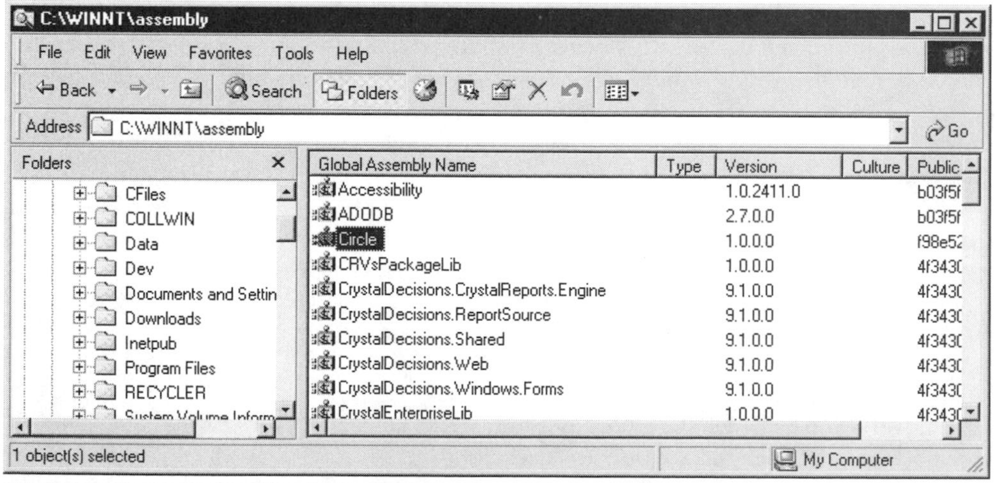

Figure 10.2   The global assembly cache viewer is part of Windows Explorer

The cache is actually a hidden directory, named *Assembly* in the Windows directory. Windows Explorer contains a viewer for this directory. To view the cache, start Windows Explorer and then maneuver to the *Windows* directory (*WinNT* on a Windows NT or Windows 2000 system). Open the Assembly directory to list the members of the cache. Notice that in detail view, the list control for Windows Explorer changes when you open this directory to display information about the assemblies.

To remove an assembly from the global assembly cache, first display the cache in Windows Explorer. Then right-click the assembly you want to remove. Select Delete from the popup menu. Alternatively, you can select the assembly to remove and then press the DELETE key.

To create a shared assembly for a module that you develop using the Visual Studio IDE, you need to add the name of the file containing the encryption keys to the *AssemblyInfo.cs* file.

1. Create the key file using the *Sn.exe* utility as described previously. You will need to provide a path to the key file, and the easiest way is to make sure this file is in the same directory as your source code files.

2. Display and expand the items in Solution Explorer to show the *AssemblyInfo.cs* file. Double click this item to display it in an editing window.

3. At the bottom of the file, you will find instructions for signing an assembly so that you can place it in the cache. Add the name of the key file to the AssemblyKeyFile attribute. An example of the instructions and the AssemblyKeyFile is shown in the following listing:

```
//
// In order to sign your assembly you must specify a key to use. Refer to
// the Microsoft .NET Framework documentation for more information on
// assembly signing.
//
// Use the attributes below to control which key is used for signing.
//
// Notes:
//   (*) If no key is specified, the assembly is not signed.
//   (*) KeyName refers to a key that has been installed in the Crypto
//       Service Provider (CSP) on your machine. KeyFile refers to a file
//       which contains a key.
//   (*) If the KeyFile and the KeyName values are both specified, the
//       following processing occurs:
//       (1) If the KeyName can be found in the CSP, that key is used.
//       (2) If the KeyName does not exist and the KeyFile does exist, the
//           key in the KeyFile is installed into the CSP and used.
//   (*) In order to create a KeyFile, you can use the sn.exe (Strong Name)
//       utility.
//       When specifying the KeyFile, the location of the KeyFile should be
//       relative to the project output directory which is
//       %Project Directory%\obj\<configuration>. For example, if your
//       KeyFile is located in the project directory, you would specify the
//       AssemblyKeyFile attribute as [assembly:
//               AssemblyKeyFile("..\\..\\mykey.snk")]
//   (*) Delay Signing is an advanced option - see the Microsoft .NET
//       Framework documentation for more information on this.
//
```

```
[assembly: AssemblyDelaySign(false)]
[assembly: AssemblyKeyFile("Circle.snk")]
[assembly: AssemblyKeyName("")]
```

4. Finally, when you build the program again, you can use a Visual Studio .NET command line to open the directory containing the executable and add it to the assembly cache with the *GacUtil.exe* utility.

Using C# Interfaces to Define an Abstraction

An interface in C# is the ultimate abstract class. Although you define it in a way that's similar to the class, all of the members of an interface are implicitly abstract. You do not provide the code to implement the properties or methods in an interface. In addition, an interface cannot contain any fields.

Because all its members are abstract, you cannot create an instance of an interface directly. You use an interface only as a base from which you may derive classes or other interfaces. Any class that inherits from an interface must implement any methods or properties in defined in the interface. In addition to being abstract, all members of an interface are implicitly *public*, and you cannot assign an access level to an interface member.

In addition, an interface may not contain constructors. Although the MSDN documentation says interfaces may contain *static* members, the compiler invariably will reject any attempt to use the *static* keyword on an interface member.

If you include a property in an interface, you must provide at least an abstract *get* or *set* accessor, or both, that you want any derived classes to implement. If, for example, you provide an abstract *get* accessor, the derived class must implement the *get* accessor. It may also implement the *set* accessor.

To define an interface, you first use the *interface* keyword and then define the interface the same way you would a class, but without implementing methods or properties. By convention, the names of interfaces begin with an uppercase *I*. The following snippet defines an interface with a method and a property:

```
interface IMyInterface
{
    void MyMethod();
    int MyValue
    {
        get;
    }
}
```

To implement this interface, a derived class must provide a body at least for the *MyMethod()* method and for the *get* accessor for the *MyValue* property:

```
class clsMyClass : IMyInterface
{
    public void MyMethod()
    {
```

```
        // Code to implement the method
    }
    public int MyValue
    {
        get {return (0);}
    }
}
```

When you implement the method and property in this code, notice that the *public* access keyword is required.

You use an interface to define a certain behavior that you want a class to exhibit. The interface provides a property that you can query using the *is* operator. If the test is true, your program knows that the class object implements the properties and methods required by the interface.

```
void SomeMethod ()
{
    clsMyClass instance = new clsMyClass();
    if (instance is IMyInterface)
    {
        // Code dependent on the IMyInterface interface
    }
}
```

For this example, the test always will be *true*, but when used with reflection (as discussed in the next two tips), you can query classes in other assemblies for which you do not have the source code.

Because all interface members are abstract, interfaces tend to be short, and they define only a few elements a class will need to implement. Some interfaces in the .NET Framework define only a single property or method.

Of course, you could provide much of the same functionality using an *abstract* class, which would also require the derived class to implement the inherited *abstract* members of the base class. A major difference, though, is that a class may inherit from only one base class, even if it is abstract. When a class inherits from an interface, it can inherit from more than one interface. To do this, you separate the names of the base interfaces with commas. The following class definition would require that the class implement the methods and properties defined in both the *ICloneable* and *IComparable*:

```
class clsClass : ICloneable, IComparable
{
    // Class members
}
```

In some ways, using an interface may be preferable to using an abstract class. An abstract class, for example, does not have to contain any abstract members, so there is no guarantee that a derived class must provide a particular method or property. The *abstract* keyword on a class definition assures only that you cannot create an instance of the class directly. An interface, on the other hand, guarantees that any defined properties or methods will be implemented by the derived class.

In addition, a class may inherit from both a base class and an interface. Assuming you had a base class named *clsBase*, which may be abstract, and an interface named *IInterface*, the following definition would inherit from both:

```
class clsClass : clsBase, IInterface
{
    // Class members
}
```

The .NET Framework defines several interfaces, many of which are used internally by .NET classes. However, you may use these interfaces to implement your own classes. For example, to implement sorting in the ListView control's details view, you need to provide a class that is derived from the *IComparable* interface. You will use this interface in Chapter 15 to sort the items in a ListView.

USE IT Considering the number and range of purpose of the .NET interface definitions, you may never have to create your own interfaces. The following example, *IntrFace.cs*, defines two interfaces, *IPlane* and *ISolid* and then derives classes from them. The *ISolid* interface guarantees that the derived class will implement a *Volume* property, and the *IPlane* interface guarantees the derived class will implement an *Area* property.

```
// IntrFace.cs -- demonstrates the use of a simple interface
//
//              Compile this program with the following command line:
//                    C:>csc IntrFace.cs
using System;

namespace nsInterface
{
    interface IPlane
    {
        double Area
        {
            get;
        }
    }
    interface ISolid
    {
        double Volume
        {
            get;
        }
    }

    public class clsCircle : IPlane
```

```
{
    public clsCircle (double radius)
    {
        m_Radius = radius;
    }
    public double Area
    {
        get {return (3.14159 * m_Radius * m_Radius);}
    }
    private double m_Radius;

    public override string ToString ()
    {
        return ("Area = " + Area);
    }
}
public class clsSphere : IPlane, ISolid
{
    public clsSphere (double radius)
    {
        m_Radius = radius;
    }
    public double Area
    {
        get {return (4 * 3.14159 * m_Radius * m_Radius);}
    }
    public double Volume
    {
        get {return (4 * 3.14159 * m_Radius * m_Radius * m_Radius / 3);}
    }
    private double m_Radius;

    public override string ToString ()
    {
        return ("Area = " + Area + ", " + "Volume = " + Volume);
    }
}

class clsMain
{
    static public void Main ()
    {
        clsCircle circle = new clsCircle (14.2);
        clsSphere sphere = new clsSphere (16.8);
```

```
        Console.WriteLine ("For the circle: " + circle);
        Console.WriteLine ("For the sphere: " + sphere);
    }
  }
}
```

The *clsSphere* class inherits from both *IPlane* (because a sphere does have a surface area) and from *ISolid*. However, the volume of a circle is meaningless, so it inherits only from *IPlane*. In C#, you cannot have this sort of multiple inheritance using abstract classes.

Getting Runtime Information Using Reflection

Within the world of .NET, *reflection* is the means by which you can discover information about an object at runtime. You have used the Intermediate Language Disassembler, *IlDasm.exe*, to look at the information in an assembly. By using reflection, you can obtain this same information from within a program.

The key to discovering type information, and to begin exploring reflection, is the *Type* class, which is a member of the *System.Reflection* namespace. The *Type* class contains methods for extracting information about a given object, including the methods, properties, and fields, along with the interfaces an object supports. The *Type* class is abstract, so you cannot create an instance of it directly.

In C#, every class or structure that you define ultimately derives from the *Object* class, and thus inherits a *GetType()* method. When you call *GetType()*, the method returns a reference to a *Type* object. From this object, you can call a rich set of methods to get information about a class or structure. Assuming you have a class name *clsClass*, the following snippet shows how to get a *Type* object:

```
clsClass cls = new clsClass();
Type t = cls.GetType();
```

The *Type* class also has a static method, *GetType()*, that allows you to get a *Type* object without having to create an instance of a class or structure. You need only pass the method the quoted name of the class:

```
Type t = Type.GetType ("clsClass");
```

Yet another method of obtaining a *Type* object is to use the *typeof* operator, passing the name of the class as a parameter:

```
Type t = typeof (clsClass);
```

USE IT Once you have the *Type* object, you can use member methods to extract information about the class. The following program, *GetType.cs*, uses a *Type* object to list the methods, properties, and fields in a class named *clsEmployee*:

```csharp
// GetType.cs -- Demonstrates using Type class to discover
//                information about a class
//
//                Compile this program with the following command line:
//                      C:>csc GetType.cs
using System;
using System.Reflection;

namespace nsReflection
{
    public class clsEmployee
    {
        public clsEmployee (string First, string Last, string Zip, int ID)
        {
            FirstName = First;
            LastName = Last;
            EmployeeID = ID;
            ZipCode = Zip;
        }
        public string  FirstName;
        public string  LastName;
        public string  ZipCode;
        public int     EmployeeID;

        public string Name
        {
            get {return (FirstName + " " + LastName);}
        }
        public string Zip
        {
            get {return (ZipCode);}
        }
        public int ID
        {
            get {return (EmployeeID);}
        }
        static public int CompareByName (object o1, object o2)
        {
            clsEmployee emp1 = (clsEmployee) o1;
            clsEmployee emp2 = (clsEmployee) o2;
            return (String.Compare (emp1.LastName, emp2.LastName));
        }
        static public int CompareByZip (object o1, object o2)
        {
```

```
            clsEmployee emp1 = (clsEmployee) o1;
            clsEmployee emp2 = (clsEmployee) o2;
            return (String.Compare (emp1.ZipCode, emp2.ZipCode));
        }
        static public int CompareByID (object o1, object o2)
        {
            clsEmployee emp1 = (clsEmployee) o1;
            clsEmployee emp2 = (clsEmployee) o2;
            return (emp1.EmployeeID - emp2.EmployeeID);
        }
    }


    class clsMain
    {
        static public void Main ()
        {
            Type t = typeof(clsEmployee);
            if (t == null)
            {
                Console.WriteLine ("t is null");
                return;
            }
// Show what namespace the class is in
            Console.WriteLine ("Class clsEmployee is a member of " +
                                "the {0} namespace", t.Namespace);
            Console.WriteLine ("\r\nMethods in clsEmployee:");
            MethodInfo [] methods = t.GetMethods ();
// Show the methods in the class
            foreach (MethodInfo m in methods)
                Console.WriteLine ("\t" + m.Name);
            Console.WriteLine ("\r\nProperties in clsEmployee:");
            PropertyInfo [] props = t.GetProperties ();
// Show the properties in the class
            foreach (PropertyInfo p in props)
                Console.WriteLine ("\t" + p.Name);
            Console.WriteLine ("\r\nFields in clsEmployee:");
            FieldInfo [] fields = t.GetFields ();
// Show the fields in the class
            foreach (FieldInfo f in fields)
                Console.WriteLine ("\t" + f.Name);
        }
    }
}
```

Running *GetType.cs* will list the namespace for the *clsEmployee* class along with the member methods, properties, and fields. Notice that the methods return only information about members to which you have access. To prove this, in the preceding code, try changing the member fields for the employee's name to *protected* or *private*.

You also can use reflection to obtain information about an entire assembly. If you did not add the *Circle* assembly to the global assembly cache (see the tip "Creating a Shared Assembly" earlier in this chapter), use the *GacUtil.exe* utility to add it.

The following program, *Asy.cs*, will load the assembly from the global assembly cache and list information about the assembly, plus information about the structure and class that it contains. To get the assembly information, you use the *Assembly* class, which is also a member of the *System.Reflection* namespace. Calling the static member *Load* will return a reference to the assembly information.

```
// Asy.cs -- Demonstrates using reflection to get information
//           about an assembly.
//
//           Compile this program with the following command line:
//               C:>csc Asy.cs
using System;
using System.Reflection;

class clsMain
{
    static public void Main ()
    {
        Assembly asy = null;
        try
        {
            asy = Assembly.Load ("Circle");
        }
        catch (Exception e)
        {
            Console.WriteLine (e.Message);
            return;
        }
        Type [] types = asy.GetTypes();
        foreach (Type t in types)
            ShowTypeInfo (t);
    }
    static void ShowTypeInfo (Type t)
    {
            Console.WriteLine ("{0} is a member of the {1} namespace",
                                t.Name, t.Namespace);
            Console.WriteLine ("\r\nMethods in {0}:", t.Name);
```

```
        MethodInfo [] methods = t.GetMethods ();
        foreach (MethodInfo m in methods)
            Console.WriteLine ("\t" + m.Name);
        Console.WriteLine ("\r\nProperties in {0}:", t.Name);
        PropertyInfo [] props = t.GetProperties ();
        foreach (PropertyInfo p in props)
            Console.WriteLine ("\t" + p.Name);
        Console.WriteLine ("\r\nFields in {0}:", t.Name);
        FieldInfo [] fields = t.GetFields ();
        foreach (FieldInfo f in fields)
            Console.WriteLine ("\t" + f.Name);
    }
}
```

When you run *Asy.cs*, you should see the *POINT* structure and the *clsCircle* class, along with their member properties, methods, and fields.

Dynamically Invoking an Object

Now that you have discovered information about an assembly and the types it contains, the next step is to create an object and invoke its properties or methods from that information. The .NET Framework provides the means to create an object and to invoke its members dynamically.

The key to doing this is the *Activator* class, which is a member of the *System.Reflection* namespace. The *Activator* class contains only static methods, so you never have to declare an instance of the class. Using the *Activator* class involves *late binding*, in which the exact type of the object is not known until runtime. The opposite is *early binding*, which you use when you create an object using the *new* keyword.

Early binding is always preferable to late binding, because early binding ensures that errors will be determined when you compile the program. Early binding usually results in faster program load times as well. Late binding, however, allows you to create an object without knowing its type.

USE IT   The following program, *Invoke.cs*, extends the *Asy.cs* program and creates objects of the *POINT* structure and the *clsCircle* class in the *Circle* assembly:

```
// Invoke.cs -- Demonstrates dynamically invoking an object
//
//              Compile this program with the following command line:
//                  C:>csc Invoke.cs
using System;
using System.Reflection;

namespace nsReflection
```

```
{
    class clsMain
    {
        static public void Main ()
        {
// Load the Circle assembly.
            Assembly asy = null;
            try
            {
                asy = Assembly.Load ("Circle");
            }
            catch (Exception e)
            {
                Console.WriteLine (e.Message);
                return;
            }
// Parameter array for a POINT object.
            object [] parmsPoint = new object [2] {15, 30};
// Parameter array for a clsCircle object.
            object [] parmsCircle = new object [3] {100, 15, 30};
// Get the type of clsCircle and create an instance of it.
            Type circle = asy.GetType("nsCircle.clsCircle");
            object obj = Activator.CreateInstance (circle, parmsCircle);
// Get the property info for the area and show the area.
            PropertyInfo p = circle.GetProperty ("Area");
            Console.WriteLine ("The area of the circle is " +
                                p.GetValue(obj, null));
// Get the POINT type and create an instance of it.
            Type point = asy.GetType("nsCircle.POINT");
            object pt = Activator.CreateInstance (point, parmsPoint);
// Show the point using object's ToString() method.
            Console.WriteLine ("The point is " + pt.ToString ());
        }
    }
}
```

Compiling and running *Invoke.cs* results in the following output:

```
The area of the circle is 31415.9
The point is (15, 30)
```

Assuming that you do not have the source code for the *Circle* assembly, you now have discovered information about the assembly and its types, and you've created objects indirectly using the *Activator* class.

Creating Threads of Execution

Windows is a *multi-threaded* operating system. Normally, when you run a program, the program code executes one statement at a time. Actually, when it is converted to the binary instruction code the central processor chip understands, it executes one instruction at a time.

Sometimes it is convenient to execute a part of the code separately from the main execution path to provide background processing. In this case, you can start additional threads in your program.

Threads are represented in the .NET Framework by the *Thread* class in the *System.Threading* namespace. To start a thread, you must provide it a starting method in the form of a *ThreadStart* object. The *ThreadStart* is a delegate method, must have a return type of *void,* and takes no parameters.

The *Thread* class contains several static methods that you can invoke without creating an instance of the class. One of these that you have encountered is *Sleep( )*, which causes the current thread to pause for a designated number of milliseconds.

The following program, *Thread.cs*, implements a thread that prints to the console. The main program thread calls the secondary thread's *Join( )* method to wait for the secondary thread to terminate:

```
// Thread.cs -- Demonstrates starting and waiting on a thread
//
//              Compile this program with the following command line:
//                    C:>csc Thread.cs
using System;
using System.Windows.Forms;
using System.Threading;


namespace nsThreads
{
    class clsMain
    {
        static public void Main ()
        {
// Create the new thread object
            Thread NewThread = new Thread (new ThreadStart (RunThread));
// Show a message box.
            MessageBox.Show ("Click OK to start the thread", "Thread Start");
// Start the new thread.
            NewThread.Start ();
// Inform everybody that the main thread is waiting.
            Console.WriteLine ("Waiting . . .");
// Wait for NewThread to terminate.
            NewThread.Join ();
// And it's done.
```

```
                        Console.WriteLine ("\r\nDone . . .");
            }


// Method to assign to the new thread as its start method
        static public void RunThread ()
            {
// Sleep for a second, print message and repeat.
            for (int x = 5; x > 0; --x)
                {
                    Thread.Sleep (1000);
                    Console.Write ("Thread is running. {0} second{1}  \r",
                              x, x > 1 ? "s" : "");              }
// The thread will terminate at this point. It will not return to
// the method that started it.
            }
        }
}
```

You can use a thread for performing lengthy background processing, such as computing the values for a table or reading a lengthy file while still letting your main program thread interact with the user.

Additionally, you can use threads to run multiple instances of an object. An example of this might be a Web proxy server, in which case you want multiple users to be able to access the Web at the same time. If you simply wait for a user to connect and then head off to process the proxy request, other users would be blocked until the first user finishes.

USE IT   You might implement such a proxy server using code similar to the following program, *Proxy.cs*.

```
// Proxy.cs -- Implements a multi-threaded Web proxy server
//
//              Compile this program with the following command line:
//                  C:>csc Proxy.cs
using System;
using System.Net;
using System.Net.Sockets;
using System.Text;
using System.IO;
using System.Threading;

namespace nsProxyServer
{
    class clsMain
    {
        static public void Main (string [] args)
```

```csharp
        {
            int Port = 3125;
            if (args.Length > 0)
            {
                try
                {
                    Port = Convert.ToInt32 (args[0]);
                }
                catch
                {
                    Console.WriteLine ("Please enter a port number.");
                    return;
                }
            }
            try
            {
// Create a listener for the proxy port.
                TcpListener sockServer = new TcpListener (Port);
                sockServer.Start ();
                while (true)
                {
// Accept connections on the proxy port.
                    Socket socket = sockServer.AcceptSocket ();
// When AcceptSocket returns, it means there is a connection. Create
// an instance of the proxy server class and start a thread running.
                    clsProxyConnection proxy =
                                        new clsProxyConnection (socket);
                    Thread thrd = new Thread (new ThreadStart (proxy.Run));
                    thrd.Start ();
// While the thread is running, the main program thread will loop around
// and listen for the next connection request.
                }
            }
            catch (IOException e)
            {
                Console.WriteLine (e.Message);
            }
        }
    }

    class clsProxyConnection
    {
        public clsProxyConnection (Socket sockClient)
        {
```

```csharp
            m_sockClient = sockClient;
        }
        Socket m_sockClient; //, m_sockServer;
        Byte [] readBuf = new Byte [1024];
        Byte [] buffer = null;
        Encoding ASCII = Encoding.ASCII;

        public void Run ()
        {
            string strFromClient = "";
            try
            {
// Read the incoming text on the socket.
                int bytes = ReadMessage (m_sockClient,
                                    readBuf, ref strFromClient);
// If it's empty, it's an error, so just return.
// This will terminate the thread.
                if (bytes == 0)
                    return;
// Get the URL for the connection. The client browser sends a GET command
// followed by a space, then the URL, then an identifier for the HTTP version.
// Extract the URL as the string between the spaces.
                int index1 = strFromClient.IndexOf (' ');
                int index2 = strFromClient.IndexOf (' ', index1 + 1);
                string strClientConnection =
                        strFromClient.Substring (index1 + 1, index2 - index1);

                if ((index1 < 0) || (index2 < 0))
                {
                    throw (new IOException ());
                }
// Write a messsage that we are connecting.
                Console.WriteLine ("Connecting to Site " +
                                    strClientConnection);
                Console.WriteLine ("Connection from " +
                                    m_sockClient.RemoteEndPoint);
// Create a WebRequest object.
                WebRequest req = (WebRequest) WebRequest.Create
                                                (strClientConnection);
// Get the response from the Web site.
                WebResponse response = req.GetResponse ();
                int BytesRead = 0;
                Byte [] Buffer = new Byte[32];
                int BytesSent = 0;
```

```csharp
// Create a response stream object.
                Stream ResponseStream = response.GetResponseStream();
// Read the response into a buffer.
                BytesRead = ResponseStream.Read(Buffer,0,32);
                StringBuilder strResponse = new StringBuilder("");
                while (BytesRead != 0)
                {
// Pass the response back to the client.
                    strResponse.Append(Encoding.ASCII.GetString(Buffer,
                                        0, BytesRead));
                    m_sockClient.Send(Buffer, BytesRead, 0);
                    BytesSent += BytesRead;
// Read the next part of the response.
                    BytesRead = ResponseStream.Read(Buffer, 0, 32);
                }
            }
            catch (FileNotFoundException e)
            {
                SendErrorPage (404, "File Not Found", e.Message);
            }
            catch (IOException e)
            {
                SendErrorPage (503, "Service not available", e.Message);
            }
            catch (Exception e)
            {
                SendErrorPage (404, "File Not Found", e.Message);
                Console.WriteLine (e.StackTrace);
                Console.WriteLine (e.Message);
            }
            finally
            {
// Disconnect and close the socket.
                if (m_sockClient != null)
                {
                    if (m_sockClient.Connected)
                    {
                        m_sockClient.Close ();
                    }
                }
            }
// Returning from this method will terminate the thread.
        }
// Write an error response to the client.
```

```
        void SendErrorPage (int status, string strReason, string strText)
        {
            SendMessage (m_sockClient, "HTTP/1.0" + " " +
                        status + " " + strReason + "\r\n");
            SendMessage (m_sockClient, "Content-Type: text/plain" + "\r\n");
            SendMessage (m_sockClient, "Proxy-Connection: close" + "\r\n");
            SendMessage (m_sockClient, "\r\n");
            SendMessage (m_sockClient, status + " " + strReason);
            SendMessage (m_sockClient, strText);
        }
// Send a string to a socket.
        void SendMessage (Socket sock, string strMessage)
        {
            buffer = new Byte [strMessage.Length + 1];
            int len = ASCII.GetBytes (strMessage.ToCharArray(),
                            0, strMessage.Length, buffer, 0);
            sock.Send (buffer, len, 0);
        }
// Read a string from a socket.
        int ReadMessage (Socket sock, byte [] buf, ref string strMessage)
        {
            int iBytes = sock.Receive (buf, 1024, 0);
            strMessage = Encoding.ASCII.GetString (buf);
            return (iBytes);
        }
    }
}
```

To test this program, you should have a shared Internet connection and run the proxy server on the machine that you use for a firewall. When the program gets a connection request, it creates a new instance of the *clsProxyConnection* class and then starts a thread to handle the connection. Then it loops back and waits for another request while the new thread processes the Web request. Thus, multiple users may connect using only a single proxy server program.

CHAPTER 11

Using Arrays

TIPS IN THIS CHAPTER

A *variable* is a symbol—an identifier—that you and the language compiler use to represent a memory location where a piece of data is stored. Naming a variable is a convenience for the programmer. To the computer, it is much easier to keep track of the memory addresses.

As a strongly typed language, the C# compiler uses the information that you connect with the variable name, the *data type*, to set aside exactly enough memory to hold a value of that data type. You cannot, for example, store the 8 bytes of a *long* data type in the 4 bytes that the compiler sets aside for an *int* data type.

It is not always possible, even using the same data type, to store all the information you need in a single variable. For example, if you need to store a list of hourly temperatures from your local airport, you would need to create 24 different variables.

Most languages—at least those advanced enough on the programming chain to be called "high level"—provide a data structure called an *array* to link multiple values to a single variable name. Usually the *elements*—the individual values—of an array are arranged in memory one after the other in a *contiguous* fashion. You can access the individual values using an offset, or *index*, into the array.

The concept of an array and using an index to access elements is what makes using loops in programming so handy. By using an index to access the members in a loop, you can process every element in a large array with a relatively small number of program statements.

C# implements an array as a reference-type variable using the abstract *Array* class. When you declare an array, you actually are creating a new data type derived from the *Array* class. For the temperature example, instead of declaring 24 different variables to hold the temperatures, which would result in a lengthy program, you can reduce the process of collecting and displaying the temperatures to a relatively few lines of code. The following program, *GetTemps.cs*, does just that:

```
// GetTemps.cs -- Stores a sequence of temperatures in an array
//
//                  Compile this program with the following command line:
//                          C:>csc GetTemps.cs
//
namespace nsTemperatures
{
    using System;
    class clsMain
    {
        static public void Main ()
        {
            int [] Temps = new int [24];
            for (int x = 0; x < 24; ++x)
            {
                while (true)
                {
                    Console.Write ("Enter the temperature for " +
                                    (x == 0 ? "Midnight"
                                    : (x == 12 ? "Noon"
```

```
                                       : ((x < 12 ? x.ToString() + " a."
                                       : ((x - 12).ToString() + " p."))
                                       + "m."))) + ": "
                               );
                    try
                    {
                        Temps[x] = Convert.ToInt32 (Console.ReadLine ());
                        break;
                    }
                    catch
                    {
                        Console.WriteLine
                                ("\r\nPlease enter a number value.");
                    }
                }
            }
            Console.WriteLine ("The daily temperature report:");
            for (int x = 0; x < 24; x += 4)
            {
                Console.WriteLine ("{0,4:D4} : {1,3:D}\t{2,4:D4}: {3,3:D}\t" +
                                "{4,4:D4}: {5,3:D}\t{6,4:D4}: {7,3:D}",
                                x * 100, Temps[x],
                                (x + 1) * 100, Temps[x + 1],
                                (x + 2) * 100, Temps[x + 2],
                                (x + 3) * 100, Temps[x + 3]);
            }
        }
    }
}
```

After getting the temperatures, *GetTemps.cs* places them in an array, and a second loop displays the following (which depends on the temperatures you entered):

```
The daily temperature report:
0000:  48     0100:  47     0200:  45     0300:   45
0400:  44     0500:  45     0600:  48     0700:   54
0800:  59     0900:  64     1000:  70     1100:   75
1200:  86     1300:  92     1400:  98     1500:  101
1600:  99     1700:  97     1800:  96     1900:   91
2000:  82     2100:  70     2200:  63     2300:   55
```

Without the array, the loops would have been useless and you would have had to print each of the 24 temperature variables one by one.

An array is a random-access data structure. To access a single element in an array, you do not need to start at one end and work your way toward the element you want to set or retrieve. You simply specify the index inside a set of square brackets of the element you want to set or retrieve.

Declaring Arrays

When you declare an array variable, you do not actually create the array. An array is a new data type derived from the *abstract* class *System.Array*. Because the array is a class, declaring and creating it is a two-step process that you can combine into a single statement.

To declare an array, you must first signal the compiler that the new variable is an array. You do this by placing an *empty* set of brackets between the data type and the variable name when you declare the array:

```
int [] Arr;
```

This declares a reference-type variable that will hold a pointer to the array in the heap. You have not created the array, and the compiler does not yet know how large the array will be. The brackets simply tell the compiler to create a new data type derived from *System.Array*.

To create the array, you must use the *new* operator followed by the data type once again, and finally add the size of the array inside another set of brackets.

The following example creates an array of 12 integers in the heap and places a reference to the array in the variable *Arr*:

```
Arr = new int [12];
```

As with other declarations in C#, you may declare and assign an array in a single declaration assignment:

```
int [] Arr = new int [12];
```

Arrays in C# are type-safe, so you cannot assign an array of one data type to an array variable of another data type. The C# compiler will not even let you perform an explicit cast to make such an assignment. The following snippet declares and creates arrays of different data types and attempts to assign one to the other:

```
int [] IntArr = new int [10];
long [] LongArr = new long [10];
string [] StringArr = new string [10]
StringArr = (string []) LongArr
LongArr = (long []) IntArr;
```

In each case, the compiler will tell you that it cannot convert one array type to another array type. This is a vast improvement over C++, which does not guarantee type-safety. The C++ compiler sees the following declarations and assignments as perfectly legal and will not so much as display a warning:

```
int *IntArr = new int [10];
long *LongArr = new long [10];
char *StringArr = new char [10];
StringArr = (char *) LongArr;
LongArr = (long *) IntArr;
```

Just because the C++ compiler does not object to the operations does not mean they are not going to cause you problems, though. Of course, the fact that C++ allows such code also lets you to create a powerful *jagged* array using different data types, like so:

```
void *Jagged[3];
Jagged[0] = (void *) new int [15];
Jagged[1] = (void *) new long [6];
Jagged[2] = (void *) new char [36];
```

This is a powerful and occasionally useful construction in C++ that is not available in C# because of the limits of type-safety. In fact, in C# you cannot even create an array of the *void* data type. C# does allow you to implement jagged arrays, but all member arrays must be of the same data type.

To ensure type-safety, C# performs bounds checking when you attempt to access an array element. This assures that your program does not attempt to read from memory to which it does not have access—or, worse, that it does not attempt to write to memory that it does not own. Neither C nor C++ provides this kind of protection.

When you create an array, C# automatically initializes the members to 0, or *null* (*nothing* in Visual Basic). Not only is this convenient for programmers, but it is an important security precaution, especially for components that might run on another computer on a network. A common trick is to create a very large array in the heap. Most languages do not initialize arrays in the heap, so once you create the array, you can begin reading the contents of the elements. Early computers had limited memory, so often this memory contained data from programs that once owned the memory. It was possible to obtain account passwords in this way.

Although modern computers usually have more than adequate memory, arrays that have not been initialized present a security risk. Still, using languages such as C and C++, it is possible to read memory that once was owned by a system process. By initializing the array when it is created, C# avoids this risk.

In addition, you may initialize an array to your own values, and the *System.Array* class contains methods to fill all or part of an array with values.

Every array inherits from the *System.Array* class and has access to the *protected* and *public* members. Of course, because you do not actually create a class object yourself, you cannot provide additional methods to access the *protected* members of the parent class. The *System.Array* class does have a number of useful member methods and properties.

One such important property is the *Length* property. This is a read-only property, so you cannot modify its value. Once you create an array, you cannot change its size. (The *Array* class has a virtual property titled *IsFixedSize*, which is always *true*. Because this property is *virtual*, you may derive a class from *Array* to provide an implementation that may vary in size.)

The *Length* property is a count of the number of elements in an array. For a one-dimensional array, it has the same value returned by the *GetLength( )* method. Your program should take care that it never tries to access any array element with an index of *Length* or greater. This makes the *Length* property safe to use in the conditional expression of a *for* loop:

```
for (int x = 0; x < Arr.Length; ++x)
{
    // x will always be a valid index into Arr
    // Statements here that access the array using x as an index
}
```

The first element in an array is always element *0*, and the index of the last element is always *Length – 1*. If you attempt to access an element using an index less than 0 or greater than *Length – 1*, your program will throw an *IndexOutOfRangeException*. By testing any index value to make sure it is less than *Length*, this is not likely to happen—unless you are careless. However, C# does provide a special case of the *for* loop that you may use with arrays.

Arrays and the *foreach* Loop

The *foreach* statement provides safe, read-only, sequential access to the elements in an array. You can use the statement to read the array values, but you cannot set values in the loop.

To use the *foreach* loop, use the *foreach* keyword followed by a set of parentheses. Inside the parentheses, add the data type of the array, followed by the name of a variable and the identifier of the array. Write the body of the loop inside a set of braces:

```
int [] Arr = new int [10];
foreach (int x in Arr)
{
    // Statements in here that use x as a read-only variable
}
```

The construction of the *foreach* loop declares a new variable; in the preceding example, it's *int x*. This variable may not duplicate another variable in use in the method, and you may not use it outside the loop block.

When the loop executes, C# sequentially assigns the value of the array elements to the variable in the loop statement, starting with the 0 element and continuing to the last element. Remember that the variable contains the value of the array element, not the index, because there is no indexer available inside the loop:

```
// ForEach.cs -- Sums the values in an array using a foreach loop
//
//              Compile this program with the following command line
//                    C:>csc ForEach.cs
//
namespace nsForEach
```

```
{
    using System;
    class clsMain
    {
        static public void Main ()
        {
            DateTime now = DateTime.Now;
            Random rand = new Random ((int) now.Millisecond);
            int [] Arr = new int [10];
            for (int x = 0; x < Arr.Length; ++x)
            {
                Arr[x] = rand.Next () % 100;
            }
            int Total = 0;
            Console.Write ("Array values are ");
            foreach (int val in Arr)
            {
                Total += val;
                Console.Write (val + ", ");
            }
            Console.WriteLine ("and the average is {0,0:F1}",
                            (double) Total / (double) Arr.Length);
        }
    }
}
```

Because the *foreach* loop provides a read-only value, this code first sets the values of the array to a random value in a *for* loop. After initializing a *Total* variable, the program then executes a *foreach* loop to total all the values in the array.

The output should be different for every run, but it should appear similar to the following:

```
Array values are 67, 84, 75, 86, 39, 71, 61, 46, 76, 32,
and the average is 63.7
```

Because it has no index, provides only a read-only variable, and is inflexible in its execution, the *foreach* loop is more limited than the more common *for* loop. It is, however, a convenient shorthand when you need to iterate all the elements in an array.

Initializing an Array

C# initializes the elements of an array to 0, or *null* in the case of an array of objects, for security purposes among other reasons. The result often is a convenience to the programmer. Very often you will want to start out with the array initialized to 0.

That will not *always* be the case, however. In some cases, because you will have a set of initial values for the array elements, it would be more convenient to start out with those values rather than set them in a *for* loop. If the values have no obvious arithmetic or mathematical relationship, using a *for* loop would probably do you no good anyway.

You may initialize the elements of an array by enclosing the values, separated by commas, inside a set of braces immediately following the *new* statement that creates the array. Do not include an equals sign (that's C++ syntax), but do add a semicolon following the closing brace:

```
int [] Arr = new int [10] {67, 84, 75, 86, 39, 71, 61, 46, 76, 32};
```

If you initialize an array in this way, you must provide *exactly* as many values as there are elements in the array. This example declares an array of 10 elements, so exactly 10 values must reside inside the set of braces. Too few or too many will result in a compiler error.

> **QUICK TIP**
>
> *C++ programmers must be careful to provide the same number of values as elements in the array. C++ compilers let you provide fewer values than array elements, in which case the compiler assigns as many values as possible and then fills the remaining elements with the last value.*

As with C++, however, you can let the compiler figure the size of the array from the number of values that you provide:

```
int [] Arr = new int [] {67, 84, 75, 86, 39, 71, 61, 46, 76, 32};
```

The last two examples achieve the same result—a single-dimension array initialized with the 10 values. Considering the requirement for a one-to-one match between elements and initializing values, it's probably better to write your code in the second way. If you use the first method and later add a value, you may forget to update the array size and cause a compiler error.

USE IT An array's initializing values do not have to be literal values. They may be any expression that results in a value of the same data type as the array. Using this knowledge, you can rewrite the *ForEach.cs* program as a new program named *InitArr.cs*, as follows:

```
// InitArr.cs -- Sums the values in an array using a foreach loop
//
//                  Compile this program with the following command line:
//                      C:>csc InitArr.cs
//
namespace nsForEach
{
    using System;
    class clsMain
    {
```

```
static public void Main ()
{
    DateTime now = DateTime.Now;
    Random rand = new Random ((int) now.Millisecond);
    int [] Arr = new int []
                {rand.Next () % 100, rand.Next () % 100,
                 rand.Next () % 100, rand.Next () % 100,
                 rand.Next () % 100, rand.Next () % 100,
                 rand.Next () % 100, rand.Next () % 100,
                 rand.Next () % 100, rand.Next () % 100
                };
    int Total = 0;
    Console.Write ("Array values are ");
    foreach (int val in Arr)
    {
        Total += val;
        Console.Write (val + ", ");
    }
    Console.WriteLine ("and the average is {0,0:F1}",
                    (double) Total / (double) Arr.Length);
}
}
}
```

The *InitArr.cs* program should produce a result similar to the *ForEach.cs* program. You do not reduce the number of statements code in this program, but you do avoid having the compiler first initialize the values, only to have you immediately write over them.

Using Multi-Dimensional Arrays

In addition to an arithmetic or mathematical relationship, elements of an array may have a *positional* relationship. Back to the temperature example, you know that for every day of the month, 24 hourly temperatures are available from the local airport. Each day, then, relates to the position of 24 different temperatures.

For the sake of simplicity, consider another example: Assume a class of 10 students are studying interdimensional widget analysis. During the course of the semester, each student takes five examinations. The grades in an array then have a positional relationship to the students, which have indexes assigned to them (anyone who studies interdimensional widget analysis deserves to be indexed). The grades fill a block in which the student index is along the horizontal side and the examination number is on the vertical side, as shown in Figure 11-1.

The only values in the block are the examination results, but the relationship is two-dimensional. You can represent this relationship in C# by declaring an array with two dimensions. To declare a

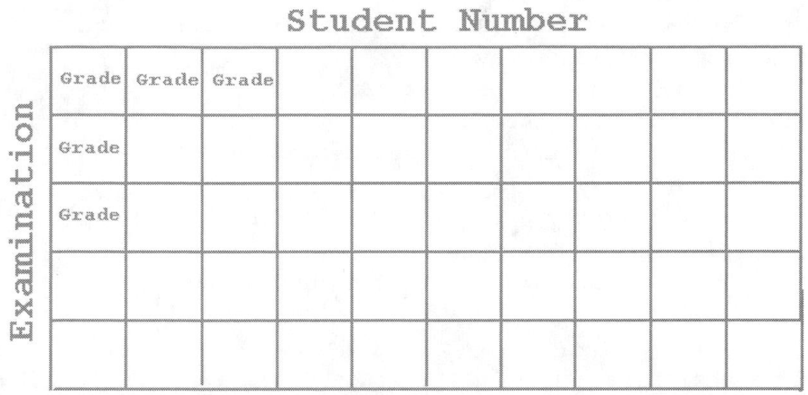

Student Number

Figure 11.1 The positional relationship of the grades and the student number make up
a two-dimensional array

two-dimensional array, type the first set of brackets with a single comma between them. Inside
the second set of brackets, write the size of the first dimension, a comma, and the size of the
second dimension:

```
int [,] Grades = new int [5,10];
```

You access an array element by adding the variable name followed by a set of brackets. Inside the
brackets, type in the index of the first dimension—often called the *row*—followed by a comma, and
then the index for the second dimension—called the *column*. The following statement would retrieve
the grade of the seventh student on the third exam:

```
int Result = Grades [2, 6];
```

USE IT   Put to practical use, the following program, *Grades.cs*, creates a two-dimensional array
and assigns each student a score between 70 and 100 on each exam (interdimensional
widget analysis students are all bright):

```
//  Grades.cs -- Uses a two-dimensional array to store grades for students
//
//              Compile this program with the following command line:
//                      C:>csc Grades.cs
namespace nsGrades
{
    using System;
    class clsMain
    {
        static public void Main ()
        {
```

```
            DateTime now = DateTime.Now;
            Random rand = new Random ((int) now.Millisecond);
// Declare a two-dimension array
            int [,] Grades = new int [5,10];
// Assign random grades to the array
            for (int x = 0; x < Grades.GetLength (0); ++x)
            {
                for (int y = 0; y < Grades.GetLength(1); ++y)
                {
                    Grades [x, y] = 70 + rand.Next () % 31;
                }
            }

// Declare another array to hold the student averages.
            int [] Average = new int [10];
            Console.WriteLine ("Grade summary:\r\n");
            Console.WriteLine ("Student   1   2   3   4   5   " +
                               "6   7   8   9  10");
            Console.WriteLine ("        --------------------" +
                               "------------------");
            for (int x = 0; x < Grades.GetLength (0); ++x)
            {
                Console.Write ("Test " + (x + 1) + " ");
                for (int y = 0; y < Grades.GetLength(1); ++y)
                {
// Save the grade to get an average
                    Average[y] += Grades[x,y];
// Show the grade
                    Console.Write ("{0,4:D}", Grades[x,y]);
                }
                Console.WriteLine ();
            }
            Console.Write ("\r\n Avg.  ");
// Show the averages
            foreach (int Avg in Average)
            {
                Console.Write ("{0,4:D}", Avg / Grades.GetLength(0));
            }
            Console.WriteLine ();
        }
    }
}
```

Notice that instead of using a *foreach* loop to read the array, you now need to use a *for* loop. The *foreach* loop would read each element in the entire array sequentially. In addition, notice that the conditional expression in the *for* loop uses the *GetLength()* method. The *Length* property in the *Array* class returns the total number of elements in the array, in this case 50. The *GetLength()* method returns only the number of elements in a single dimension of the array.

Running the *Grades.cs* program results in the following output:

```
Grade summary:


Student   1   2   3   4   5   6   7   8   9  10
          -------------------------------------------
Test 1   89  80  87  71  90  98  87  88  91  71
Test 2   70  85 100  74  81  95  86 100 100  71
Test 3   89  86  81  73  84  72  97  77  97  77
Test 4   72  77  97  80 100  94  96  99  82  77
Test 5   87  80  77  84  92  91  83  87  91  78


 Avg.    81  81  88  76  89  90  89  90  92  74
```

You can initialize a two-dimensional array when you declare it. The syntax is similar to initializing several one-dimensional arrays:

```
int [,] Grades = new int [5,10]
      {
            {89, 80,  87, 71,  90, 98, 87,  88,  91, 71},  // First row
            {70, 85, 100, 74,  81, 95, 86, 100, 100, 71},  // Second row
            {89, 86,  81, 73,  84, 72, 97,  77,  97, 77},  // Third row
            {72, 77,  97, 80, 100, 94, 96,  99,  82, 77},  // Fourth row
            {87, 80,  77, 84,  92, 91, 83,  87,  91, 78}   // Fifth row
      };
```

Notice that you must first include an open brace to enclose the entire array. Then, each row has its own set of braces, and the elements in a row are separated by commas. The closing brace for each row must be followed by a comma, except for the last row—although if you place a comma after the closing brace for the last row, the C# compiler will not consider it an error.

Arrays beyond two dimensions are less frequent in programming, but the need for them does arise. For each additional dimension, add another comma in the declaration and the size of the additional dimension when you create the array.

The following statements declare and create three- and four-dimensional arrays:

```
int [,,] Three = new int [10,10,10];
int [,,,] Four = new int [10,10,10,10];
```

When you create multi-dimensional arrays, remember that the total number of elements increases rapidly. The total is the product of all of the dimensions. A two-dimensional array with 10 elements in each dimension yields 100 elements, but a three-dimensional array with 10 element in each dimension yields 1000 elements.

Using Jagged Arrays

Using a multi-dimensional array to contain elements with a positional relationship is most convenient when all the rows are the same length. For example, all 10 students take all five examinations.

Unfortunately, life does not always dish out information to us in such convenient packages. Every year comprises 12 months, but the number of days in each month is not the same. If you wanted to create a two-dimensional array that held, for example, the sales figures for each day of the year (your company operates around the clock), you would have to declare an array of 12 rows and 31 columns. Up to three columns might be wasted in any given month.

For very large arrays with larger differences in row length, you could end up wasting a lot of memory if you create them in this way. C# provides a *jagged* array to accommodate varying amounts of data.

Jagged arrays are nothing new with C#. The C language has permitted them since the beginning as a natural consequence of the way the language manipulates data types and pointers, and C++ inherited that ability. Actually, C# jagged arrays are more restrictive than they are in C and C++ because every row in C# must be of the same data type. In fairness, however, jagged arrays are easier to use in C#.

In C#, a jagged array is a collection of arrays, each of which may be a different length. It resembles a multi-dimensional array in the way you create and use it. To create a jagged array, you do not use the comma to separate the dimensions. Instead, you write a separate set of empty brackets to indicate the dimension in the declaration. When you create the array, indicate the size of the first dimension only. The following creates a jagged array with four rows, but you do not indicate the number of columns:

```
int [][] Jagged = new int [4][];
```

If you examine the statement, you will see that the declaration and assignment creates an array to hold four references to arrays. To complete the operation, you must create the individual arrays in separate statements, and each array may be a different length:

```
int [][] Jagged = new int [4][]
Jagged[0] = new int [8];
Jagged[1] = new int [4];
Jagged[2] = new int [12];
Jagged[3] = new int [6];
```

You then access the individual elements of the array by first specifying the array inside a set of brackets and then specifying the element in that array using another set of brackets. The following statements first set and then retrieve the value of the sixth element in the third array:

```
Jagged[2][5] = 42
int Answer = Jagged[2][5];
```

You must be careful not to access any element outside the individual rows. This is where the *Length* property becomes important:

```
int [][] Jagged = new int[2][];
Jagged[0] = new int [4];
```

```
Jagged[1] = new int [8];
for (int x = 0; x < Jagged.Length; ++x)
{
    for (int y = 0; y < Jagged[x].Length; ++y)
    {
        Jagged[x][y] = rand.Next ();
    }
}
```

Each array in the jagged array is a separate array, so you may use the *foreach* loop to read the values:

```
foreach (int [] arr in Jagged)
{
    foreach (int x in arr)
    {
        Console.Write (x + ", ");
    }
    Console.WriteLine ();
}
```

The outer *foreach* loop sequentially access the arrays, and the inner loop accesses the members of each array one at a time.

Using jagged arrays does have some advantages over using multi-dimensional arrays. If the data does not fill all of the elements, or if you need to avoid empty elements for any reason, the jagged array will serve you well.

USE IT The following program, *Sales.cs*, uses a jagged array to store the sales figures for a year. When you dump the report for a single month—February, in this case—the report ends with the last day of the month:

```
// Sales.cs -- Uses a jagged array to store sales figures, then writes report
//             for one month. Demonstrates that you do not have to worry about
//             looking for empty elements.
//
//             Compile this program with the following command line:
//                  C:>csc Sales.cs
//
namespace nsSales
{
    using System;
    class clsMain
    {
        static public void Main ()
        {
            DateTime now = DateTime.Now;
```

```
        Random rand = new Random ((int) now.Millisecond);
        int [] MonthLen = new int []
                     {31, 29, 31, 30, 31, 30, 31, 31, 30, 31, 30, 31};
        double [][] Sales2000 = new double [12][];
        for (int x = 0; x < MonthLen.Length; ++x)
        {
            Sales2000[x] = new double [MonthLen[x]];
            for (int y = 0; y < Sales2000[x].Length; ++y)
            {
                Sales2000[x][y] = rand.NextDouble() * 100;
            }
        }
        Console.Write ("February Sales Report (in thousands):");
        for (int x = 0; x < Sales2000[1].Length; ++x)
        {
            if ((x % 4) == 0)
                Console.WriteLine ();
            Console.Write ("   Feb. {0,-2:D}: {1,-4:F1}",
                            x + 1, Sales2000[1][x]);
        }
    }
  }
}
```

The output from *Sales.cs* is truncated right after the last day of the month:

```
February Sales Report (in thousands):
    Feb. 1 : 18.7    Feb. 2 : 76.6    Feb. 3 : 24.2    Feb. 4 : 45.7
    Feb. 5 : 48.8    Feb. 6 : 82.5    Feb. 7 : 11.4    Feb. 8 : 38.5
    Feb. 9 : 18.9    Feb. 10: 49.3    Feb. 11: 34.6    Feb. 12: 12.7
    Feb. 13: 55.8    Feb. 14: 54.7    Feb. 15: 97.6    Feb. 16: 48.8
    Feb. 17: 86.5    Feb. 18: 10.4    Feb. 19: 27.9    Feb. 20: 92.7
    Feb. 21: 5.5     Feb. 22: 86.4    Feb. 23: 81.2    Feb. 24: 8.9
    Feb. 25: 20.7    Feb. 26: 71.1    Feb. 27: 73.9    Feb. 28: 7.2
    Feb. 29: 27.6
```

You do not need to test for an empty element, nor worry about sales for non-existent days printing as part of the report.

Using the *System.Array* Class

Declaring an array creates a new data type derived from the *System.Array* class. Each new array type inherits the method, properties, and fields in the *Array* class, which contains several useful methods and properties.

The *Array* class is *abstract*, so you cannot create an instance of it directly. However, using the *CreateInstance()* static member method, you can have the class create an instance of itself. When you create an instance in this way, the type is *Array*, and you cannot use indexes to access members of the array. Instead, you must use member methods, specifying the index as an argument.

USE IT   The following program, *CreatArr.cs*, declares an instance of *Array*. It then uses the member methods *GetLowerBound()* and *GetUpperBound()* to get the limits of the array elements:

```
//
// CreatArr.cs -- Creates and implements an instance of Array
//
//              Compile this program with the following command line:
//                   C:>csc CreatArr.cs
//
namespace nsArray
{
    using System;
    class clsMain
    {
        static public void Main ()
        {
            DateTime now = DateTime.Now;
            Random rand = new Random ((int) now.Millisecond);

// Create an instance of the Array class.
            Array Arr = Array.CreateInstance (typeof(Int32), 10);
// Initialize the elements using the SetValue() member method
// Use the GetLowerBound() and GetUpperBound() methods for safe access.
            for (int x = Arr.GetLowerBound(0);
                    x < Arr.GetUpperBound(0) + 1;
                    ++x)
            {
                Arr.SetValue (rand.Next () % 100, x);
            }
            int Total = 0;
            Console.Write ("Array values are ");
// Use the foreach loop on the Array instance
            foreach (int val in Arr)
            {
                Total += val;
                Console.Write (val + ", ");
            }
            Console.WriteLine ("and the average is {0,0:F1}",
                        (double) Total / (double) Arr.Length);
        }
    }
}
```

Another member method, *Clear()*, will reset all the elements of the array to 0, or *null* in the case of an array of objects. In addition, the *Rank()* method returns the number of dimensions in the array.

Searching and Sorting Arrays

The *System.Array* class also has several member methods that sort arrays and search for values in the elements of an array. These include methods that sort the array by element values, reverse the order of the array, and perform a binary search.

The *Array* class provides two methods for finding a particular value in the elements of an array. The *IndexOf()* method returns the index of the first occurrence of a value, and the *LastIndexOf()* method returns the index of the last occurrence. These are *static* members, so you call them using the *Array* identifier.

 USE IT In the *Index.cs* program that follows, an array has 12 members. Two members have the same value, 42, and the program uses *Array* member methods to find their indices:

```
//
// Index.cs -- Creates an array and looks for the index of a given
//             value from either end.
//
//             Compile this program with the following command line:
//                  C:>csc Index.cs
//
namespace nsArray
{
    using System;
    class clsMain
    {
        static public void Main ()
        {
            int [] Arr = new int [12]
                        {29, 82, 42, 46, 54, 65, 50, 42, 5, 94, 19, 34};
            Console.WriteLine ("The first occurrence of 42 is at index "
                                + Array.IndexOf(Arr, 42));
            Console.WriteLine ("The last occurrence of 42 is at index "
                                + Array.LastIndexOf(Arr, 42));
        }
    }
}
```

Both *IndexOf()* and *LastIndexOf()* return *−1* if the value is not found in the array. Both methods also are overloaded so that you may give the method a starting position:

```
int x = 0;
// Search Arr for the value 42, starting at position x.
```

```
while ((x = Array.IndexOf (Arr, 42, x)) >= 0)
{
    Console.WriteLine ("42 found at index " + x);
    ++x;    // Increment x to get beyond the found index
}
x = Arr.Length - 1;
while ((x = Array.LastIndexOf (Arr, 42, x)) >= 0)
{
    Console.WriteLine ("42 found at index " + x);
    --x;    // Decrement x to start before the last found index
}
```

When added to the program, these snippets will show the following results:

```
42 found at index 2
42 found at index 7
42 found at index 7
42 found at index 2
```

Sorting an array is a task that programmers don't relish. Everybody knows how to do sorting, but unless you write a lot of sort routines, it seems you always have to go back to the book or to another sample to refresh your memory. It should come as some delight, then, that *Array* contains a member method to sort the elements in an array. The *Sort()* method sorts the elements from lowest to highest value. In addition, *Array* contains a method to reverse the order, so once you sort in ascending order you need only apply the *Reverse()* method to sort in descending order:

```
// Sort.cs -- Sorts an array in ascending order, then reverses the elements
//
//              Compile this program with the following command line:
//                  C:>csc Sort.cs
//
namespace nsArray
{
    using System;
    class clsMain
    {
        static public void Main ()
        {
            DateTime now = DateTime.Now;
            Random rand = new Random ((int) now.Millisecond);

            int [] Arr = new int [12];
            for (int x = 0; x < Arr.Length; ++x)
            {
                Arr [x] = rand.Next () % 101;
```

```
    }
    Console.WriteLine ("The unsorted array elements:");
    foreach (int x in Arr)
    {
        Console.Write (x + " ");
    }
    Array.Sort (Arr);
    Console.WriteLine ("\r\n\r\nThe array sorted " +
                        "in ascending order:");
    foreach (int x in Arr)
    {
        Console.Write (x + " ");
    }
    Array.Reverse (Arr);
    Console.WriteLine ("\r\n\r\nThe array sorted " +
                        "in descending order:");
    foreach (int x in Arr)
    {
        Console.Write (x + " ");
    }
        }
    }
}
```

Depending on the results of the random number call, the output from *Sort.cs* should look something like the following:

```
The unsorted array elements:
47 26 1 4 15 29 57 59 87 41 26 24

The array sorted in ascending order:
1 4 15 24 26 26 29 41 47 57 59 87

The array sorted in descending order:
87 59 57 47 41 29 26 26 24 15 4 1
```

These sorting methods are *static* members. Thus, they are members of the class, so you use the *Array* identifier and pass the array to sort as an argument.

Using the *Copy* Method to Copy Array Values

The *static* method *Copy()* contains overloads that make it convenient to copy one array to another array or to copy a portion of one array to another array. The method also performs casting while copying the elements, so you may use it to copy an array of one data type into an array of another data type.

The casting will work only if an implicit cast is allowed on the data types. Even while copying an array, you cannot, for example, copy an array of type *double* into an array of type *int*. However, you can copy an array of type *int* into an array of type *double*, because the implicit cast is permitted.

In the first overload, you specify the source array, the destination array, and the number of elements to copy. You do not need to copy the entire array, but copying will begin with the first element:

```
Array.Copy (srcArr, dstArry, count);
```

USE IT   The *Int2Dbl.cs* program, shown in the following listing, copies the first eight elements of an integer array into the elements of an array of type *double*:

```
//
//  Int2Dbl.cs -- Uses the Array.Copy() method to copy an array of ints
//                into an array of doubles.
//
//              Compile this program with the following command line:
//                    C:>csc Int2Dbl.cs
//
namespace nsArray
{
    using System;
    class clsMain
    {
        static public void Main ()
        {
            DateTime now = DateTime.Now;
            Random rand = new Random ((int) now.Millisecond);
            int [] iArr = new int [10]
                    {
                        rand.Next() % 101, rand.Next() % 101,
                        rand.Next() % 101, rand.Next() % 101,
                        rand.Next() % 101, rand.Next() % 101,
                        rand.Next() % 101, rand.Next() % 101,
                        rand.Next() % 101, rand.Next() % 101
                    };

            double [] dArr = new double [8];
            Array.Copy (iArr, dArr, dArr.Length);
            Console.Write ("The dArr contains:\r\n    ");
            foreach (double d in dArr)
            {
                Console.Write ("{0,4:F1}  ", d);
            }
            Console.Write ("\r\n\r\nThe iArr contains:\r\n    ");
            foreach (int x in iArr)
            {
```

```
                    Console.Write (x + "   ");
                }
                Console.WriteLine ();
        }
    }
}
```

The implicit cast is permitted. If you tried to copy the *double* values into the *int* array, the compiler would not issue an error, but the program will throw an *ArryTypeMismatchException*.

In the second form, you specify a starting position for the copy operation for each array involved in the copy. Elements less than the starting position will not be affected, but you must be careful not to attempt to write outside the bounds of the destination array. The form of this overload is shown here:

```
Array.Copy (srcArr, srcStart, dstArry, dstStart, count);
```

Again, you may perform the copy only if the implicit cast is permitted.

USE IT The *CopyPart.cs* program shown in the following listing copies just a portion of the *int* array into the *double* array.

```
//  CopyPart.cs -- Uses the Array.Copy() method to copy part of an array
//                 ints into a section of an array of doubles.
//
//                 Compile this program with the following command line:
//                      C:>csc CopyPart.cs
//
namespace nsArray
{
    using System;
    class clsMain
    {
        static public void Main ()
        {
            DateTime now = DateTime.Now;
            Random rand = new Random ((int) now.Millisecond);
            int [] iArr = new int [12]
                {
                        rand.Next() % 101, rand.Next() % 101,
                        rand.Next() % 101, rand.Next() % 101,
                        rand.Next() % 101, rand.Next() % 101,
                        rand.Next() % 101, rand.Next() % 101,
                        rand.Next() % 101, rand.Next() % 101,
                        rand.Next() % 101, rand.Next() % 101
                };
```

```
            double [] dArr = new double [14];
            Array.Copy (iArr, 2, dArr, 4, 8);
            Console.Write ("The dArr contains:\r\n    ");
            for (int x = 0; x < dArr.Length; ++x)
            {
                Console.Write ("{0,4:F1}  ", dArr[x]);
                if (x == 6)
                    Console.Write("\r\n    ");
            }
            Console.Write ("\r\n\r\n\r\nThe iArr contains:\r\n    ");
            foreach (int x in iArr)
            {
                Console.Write (x + "  ");
            }
            Console.WriteLine ();
        }
    }
}
```

The output from *CopyPart.cs* shows that the copy began from the third element in the *int* array to the fifth array of the *double* array. Copying ended at the ninth element of the *int* array to the eleventh element of the *double* array:

```
The dArr contains:
    0.0   0.0   0.0   0.0  51.0   8.0  92.0
   29.0  88.0  64.0  99.0  13.0   0.0   0.0

The iArr contains:
    99   8  51   8  92  29  88  64  99  13  24  90
```

Using Arrays of Objects

You may create an array of virtually any data type in C#, including user-defined types such as structures and classes. This means that an array element may contain methods, properties, and fields rather than simply a single value.

To declare an array of objects, simply declare the array as you would for any simple data type, but use the class name as the data type. The following statement creates an array of 10 objects of type *clsClass*:

```
clsClass [] Arr = new clsClass[10];
```

If it were that simple, however, it hardly would be worth mentioning. To use the methods that manipulate the array members, such as *Sort()* or *Reverse()*, you must implement the *IComparable* interface and provide some means for one object of the class type to determine whether its value is comparable to another. If you attempt to use one of these methods without implementing *IComparable*, the compiler will issue an error.

To implement the *IComparable* interface, a class needs to provide a *CompareTo()* method, which should return a value less than 0 if the instance's value is less than that of the object it is being compared with, or a value greater than 0 if it is greater. If the comparable object's value is the same as the instance, the method should return 0.

USE IT The following program creates and array containing four instances of the *clsElement* class, which implements the *IComparable* interface:

```
// ClassArr.cs -- Creates and accesses an array of classes. Implements the
//                IComparable interface.
//
//                Compile this program with the following command line
//                     C:>csc ClassArr.cs
//
namespace nsForEach
{
    using System;
    class clsMain
    {
        static public void Main ()
        {
            clsElement [] Arr = new clsElement []
                            {
                                    new clsElement (8), new clsElement (3),
                                    new clsElement (12), new clsElement (7)
                            };
            Console.WriteLine ("Unsorted:");
            foreach (clsElement val in Arr)
            {
                Console.WriteLine ("The instance number is " + val.Instance);
            }
            Array.Reverse (Arr);
            Console.WriteLine ("\r\nIn Reverse order:");
            foreach (clsElement val in Arr)
            {
                Console.WriteLine ("The instance number is " + val.Instance);
            }
            Array.Sort (Arr);
            Console.WriteLine ("\r\nSorted:");
            foreach (clsElement val in Arr)
            {
                Console.WriteLine ("The instance number is " + val.Instance);
            }
```

```
                Console.WriteLine ();
            }
        }
    class clsElement : IComparable
    {
        public clsElement (int instance)
        {
            m_Instance = instance;
        }
        private int m_Instance;
        public int Instance
        {
            get{return (m_Instance);}
        }
        public int CompareTo (object o)
        {
            if (o.GetType() != this.GetType())
                throw(new ArgumentException());
            clsElement elem = (clsElement) o;
            return (this.Instance - elem.Instance);
        }
    }
}
```

The *CompareTo()* method uses the value passed in the constructor as the basis for comparing one instance with another. The output shows that the *Sort()* and *Reverse()* methods rely on the value returned by this method:

```
Unsorted:
The instance number is 8
The instance number is 3
The instance number is 12
The instance number is 7

In Reverse order:
The instance number is 7
The instance number is 12
The instance number is 3
The instance number is 8

Sorted:
The instance number is 3
The instance number is 7
The instance number is 8
The instance number is 12
```

If the class relies on an arithmetic value, it should return a comparison based on a number comparison. A string-based class should return a string comparison. However, there is no restriction on what you may compare as long as the *CompareTo()* method returns a value relative to zero.

For a simple *Reverse()* operation, it is enough just to provide the *CompareTo()* method; you do not need to derive the class from the *IComparable* interface. However, the *Sort()* method will throw an *InvalidOperationException* if you do not derive from *IComparable*.

Using Indexers

A class may be a container for other objects. For example, a class may be used to maintain an array of something rather than be part of an array itself. This might occur in a database class where the instance maintains a row in the database and provides a means of returning the database columns.

When you need to implement something like this, you can provide the object with an *indexer*. An indexer makes it possible to index an object as though it were an array when it actually is not. This is handy for cases in which the class object is a container for an object that actually can be indexed.

You can draw some parallels between an indexer and a property. A property looks and acts like a field to a programmer using the class, but it uses *get* and *set* accessor methods to store and retrieve a value. Similarly, an indexer uses *get* and *set* accessors to provide indexes for an internal object.

USE IT   The *Indexer.cs* program that follows shows the use of an indexer in its simplest form. The *Show()* method in the class is included simply to show that the value returned by the indexer is the same as the value in the internal array:

```
//
// Indexer.cs -- Implements an indexer in a class
//
//                Compile this program with the following command line:
//                        C:>csc Indexer.cs
//
namespace nsIndexer
{
    using System;
    class clsMain
    {
        static public void Main ()
        {
            clsIndexed idx = new clsIndexed (10);
            Console.WriteLine ("The value is " + idx[3]);
            idx.Show (3);
        }
    }
    class clsIndexed
    {
```

```
    public clsIndexed (int elements)
    {
        DateTime now = DateTime.Now;
        Random rand = new Random ((int) now.Millisecond);
        Arr = new int [elements];
        for (int x = 0; x < Arr.Length; ++x)
            Arr[x] = rand.Next() % 501;
    }
    int [] Arr;
    public int this[int index]
    {
        get {return (Arr[index]);}
    }
    public void Show (int index)
    {
        Console.WriteLine ("The value is " + Arr[index]);
    }
    }
}
```

The *clsIndexed* class is not an array itself, but after you create an instance in *Main( )*, you then treat it as an array. Doing so returns the value of the internal array using the index you provided.

How Indexers Work

An indexer is much like a property. A property does not allocate any storage to save the value passed in a *set* accessor, nor does it have to retrieve any stored value when the *get* accessor is called.

Similarly, the indexer does not have to operate on an array, as its name might suggest. You may provide any code and save values in any storage in the *set* accessor. The *get* accessor may provide code and return any value. The indexer simply makes the object *appear* to the program as an array. Like a property, you may provide error-checking code in either accessor.

USE IT   In the preceding tip, the example's constructor created an array and filled it with random numbers to show that the indexer is like an index. In the following program, *Seed.cs*, the *get* accessor returns a random number directly using the index to limit the range of the random number. In this code, it's important that you notice that the *get* accessor for an indexer has a value that is passed to it, unlike the *get* accessor for a property:

```
//
// Seed.cs -- Implements an indexer and demonstrates that an indexer
//            does not have to operate on an array
//
//            Compile this program with the following command line:
```

```
//                    C:>csc Seed.cs
//
namespace nsIndexer
{
    using System;
    class clsMain
    {
        static public void Main ()
        {
            clsIndexed idx = new clsIndexed ();
            Console.WriteLine ("The value is " + idx[900]);
        }
    }
    class clsIndexed
    {
        public int this[int Index]
        {
            get
            {
                DateTime now = DateTime.Now;
                Random rand = new Random ((int) now.Millisecond);
                return (rand.Next () % Index);
            }
        }
    }
}
```

The *get* accessor does not return any stored value. It gets a new random number, does a modulo division with the index you passed it, and returns a random number. Each time you access the "array," it returns a new random number between *0* and *Index – 1*.

Getting a random number is better accomplished with a method or even a property rather than an indexer. However, the purpose of this code example is to show that the indexer works much like a property, except that you must pass a value to the indexer.

Declaring an Indexer

You declare an indexer in much the same way that you declare a property. You may provide either a *get* or a *set* accessor, or both. You must always pass an indexer at least one parameter, but you may provide an indexer that takes more than one parameter to make it appear as a multi-dimensional array.

You always declare an indexer using the *this[ ]* syntax. Thus, an indexer always is an instance member. You can declare a *static* property but not a *static* indexer. An indexer must have a return type, and you cannot declare it to be *void*.

Indexers may be overloaded, and if you do so, the rules are the same as those for overloading methods. The return type is not a part of an indexer's signature, and you must provide a parameter list that differs in the data type or the number of parameters.

USE IT To declare an indexer, you first write the access level, which you can do using any of the access keywords that you used with any method, property, or field. Then add the return type, which may not be void. Next add the *this* keyword followed by a set of square brackets. Inside the brackets, you must provide at least one parameter. The parameters are not treated as variables, so you cannot pass an indexer a value using the *ref* or *out* keyword.

Immediately after the brackets, you must provide a set of braces to delimit the scope of the indexer. Inside the braces, you must provide either a *get* or a *set* accessor, or both. The following declares an indexer that implements both accessors:

```
public int this[int index]
{
    get
    {
        // Code to implement the get accessor
    }
    set
    {
        // Code to implement the set accessor
    }
}
```

If you do not provide a *set* accessor, the indexer may not be used as an lvalue in a statement and the indexer becomes read-only. If you do not provide a *get* accessor, the indexer may not be used in an expression or on the right side of an assignment operation.

Using the C# Indexer Wizard

Creating an indexer for a Visual Studio project is as easy as summoning the Indexer Wizard. Not surprisingly, the Indexer Wizard looks similar to the Property Wizard.

USE IT Here's how to use the Indexer Wizard.

1. With a project open in Visual Studio, display the Class View tool window. If it is not visible, press CTRL-SHIFT-C.

2. Open the tree control to display the classes in the project. Select the class to which you want to add an indexer and right-click it.

3. From the popup menu, select Add. Another popup menu will appear. Select Indexer. The Indexer Wizard should appear, as shown in Figure 11-2.

4. Add the information to the Indexer Wizard controls, as described in the section "Declaring an Indexer," earlier in this chapter. Notice that, unlike the Property Wizard, there is no control to enter the name of the indexer. An indexer always uses the name *this*. Notice, too, that unlike the Property Wizard, there is no method to select accessors. The wizard always creates an indexer with both the *get* and *set* accessors. If you want to include only one, remove the unwanted accessor from the code after the wizard creates the indexer.

5. You must provide at least one parameter or the wizard will not let you finish the operation.

6. When you're done, click Finish.

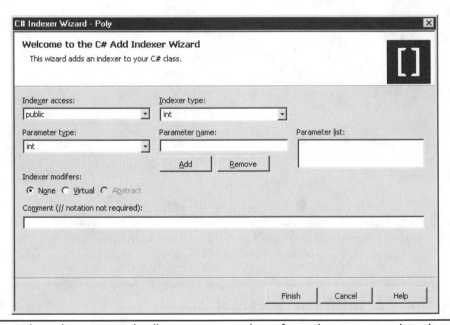

Figure 11.2   The Indexer Wizard will construct an indexer for a class in a Visual Studio project

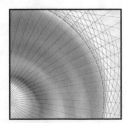

CHAPTER 12

File Operations

TIPS IN THIS CHAPTER

$\mathbf{F}$iles are the primary system of permanent storage on any computer system. The medium for storage may vary from floppy to hard disk, but the result is persistent storage of data in a named object called a *file*.

Regardless of the language, writing any kind of significant programs means that eventually you are going to have to deal with files.

The .NET Common Language Runtime (CLR) provides file support by implementing *streams*. A stream is the flow of data from one point to another. Either or both endpoints of a stream may be on the same computer, or they may be on separate computers. A stream is an abstract sequence of bytes between any two points whose endpoints are not specified.

The .NET streams classes along with support classes and enumerations are located in the *System.IO* namespace. To use the classes without having to fully qualify their names, you may add the following line to your C# program:

```
using System.IO;
```

Visual Studio does not automatically add this line when you create a project. If you plan to use streams in your program, you will have to add it manually.

Introduction to Streams

Effectively, the *endpoints* of a stream are *programs*. Data read by a program travel upstream to the source, and data written by a program travel downstream to the destination. The directions are relative—what is upstream at one end will be downstream at the other end.

An example of a stream is the *standard input*. In Windows, a *driver* program reads the characters you type on the keyboard and delivers the results to the operating system. With operating systems such as MS-DOS, it was possible for programs to read keyboard input directly, but multitasking operating systems such as Windows need to isolate the hardware from the programs.

In the C family, the keyboard driver is one end of the *standard input* stream. At the other end is the program that receives keyboard input. In C#, you open the input stream using the *Console* class and read the stream using the *Read()* and *ReadLine()* methods.

To write to the console—the display screen—your program writes to the *standard output* stream, and information flows downstream to the driver program that controls the display, which then displays the results on the screen.

There are advantages to using streams. First, a program can treat files and devices the same way. For example, a program can use the same stream methods to write to a file that it uses to write to the console. The *Console* class implements its own methods for reading and writing, but eventually these methods call stream methods.

The following program, *WriteOut.cs*, uses a common method to write the same string both to a file and to the console device:

```
// WriteOut.cs -- Writes the same string to a file and to the screen using
//                a common method.
//
```

```
//              Compile this program with the following command line:
//                    C:>csc WriteOut.cs
namespace nsStreams
{
    using System;
// When using streams, you must declare that you are using System.IO
    using System.IO;
    class clsMain
    {
        static public void Main ()
        {
            string str = "This is a line of text\r\n";
// Open the standard output stream
            Stream ostrm = Console.OpenStandardOutput ();
// Open a file. You should protect an open in a try ... catch block
            FileStream fstrm;
            try
            {
                fstrm = new FileStream ("./OutFile.txt",
                                    FileMode.OpenOrCreate);
            }
            catch
            {
                Console.WriteLine ("Failed to open file");
                return;
            }
// Call WriteToStream() to write the same string to both
            WriteToStream (ostrm, str);
            WriteToStream (fstrm, str);
// Close the file.
            fstrm.Close ();
            ostrm.Close ();
        }
        static public void WriteToStream (Stream strm, string text)
        {
            foreach (char ch in text)
            {
                strm.WriteByte ((Byte) ch);
            }
// Flush the output to make it write
            strm.Flush ();
        }
    }
}
```

The *WriteToStream()* method really doesn't care what is on the other end of the stream. It places the character in the stream, and the data flow downstream to the destination, which may be a file or a device.

You also can reassign streams to other files or devices. The stream doesn't care whether the endpoint is a file or a device. The stream must support the operation, however. For example, you cannot assign an output stream to the standard input device and write data to it. Your program will throw a *NotSupportedException* if you attempt to write to an input stream.

The following program, *Redirect.cs*, assigns the standard output stream to a file:

```
// Redirect.cs -- Demonstrates redirecting the Console output to a file
//
//                 Compile this program with the following command line:
//                       C:>csc Redirect.cs
//
using System;
using System.IO;

namespace nsStreams
{
    class clsMain
    {
        static public void Main ()
        {
            FileStream ostrm;
            StreamWriter writer;
            TextWriter oldOut = Console.Out;
            try
            {
                ostrm = new FileStream ("./Redirect.txt",
                                        FileMode.OpenOrCreate,
                                        FileAccess.Write);
                writer = new StreamWriter (ostrm);
            }
            catch (Exception e)
            {
                Console.WriteLine ("Cannot open Redirect.txt for writing");
                Console.WriteLine (e.Message);
                return;
            }
            Console.SetOut (writer);
            Console.WriteLine ("This is a line of text");
            Console.WriteLine ("Everything written to Console.Write() or");
            Console.WriteLine
                        ("Console.WriteLine() will be written to a file");
            Console.SetOut (oldOut);
            writer.Close();
```

```
        ostrm.Close();
        Console.WriteLine ("Done");
    }
  }
}
```

Before redirecting the output, the program first saves the *TextWriter* object associated with the console output. You will need this object to restore the console output when you are finished writing to the file.

The *TextReader* class is designed for character output, where a stream is designed for byte output; to prepare a stream for character output, you associate it with a *TextReader* object. The *TextReader* class is *abstract*, so you cannot create an instance of it directly. For a stream, you use the *StreamWriter* class, which is derived from *TextWriter*.

You should always open a file using a *FileStream* object in a *try ... catch* block. If the open operation fails for any reason, the *FileStream* constructor will throw an exception. There is no error code to examine.

Next, *Redirect.cs* assigns the file stream to the console output device and writes a few lines of text. Any text written to the console device will be written to the file.

Using the *TextReader* object that you saved earlier, the program then reassigns the output to the console, closes the stream and stream writer, and writes a message to the screen that says that the program is finished.

Using the *Stream* Class

In the .NET Framework, the *Stream* class is the base for all classes that implement stream objects. The *Stream* class is an *abstract* class, so you may not create an instance of it directly. Instead, you use it as a base from which to derive any new streams classes.

Some objects in the .NET library classes will return a *Stream* object that has been downcast from other classes. For example, the *Console.OpenStandardOutput()* method that you used in an earlier example returns a *BufferedStream* object that has been downcast to a *Stream* object.

A great many of the member methods and properties are *abstract* as well, and you will need to implement each of these to any derived class. Other methods and properties are *virtual*, and you may override them as needed.

Fortunately, C# provides several classes derived from *Stream*, as shown in the following table. You will rarely, if ever, have to create your own classes derived directly from *Stream*.

Stream Class	Purpose
BufferedStream	Provides buffered reads and writes to other streams. The buffer is a memory block used to store data temporarily, thus reducing calls to the operating system. Not inheritable.
FileStream	Used to read and write files. A *FileStream* object is "byte-oriented" to reflect the normal storage method of most file systems. Provides synchronous and asynchronous operations.

Stream Class	Purpose
MemoryStream	Provides a method of writing to an unsigned byte array in memory instead of to a file. Access to file objects may be restricted for some components, and often *MemoryStream* provides an alternative to temporary files.
NetworkStream	Implements a stream using a network socket. Does not support random access.
CryptoStream	Combines stream operations with cryptographic transformations. The input or output for a *CryptoStream* may be linked with another stream for file or network operations.

You also may link *Stream* objects with *TextReader* or *TextWriter* objects to provide translation between the stream and your program. For example, because strings in C# normally use Unicode and files are usually byte-oriented, you cannot directly assign the results of a read operation to a string. An object derived from *TextReader* may be attached to the stream to provide translation.

Similarly, you cannot assign a string directly to a *FileStream* write operation without breaking it down into individual bytes. A *TextWriter* object attached to the *FileStream* object provides the translation for you.

In most cases, a *FileStream* object provides for random access. You may move to any position in the file and read or write data. The *Stream* class maintains a *public* instance property called *Position* that indicates the location in the stream where the next read or write operation will take place. When you perform an operation, the *Position* value is updated to indicate the position where the operation ended. So, for example, if *Position* is 64 and you read 8 bytes, the *Position* property will contain a value of 72.

An important member of the *Stream* class is the *Seek()* method. Except under certain conditions, such as when you open a stream for appending, you can adjust the *Position* property using *Seek()*. The *Seek()* method requires two arguments: the number of bytes to move and the starting position for the seek operation. A value of *SeekOrigin.Begin* will seek from the beginning of a file, *SeekOrigin.End* will seek from the end of the file, and *SeekOrigin.Current* will seek from the current value of *Position*. A negative value moves backward in a file (toward the beginning of the file), and a positive value moves forward (toward the end of the file).

The following program, *Seek.cs*, opens a file for reading and writing and then writes a couple of lines to the file. Then, using *Seek()*, it moves the pointer to read portions of the file:

```
// Seek.cs -- Demonstrates seeking to a position in a file from the end,
//            middle, and beginning of a file
//
//            Compile this program with the following command line:
//                 C:>csc Seek.cs
using System;
using System.IO;
using System.Text;

namespace nsStreams
{
```

```csharp
class clsMain
{
    const string str1 = "Now is the time for all good men to " +
                        "come to the aid of their Teletype.\r\n";
    const string str2 = "The quick red fox jumps over the " +
                        "lazy brown dog.\r\n";
    static public void Main ()
    {
        FileStream strm;
        try
        {
            strm = new FileStream ("./StrmSeek.txt",
                        FileMode.Create,
                        FileAccess.ReadWrite);
        }
        catch (Exception e)
        {
            Console.WriteLine (e);
            Console.WriteLine ("Cannot open StrmSeek.txt " +
                            "for reading and writing");
            return;
        }
        foreach (char ch in str1)
        {
            strm.WriteByte ((byte) ch);
        }
        foreach (char ch in str2)
        {
            strm.WriteByte ((byte) ch);
        }
// Seek from the beginning of the file
        strm.Seek (str1.Length, SeekOrigin.Begin);
// Read 17 bytes and write to the console.
        byte [] text = new byte [17];
        strm.Read (text, 0, text.Length);
        ShowText (text);
// Seek back 17 bytes and reread.
        strm.Seek (-17, SeekOrigin.Current);
        strm.Read (text, 0, text.Length);
        ShowText (text);
// Seek from the end of the file to the beginning of the second line.
        strm.Seek (-str2.Length, SeekOrigin.End);
```

```
            strm.Read (text, 0, text.Length);
            ShowText (text);
        }
        static void ShowText (byte [] text)
        {
            StringBuilder str = new StringBuilder (text.Length);
            foreach (byte b in text)
            {
                str.Append ((char) b);
            }
            Console.WriteLine (str);
        }
    }
}
```

In this example, all three seek operations take you to the same position in the file.

You cannot use the *Seek()* method on all streams. For example, if you have opened the stream in append mode, or if the endpoint of the stream is a socket or serial port, you cannot move the file position. You can test whether you can use *Seek()* by testing the *CanSeek* property. If *CanSeek* is *true*, you can move the file position.

Using the *FileStream* Class

The *FileStream* class is the workhorse of the stream classes. It performs byte-oriented operations directly on files, and when coupled with a *TextReader* or *TextWriter* object, it can use strings for reading and writing operations.

The nine overloaded constructors let you open a file directly, connect a stream to a file that is already open using a file handle, specify the buffer size, and open the file for asynchronous operations.

At the least, you will have to specify either a *FileAccess* or a *FileMode* in the constructor. The *FileAccess* provides enumerated constants for opening a file for read, write, or read and write access, as shown in the following table.

File Access	Meaning
FileAccess.Read	Opens the file for read access. Data cannot be written to a file using this access.
FileAccess.Write	Opens the file for write access. Data cannot be read from a file using this access.
FileAccess.ReadWrite	Opens the file for both read and write access. This is the same as *FileAccess.Read* | *FileAccess.Write*.

The file mode argument determines whether the constructor will create a file if it does not already exist or throw an exception if the file cannot be opened with the specified access and mode.

The file mode is expressed as a *FileMode* enumerated value, as shown in the following table:

File Access	Operation
Open	Opens an existing file. Throws a *FileNotFoundException* if the file does not exist.
Create	Creates a new file. If the file already exists, it will be overwritten.
OpenOrCreate	Opens a file if it exists or creates a new file if it does not exist.
CreateNew	Specifies that the operating system should create a new file.
Append	Opens the file if it exists and seeks to the end of the file, or creates a new file. May be used only with *FileAccess.Write*. Any attempt to read fails and throws an *ArgumentException*.
Truncate	Opens an existing file and truncates the file to 0 bytes.

To use several of the *FileStream* constructors, you must specify a value to indicate how you want to share the file. The share is also an enumerated value. A value of *FileShare.None* would prevent any other process from opening the file while your program has it open. A value of *FileShare.Read* or *FileShare.Write* will let any other process—or even your own program—open the file for reading or writing, respectively, while your program has the file open. The value *FileShare.ReadWrite* combines the reading and writing sharing.

USE IT Several combinations of access and mode are available, but some of them are mutually exclusive. For example, *FileAccess.Truncate* implies that you have opened the file for writing. If you specify *FileMode.Read* with *FileAccess.Truncate*, your program will throw an *ArgumentException*.

The *Truncate* value also implies that you are opening an existing file. The value takes precedence over the *OpenOrCreate* value, so if you use the two values together and the file does not already exist, the open operation will fail. If you need to use the *OpenOrCreate* flag, you can use the *Stream* class *SetLength()* method to truncate the file once you have opened it—*SetLength()* is an *abstract* method in *Stream* and is overridden by the *FileStream* class:

```
strm.SetLength (0);
```

So far, you have seen many examples of opening a file for reading. The following program, *StrmWrit.cs*, opens a file for writing and truncates it using the *SetLength()* method. Then it accepts text from the keyboard, which it writes to the file, *Write.txt*:

```
// StrmWrit.cs -- Demonstrates opening/creating a file for writing and
//                truncating its length to 0 bytes.
//                Compile this program with the following command line:
//                     C:>csc StrmWrit.cs
using System;
using System.IO;

namespace nsStreams
{
```

```
    class clsMain
    {
        static public void Main ()
        {
            FileStream strm;
// Open or create the file for writing
            try
            {
                strm = new FileStream ("./write.txt",
                                        FileMode.OpenOrCreate,
                                        FileAccess.Write);
            }
// If the open fails, the constructor will throw an exception.
            catch (Exception e)
            {
                Console.WriteLine (e.Message);
                Console.WriteLine ("Cannot open write.txt for writing");
                return;
            }
// Truncate the file using the SetLength() method.
            strm.SetLength (0);
            Console.WriteLine ("Enter text. Type a blank line to exit\r\n");
// Accept text from the keyboard and write it to the file.
            while (true)
            {
                string str = Console.ReadLine ();
                if (str.Length == 0)
                    break;
                byte [] b; // = new byte [str.Length];
                StringToByte (str, out b);
                strm.Write (b, 0, b.Length);
            }
            Console.WriteLine ("Text written to write.txt");
// Close the stream
            strm.Close ();
        }
//
// Convert a string to a byte array, adding a carriage
// return/linefeed to it
        static protected void StringToByte (string str, out byte [] b)
        {
            b = new byte [str.Length + 2];
            int x;
            for (x = 0; x < str.Length; ++x)
```

```
        {
            b[x] = (byte) str[x];
        }
// Add a carriage return/linefeed
        b[x] = 13;
        b[x + 1] = 10;
    }
  }
}
```

If you open the file with the *OpenOrCreate* mode and the file already exists, any text in the file will remain. If you do not write over all of it, any remaining text will persist in the file as "garbage" text. Using *SetLength(0)* assures that any old text is removed.

Using the *MemoryStream* Class to Create Temporary Storage

The *MemoryStream* class is useful when you need temporary storage in your program. Rather than create a temporary file to hold data, the *MemoryStream* class provides faster access. In addition, a system administrator can prevent some applications from creating or opening files, so a temporary file may not be practical.

Using *MemoryStream*, you create a memory-based file on which you may apply stream-type methods including the *Seek()* method. For rapidly changing information, operating on a memory file is much faster than saving the information in a disk-based file. When you are finished updating the information, the *MemoryStream* class includes methods for transferring the contents to a *byte* array or for writing the contents to another stream.

USE IT The *MemoryStream* constructors allow you to create a memory file that initially has a size of 0, or to attach the *MemoryStream* object to an existing *byte* array or to a portion of an existing *byte* array. When you attach the stream to an existing *byte* array, you can set the *CanWrite* property to *false*, thus making the stream read-only.

In addition, you can use the *MemoryStream* object's buffer as the target for a read operation from another stream. The following program, *MemStrm.cs*, opens a configuration file and then creates a *MemoryStream* object to hold the contents. It then reads the file into the *MemoryStream* object:

```
// MemStrm.cs -- Demonstrates reading a file into memory, attaching it to a
//                MemoryStream and using stream methods to access the contents
//
//                Compile this program with the following command line:
//                     C:>csc MemStrm.cs
using System;
```

```csharp
using System.IO;

namespace nsStreams
{
    class clsMain
    {
        const string USA = "[USA]";
        const string PhoneEntry = "Phone_number=";
        static public void Main ()
        {
            FileStream cfg;
            try
            {
                cfg = new FileStream ("./config.ini",
                                    FileMode.Open,
                                    FileAccess.ReadWrite);
            }
            catch (FileNotFoundException)
            {
                Console.WriteLine ("Cannot find ./config.ini");
                return;
            }
            catch (Exception e)
            {
                Console.WriteLine (e.Message);
                Console.WriteLine ("Cannot find ./config.ini");
                return;
            }
            MemoryStream mem = new MemoryStream ((int) cfg.Length);
            cfg.Read (mem.GetBuffer(), 0, (int) cfg.Length);
            int pos = FindInBuffer (USA, 0, mem.GetBuffer());
            if (pos < 0)
            {
                Console.WriteLine ("Could not find match in buffer");
            }
            else
            {
                pos = FindInBuffer (PhoneEntry, pos, mem.GetBuffer());
                if (pos < 0)
                {
                    Console.WriteLine ("Could not find phone number");
                }
                else
                {
```

```
                    string NewPhone = "1888555-9876";
                    mem.Seek (pos + PhoneEntry.Length, SeekOrigin.Begin);
                    for (int x = 0; x < NewPhone.Length; ++x)
                    {
                        mem.WriteByte ((byte) NewPhone[x]);
                    }
                    cfg.SetLength (0);
                    cfg.Write (mem.GetBuffer(), 0,
                            (int) mem.GetBuffer().Length);
                }
            }
            cfg.Flush ();
            cfg.Close ();
            mem.Close ();
        }
//
// Find a string of characters in a buffer of type byte
        static int FindInBuffer (string ToFind, int start, byte [] buf)
        {
            for (int x = start; x < buf.Length; ++x)
            {
                if (buf[x] == (byte) ToFind[0])
                {
                    int y;
                    for (y = 1; y < ToFind.Length; ++y)
                    {
                        if ((x + y) >= buf.Length)
                            break;
                        if (buf[x + y] != (byte) ToFind[y])
                            break;
                    }
                    if (y == ToFind.Length)
                    {
                        return (x);
                    }
                }
            }
            return (-1);
        }
    }
}
```

After reading the configuration file contents into the *MemoryStream* object's buffer, the program searches for a phone number entry and changes it. Then it writes the configuration file back to disk.

Using the *NetworkStream* Class to Create a Network Connection

The *NetworkStream* class provides much the same services as the *MemoryStream* class, except it provides services for a network connection rather than for storage. Unlike the other *Stream*-derived classes, however, you cannot use the *Position* property. Any attempt to read or set the stream position will throw a *NotSupportedException*.

The MSDN does not provide much information about implementing the *NetworkStream,* and examples of it are extremely rare, and perhaps non-existent. Even some books that claim to be professional-level books skirt by this class. However, you can apply standard socket concepts to create a connection with a server and then open the stream and write data to it.

 To demonstrate the *NetworkStream* class, you will need two programs: a server program to listen for a connection and a client program to send data to the client. The following program is also a good example of how to set up a client/server relationship in C#.

NStrSvr.cs is the server program. It creates a socket on port 2048 and then waits for a connection. Once the connection has been established, it opens a *NetworkStream* object on the socket.

```
// NStrSvr.cs -- Acts as a server program to demonstrate the use of
//               the NetworkStream class.
//
//               Compile this program with the following command line:
//                   C:>csc NStrSvr.cs
//
// To use this program with the companion client program, first start
// the server (this program), then connect to it using the client program
// in a separate console window.
// As you enter lines from the client, they will appear in the server
// console window. To end the session, press <Enter> on a blank line.
//
using System;
using System.IO;
using System.Net;
using System.Net.Sockets;

namespace nsStreams
{
    class clsMain
    {
        static public void Main ()
        {
            IPAddress hostadd = Dns.Resolve("localhost").AddressList[0];
            Console.WriteLine ("Host is " + hostadd.ToString());
```

```csharp
        IPEndPoint EPhost = new IPEndPoint(hostadd, 2048);

        Socket s = new Socket(AddressFamily.InterNetwork,
                              SocketType.Stream,
                              ProtocolType.Tcp );
        s.Bind (EPhost);
        s.Listen (0);
        Socket sock = s.Accept();
        NetworkStream strm =
                      new NetworkStream (sock, FileAccess.ReadWrite);
        byte [] b = new byte [256];
        while (true)
        {
            for (int x = 0; x < b.Length; ++x)
               b[x] = 0;
            strm.Read (b, 0, b.Length);
            if (b[0] == 4)
                break;
            string str = ByteToString (b, 0);
            Console.WriteLine (str);
        }
        strm.Close ();
        sock.Close ();
        s.Close ();
    }
//
// Convert a buffer of type byte to a string
    static string ByteToString (byte [] b, int start)
    {
        string str = "";
        for (int x = start; x < b.Length; ++x)
        {
            if (b[x] == 0)
                break;
            str += (char) b [x];
        }
        return (str);
    }
  }
}
```

To create the *NetworkStream* object, you must first establish a connection on a valid socket. The stream object does not own the socket, so closing the stream does not close the socket. You need to perform these operations in separate statements.

You will use the client program, *NStrCli.cs*, to type strings that will be passed to the server program. Each time you type a line and press the ENTER key, the string will appear in the server window. The client listing follows:

```csharp
// NStrCli.cs -- Acts as a client program to demonstrate the use of
//               the NetworkStream class.
//
//               Compile this program with the following command line:
//                    C:>csc NStrCli.cs
//
// To use this program with the companion server program, first start
// the server, then connect to it using the client program (this program)
// in a separate console window.
// As you enter lines from the client, they will appear in the server
// console window. To end the session, press <Enter> on a blank line.
//
using System;
using System.IO;
using System.Net;
using System.Net.Sockets;

namespace nsStreams
{
    class clsMain
    {
        static public void Main ()
        {
            IPAddress hostadd = Dns.Resolve("localhost").AddressList[0];
            Console.WriteLine ("Host is " + hostadd.ToString());
            IPEndPoint EPhost = new IPEndPoint(hostadd, 2048);

            Socket s = new Socket(AddressFamily.InterNetwork,
                              SocketType.Stream,
                              ProtocolType.Tcp );
            string str = "Hello, World!";
            byte [] b;
            StringToByte (out b, str);
            s.Connect (EPhost);
            NetworkStream strm = new NetworkStream (s, FileAccess.ReadWrite);
            if (!s.Connected)
            {
                Console.WriteLine ("Unable to connect to host");
                return;
            }
            strm.Write (b, 0, b.Length);
```

```
            while (b[0] != 4)
            {
                string text = Console.ReadLine ();
                if (text.Length == 0)
                {
                    b[0] = 4;
                    strm.Write (b, 0, 1);
                    break;
                }
                StringToByte (out b, text);
                strm.Write (b, 0, text.Length);
            }
            strm.Close ();
            s.Close ();
        }
//
// Convert a buffer of type byte to a string
        static string ByteToString (byte [] b, int start)
        {
            string str = "";
            for (int x = start; x < b.Length; ++x)
            {
                str += (char) b [x];
            }
            return (str);
        }
//
// Convert a buffer of type string to byte
        static void StringToByte (out byte [] b, string str)
        {
            b = new byte [str.Length];
            for (int x = 0; x < str.Length; ++x)
            {
                b[x] = (byte) str [x];
            }
        }
    }
}
```

These programs both assume they are running on the same machine. When you start either program, you should see a line identifying the host address as 127.0.0.1, which is the localhost feedback address.

To run these programs, you should open two console windows. They do not have to be Visual Studio console windows. Start the server program first. Without the server program running, the client will be unable to establish a connection and will throw an exception. To keep the programs short, no exception handling is included.

When the client makes a connection with the server, it will send the string "Hello, World!" This string should appear in the server console window to let you know the connection is ready.

Using the *BufferedStream* Class to Buffer a Stream's Input or Output

The *BufferedStream* class provides intermediate storage for another stream. You may read and write a buffered stream as though it were an ordinary stream, but nothing is transferred to the underlying stream until you flush the buffered stream. This allows you to commit data to a stream, yet still be able to edit the contents of the stream before you actually write the information to disk or to a device at the other end of the underlying stream.

The *Console* class uses buffered streams to interact with the user. As you type a line in response to the *Console.ReadLine()* method, the *Console* class provides for command-line editing. The data is not passed back to the calling program until you press the ENTER key.

USE IT   The following program, *BufStrm.cs*, writes two strings to a buffered stream. The second line begins with a lowercase letter, so before committing the text to a file, the program backs up and corrects the error:

```
// BufStrm.cs -- Demonstrates the use of a buffered stream to serve
//               as intermediate data holder for another stream.
//
//               Compile this program with the following command line:
//                     C:>csc BufStrm.cs
using System;
using System.IO;

namespace nsStreams
{
    class clsMain
    {
        static public void Main ()
        {
            FileStream strm;
            try
            {
                strm = new FileStream ("./BufStrm.txt",
```

```
                                     FileMode.OpenOrCreate,
                                     FileAccess.Write);
        }
        catch (Exception e)
        {
            Console.WriteLine (e.Message);
            Console.WriteLine ("Cannot open ./BufStrm.txt");
            return;
        }
        strm.SetLength (0);
        BufferedStream bstrm = new BufferedStream (strm);
        string str = "Now is the time for all good men to " +
                     "come to the aid of their Teletype.\r\n";
        byte [] b;
        StringToByte (out b, str);
        bstrm.Write (b, 0, b.Length);
// Save the current position to fix an error.
        long Pos = bstrm.Position;
        Console.WriteLine ("The buffered stream position is "
                           + bstrm.Position);
        Console.WriteLine ("The underlying stream position is "
                           + strm.Position);
        str = "the quick red fox jumps over the lazy brown dog.\r\n";
        StringToByte (out b, str);
        bstrm.Write (b, 0, b.Length);
        Console.WriteLine ("\r\nThe buffered stream position is " +
                           bstrm.Position);
        Console.WriteLine ("The underlying stream position is still "
                           + strm.Position);
// Fix the lowercase letter at the beginning of the second string
        bstrm.Seek (Pos, SeekOrigin.Begin);
        b[0] = (byte) 'T';
        bstrm.Write (b, 0, 1);
// Flush the buffered stream. This will force the data into the
// underlying stream.
        bstrm.Flush ();
        bstrm.Close ();
        strm.Close ();
    }
//
// Convert a buffer of type string to byte
    static void StringToByte (out byte [] b, string str)
    {
        b = new byte [str.Length];
        for (int x = 0; x < str.Length; ++x)
```

```
                {
                    b[x] = (byte) str [x];
                }
            }
        }
    }
}
```

By examining the data file *BufStrm.txt*, you will see that the lowercase letter at the beginning of the second line was corrected before the text was written to the file.

Performing Asynchronous I/O

Stream reading and writing may be done *synchronously* or *asynchronously*. The default is to perform synchronous reading and writing when you open a stream.

Reading from and writing to the console is an example of synchronous I/O. Your program calls a method to write to the console, *Console.Write()* or *Console.WriteLine()*, or a method to read from the keyboard such as *Console.ReadLine()*. The program waits in the method call until the operation completes; then it returns to the next statement in the program.

Most reading and writing can be done synchronously, but that is not always the case. Often you will want your program to perform other tasks while the operation is being performed. Synchronous I/O is particularly undesirable when you open a device for which the incoming data may be unpredictable, such as a serial port with which you are accessing a modem.

When you are using a modem line, you need to monitor the line continuously, yet still make your program responsive to the user. You can do this with asynchronous reads and writes using the *BeginRead()* and *BeginWrite()* methods.

 The following program, *Async.cs*, reads a file asynchronously and then writes the data read to the screen. The program first starts a read operation using the *BeginRead()* method, and then it continues with the next statement. When the read completes, the method calls a completion method. To simulate other tasks, the program sleeps for a quarter of a second before successive reads:

```
// Async.cs -- Asynchronously reads a stream
//
//              Compile this program with the following command line:
//                   C:>csc Async.cs
//
using System;
using System.IO;
using System.Threading;

namespace nsStreams
{
    class clsMain
```

```csharp
{
    static Byte [] data;
    static bool bDone = true;

    static public void Main (string [] args)
    {
        if (args.Length == 0)
        {
            Console.WriteLine ("Please enter a file name");
            return;
        }
        FileStream istrm;
        try
        {
            istrm = new FileStream (args[0], FileMode.Open,
                                    FileAccess.Read, FileShare.Read,
                                    64, true);
        }
        catch (FileNotFoundException)
        {
            Console.WriteLine (args[0] + " was not found");
            return;
        }
        catch (Exception)
        {
            Console.WriteLine ("Cannot open " + args[0] +
                               " for reading");
            return;
        }
        data = new Byte[64];
        AsyncCallback cb = new AsyncCallback (ShowText);
        long Length = istrm.Length;
        int count = 0;
        while (true)
        {
            if (Length == istrm.Position)
                break;
            if (bDone)
            {
                bDone = false;
                istrm.BeginRead (data, 0, data.Length, cb, count);
                ++count;
            }
            Thread.Sleep (250);
        }
```

```
            istrm.Close ();
        }
        static public void ShowText (IAsyncResult result)
        {
            for (int x = 0; x < data.Length; ++x)
            {
                if (data[x] == 0)
                    break;
                Console.Write ((char) data[x]);
                data[x] = 0;
            }
            bDone = true;
        }
    }
}
```

When you compile and run *Async.cs*, the output will appear to be jerky because of the quarter-second sleep. Instead of merely sleeping, however, your program could be performing other tasks.

To use asynchronous operations, you should open the file with the asynchronous flag set to *true*. This is done in the constructor. Then you need to create an *AsyncCallback* delegate, which is accomplished using the following statement:

```
AsyncCallback cb = new AsyncCallback (ShowText);
```

The argument to the *AsyncCallback* constructor is the name of the method that the asynchronous operation will call when it completes. C++ programmers may recognize this as being similar to *overlapped I/O*.

Writing to the console is performed in the callback method. When it finishes writing, the method sets a flag indicating that it is done, and the operation ends.

There are some variations on the same operation. The *BeginRead()* and *BeginWrite()* methods return an *IAsyncResult* object, which you can then pass to a *EndRead()* or *EndWrite()* method call. This will make your program wait for the operation to complete. In addition, these methods return the number of bytes actually read or written. Add a variable for this object and change the loop so that it reads as follows:

```
IAsyncResult result = null;
while (true)
{
    bDone = false;
    result = istrm.BeginRead (data, 0, data.Length, cb, count);
    ++count;
    Thread.Sleep (250);
    if (istrm.EndRead (result) == 0)
        break;
}
```

Now your program will sleep only once and then wait for the operation to complete. The output will still be jerky, but you can remove the *Thread.Sleep()* call and the operation will complete. In practice, your program would perform some other operations instead of sleeping. In addition, instead of testing whether the stream pointer is at the end of the file, the last *BeginRead()* operation will return *0 bytes read* when it is at the end of the stream and your program knows the entire file has been read.

The last parameter to the *BeginRead()* and *BeginWrite()* methods accepts any object derived from the *object* class, so you can use it effectively to pass any object to the operation. The object is available in the callback function as *IAsyncResult.AsyncState*. According to the MSDN documentation, this object should distinguish one read from other. The preceding sample code simply passes a different number for this argument, which would allow you to have multiple asynchronous operations pending.

Discarding Unnecessary Data Using the *Null* Field as a Bit Bucket

Although the *Stream* class is *abstract* and you cannot create an instance of it directly, it does contain methods and fields that are inherited by derived classes. In addition, it contains a *static* field that incorporates a special stream, named the *Null* field—the perennial "bit bucket," or black hole, of data. Everything can go into it, but nothing can come out.

You can write to the *Null* stream as you would any other stream, and the data will not appear anywhere. You can read from it, it always will return nothing, and your program will not wait for any data to be returned. UNIX buffs will recognize the *Null* stream as similar to the */dev/null* device.

USE IT ▸ The stream is a *static* member of *Stream*, so you identify it as *Stream.Null*. The following program, *NullStrm.cs*, shows how to read to and write from this special stream:

```
// NullStrm.cs -- Demonstrates the use of the Null stream as a bit bucket.
//
//              Compile this program with the following command line:
//                   C:>csc NullStrm.cs
//
using System;
using System.IO;
namespace nsStreams
{
    class clsMain
    {
        static public void Main ()
        {
            byte [] b = new byte [256];
            int count = Stream.Null.Read (b, 0, b.Length);
            Console.WriteLine ("Read {0} bytes", count);
            string str = "Hello, World!";
```

```
        StringToByte (out b, str);
        Stream.Null.Write (b, 0, b.Length);

// Attach a reader and writer to the Null stream
        StreamWriter writer = new StreamWriter (Stream.Null);
        StreamReader reader = new StreamReader (Stream.Null);
        writer.Write ("This is going nowhere");
        str = reader.ReadToEnd ();
        Console.Write ("The string read contains {0} bytes", str.Length);
    }
//
// Convert a buffer of type string to byte
    static void StringToByte (out byte [] b, string str)
    {
        b = new byte [str.Length];
        for (int x = 0; x < str.Length; ++x)
        {
            b[x] = (byte) str [x];
        }
    }
  }
}
```

Even attaching *StreamReader* and *StreamWriter* objects to the stream has no effect. The program neither hangs waiting for input nor writes the information anywhere. The *Null* stream is handy for temporarily redirecting stream input and output when you do not need to use the information.

Exploiting the *TextReader* and *TextWriter* Abstract Classes

Streams are byte-oriented objects. The 8-bit byte is the basic unit of storage on a personal computer. You count the size of your hard drive in bytes (lately, *giga*bytes) and the amount of memory in your computer in bytes. You do not count these sizes in, say, characters, because the size of a character is not constant.

C# uses a 16-bit character, and strings store text in 16-bit units. The union of characters and strings with stream objects does not come easily. To write a string to a stream, you have to convert it to an array of bytes. Similarly, to retrieve a string from a stream, you convert an array of bytes to characters.

To help overcome this dichotomy between the bytes of the real world and the larger character size, C# provides a set of classes to make the translation easier. The *TextReader* class is designed to process input in terms of C# characters, and the *TextWriter* class is designed to work in the reverse direction.

Both the *TextReader* and *TextWriter* classes are *abstract*, so you may not create instances of them directly. They do, however, provide containers for the underlying methods that you will need to interface streams and strings.

USE IT To derive a class from *TextReader*, you need to implement the *Read()* and *Peek()* methods. The *Peek()* method looks ahead one character in the text stream and returns it without actually reading it from the stream.

To derive a class from *TextWriter*, you need implement only the *Write()* method.

Unless you have some specific translation and manipulations to perform, you will not often need to derive your own classes. The .NET Framework provides a connection between strings and streams with the *StreamReader* and *StreamWriter* classes.

Using *StreamReader* and *StreamWriter*

The classes derived from *TextReader* and *TextWriter* make operating on strings much more convenient. For streams, the classes of interest are *StreamReader* and *StreamWriter*.

These classes also make connecting streams and strings easier, but they also provide the basis for converting between various character encoding systems. C# was designed to be an international language, and not all of the characters in use throughout the world can be described in the 7-bit character encoding used for the ASCII character set.

A character set is not the same as character encoding, although for the ASCII characters they are virtually the same. For example, the Unicode encoding scheme can describe more than 65,000 characters, but it is unlikely that you would find any personal computers making use of all of these characters. More than likely, a group of selected characters—the character set—will be available for use on the keyboard and display.

To use *StreamReader* and *StreamWriter*, you first open a stream, which may be constructed from any of the classes derived from *Stream* or your own derived class. Then you construct a *StreamReader* or *StreamWriter* object, specifying the stream in the constructor:

```
FileStream strm = new FileStream (<file name>, <file mode>, <file access>);
StreamReader reader = new StreamReader (strm);
StreamWriter writer = new StreamWriter (strm);
```

You also can include an encoding system in the constructor. The encoding does not have to be the same for both the *StreamReader* and *StreamWriter* objects.

USE IT The following program, *StrmRdr.cs*, implements a *StreamReader* object to read text directly from a file into a string:

```
// StrmRdr.cs -- Demonstrates attaching a StreamReader object to a stream
//
//          Compile this program with the following command line:
//              C:>csc StrmRdr.cs
```

```csharp
using System;
using System.IO;

namespace nsStreams
{
    class clsMain
    {
        static public void Main (string [] args)
        {
            if (args.Length == 0)
            {
                Console.WriteLine ("Please enter a file name");
                return;
            }
            FileStream strm;
            StreamReader reader;
            try
            {
// Create the stream
                strm = new FileStream (args[0], FileMode.Open,
                                            FileAccess.Read);
// Link a stream reader to the stream
                reader = new StreamReader (strm);
            }
            catch (Exception e)
            {
                Console.WriteLine (e.Message);
                Console.WriteLine ("Cannot open " + args[0]);
                return;
            }
            while (reader.Peek () >= 0)
            {
                string text = reader.ReadLine ();
                Console.WriteLine (text);
            }
            reader.Close ();
            strm.Close ();
        }
    }
}
```

Now that is a lot easier than reading the file into a byte array and then having to convert it to a string.

The *StreamReader* class also contains a method to read the entire contents of a file in one statement:

```csharp
string str = reader.ReadToEnd ();
```

This is a handy method if you are reading the file to add text to an edit control. The entire contents of the file are contained in a single *string* object.

Using the *StreamWriter* is just as easy and simplifies your programming even more, as shown in the following program, *StrmWrtr.cs*:

```csharp
// StrmWrtr.cs -- Demonstrates attaching a StreamWriter object to a stream
//
//                Compile this program with the following command line:
//                      C:>csc StrmWrtr.cs
using System;
using System.IO;


namespace nsStreams
{
    class clsMain
    {
        static public void Main (string [] args)
        {
            if (args.Length == 0)
            {
                Console.WriteLine ("Please enter a file name");
                return;
            }
            FileStream strm;
            StreamWriter writer;
            try
            {
// Create the stream
                strm = new FileStream (args[0], FileMode.OpenOrCreate,
                                        FileAccess.Write);
// Link a stream reader to the stream
                writer = new StreamWriter (strm);
            }
            catch (Exception e)
            {
                Console.WriteLine (e.Message);
                Console.WriteLine ("Cannot open " + args[0]);
                return;
            }
            strm.SetLength (0);
            while (true)
            {
                string str = Console.ReadLine ();
                if (str.Length == 0)
                    break;
                writer.WriteLine (str);
```

```
                }
                writer.Close ();
                strm.Close ();
            }
        }
    }
}
```

As mentioned, you can attach an encoding scheme when you create the *StreamReader* or *StreamWriter* object. You can attach both a reader and a writer object to the same stream if you opened the stream for reading and writing.

USE IT   By opening two streams, you can use the reader and writer objects to convert from one character encoding scheme to another. The following program, *StrmCnvt.cs*, opens a file in ASCII encoding and writes it to another file in Unicode encoding:

```
// StrmCnvt.cs -- Uses StreamReader and StreamWriter object using different
//                encoding to translate a file from one to another
//
//                Compile this program with the following command line:
//                      C:>csc StrmCnvt.cs
using System;
using System.IO;
using System.Text;

namespace nsStreams
{
    class clsMain
    {
        static public void Main ()
        {
            FileStream istrm;
            FileStream ostrm;
            StreamReader reader;
            StreamWriter writer;
            try
            {
// Open the input file
                istrm = new FileStream ("./StrmRdr.txt", FileMode.Open,
                                                    FileAccess.Read);
// Link a stream reader to the stream
                reader = new StreamReader (istrm, Encoding.ASCII);
            }
            catch (Exception e)
            {
                Console.WriteLine (e.Message);
                Console.WriteLine ("Cannot open ./StrmRdr.txt");
```

```
                    return;
              }
              try
              {
// Open the output file
              ostrm = new FileStream ("./StrmRdr.Uni",
                                      FileMode.OpenOrCreate,
                                      FileAccess.Write);
// Link a stream reader to the stream
              writer = new StreamWriter (ostrm, Encoding.Unicode);
              }
              catch (Exception e)
              {
                  Console.WriteLine (e.Message);
                  Console.WriteLine ("Cannot open ./StrmRdr.Uni");
                  return;
              }
              ostrm.SetLength (0);
              while (reader.Peek () >= 0)
              {
                  string str = reader.ReadLine ();
                  writer.WriteLine (str);
              }
              reader.Close ();
              istrm.Close ();
              writer.Close ();
              ostrm.Close ();
          }
      }
}
```

When you run this program, it will read the file named *StrmCnvt.txt* in ASCII encoding format and rewrite it to *StrmCnvt.Uni* in Unicode encoding. The encoding conversion is almost automatic, and it's certainly easier than anything you will find in most C++ class libraries.

Opening a File Using the *FileOpen* Common Dialog

In the preceding program, the user must enter a file name on the command line. If the user does not enter a file name, the programs sends a message telling the user to type a file name as part of the command, and then the program ends.

Instead of having the program exit when the user forgets to enter a file name, you could write a prompt to give the user a chance to enter a file name before closing the program. In Windows, however, such prompts are counterintuitive. Users expect Windows programs to prompt them with Windows objects, such as dialog boxes or message boxes.

Every Windows system has a library of dialog boxes that any program may access, called the *common dialogs*. These include those that prompt the user to enter a file name to open or save, that help the user print, and that provide searching options. The .NET Framework supports the common dialogs through a set of classes that implement the dialog boxes and return information entered by the user to your program.

All the common dialog boxes are derived from the *abstract* class *CommonDialog* in the *System.Windows.Forms* namespace. The *FileDialog* class is the base class for the *OpenFileDialog* and *SaveFileDialog* classes.

USE IT   The common dialogs are a topic for Chapter 17, but the file dialog boxes contain methods for opening files and returning streams to the open files that you can learn about now. The *OpenFile* method in the *OpenFileDialog* opens a read-only file and returns a *Stream* object. The *OpenFile* method in the *SaveFileDialog* class opens the file in read/write mode and returns a *Stream* object.

The method is similar in both dialog boxes. Once you open the file, you can attach a *StreamReader* object to the stream or, in the case of the *SaveFileDialog*, you can attach a *StreamWriter* object as well. Figure 12-1, for example, illustrates the Open dialog box displayed by the *OpenFileDialog* class *ShowDialog*.

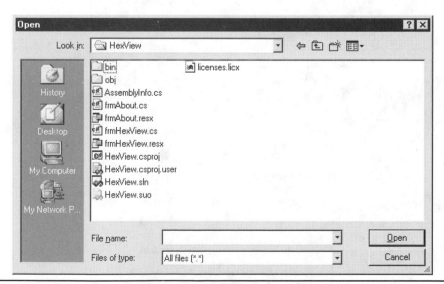

Figure 12.1   Using a common dialog to prompt the user for a file name

The following command-line program, *ReadIn.cs*, uses an *OpenFileDialog* to prompt the user for a file name and uses the *FileOpen* method to open a stream and read the file:

```
// ReadIn.cs -- Demonstrates using an OpenFileDialog to prompt for a
//              file name and to open a file
//
//              Compile this program with the following command line:
//                  C:>csc ReadIn.cs
using System;
using System.IO;
using System.Windows.Forms;

namespace nsStreams
{
    class clsMain
    {
        static public void Main (string [] args)
        {
            OpenFileDialog fileOpen = new OpenFileDialog ();
            if (args.Length == 0)
            {
                fileOpen.InitialDirectory = ".\\";
                fileOpen.Filter = "Text files (*.txt)|*.txt|" +
                            "All files (*.*)|*.*";
                fileOpen.FilterIndex = 1;
                fileOpen.RestoreDirectory = true;
                if (fileOpen.ShowDialog () == DialogResult.Cancel)
                {
                    return;
                }
            }
            else
            {
                fileOpen.FileName = args[0];
            }
            Stream strm;
            StreamReader reader;
            try
            {
                strm = fileOpen.OpenFile ();
                reader = new StreamReader (strm);
            }
```

```
            catch (Exception e)
            {
                string Message = e.Message + "\n\nCannot open "
                                    + fileOpen.FileName;
                MessageBox.Show (Message, "Open error",
                                    MessageBoxButtons.OK,
                                    MessageBoxIcon.Error);
                return;
            }
            Console.Write (reader.ReadToEnd ());
            reader.Close ();
            strm.Close ();
        }
    }
}
```

The *OpenFileDialog* will return the full path for the file, so you do not have to build the path once the user selects a file. You should, however, check to determine whether the user clicks the Cancel button. In this case, the dialog box will return *DialogResult.Cancel* and you can abort the operation. The only other possible value for the dialog's return value is *DialogResult.OK*.

The filter property gives you the means to separate certain file types or to restrict the user's access to certain file types. For example, if you do not want the user to be able to open anything other than files with a *.txt* extension, you could eliminate the portion of the filter that lists all file types (*.*). The resulting filter would look like the following:

```
fileOpen.Filter = "Text files (*.txt)|*.txt"
```

To add an entry to the filter, make it a part of the *Filter* string using the following syntax:

```
"<Display Text>|<File Specification>"
```

Each entry is displayed as a selection in the Files of Type selection box (a combo box). You separate entries in the string with a vertical bar (|), but do not place a vertical bar at the beginning or end of the entire string. If you do, the program will throw an *ArgumentException*.

To add a line for C# files to the dialog box as the second entry, change the line in the preceding example to read as follows:

```
fileOpen.Filter = "txt files (*.txt)|*.txt" +
                "|C# files (*.cs)| *.cs" +
                "|All files (*.*)|*.*";
```

The *FilterIndex* property determines which of the entries will be displayed when the dialog box first appears. The first entry in the string has an index of 1, which is the default. If you enter 0 for this property, the first entry will be displayed.

Using the *File* and *FileInfo* classes

The introduction to the *StreamReader* and *StreamWriter* classes makes reading from and writing to files much easier than using arrays. For manipulating files—such as copying or renaming, checking whether a file exists, or getting its status—the *File* class is another object that is nice to know about.

The *File* class is a *sealed* class, so you cannot derive any new classes from it. All of its members are *static* methods (it contains no properties), so you do not even need to create an instance of *File* to use its members.

In the previous examples, you created a *FileStream* object and later created a reader or writer object to attach to it. The *File* class lets you first check whether a file exists, and then you can open it, create the stream, and attach a *StreamReader* or *StreamWriter* object at the same time.

USE IT   The following program, *Exists.cs*, shows how you can test whether a file exists before trying to open it. As with any other file open, it is a good idea to perform the operation in a *try ... catch* block.

```
// Exists.cs -- Uses methods in the File class to check whether a file exists.
//              If it exists, it then opens and reads the file to the console.
//
//              Compile this program with the following command line:
//                   C:>csc Exists.cs
using System;
using System.IO;

namespace nsStreams
{
    class clsMain
    {
        static public void Main (string [] args)
        {
            if (args.Length == 0)
            {
                Console.WriteLine ("Please enter a file name");
                return;
            }
            if (!File.Exists (args[0]))
            {
                Console.WriteLine (args[0] + " does not exist");
                return;
            }
            StreamReader reader;
// Open the file using the File class method. This will create the
// stream and reader objects.
            try
            {
```

```
                    reader = File.OpenText (args[0]);
                }
                catch (Exception e)
                {
                    Console.WriteLine (e.Message);
                    Console.WriteLine ("Cannot open " + args[0]);
                    return;
                }
                while (reader.Peek() >= 0)
                {
                    Console.WriteLine (reader.ReadLine ());
                }
                reader.Close ();
            }
        }
    }
```

To copy a file, you don't even need to open the file and read it. The *File.Copy()* method takes care of all of the details, as shown in the following program, *cp.cs*:

```
// cp.cs -- Uses methods in the File class to check whether a file exists.
//          If it exists, it then opens and reads the file to the console.
//
//          Compile this program with the following command line:
//              C:>csc cp.cs
using System;
using System.IO;

namespace nsStreams
{
    class clsMain
    {
        static public void Main (string [] args)
        {
            if (args.Length < 2)
            {
                Console.WriteLine ("usage: cp <copy from> <copy to>");
                return;
            }
            if (!File.Exists (args[0]))
            {
                Console.WriteLine (args[0] + " does not exist");
                return;
            }
// If the destination file already exists, check whether its OK
```

```
// to overwrite it.
            bool bOverwrite = false;
            if (File.Exists (args[1]))
            {
                Console.Write (args[1] +
                                " already exists. Overwrite [Y/N]? ");
                string reply = Console.ReadLine ();
                char ch = (char) (reply[0] & (char) 0xdf);
                if (ch != 'Y')
                    return;
                bOverwrite = true;
            }
            File.Copy (args[0], args[1], bOverwrite);
        }
    }
}
```

On UNIX and 32-bit versions of Windows, the directory entry for a file records three important times. The time the file was created is permanently stored with the directory entry. Each time you access a file, the time of the access is recorded as well. If you change a file, the time you modified it is saved as part of the directory entry.

The *File* class has *static* methods to retrieve these times. The following program, *Status.cs*, shows examples of reading and displaying the times:

```
// Status.cs -- Uses methods in the File class to check the
//              status of a file.
//
//              Compile this program with the following command line:
//                  C:>csc Status.cs
using System;
using System.IO;

namespace nsStreams
{
    class clsMain
    {
        static public void Main (string [] args)
        {
            if (args.Length == 0)
            {
                Console.WriteLine ("Please enter a file name");
                return;
            }
            if (!File.Exists (args[0]))
```

```
            {
                Console.WriteLine (args[0] + " does not exist");
                return;
            }
            DateTime created = File.GetCreationTime (args[0]);
            DateTime accessed = File.GetLastAccessTime (args[0]);
            DateTime written = File.GetLastWriteTime (args[0]);
            Console.WriteLine ("File " + args[0] + ":");
            string str = created.ToString();
            int index = str.IndexOf (" ");
            Console.WriteLine ("\tCreated on " + str.Substring (0, index)
                            + " at " + str.Substring (index + 1));
            str = accessed.ToString();
            index = str.IndexOf (" ");
            Console.WriteLine ("\tLast accessed on "
                            + str.Substring (0, index) + " at "
                            + str.Substring (index + 1));
            str = written.ToString();
            index = str.IndexOf (" ");
            Console.WriteLine ("\tLast written on "
                            + str.Substring (0, index)
                            + " at " + str.Substring (index + 1));
        }
    }
}
```

Using the *FileStream* class, you must first create a stream and then attach a *TextReader* or *TextWriter* object to the stream after you open the file. The *File* and *FileInfo* classes bypass that step and let you create a reader or writer object directly when you open a file. Like the *File* class, *FileInfo* also provides methods for manipulating files, such as copying, deleting, renaming, and moving files.

The *FileInfo* is a companion class to the *File* class. The *File* class contains only *static* members, and the *FileInfo* class contains only instance members. Therefore, you must create a *FileInfo* object before using any of the members.

Many of the methods in the *File* and *FileInfo* classes are the same and perform identical functions, but for repeated operations on a single file, the *FileInfo* class is usually more efficient. Because it contains only *static* members, the *File* class performs security checks each time you use a method to make sure you have proper access to a file. The *FileInfo* normally performs the security checks when you create an instance of the class. Until you destroy the *FileInfo* object and re-open a file with a new object, the security checks are usually not needed on each method.

Some of the methods in *File* are implemented as properties in *FileInfo*. For example, to get the creation time for a file using *File*, you must call the *File.GetCreationTime()* method. In the *FileInfo* class, you get the *CreationTime* property. The same is true for the time of last access and the time the file was last written.

Getting and Setting the Directory

The .NET Framework also contains classes for manipulating and operating on directories similar to the *File* and *FileInfo* classes.

The *Directory* class contains only *static* methods and no properties. The *DirectoryInfo* class contains only instance methods and properties. Like the *File* class, the *Directory* class performs security checks each time you call one of its methods. The *DirectoryInfo* performs security checks only as needed, so if you are performing multiple operations on a directory, it is more efficient to create an instance of *DirectoryInfo*.

USE IT   If you attempt to access a directory that does not exist, the program will throw a *DirectoryNotFoundException*. In addition, on some Windows versions, you may not be able to access certain directories and your program will throw an *UnauthorizedAccessException*. To guard against this, you should open the directory in a *try ... catch* block or check whether the directory actually exists by calling the *Directory.Exists()* method. You will need to catch the *UnauthorizedAccessException* in a guarded block.

▶ *NOTE*

According to the MSDN documentation, SetCurrentDirectory() should throw a DirectoryNotFoundException if you try to change to a nonexistent directory. The program actually throws a FileNotFoundException. In addition, the MSDN says the method will throw a SecurityException, which does not exist, rather than an UnauthorizedAccessException if the user does not have access to a directory. These issues likely will be resolved by the time Microsoft releases the commercial product.

If you need to change the current working directory in your program, you can use the *Directory.SetCurrentDirectory()* method, passing it the name of the new directory as an argument. The following short program, *ShowDir.cs*, accepts a directory from the command line and then changes to that directory before listing the files.

```
//  ShowDir.cs -- Changes the current working directory and then lists
//                the files in the directory.
//
//                Compile this program with the following command line:
//                     C:>csc ShowDir.cs
using System;
using System.IO;

namespace nsStreams
{
    class clsMain
    {
```

```csharp
        static public void Main (string [] args)
        {
            if (args.Length > 0)
            {
// Build the directory name from the arguments (a directory name may
// contain spaces).
                string DirName = "";
                foreach (string str in args)
                {
                    DirName += str;
                    DirName += " ";
                }
// Strip any trailing spaces from the directory name
                DirName = DirName.Trim ();
// Check whether the directory exists
                if (!Directory.Exists(DirName))
                {
                    Console.WriteLine ("No such directory: " + DirName);
                    return;
                }
// Set the current working directory
                try
                {
                    Directory.SetCurrentDirectory (DirName);
                }
                catch (UnauthorizedAccessException)
                {
                    Console.WriteLine ("Not authorized to access "
                                        + DirName);
                    return;
                }
            }
// List the files in the selected directory
            string [] files = Directory.GetFiles (".");
            foreach (string str in files)
            {
                int index = str.LastIndexOf ("\\");
                Console.WriteLine (str.Substring (index + 1));
            }
        }
    }
}
```

The program first assembles the arguments into a single directory name so that you do not have to quote a directory name that contains spaces. The program uses the *Exists()* method to determine whether the directory exists, but you could add a catch statement after the *try* block:

```
catch (DirectoryNotFoundException)
{
    Console.WriteLine ("No such directory: " + DirName);
    return;
}
```

To use the *DirectoryInfo* methods and properties, you first must create an instance of *DirectoryInfo*, passing the directory name to the constructor. This reduces the overhead of security checks on each method or property access. It is also useful for recursively getting the contents of a directory.

The following program, *Dirs.cs*, uses the *DirectoryInfo* structure to recursively list the subdirectories in a directory:

```
//  Dirs.cs -- Uses the DirectoryInfo class to recursively show
//             subdirectories.
//
//             Compile this program with the following command line:
//                   C:>csc Dirs.cs
using System;
using System.IO;

namespace nsStreams
{
    class clsMain
    {
        static public void Main (string [] args)
        {
            string StartDir = "";
// Build the directory name from any arguments
            if (args.Length > 0)
            {
                foreach (string str in args)
                {
                    StartDir += str;
                    StartDir += " ";
                }
// Strip any trailing spaces from the directory name
                char [] trim = new char[1] {' '};
                StartDir.TrimEnd (trim);
            }
            else
            {
```

```
        StartDir = ".";
    }
    DirectoryInfo d;
    try
    {
        d = new DirectoryInfo (StartDir);
    }
    catch (DirectoryNotFoundException)
    {
        Console.WriteLine ("Cannot open directory " + StartDir);
        return;
    }
    DirectoryInfo [] dirs;
    try
    {
        dirs = d.GetDirectories ();
    }
    catch (UnauthorizedAccessException)
    {
        Console.WriteLine ("Not authorized to access " + StartDir);
        return;
    }
    catch (DirectoryNotFoundException)
    {
        Console.WriteLine ("Cannot open directory " + StartDir);
        return;
    }
    foreach (DirectoryInfo dir in dirs)
    {
        try
        {
            ShowDirectories (dir, 0);
        }
        catch (UnauthorizedAccessException)
        {
            continue;
        }
    }
}
static public void ShowDirectories (DirectoryInfo d, int level)
{
    int spaces = level;
    while (spaces-- >= 0)
        Console.Write (" ");
```

```
        Console.WriteLine (d);
        DirectoryInfo [] dirs = d.GetDirectories ();
        if (dirs.Length > 0)
        {
            foreach (DirectoryInfo dir in dirs)
            {
                try
                {
                    ShowDirectories (dir, level + 2);
                }
                catch (UnauthorizedAccessException)
                {
                    continue;
                }
            }
        }
    }
}
```

You should note that the *UnauthorizedAccessException* will be thrown when you try to access a restricted directory rather than when you create the *DirectoryInfo* object.

PART III

Windows Programming in C#

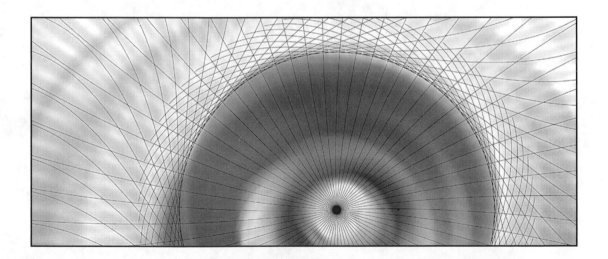

CHAPTER 13

Writing Windows Forms Applications

TIPS IN THIS CHAPTER

C onsole-based applications aside, most users expect to interact with Windows programs through windows, which may range from a full-screen application to a simple message box or dialog box.

The ultimate purpose of Visual Studio is to help you to write programs and components for Windows. Not surprisingly then, the .NET platform provides considerable support for developing traditional Windows applications.

The Windows *form* is the beginning point and the building block for Windows applications you develop using Visual Studio and C#. When you create a Windows application project using Visual Studio, the integrated development environment (IDE) includes one form in the project. You may add more forms to the project as needed.

Forms and Windows Programming

Visual Basic programmers are probably more familiar with forms than are Visual C++ programmers. When you create a Windows project in Visual Basic, you are provided with a single form. A forms-based program is similar to what Visual C++ programmers would consider a dialog box–based application, although forms capabilities go beyond those normally associated with dialog boxes.

Creating a form is as simple as declaring an instance of the *System.Windows.Form* class and then calling *Application.Run()*. The *Form* class is neither *abstract*, so you may declare an instance of it directly, nor *sealed*, so you may derive a new class from it. Although Visual Studio contains a number of tools that help you build and manipulate forms, you can create a form in a console-based program.

The following program. *Form.cs*, creates a basic, albeit not very exciting, form:

```
// Form.cs -- Demonstrates creating a form in a console program
//
//              Compile this program with the following command line:
//                  C:>csc Form.cs
using System;
using System.Windows.Forms;

namespace nsForm
{
    class clsMain
    {
        static public void Main ()
        {
            Application.Run(new Form());
        }
    }
}
```

The form created here is essentially blank. It does, however, contain a title bar with a system menu and buttons to maximize, minimize, and close the form; these elements are built into the *Form* class.

The *Run()* method is a *static* member of the *Application* class. The method starts a message loop on the current thread and makes the specified form visible.

A form is a convenient container for *controls*. Originally, a Windows control was a graphical object that displayed on the screen and that you used to provide feedback from the user. Lately, however, the word *control* has come to include objects that you cannot see, such as timers. The most commonly used example of a control is a button. The button displays text on its surface to let the user know its purpose, and when the user clicks the button with the mouse, the click generates a system *event* that can cause a function or method to execute.

(To demonstrate some of the form operations in this chapter, you will need to add *event handlers* to respond to events. You have done this in projects in earlier chapters, but more detailed information on adding event handlers for controls appears in Chapter 16, beginning with the tip on "Responding to Control Messages.")

When you add controls to a form, the complexity of the code increases rapidly. In C#, you need to derive your own class from *Form* and build the controls directly in the class, as shown in the following program, *Button.cs*:

```
// Button.cs -- Adds a button to a simple form
//
//            Compile this program with the following command line:
//                 C:>csc Button.cs
using System;
using System.Windows.Forms;

namespace Form
{
    public class clsForm : System.Windows.Forms.Form
    {
        private Button button1;
        public clsForm()
        {
            Text = "A Simple Form";
            button1 = new Button ();
            button1.Text = "Cancel";
            button1.Name = "button1";
            button1.Size = new System.Drawing.Size (72, 30);
            button1.Location = new System.Drawing.Point (
                                       ClientRectangle.Width / 2 - 36,
                                       ClientRectangle.Height - 35);
            Controls.AddRange(new System.Windows.Forms.Control[]
                                             {this.button1});
            button1.Click += new System.EventHandler(OnClickButton1);
        }
        static public void Main()
        {
            Application.Run(new clsForm());
```

```
        }
        void OnClickButton1 (object sender, System.EventArgs e)
        {
            Application.Exit ();
        }
    }
}
```

This is the code you need to create, label, display, and enable a single button on a form, and a button is one of the *simpler* controls to program. With a couple of buttons, an edit box or two, a list control, and a few other controls, you could quickly become overwhelmed with calculating positions and sizes. Certainly, many good programs are written in this way, but it does make you appreciate the work performed for you by the Visual Studio Forms Designer. As you move or resize a control using the Forms Designer, the IDE will keep track of the new values and insert them into your program.

Using the *System.Windows.Forms* Namespace

The .NET Framework provides two different graphical user interfaces (GUIs). The Windows Forms GUI contains classes in the *System.Windows.Forms* namespace to implement traditional Windows desktop applications. The second GUI, Web Forms, is the platform you use to develop ASP.NET applications. Most of the Web Forms classes are contained in the *System.Web.UI* and *System.Web.UI.WebControls* namespaces.

The *System.Windows.Forms* namespace contains a large number of types, such as classes, structures, interfaces, and delegates, that are aimed at helping you build Windows applications. Forms objects use properties to define their appearance, and they use methods to define their behavior. The methods may include event handlers—essentially message handlers—to help your program respond to user input. The *Forms* classes hide much of the underlying details.

To use the *System.Windows.Forms* namespace and thus make it easier to derive your own classes from the *Form* class, you must first declare that you are using the namespace. To do this, include the following line in your program, usually at the top of the source file:

```
using System.Windows.Forms;
```

This declaration gives you access to a rich set of classes that implement forms and controls for building Windows applications. Certainly, you could create a button by referring to the fully qualified name of the class, *System.Windows.Forms.Button*, but the *using* namespace declaration lets you refer to it simply as *Button*.

The first stop toward building a Windows application using the *Forms* namespace is the *Application* class. You used a member of this class in the preceding examples to create the basic form. The *Application* class is *sealed* so you cannot derive other classes from it, but the class contains only *static* methods and properties, so you do not need to declare an instance of the class.

Before you begin, you need to understand two methods in the *Application* class. The first is the *Run()* method, which starts a traditional Windows message loop for the application and optionally creates the first form for your application. When you create a forms-based application using

Visual Studio, the IDE wizard adds the *Main()* method as a member of the default form and inserts a call to this method as the only statement in the *Main()* method:

```
static void Main()
{
Application.Run(new clsForm());
}
```

If your program needs to perform any processing before the form displays, you can insert the code before the call to the *Run()* method. You should keep any such code to a minimum, however. Users tend to get impatient if it takes more than a few seconds between the time when they start a program and when they see results.

You may also create a form before you call the *Run()* method and pass the form instance as a parameter to the method. In addition, you may create an *ApplicationContext* object and assign a form that will display on startup.

Finally, you may call *Run()* without passing any parameters. This will start the main application message loop, but it will not display any form on startup. There are, however, some pitfalls to this type of call. For example, closing the startup form will not stop your application. This issue will be addressed later in the chapter, in the tip on "Hiding and Showing Forms," when you start a form-based application without displaying the form.

The other important method in the *Application* class is *Exit()*. When you call *Application.Exit()*, the method notifies all message loops that have been started to terminate, and then it closes all windows that the application has open. The *Exit()* method takes no parameters and does not return an exit code to the operating system.

Using the *Exit()* method will be the normal method for exiting a Windows application in C#. You can call the *Close()* method on the form that you passed to *Run()* to close an application. The downside of calling *Close()* on a form, however, is that if you later change the startup form, the method will simply close the one form and not stop the application. You'd then need to remember to call *Close()* in the new startup form.

The *System.Windows.Forms* namespace also contains the classes for implementing the Windows common controls library. These include the buttons, edit boxes, labels, list boxes, tree and list controls, and other objects that you will use to build an interface that allows your program to interact with the user. You will use some of these controls in this chapter to build form-based projects, and other types of controls will be covered in Chapter 16.

Menu controls, discussed in Chapter 15, are a part of the *System.Windows.Forms* namespace. They include the main menu for an application, drop-down menus, and context-sensitive (popup) menus.

The classes that give you access to the Windows common dialog library also belong to the *System.Windows.Forms* namespace. These are the dialog boxes that open and close a file, select colors and fonts, and control printing. The common dialogs will be covered in Chapter 17.

Utility classes are used to implement the system clipboard and timers, provide access to the display, control cursors, hold image lists for other controls, and implement tool tips, the small popup windows with descriptive text that appear when the cursor hovers above a control or object. These will be covered in this and other chapters as needed.

Creating a Form-Based Application

If you have read through the preceding chapters of this book, you have slugged your way through a number of small applications, most of them generally aimed at demonstrating a particular topic or aspect of C# programming. Most of these programs have been console-based programs, but a few of them, such as the clock project from Chapter 3 and the simple drawing program from Chapter 8, have been based on Windows forms.

USE IT   So far in this chapter, you have seen how easy it is to create a form. Now it is time for you to create a form-based project in Visual Studio and take a look at the preparatory steps the application wizard does for you. In addition to creating a source file and deriving a new class from *System.Windows.Forms.Form*, the application wizard will set up the compiler options, create a "solution," and create several files by which Visual Studio will manage your project. In the following procedure, you'll work your way through setting up a new project.

1. Start Visual Studio.

2. Select File | New | Project. Or, if you configured Visual Studio to display the Start page when you first run it (this is the default), click the New Project button on the Start page. Either method will display the New Project dialog box shown in Figure 13-1.

3. Whether your project is in Visual C#, Visual C++, Visual Basic, or any other project types supported by Visual Studio, a new project starts from the New Project dialog when you use the application wizard. On the left side of the dialog, in the Project Types panel, select the Visual C# Projects item.

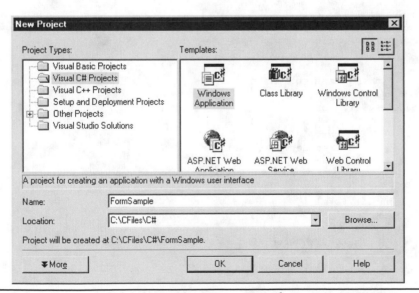

Figure 13.1   The New Project dialog box is the starting point for creating projects in Visual Studio

4. On the Templates panel at the right, you'll see the application workspaces you can create using the language you selected in the Project Types panel. Click Windows Application.

5. At the bottom of the New Project dialog box is a Location text box. The default path for projects is the one you set earlier in the Options dialog box, but you can enter a new path here. If you select a new path, Visual Studio will remember the path. This box is a combo box, so you can click the arrow to the right of it to display other paths you might have used to create projects. If you want a path other than the default path or those included in the combo box list, type it in this box.

6. In the Name box, Visual Studio will display a default name based on the project type and a sequence number—something like *WindowsApplication1* for a Windows application. You probably will want to give your projects names that more or less describe their functions. For this project, type **FormSample** in the Name box.

7. Click the OK button and give the application wizard a few seconds to do its job. A form template will appear in Visual Studio, which is a representation of the form that will appear when you run the program. Although Visual Studio does not identify it as such, this is the Forms Designer template that you will use to add objects to the form.

8. For now, however, you want to look at the code the application wizard created for you. Right-click anywhere on the form template and select View Code from the popup menu. You should see the source file that creates the form, similar to the following:

```
using System;
using System.Drawing;
using System.Collections;
using System.ComponentModel;
using System.Windows.Forms;
using System.Data;

namespace FormSample
{
    /// <summary>
    /// Summary description for Form1.
    /// </summary>
    public class Form1 : System.Windows.Forms.Form
    {
        /// <summary>
        /// Required designer variable.
        /// </summary>
        private System.ComponentModel.Container components = null;

        public Form1()
        {
            //
            // Required for Windows Forms Designer support
            //
            InitializeComponent();
```

```
        //
        // TODO: Add any constructor code after InitializeComponent call
        //
    }

    /// <summary>
    /// Clean up any resources being used.
    /// </summary>
    protected override void Dispose( bool disposing )
    {
        if( disposing )
        {
            if (components != null)
            {
                components.Dispose();
            }
        }
        base.Dispose( disposing );
    }

    #region Windows Forms Designer generated code
    /// <summary>
    /// Required method for Designer support - do not modify
    /// the contents of this method with the code editor.
    /// </summary>
    private void InitializeComponent()
    {
        this.components = new System.ComponentModel.Container();
        this.Size = new System.Drawing.Size(300,300);
        this.Text = "Form1";
    }
    #endregion

    /// <summary>
    /// The main entry point for the application.
    /// </summary>
    [STAThread]
    static void Main()
    {
        Application.Run(new Form1());
    }
    }
}
```

The basic code that you used to create a form is contained in this listing, with some important and notable additions. First, the code contains *using* statements for the various namespaces you will need for a form-based project. In addition to numerous comments, the code also contains a constructor for the *Form1* class and an *InitializeComponents()* method that is called from within the constructor. You may add code to the constructor, but you should add it after the call to *InitializeComponents()*. This will assure that the form and any controls that you have placed on the form have been created and initialized.

The *InitializeComponents()* method is the private property of the Visual Studio tools. As you add controls to the form and set their properties, you will see statements appear in this method to implement the controls and settings. It may be tempting to make modifications to this code, but you run a significant risk of losing those modifications. When you add, remove, or change the properties of a control, Visual Studio will rewrite this method and any changes you have made will be lost permanently.

Notice that the *InitializeComponents()* method is enclosed within a *#region* and *#endregion* block. Occasionally, you may want to look at this code, but this method has a way of growing very large very quickly, making it time-consuming to scroll through, so you probably will want to keep the region hidden. To do this, click on the minus (−) symbol next to the line containing the *#region* statement. The block will collapse and the symbol will change to a plus (+) symbol, which you can click to expand the code again if you need to do so.

After the *InitializeComponents()* method, examine the *Main()* method. The application wizard has marked *Main()* with an *STAThread* attribute. This sets the *apartment* thread model for the application. You do not need this attribute to run multiple threads in a program, but if you intend to use certain controls and OLE objects such as the system clipboard, you will need to include the *STAThread* attribute in the *Main()* method. The attribute has meaning only when placed in the *Main()* method.

▶ **NOTE**

A thread is an execution point within a program. Every program has at least one thread, but you may create other threads within a program. Each thread has its own instruction pointer and stack space. When a program with more than one thread runs, the Windows scheduler gives each thread its own processor time, and thus it appears that more than one program is running in the same program space.

Hiding and Showing Forms

When you use Visual Studio to create a Windows application, the application wizard always creates a form. The form and the class derived from *System.Windows.Forms.Form* is the starting point for your program. One of the advantages of this method is that the *Run()* method starts a Windows message loop using the form as the target window for the system messages.

It is not always desirable to show the form, or sometimes you may want to delay the form display until your program completes initialization or some other processing. If your program performs some background processing for another application, you may not want to display the form at all.

Each form has a property named *Visible* that you can use to control the display. If you set it to *true*, the form will display. Setting it to *false* will hide the form.

One of the things *Application.Run()* does is to display the form that you pass it as a parameter. If you pass a form instance through the constructor, setting the *Visible* property to *false* in the form's constructor has no effect, and the form still will display.

The MSDN documentation suggests creating the form in the *Main()* method and then setting the *Visible* property to *true* when you want the form to display. However, in a note, the documentation reminds you of the importance of calling *Application.Run()* to start the application's main message loop. The catch here is that if you create an invisible form and then call *Application.Run()*, you'll have no way of displaying the form.

USE IT   You can handle such a predicament in two ways. First, you can do whatever processing
          your program needs and then call *Application.Run()* using the form instance as an argument,
as shown in the following snippet:

```
static public void Main()
{
    Form1 form = new Form1();
// Preliminary processing here
    Application.Run (form);
}
```

However, there's not much advantage to doing this over simply passing the form instance as an
argument to *Run()*.

Another method entails starting a second thread in your program to perform the background
processing and then calling *Run()* with no arguments. This will start the application's message
loop, and your code can decide when or whether to display the form.

The disadvantage to this method is that closing the form will not cause the *Run()* method to
return, thus ending your program. You need to provide an event handler for the *Closed* event and
call *Application.Exit()* in the event handler. The following program, *HideForm.cs*, starts a thread that
does nothing but wait two and a half seconds and then ask if you want to display the form. Answering
No will keep the form hidden. Answering Yes will display the form and terminate the second thread.
Clicking the Cancel button will end the program.

```
// HideForm.cs -- Demonstrates hiding a form and then doing background
//                processing in a second thread.
//
//                Compile this program with the following command line:
//                    C:>csc HideForm.cs
using System;
using System.Windows.Forms;
using System.Threading;


namespace HideForm
{
    public class Form1 : System.Windows.Forms.Form
    {
        private System.Windows.Forms.Button button1;
        public Form1()
        {
            Text = "A Simple Form";
            button1 = new Button ();
            SuspendLayout();
            button1.Text = "Cancel";
            button1.Name = "button1";
```

```
        button1.Size = new System.Drawing.Size (72, 30);
        button1.Location = new System.Drawing.Point (
                    (ClientRectangle.Width - button1.Size.Width) / 2,
                    ClientRectangle.Height - 35);
        Controls.AddRange(new System.Windows.Forms.Control[]
        {this.button1});
        button1.Click += new System.EventHandler(OnClickButton1);
        this.Closed += new System.EventHandler(OnClickButton1);
        ResumeLayout (false);
        this.Visible = false;
    }
    [STAThread]
    static void Main()
    {
        Form1 form = new Form1();
        Thread delay = new Thread (new ThreadStart(form.DelayVisible));
        delay.Start ();
        Application.Run();
    }

    public void DelayVisible ()
    {
        while (true)
        {
            Thread.Sleep (2500);
            DialogResult result = MessageBox.Show (
                            "Display Form?", "Display",
                            MessageBoxButtons.YesNoCancel);
            switch (result)
            {
                case DialogResult.Yes:
                    this.ShowDialog();
                    return;
                case DialogResult.No:
                    continue;
                case DialogResult.Cancel:
                    Application.Exit ();
                    break;
            }
            return;
        }
    }
```

```
    private void OnClickButton1(object sender, System.EventArgs e)
    {
        Application.Exit ();
    }
  }
}
```

When you run the program, nothing happens at first. In a couple of seconds, though, a message box will appear asking whether you want to display the form. If you click No, the message box will continue to appear every couple of seconds until you click Yes to display the form or click Cancel to end the program.

Notice in the constructor that the event handler for the *Closed* event is set to the same event handler for the *Click* event for the button:

```
button1.Click += new System.EventHandler(OnClickButton1);
this.Closed += new System.EventHandler(OnClickButton1);
```

This event handler does nothing but close the application when you click the button or close the form using the Close button on the title bar. You could provide separate methods for the events.

Adding Controls to a Form

The primary purpose of a form is to hold Windows controls that allow you to display information to the user and respond to user actions. The *System.Windows.Forms* namespace contains classes to implement the Windows common controls, and Visual Studio provides tools to help you add controls to forms.

Using the Forms Designer, you can select controls from the Visual Studio Toolbox window, place them on the form, and size and position the controls. Then, from the Properties tool window, you can manipulate the appearance and the way the controls operate.

USE IT   Now create a new Windows application called *AddControls* using the steps from "Creating a Form-Based Application" earlier in this chapter. For this project, you will add a list box, a text box, and a couple of buttons to the form, and then you'll size and position the controls.

1. When the Forms Designer template appears, select the Windows Forms item in the Toolbox. By default, the Toolbox appears to the left of the Visual Studio screen. If you have the Toolbox set to Auto Hide, it may appear as a tab at the right. Move the mouse cursor over this tab and the Toolbox should appear. If neither the Toolbox or the tab are visible, choose View | Toolbox. The Visual Studio frame should appear as shown in Figure 13-2.

2. Because the Toolbox has no visible scroll bar, scrolling is accomplished using the up and down arrows that appear on the right side of the Toolbox. If you need to scroll, click the up and down arrow buttons to locate the Button entry in the Toolbox and click the icon next to it.

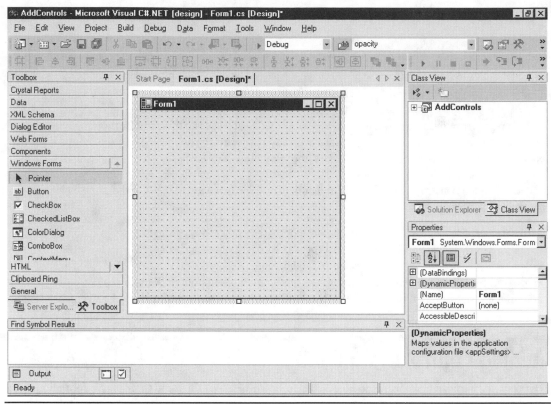

Figure 13.2 The blank form template appears in the center of the Visual Studio frame. The Toolbox is to the left of the template, and the Properties tool window is to the lower right.

Notice that the cursor has changed to a plus symbol with the object's icon attached to the lower right of the symbol. Drag the cursor over the form template.

3. Move the cursor to the location at which you want the button to appear—at the bottom of the form, for this example. When the cursor is at the upper-left corner of the spot where you want the button to appear, click and hold down the mouse button. Drag the cursor to the right and down to draw a rectangle, which will appear to show the location of the button. Release the mouse button and the button object will appear on the form template.

After you click the icon in step 2, you can also simply click on the form where you want the object to appear and then move and resize it. To move the object, click and drag it to the proper location and release the mouse button. To resize an object, grab a corner or side of the object and drag it to the proper size, and then release the mouse button.

4. Now add a second button to the form using the same technique, again placing it at the bottom of the form.

5. Drag the TextBox item from the Toolbox to add a text box to the form. Place the edit box just above the buttons.

6. Drag the ListBox item from the Toolbox to add a list box to the form. Make the list box fairly large and place it just above the text box. The form should appear similar to the one shown in Figure 13-3 (which also shows the button names on the form that will be added in step 12).

7. Now make the buttons the same size. Select one of the buttons and resize it to appear the way you want both buttons to appear. Click the other button to select it, and SHIFT-click the button you just resized; both buttons should now be selected.

8. Choose Format | Make Same Size | Both. When you select multiple objects in this way, the *last item you selected* will be used as the pattern for the Format command. Choose Format | Align | Tops. The buttons should appear the same size and the tops should be aligned on the form template.

9. With both buttons still selected, left-click and hold down the mouse button on one of the form buttons. Drag both buttons where you want them to appear. With both buttons selected, you can move them in a single operation.

10. Try moving the controls around the form template until you are comfortable with the operation. Developing some agility at these operations will greatly speed up your program development time. If you make a mistake, press CTRL-Z to undo the last operation.

11. Now make the text box and the list box the same width. First size the list box, and then select the text box. SHIFT-click the list box to select it. Choose Format | Make Same Size | Width. Align the left sides of the two boxes by choosing Format | Align | Lefts.

12. Now you can set the text for the buttons using the Properties tool window as shown next. Select the leftmost button on the form template, scroll through the Properties window until you find

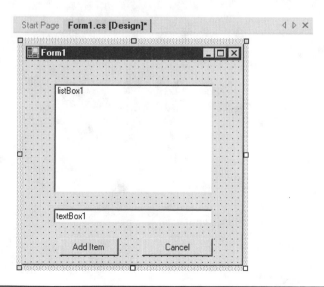

Figure 13.3   The form template should contain two buttons, a text box and a list box

the *Text* property, and select it. Change the text to **Add Item**. Do the same for the right button to read **Cancel**.

13. Now set the *Text* property for the text box in the same way, except you'll erase the text *textBox1* and leave the property blank.

14. Double-click the leftmost button in the form template to add an event handler for the Click event. Visual Studio will open the source code file and move the caret to the event handler it adds to the file. Return to the Forms Designer and do the same for the rightmost button. Chapter 16 will discuss the steps for adding named methods for the events, but for now the default event handler names will suffice.

15. Add the following code to these event handlers. The is the only code you will need to add for this project:

```
private void button1_Click(object sender, System.EventArgs e)
{
    if (textBox1.Text == "")
        return;
    string strAdd = textBox1.Text;
    if (listBox1.FindString (strAdd, -1) < 0)
    {
        listBox1.Items.Add (strAdd);
        textBox1.Text = "";
        textBox1.Focus();
        return;
    }
    MessageBox.Show ("\"" + strAdd + "\" is already in the list box",
                "Duplicate");
}

private void button2_Click(object sender, System.EventArgs e)
{
```

```
          Application.Exit();
  }
```

16. Finally, build the project by pressing CTRL-SHIFT-B; then run it in the debugger by pressing the F5 key. Type some text into the list box and click the Add Item button to see what happens.

Adding Forms to an Application

For many applications, a single form will be all that you need. Sometimes, however, you will need to use a second form to display supplemental information to the user or to provide a way to get additional information for the startup form.

In the preceding example, you simply typed a line of text and clicked a button to add a string to the list box. Suppose, however, that the data behind the item in the list box was an employee record that contained fields for the employee's first and last names along with address information. You could enlarge the form and add fields to display all this information before adding a name to the list.

But that would clutter the form with fields that are unnecessary except when adding or editing an employee record. A better method would be to place these fields on a second form that you could summon by clicking the Add Item button.

USE IT Now you'll create another Windows application project named *Employee*.

1. Prepare a form in the same way that you did in the last project, except do not add a text box.

2. Create an event handler for the list box to handle the *DoubleClick* event. The list box does not have a default event, so double-clicking on it will not work. To add the event, select the Events button on the Properties tool window (the button with the lightning flash). Scroll through the events until you find the *DoubleClick* item; select it, and enter **listBox1_OnDoubleClick**.

3. Press the ENTER key and Visual Studio adds the event handler to the *Form1* class. (After you do this, click on the Properties button to reset the Properties tool window to display the properties list.)

4. Before you add code to the source file, add a second form to the project. Select the Solution Explorer tab at the right side of the Visual Studio frame. If the Solution Explorer is not visible, choose View | Solution Explorer.

5. In the Solution Explorer, right-click the second line, which contains the name of the project.

6. From the popup menu, select Add | Add Windows Form to display the Add New Item dialog box shown in Figure 13-4.

7. Select Windows Form in the Templates panel.

8. In the Name box at the bottom of the dialog box, type **EmpForm.cs**.

9. Click Open to close the dialog box and create the new form. Visual Studio will create another source code file to hold the code for the *EmpForm* class.

10. Add two buttons and six text boxes to the new form so that it looks like the one shown here:

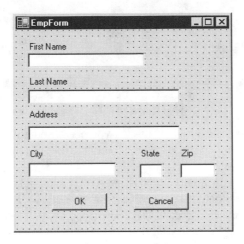

11. Use the Label item on the Toolbox to place labels above each of the text boxes. Use the *Text* property to set the text for the labels.

12. Set the text for the left button to **OK** (the *button1* object) and **Cancel** for the right button (the *button2* object).

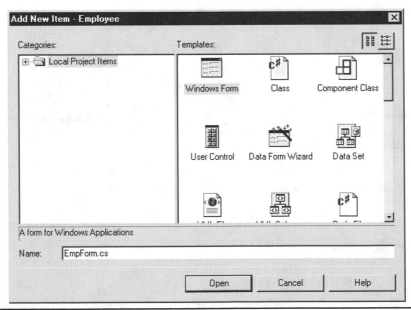

Figure 13.4   Add a form to a project by displaying the Add New Item dialog box from the Solution Explorer

13. Click a blank area of the form to make the Properties tool window display properties for the form. Set the *CancelButton* property for the form to *button2*. This will make it unnecessary to add an event handler for the Cancel button.

14. Double-click on the OK button (*button1*) to an event handler for the *Click* event.

15. Because this form needs to return a result to the first form, set the *DialogResult* property for the two buttons. Select the first button and scroll through the Properties until you find the DialogResult entry. Set this property to OK. Do the same for the second button but set the property to Cancel.

16. Open the source file for the *EmpForm* class. If necessary, right-click the form and select View Code from the popup menu. The listing for this class is shown here—for brevity, the *InitializeComponent()* method is not shown:

```
using System;
using System.Drawing;
using System.Collections;
using System.ComponentModel;
using System.Windows.Forms;

namespace Employee
{
    public struct EMPLOYEE
    {
        public string     FirstName;
        public string     LastName;
        public string     Address;
        public string     City;
        public string     State;
        public string     Zip;
        public override string ToString ()
        {
            return (LastName + ", " + FirstName);
        }
    }
    /// <summary>
    /// Summary description for EmpForm.
    /// </summary>
    public class EmpForm : System.Windows.Forms.Form
    {
        private System.Windows.Forms.TextBox textBox1;
        private System.Windows.Forms.TextBox textBox2;
        private System.Windows.Forms.TextBox textBox3;
        private System.Windows.Forms.TextBox textBox4;
        private System.Windows.Forms.TextBox textBox5;
        private System.Windows.Forms.TextBox textBox6;
        private System.Windows.Forms.Label label1;
        private System.Windows.Forms.Label label2;
        private System.Windows.Forms.Label label3;
        private System.Windows.Forms.Label label4;
        private System.Windows.Forms.Label label5;
        private System.Windows.Forms.Label label6;
        private System.Windows.Forms.Button button1;
```

```csharp
    private System.Windows.Forms.Button button2;
    /// <summary>
    /// Required designer variable.
    /// </summary>
    private System.ComponentModel.Container components = null;

    public EmpForm(EMPLOYEE emp)
    {
        //
        // Required for Windows Form Designer support
        //
        InitializeComponent();

        //
        // TODO: Add any constructor code after InitializeComponent call
        //
        textBox1.Text = emp.FirstName;
        textBox2.Text = emp.LastName;
        textBox3.Text = emp.Address;
        textBox4.Text = emp.City;
        textBox5.Text = emp.State;
        textBox6.Text = emp.Zip;
    }


    /// <summary>
    /// Clean up any resources being used.
    /// </summary>
    protected override void Dispose( bool disposing )
    {
        if( disposing )
        {
            if(components != null)
            {
                components.Dispose();
            }
        }
        base.Dispose( disposing );
    }


    #region Windows Form Designer generated code
// [The InitializeComponent() method is here
    #endregion

    public void GetEmployeeData (out EMPLOYEE emp)
    {
        emp.FirstName = textBox1.Text;
        emp.LastName = textBox2.Text;
        emp.Address = textBox3.Text;
        emp.City = textBox4.Text;
        emp.State = textBox5.Text;
        emp.Zip = textBox6.Text;
    }
```

```
        private void button1_Click(object sender, System.EventArgs e)
        {
            this.Close ();
        }
    }
}
```

17. Return to the *Form1.cs* source code file (click on the tab labeled "Form1.cs" at the top of the client area). Add code for the event handlers that you placed in the *Form1* class. The code for these methods is shown here:

```
private void button1_Click(object sender, System.EventArgs e)
{
    EMPLOYEE emp = new EMPLOYEE();
    EmpForm eform = new EmpForm (emp);
    if (eform.ShowDialog (this) == DialogResult.Cancel)
        return;
    eform.GetEmployeeData (out emp);
    listBox1.Items.Add (emp);
}

private void button2_Click(object sender, System.EventArgs e)
{
    Application.Exit ();
}

private void listBox1_OnDoubleClick(object sender, System.EventArgs e)
{
    int index = listBox1.SelectedIndex;
    if (index < 0)
    {
        return;
    }
    EMPLOYEE emp = (EMPLOYEE) listBox1.Items[index];
    EmpForm eform = new EmpForm (emp);
    if (eform.ShowDialog (this) == DialogResult.Cancel)
    {
        return;
    }
    eform.GetEmployeeData (out emp);
    listBox1.Items.RemoveAt (index);
    listBox1.Items.Insert (index,emp);
}
```

Build and run the program. When the first form appears, click the Add Item button to create and display the second form. Two forms, similar to Figure 13-5, should appear on the screen.

Create an employee record by entering the information in the text boxes on the second form. Enter something in each of the text boxes. When you click OK, the employee's first and last names should appear in the list box on the first form. You can change the information that displays in the list box by modifying the *ToString()* method in the *EMPLOYEE* structure.

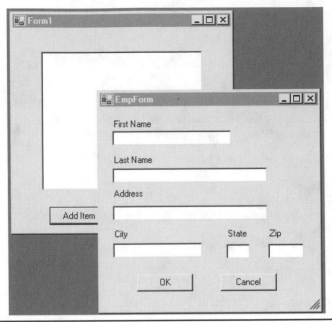

Figure 13.5 The text boxes on the second form provide fields for entering data without making the main form unnecessarily busy

Add a few more employee records to the list box. After you have added three or four items to the list box, double-click one of the items. The second form should appear with all of the text boxes containing information for that item.

Setting the Tab Order

When you lay out the controls on a form, Visual Studio creates a *tab order* according to the order that you added the controls. When you display the form, the focus will be on the first control that you placed on the form (some controls, however, such as the Label control do not accept user input and thus do not get the focus).

After giving the first control the focus, the form uses the tab order to respond to TAB key presses. When you press the TAB key, the second control you placed on the form will get the focus. With the next TAB key press, the third control will get the focus. This continues until the focus is on the last control, at which time the next TAB press will return the focus to the first control.

If you added the controls in order, the tab order will be correct. However, if you did not add them in order, or if you returned to the form and added or moved controls, the tab order will no longer be correct. Users rightfully expect the TAB key to move them through the controls in a logical order, one after another.

USE IT ▶ You can display and change the tab order by selecting the form and then choosing View | Tab Order. (Make sure that you click a blank area of the form. If you click a control, Tab

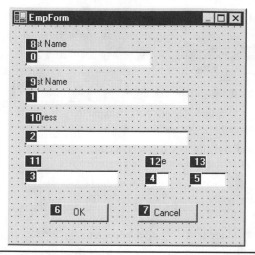

Figure 13.6   Displaying the tab order for a form allows you to set the sequence in which the controls will receive the focus

Order will not appear on the menu.) The form will number each control to indicate the current tab order, with 0 being the control that will get the focus when you first display the form. The tab order for the second form, the EmpForm, in the previous project is shown in Figure 13-6.

To change the tab order, simply click the controls in the appropriate order of focus. With each click, the box containing the tab number will change from blue to white, indicating that you have set the order for that control. The label controls display numbers as well, but you do not have to set the tab order for them.

You can eliminate a control from the tab order by setting its *TabStop* property to *false*. Select the control, and scroll through the properties until you find *TabStop*. Notice that label controls do not contain this property.

When you group controls using the GroupBox control, you can set the tab order for the group independently. This will be covered in Chapter 16.

Setting Form Properties

One of the problems with using a form as a dialog box is that the form is a "do-all" object. In addition to dialog boxes, you can use a form with controls that automatically resize if the user changes the form size. An example of such a form is a view project that contains an editing control for displaying and modifying the contents of files. Having a form the user can resize is not desirable when you're using a form as a dialog box. If the user maximizes the form, the control will appear in the upper-left corner and a large blank gray area will dominate the form.

USE IT   You can prevent this from happening by disabling the maximize and minimize buttons on the form's title bar and by setting the maximum and minimum size of the form so that it cannot be resized. You also can set the *FormBorderStyle* property to *FixedDialog* to prevent resizing.

The properties that you may use on forms are shown in the following table.

Property	Description
FormBorderSize	Set to *FixedDialog* to prevent resizing.
MaximizeBox	Set to *false* to disable the maximize box on the title bar.
MinimizeBox	Set to *false* to disable the minimize box on the title bar. If you set both the *MaximizeBox* and *MinimizeBox* properties to *false*, the sizing boxes will be removed from the title bar.
MaximumSize	If you allow resizing, you can set the maximum size for the dialog box using this property. Setting to 0,0 does not restrict the maximum size.
MinimumSize	Sets the minimum size for the form if you allow resizing. Setting to 0,0 does not restrict the minimum size.

By default, whenever you create and display a form, an icon appears in the Windows task bar. If two or three forms are open in a project, the same number of icons will be visible in the task bar. You don't need more than one task bar item for a single project, and the multiple icons could lead to user confusion. To prevent this from happening, set the *ShowInTaskBar* property for additional forms to *false*.

Using Modal and Modeless Forms

In the Employee project example from earlier in this chapter, you created and displayed a second form to allow the user to enter information about an employee. After the second form is displayed, however, a user cannot return to the main form until the second form is dispatched by clicking OK or Cancel.

This is an example of a *modal* dialog box. Once the parent form creates the second form, control passes to the new form, which will not relinquish control back to the parent until it closes. The *MessageBox* class is also an example of a modal form. After you display the message box, you must close it before you can return to your program. If you click the parent form, your computer will simply beep at you.

Forms also may be *modeless*, in which case the user determines which form will have the focus. Whether a form is modal or modeless depends on the method you use to create the form.

You create a modal form by calling the form's *ShowDialog()* method. The calling method stops at this statement, and the next statement does not execute until the new form exits.

The *Show()* method is used to create a modeless dialog box. When this statement executes, the method continues to the next statement without waiting for the spawned form to close. Modeless forms usually take more care in setting up because it is possible to call the spawning method repeatedly, thus creating multiple instances of a modeless form.

USE IT   The following Windows application project, *Modeless*, demonstrates the use of a modeless form. After you create the project, create a second form named *AddItemForm*. The two forms are shown in Figure 13-7.

1. First, change the name of the *Form1* class to **MainForm**. Right-click the *Form1.cs* item in the Solution Explorer. Select Rename from the popup menu and change the name to **MainForm**. Click the form.

2. Scroll through the Properties tool window to find the *Name* property for the *Form1* object and change it to **MainForm**. The *Text* property is the name displayed in the title bar, and you can set it to anything you want.

3. Add the controls to the two forms so that they look similar to those shown in Figure 13-7.

4. Set the *Text* properties for each button. On the first form, the left button text should be **Add Item**, the middle button text should be **Delete Item**, and the third button text should be **Close**. For the second form, the left button text should be **Add** and right button text **Close**. Add messages for the *Click* event for each button (double-click a button to use the default event handler name).

5. Add a *public* method named *AddItemToList( )*. This method will give the modeless form access to the list box. Add a field to the *MainForm* class to hold an instance for the modeless form and initialize it using the *new* operator in the *MainForm* constructor. Simply creating the second form will not display it. When you click the Add Item button on the first form, the event

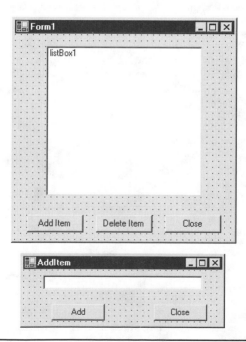

Figure 13.7   The main form (top) contains a button to spawn the modeless dialog box plus a button to delete items from the list. The *AddItemForm* (bottom) contains a text box and button to add items to the list box on the main form.

handler calls the second form's *Show()* method to display the form. The code for the *MainForm* class is shown in the following listing:

```csharp
using System;
using System.Drawing;
using System.Collections;
using System.ComponentModel;
using System.Windows.Forms;
using System.Data;

namespace Modeless
{
    /// <summary>
    /// Summary description for MainForm.
    /// </summary>
    public class MainForm : System.Windows.Forms.Form
    {
        private System.Windows.Forms.ListBox listBox1;
        private System.Windows.Forms.Button button1;
        private System.Windows.Forms.Button button2;
        private System.Windows.Forms.Button button3;
        /// <summary>
        /// Required designer variable.
        /// </summary>
        private System.ComponentModel.Container components = null;

// Create an instance of the second form.
        AddItemForm frmAdd = new AddItemForm (this);

        public MainForm()
        {
            //
            // Required for Windows Forms Designer support
            //
            InitializeComponent();

            //
            // TODO: Add any constructor code after InitializeComponent call
            //
            frmAdd = new AddItemForm (this);

        }

        /// <summary>
        /// Clean up any resources being used.
        /// </summary>
        protected override void Dispose( bool disposing )
        {
            if( disposing )
            {
                if (components != null)
                {
                    components.Dispose();
                }
```

```
        }
        base.Dispose( disposing );
    }

    #region Windows Forms Designer generated code
    /// <summary>
    /// Required method for Forms Designer support - do not modify
    /// the contents of this method with the code editor.
    /// </summary>
    private void InitializeComponent()
    {
        this.listBox1 = new System.Windows.Forms.ListBox();
        this.button1 = new System.Windows.Forms.Button();
        this.button2 = new System.Windows.Forms.Button();
        this.button3 = new System.Windows.Forms.Button();
        this.SuspendLayout();
        //
        // listBox1
        //
        this.listBox1.Location = new System.Drawing.Point(42, 16);
        this.listBox1.Name = "listBox1";
        this.listBox1.Size = new System.Drawing.Size(208, 199);
        this.listBox1.TabIndex = 0;
        //
        // button1
        //
        this.button1.Location = new System.Drawing.Point(17, 240);
        this.button1.Name = "button1";
        this.button1.TabIndex = 1;
        this.button1.Text = "Add Item";
        this.button1.Click +=
                    new System.EventHandler(this.button1_Click);
        //
        // button2
        //
        this.button2.Location = new System.Drawing.Point(109, 240);
        this.button2.Name = "button2";
        this.button2.TabIndex = 2;
        this.button2.Text = "Delete Item";
        this.button2.Click +=
                    new System.EventHandler(this.button2_Click);
        //
        // button3
        //
        this.button3.DialogResult =
                        System.Windows.Forms.DialogResult.Cancel;
        this.button3.Location = new System.Drawing.Point(201, 240);
        this.button3.Name = "button3";
        this.button3.TabIndex = 3;
        this.button3.Text = "Close";
        this.button3.Click +=
                    new System.EventHandler(this.button3_Click);
        //
```

```csharp
        // MainForm
        //
        this.AutoScaleBaseSize = new System.Drawing.Size(5, 13);
        this.CancelButton = this.button3;
        this.ClientSize = new System.Drawing.Size(292, 273);
        this.Controls.AddRange(new System.Windows.Forms.Control[] {
                                            this.button3,
                                            this.button2,
                                            this.button1,
                                            this.listBox1});
        this.Name = "MainForm";
        this.Text = "MainForm";
        this.ResumeLayout(false);

    }
    #endregion

    /// <summary>
    /// The main entry point for the application.
    /// </summary>
    [STAThread]
    static void Main()
    {
        Application.Run(new MainForm());
    }

    private void button1_Click(object sender, System.EventArgs e)
    {
        if (frmAdd.IsDisposed == true)
            frmAdd = new AddItemForm (this);
        frmAdd.Show ();
    }

    private void button2_Click(object sender, System.EventArgs e)
    {
        if (listBox1.SelectedIndex < 0)
            return;
        object obj = listBox1.Items[listBox1.SelectedIndex];
        listBox1.Items.Remove (obj);
    }

    private void button3_Click(object sender, System.EventArgs e)
    {
        Application.Exit ();
    }

    public string AddItemToList (string strAdd)
    {
        if (strAdd == "")
            return ("");
        if (listBox1.FindString (strAdd, -1) < 0)
        {
            listBox1.Items.Add (strAdd);
```

```
                    return ("");
                }
                MessageBox.Show ("\"" + strAdd +
                        "\" is already in the list box", "Duplicate");
                return (strAdd);
            }
        }
    }
```

Instead of adding an item to the list box directly, the Add Item button will display the second form as a modeless form. The Delete Item button will remove the selected item from the list box.

You will enter text for the list box items using the text box on the second form. When you click the Add button on the second form, the event handler will call the *AddItemToList()* method in the *MainForm* class. The code for the *AddItemForm* class is shown here:

```
using System;
using System.Drawing;
using System.Collections;
using System.ComponentModel;
using System.Windows.Forms;

namespace Modeless
{
    /// <summary>
    /// Summary description for AddItemForm.
    /// </summary>
    public class AddItemForm : System.Windows.Forms.Form
    {
        private System.Windows.Forms.TextBox textBox1;
        private System.Windows.Forms.Button button1;
        private System.Windows.Forms.Button button2;
        /// <summary>
        /// Required designer variable.
        /// </summary>
        private System.ComponentModel.Container components = null;
        MainForm parent;
        public AddItemForm(MainForm parent)
        {
            //
            // Required for Windows Forms Designer support
            //
            InitializeComponent();

            //
            // TODO: Add any constructor code after InitializeComponent call
            //
            this.parent = parent;
        }
```

```csharp
/// <summary>
/// Clean up any resources being used.
/// </summary>
protected override void Dispose( bool disposing )
{
    if( disposing )
    {
        if(components != null)
        {
            components.Dispose();
        }
    }
    base.Dispose( disposing );
}


#region Windows Forms Designer generated code
/// <summary>
/// Required method for Forms Designer support - do not modify
/// the contents of this method with the code editor.
/// </summary>
private void InitializeComponent()
{
    this.textBox1 = new System.Windows.Forms.TextBox();
    this.button1 = new System.Windows.Forms.Button();
    this.button2 = new System.Windows.Forms.Button();
    this.SuspendLayout();
    //
    // textBox1
    //
    this.textBox1.Location = new System.Drawing.Point(28, 8);
    this.textBox1.Name = "textBox1";
    this.textBox1.Size = new System.Drawing.Size(224, 20);
    this.textBox1.TabIndex = 1;
    this.textBox1.Text = "";
    //
    // button1
    //
    this.button1.Location = new System.Drawing.Point(40, 48);
    this.button1.Name = "button1";
    this.button1.TabIndex = 2;
    this.button1.Text = "Add";
    this.button1.Click +=
                    new System.EventHandler(this.button1_Click_1);
    //
    // button2
    //
    this.button2.Location = new System.Drawing.Point(184, 48);
```

```
            this.button2.Name = "button2";
            this.button2.TabIndex = 3;
            this.button2.Text = "Close";
            this.button2.Click += new System.EventHandler(this.button2_Click);
            //
            // AddItemForm
            //
            this.AutoScaleBaseSize = new System.Drawing.Size(5, 13);
            this.ClientSize = new System.Drawing.Size(280, 77);
            this.Controls.AddRange(new System.Windows.Forms.Control[] {
                                        this.button2,
                                        this.button1,
                                        this.textBox1});
            this.Name = "AddItemForm";
            this.Text = "AddItem";
            this.ResumeLayout(false);

        }
        #endregion

        private void button1_Click_1(object sender, System.EventArgs e)
        {
            textBox1.Text = parent.AddItemToList (textBox1.Text);
        }

        private void button2_Click(object sender, System.EventArgs e)
        {
            this.Dispose ();
            this.Close ();
        }
    }
}
```

Compile and run the program. Check that the Add Item button on the first form displays the second form. With the second form displayed, enter some text in the text box and click on the Add button. The text should appear in the list box on the first form. Without closing the second form, add three or four items to the list box.

Notice that you can return to the first form without closing the second form. Simply click on the first form to activate it. Again, without closing the second form, select an item in the list box and press the Delete Item button.

When you click the Close button on the second form, the form's *Dispose()* method is called. This method is a member of the *System.Windows.Forms.Form* class, and frees system resources used by the form. When you call this method, it sets the *IsDisposed* property to *true*, and you can use the property to prevent multiple instances of the second form from being created. When you click the Add Item button on the first form, the event handler looks at this property. If the property is *true*, the event handler creates a new instance of the form.

CHAPTER 14

Debugging C# Programs

TIPS IN THIS CHAPTER

"One dollar and eighty-seven cents. That was all. And sixty cents of it was in pennies."

– William Sydney Porter

Everybody makes mistakes. You might have recognized the quote as the opening of author O'Henry's *The Gift of the Magi*. O'Henry, of course, was William Sydney Porter's pen name, and that slight arithmetic incongruity did not stop *The Gift of the Magi* from becoming one of the most widely read short stories in the world.

The point is that no matter how good you are at the art of programming, or how carefully you write your code, errors are going to creep in. If you mistype the name of a variable or make a mistake in syntax, the compiler usually will catch the error before your code makes it to the executable state.

The compiler, however, is not going to perform your arithmetic for you. It will not know that a loop is being performed one time too many or one time too few. The compiler is concerned only with whether you use the language properly, and it will not detect when a method returns the wrong object or value, as long as the return can be cast properly.

Visual C# is designed to minimize programming errors. It is pickier than compilers for most languages, and it will issue an error in many cases where another language compiler might issue only a warning, if that much. It is much less likely that a C# program will achieve executable status with many of the common errors that weary programmers make.

When errors do creep into your programs—and they will—you move from the coding stage to the debugging stage. Debugging may be as simple as scanning the lines of your code looking for obvious problems, or it may be as complex as stepping through your code line by line in a debugger, examining the values of each variable, property, and method return as you encounter them.

The .NET Framework and Visual Studio contain a number of tools that can help you during the debugging process. Visual Studio .NET includes a number of new debugging features, including cross-language debugging, multiple-program debugging, multi-threaded debugging, and the ability to attach to a running process and examine it in a debugger. The .NET library contains a number of classes that are intended to assist in the debugging process.

These tools range from a trusty command line debugger, *cordbg.exe*, to graphical debuggers in the .NET Framework and Visual Studio. Just-In-Time debuggers, not new with .NET or Visual Studio .NET, give you the ability to break into a running process when the process encounters an error and throws an exception.

Creating a Debug Version of Your Program

The first step in the debugging process is to build a *debug version* of your program. For command-line programs, you do this using the */debug* compiler switch, which causes the compiler to write debug information to the executable file. Using this switch, the compiler also creates a *program database* file, with an extension of *.pdb,* along with the executable file.

The */debug* switch has a few options. Specifying */debug*, */debug+*, or */debug:full* produces essentially the same result: each causes the compiler to create the *.pdb* file and to write debugging information to the executable. On the other hand, specifying */debug–* is the same as *not* using the switch; it tells the compiler not to emit debugging information and not to create the program database file.

The program database file must have the same name as the executable file, but with a *.pdb* extension instead of *.exe*. You cannot specify a different program database file for the debuggers. In addition, the debuggers look for the program database file in the same directory as the executable. However, if the Visual Studio debugger cannot find the program database file in that directory, you can specify additional search directories.

A program's *.pdb* file contains full debugging information, including function prototypes. The file contains more information than Visual C++ programmers may be used to, and the compiler can add to the file incrementally as you develop your program. Incremental additions mean the compiler can add only information that has changed, without wasting a lot of its time rewriting the entire file.

You can specify that you want the compiler to generate the program database file but not to write any debugging information in the executable file. The command-line option is */debug:pdbonly*. With this option, you enable full source-code debugging when you start the program in a debugger. However, if the program is already running and you attach a debugger to it, you will not have the benefit of source-code debugging. Instead, the debugger will display the code in assembler statements.

Command-line debuggers are not as prevalent as they used to be. A great many programmers have never used a command-line debugger, so this chapter will not explore *cordbg.exe* too extensively. For detailed information on the debugger commands, look in the MSDN documentation under the topic "Cordbg.exe" (note the lowercase *d*). Nevertheless, you need to be aware of the command-line debugger, and you should have some idea of how it works.

Compile the following program, *dbTest.cs*, using the */debug:full* compiler switch:

```
// dbTest.cs -- Sample program to be used with cordbg.exe
//
//              Compile this program with the following command line:
//                  C:>csc /debug:full dbTest.cs
//
using System;

namespace nsDebug
{
    class clsMain
    {
        static public void Main ()
        {
            double x = 7.0;
            while (true)
            {
                Console.Write ("\r\nPlease enter a number: ");
                string str = Console.ReadLine ();
                if (str.Length == 0)
                    break;
                double val = 0;
                try
                {
                    val = Convert.ToDouble (str);
```

```
                }
                catch (Exception)
                {
                    Console.WriteLine ("\r\nInvalid number");
                    continue;
                }
                Console.WriteLine (x + " X " + val +
                                    " = {0,0:F6}", val / x);
            }
        }
    }
}
```

In the same directory where you compile the program, start the *cordbg.exe* command-line debugger. At the debugger prompt, enter **run dbtest.exe**. Your screen should contain code like the following:

```
Microsoft (R) Common Language Runtime Test Debugger Shell.
Version 1.0.2914.16 Copyright (C) Microsoft Corp. 1998-2001. All rights
reserved.

(cordbg) run dbtest.exe
Process 1168/0x490 created.
Warning: couldn't load symbols for
c:\winnt\microsoft.net\framework\v1.0.2914\mscorlib.dll
[thread 0x590] Thread created.

014:                double x = 7.0;
(cordbg)
```

Use the *next* command (which you enter at the *cordbg* prompt) to step through the program statements. When you come to a method that is contained in a system assembly, you can step over it with the *next* command, or you can use the *step* command to display the method's assembly instructions. Type **help** to get a list of the available commands. End the debugging process by typing **exit** or **quit** at the prompt.

To attach the debugger to a running process, you must first know the *process id* (PID) of the process. To attach the debugger to a process, first start the program and let it run to the point where you want to start debugging.

Type **pro** to get a list of the .NET processes running on the computer, similar to the following:

```
Microsoft (R) Common Language Runtime Test Debugger Shell.
Version 1.0.2914.16 Copyright (C) Microsoft Corp. 1998-2001. All rights
reserved.

(cordbg) pro
PID=0x604 (1540)   Name=C:\CFiles\DBTEST\DBTEST.EXE
```

```
    ID=1   AppDomainName=DBTEST.EXE

PID=0x534 (1332)  Name=C:\Program Files\Microsoft Visual
Studio.NET\Common7\IDE\devenv
    ID=1   AppDomainName=DefaultDomain
(cordbg)
```

In this case, the only .NET programs running on this computer are *dbTest.exe* and one instance of Visual Studio .NET. The PID for *dbTest.exe* is *1540*.

On Windows NT systems, you can get the PID from the Windows Task Manager. Right-click a blank area of the task bar. Select Task Manager from the popup menu. When the Task Manager window appears, select the Processes tab as shown in Figure 14-1.

Search through the process list for the name of the program you want to debug. The PID is the number in the second column. Use this number in *cordbg.exe* to attach to the process using the following command. (*1540* is the PID of *dbTest.exe* shown in Figure 14-1.) You may have to start another command window to run *cordbg*.

```
(cordbg) attach 1540
```

If the debugger successfully attaches to the process, it will show you the address where it attached. Use the same commands to step through the program.

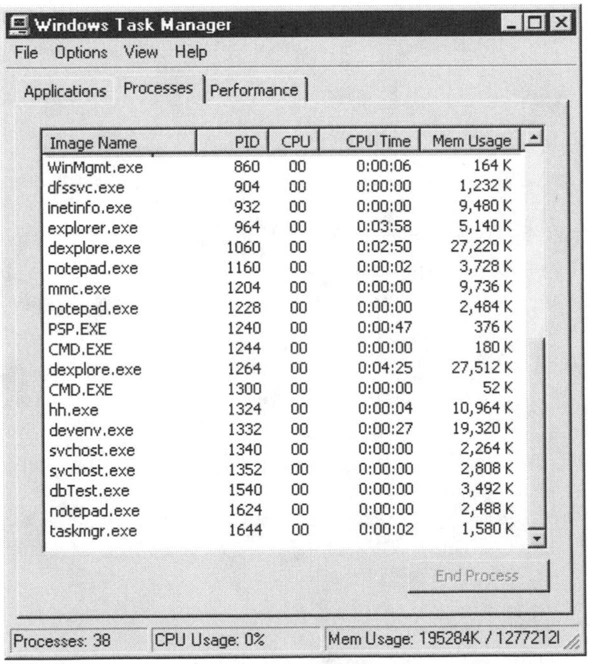

Figure 14.1 The Windows Task Manager lists all the processes running on an NT system, along with their process ids

It is more likely that you would prefer to use a graphical user interface (GUI)-based debugger such as *DbgCLR.exe* or the Visual Studio .NET debugger. The *DbgCLR* program is the Microsoft part of the .NET Software Development Kit (SDK), and you can use it even if you do not have Visual Studio .NET. *DbgCLR*, however, will not compile any changes you make to a program.

Debugging C# and .NET Applications Using *DbgCLR.exe*

Whether you use the command-line debugger or the GUI-based *DbgCLR.exe*, you still must compile your programs using the */debug* flag to produce a program database file. The *DbgCLR* debugger looks similar to the Visual Studio .NET debugger.

The .NET SDK installation program puts *DbgCLR.exe* in its *FrameworkSDK\GuiDebug* subdirectory. If you used the defaults when you installed the SDK, you should find the *DbgCLR.exe* program file in the *C:\Program Files\Microsoft.NET\FrameworkSDK\GuiDebug* directory. If you intend to use the debugger often, you might add it to your system's *PATH* environment variable or create a shortcut to it in a more convenient location.

 You can start a program in a debugging session from within the debugger, as shown next, or you can attach it to a running process, which is described a bit later.

1. To start a debugging session, start *DbgCLR*.

2. When the debugger starts, open the Debug menu. The only item on this menu at this point is Program To Debug. Select this item to open the Program To Debug dialog box, where you can enter the program file name, any arguments you want to pass to the program, and the working directory, as shown here.

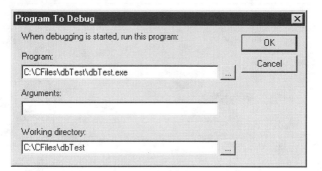

3. The ellipse (…) buttons next to the Program and Working directory boxes are browse buttons. Click them to find and set up a path to the target program.

4. Locate and select the *dbTest.exe* program and click OK to close the dialog box. The debugger window will not change much, but you should notice that the program name appears in the Solution Explorer panel on the right side of the screen. If you now examine the Debug menu, you should see a list of commands to start, break, and step through the program, among other tasks.

5. Press the F5 key to start the program in the debugger.

6. Now select the debugger window and press CTRL-ALT-BREAK to break the program. The debugger will display the source file, as shown in Figure 14-2. Notice that the title bar indicates that the file is open in read-only mode. The debugger contains no compiler, so you cannot change and recompile the program from *DbgCLR*.

Alternatively, you may attach a debugger to a running process using *DbgCLR*.

1. Close the program you are debugging by choosing File | Close Solution. You can save the solution file for later debugging sessions if you want.

2. Without leaving the debugger, start *dbTest.exe* in a command window. Return to the debugger window and choose Tools | Debug Processes. This will display the Processes dialog box shown in Figure 14-3.

3. Unlike the *pro* command in *cordbg*, which listed only .NET programs, the Processes dialog box will list all the programs you are running on the computer. A check box option allows you to

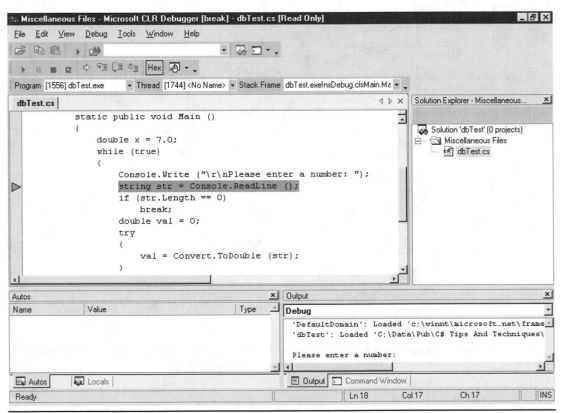

Figure 14.2   Breaking the program will display the source file in the debugger

display system processes as well. If you select a process that is not a .NET program, the debugger will create a solution but will not add the program to the solution.

4. Search through the list of processes and select the *dbTest.exe* program. Click the Attach button to attach the debugger to the process. You may add multiple processes to a debugging session.

5. When you have added all the processes you want to debug, click the Close button to dispatch the Processes dialog box.

6. The program now is attached to the debugger. If you break the program using CTRL-ALT-BREAK, you should see the debugging window shown in Figure 14-2. The *dbTest.exe* program is waiting for you to enter a number.

To detach the debugger from a process, choose Debug | Detach All. If you have attached it to multiple processes, this will end debugging on all the processes.

To detach just from one process, choose Debug | Processes. This will return you to the Processes dialog box in Figure 14-3. At the bottom of the dialog box is a list of processes to which the debugger is attached. Select the one you want to detach, and then click the Detach button.

You may have noticed that the command-line debugger, *CorDBG.exe*, terminated the program when you exited the debugger. However, when you ended the debugging session in *DbgCLR*, the program you were debugging is still running. In fact, if you type *CorDBG* before leaving *DbgCLR* and then enter the *pro* command, you will see another instance of *dbTest.exe* running.

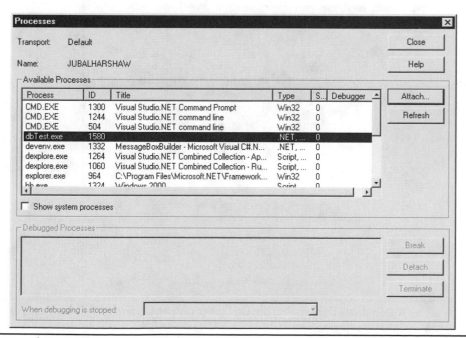

Figure 14.3   The Processes dialog box lists program that you are running on your computer

Troubleshooting .NET Applications Using Just-In-Time Debugging

You also can start the *DbgCLR* debugger after a program throws an exception, in which case, the debugger serves as a Just-In-Time debugger. *Just-In-Time* denotes an action that is performed on demand. The demand in this case is an unhandled exception, and the CLR asks you whether you want to start a debugging session and attach the program to it.

USE IT

1. To demonstrate this, you can remove or comment out the *try* statement in *dbTest.cs*, and remove or comment out the entire *catch* block.

2. Recompile the program, again using the */debug:full* switch, and run it.

3. Enter a non-numeric value, such as **xyz**, and press ENTER. Almost immediately, you will see a Just-In-Time Debugging dialog box, as shown in Figure 14-4.

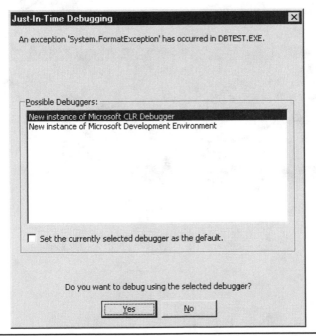

Figure 14.4   The Just-In-Time Debugging dialog box is an entry point to the .NET and Visual Studio debuggers

4. If you have not installed Visual Studio, only the .NET debugger will appear in this list. (It is possible to write and compile programs on one computer and debug them on another.) Select the line that reads New Instance Of Microsoft CLR Debugger and click the Yes button to start the debugger and automatically attach to the process.

5. After you are in the debugger, you will see a dialog box similar to the one shown here, which notifies you of the exception and gives you any additional information available.

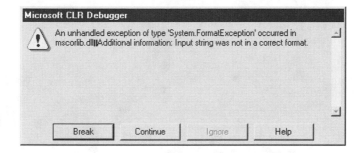

6. Click the Break button to pause the program at the point where the program threw the exception. You can now examine the variables and statements to determine what caused the exception.

Running a Program in the Visual Studio Debugger

The Visual Studio debugger is similar to the *DbgCLR.exe* program, so much so that sometimes you might have to look twice to see which debugger you are running. The Visual Studio debugger, however, offers many more tools and has more capability than the *DbgCLR* program.

USE IT   The first thing you will notice is that the Visual Studio debugger will attach to non-.NET processes as well as .NET processes. When you attach to a process, you will see the same Processes dialog box that you saw in *DbgCLR*. However, when you click the Attach button, you will see a second dialog box, shown in Figure 14-5, that asks you what type of processes you want to debug.

If you remove the checkmarks from the check boxes for all types except Common Language Runtime, the debugger will not be able to break into non-.NET programs, which is similar to the actions of *DbgCLR*.

Another major difference in this Processes dialog box is that the Transport and Name fields are combo box controls rather than just label fields. Using the Visual Studio debugger, you can attach to a program running on other computers across a network using whatever transports (such as TCP/IP) that are available. Clicking the arrow button next to the Processes dialog box's Name control will

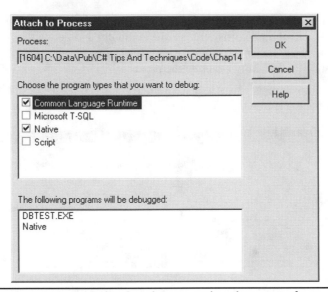

Figure 14.5   The Attach to Process dialog box lets you select the types of programs to debug

display the Browse For Computer dialog box, shown next. You can select another computer to attach to a process from here.

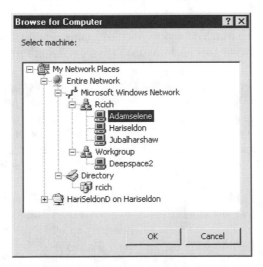

This dialog box shows three computers running in the RCICH domain (actually named rcich.org) and a fourth computer named Deepspace2—a firewall—that is not a member of the domain.

To use remote debugging, you need to install the remote debugging components on the machines to which you want to attach. The installation is included on the Visual Studio CDs and can be run separately without installing Visual Studio on the remote machine(s).

In addition to Just-In-Time debugging, Visual Studio contains the tools you need to create and test projects. To debug a Visual Studio project, you load the project, or solution, file in the IDE and then use the same debugging commands available in Just-In-Time debugging. You can run the program directly in the debugger without having to attach to it, however.

Setting Breakpoints to Suspend a Program's Execution

A *breakpoint* is a position you set in a program that will cause the debugger to pause the program. With the program paused, you can inspect the contents of variables and single-step through the program code.

You can set conditions on breakpoints so that the program pauses only when a certain condition occurs, such as a value of a variable.

 USE IT   To demonstrate breakpoints, open the *AddControls* project from Chapter 13.

1. Locate a line in the source file where you want the program to break, and click in the left margin. The IDE will place a maroon circle in the margin and highlight the code line in maroon.

2. With the *AddControls* project open, scroll down to line 126 and click in the left margin. The IDE should appear as shown in Figure 14-6.

3. Start the program running in the debugger by pressing the F5 key.

4. When the form appears, type something in the text box and click the Add Item button. Immediately after you click, the program should pause, the source file will appear, and the line where you set the breakpoint will appear in yellow. The yellow highlight indicates the current execution point of a program paused in the debugger.

   This is an example of placing an *unconditional* breakpoint. When the program executes the statement in the debugger, the program will pause. At this point, you can examine variables, add objects to the Watch window, and single-step through the program using the F10 and F11 keys.

5. Now move the cursor over the *strAdd* variable in the line containing the breakpoint. The statement has not executed yet, so a tool tip window should pop up showing that the value is null.

6. Move the cursor to the *Text* property of the text box at the end of the same line. The tool tip window should show that it contains the text you entered in the text box.

7. Press the F10 key and look again at the *strAdd* variable. Pressing F10 executes the current line and moves the current instruction marker, the yellow highlight, to the next line. Now the *strAdd* variable should show the same value as the text you typed.

The F10 key invokes the *Step Over* command and the F11 key invokes the *Step Into* command. When you press the F10 key on a line containing a method call, the program will execute the method and return, moving the current execution point to the next line. If you want to step into the method and examine the statements there, press the F11 key instead.

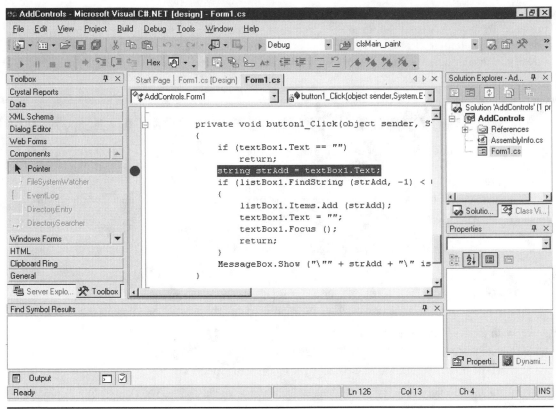

Figure 14.6 The *AddControls* project in Visual Studio showing a breakpoint at line 126

With the program paused, you can add a variable to the Watch window as well.

1. If the Watch window is not open, choose Debug | Windows | Watch. A submenu should appear, giving you the option of viewing any of four watch windows. You can store different sets of variables in each watch window to keep track of them more easily. Select one of the windows, and it should appear at the bottom left of the screen.

2. Click the blank area in the Name column in the Watch window and begin typing the name of the *strAdd* variable.

3. Press ENTER. The contents of the variable should appear in the Value column and the data type should appear in the Type column.

4. You can change the value at this point. Double-click the value and it will open as an editable field.

Another method of adding a variable to the Watch window is to drag it from the source code window and drop it in the Watch window.

1. Highlight the variable name as you would highlight text in any text editor.
2. Click and hold down the left mouse button on the highlighted text. Drag the mouse cursor and the text to the Watch window and release the mouse button. The information about the variable will appear as if you had typed it in.

You can set conditions on breakpoints. You may want the breakpoint to halt the program only when a variable has reached 0, or perhaps you may want the break to occur after the statement containing the breakpoint has executed 10 times.

1. Choose Debug | New Breakpoint to display the New Breakpoint dialog box. Note that the name of this dialog is a little misleading, because you can edit the properties of an existing breakpoint as well as add new breakpoints from here. In fact, it is easier to set the breakpoint first and then edit it from this dialog box than it is to enter all of the information for a new breakpoint into these fields. If you have more than one breakpoint set, click the line containing the breakpoint before opening the dialog box. When the dialog box appears, it will already have entered the information about the breakpoint.
2. To set a condition on a breakpoint, click the Condition button to display the Breakpoint Condition dialog box.
3. You can enter any value, variable name, or expression that is valid to the compiler in the Condition box. A variable name must be in scope at the line where you place the breakpoint. If you check the Is True check box, however, the expression, variable, or value must evaluate to *true* or *false*. The Breakpoint Condition dialog box will let you set an invalid condition, but you will get an error when the IDE attempts to evaluate it. You also may select the Has Changed check box to cause the program to break when the value of the variable changes.
4. To disable the condition without removing any of the information about the breakpoint, uncheck the Condition box.
5. Finally, you can cause the breakpoint to pause the program only after the program has executed the statement a certain number of times. Click the Hit Count button and enter the information in the boxes.
6. Select a breakpoint frequency and enter a value in the box to the right.

To remove a breakpoint, click the maroon circle in the debugger code's margin. The line will return to normal.

Setting Conditions on Methods

You can selectively include or exclude methods from a program by using *conditional methods*. The compilation of a conditional method, including any calls to the method elsewhere in the code, will depend on whether you have defined a symbol using the *#define* preprocessor directive.

The conditional attribute is part of the *System.Diagnostics* namespace, so to use conditional methods you must include the following *using* statement in your program:

```
using System.Diagnostics;
```

To declare a method as conditional, use the *Condition* attribute when you define the method. You also must include a symbol in the attribute, as in the following snippet:

```
[Condition("<symbol>")]
private void Method(<params>)
{
//  Method statements
}
```

If *<symbol>* has been defined, the method and all calls to the method will be included in the compiled code. If *<symbol>* has not been defined, the method and any calls to it elsewhere in the code will not be included in the compilation. In C++, you would accomplish selective compilation by setting a function name to a function that does nothing, or a *null* function, when a symbol has or has not been defined. The conditional method is even better. If the symbol has not been defined, the method and all calls to it simply disappear from the compiled code. Although it still appears in the source code, you cannot even set a breakpoint in it or on any line containing a call to the conditional method.

There are, however, some conditions in regard to using conditional methods:

- A conditional method must have a *void* return type.

- A conditional method cannot override another method in a base class. It can, however, be marked as *virtual* and be overridden in a derived class. In the latter case, the derived class method inherits the conditional attribute.

- You cannot use the conditional attribute on a method that implements a method defined in an interface.

The MSDN documentation also notes that a conditional method must be part of a class definition. However, it will work as a member of a structure.

USE IT   The following program, *CondMeth.cs*, implements a conditional method that will be included in the compilation only when the symbol *MY_CONDITION* has been defined. The method displays the value passed to the constructor of a class:

```
// CondMeth.cs -- demonstrates the use of a conditional method
//
//              Compile this program with the following command line:
//                    C:>csc CondMeth.cs
//
#define MY_CONDITION

using System;
```

```
using System.Diagnostics;

namespace nsConditional
{
    class clsMain
    {
        static public void Main ()
        {
            clsTest test = new clsTest(42);
            test.ShowValue ();
        }
    }
    class clsTest
    {
        public clsTest (int num)
        {
            m_Num = num;
        }
        int m_Num;

        [Conditional("MY_CONDITION")]
        public void ShowValue()
        {
            if (m_Num < 50)
            {
                Console.WriteLine (m_Num + " is less than 50");
            }
        }
    }
}
```

Compile and run the program to verify that the method is being called. The program should print out a message telling you that the value passed to the constructor is less than 50.

Now remove the *#define* directive at the top of the source code file. Recompile and run the program again, and you will not see the message.

You also can control the definition of a symbol using the */define* or */d* compiler switch. Make sure the *#define* directive in the source file has been removed or commented out, and then compile the program using the following command line:

```
C:>csc /d:MY_CONDITION CondMeth.cs
```

Now when you run the program, the method will execute.

In Visual Studio projects, you typically will use conditional expressions with the *DEBUG* definition to help you diagnose code in your programs. When you compile the debug version of a project in Visual Studio, the IDE defines *DEBUG*. To take advantage of this, you can mark conditional expressions with the following condition:

```
[Conditional("DEBUG")]
```

Methods marked with this condition will be included only in debug builds of your program. When you build the release version, the compiler will remove the method and all calls to the method. Be sure to add the *using* statement for *System.Diagnostics*; the application wizard does not automatically include this statement.

Compiling a command-line program with the */debug* flag does not automatically define the *DEBUG* symbol; it creates the program database file, places debugging information in the program, and causes the compiler not to "optimize" the code. You may define the symbol by adding a *#define* directive at the top of the source code file or by using the */d:DEBUG* compiler flag.

Recovering the *StackTrace*

When your program throws an exception, the Common Language Runtime (CLR) begins unwinding the stack looking for an exception handler. In the process, the *Exception* object, or an object created from a class derived from *Exception*, collects important information about the methods on the stack and keeps it in an internal property named *StackTrace*.

Normally, the stack is captured just before the exception is thrown and the stack begins unwinding. It is then saved in the *StackTrace* property. This is a *string* property and you may print it directly to the console.

USE IT   The following program, *StakTrce.cs*, throws an exception when it is four method calls deep. In the second method, it catches the exception and prints the *StackTrace* property in the exception object.

```
// StakTrce.cs -- demonstrates printing the stack trace when an
//                exception is thrown.
//
//                Compile this program with the following command line:
//                    C:>csc /debug:full StakTrce.cs
using System;

namespace nsExceptions
{
    class clsMain
    {
        static public void Main ()
        {
            clsTest test = new clsTest();
            test.TestStackTrace ();
```

```
        }
    }
    public class clsTest
    {
        public void TestStackTrace ()
        {
            try
            {
                CauseTrouble(1.7);
            }
            catch (Exception e)
            {
                Console.WriteLine (e.StackTrace);
            }
        }
        void CauseTrouble (double val)
        {
            clsAnother nudder = new clsAnother ();
            nudder.MakeProblem ((int) val);
        }
    }
    class clsAnother
    {
        public void MakeProblem (int x)
        {
            throw (new Exception());
        }
    }
}
```

Compiling and running *StakTrce.cs* will print the series of method calls that lead back from the point where the exception was thrown to the point where it was caught:

```
   at nsExceptions.clsAnother.MakeProblem(Int32 x) in
C:\CFILES\C#\STAKTRCE\StakTrce.cs:line 41
   at nsExceptions.clsTest.CauseTrouble(Double val) in
C:\CFILES\C#\STAKTRCE\StakTrce.cs:line 34
   at nsExceptions.clsTest.TestStackTrace() in
 C:\CFILES\C#\STAKTRCE\StakTrce.cs:line 24
```

This detailed information is available only when you compile a program using the */debug* flag. Simply defining the *DEBUG* symbol will not cause the compiler to create the program database file. In fact, without the */debug* flag, the compiler will "optimize" the intermediate language code, and the trace may be entirely different, as the next bit of code will demonstrate.

Recompile *StakTrce.cs* without the */debug* flag and run it again, and you will see the following output:

```
at nsExceptions.clsAnother.MakeProblem()
at nsExceptions.clsTest.TestStackTrace()
```

So what happened to the call to *CauseTrouble()*? The method performs no useful processing. It simply creates an object of the *clsAnother* class and calls a member method, *MakeProblem()*. Apparently, the compiler has optimized the code to make it more efficient, simply creating the object and calling the method.

You might also notice that the stack trace in either case tells you nothing about how the program got to the method where it caught the exception. So you do not know where the call to *TestStackTrace()* was actually performed.

This information is available on the stack, and you can recover it at any time by calling the stack trace from the *Environment* class. All the methods and properties of *Environment* are *static*, so you do not have to create an instance of the class. In addition, you can see the trace information even if no exception is thrown. In *StakTrce.cs*, modify the *MakeProblem()* method so that it does not throw an exception. Replace the *throw* statement with the following line:

```
Console.WriteLine (Environment.StackTrace);
```

Now compile the program using the */debug:full* compiler flag. When you run the program, you will see a full trace of the method calls on the stack, including the call to get the stack trace itself:

```
at System.Environment.GetStackTrace(Exception e)
at System.Environment.GetStackTrace(Exception e)
at System.Environment.get_StackTrace()
at nsExceptions.clsAnother.MakeProblem(Int32 x) in
C:\CFILES\C#\STAKTRCE\EnvTrace.cs:line 42
at nsExceptions.clsTest.CauseTrouble(Double val) in
C:\CFILES\C#\STAKTRCE\EnvTrace.cs:line 36
at nsExceptions.clsTest.TestStackTrace() in
C:\CFILES\C#\STAKTRCE\EnvTrace.cs:line 16707566
at nsExceptions.clsMain.Main() in
C:\CFILES\C#\STAKTRCE\EnvTrace.cs:line 16
```

In this example, the program has been copied to *EnvTrace.cs* before making the modifications.

Using the *Debug* Class

The .NET Framework contains a number of classes in the *System.Diagnostics* namespace to help you debug a program. There are some 50 classes in this namespace, all aimed at helping you find and fix problems in your applications.

An important and useful member of this namespace is the *Debug* class. All the members of *Debug* are *static*, so you do not need to declare an instance of the class to use the methods and properties.

However, you cannot just insert calls to the *Debug* class methods in your code. Instead, you first must define the *DEBUG* symbol using the */d:DEBUG* compiler option or placing a *#define* directive at the top of your source file.

Then you must provide a *trace listener* for the *Debug* methods. The next tip in this chapter covers listeners, but to enable the code used in this tip you will need to create a listener to cause the *Debug* class to write to the console. A trace listener directs debug and tracing output to a specified object. The trace listener collection is contained in the *Listeners* property of the *Debug* class.

USE IT To show how the trace listener works for the *Debug* class, enter the following program, *DebugTst.cs*, and compile it with the flags shown at the top of the program:

```
// DebugTst.cs -- A simple demonstration of the Debug class.
//
//                  Compile this program with the following command line:
//                      C:>csc /debug:full /d:DEBUG DebugTst.cs
using System;
using System.Diagnostics;
using System.IO;

namespace nsDebugTest
{
    class clsMain
    {
        static void Main()
        {
            Debug.WriteLine ("Debug is on");
            clsTest test = new clsTest(42);
            test.ShowValue();
        }
    }
    class clsTest
    {
        public clsTest (int num)
        {
            m_Num = num;
        }
        int m_Num;

        public void ShowValue()
        {
            try
            {
                DoSomething ();
            }
            catch (Exception e)
```

```
            {
                Console.WriteLine (e.StackTrace);
            }
            if (m_Num < 50)
            {
                Debug.WriteLine (m_Num + " is less than 50");
            }
        }
        void DoSomething ()
        {
            Debug.WriteLine (Environment.StackTrace);
        }
    }
}
```

When you run the program, it does absolutely nothing. It simply runs and then returns, although you compiled it with the *DEBUG* symbol defined. The calls to *Debug.WriteLine( )* execute, but the output has nowhere to go.

Now modify the Main() method to create a trace listener for the console. The method should look like the following listing:

```
static void Main()
{
    Debug.Listeners.Clear();  // Dump any existing listeners.
    Debug.Listeners.Add (new TextWriterTraceListener(Console.Out));
    Debug.AutoFlush = true;
    Debug.WriteLine ("Debug is on");
    clsTest test = new clsTest(42);
    test.ShowValue();
}
```

Recompile the program using the command line in the program. When you run it now, the program prints several lines of debugging information.

The *Debug.AutoFlush* property tells the *Debug* class methods to flush the stream on every write. Flushing on every write is not so important for the *Console.Out* object, because it normally flushes the stream on every line, but it does become important when you use the methods to output debug information to files. The *AutoFlush* property is *false* by default. If you do not set it to *true*, you can call *Debug.Flush( )* at any time to flush the listener streams.

The *Debug.WriteLine( )* method is similar to the *Console.WriteLine( )* method except that it writes to the listener rather than directly to the console. The *Debug* class also provides a similar *Write( )* method, but it also contains conditional write methods.

The *Debug.WriteIf( )* method writes to the listener collection only if a given condition is *true*. The first parameter to the method must be a value, variable, or expression that evaluates to a Boolean *true* or *false*, as in the following snippet:

```
int var = 2;
Debug.WriteIf (var == 0, "The variable is 0");
```

This would cause *WriteIf()* not to write anything to the output because the test expression is *false*. If the test expression evaluated to *true*, the message would be written. The *Debug.WriteLineIf()* performs in the same way, except that it appends a line-ending sequence to the output.

The *Debug.Assert()* method uses the reverse logic. It will print the message if the test expression is *false*, and it will inhibit any output when the expression is *true*:

```
int var = 2;
Debug.Assert (var == 0, "The variable is not 0");
```

In addition, the *Assert()* method will include the string *Fail:* in front of the message. When inserted into code, the preceding snippet will produce the following output:

```
Fail: The variable is not 0
```

The *Assert()* method provides more than just reverse logic for output, however. A statement using *Assert()* will work even if you did not add the *Console.Out* stream to the listener collection. Without a listener, the *Assert()* method will display a message box if the test expression is *false*. Modify the *Main()* method in the previous project so that it looks like the following:

```
static public void Main ()
{
    int var = 2;
    Debug.Assert (var == 0, "The variable is not 0");
}
```

Compile and run the program. When the *Debug.Assert()* statement executes, you will see a message box similar to that shown here.

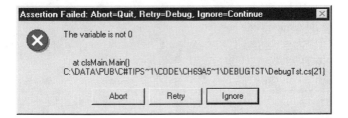

The message box contains the message you included in the method call plus the stack trace. If you click Abort, the program will end. Clicking Ignore will cause the program to continue normally. Clicking Retry will cause the program to perform the test again. If the test fails a second time, it will throw an exception and you will be asked whether you want to debug the program.

The *Debug* class also contains properties to control the indentation of debug messages. The *IndentSize* property determines the number of spaces to write to the listener streams before printing the debug messages. The default value is four spaces. The *IndentLevel* determines how many times these spaces are printed before the debug message prints. Calling the *Debug.Indent()* or *Debug.Unindent()* method increments or decrements the *IndentLevel* property by one, the same as executing *++Debug.IndentLevel* or *--Debug.IndentLevel*.

Indenting lines of code gives a visual indication of how deep into your program a problem occurs. The following program, *Indent.cs*, shows an example of indenting:

```
// Indent.cs -- Demonstrates indenting debug messages.
//
//              Compile this program with the following command line:
//                  C:>csc /debug:full /d:DEBUG Indent.cs
using System;
using System.Diagnostics;

namespace nsDebugging
{
    class clsMain
    {
        static public void Main ()
        {
            Debug.Listeners.Clear ();
            Debug.Listeners.Add (new TextWriterTraceListener(Console.Out));
            Debug.AutoFlush = true;
            Debug.IndentSize = 5;
            Debug.WriteLine ("First level debug message.");
            FirstMethod ();
            Debug.WriteLine ("Return to first level debug message.");
        }
        static private void FirstMethod ()
        {
            Debug.Indent ();
            Debug.WriteLine ("Second level debug message");
            SecondMethod ();
            Debug.WriteLine ("Return to second level debug message");
            Debug.Unindent ();
        }
        static private void SecondMethod ()
        {
            Debug.Indent ();
            Debug.WriteLine ("Third level debug message.");
            Debug.Unindent  ();
        }
    }
}
```

Each method call increments the indent level upon entering and decrements it upon leaving. Thus, its message will always be shown indented relative to the method that called it. The following shows the output from this program:

```
First level debug message.
     Second level debug message
          Third level debug message.
     Return to second level debug message
Return to first level debug message.
```

Debug contains two other methods that are useful. The *Close()* method flushes all the output buffers and then closes the listeners. When you execute this method, no more debugging messages will be printed through the *Debug* class.

The *Fail()* method provides an assertion that will always fail. Unlike *Debug.Assert()*, it does not need to be passed a test expression because it can never succeed. You need only pass it the error message to print or to display on the assertion message box.

The *Trace* class provides methods and properties identical to the *Debug* class. Implementing the *Trace* class, however, requires that you define a *TRACE* symbol using the */d:TRACE* compiler option or adding a *#define TRACE* line to your source file.

By providing identical methods and properties in two different classes, you can provide alternative debugging steps in a program. For example, in a debugging session, you may want to see the debugging message on the console. In a release version of the program, one compiled without the */debug* compiler flag, you may want to write the messages to a log file. You can maintain a single source code file for debugging and for the release version.

In projects you create using Visual Studio .NET, trace is enabled by default in both the debug and release versions of the program.

Using Trace Listeners

A *trace listener* is an object created from an instance of a class derived from the *TraceListener* class. Trace listeners collect and store trace and debug information and then route the information to the proper targets.

The *Debug* and *Trace* classes both require listeners before you can use most of the methods and properties in the classes. The *TraceListener* class itself is an *abstract* class, so you cannot create an instance of it directly. However, the .NET Framework provides three classes derived from *TraceListener*, so you may never have to implement a derived class yourself.

Directing debugging information through listeners provides alternative methods of *instrumentation*. In Microsoft parlance, *instrumentation* refers to the ability to embed in an application the means to monitor, measure, and control the application's performance. You can write trace code in your program but not provide listeners, for example. If a situation arises in which you need to monitor an application, you can provide the listeners in a configuration file, thus enabling the trace code.

In addition, using multiple listeners allows the debug and trace information to be written to multiple locations. The three trace listener classes provided by the .NET Framework are as follows:

- **TextWriterTraceListener** Redirects an instance of a class derived from *TextWriter* to the console or to a file. You also may implement this class using a *Stream* object.
- **EventLogTraceListener** Redirects the output to an object created from the *EventLog* class.
- **DefaultTraceListener** Redirects the output to the Visual Studio Output window. A listener of this type is implemented automatically with every trace listener collection. Calling the *Trace.Clear()* or *Debug.Clear()* method will remove it.

You can provide multiple listeners in the same collection, and each listener will receive the same messages. Each will write the same message to its own target. You used a *TextWriterTraceListener* in the preceding tip to write debug messages to the console. In this tip, you will look at using the *TextWriterTraceListener* to write to a file as well, and you'll examine the *DefaultTraceListener* in a Visual Studio project. The *EventLogTraceListener* is covered in the next tip.

You can use *TextWriterTraceListener* to write the debug results to a file, to the screen, or to both. You can add listeners as you need them, and you can selectively remove them if you keep a reference to them in a variable or assign names to the listeners.

USE IT The following program adds a listener to write the trace results to a file named *Trace.Out* as well as to the console. It creates the listeners in the *EnableDebugging()* method.

```
// Listener.cs -- Demonstrates routing debug messages to a file.
//
//              Compile this program with the following command line:
//                   C:>csc /debug:full /d:TRACE Listener.cs
using System;
using System.Diagnostics;
using System.IO;

namespace nsDebugTest
{
    class clsMain
    {
        static void Main(string[] args)
        {
            EnableDebugging();
            Trace.AutoFlush = true;
            Trace.WriteLine ("Debug is on");
            int Num = 1;

            Trace.Assert (Num == 0, "Num is not equal to 0");
            clsTest test = new clsTest(42);
```

```csharp
            test.ShowValue();
        }
    static void EnableDebugging ()
    {
        Trace.Listeners.Clear();
        Trace.Listeners.Add (new TextWriterTraceListener
                                        (Console.Out));
        FileStream strm = new FileStream ("./Trace.Out", FileMode.Create);
        StreamWriter writer = new StreamWriter (strm);
        Trace.Listeners.Add (new TextWriterTraceListener(writer));
    }
}
class clsTest
{
    public clsTest (int num)
    {
        m_Num = num;
    }
    int m_Num;

    public void ShowValue()
    {
        try
        {
            DoSomething ();
        }
        catch (Exception e)
        {
            Console.WriteLine (e.StackTrace);
        }
        if (m_Num < 50)
        {
            Debug.WriteLine (m_Num + " is less than 50");
            Console.WriteLine (m_Num + " is less than 50");
        }
    }
    void DoSomething ()
    {
        Trace.WriteLine (Environment.StackTrace);
    }
}
}
```

When you run the program, all the trace messages will appear on the screen, but if you examine the directory in which you ran the program, you will find the *Trace.Out* file containing a duplicate of the messages you wrote to the console.

To selectively add or remove a listener, you can keep its reference in a variable. Add the following lines to the *Main()* method so the method looks like the following:

```
static void Main(string[] args)
{
    EnableDebugging();
    Trace.AutoFlush = true;
    Trace.WriteLine ("Debug is on");
// Add the following three lines:
    FileStream strm = new FileStream ("Once.txt", FileMode.Create);
    TextWriterTraceListener listen = new TextWriterTraceListener (strm);
    Trace.Listeners.Add (listen);
// The next two lines already exist.
    int Num = 1;
    Trace.Assert (Num == 0, "Num is not equal to 0");
// Add the next three lines to remove the listener.
    listen.Flush ();     // Flush the listener
    Trace.Listeners.Remove (listen);
    strm.Close ();        // Close the stream.

    clsTest test = new clsTest(42);
    test.ShowValue();
}
```

Compile and run the program again. You should find another file, *Once.txt*, that contains only the *Trace.Assert()* call.

You also can add a listener and give it a name. From that point, you may reference the listener by its name. This is handy when you want to close a listener that you created in another method. Modify the *EnableDebugging()* method so that it looks like the following listing:

```
static void EnableDebugging ()
{
    Trace.Listeners.Clear();
    Trace.Listeners.Add (new TextWriterTraceListener
                                        (Console.Out, "Console"));
    FileStream strm = new FileStream ("./Trace.out", FileMode.Create);
    StreamWriter writer = new StreamWriter (strm);
    Trace.Listeners.Add (new TextWriterTraceListener(writer));
}
```

This adds the name *Console* to the listener that writes debugging information to the screen. Now add the following two lines at the end of the *Main()* method:

```
Trace.Listeners.Remove ("Console");
Trace.WriteLine ("\r\nConsole output has been disabled");
```

The first line removes the console listener and the second writes another line to the other listeners. The line does not write to the screen, but if you look at the *Trace.Out* file, you will see the message "Console output has been disabled."

The *Debug* and *Trace* classes automatically create an instance of *DefaultTraceListener*, which Visual Studio uses to write to the Output window. You do not have to create any listeners to use *Debug* and *Trace* when you create and compile your programs in Visual Studio .NET.

Now create a new application in Visual Studio. It can be a Windows application or a console application. Either will write to the Output window. The following listing shows a console application created, compiled, and run within Visual Studio:

```
using System;
using System.Diagnostics;

namespace VSTrace
{
    /// <summary>
    /// Summary description for Class1.
    /// </summary>
    class Class1
    {
        static void Main(string[] args)
        {
            Trace.WriteLine ("This should appear in the Output window");
        //
        // TODO: Add code to start application here
        //
        }
    }
}
```

When you run this program, it will start and exit almost immediately. Examining the Output window, however, shows that the line was written:

```
'VSTrace.exe': Loaded
'c:\winnt\assembly\gac\system.xml\1.0.2411.0__b77a5c561934e089\system.xml.dll',
No symbols loaded.
This should appear in the Output window
The program '[1164] VSTrace.exe' has exited with code 0 (0x0).
```

The line will be written in both the debug and release versions. Notice, however, that the same is not true for the *Debug* class. Change the code to call *Debug.WriteLine( )* rather than *Trace.WriteLine( )*, and then recompile and run the program in both debug and release versions. The line is written to the Output window only in the debug version.

Writing Messages to Event Logs

Windows NT systems maintain a set of event logs to which system processes and applications can write messages. You then can view the messages by using the EventViewer program that is installed as part of the Windows NT installation.

By default, three event logs are created: an application log, a security log, and a system log. The system writes its messages to the system log and applications use the application log. If you are lucky, nothing ever gets written to the security log.

In the past, using the event logs was a tedious and often frustrating task. First you had to create a message file in which you identified all your messages by number and then entered the text for them. You then compiled it with a message compiler. This generated a binary file containing the message information, which you included as a resource item in your project. Your program then had to make sure it was registered as an event message source. If anything went wrong in the process, as it often did, the event log would display a message that it could not find the text and show whatever string you passed it.

The .NET Framework makes this process a lot easier. The message compiler and resource item are gone. You need only create an object using the *EventLog* class, specifying what log you want to write to, and then start writing your messages. You can even create your own event logs, which then can be examined with the Event Viewer program.

The default is to write an information message to the event logs. However, the *EventLogEntryType* enumeration defines five different message types that you may write, as shown in the following table.

Message Type	Description
Error	An error event that indicates a significant problem the user should know about.
FailureAudit	A security event that indicates a failed audit event. For example, a failed attempt to open a file failed for security reasons.
Information	An information event that indicates a significant, successful operation.
SuccessAudit	A security event that indicates an audited access attempt was successful. For example, logging on successfully.
Warning	An information event that indicates a problem that is not immediately significant. Warnings may indicate conditions that could cause problems.

The entry type will determine the icon the event log displays. If you do not specify a type, *EventLogEntryType.Information* type will be used.

USE IT   The following program, *AppLog.cs*, writes a warning message to the application log:

```
// AppLog.cs -- Demonstrates registering an event source and writing to the
//              application log.
//
//              Compile this program with the following command line:
//                   C:>csc AppLog.cs
using System;
using System.Diagnostics;
using System.IO;

namespace nsEventLogs
{
    class clsMain
    {
        static public void Main ()
        {
// Create the EventLog object
            EventLog EvLog = new EventLog ();
// Register the source if it has not already been registered.
            if (!EventLog.SourceExists ("AppLog.exe"))
            {
                Console.WriteLine ("Creating event log source");
                EventLog.CreateEventSource ("AppLog.exe", "Application");
            }
// Set the source for the messages to be display in the Event Viewer.
            EvLog.Source = "AppLog.exe";
// Throw an exception. You don't have to do this, but it's a good reason
// to write to the log.
            try
            {
                CauseTrouble ();
            }
            catch (IOException)
            {
// Write the information to the application log.
                EvLog.WriteEntry("IO exception was thrown",
                                     EventLogEntryType.Warning);
            }
        }
        static void CauseTrouble ()
        {
```

```
        throw (new IOException());
    }
  }
}
```

To see the log, choose Start | Programs | Administrative Tools from the Windows task bar. Click the Event Viewer item to display the event log viewer shown in Figure 14-7. The message you just wrote should appear at the top. (This figure is from a Windows 2000 system; the Event Viewer for Windows NT 4.0 will appear differently).

To view details about the message, double-click the item in the Application Log panel on the right side of the Event Viewer. An Event Properties dialog box similar to Figure 14-8 should appear.

You do not need to use the name of your program as the event source, but it is a convenient identifier. The event source identifies a particular program that contains the messages that will display in the Event Viewer. If you use a common name for more than one program, you will have to provide one program, or a dynamic link library (DLL), that contains all the error messages you write.

Before continuing, a word of caution is in order. When you register an event source, the program writes an entry into the system registry. If you use event sources willy-nilly on a lot of test programs, you will clog up the registry and possibly slow down your computer. Always remember to delete any unused event sources.

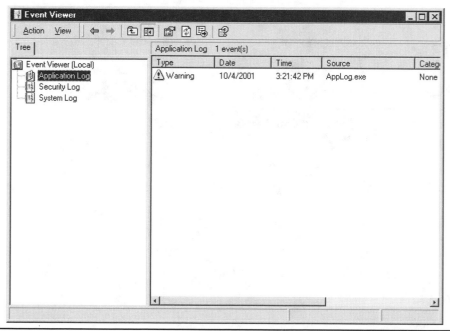

Figure 14.7   The Windows 2000 Event Viewer window shows the message you just wrote

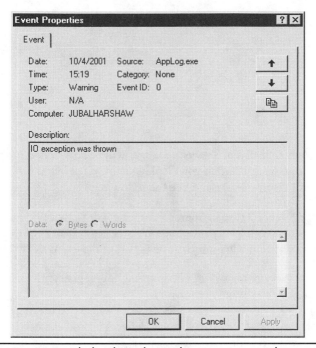

Figure 14.8   The Event Properties dialog box shows the source name that you registered with the message displayed in the Description box

The following short program, *RemSrc.cs*, removes an event source:

```
// RemSrc.cs -- Removes the registration for an event source if
//              it has been registered.
//
//              Compile this program with the following command line:
//                  C:>csc RemSrc.cs
using System;
using System.Diagnostics;

namespace nsEventLogs
{
    class clsMain
    {
        static public void Main (string [] args)
        {
            if (args.Length == 0)
            {
                Console.WriteLine ("Please enter an event source to remove.");
                Console.WriteLine ("Usage: RemSrc [source]");
                return;
            }
```

```
            if (EventLog.SourceExists (args[0]))
            {
                Console.WriteLine ("Deleting event log source " + args[0]);
                EventLog.DeleteEventSource (args[0]);
            }
        }
    }
}
```

After you delete a source, the Event Viewer no longer will be able to find the program to display the error message information. Instead, when you display the message in the Event Properties dialog box, the Description field will display a message like the following:

The description for Event ID (0) in Source (AppLog.exe) cannot be found. The local computer may not have the necessary registry information or message DLL files to display messages from a remote computer. The following information is part of the event: IO exception was thrown.

This is normal, and it is better than clogging up the system registry. Eventually, the events will be overwritten anyway, so the entry is only temporary.

You can create an instance of *EventLogTraceListener* to write error messages to the event log when you use tracing. Add the instance to the trace listener collection. You can use this listener in addition to any other listeners that write to a file or to the console.

To create the *EventLogTraceListener* object, you first register the event source and then attach it when you create the *EventLogTraceListener* object, as shown in the following program, *LogTrace.cs*:

```
// LogTrace.cs -- Demonstrates adding a EventLogTraceListener to the listener
//                collection and writing error messages to the application
//                log.
//                Compile this program with the following command line:
//                     C:>csc /debug:full /d:TRACE LogTrace.cs
using System;
using System.Diagnostics;

namespace nsEventLogs
{
    class clsMain
    {
        static public void Main ()
        {
// Create the EventLog object
            EventLog EvLog = new EventLog ();
// Register the source if it has not already been registered.
            if (!EventLog.SourceExists ("AppLog.exe"))
            {
                Console.WriteLine ("Creating event log source");
                EventLog.CreateEventSource ("AppLog.exe", "Application");
            }
```

```
        EvLog.Source = "AppLog.exe";
        Trace.Listeners.Add (new EventLogTraceListener (EvLog));
        Trace.Listeners.Add (new TextWriterTraceListener (Console.Out));
        Trace.WriteLine ("Debugging to the event log");
// Set the source for the messages to be displayed in the Event Viewer.
        EvLog.Source = "AppLog.exe";
    }
  }
}
```

This program will display the message "Debugging to the event log" on the console, and it will write it to the application log as well.

CHAPTER 15

Building the User Interface

TIPS IN THIS CHAPTER

A great many programs that you write may be utility programs or programs that are run from the command line. For these programs, you can write a prompt that will appear on the console when user input is required. Then you can have the program read the input line and parse it to extract the information entered by the user.

Windows applications that operate through forms or windows, however, have no console device to prompt a user and accept additional input. Those who use Windows programs have become accustomed to interacting with a program through graphical objects in an interface (the GUI), which may include forms (dialog boxes) that prompt users for additional information, toolbars that contain buttons that may be clicked with the mouse, or status bars that display messages and program information.

The objects that your program uses to interact with a user make up the program's user interface. Even the method that you choose to display program information such as the contents of a file is part of the user interface. For example, you must consider whether your program should display information in list form, in a hierarchical tree, or in an editing window.

The best way to display the contents of a database record, for example, is usually through a form that contains controls for each field in the record. You can provide text boxes that will let the user modify the record's contents and then rewrite the information to the database when the user closes the form.

When you design the form, however, you need to take into account how the user will *use* the form. If the form displays an employee record, as in the sample form application from Chapter 13, you probably would place the text boxes for the first and last names together on the form. Your program would only confuse the user if, for example, you placed the first name at the top of the form and the last name at the bottom (unless, of course, you had a logical reason for doing so). Following the natural sequence of how one would enter an address, the next fields, in order, would contain the address, city, state, and finally Zip code.

The tab order is another important consideration in designing the user interface. In the employee form from Chapter 13, the user rightfully expects that a press of the TAB key will move the cursor from the current field to the next one in order. If the TAB key were to cause the focus to move from the first name to the state or Zip code box, users would likely be frustrated.

The particular design that you use to display the information in a file or other source is referred to as the *view*. Typically, a view contains one or more controls that present information to the user. At least a couple of the controls in the Visual Studio Forms Designer—the ListView and the TreeView— have been renamed in Visual Studio .NET to reflect the concept of a view.

You can think of a view as a window into an object, such as a file or a database. It represents a particular perspective into the object, and it is by no means the only way to display information for a given type.

In this chapter, you will look at other objects that you can use to build a user interface for a program. First, you will build a simple text editor program that users will interact with via a menu. You will use the *Editor* project to add enhancements to the menus. After that, you will look at the ListView and TreeView controls and build a Windows Explorer-style application.

Adding a Menu to a Form

For the most part, users take for granted many of the user interface objects that have become common in Windows applications. They may expect to see a toolbar, for example, but they won't feel short-changed if it is not present.

The menu, though, is one of the oldest of the Windows interface objects, and most users have come to expect Windows applications to include menus. It is a rare user who will forgive the lack of a menu on an application such as a text editor.

Visual Studio contains considerable support for designing and building a user interface, including controls to implement both regular menus and popup context menus. To add a menu to a form using Visual Studio, you simply click the *MainMenu* control item on the Toolbox window. This doesn't add items to the menu, but it does give you a start on building one.

 Now you'll build an application with a menu.

1. Create a new Windows application using Visual Studio. Name the project **FormMenu**.

2. When the project appears, display the Toolbox. Select the Windows Forms bar and scroll through until you find the *MainMenu* item. Click *MainMenu* and move to the form and click again. (You also may double-click *MainMenu* to add the item to the form.)

3. Notice two things about the Visual Studio display. First, a panel appears under the form with an icon labeled *mainMenu1,* as shown in Figure 15-1.

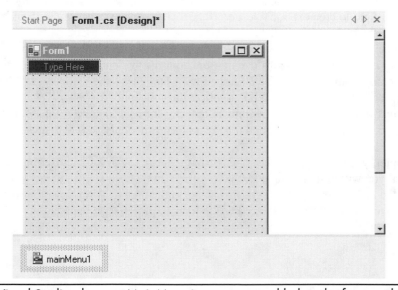

Figure 15.1   Visual Studio places a *MainMenu* item on a panel below the form and an area at the top of the form where you may add menu items

The *mainMenu1* item represents an object derived from the *MainMenu* class. The object has few properties to modify, but you can change the name from *mainMenu1* to something more meaningful if you like. The Forms Designer will use this object as you add items to the menu.

Second, a blank menu appears at the top of your form. This is where you will add menu items. The *Type Here* item is a template for a menu item. Visual Studio does not add the menu item to the program until you type something in the box.

4. Click the Type Here item and an editing box will open, where you can type the menu name. Type **&File** in this box. The ampersand indicates that the letter following it is an *access* key to the menu—in this case, it indicates that the user can open the File menu by typing ALT-F. Many users prefer to use access keys to execute menu items rather than move from the keyboard to the mouse.

5. Press ENTER and Visual Studio will open two more menu items with the text *Type Here*— one below the File menu item and another to the right of the item. The menu items arranged horizontally across the top represent top-level menus that will appear on your form, and the items arranged vertically represent submenu items that will appear only when the user opens a top-level menu.

6. Before continuing, click one of the items you just added and examine the Properties tool window. By default, the menu editor names menu items using the base *menuItem* and adds a number to it, similar to the manner in which it names other controls such as *button1* and *button2*.

QUICK TIP

Although it seems easy to go with the default naming scheme in the Properties tool window, if you went with the default names and added, say, 20 menu items, you'd have menuItem1 through menuItem20, and it would be easy to lose track of which menu item belongs to which menu, particularly if you do not add them in order. To identify menu items, you can prefix them with mnu *or* menu. *The File menu item, then, becomes mnuFile. When you add an submenu item to include in the top-level menu, you include the top-level name with the item name. So, for example, if you add an Open item to the File menu, its name would be mnuFileOpen. You don't have to use this scheme, but it makes it easier for you or other programmers to maintain the code if you do it this way.*

---

7. Return to the form and click the Type Here item that appears below the File menu item. Type **E&xit** in this box and press the ENTER key to add an item to the File menu. In the Properties tool window, name this item *mnuFileExit*.

8. Double-click the Exit menu item to add an event handler for the *Click* event. Visual Studio will add an *mnuFileExit_Click()* method and display the source file. You will use this event to call the *Application.Exit()* method and end the program. The following listing shows the code for *Form1.cs*:

```
using System;
using System.Drawing;
using System.Collections;
using System.ComponentModel;
using System.Windows.Forms;
```

```csharp
using System.Windows.Forms;
using System.Data;

namespace FormMenu
{
    /// <summary>
    /// Summary description for Form1.
    /// </summary>
    public class Form1 : System.Windows.Forms.Form
    {
        private System.Windows.Forms.MainMenu mainMenu1;
        private System.Windows.Forms.MenuItem mnuFile;
        private System.Windows.Forms.MenuItem mnuFileExit;
        /// <summary>
        /// Required designer variable.
        /// </summary>
        private System.ComponentModel.Container components = null;

        public Form1()
        {
            //
            // Required for Windows Forms Designer support
            //
            InitializeComponent();

            //
            // TODO: Add any constructor code after InitializeComponent call
            //
        }

        /// <summary>
        /// Clean up any resources being used.
        /// </summary>
        protected override void Dispose( bool disposing )
        {
            if( disposing )
            {
                if (components != null)
                {
                    components.Dispose();
                }
            }
            base.Dispose( disposing );
        }

        #region Windows Forms Designer generated code
        /// <summary>
        /// Required method for Forms Designer support - do not modify
        /// the contents of this method with the code editor.
        /// </summary>
        private void InitializeComponent()
        {
            this.mainMenu1 = new System.Windows.Forms.MainMenu();
```

```csharp
        this.mnuFile = new System.Windows.Forms.MenuItem();
        this.mnuFileExit = new System.Windows.Forms.MenuItem();
        //
        // mainMenu1
        //
        this.mainMenu1.MenuItems.AddRange
                            (new System.Windows.Forms.MenuItem[]
                              {this.mnuFile}
                            );
        //
        // mnuFile
        //
        this.mnuFile.Index = 0;
        this.mnuFile.MenuItems.AddRange
                            (new System.Windows.Forms.MenuItem[]
                              {this.mnuFileExit}
                            );
        this.mnuFile.Text = "&File";
        //
        // mnuFileExit
        //
        this.mnuFileExit.Index = 0;
        this.mnuFileExit.Text = "E&xit";
        this.mnuFileExit.Click +=
                  new System.EventHandler(this.mnuFileExit_Click);
        //
        // Form1
        //
        this.AutoScaleBaseSize = new System.Drawing.Size(5, 13);
        this.ClientSize = new System.Drawing.Size(292, 273);
        this.Menu = this.mainMenu1;
        this.Name = "Form1";
        this.Text = "Form1";

    }
    #endregion

    /// <summary>
    /// The main entry point for the application.
    /// </summary>
    [STAThread]
    static void Main()
    {
        Application.Run(new Form1());
    }

    private void mnuFileExit_Click(object sender, System.EventArgs e)
    {
        Application.Exit ();
    }
  }
}
```

9. Compile and run the program. Try pressing the access keys to open the menu from the keyboard—type ALT-F and then ALT-F-X to exit the program.

▶ **NOTE**

An access key is not the same as a shortcut key. Later in this chapter in "Adding Shortcut Keys (Accelerators)," you will add shortcuts to the menu items.

Using the Menu Designer

Of course, including only a single menu in a program does not add a lot of functionality to an application, but doing so does demonstrate the steps required to add a single menu to a program. These steps can be tedious—first adding the menu item and then switching to the Properties tool window to modify the *Name* property—especially if you have to do this for a lot of menu items.

Microsoft recognized the unique nature of naming menu controls when it created the Menu Designer, the tool you used in the preceding example to add the menu to a form. The Menu Designer contains shortcuts to help you build menus faster. This fits into the principle of rapid application development that is one of the primary benefits of C# and Visual Studio .NET.

USE IT The ease of using the Menu Designer will become more apparent when you build a menu with more than one item on it. Now you'll create a new Windows application named *Editor*, a simple text editor that demonstrates building menus and responding to the events generated by menu items.

1. After you create the project in Visual Studio, expand the form so that it is about two-thirds as high as it is wide. This is a good aspect ratio for editing views.

2. Using the Toolbox, add *MainMenu*, *StatusBar*, *OpenFileDialog*, and *SaveFileDialog* controls to the form.

3. Add a *TextBox* control to the form. Place the control between the menu and the status bar, but don't worry about drawing it to size.

4. Set the *Multiline* property for the text box to *true*. Set the *Dock* property to *Fill*; this will make the control expand or shrink to fill the center part of the form when the user resizes the form. Set the *AcceptsReturn* and *AcceptsTab* properties to true. When the text box has the focus, this will send the ENTER and TAB keystrokes to the text box.

5. Set the *ScrollBars* property to *Both*.

6. Set the *Font* property to another font or just use the default font. (The default font, while fine for smaller text boxes on a dialog box, does not look good in a large text box, nor is it very readable.)

7. Click in a blank area of the form and set the *Text* property to *Editor*. The *Text* property is the text that will appear in the program's title bar.

8. Select the main menu object and add three top-level menus to it. Name them *&File*, *&Edit*, and *&View*. Do not change the *Name* property for the menu items yet. Under each top menu, add the following items. Once again, do not change the *Name* property yet.

   - **File**   Add New, Open, Save, Save As, and Exit.

   - **Edit**   Add Cut, Copy, and Paste.

   - **View**   Add Status Bar.

9. Now *right-click* one of the top-level menu items and select Edit Names from the popup menu. The appearance of the menus will change and their *Name* properties will be displayed along with the text of the menu item, as shown in Figure 15-2.

10. Click the name for each menu item to change it in the Properties tool window, according to the scheme you used in the preceding tip. The New item on the File menu is named *mnuFileNew* and the Cut item on the Edit menu is named *mnuEditCut*, for example.

11. After setting the names, double-click each menu item to add event handlers to the code.

12. Before compiling the project, add an event handler for the *Closing* event for *Form1*. You will be using stream objects, so add a line at the top indicating that you are *using System.IO*. The event handler for the *Closing* event receives as a parameter a *CancelEventArgs* object. If you set the *Cancel* member of this object to *true* before returning from the event handler, you can

Figure 15.2   Rather than return to the Properties tool window to set the name of each menu item, you can modify the names directly in the Menu Designer

stop the form from closing. The code for the *Form1* class is shown in the following listing. For brevity, the *InitializeComponent( )* method is not listed.

```csharp
using System;
using System.Drawing;
using System.Collections;
using System.ComponentModel;
using System.Windows.Forms;
using System.Data;
using System.IO;

namespace Editor
{
    /// <summary>
    /// Summary description for Form1.
    /// </summary>
    public class Form1 : System.Windows.Forms.Form
    {
        private System.Windows.Forms.StatusBar statusBar1;
        private System.Windows.Forms.MainMenu mainMenu1;
        private System.Windows.Forms.TextBox textBox1;
        private System.Windows.Forms.MenuItem mnuFile;
        private System.Windows.Forms.MenuItem mnuEdit;
        private System.Windows.Forms.MenuItem mnuView;
        private System.Windows.Forms.MenuItem mnuFileOpen;
        private System.Windows.Forms.MenuItem mnuFileSave;
        private System.Windows.Forms.MenuItem mnuFileSaveAs;
        private System.Windows.Forms.MenuItem mnuFileNew;
        private System.Windows.Forms.MenuItem mnuFileExit;
        private System.Windows.Forms.MenuItem mnuEditCut;
        private System.Windows.Forms.MenuItem mnuEditCopy;
        private System.Windows.Forms.MenuItem mnuEditPaste;
        private System.Windows.Forms.MenuItem mnuViewStatusBar;
        private System.Windows.Forms.OpenFileDialog openFileDialog1;
        private System.Windows.Forms.SaveFileDialog saveFileDialog1;
        /// <summary>
        /// Required designer variable.
        /// </summary>
        private System.ComponentModel.Container components = null;

        public Form1()
        {
            //
            // Required for Windows Form Designer support
            //
            InitializeComponent();

            //
            // TODO: Add any constructor code after InitializeComponent call
            //
        }

        /// <summary>
```

```
        /// Clean up any resources being used.
        /// </summary>
        protected override void Dispose( bool disposing )
        {
            if( disposing )
            {
                if (components != null)
                {
                    components.Dispose();
                }
            }
            base.Dispose( disposing );
        }


        #region Windows Form Designer generated code
// InitializeComponent() method appears here
        #endregion

        /// <summary>
        /// The main entry point for the application.
        /// </summary>
        [STAThread]
        static void Main()
        {
            Application.Run(new Form1());
        }
        string m_strFileName = "";
        bool m_bReadOnly = false;
// Event handler for the New item on the File menu
        private void mnuFileNew_Click(object sender, System.EventArgs e)
        {
// If the text has changed since last save, ask before clearing the text
            if (textBox1.Modified == true)
            {
                string str;
                if (m_strFileName.Length > 0)
                {
                    str = m_strFileName;
                }
                else
                {
                    str = "The text in the edit control ";
                }
                str += " has changed. Do you want to save it?";
                if (MessageBox.Show(str, "TextChanged",
                    MessageBoxButtons.YesNo) == DialogResult.Yes)
                {
                    mnuFileSave_Click (sender, e);
                }
            }
// Erase any text in the text box.
            textBox1.Clear ();
// and set the modified flag to false
```

```
                    textBox1.Modified = false;
// Empty the file name
                    m_strFileName = "";
                    statusBar1.Text = "";
        }
// Event handler for the Open item on the File menu
        private void mnuFileOpen_Click(object sender, System.EventArgs e)
        {
// Intialize with the last file name used.
                    openFileDialog1.FileName = m_strFileName;
// Set the filter for text files
                    openFileDialog1.Filter =
                            "Text files (*.txt)|*.txt|C# files (*.cs)|*.cs";
// Show the Read Only check box on the dialog box
                    openFileDialog1.ShowReadOnly = true;
// The default extension is for text files
                    openFileDialog1.DefaultExt = ".txt";
                    if (openFileDialog1.ShowDialog () ==
                        DialogResult.Cancel)
                    {
                        return;
                    }
                    this.m_strFileName = openFileDialog1.FileName;
                    FileStream strm;
                    try
                    {
                        strm = new FileStream (m_strFileName,
                            FileMode.Open,
                            FileAccess.Read);
                        StreamReader reader = new StreamReader(strm);
                        textBox1.Text = reader.ReadToEnd ();
// Save the state of the read only box
                        m_bReadOnly = openFileDialog1.ReadOnlyChecked;
                        strm.Close ();
// Set the selection so the caret is at the top of the file
                        textBox1.SelectionStart = 0;
                        textBox1.SelectionLength = 0;
// Adding text to the text box sets its Modified property to true. The
// file has not actually been modified, so reset the Modified property.
                        textBox1.Modified = false;
                        statusBar1.Text = m_strFileName;
                    }
// Catch the exception when the file cannot be found.
                    catch (FileNotFoundException)
                    {
                        MessageBox.Show ("Cannot open file", "Warning");
                    }
        }
// Event handler for the Save item on the File menu
        private void mnuFileSave_Click(object sender, System.EventArgs e)
        {
                    if (m_bReadOnly)
                    {
```

```
            MessageBox.Show ("File is open as Read-Only",
                "Warning");
            return;
        }
        if (m_strFileName.Length == 0)
        {
            mnuFileSaveAs_Click (sender, e);
            return;
        }
        if (textBox1.Modified == false)
        {
            return;
        }
        if (m_strFileName.Length == 0)
        {
            return;
        }
        FileStream strm;
        try
        {
            strm = new FileStream (m_strFileName,
                FileMode.Open,
                FileAccess.Write);
            StreamWriter writer = new StreamWriter(strm);
            writer.Write (textBox1.Text);
            writer.Flush ();
// Chop off any straggler text in the file.
            strm.SetLength (textBox1.Text.Length);
            strm.Close ();
            textBox1.Modified = false;
        }
        catch (FileNotFoundException)
        {
            MessageBox.Show ("Cannot open file", "Warning");
        }
        catch (NotSupportedException)
        {
            MessageBox.Show ("Cannot write to file", "Warning");
        }
        catch (UnauthorizedAccessException)
        {
            MessageBox.Show ("Not authorized to write to file",
                "Warning");
        }
    }
// Event handler for the Save As item on the File menu
    private void mnuFileSaveAs_Click(object sender, System.EventArgs e)
    {
        if (m_strFileName.Length > 0)
        {
            saveFileDialog1.FileName = m_strFileName;
        }
        if (saveFileDialog1.ShowDialog () ==
```

```
              DialogResult.Cancel)
        {
            return;
        }
        if (saveFileDialog1.FileName.Length == 0)
        {
            return;
        }
        string fn = saveFileDialog1.FileName;
        FileStream strm;
        try
        {
            strm = new FileStream (fn, FileMode.OpenOrCreate,
                FileAccess.Write);
            StreamWriter writer = new StreamWriter(strm);
            writer.Write (textBox1.Text);
            writer.Flush ();
            // Chop off any straggler text in the file.
            strm.SetLength (textBox1.Text.Length);
            strm.Close ();
            textBox1.Modified = false;
            m_strFileName = fn;
            statusBar1.Text = m_strFileName;
        }
        catch (FileNotFoundException)
        {
            MessageBox.Show ("Cannot open file", "Warning");
        }
        catch (NotSupportedException)
        {
            MessageBox.Show ("Cannot write to file", "Warning");
        }
        catch (UnauthorizedAccessException)
        {
            MessageBox.Show ("Not authorized to write to file",
                "Warning");
        }
    }
// Event handler for the Exit item on the File menu
    private void mnuFileExit_Click(object sender, System.EventArgs e)
    {
        Application.Exit ();
    }
// Event handler for the three items on the Edit menu
    private void mnuEditCut_Click(object sender, System.EventArgs e)
    {
        textBox1.Cut();
    }
    private void mnuEditCopy_Click(object sender, System.EventArgs e)
    {
        textBox1.Copy();
    }
    private void mnuEditPaste_Click(object sender, System.EventArgs e)
```

```
                        {
                            textBox1.Paste();
                        }
        // Event handler for the Status Bar item. Toggle the status bar on and off
                private void mnuViewStatusBar_Click(object sender, System.EventArgs e)
                        {
                            statusBar1.Visible ^= true;
                            mnuViewStatusBar.Checked = statusBar1.Visible;
                        }
        // Check whether the file needs to be saved before closing the form
                private void Form1_OnClosing(object sender,
                                            System.ComponentModel.CancelEventArgs e)
                        {
                            if (textBox1.Modified == false)
                                return;
                            DialogResult mbResult = MessageBox.Show(
                                            "The text has been modified. " +
                                            "Do you want to save it first?",
                                            "Text Changed",
                                            MessageBoxButtons.YesNoCancel,
                                            MessageBoxIcon.None,
                                            MessageBoxDefaultButton.Button1);
                            switch (mbResult)
                            {
                                case DialogResult.Yes:
                                    mnuFileSave_Click (sender, e);
                                    break;
                                case DialogResult.No:
                                    break;
                                case DialogResult.Cancel:
                                    e.Cancel = true;
                                    return;
                            }
                        }
                }
            }
        }
```

13. Build and test run the *Editor* program. This is not, nor will it be, a full document editor, but it demonstrates a project in which you provide a method for a user to create or insert text.

Adding Menu Adornments

You can add some preset images to menu items to indicate that some action has been taken. To use these images, you need only set their corresponding properties to *true*.

USE IT   The images include a check mark, which is placed to the left of the menu item when the menu is displayed. You can turn the check mark on or off by setting the *Checked* property to on or off. In addition, you can make the check mark appear as a solid bullet by setting the *RadioCheck* property to *true*. If you use the *RadioCheck* property, you must also use the *Checked* property to display or hide the bullet.

1. In the *Editor* project, select the form in the Forms Designer and click on the View menu item so that the Status Bar item is displayed; then select that item.

2. Set the *Checked* property to *true*. Return to the code and add a line to make the *Checked* property track the *Visible* property, as shown in the following:

```
// Event handler for the Status Bar item. Toggle the status bar on and off.
        private void mnuViewStatusBar_Click(object sender, System.EventArgs e)
        {
            statusBar1.Visible ^= true;
            mnuViewStatusBar1.Checked = statusBar1.Visible;
        }
```

3. Rebuild and run the *Editor* project. Toggle the status bar on and off using the menu item. The check mark should appear only when the status bar is visible.

When you include items on a menu that are only slightly similar to other items on a menu, you can separate them using a menu *separator*—which literally provides a horizontal separator line in the menu. For example, the Exit item usually appears on the File menu, but it is not really a file operation. Commonly, this item is set off from the rest of the menu by a separator. Here's how you can add a separator.

1. Select the form in the Forms Designer.

2. Open the File menu, and right-click the Exit item in the Menu Designer.

3. From the popup menu, select Insert Separator. The Menu Designer will insert the separator above the selected item.

Adding Shortcut Keys (Accelerators)

A *shortcut key* provides a method for the user to perform a menu action without having to open a menu and select an item with the mouse. Many users prefer this method rather than having to move their hands from the keyboard to use the mouse.

In previous versions of Visual Studio, you set up shortcut keys by creating an *accelerator table*. In Visual Studo .NET, the shortcut key is a menu item *property*.

USE IT Now add a shortcut key to a menu item in the *Editor* project.

1. Select the menu item in the Menu Designer. In the Properties tool window, scroll through the properties until you find the *Shortcut* property. Click in the editable area next to this property.

2. A button with an ellipsis (...) will appear. Click this button and scroll through the popup list until you find the key combination that you want to use for the menu item.

3. In the *Editor* project, select CtrlN as the shortcut key for the New item. Then add CtrlO for the Open item and CtrlS for the Save item.

4. You do not need to add any code for the shortcut keys. Rebuild and run the editor once again and test the shortcut keys.

Adding Images

The next step is to add a simple toolbar to the *Editor* project. Before you do this, you need to prepare an image list as a source for images to display on the toolbar buttons.

The ImageList control is a support control. You do not display it separately. Instead, you assign it to various other controls, such as a Toolbar, ListView, or TreeView control.

 Now add an image list to the *Editor* project.

1. Open the form in the Forms Designer and display the Toolbox. Scroll through the Windows Forms list until you find the ImageList item. (Hint: if you right-click the Toolbox and choose Sort Items Alphabetically, you'll find it easier to locate many of the controls.)

2. Double-click the ImageList item. This is a hidden control, so you do not need to position it on the form. An icon representing the image list will appear in the panel just below the form.

3. Select the icon and locate the *ImageSize* property. Set the size to 16 by 16.

4. Locate the *Images* property. This is a collection, so selecting it in the Properties tool window will display a button with an ellipsis to the right. Click the button to display the Image Collection Editor shown in Figure 15-3 (the image list will be empty at this point).

   You can add images from any image file on your system, but it is usually convenient to collect the images and copy them in your project directory. You can find a number of stock images in the *Common7\Graphics* directory, where you installed Visual Studio .NET. The book's Web site contains the images used in this project. For the ImageList control, the images do not need to be the same size. The control will resize them all to be the same size.

5. Now click the Add button to display the File Open dialog box.

6. Select the image file for the first image. It is best to add the images in the same order that you plan to use them. For the toolbar that you will add, add images for the New, Open, and Save menu items. (The sample project shows a button for an About item, but this project will not implement an About box.)

7. Repeat the Add process until you have added all the images you will use.

8. Click OK to close the Image Collection Editor. If you click Cancel, the dialog box will close without adding the images to your image list.

You can rearrange the order of the images by selecting an image in the left panel and clicking the up or down arrow buttons to move the image.

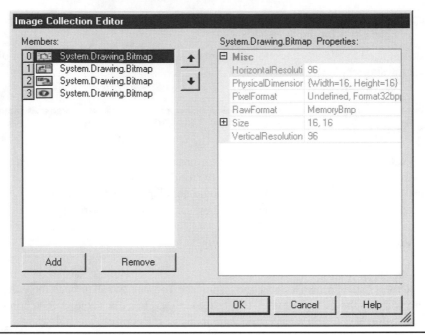

Figure 15.3   Use the Image Collection Editor to read the images from the bitmap files

Adding a Toolbar

Now that you have created an image list, you can add a toolbar to the *Editor* project. Toolbars generally duplicate menu items, allowing the user to click a toolbar button rather than choosing a menu and then selecting an item.

USE IT   To add a toolbar to the *Editor* project:

1. With the form open in the Forms Designer, scroll through the Toolbox until you find the ToolBar item. Double-click it and the Forms Designer will add the toolbar to the top of the form, just under the menu bar.

2. In the Properties tool window, find the *ImageList* property and set it to the name of the image list you just created. For this project, the image list is *imageList1*.

3. Scroll up to the *ButtonSize* property. You need to set the size at least as large as the images in the image list, 16 by 16. If you plan to add text to the toolbar, you will need to set a larger size. About 36 by 36 will accommodate a single short word.

4. Move to the *Buttons* property and select it. This is a collection as well, and clicking the ellipsis button will open the ToolBarButton Collection Editor dialog box. The dialog box looks similar to the Image Collection Editor.

5. Click the Add button on the dialog box to add a button to the toolbar. A list of properties for the new button will appear in the right panel of the dialog box.

6. Name the button. You might find it handy to use the same name as the menu item, prefixing it with a *tb*, for example, so the first button that will be used with the *mnuFileNew* menu item becomes *tbFileNew*.

7. If you want text to appear on the button, type it in the *Text* property, keeping it short. If the text will not fit in the button, none of it will display.

8. Finally, type a short description in the *ToolTipText* property. This text will appear as a tool tip when the user hovers the mouse over the button.

9. Repeat the process until you have added all the buttons to the toolbar. As you can with the Image Collection Editor, you can change the order by selecting a button in the left panel and using the up and down arrow buttons to move it.

10. Add an item named *Toolbar* to the View menu. Name it **mnuViewToolbar**. This item will be used to show and hide the toolbar.

11. In the Properties tool window, set the *Checked* property to *true*. Add the following event handler to the code to toggle the toolbar on and off:

```
private void mnuViewToolbar_Click(object sender, System.EventArgs e)
{
    toolBar1.Visible ^= true;
    mnuViewToolbar.Checked = toolBar1.Visible;
}
```

12. In the current version of Visual Studio .NET, there is no way to add event handlers for individual buttons. Normally, you would use the same event handlers that you added for the matching menu items. You need to add a single event handler for the *ButtonClick* event. In addition, there's no index for the button to easily identify it. Fortunately, you can use the image list index for the button to simplify coding. Add the following event handler for the *ButtonClick* event:

```
private void toolBar1_ButtonClick(object sender,
                    System.Windows.Forms.ToolBarButtonClickEventArgs e)
{
    switch (e.Button.ImageIndex)
    {
        case 0:
            mnuFileNew_Click(sender, (System.EventArgs) e);
            break;
        case 1:
            mnuFileOpen_Click(sender, (System.EventArgs) e);
```

```
 ▣ Editor                                                    _ □ ✕
 File  Edit  View
 ┌──────┬──────┬──────┬──────┐
 │  🗋   │  📂   │  💾   │  ❓   │
 │ New  │ Open │ Save │About │
 └──────┴──────┴──────┴──────┘
 using System;                                              ▲
 using System.Drawing;
 using System.Collections;
 using System.ComponentModel;
 using System.Windows.Forms;
 using System.Data;

 namespace AddControls
 {
         /// <summary>
         /// Summary description for Form1.
         /// </summary>
         public class Form1 : System.Windows.Forms.Form  ▼
 C:\CFiles\C#\AddControls\Form1.cs
```

Figure 15.4   The *Editor* program provides simple text editing capability

```
            break;
        case 2:
            mnuFileSave_Click(sender, (System.EventArgs) e);
            break;
    }
}
```

13. Rebuild and run the *Editor* program and you should see a window similar to that shown in Figure 15-4.

Adding a Context Menu

One of the convenient aspects of popup menus is that a user can open a menu and perform an action without having to move to the tool bar or main menu. The popup menus are context menus, and they are easy to add using Visual Studio .NET.

 You can add context menus to most of the controls available in the Forms Designer. Context menus are displayed when the user right-clicks a control.

1. With the *Editor* project form open, scroll through the Toolbox until you find the ContextMenu control. Double-click it to add it to your project.

2. Select the icon in the panel below the form to open it in the Menu Designer. Notice on the form that "Context Menu" is displayed at the top rather than on the main menu. Click this label to open the context menu in the Menu Designer.

3. Add the following items to the menu: New, Open, Save, a separator, Cut, Copy, and Paste.

4. Right-click and select Edit Names to name the menu items. Although context menu commands often duplicate main menu items, each context menu item must have a unique name. You might find it handy to use the same name as the main menu item and prefix it with a letter, such as *c*, for example. The main menu New item would then become *cmnuFileNew*.

5. Name all the context menu items according to whatever scheme you prefer. If you include context menus for more than one control, you might want to include the control name in the context menu name. For example, the name for a context menu on a text box might become *cmnuTextBox1FileNew*.

6. Select each context menu item and set the *Click* event for it to the same event handler as the main menu item. In the Properties tool window, click the editing area next to the *Click* event entry and a combo box drop-down arrow will appear. Click the arrow to reveal a list of existing event handlers.

7. Select the event handler from the list. Repeat this for each of the context menu items, selecting an event handler to match the corresponding main menu item.

8. Finally, select the text box in the Forms Designer and scroll through the Properties box until you find the *ContextMenu* property. Enter the name of this context menu, **contextMenu1**.

9. It's as easy as that. You don't even have to write any code unless you included items that are not on the main menu. Rebuild the *Editor* project and run it. Right-click the text box and the context menu will appear as shown here.

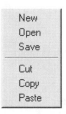

Displaying Items in a TreeView Control

Two commonly used view controls are the TreeView and the ListView controls. The TreeView control presents items in a hierarchical form, usually with node buttons that you can use to expand and collapse the items as needed. The ListView control displays items in one of four different views, making it a very flexible control. (The ListView control will be discussed later in the chapter, in "Displaying Items in a ListView Control.")

Visual Studio uses TreeView controls in several of its tool windows, such as the Solution Explorer and the Class View panels. A Windows form project using a TreeView control is shown in the Choose

Directory dialog box (which you'll create next). The directory panels in Windows display a ListView control when you open a folder from the desktop.

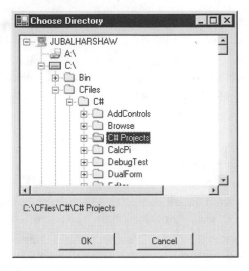

USE IT   In this tip, you will build a form that displays the drives and directories on your computer in a TreeView control. You can use this project as a component in other projects where you want the user to select a folder.

1. First, create a new Windows application project named *Tree*.

2. In the form, add two buttons at the bottom and label them "OK" and "Cancel." (The OK button will copy the selected directory to the clipboard, where you may retrieve it in another application. The Cancel button exits the program.)

3. Just above the buttons, add a Label control large enough to hold at least two lines (some directory paths may be long).

4. Scroll through the Toolbox to find the TreeView item. Select this item, drag it to the form, and make it fairly large on the form, as shown in Figure 15-5.

5. Add an ImageList control to the form. You do not need to use an image list with a tree control, but such lists are easy to prepare and give a better appearance to the tree.

6. Give the form a name to display in the title bar; for this example, name it **Choose Directory**.

7. You can remove the minimize and maximize boxes and set the *FormBorder* property to a fixed value to keep the user from resizing the form.

The TreeView displays a collection of nodes created from instances of the *TreeNode* class. To create the hierarchical display, you start out with one or more root nodes. Each node has a *Parent* property that identifies the node to which it is attached. Root nodes have a value of *null* for this property. The new node is a *child* node of its attached *parent* node. Each node contains a *Nodes* property and an instance of *TreeNodeCollection*, which contains the nodes that are attached to it.

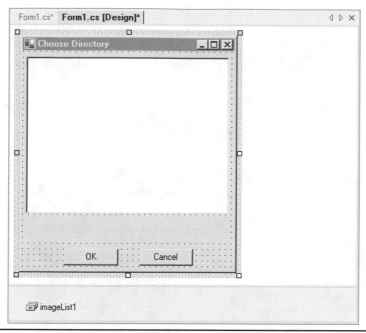

Figure 15.5   The *Tree* project form after the controls have been added

The TreeView handles the details of expanding or collapsing a node when the user clicks it. Once you understand the sequence of adding nodes to nodes, TreeView is an easy control to use.

In this project, you'll use the same recursive method that you used in the *Dirs* program in Chapter 12. However, instead of writing the directory names to the screen, you will use them to label the nodes in the tree.

Before getting started on the coding, create an image list for this project using the steps from "Adding Images" earlier in this chapter. The following project uses icons for an open and close folder, which the TreeView control will automatically select; it also uses icons for the local machine, a floppy drive, and the hard drives. You can draw these images or collect them from the Visual Studio .NET graphics directory. The size for images in the image list should be 16 by 16 to match the line size in the TreeView control.

1. Add the following namespaces to the project:

```
using System.IO;
using System.Text;
```

2. Add two methods to the *Form1* class named *PopulateTree()* and *LoadDirectories()*.

3. In the *Form1* constructor, call the *PopulateTree()* method to initialize and load the tree. The code for the constructor and these two methods is shown in the following listing:

```
public Form1()
{
    //
```

```csharp
        // Required for Windows Forms Designer support
        //
        InitializeComponent();
        //
        // TODO: Add any constructor code after InitializeComponent call
        //
        PopulateTree ();
    }
    //
    // Initializes and populates the TreeView control.
    protected void PopulateTree()
    {
        TreeNode tnRootNode;
// Clear any residual nodes from the tree. You do not have
// to do this for a new tree, but if you want to add a refresh
// button later you will need to do this.
        treeView1.Nodes.Clear();
// Get the machine name from the Environment class. This will
// be the root node.
        tnRootNode = new TreeNode(Environment.MachineName, 2, 2);
        treeView1.Nodes.Add(tnRootNode);
// Get the node collection for the root node. The drives will be
// added to this node.
        TreeNodeCollection tncDrives =  tnRootNode.Nodes;

// Get the logical drives from the Environment class.
        string[] strLogicalDrives = Environment.GetLogicalDrives();
        string strCurrentDrive = "";
// Add the drives to the machine name node.
        foreach (object obj in strLogicalDrives)
        {
            strCurrentDrive = (string) obj;
// Create a root node for the drive. Use a different image
// for the floppy and hard drives.
            if (strCurrentDrive == "A:\\")
            {
// The floppy drive image index is 3
                TreeNode tnDriveNode = new TreeNode(strCurrentDrive, 3, 3);
                tncDrives.Add(tnDriveNode);
                continue;
            }
            else
            {
// Add the directories on this drive. First create a node object.
                TreeNode tnDriveNode = new TreeNode(strCurrentDrive);
// Get the directory info for the current drive.
                DirectoryInfo d = new DirectoryInfo (strCurrentDrive);
// Add the directories to the node.
// The hard drive image index is 4
```

```
                        ShowDirectories(d, tncDrives, 4, 4);
            }
        }
// Expand the root node to show the drives.
        tnRootNode.Expand ();
}
//
// Recursively add directories to the tree.
public void ShowDirectories (DirectoryInfo d,
                              TreeNodeCollection tncCollection,
                              int iImageIndex, int iSelectedImage)
{
// Create a node for this entry.
        TreeNode tnCurNode = new TreeNode(d.Name, iImageIndex, iSelectedImage);
// Add the new node to the current node (passed as an argument).
        tncCollection.Add(tnCurNode);
// Get the subdirectories for this directory and call this
// method recursively to add the nodes. If a CD or DVD drive is empty
// the CLR will throw an exception. Catch it and just return.
        DirectoryInfo [] dirs;
        try
        {
            dirs = d.GetDirectories ();
        }
        catch (Exception)
        {
            return;
        }
        foreach (DirectoryInfo dir in dirs)
        {
            try
            {
// Call this method passing the node collection as an argument.
// The closed folder image index is 0; the open folder index is 1.
                ShowDirectories (dir, tnCurNode.Nodes, 0, 1);
            }
// If we cannot access this directory, just pass on it.
            catch (UnauthorizedAccessException)
            {
                continue;
            }
        }
}
```

4. That's pretty simple coding for a control as complex as the TreeView control. Now add event handlers for the *Click* event for the two buttons.

5. Add an event handler for the TreeView *AfterSelect* event.

6. The OK button event handler will copy the selected directory to the clipboard and the Cancel button event handler will close the form. The *AfterSelect* event handler will build a string representation of the selected directory and display it in the Label control. The code for these event handlers is shown here:

```
private void button1_Click(object sender, System.EventArgs e)
{
// Copy the result to the clipboard.
// If used as a choose directory form, use label1.Text
// to retrieve the selected directory instead of the
// clipboard.
    Clipboard.SetDataObject (label1.Text, true);
    Application.Exit ();
// Use the following line if this is a form inside another application.
//  Close ();
}

private void button2_Click(object sender, System.EventArgs e)
{
    Application.Exit ();
// Use the following line if this is a form inside another application.
//  Close ();
}

// Build the string for display. Start with the selected node and
// move upward, inserting the node name at the beginning of the string
// as you move up.
private void treeView1_AfterSelect(object sender,
                                    System.Windows.Forms.TreeViewEventArgs e)
{
    StringBuilder str = new StringBuilder();
    str.Insert (0, treeView1.SelectedNode.Text);
    TreeNode tcNode = treeView1.SelectedNode;
    while ((tcNode = tcNode.Parent) != null)
    {
        if (tcNode.Text.IndexOf ('\\') >= 0)
        {
            string temp = tcNode.Text;
            int index = temp.IndexOf ('\\');
            temp.Remove (index, 1);
            str.Insert (0, temp);
            continue;
        }
        if (tcNode.Text == Environment.MachineName)
            break;
        str.Insert (0, tcNode.Text + "\\");
    }
    label1.Text = str.ToString();
}
```

7. Build and test drive the application. Depending on the speed of your machine and the number of drives, it might take a few seconds for the form to display. You can collect and add additional icons to the image list to represent special directories. For example, you can use the icon for the Recycle directory instead of the normal open and close folder icons.

Displaying Items in a ListView Control

ListView is another commonly used view for building a user interface. The ListView control can display items in four different modes—large icon, small icon, list, and detail (or report)—which makes it a flexible control. As with the TreeView, Visual Studio and the C# classes make this control much easier to use than the corresponding control in Visual C++.

The large icon mode presents a view that the user can quickly scan with the icons arranged in rows. The small icon view allows more items to be displayed in the control because the items are smaller. The list mode looks like the small icon view, but the items are arranged in columns rather than rows. In the detail view, which used to be called the report view, the items are arranged vertically, and you can create columns to display other information about each item. The four views are shown in Figure 15-6.

USE IT Adding items to a ListView is considerably easier than performing the same operation for the TreeView. The ListView contains only one collection, called *Items*, and it is created as part of the control. You need only add items to that one collection. The downside is that you have to provide a custom class definition to sort the items in the ListView. The *ListViewItemSorter* property must be a class that inherits from the *IComparer* interface, so it isn't just a matter of using a callback function.

1. Create a new Windows form project and name it *List*.

2. Add a toolbar at the top, a button at the bottom, and a label just above the button.

3. Draw a ListView control between the label and the toolbar, as shown in Figure 15-7. Draw the initial positions carefully; rather than dock the controls, for the sake of doing things differently, this project will adjust the size and position in code. You will need three image lists for this project, one for the large image view, another for the small image view, and a third for the toolbar. The image lists in this project are named *imgLargeIcon*, *imgSmallIcon*, and *imgToolbar*.

4. Create the image lists first. This project uses 50 images for the state flags. By coincidence, a collection of flag images is handily located on the Web site for this book. (When you add these images to the lists, be sure to skip the *OregonBackLarge.bmp* file. Oregon is the only state that has a flag with different obverse and reverse sides, and you won't be using both sides in the project.)

5. You can use the same images for both the large and small image lists because the ImageList control will resize them to fit. Set the size for the small image list to 24 by 16 and the large image list to 48 by 32. The toolbar image list is 16 by 16.

6. Add the following namespace to the project so you will be able to open a stream for the data file:

```
using System.IO;
```

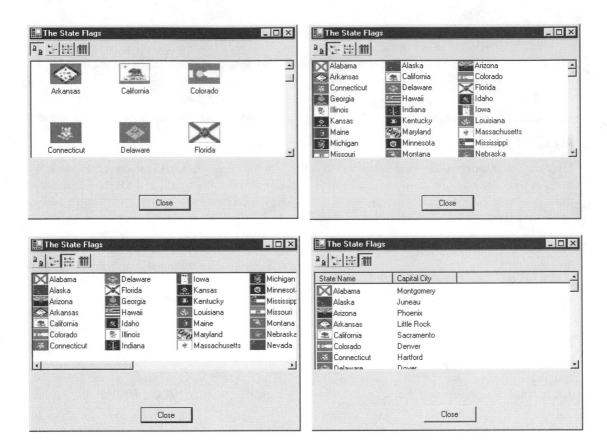

Figure 15.6 The ListView control offers users four different views of items: large icon at top left, small icon at upper right, list at lower left and detail (or report) at lower right

7. Now add four buttons for the toolbar. The four images you will need for the toolbar also are on the book's Web site.

8. Set the properties for the ListView control: Set *BorderStyle* to *Fixed3D*, *FullRowSelect* to *true*, *MultiSelect* to *false*, and the *SortOrder* to *Descending*. Set the *LargeImageList* property to *imgLargeIcon* and the *SmallImageList* property to *imgSmallIcon*.

   Setting the *FullRowSelect* property to *true* accomplishes two things. When the ListView is in the details mode, the user can click anywhere on a row to select a line. With it set to *false*, you will have to add a mouse click event handler and do a hit test. Also, setting the property to *true* makes an entire selected row appear highlighted. When *FullRowSelect* is set to *false*, only the first column is highlighted. A short string, say just a single character or number, could easily be missed.

9. Use the ListView's *Column* property to access the ColumnHeader Collection Editor dialog box. The dialog box is similar to the image list's Image Collection Editor dialog box that you used earlier in the chapter. Add two columns to the control. Label one *State Name* and the other *Capital City*. Make both columns about 120 units wide.

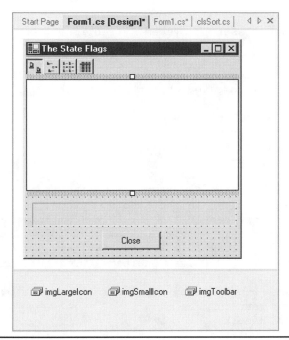

Figure 15.7   The layout of the *List* project

10. Click OK to save the columns and exit the dialog box.

11. Now add message handlers for the toolbar and button *Click* events and for the ListView's *SelectedIndexChanged* and *ColumnClick* events.

12. Use the Class Wizard to add a new class to the project. When the Class Wizard dialog box appears, enter the name of the class, *clsSort*, in the Class Name field. Then, click on the Inheritance item on the left side of the Class Wizard. In the Current Namespace item, select *System.Collections* namespace. A list of interfaces will appear in the Available Interfaces box. Select *IComparer* and click Add. Click the Finish button to add the class to the project.

13. The code for *clsSort* is shown in the following listing. The wizard does not add the *System.Collections* or *System.Windows.Forms* namespace at the top, so you will have to do that manually. You do not need the constructor that the wizard added, so you can remove or leave it.

```
using System;
using System.Collections;
using System.Windows.Forms;

namespace List
{
    /// <summary>
    ///
```

```
    /// </summary>
    public class clsSort : System.Collections.IComparer
    {
//
// Compare() is a required method when using the ICompare interface.
    public int Compare (object o1, object o2)
    {
        if (!(o1 is ListViewItem))
            return (0);
        if (!(o2 is ListViewItem))
            return (0);
//
// Get the listview items and extract the subitem text
// using the value saved in the ByColumn property.
        ListViewItem lvi1 = (ListViewItem) o2;
        string str1 = lvi1.SubItems[ByColumn].Text;
        ListViewItem lvi2 = (ListViewItem) o1;
        string str2 = lvi2.SubItems[ByColumn].Text;
//
// Compare the strings according to the sort order property
// and save the result.
        int result;
        if (lvi1.ListView.Sorting == SortOrder.Ascending)
            result = String.Compare (str1, str2);
        else
            result = String.Compare (str2, str1);
//
// Saving the sort information lets you do a reverse sort
// on the column if it is clicked a second time. The OnColumnClick
// event handlers sets and uses these properties.
        LastSort = ByColumn;
// Return the result to the ListView.
        return (result);
    }
    /// <summary>
    /// Column number to sort by
    /// </summary>
    public int ByColumn
    {
        get {return Column;}
        set {Column = value;}
    }
    int Column = 0;
//
// Set and get the column used in the last sort.
    public int LastSort
    {
        get {return LastColumn;}
        set {LastColumn = value;}
```

```
        }
        int LastColumn = 0;
    }
}
```

14. With the sorter class finished, add a field to the *Form1* class to declare an instance of the class. You will assign it to the ListView control in the constructor:

```
// Instance fields.
clsSort Sorter = new clsSort();
```

15. The data for the control comes from a text file, *States.txt*. You can edit the file to add more information and add columns to the ListView to display it. The data is simply an alphabetical listing of the states. To create it yourself, type in the name of the state, a comma, and the capital city. The file is read in the constructor. The code for the constructor and the event handlers is shown in the following listing:

```
//
// Instance fields.
clsSort Sorter = new clsSort();
//
// The Form1 constructor.
public Form1()
{
    //
    // Required for Windows Form Designer support
    //
    InitializeComponent();
    //
    // TODO: Add any constructor code after InitializeComponent call.
    //
    int index = 0;
// Read the data file.
    FileStream strm;
    try
    {
        strm = new FileStream ("States.txt", FileMode.Open, FileAccess.Read);
        StreamReader reader = new StreamReader (strm);
        while (reader.Peek() > 0)
        {
// Split the string using the comma as a field separator.
            string State = reader.ReadLine();
            string [] Data = State.Split (new char [] {','});
// Create a ListViewItem to hold the data.
            ListViewItem item = new ListViewItem (Data);
// The data file is in alphabetical order. If you added the flag images
// to the image list alphabetically, you can just use the index value.
            item.ImageIndex = index++;
// Add the item to the control.
            listView1.Items.Add (item);
        }
        strm.Close ();
    }
```

```csharp
        catch (FileNotFoundException)
        {
            MessageBox.Show ("Cannot open file", "Warning");
        }
// Assign the clsSort object to the item sorter.
        listView1.ListViewItemSorter = Sorter;
    }


//
// Process a button click on the toolbar.
    private void toolBar1_ButtonClick(object sender,
                        System.Windows.Forms.ToolBarButtonClickEventArgs e)
    {
// Put all buttons in the raised state. You don't know which
// button was down prior to this event unless you save it in
// an instance variable.
        for (int x = 0; x < 4; ++x)
        {
            toolBar1.Buttons[x].Pushed = false;
        }
// Put the button that was just pressed into a down state.
        toolBar1.Buttons[e.Button.ImageIndex].Pushed = true;
//
// Use the image index to determine which button was pressed, then
// set the ListView's View property to that state.
        switch (e.Button.ImageIndex)
        {
            case 0:
                listView1.View = View.LargeIcon;
                break;
            case 1:
                listView1.View = View.SmallIcon;
                break;
            case 2:
                listView1.View = View.List;
                break;
// For the report view, clear the sorting variables.
            case 3:
                listView1.View = View.Details;
                if (listView1.Sorting == SortOrder.None)
                    listView1.Sorting = SortOrder.Ascending;
                else
                    listView1.Sorting = SortOrder.None;
                break;
        }
    }


    private void button1_Click(object sender, System.EventArgs e)
    {
        Application.Exit ();
    }
//
// Manually resize and reposition the controls on the form when the
```

```csharp
// user changes the form size. The docking properties are not reliable.
private void Form1_OnResize(object sender, System.EventArgs e)
{
    if (!(sender is Form1))
        return;
//
// The movement of the button will determine positions
// for the other controls.
    int btnTop = button1.Bounds.Y;
//
// Reposition the button at the bottom.
    Rectangle rcButton = button1.Bounds;
    rcButton.X = (this.Bounds.Width - rcButton.Width) / 2;
    rcButton.Y = this.Bounds.Height - 5 * button1.Bounds.Height / 2;
    button1.Bounds = rcButton;
    int cy = button1.Bounds.Y - btnTop;
//
// Reposition and resize the Label control.
    Rectangle rcText;
    rcText = label1.Bounds;
    rcText.Y += cy;
    rcText.Height = label1.Bounds.Height;
    rcText.Width = this.Bounds.Width - 2 * rcText.Left - 8;
    label1.Bounds = rcText;
//
// Resize the ListView control. The upper left will not change.
    Rectangle rcView;
    rcView = listView1.Bounds;
    rcView.Width = this.Bounds.Width - 2 * rcView.Left - 8;
    rcView.Height += cy;
    listView1.Bounds = rcView;
}
//
// Process the column click event. This will happen only
// in report (details) mode.
private void listView1_OnColumnClick(object sender,
                            System.Windows.Forms.ColumnClickEventArgs e)
{
// Make sure the sorter is valid.
    if (!(listView1.ListViewItemSorter is clsSort))
        return;
// Extract the sorter and recast it to clsSort.
    clsSort Sorter = (clsSort) listView1.ListViewItemSorter;
// If this click was on the same column as the last one, reverse the
// sort order by setting the property in clsSort.
    if (Sorter.LastSort == e.Column)
    {
        if (listView1.Sorting == SortOrder.Ascending)
            listView1.Sorting = SortOrder.Descending;
        else
            listView1.Sorting = SortOrder.Ascending;
    }
    else
```

```
        listView1.Sorting = SortOrder.Descending;
// Save the column that was clicked.
    Sorter.ByColumn = e.Column;
// And tell the control to re-sort.
    listView1.Sort ();
}
//
// Use the SelectedIndexChanged event to read the item's information
// and display it in the label control.
private void listView1_OnSelectedIndexChanged(object sender,
                                        System.EventArgs e)
{
    if (listView1.SelectedItems.Count == 0)
    {
        label1.Text = "";
        return;
    }
// Retrieve the text from the ListView control.
    string State = listView1.SelectedItems[0].SubItems[0].Text;
    string Capital = listView1.SelectedItems[0].SubItems[1].Text;
// Display the text in the label control.
    if (State.Length > 0)
    {
        label1.Text = "The capital of " + State + " is " + Capital;
    }
}
```

Compared with creating a similar view in Visual C++, relatively little coding is needed to produce a flexible control that can display the information in different ways. Build and run the project. (By the way, there's no guarantee of the accuracy of all of the flag details or the capital cities.)

An Explorer-Style Application

A common method of displaying data is to use and explorer-style application. The Windows Explorer is an example of this type of application, and it's the program from which the style gets its name.

An explorer application involves placing one control on the left side of a form and adding a second control on the right. A splitter bar separates the two, and the controls resize themselves to fit the portion of the form bounded by the splitter bar.

Usually the control on the left side is a TreeView control, and the control on the right is a ListView. Actually, you can use any control types, within reason—an edit box would be appropriate for one of the panels, but it wouldn't look good to have a button filling half of the form.

You are not limited to just two panes in an explorer-style application, and you can split a form horizontally as well as vertically. The order in which you create the controls and the splitters is important, however. This tip will not go through the process of setting up TreeView and ListView controls, but it will show the sequence to set up splitter forms.

The most common approach is to split a form vertically. This topic will not end up with a usable program, so you can call it anything you want.

1. In a new Windows application, widen the form to make it about twice as wide as it is deep.

2. If you want to include a menu, toolbar, or status bar on the form, add them first.

3. Add a TreeView item on the left side of the form. You do not have to draw the controls to size; just make sure they are in the general area of the form.

4. Set the *Dock* property of the TreeView to *Left*.

5. Now add a Splitter control, which should align itself on the right side of the TreeView control.

6. Add another control such as text box or a ListView control. Set its *Dock* property to *Fill*. (If you use a text box, be sure you set the *Multiline* property to *true*.)

7. Build and run the program. You should see a form filled with a TreeView on the left and the other control on the right, with a splitter bar between them. Grab the splitter bar with the mouse and move it from side to side and the controls should resize themselves to fit.

If you choose to split a form horizontally, the sequence is basically the same except for the docking.

1. Delete all the controls on the form. Add a ListView control near the top of the form and set its *Dock* property to *Top*.

2. Add a splitter control. The splitter should attach to the left side of the form, but if you set its *Dock* property to *Top*, it will align itself below the ListView.

3. Finally, add another control, such as a text box or rich text box (set the *Multiline* property to *true*) at the bottom and set its *Dock* property to *Fill*.

4. Build and run the application and you should again see a splitter window. This time, however, the split will be horizontal. Grab the splitter bar between the controls and move it up and down to see how the controls resize themselves.

Splitting a form three ways is a combination of the preceding steps, but it's a bit more involved. When you finish a three-way split, you'll have a window that looks like Figure 15-8.

1. Delete the controls you just added to the form.

2. Add a TreeView on the left and dock it on the left side.

3. Add the first splitter control. It should dock on the left automatically.

4. Add a ListView control at the upper right and set its *Dock* property to *Top*.

5. Add a second splitter bar. It will automatically dock on the left and attach to the side of the TreeView, but its *Dock* property should be set to *Top* and it will attach to the bottom of the ListView control.

6. Add a third view control (a text box or rich text box) on the lower right side of the form and set its *Dock* property to *Fill*.

7. Build and run the program. Try moving both splitter bars and you will see that all three view controls resize themselves to fill the space. Also, try resizing the form itself and the view windows will expand to fit.

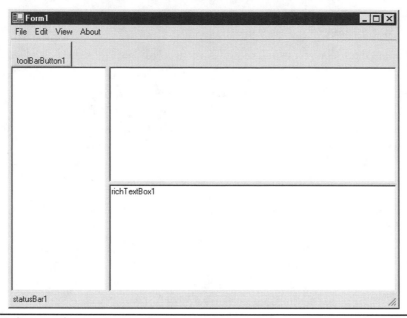

Figure 15.8   Splitting a form twice produces a window with three view controls

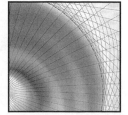

CHAPTER 16

Using Windows Controls

TIPS IN THIS CHAPTER

A Windows form is the starting point for building a Windows-based application using C#. By itself, however, a form represents little more than a moveable surface. You can draw objects and text directly on a form, but the real power of a form lies in its power to serve as a container for Windows controls.

A control is an object through which you can display and accept information from a user. A control usually fulfills a specific function of input or output. For example, a button control responds to a mouse button click, but a text box accepts keyboard input from the user. Each control contains its own set of properties and methods and generates a particular set of events in response to user or program actions.

Starting with Forms and Controls

In Windows applications, a control is a child window that provides basic input and output function. Normally, an application uses controls within a dialog box or in a form in the .NET Framework, but you can create controls to use with other windows. When you create a dialog box, it becomes the parent window for the controls inside it. This parent/child relationship is important because the controls send "messages" to the parent window, notifying the parent when a significant event occurs, such as a mouse click or a key press. In C#, you can intercept these events in the same class that you use to implement a form or dialog box.

While C# handles the details, the form communicates back to the control using messages. For example, if you set the *CheckState* property of a check box control to *false*, the form sends a message to the control telling it to remove the check mark in the box and then redraw itself. In conventional Windows programming, these messages are sent from code that you write.

Controls are not limited to the objects you place on a form. A menu is also a control, and each item on the menu also represents a control.

A control can take different forms. The radio button and check box controls, for example, are alternate incarnations of the basic button control. You use the radio button to accept a one-of-many selection and the check box to accept a true or false condition (or, in some cases, an indeterminate condition).

Many of these controls are represented in the Windows *common controls library*, a collection of Windows operating system files that are available to any language used to program applications for Windows. Microsoft updates this library periodically, introducing new controls and updating and fixing bugs in existing controls.

Originally called *predefined controls*, the common controls library grew out of a need to present a consistent user interface for applications. These basic controls, listed in the following table along with their .NET class names, predate most versions of the Windows operating systems now in use.

Control	.NET Class	Description
Button	Button	Provides a selection mechanism such as buttons, check boxes, or radio buttons.
Listbox	ListBox	Displays a list from which the user can select one or more items.

Control	.NET Class	Description
Edit	TextBox	Used to display text and to allow the user to edit text.
Combobox	ComboBox	Combines the edit and list box controls so the user can select and edit an item.
Scrollbar	ScrollBar	Provides a means through which the user may select the direction and distance to scroll information in a window.
Static	Label	A read-only text control often used to provide labels for other controls.

You will use these basic controls a lot as you write Windows form applications. Certainly you can design a form without using any of them, but they form the nucleus around which you will use other controls. It is a rare form that will not contain one or more basic controls.

In addition to the basic controls, a number of advanced controls were introduced with Windows 95, and several have been added to the collection in the years since Windows 95 was released. These include the list and tree controls, the animation control, and the tab control. The advanced controls are not available on versions of Windows prior to Window 95. Some of them, such as the animation control, require a multi-threaded environment.

All these controls are represented by classes in the .NET Framework. Where a control has more than one form, each is represented by its own class. For example, the *Button*, *CheckBox*, and *RadioButton* classes represent the three forms of the Button control.

In Visual C#, you will find the control objects in the Toolbox. You can double-click items in the Toolbox to add controls to your form, or you can click a control and draw it on the form at the size you need.

The Toolbox also contains items that technically are not controls, such as dialog boxes to open and save file, font, and color controls and various printing items. These items are part of the *common dialogs library*, which will be covered in Chapter 17. In addition, the Toolbox contains items to add menus to your forms, which is covered in Chapter 15.

As you design a form, you'll add and position various controls on the form. To set the appearance and initial contents of the controls, you use the Properties tool window. Then, to respond to user input from the controls, you add *event handler* methods to your code. Control events are the C# equivalent of message handler functions that are invoked when a control sends a message to its parent window, which is usually the Windows form.

Adding Controls to a Form

To add and position the controls on a form in Visual Studio, you must have the form open in the IDE's Forms Designer. You must also display the Toolbox, which you can open by pressing CTRL-ALT-X. If the Toolbox is already visible, this will give it the focus. While you are working with controls, you might find it handy to turn off the AutoHide feature in the Toolbox. To do this, click the push pin icon on the right side of the Toolbar's title bar to make the pin point downward.

As with many operations in Visual Studio, you can add controls to a form in several ways:

- *Double-click the Toolbox control.* This will create the control on the upper-left of the form in a default size. If you have a control selected in the form, the new control will usually be drawn on top of the selected control. You will have to move the new control to the correct position and resize it as necessary.

- *Click the Toolbox item, and then click at the location on the form where you want the control to appear.* Click and hold down the left mouse button and draw the rectangle to the size you want. This is the most accurate method, and it requires the least repositioning and resizing of controls.

- *Drag and drop the control.* Click and drag the control item to the point where you want the upper-left corner of the control to appear on the form. Release the mouse button and the control will be drawn in a default size. You will have to resize the control as necessary.

There is no best method for adding a control to a form. The best way is the one that works for you. Microsoft provides these alternatives to accommodate individual preference. If you are unsure which method to use, create a Windows application project and try all three.

To move a control on the form, click it with the left mouse button and drag it to the proper location. You also can select it on the form and use the keyboard cursor keys to move the control. One press of a cursor key moves the control 8 dialog units. For fine adjustments, hold the CTRL key down while you press the cursor key; this will make the control move only 1 unit per key press. You also can make fine adjustments using the *Location* property in the Properties tool window.

To resize a control, grab one side or a corner with the mouse and drag the rectangle to the desired size. The CTRL key does not work with resizing, so for fine adjustments you will need to modify the *Size* property.

Visual Studio also provides a Format menu to help you in sizing and positioning controls, and a Layout toolbar contains buttons for common operations. The Layout toolbar normally appears just above the Toolbox and Forms Designer areas and is shown in Figure 16-1. If you can't find it, right-click in the toolbar area and select Layout. If you do this repeatedly, the Layout toolbar will appear and disappear.

Unless you have one or more controls selected in the Forms Designer, all the Format menu items and Layout toolbar buttons will be disabled. Many of these items and buttons deal with aligning and sizing controls in relation to other controls, and they require that you have more than one control selected. To select more than one control, click on a control to select it, and then CTRL-click each of the other controls that you want to select.

The order in which you select the controls to apply menu and toolbar options is important. The Forms Designer will use the *last* control that you select as the *pattern* control. This means, for example, that if you select three controls and then select Format | Make Same Size | Both, the Forms Designer will make all the controls the same size as the last control that you selected.

When you select multiple controls, you'll see black resizing boxes around the last control you selected; the others will have white boxes. In Figure 16-2, the four buttons along the top have been selected, but only the last button, the one labeled "System," has black boxes, so you know that it is the control the Forms Designer will use as a pattern for sizing and alignment operations.

The form uses a grid pattern to help you in laying out controls. Normally, the dots that form the grid are placed 8 dialog units apart, but you can modify the spacing. To do so, select Tools | Options to display the Options dialog box. In the left panel, click Windows Forms Designer and the grid options will appear in the right panel. Set the grid spacing as necessary. You can set different vertical and horizontal grid spacing.

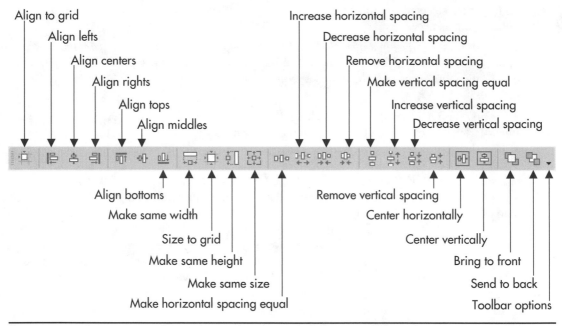

Figure 16.1 The Layout toolbar contains buttons to help you to align and position controls on a form

The grid spacing determines how two menu items (and two corresponding buttons on the Layout toolbar) perform. Select Format | Align, and you will see a To Grid item; if you select Format | Make Same Size, you will see a Size To Grid item. When you select these items, the Forms Designer will use the grid spacing to align and size the controls, moving the edges of the controls to the nearest grid point.

When you have positioned and sized all the controls, you can lock them in place to prevent them from being accidentally moved or resized. Choose Format | Lock Controls. When the controls are

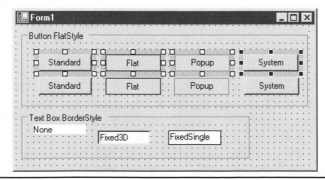

Figure 16.2 When selecting multiple controls, the last, or pattern, control will have black resizing boxes around it

locked and you select one, the control will display with a white rectangle around it rather than show the resize boxes. You cannot move or resize any of the controls when the lock is on. To turn off the lock, simply repeat the Format | Lock Controls sequence.

On the Format menu, you will also find an Order item, which drops down a submenu containing only two items, Bring To Front and Send To Back. You use these command when *layering* controls—that is, when placing one control on top of another. This situation occurs frequently when you use the GroupBox and Panel controls. Selecting Bring To Front places a control "on top" of the other controls in a layer. Send To Back places the control "under" the other layered controls.

Layering controls and placing them within a group will be covered later in this chapter in the tip on "Using the GroupBox Control."

Setting Properties for Controls

When you lay out your controls on the Windows form, you may have to change their properties so that the controls appear and perform the way you want. The Forms Designer provides some default properties, but you will often need to change them.

For example, the default value for a text box's *MultiLine* property is *false*, meaning that it can accommodate only one line of text at a time. If you need to display several lines in a text box, you will need to change this property to *true*.

The settings you give the initial properties for a control will determine how that control will appear when it first displays on a form. For example, Figure 16-3 shows the four different *FlatStyle* settings for a button control in both the up and down states and the three different *BorderStyle* settings for a text box. All the controls are drawn the same size.

To set the properties for a control, you select the control on the form and then access the Properties tool window. Only the *public* properties—the properties that you can modify—for a control appear in this window. Although you can change most of the properties listed for a control in your code, it's much easier to do so using the Properties tool window. When you set the properties using the Properties tool window, Visual Studio automatically adds the code to the *InitializeComponent( )* method in the form class.

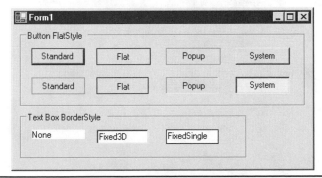

Figure 16.3   You can change the initial appearance of a control by setting its styles. The button is shown in its various styles in both the up and down states, and the text box control shows its border styles.

USE IT   In this example, you will use the Properties tool window to create a button that will stay "down" when you click it. The standard button control cannot be used in this way, but it is easy to convert a check box control to look like a button.

1. Create a C# Windows forms application using Visual Studio. The project on the Web site is named *CheckButton*, but you can give it any name. You will use it to experiment with various styles.

2. Add CheckBox and Button controls to the form, similar to that shown here. The check box on this form will soon resemble the button control, but it will "toggle" up and down when you click it.

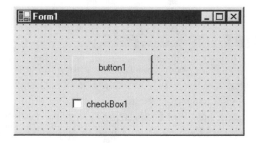

3. Make the two controls about the same size. Compile and run the program to see that the button always returns to its up state after you click it. There is no way to change that action using properties.

4. Return to the Forms Designer and click the CheckBox control to select it. Move to the Properties tool window at the lower right of the Visual Studio frame. If the Properties tool window is not visible, press the F4 button to make it visible.

5. Scroll through the properties until you find the *Appearance* property. Click this property to select it and a drop-down arrow should appear to the right, as shown in Figure 16-4.

Figure 16.4   Scroll through the Properties tool window list to find the property that you want to modify

6. Click the arrow and select *Button*. When you do this, notice that the appearance of the check box changes so that it looks similar to the button.

7. Find the *FlatStyle* property and select it. Press the drop-down arrow that appears at the right and change the property to *System*. This will make the button appear distinctly different in its up and down states.

8. To center the text in the check box button, scroll through the properties list until you find the *TextAlign* property and select it. Notice once again that a drop-down arrow appears to the right. However, when you click this arrow, an image similar to the following appears rather than a selection list. You'll find a number of these popup images throughout the Properties tool window as you experiment with the properties of various controls. They are not always self-explanatory, and you may have to experiment at first to determine what the images mean.

9. The button at the left center is depressed to indicate that the text alignment property is *CenterLeft*. Click the center of the image to change the text alignment to *Center*.

10. Build and run the project again and you should see two similar buttons. However, the one at the bottom actually is a check box, and the button state will toggle up and down when you click it.

You could have changed all these properties in your program code. To show this, change the properties back to their original states (*Appearance* to *Normal*, *FlatStyle* to *Flat*, and *TextAlign* to *CenterLeft*). Add the following lines to the *Form1* constructor *after* the call to the *InitializeComponent()* method:

```
checkBox1.Appearance = Appearance.Button;
checkBox1.FlatStyle = FlatStyle.System;
checkBox1.TextAlign = ContentAlignment.MiddleCenter;
```

To guide you in selecting property states, the Properties tool window contains a small description box that you can display. Right-click the Property Pages button of the toolbar above the Properties tool window (the button on the far right) and make sure the Description item on the popup menu is checked (Figure 16-5).

Select different properties in the list, and the description will change to reflect each new selection.

The more Windows programming you do, the more you will use controls, and you should familiarize yourself with the various properties of the controls. There are far too many to list here, but you can look up the modifiable properties in the MSDN help file by entering the class name in the Look For box of the Index tab, and then selecting Properties from the index, as shown in Figure 16-6.

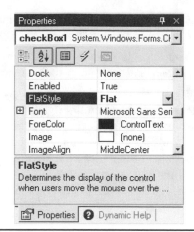

Figure 16.5 The Properties tool window can be configured to display a brief description of the selected property

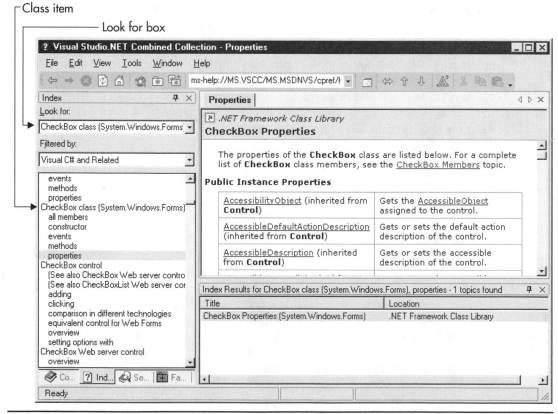

Figure 16.6 The MSDN will lead you to a listing of the variable properties available for a Windows control

Double-click the Properties item to display a list of properties in the Help window. Look under the Public Instance Properties topic for those that you can access. Notice that some of the properties in this list are read-only and do not appear in the Properties tool window.

When multiple controls have the same property, you can set the property for all of the controls to the same value by using the multiple selection capability of the Forms Designer. Here's how.

1. Assuming that you have a group of buttons that you want to set the *Appearance* property to *System*, click the first button to select it.

2. Hold down the CTRL key, and click the other buttons one at a time.

3. When you have selected all the controls, set the property value in the Properties tool window to the desired value.

Using Invisible Controls

Not all the objects on the Toolbox fit the *technical* definition of a control. Microsoft defines a control as "a child window an application uses in conjunction with another window to carry out simple input and output (I/O) tasks."

Earlier in this chapter, you learned that some of the items on the Toolbox are actually common dialogs. Even so, other objects on the Toolbox, such as the ImageList and Timer objects, do not fit this definition because they do not produce "child windows."

Microsoft calls these objects *invisible controls.* They do not provide a user interface that displays on the dialog box or form. When you add these objects to a form, the Forms Designer opens a tray just below the form to display invisible controls. Figure 16-7 shows the invisible control tray display containing Timer and ImageList controls.

Invisible controls do not require alignment or positioning on the form, and the Forms Designer tends to add the icons for these controls to the invisible control tray wherever they will fit. After you have added several controls, the Forms Designer will place one control on top of another. If this happens and you cannot see an invisible control that you know you have added, right-click the invisible control tray and select Line Up Icons from the popup menu. This will make the Forms Designer distribute the controls evenly so you can see all the icons.

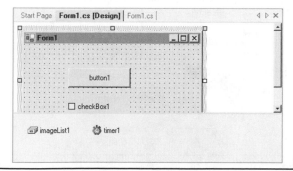

Figure 16.7   When you add invisible controls to a form, the Forms Designer opens a tray below the form to hold the icons representing the controls

USE IT One obvious advantage of adding invisible controls to the tray is that it gives you an identifiable object in the Forms Designer that you can select using the mouse. When you select an invisible control, the Properties tool window changes to display the properties for the invisible control.

Using the project from the preceding tip, add a Timer control to the project. Click the icon in the invisible control tray to select the timer that you just added, and then examine the Properties tool window, as shown in Figure 16-8.

Because invisible controls do not require positioning on the form, programmers often create these objects in code as they are needed rather than adding them as invisible controls. For example, you could have added a timer in your code using the following statements:

```
Timer timer1 = new Timer();
timer1.Interval = 1000;
```

Controls such as the Timer control often have few properties to set, and it is easy to create them in code. However, if you create an object repeatedly, you need to remember that each instance creates a new object in the heap memory. This tends to increase the load on the garbage collection process, which must determine when an object is no longer accessible and then remove the object from memory.

Responding to Control Messages

In traditional Windows programming, a control communicates with its parent window through a series of Windows notification messages. In a Windows application created using C#, the control's parent is the form that contains the control.

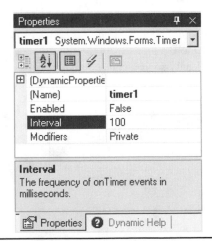

Figure 16.8 Clicking an invisible control icon gives you the same access to its properties as clicking a visible control

For example, when the user clicks a button on a dialog box, it causes the button to send a *BN_CLICKED* notification to the dialog box using the general Windows message *WM_COMMAND*. In traditional Windows programming, you need to add a message handler to detect the message and perform whatever action is necessary for a button click. In C#, however, the message handling process is simplified by handling messages from controls as *events*. Generally, the events a control may generate correspond to the messages that the control sends in a traditional Windows application.

Windows programs generally are *event-driven*. You cannot predict, for example, when the user will click a button or perform some other action. Your program needs to provide some means of responding to the actions when they occur. You accomplish this by adding *event handlers* to your program.

Each control has a specific set of events that it will generate, although some events may be common to most or all controls. For example, all the controls generate a *Click* event when the mouse clicks the control. The class definition for the control includes a *delegate* for each event that you may use to attach your event handler methods. (Delegates are covered in detail in Chapter 18. Essentially, a delegate is a *pointer* to a method. In normal coding, however, C# does not permit pointers, so a delegate holds references to one or more methods that will be called when the delegate's event is triggered.)

Event handlers for control events always have a return type of *void*. You can add an event handler yourself, but unless you have an eidetic memory you invariably will have to look up the event handler in the MSDN help file to determine what parameters it requires.

A far easier way is to use the Events page of the Properties tool window. You select this page by clicking the Events button on the Properties window toolbar. The Events button is the one with an icon depicting a lightning bolt.

The Events page lists all the *public* events that you may handle in your code. You simply type in the name of the event handler you want to use and Visual Studio will add the method to your program code. Alternatively, you can select an existing method to use as an event handler. The latter is handy for groups of related controls, such as radio buttons.

USE IT To demonstrate adding an event using the Properties tool window, create a new Windows application named *Events*. You can shrink the form to a convenient size, but leave it large enough to add controls later. You will use this project for several of the following tips.

1. Add two buttons near the bottom of the form. By default, the Forms Designer will name one of the buttons *button1* and the other *button2*, but those names are not very descriptive.

2. Use the Properties window to change the *Name* property of one button to *btnOK* and the *Text* property to *OK*. Change the name of the second button to *btnCancel* and the *Text* property to *Cancel*.

3. Select the button you named *btnOK*, and then click the Events button on the Properties tool window. In previous projects, you have double-clicked a button to add an event handler for the *Click* event and then simply used the default event handler name. For this example, you will select the name of the event handler.

4. Find the *Click* event in the list and select the blank box to the right. Notice that a drop-down arrow appears in the box. At this point, no event handlers are in your code, so the list will be empty.

5. In the blank area of this box, type **btnOK_OnClick** and press the ENTER key. Visual Studio will respond by opening the code window for the *Form1* class and adding the event handler to the code.

6. Return to the Forms Designer and do the same for the second button, except name the event handler **btnCancel_OnClick**. Before you press ENTER, however, select the drop-down arrow and examine the event handler list, which should contain the name of the first event handler that you added. You just want to look at the list, so don't select the event handler now.

7. Name the event handler methods using any scheme you want. To simplify things after you have added a number of event handlers to your code, the event handler name should contain the name of the control along with the name of the event. This will make them easier to identify in your code. A good scheme is to use the control name, an underscore character, the word *On* to indicate an event, and finally the name of the event. Thus, the name of the event handler for the Cancel button's *Click* event becomes *btnCancel_OnClick*.

8. Add code to display a message box for each event handler. The code for the two methods should look like the following:

```
private void btnOK_OnClick(object sender, System.EventArgs e)
{
    MessageBox.Show ("OK button clicked", "Events");
}
private void btnCancel_OnClick(object sender, System.EventArgs e)
{
    MessageBox.Show ("Cancel button clicked", "Events");
}
```

9. Build the project and run the program. Each button should display its own message box. Many applications use event handlers to validate the information on the form and to close the form.

Using One Event for Multiple Controls

You often will find that the event handlers for different controls will need to execute the same or similar code. In such a case, you can assign a single event handler to handle events from multiple controls, and then you can sort out the individual control in your code.

In the last tip, you might have noticed that the event handler used two parameters. The first, *sender*, is an *object* that represents the control that generated the event. You can use the *is* operator to test for the control type or use the equality operator (= =) to test for a particular control.

The second object is a *System.EventArgs* object. By itself, this object contains little information, and you may not find much use for it. However, control events always pass an object created from *System.EventArgs* or a class derived from it. Many of the derived types contain useful information or properties. For example, the *Closing* event from a form passes an object created from *CancelEventArgs*, which contains a *Cancel* property. By setting *Cancel* to *true*, you can stop the form from closing.

USE IT   In this example, you will add common event handlers for the *MouseEnter* and *MouseLeave* events to change the appearance of the buttons when you move the mouse cursor over one of them.

1. Using the *Events* project from the preceding tip, select one of the buttons and then click the Events button on the Properties tool window.

2. Locate the *MouseEnter* event in the list, type **OnMouseEnter** (this method will be used by more than one control, so the event handler name does not include the control name), and press the ENTER key. Visual Studio will add an event handler for the button to your source code file.

3. Locate the *MouseLeave* event and type **OnMouseLeave**.

4. Return to the form and select the other button. Move to the Events page on the Properties tool window and locate the *MouseEnter* event for this button. Instead of typing in the name of the event handler, select the drop-down button and choose the OnMouseEnter item from the list. Do the same for the *MouseLeave* event, selecting the OnMouseLeave item from the drop-down list.

The following code implements the event handlers for both buttons:

```
private void OnMouseEnter(object sender, System.EventArgs e)
{
// Test whether the sender is a button
    if (sender is Button)
    {
// Change the button style to Flat
        ((Button) sender).FlatStyle = FlatStyle.Flat;
        return;
    }
// Add code here to handle MouseEnter event for other controls
}

private void OnMouseLeave(object sender, System.EventArgs e)
{
// Test whether the sender is a button
    if (sender is Button)
    {
// Change the button style back to Standard
        ((Button) sender).FlatStyle = FlatStyle.Standard;
        return;
    }
// Add code here to handle MouseLeave event for other controls
}
```

You can use the same event handler for other type controls. For example, if you want to change the appearance of a check box when the mouse is over the control, add the following code:

```
if (sender is CheckBox)
{
```

```
        // Code to change the appearance of a checkbox
}
```

By using the equality operator to test for a particular control, you could make the *MouseEnter* and *MouseLeave* events perform different actions for the two buttons. The following code toggles the appearance of the OK button between *Flat* and *Standard*, and it toggles the Cancel button's background color from light to normal:

```csharp
private void OnMouseEnter(object sender, System.EventArgs e)
{
// Test whether the sender is a button
    if (sender is Button)
    {
// Change the OK button style to Flat, but then
// change the background color of the Cancel button
        if (sender == btnOK)
            ((Button) sender).FlatStyle = FlatStyle.Flat;
        else if (sender == btnCancel)
            ((Button) sender).BackColor = SystemColors.ControlLightLight;
        return;
    }
// Add code here to handle MouseEnter event for other controls
}

private void OnMouseLeave(object sender, System.EventArgs e)
{
// Test whether the sender is a button
    if (sender is Button)
    {
// Change the OK button style to Flat, but then
// change the background color of the Cancel button
        if (sender == btnOK)
            ((Button) sender).FlatStyle = FlatStyle.Standard;
        else if (sender == btnCancel)
            ((Button) sender).BackColor = SystemColors.Control;
        return;
    }
// Add code here to handle MouseLeave event for other controls
}
```

Enabling and Disabling Controls Using Idle Processing

The *Enabled* property is an important property of any control. If this property is *false*, the control will be *grayed out,* or *disabled,* and will not accept user input. A disabled control will not generate events, even those caused by moving the mouse cursor over the control.

Sometimes you will want to prevent the user from performing a particular action until some condition becomes true. For example, you may want to disable the OK button until the user types something in a text box.

You could use the *TextChanged* event for a text box to test whether something has been entered into the text box. However, that would work for just one control and one event. If you needed to enable or disable a number of controls based on other conditions, you would have to add multiple event handlers to test for those conditions.

You can, however, take advantage of the fact that an application generates an *Idle* event whenever it finishes processing and enters an idle state. This event occurs rapidly after every user event, and you can use it to test existing conditions in your program to enable or disable controls selectively. The *Idle* event is roughly equivalent to the undocumented *WM_KICKIDLE* message provided in Visual C++.

USE IT You will need to add this event manually to your program, as there doesn't seem to be any way to add it using the Properties tool window. The delegate for the event is a member of the *Application* class, which is the same class you use to run a forms-based application by calling its *Run( )* member method. The class contains only *static* members, so you do not have to create an instance of the class to use the *Idle* event.

1. Add a TextBox control to the *Events* project that you created in the "Responding to Control Messages" tip earlier in this chapter. You can use the default name *textBox1*.

2. Change the *Text* property for the text box so that it is empty.

3. Manually add the following event handler to the source code:

```
private void OnIdle (object sender, EventArgs e)
{
    btnOK.Enabled = textBox1.Text.Length > 0;
// Add code here to test other conditions to enable or disable
// controls as needed.
}
```

4. Now modify the *Form1* class constructor to add the event handler to the *Application.Idle* delegate. The constructor code should look like the following listing:

```
public Form1()
{
    //
    // Required for Windows Forms Designer support
    //
    InitializeComponent();
    //
    // TODO: Add any constructor code after InitializeComponent call
    //
    // Add the following line to the constructor
    Application.Idle += new System.EventHandler(OnIdle);
}
```

5. Build the application and run the program. Assuming you removed any text from the text box's *Text* property, the application should start up with the text box empty and the OK button disabled.

6. Select the text box and type a character. As soon as you enter the character, the text length becomes greater than 0. Before you can type a second character, the application enters an idle state and calls the *Idle* event handler, thus enabling the OK button.

The reverse happens when you remove text from the text box. When the text becomes empty, the *Idle* event handler disables the OK button.

Using the GroupBox Control

The GroupBox control is used to set off related controls. Normally, it will draw a frame around a group of associated controls, and you can add an optional label or title to the box.

If you have programmed in Visual C++, you may remember the group box as little more than a static control used to draw a border around a group of controls. In C#, the GroupBox control has some extended capabilities. You can use the GroupBox control to enable or disable the block of controls as a single unit. You can hide or reveal all the controls in a group by using the control's *Visible* property. You also can arrange the tab order of controls in a GroupBox control independently of the other controls on a dialog box. Essentially, in C# the GroupBox control becomes a controller for other controls, whereas in C++ it is little more than a dialog box adornment.

USE IT   Create a new Windows application named *Group*. First, you will look at what happens when you add controls to a group box, which is the normal method of using the control. At the end of this tip, you'll see what happens when you add a group box to a set of existing controls, which is likely to happen at some point in your programming.

1. Select the GroupBox control in the Toolbox. Click it just once, and then draw it on the upper half of the form.

2. Add a few controls inside the GroupBox control, such as a text box and a couple of check boxes. It is important that you draw the GroupBox control first, and then draw the other controls inside it.

3. Draw another check box *outside* the GroupBox control.

4. After you have drawn the controls, display the tab order for the controls. Choose View | Tab Order. The form should look similar to Figure 16-9.

5. Notice that the tab index for the GroupBox control is 0, but the index for controls within the group is displayed in decimal notation. You can set the tab index for controls within the group without altering the order of other controls on the form.

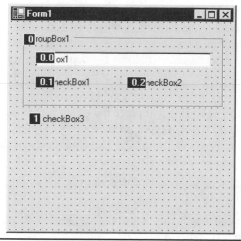

Figure 16.9   The GroupBox control contains its own tab order that you can set independently of other controls

6. Displaying the tab order is a toggle operation. You need to turn off the tab order display before proceeding. To do this, just repeat the steps you used to show the tab order.

7. Next, using the technique from the preceding tip, add the following *Idle* event handler to the program. Use the check box that you drew outside the group to enable or disable the group. Remember to add the method to the *Application* class delegate in the *Form1* constructor:

```
private void OnIdle (object sender, EventArgs e)
{
    groupBox1.Enabled = checkBox3.Checked;
}
```

8. Build the application and run the program. The form should display with the GroupBox control and all the controls inside it disabled. Checking and unchecking the check box that is not a member of the group should alternately enable and disable the entire group of controls.

That was relatively painless. In an ideal world, this is how you will use the GroupBox control. You'll draw the GroupBox object first and then add the controls to it. In the real world, however, you'll be in the midst of designing your form when you realize that several of the controls you've already drawn need to be grouped. Things get a bit less friendly at that point.

To show what happens in such a case, add another group of controls to the bottom of the form but *do not* draw the GroupBox control.

1. Draw another text box and a couple of check boxes close together.

2. After the controls are in place, draw a GroupBox control around them. When you release the mouse button after drawing the group box, the controls included in the GroupBox control

disappear—they're actually behind the group box. The Forms Designer layers the controls when you draw them, placing the most recently drawn control at the top of the *z order*. If you imagine the width of your monitor screen as the x-axis and the height as the y-axis of a three-dimensional system, the z-axis would be the depth of the screen. The most recently drawn control—the GroupBox control—is at the top of the z-axis and thus covers the other controls.

3. To reveal the other controls, make sure the group box you just drew is selected. Then choose Format | Order | Send to Back. This will place the group box under the other controls on the z-axis. But this still doesn't solve all your problems. If you reveal the tab order, you'll see that the controls are not actually in the group box. The tab indexes of the controls do not have the decimal notation that you saw in the first group.

4. Hide the tab order, and then select each of the controls one at a time, dragging it outside the group box boundary.

5. Grab each control again and drag it back to its original location. Reveal the tab order again and you will see the decimal notation, indicating that the controls are now associated with the group box.

▶ **NOTE**

According to the documentation, you should be able to place the controls on the clipboard (by pressing CTRL-INSERT), delete them, and then reinsert them from the clipboard (SHIFT-INSERT). However, this does not appear to work in the current version.

At this point, you should understand that the Panel control works similarly to the GroupBox control, except that with the *BorderStyle* property set to *none*, the Panel control is invisible on the form (it will display in the Forms Designer as a rectangle, but when the program runs the rectangle will not display). This allows you to group controls without having to display a border around them, an important fact to know when you group radio button controls in the next tip.

Grouping Radio Button Controls

The radio button control provides a *one-of-many* selection mechanism. Only one member of a group of radio buttons may be selected at a given time. When you click another radio button in the group, the selection moves to the button you just clicked.

In traditional Windows programming, you set the *Group* property of the first radio button to *true* and then set the property for the remaining members of the group to *false*. Then you set the *Group* property of the first control after the radio buttons to *true*. This forces the resource compiler to place the radio buttons in a single group. You can form several groups of radio buttons on a single dialog box using this technique.

The .NET RadioButton object, however, does not have a *Group* property, so this scheme does not work. Every RadioButton control that you add to a form becomes a member of a single group.

USE IT You can force radio buttons into smaller groups by placing them in GroupBox or Panel controls. Use the GroupBox control if you want a border placed around the group of radio buttons. Use a Panel control if you want to set an invisible boundary.

1. Create a new Windows application named *Radio*.

2. Locate the RadioButton control object on the Toolbox and use it to draw six radio buttons on the form, three on the right and three on the left, as shown here.

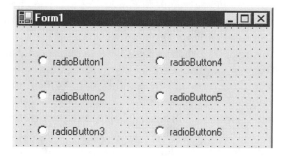

3. Build the project and run the program to confirm that all the radio buttons are members of a single group. When you select a button, the dot indicating the selection will disappear from the previous control and move to the one you just selected. All six buttons work together as a single group.

4. End the program and return to the Forms Designer.

5. Delete all the radio buttons.

6. Locate the Panel control object on the Toolbox and draw two panels on the form, one on the left and another on the right. Draw three radio buttons inside each panel, like this:

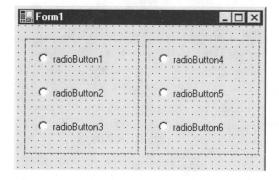

7. Build the project again and run the program. Although the form appears the same as it did earlier, the radio buttons now should function as two groups of three buttons each. Changing the selection in the group at the right does not alter the selection in the group on the left.

Anchoring Controls on Forms

A Windows form application looks similar to a dialog box application. However, a user can resize a form by grabbing a side or corner and expanding or shrinking the form. You can carefully size your form and lay out the controls on it, but when the user resizes the form, it creates a blank area with no controls. Or worse, if the user shrinks the form size, it can result in some controls falling off the form.

You can prevent the user from resizing the form by setting the *FormBorderStyle* for the form to one of three fixed styles: *FixedSingle*, *Fixed3D*, or *FixedDialog*. If you choose to allow the user to resize the form, you can set properties for the controls to make the form adjust to the resizing operation.

You can make the controls retain their relative positions to one another and to the sides of the form by *anchoring* them to one or more edges of the form. Anchoring is the process of creating a relationship between one part of the form and the control itself. As the form expands or contracts, the control and the form will maintain that relationship.

A control can be anchored to one, two, three, or all four edges of a form. Anchoring a control to opposite sides causes its size in that dimension to increase or decrease as the form grows or shrinks. For example, if you anchor a text box to the top and bottom of a form, the text box will become taller or shorter as the form becomes taller or shorter.

USE IT To see how anchoring affects the position of controls, create a new Windows application named *Anchor*.

1. Add a TextBox control to the middle of the form and set its *Multiline* property to *true*. Add other controls around the edge, three controls to on a side and, of course, one in each corner, similar to Figure 16-10. (Note that these can be any type of controls that display on the form; the purpose here is to show the effects of anchoring.) In this sample, the *Text* property of each control is set to show its anchor points.

2. Before you begin anchoring the controls, build the project and run the program to see how resizing the form without anchored controls appears.

3. When the form displays, grab the lower right corner with the mouse and make the form larger and smaller. Notice that the controls do not move, and some of them disappear when the form gets smaller. Expanding the form causes large blank areas on the right and bottom.

4. Exit the program. Now select each control in order and set its *Anchor* property as shown in Figure 16-10. When you select the *Anchor* property in the Properties tool window and select the drop-down arrow, you will see an image like this:

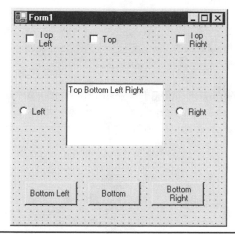

Figure 16.10   Anchoring controls will make them retain their relative positions on the form as the user resizes the form

5. The bars indicate the sides to which the control is to be anchored. A gray bar indicates the control is anchored to that side, and a white bar indicates it is not anchored. Clicking a bar toggles the anchor state for that side. To anchor a control to the top only, make sure that only the bar at the top is gray.

6. When you have set the anchor point for each control, build the project and run the program again. Repeat the process of enlarging and shrinking the form. This time, enlarging the form causes the controls to keep their relative positions. Because the text box is anchored to all four sides, its size grows or shrinks according to the form size.

7. At some point when you shrink the form, the controls begin to overlap. You can stop this from happening by setting the *MinimumSize* property for the form. Determine the minimum size by shrinking the form in the Forms Designer, and then copy the *Size* property values to the *MinimumSize* property.

Docking Controls on Forms

Anchoring controls makes them retain their relative positions along the sides of a form. However, unless you anchor opposite sides of a control, resizing the form will not make the size of the control change.

At times you will need to make a control fill one side of the form. You can do this by docking the control. Unlike anchoring, you cannot dock a control to two or three sides. You may dock to none, one, or all sides of a form.

Docking a control to a side of a form causes the control to resize to fill the side of the form to which it is docked. If you dock more than one control to a side, the controls will be placed one above another if they are docked to the top or bottom, or side to side if they are docked to the left or right sides of the form. Docking to all four sides of a form is *fill* docking and causes the control to expand to fit the size of the form.

When you select the *Dock* property in the Properties tool window and click the drop-down arrow, Visual Studio will display a panel containing a group of buttons, as shown here. Clicking the center button selects fill docking, and clicking the None button selects no docking. The other buttons set the docking to one of the four sides of the form.

For most controls, the *Dock* property is set to *None* by default. However, some controls are created docked to one side of the form. A StatusBar control, for example, by default docks to the bottom of the form. A ToolBar control by default docks to the top of a form.

USE IT   Docked controls will not resize themselves so that they cover other docked controls. They will, however, cover other controls that are not docked. For this reason, you probably will want to limit the number of controls you include on a form containing a docked control, and you probably will have to dock all the controls to keep them from covering one another.

1. Create a new Windows application named *Docking*.

2. Place a Label control near the top. Make it deep enough to display a single line of text, but don't worry about sizing it otherwise.

3. Set the *Dock* property for the Label control to *Top*.

4. Then set the *TextAlign* property to *MiddleCenter*. Set the *Text* property to something like *Docking Sample*.

5. Add a StatusBar control, which will dock to the bottom of the form by default. This control also contains a "grabber" panel on the right, which makes it easier to resize the form.

6. Add a TextBox control somewhere near the middle of the form. Set the *Multiline* property to *true*. Set the *Dock* property to *Fill*. This will make the text box area fill the space between the Label and StatusBar controls, as shown in Figure 16-11.

7. Build the project and run the program. Use the grabber on the StatusBar control to resize the form. As the size changes, each control resizes itself to fill the side to which it is docked. The Label control at the top maintains the text at the center top of the form, and the StatusBar control fills the bottom edge of the form.

Because all the controls are docked, they will not cover one another. The TextBox control fills the space between the text at the top and the status bar at the bottom.

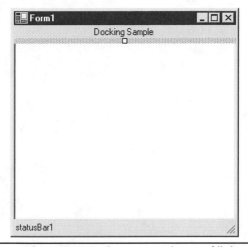

Figure 16.11   By setting the *Dock* properties, three controls now fill the entire form

CHAPTER 17

Using the Common Dialogs

TIPS IN THIS CHAPTER

E very Windows system has a library of dialog boxes used for common operations such as opening and saving files, choosing fonts and colors, and printing. These dialog boxes are contained in a dynamic link library (DLL) that was installed when you installed the Windows operating system.

Providing a set of dialog boxes for common operations presents the user with a consistent interface. It shortens the learning curve for users of an application, and it frees the programmer from having to create the dialog boxes from scratch for every program. If the common dialogs library did not exist, most programmers would want to create one just to save time.

On the same computer, the common dialogs appear the same whether you create them using C#, Visual C++, Visual Basic, or any other language that can call the Windows application programming interface.

For this chapter, you will resurrect the *Editor* project from Chapter 15. The project already uses common dialog boxes to open and save files, but in this chapter you will look at some of the advanced options available for these operations. By the end of the chapter, the *Editor* project will contain menu commands to set the font for the text box, set the background and foreground colors, print the contents of the text box, display a print preview, and set up the printer. The code in this chapter will use menu items to access the common dialogs. You can add toolbars to the editor if desired.

The .NET Framework defines a *CommonDialog* class from which it derives the common dialogs, as summarized in the following table.

Dialog	Description
ColorDialog	Allows the user to select a color and optionally define custom colors.
OpenFileDialog	Allows the user to select a file to open. The user optionally may select other directories to find the file.
SaveFileDialog	Allows the user to save a file.
FontDialog	Displays a list of fonts available on the system and allows the user to select one. The programmer may limit the fonts that are displayed.
PageSetupDialog	Allows the user to set page options such as margins and orientation (landscape or portrait) for printing.
PrintDialog	Allows the user to select print options.

In addition, the .NET Framework provides a *PrintPreviewDialog* derived from *System. Windows.Forms.Form*. This dialog is not part of the common dialogs library, but it implements *PrintPreviewControl* and provides default actions. You can use *PrintPreviewDialog* instead of *PrintPreviewControl*. The dialog box contains all the toolbar buttons and controls that you will need to implement a full print preview. Using this dialog box, it is unlikely that you'll ever need to use the preview control directly.

As a programmer, you need to remember that the common dialogs do not perform any actions for you. They are simply information collecting devices. For example, if the user displays the Font dialog box and selects a new font, *FontDialog* returns information to the program about the user's selection. *SaveFileDialog* does not actually save a file, but returns the file name entered by the user. It is your responsibility to write a program that takes action based on that user information.

All the common dialog boxes contain a Cancel button and return *DialogResult.Cancel* when the user clicks this button. Because it's possible that the user may have made some changes in the dialog box before clicking the Cancel button, you should always check for this value and abort any changes to your program.

To give you a preview of what the various common dialogs, and the Print Preview dialog box, look like, the following program will step through each one. The information they return will not be used, so you can experiment with the controls to get a feel of how the dialog boxes work. You can dispatch them by pressing the ESCAPE key, except for the Print Preview dialog box, for which you must click the Close button to exit the Print Preview dialog box.

```csharp
// CmnDlgs.cs -- steps through the common dialogs. Does nothing else useful.
//
//               Compile this program with the following command line:
//                    C:>csc CmnDlgs.cs
using System;
using System.Windows.Forms;
using System.Drawing.Printing;

namespace clsCommonDialogs
{
    class clsMain
    {
        static public void Main ()
        {
// Create and display a Choose Color dialog box.
            ColorDialog cd = new ColorDialog ();
            cd.ShowDialog ();
            cd.Dispose ();
// Create and display a Choose Font dialog box.
            FontDialog fd = new FontDialog ();
            fd.ShowDialog ();
            fd.Dispose ();
// Create and display an Open File dialog box.
            OpenFileDialog ofd = new OpenFileDialog ();
            ofd.ShowDialog ();
            ofd.Dispose ();
// Create and display a Save File dialog box.
            SaveFileDialog sfd = new SaveFileDialog();
            sfd.ShowDialog ();
            sfd.Dispose ();
// Create and display a Page Setup dialog box.
            PrintDocument printDoc = new PrintDocument();
            PageSetupDialog psd = new PageSetupDialog ();
            psd.Document = printDoc;
            psd.ShowDialog ();
            psd.Dispose ();
```

```
// Create and display a Print dialog box.
        PrintDialog pd = new PrintDialog ();
        pd.Document = printDoc;
        pd.ShowDialog ();
        pd.Dispose ();
// Create and display a Print Preview File dialog box.
// This dialog is not a part of the common dialogs library.
        PrintPreviewDialog ppd = new PrintPreviewDialog ();
        ppd.ShowDialog ();
        ppd.Dispose ();
        printDoc.Dispose ();
    }
  }
}
```

You should note a couple of things about this code. First, after dispatching the dialog boxes, the code calls the member *Dispose()* method. Some dialog boxes use considerable system resources, so you should call this method when you no longer need the dialog box.

Second, the printing dialog boxes all require an object derived from *PrintDocument*. Without this object, or if the object is *null*, all printing dialog boxes will throw an exception. The *PrintDocument* object contains important information these dialog boxes need, such as a *PageSetup* object and a *PrinterSettings* object. Just creating the *PrintDocument* object will fill these other objects with basic information about the default printer.

The MSDN documentation is sketchy on some of the printing operations, and because C# is new there is little in the literature on using these classes. To present the dialog boxes in a usable form in a complete program rather than in just snippets, you'll again use the *Editor* project to demonstrate how the dialog boxes work.

You can implement most of the common dialogs by adding a control object from the Toolbox, or you can create the control object in memory as needed by creating an object of the class. Using the Toolbox controls has some advantages, however. You can set the properties that you want to remain constant using the Properties tool window, thus freeing you from the need to do this every time you use the dialog. In addition, if you use a dialog box often, using a control object tends to reduce the load on the garbage collector because the object persists for the life of the process.

The "Choosing a Color" tip that deals with the *ColorDialog* implements dialog boxes in both ways. For the foreground color, the method creates a ColorDialog on the fly and sets the properties in code. For the background color, a ColorDialog control is used.

Choosing a Color

ColorDialog presents a constant interface through which the user can select from a group of preset colors or select a custom color using a graduated scale. In its basic form, shown in Figure 17-1, the dialog displays 48 colors from the current palate and 16 boxes for custom colors. ColorDialog is represented in the .NET Framework by the *ColorDialog* class and is an easy object to learn and use.

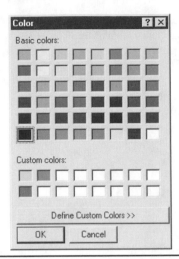

Figure 17.1   The basic form of the ColorDialog display

Clicking the Define Custom Colors button opens the second half of the display, as shown in Figure 17-2. On the Custom Colors portion of the dialog box, the user can define a custom color from a continuously graduated control and then add it to the 16 custom color boxes.

The display is under programmer control. By setting the *AllowFullOpen* property to *false*, the programmer can prevent the user from opening the Custom Colors portion of the dialog box, and

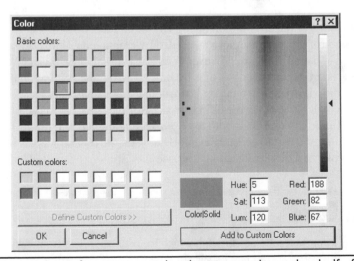

Figure 17.2   Clicking on the Define Custom Colors button reveals another half of the ColorDialog display

the user cannot add any colors to the Custom Colors boxes. The programmer can also choose whether to display any colors in the Custom Colors boxes.

USE IT You can create ColorDialog in memory by creating an object of the *ColorDialog* class. The object sets the properties to default values, which you can then set to your own values. Alternatively, using the Visual Studio Forms Designer, you can add a ColorDialog control from the Toolbox and set the properties in the Properties tool window.

1. Open the *Editor* project from Chapter 15. Display the form in the Forms Designer, and scroll through the Toolbox until you find the ColorDialog item. Double-click it to add a ColorDialog control to the form.

2. Using the Menu Designer, add a top-level Format menu. For submenu items, add Set Text Color and Set Background Color. Name the items *mnuFormatSetTextColor* and *mnuFormatSetBackgroundColor*. Double-click each of the menu items to add event handlers to your code.

3. You could use the same ColorDialog control to set both the text and background colors, but for illustrative purposes, the dialog to set the text color will be created in memory, and the ColorDialog control will be used to set the background color. In the Properties tool window, set the *colorDialog1* properties *AllowFullOpen* and *ShowFullOpen* to *true*, and set the *ShowHelp* property to *false*. You can experiment with the other properties based on the descriptions in the code that follows.

4. Add an array of 16 integers to the *Form1* class and name it *clrCustom*. The array is of type *int* because the dialog box in the common dialogs library is used by other languages as well, and it expects an integer array for the custom colors:

```
// Set up some permanent storage for the custom colors
int [] clrCustom = new int [16]
            {
              0x00ffffff, 0x00ffffff, 0x00ffffff, 0x00ffffff,
              0x00ffffff, 0x00ffffff, 0x00ffffff, 0x00ffffff,
              0x00ffffff, 0x00ffffff, 0x00ffffff, 0x00ffffff,
              0x00ffffff, 0x00ffffff, 0x00ffffff, 0x00ffffff
            };
```

5. The values initialize the custom colors to all white. The values encode the red, green, and blue components of the colors. Using hexadecimal format, you can code custom colors using the scheme shown here:

6. Add code to the event handlers, as shown next. The method to set the text color is considerably longer because you need to set the properties in code and because it includes comments for each of the properties.

```csharp
private void mnuColorSetTextColor_Click(object sender, System.EventArgs e)
{
    ColorDialog cd = new ColorDialog ();
// Setting FullOpen to true will display the custom color portion
// when the dialog box first opens.
    cd.FullOpen = false;
// Setting the Color property will select the color in the dialog
    cd.Color = textBox1.ForeColor;
// Setting AnyColor to true will cause the dialog box to display
// all available colors
    cd.AnyColor = false;
// Setting AllowFullOpen to false will prevent the user from
// displaying the custom color section. This overrides FullOpen.
    cd.AllowFullOpen = true;
// Setting CustomColors to an array of int will initialize the
// 16 custom color boxes.
    cd.CustomColors = clrCustom;
// Setting ShowHelp to true will display a help button. You are
// responsible for writing the help file, however.
    cd.ShowHelp = false;
// Setting SolidColorOnly to false will restrict the selection to
// a solid color. This has meaning only when the palette contains less than
// a full set.
    cd.SolidColorOnly = false;
    if (cd.ShowDialog () == DialogResult.Cancel)
        return;
    textBox1.ForeColor = cd.Color;
    clrCustom = cd.CustomColors;
}


private void mnuColorSetBackgroundColor_Click(object sender,
                                              System.EventArgs e){
// Intialize the color for the dialog box.
    colorDialog1.Color = textBox1.BackColor;
// Set the custom colors to the member array.
    colorDialog1.CustomColors = clrCustom;
// Show the colors.
    if (colorDialog1.ShowDialog () == DialogResult.Cancel)
        return;
// Save any custom colors the user selected.
    clrCustom = colorDialog1.CustomColors;
// Set the text box background color.
    textBox1.BackColor = colorDialog1.Color;
}
```

7. Compile and run the *Editor* program. Try setting different combinations of text and background colors.

On a laptop computer, you might want the user to be able to adjust the colors for different lighting conditions. The lighting on a football field, for example, probably would be very different from that in a city council meeting.

Selecting a Text Style with *FontDialog*

The *FontDialog* object is more complicated than the *ColorDialog* object, although it is not by any means difficult to learn and use. You have to deal with more properties, and more information is returned when the user closes the dialog box.

A font dialog box is shown in Figure 17-3.

As with *ColorDialog*, you can create the *FontDialog* object in memory or you can add a FontDialog control from the Toolbox. Because of the large number of properties, it is usually easier to use the Toolbox control and set the default properties, changing only those that need adjusting in code.

USE IT   Now that you are adding a number of hidden controls in the *Editor* project, you might find it more convenient to drag and drop new controls where you want them. Simply double-clicking a control lets the Forms Designer place it anywhere, often causing one control's icon to cover another. In addition, after you close a project containing a number of items in this panel and later reopen it, it may appear that some of the icons are missing. They are still there, though; you can use the Line Up Icons menu item to reveal them.

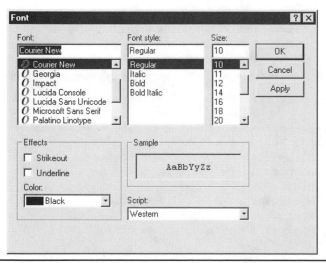

Figure 17.3   The *FontDialog* object offers a number of options for selecting a font

> ▶ **QUICK TIP**
>
> *Right-click a blank area of the panel below the form and select the Line Up Icons item. This will uncover any icons that already have been covered.*

1. Now add a Set Font item to the Format menu. Name the item *mnuFormatSetFont*.

2. Select the Events icon on the Properties tool window and add an event handler named *mnuFormatSetFont_Click()* for the *Click* event.

3. Drag and drop a FontDialog control from the Toolbox to the editor form. Set the *FontMustExist* property to *true*. The Font Name item on the dialog box is editable, and this will make the dialog box pop up an error message if the user types in a font that does not exist.

4. Set the *ShowColor* property to *true*. The dialog box contains a limited color selection, which you can use to set the text box *ForeColor* property.

5. Set the *ShowHelp* property to *false*. If you set this to *true*, the dialog will contain a Help button, but you are responsible for writing the help file.

6. Next, set the *ShowEffects* property to *true*. This will make the dialog box display check boxes where the user can select underline and strikeout text effects.

7. Set the *ScriptsOnly* property to *false*. This property will selectively hide OEM, Symbol, and ANSI character set fonts. Setting it to *false* displays all fonts.

8. Finally, set the *ShowApply* property to *true*. This will display an Apply button. When the user clicks this button, the dialog box will generate an *Apply* event, which you can catch to set the editor font even before the user closes the dialog box.

9. The coding for the *FontDialog* object is fairly straightforward. Most of the work is handled by the dialog box class itself. Before coding, however, you should select the Events button on the Properties tool windows and add an event handler named *fontDialog1_OnApply* for the *Apply* event. The code for the menu item handler and the *Apply* event is shown in the following listing:

```
private void mnuFormatSetFont_Click(object sender, System.EventArgs e)
{
// Initialize the font display to the text box font.
    fontDialog1.Font = textBox1.Font;
// Initialize the font display color to the text box text color. This
// will be an approximate value because the font dialog has a limited
// color display.
    fontDialog1.Color = textBox1.ForeColor;
// Show the font dialog. Do nothing if the user presses Cancel.
    if (fontDialog1.ShowDialog () == DialogResult.Cancel)
        return;
// Call the OnApply method to set the text box values. Calling the
// same method as the Apply event means you need to maintain code in
// only one location.
    fontDialog1_OnApply (sender, e);
}
```

```
private void fontDialog1_OnApply(object sender, System.EventArgs e)
{
// Set the text box font.
   textBox1.Font = fontDialog1.Font;
// Set the text box text color.
   textBox1.ForeColor = fontDialog1.Color;
}
```

Although there are more properties available than the number used for the color dialog box, the font dialog box is easy to code. You don't even have to create the font; the dialog box takes care of that chore.

Opening and Saving Files

The *Editor* project already sports *OpenFileDialog* and *SaveFileDialog*. You added those to the form when you built the original project in Chapter 15. However, at that point, you were more concerned about the dialog boxes as part of the user interface. A number of options and properties were not covered in that chapter.

Both *OpenFileDialog* and *SaveFileDialog* are derived from *FileDialog* rather than directly from *CommonDialog*, so it is not surprising that both dialog box classes share a number of common properties. The properties common to both dialog boxes are summarized in the following table.

Property	Access	Description
AddExtension	Get and *Set*	Indicates whether the dialog box adds an extension to the file name if the user does not enter an extension.
DefaultExt	Get and *Set*	Under some conditions, the dialog box will add this extension to a selected file name.
CheckFileExists	Get and *Set*	Indicates whether the dialog box will display a warning if the user enters a file name that does not exist.
CheckPathExists	Get and *Set*	Indicates whether the dialog box will display a warning if the user enters a path that does not exist.
FileName	Get and *Set*	When you show the dialog box, the name in this property will be display in the File Name control. When the dialog box closes, this property will contain the full path name of the selected file.
FileNames	Get	An array of strings containing the full path of the selected file names when the *Multiselect* property is set to *true*. (The *SaveFile* dialog class does not have a *Multiselect* property, so this will contain only one file name.)
Filter	Get and *Set*	Determines the choices available in the Files of Type box.

Property	Access	Description
FilterIndex	Get and *Set*	On show, determines the filter the dialog box will display in the Files of Type box. On close, contains the one-based index of the filter the user has selected.
RestoreDirectory	Get and *Set*	A user can change directories when searching for a file name. If this property is *true*, the dialog box will restore the working directory before closing.
ShowHelp	Get and Set	Displays a Help button on the dialog box. You must provide the help file and a *GetHelp* event handler.
Title	Get and *Set*	String to use for the title bar of the dialog box.
ValidateNames	Get and *Set*	Determines whether the dialog box will accept only Window file names.

You should choose combinations of the *DefaultExt*, *AddExtension*, *CheckFileExists*, and *CheckPathExists* properties carefully. The *DefaultExt* and *AddExtension* properties will work properly only if you set the *CheckFileExists* and the *CheckPathExists* properties to *false*. However, it is possible for the user to type a file name or path in the File Name box if you set the *CheckFileExists* and the *CheckPathExists* properties to *false*. You will need to verify the name and path in your code before attempting to open a file.

If you set *CheckPathExists* to *true* and *CheckFileExists* to *false*, the dialog box will verify that the directory path exists but not the file itself. The dialog box will return when the user clicks the Open button even if the user typed in a nonexistent file name with a path that *does* exist.

The *DefaultExt* and *AddExtension* properties will work properly only if you set the *CheckFileExists* property to *false*. If you set the *DefaultExt* to *true* and use *txt* (note that there is no period before the extension) for the *AddExtension* property, and the user types a name such as **Stuff** without an extension, the dialog box will return *Stuff.txt* as the selected file name. If you set *CheckFileExists* to *true*, the dialog box will attempt to verify that the file *Stuff*, without the extension, exists before returning.

OpenFileDialog contains a check box labeled "Open as read-only" that you can selectively display and hide using the *ShowReadOnly* property. If you set this property to *true*, you can set the check mark by setting the *ReadOnlyChecked* value to *true* or *false*. When the dialog box closes, the *ReadOnlyChecked* property will contain *true* if the box is checked and *false* if the box is unchecked.

The *SaveFileDialog* class contains two properties not in the *OpenFileDialog* class. The *CreatePrompt* property is a Boolean value that determines whether the dialog will prompt the user to create a file if it does not exist. If the user selects Yes, the dialog box will close. Otherwise, the dialog box will remain open to accept another file name. The *OverwritePrompt* is also a Boolean property. If *true* and the user enters the name of a file that exists, it will display a prompt asking whether it is OK to overwrite the file. If the user selects No, the dialog box will not close.

Both *OpenFileDialog* and *SaveFileDialog* contain a couple of events that are usable with your code. When the user clicks the OK button (labeled "Open" on the OpenFile dialog box and "Save" on the SaveFile dialog box), the dialog box generates a *FileOK* event. You can add your own event handler method to the dialog box, examine the current contents of the dialog box, and decide whether to let the dialog box close.

In addition, if you display the Help button, the dialog box generates a *HelpRequest* event, which you can use to display your help file for the dialog box.

USE IT   The following program, *DlgSamp.cs*, shows several of the properties and events used to implement an *OpenFileDialog* object:

```
// DlgSamp.cs -- Shows the use of some of the OpenFile dialog box.
//
//               Compile this program with the following command line:
//                    C:>csc DlgSamp.cs
using System;
using System.Windows.Forms;
using System.ComponentModel;


class clsMain
{
    static public void Main ()
    {
// Create the dialog box object.
        OpenFileDialog ofd = new OpenFileDialog ();
// Allow multiple file selection.
        ofd.Multiselect = true;
// Set the text for the title bar.
        ofd.Title = "Concatenate files";
// Do not verify that the file exists.
        ofd.CheckFileExists = false;
// Do verify that the path exists.
        ofd.CheckPathExists = true;
// Add a default extension if the user does not type one.
        ofd.AddExtension = true;
// Set the default extension.
        ofd.DefaultExt = "txt";
// Show the read-only box.
        ofd.ShowReadOnly = true;
// Show the Help button.
        ofd.ShowHelp = true;
// Call this method when the user clicks the OK (Open) button.
        ofd.FileOk += new CancelEventHandler (CancelOpenFile);
// Call this method when the user clicks the Help button.
        ofd.HelpRequest += new EventHandler (ShowOpenHelp);
// Show the dialog box.
        if (ofd.ShowDialog () == DialogResult.Cancel)
            return;
// Display a list of the selected files.
        foreach (string str in ofd.FileNames)
```

```
                    Console.WriteLine (str);
        }
// Delegate called when the user clicks the OK (Open) button.
        static private void CancelOpenFile (object sender, CancelEventArgs e)
        {
// Cast the object to an OpenFileDialog object.
            OpenFileDialog dlg = (OpenFileDialog) sender;
// Show the selected files.
            Console.WriteLine ("The selected files are:");
            foreach (string str in dlg.FileNames)
                Console.WriteLine ("\t" + str);
// Ask whether to cancel the close event.
            Console.Write ("\r\nCancel event? [y/n]: ");
            string reply = Console.ReadLine ();
            if (reply[0] == 'y')
                e.Cancel = true;
        }
// Delegate called when the user clicks the Help button.
        static private void ShowOpenHelp (object sender, EventArgs e)
        {
            Console.WriteLine
                        ("Open your help file to the File Open topic here.");
        }
}
```

When you compile and run this program, an *OpenFile* dialog box will appear with the text "Concatenate file" in the title bar. Click the Help button and the method will write a line to the console screen from which you ran the program. Select one or more files and click the Open button. The console will show a list of the selected files and prompt whether you want to cancel the operation. If you enter **y**, the dialog box will not close.

A Word About Printing

Converting the contents and information in a project to a form that can be displayed on the printed page sometimes can be a daunting task. What is suitable for display on a screen does not always make sense on a piece of paper.

In Visual C++, when you use the Microsoft Foundation Class (MFC) library to create a project with some of the "view" classes such as *CEditView* or *CRichEditView*, the MFC framework takes care of the details of printing for you. Almost certainly such view classes eventually will be available in C#. If Microsoft does not develop them, a third-party source will do so when C# becomes popular enough to support a commercial class library.

In other views, such as the *CFormView* or the *CListView* classes, you have to provide your own printing code. On the printed page, nobody really cares about the form itself. The paper object becomes the form, and the focus turns to the data.

Usually, drawing for a printer involves getting down and dirty with the printer *device context* (the DC). You need to calculate the position of text and objects and draw them yourself. In addition, a text box on a form can position lines, and if a line is too long to fit the display, it can wrap the text to the next line. If the text depth is too much for the text box, it will add a scroll bar so you can access the additional text.

When drawing on a sheet of paper, however, simply writing a line in the device context will not cause it to break. If it is too long, it will extend into the page's right margin. If it is longer still, it will draw right off the page (actually the text will be "clipped"; it can't really draw off the page). In addition, sheets of paper do not come with scroll bars, so you must split the text into pages and print the pages one at a time.

USE IT The device context in C# is represented in the *Graphics* class. A number of methods in this class assist you in drawing text and shapes on a device, whether it is a computer screen, a plotter, or a laser printer. The idea behind the device context is to separate the programmer from the details of the output device. The programmer draws text or shapes without worrying about how the output device actually performs the operations. The device context then takes care of the details of translating the drawing command to the output device commands through the device driver.

You can draw text and graphics on a printer in a number of ways. The code in this tip presents one such method that you can adapt to other output functions. The code draws text on the printer by breaking it down into shorter pieces of text that will fit on a line. It attempts to break a line on a space, but if there are no spaces it will break the line on a whole character.

1. In the *Editor* project, add three new items to the File menu: Print, Print Preview, and Page Setup. Place them below the Save As item after adding a separator below Save As.

2. Name the three items *mnuFilePrint*, *mnuFilePrintPreview*, and *mnuFilePageSetup*. The new and improved File menu now contains printing items, as shown here. It would be convenient at this time to add CTRL-P as a shortcut key for the Print item.

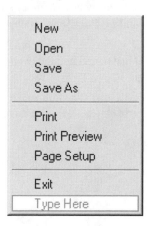

3. Double-click the *mnuFilePrint* item to add an event handler for its *Click* event. You can also add event handlers in the same way for the other two items. (You will use them later in this chapter.)

4. At the top of the *MainForm.cs* source file, add the following lines:

```
using System.Drawing.Printing;
using System.Text;
```

5. Add the following methods to the *MainForm* class, using the return types and parameters shown:

```
void OnPrintPage(object sender, PrintPageEventArgs e)
{
}
byte [] StringToByte (string str)
{
}
void ExpandTabs (ref string text)
{
}
```

The *OnPrintPage()* method is a delegate method that the *PrintDocument* object will call to print the text to the printer. The *StringToByte()* method will convert the string text in the text box control to a *byte* array for use by the print stream. Some printer drivers do not automatically expand the tabs to spaces, so the *ExpandTabs()* method will expand each tab in the string from one to eight spaces.

6. Finally, add the following fields to the *MainForm* class:

```
string m_strRemaining = "";
StreamReader m_PrintReader;
PrinterSettings m_PrinterSettings = new PrinterSettings ();
PageSettings m_PageSettings = new PageSettings();
```

The *strRemaining* field will hold any excess text that will not fit on a page. The *StreamReader* object *m_PrintReader* will read a *byte* array as a memory stream and hand it to the *OnPrintPage()* method. (The *m_PrinterSettings* and *m_PageSettings* objects will be used later to save changes to the printer setup.)

The code for the two methods you just added and the event handler for the Print item *Click* event are shown in the following listing:

```
// Event handler for the Print click event.
private void mnuFilePrint_Click(object sender, System.EventArgs e)
{
    if (textBox1.Text.Length == 0)
        return;
    byte [] bytestrm;
    try
    {
        PrintDocument pd = new PrintDocument ();
```

```csharp
            pd.PrinterSettings = (PrinterSettings) m_PrinterSettings.Clone();
            pd.DefaultPageSettings = (PageSettings) m_PageSettings.Clone();
            bytestrm = StringToByte (textBox1.Text);
            MemoryStream strm = new MemoryStream (bytestrm);
            m_PrintReader = new StreamReader (strm);
            try
            {
                m_PrinterSettings = pd.PrinterSettings;
                m_PageSettings = pd.DefaultPageSettings;
// The Document Name property is displayed in the Windows spooler.
                if (m_strFileName == "")
                    pd.DocumentName = "Untitled";
                else
                    pd.DocumentName = m_strFileName;
                pd.PrintPage += new PrintPageEventHandler
                    (this.OnPrintPage);
                pd.Print();
            }
            finally
            {
                m_PrintReader.Close();
            }
        }
        catch(Exception e2)
        {
            MessageBox.Show(e2.Message);
        }
        bytestrm = null;
}
// Return a byte array from a string.
byte [] StringToByte (string str)
{
    byte [] b = new byte [str.Length];
    for (int x = 0; x < str.Length; ++x)
        b[x] = (byte) str[x];
    return (b);
}
// The print page delegate used by the PrintDocument object.
void OnPrintPage(object sender, PrintPageEventArgs e)
{
// Create your own printer font in mnuFilePrint_Click()
// or use the one in textBox1
    Font fontPrint = textBox1.Font;
    float linesPerPage = 0;
    float yPos = 0;
    int count = 0;
    float leftMargin = e.MarginBounds.Left;
    float topMargin = e.MarginBounds.Top;
    string line = null;
```

```csharp
// Declare some layout objects.
// A SizeF structure to hold the size of the line
    SizeF size = new SizeF();
// StringFormat to tell the MeasureString() method that
// We want the line to break on a character
    StringFormat sf = new StringFormat ();
    sf.Trimming = StringTrimming.Character;
    SizeF layout = new SizeF (-1, fontPrint.GetHeight ());


// Calculate the number of lines per page.
    linesPerPage = e.MarginBounds.Height /
        fontPrint.GetHeight (e.Graphics);
// Print each line of the file.
    while(count < linesPerPage)
    {
// Pick up any residual text from the previous page/line
// that wouldn't fit on a line
        if (m_strRemaining.Length != 0)
        {
            line = m_strRemaining;
            m_strRemaining = "";
        }
// If no residual text, get a new line.
        else
        {
            if ((line = m_PrintReader.ReadLine()) == null)
                break;
            ExpandTabs (ref line);
        }
// Calculate the y position on the page
        yPos = topMargin + (count * fontPrint.GetHeight(e.Graphics));
// Save the line in a temporary variable
        string first = line;
// Measure the string in the selected font
        size = e.Graphics.MeasureString (first, fontPrint, layout, sf);
        int index = first.Length - 1;
        if (size.Width > e.MarginBounds.Width)
        {
// If there is no space in the line, break on a character
            if (first.LastIndexOf (" ", first.Length - 1) < 0)
            {
                while (size.Width > e.MarginBounds.Width)
                {
                    first = line.Substring (0, --index);
                    size = e.Graphics.MeasureString (first, fontPrint,
                                                        layout, sf);
                }
            }
            else
// Step back through the line word by word until it fits
```

```
            {
                while (size.Width > e.MarginBounds.Width)
                {
                    index = first.LastIndexOf (" ", first.Length - 1);
                    first = line.Substring (0, index);
                    size = e.Graphics.MeasureString (first, fontPrint,
                                                     layout, sf);
                }
                ++index;
            }
// Save any remaining text
            m_strRemaining = line.Substring (index);
        }
// Draw the text on the page
        e.Graphics.DrawString(first, fontPrint, Brushes.Black,
            leftMargin, yPos, new StringFormat());
        count++;
    }
// Continue to the next page if the last line was not null.
// Note: the PrintDocument.Print() method will issue a form feed
// each time you return from this method with e.HasMorePages
// set to true.
    if(line != null)
        e.HasMorePages = true;
// Otherwise it is the end of the file as we know it.
// Note: returning with e.HasMorePages set to false will
// end the print job and send it to the spooler.
    else
        e.HasMorePages = false;
}


// Expand tabs to eight spaces. This is the setting for the text box.
private void ExpandTabs (ref string text)
{
    string str = text;
    int index = str.IndexOf ('\t');
    if (index < 0)
        return;
    StringBuilder untabbed = new StringBuilder (str);
    do
    {
        int spaces = 8 - index % 8;
        untabbed.Remove (index, 1);
        untabbed.Insert (index, " ", spaces);
        str = untabbed.ToString();
        index = untabbed.ToString().IndexOf ('\t');
    } while (index > 0);
    text = str;
}
```

The .NET Framework classes support an advanced graphics device interface. One of the advantages of this is that you can use the same font to write text to the printer that you use for the text box. In Visual C++, you must create the font for a particular device context.

Now build and run the *Editor* program. Type some text or open a file in the editor. Make sure at least one line is too long for the printer to verify that the line break code is working. For openers, you might start with a short file or just a few lines of text to make sure the code performs as it should.

You should pay attention to the nested *try* blocks in the *mnuFilePrint_Click()* method. The inner block provides a *finally* block that will close the stream regardless of the result of the printing operation. The outer block will catch any exceptions thrown in the process of opening the stream and in the printing operation. If, for example, the *OnPrintPage* method throws an exception, the outer block will catch it and display a message block.

Selecting a Printer

One of the problems with the code in the preceding tip is that the user has no opportunity to select a printer. The *PrintDocument* object simply pops up a quick status window announcing that it is printing the document. In addition, there is no way for the user to cancel the operation if the item was selected accidentally.

This is the way earlier versions of Notepad worked, but that changed in Windows 2000. The new version of Notepad, and other programs such as Visual Studio, intercept the print command and the actual printing operation with a print dialog box. Many programs also allow you to define a block of text and then just print the selected block. You'll see different versions of the print dialog box around, but the version created by the .NET Framework looks similar to Figure 17-4.

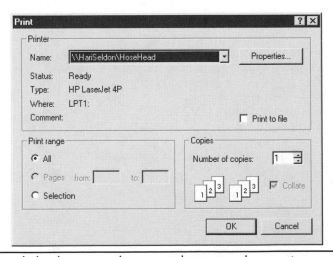

Figure 17.4   The Print dialog box gives the user a chance to select a printer and set options

USE IT   To intercept the printing process, you need to provide a *PrintDialog* object and display it before the printing begins. The *PrintDialog* class contains several properties for enabling controls on the dialog box.

1. Add a PrintDialog control to the *Editor* project using the Toolbox. You can create the object in memory, but to save loading up the garbage collector, it is preferable to create an object as a member of the class.

2. Enable the Print dialog box at the beginning of the event handler for the Print menu item. This will give the user a chance to abort the operation. In addition, you should place it before you create the stream to read the text. If the text box contains a selection, you can enable the Selection button on the dialog box and then just print the selected portion of text.

3. Oddly, you set the flag to enable the Selection box in the *PrintDialog* object, but you retrieve it from the *PrinterSettings* object member of the *PrintDialog* class.

4. Modify the *mnuFilePrint_Click()* method so that it looks like the following listing:

```
private void mnuFilePrint_Click(object sender, System.EventArgs e)
{
    if (textBox1.Text.Length == 0)
        return;
    byte [] bytestrm;
    try
    {
        PrintDocument pd = new PrintDocument();
        pd.PrinterSettings = (PrinterSettings) m_PrinterSettings.Clone();
        pd.DefaultPageSettings = (PageSettings) m_PageSettings.Clone();
// Beginning of added code.
        printDialog1.PrinterSettings = m_PrinterSettings;
        printDialog1.Document = pd;
// If the text box contains selected text, enable the Selection box
        if (textBox1.SelectionLength > 0)
            printDialog1.AllowSelection = true;
        else
            printDialog1.AllowSelection = false;
        if (printDialog1.ShowDialog () == DialogResult.Cancel)
            return;
// End of added code.
// Modify the code that creates the memory stream.
// If the PrintRange property of the printer settings is Selection,
// get just the selected text in the text box.
        if (printDialog1.PrinterSettings.PrintRange == PrintRange.Selection)
            bytestrm = StringToByte (textBox1.SelectedText);
// Otherwise, get all of the text in the text box.
        else
```

```
                    bytestrm = StringToByte (textBox1.Text);
// Create the stream.
            MemoryStream strm = new MemoryStream (bytestrm);
            m_PrintReader = new StreamReader (strm);
            try
            {
                m_PrinterSettings = pd.PrinterSettings;
                m_PageSettings = pd.DefaultPageSettings;
// The Document Name property is displayed in the Windows spooler.
                if (m_strFileName == "")
                    pd.DocumentName = "Untitled";
                else
                    pd.DocumentName = m_strFileName;
                pd.PrintPage += new PrintPageEventHandler
                    (this.OnPrintPage);
                pd.Print();
            }
            finally
            {
                m_PrintReader.Close();
            }
        }
        catch(Exception e2)
        {
            MessageBox.Show(e2.Message);
        }
        bytestrm = null;
    }
```

5. Rebuild and run the *Editor* project. Open a file and test-drive the printing code to make sure that you may cancel an operation using the *PrintDialog* object. Select a block of text in the text box and verify that you can print just the selected portion of text.

Setting Page Options

Setting the printing options using the *PrintDialog* object requires that the user input some text in the text box that summons the print process. If the user then cancels the operation, any changes to the printer setup made in the *PrintDialog* object are not saved.

The .NET Framework provides a common dialog box class that you can use to permit the user to set printer options ahead of time, before they are needed for a print operation. The class is the *PageSetupDialog* class, and the dialog box is shown in Figure 17-5.

Clicking the Printer button on the Page Setup dialog box displays a second dialog box, where the user can select a printer.

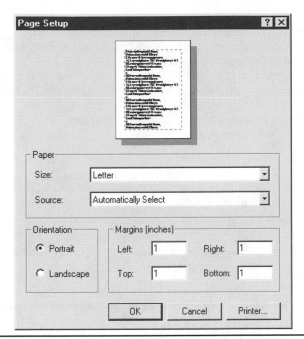

Figure 17.5   *PageSetupDialog* is used to set printer options in advance

You can disable the Printer button by setting the *AllowPrinter* property to *false*. In addition, you can selectively enable or disable any other controls on the dialog box.

USE IT   Now add *PageSetupDialog* to the *Editor* project.

1. Add a *PageSetupDialog* control to the project using the Toolbox. If you did not create an event handler for the Page Setup item on the File menu, add it now.

   Most of the properties in this project deal with enabling or disabling the various controls on the dialog box. You will not need to create a document to use this dialog box. The only event generated is the *HelpRequest* event, where you can provide a help file.

2. Add the following code to the *mnuFileSetup_Click()* event handler in the *MainForm* class:

```
private void mnuFilePageSetup_Click(object sender, System.EventArgs e)
{
// Clone the PageSettings so change can be aborted.
    PageSettings pageSettings = (PageSettings) m_PageSettings.Clone ();
    pageSetupDialog1.PageSettings = pageSettings;
// To disable the printer button on the dialog, remove the following
// two lines and the last line in this method.
    PrinterSettings printerSettings =
```

```
                                          (PrinterSettings) m_PrinterSettings.Clone ();
            pageSetupDialog1.PrinterSettings = printerSettings;
// Set the following property to false to disable the Printer button
//            pageSetupDialog1.AllowPrinter = false;
// If the user presses the Cancel button, don't save any changes.
    if (pageSetupDialog1.ShowDialog () == DialogResult.Cancel)
        return;
// Save the new settings in the instance members.
    m_PageSettings = pageSettings;
    m_PrinterSettings = printerSettings;
}
```

3. Build the project and run the Page Setup dialog through its paces. Try changing the margins and close the box by clicking the OK button. Reopen the dialog box to make sure the new margins were changed. Try this with the various controls on the dialog box.

When you are satisfied with the operation of the dialog box, try printing some text to see if the settings are carried through to the printing process.

Previewing the Print Output

The Print Preview dialog is not a common dialog, but it's included here because it goes along with the printing functions you have already added to the *Editor* project. It is derived directly from the *System.Windows.Forms.Form* class rather than from the *CommonDialog* class.

A print preview gives the user a sneak peek at how the printed output will look before the user commits the text or drawing to print. The dialog box uses the same print delegate method used by *PrintDocument*.

USE IT The Print Preview dialog box requires a separate controller to display the pages on the screen as a series of images. You do not have to do anything but create the controller to use it.

1. From the Toolbox, add a PrintPreviewDialog control to the *Editor* project. Be careful not to select *PrintPreviewControl*. The latter is an object that appears on your form, and you use it to create your own custom print previews.

2. If you did not already add an event handler for the Print Preview menu item, do so now.

3. Add the following code to the *mnuFilePrintPreview_Click* method:

```
private void mnuFilePrintPreview_Click(object sender, System.EventArgs e)
{
// Create a byte stream just as you did for printing.
    byte [] bytestrm;
    bytestrm = StringToByte (textBox1.Text);
    MemoryStream strm = new MemoryStream (bytestrm);
    m_PrintReader = new StreamReader (strm);
```

```
// This dialog box requires a PrintDocument.
   PrintDocument pd = new PrintDocument ();
// Get the current page settings.
   pd.DefaultPageSettings = m_PageSettings;
// Add a preview controller. This displays the pages on the screen
// as a series of images.
   pd.PrintController = new PreviewPrintController ();
// Use the OnPrintPage method as the page event handler.
   pd.PrintPage += new PrintPageEventHandler (this.OnPrintPage);
// Add the document to the dialog.
   printPreviewDialog1.Document = pd;
// Show the dialog. Don't need to test for Cancel here.
   printPreviewDialog1.ShowDialog ();
// Dispose of the document and the byte array.
   pd.Dispose ();
   bytestrm = null;
}
```

4. Build and test run the project. Open a file and select the Print Preview item on the File menu to make sure the preview appears properly.

The little *Editor* project is starting to take on a little bit of power. Of course, one *Notepad.exe* per universe is all that is needed, but this project can be the start of a more powerful program, or just a component that you use with a larger project.

CHAPTER 18

Using Events and Delegates

The .NET Framework and C# define processes through which objects may talk to one other. Obviously, a method in one class may call a method in another class, passing it values through the argument list. Or a method may access fields and properties that another class exposes.

It is possible, however, for an object to respond to another object that created it without knowing the specific instance of the other object. This is accomplished using *events* and *delegates*. For example, a method may not know which mathematical operation to perform, such as getting the area of a circle or of a sphere, until the program actually runs. In another case, a sort routine may not know the sort method or sort order until runtime.

In these types of cases, the exact method to execute can be determined at runtime and assigned to a delegate. C++ programmers can compare delegates to function pointers, but delegates in C# are much more versatile than C++ function pointers.

Delegates sometimes are called *safe function pointers* because they are guaranteed to return a value of the type declared and to match the delegate declaration. If you attempt to assign a function that does not match the delegate declaration, the compiler will issue an error and reject the assignment.

Function pointers often are used when calling Windows application programming interface (API) functions that need to respond to an application's request. For example, the list control has a method to sort the contents of the control, but it needs to know how the program wants to sort the items. You pass the control the address of your comparison function as a *callback* function. The list control then calls your comparison function, you return the result, and the list control sorts its contents according to the results you give it.

In C++, such callback methods must be declared *static*. The C# delegate is more versatile in that the method can be an instance member of a class. The *Delegate* class is capable of storing the instance of an object as well as the address of the method.

You declare a delegate using the *delegate* keyword and then define the function type that you want to call. The definition looks much like a C++ prototype except for the *delegate* keyword:

```
public delegate <type> DelegateMethod (<parameters>);
```

The declaration specifies only the form of the delegate. A delegate declaration actually creates a new class derived from the *System.MulticastDelegate* class.

The preceding declaration would create a new class like the following:

```
public DelegateMethod : System.MulticastDelegate
{
    DelegateMethod (<parameters>);
// Invoke synchronously
    public virtual void Invoke (<parameters>);
// Invoke asynchronously
    public virtual IAsyncResult BeginInvoke (<parameters>,
                                             AsyncCallback cb, object o);
    public virtual void EndInvoke (IAsyncResult result);
}
```

Invoking the delegate asynchronously is similar to invoking the asynchronous methods that you encountered in Chapter 12 when dealing with streams. Most commonly, you will use the synchronous method in which a statement will call the delegate and wait for it to complete.

Because it creates a new class definition, a delegate declaration does not have to be a member of a class or structure. You cannot call it because the delegate declaration does not provide a body of code for the method.

The next task is to create a variable to hold a function pointer:

```
public DelegateMethod DelegateVar;
```

The following program, *SimpDlgt.cs*, implements a simple delegate that calls a single function:

```
// SimpDlgt.cs -- Demonstrates a simple form of a delegate
//
//                 Compile this program using the following command line:
//                     C:>csc SimpDlgt.cs
using System;

namespace nsDelegate
{
// Declare the delegate. This actually creates a new class definition.
    delegate double MathOp (double value);

    class clsMain
    {
        static public void Main ()
        {
// Declare an object of the delegate type.
            MathOp DoMath;
// Create the delegate object using a method name.
            DoMath = new MathOp (GetSquare);
// Execute the delegate. This actually calls the Invoke() method.
            double result = DoMath (3.14159);
// Show the result.
            Console.WriteLine (result);
// Assign another method to the delegate object.
            DoMath = new MathOp (GetSquareRoot);
// Call the delegate again.
            result = DoMath (3.14159);
// Show the result.
            Console.WriteLine (result);
        }
// Return the square of the argument.
        static double GetSquare (double val)
        {
```

```
            return (val * val);
        }
// Return the square root of the argument.
        static double GetSquareRoot (double val)
        {
            return (Math.Sqrt (val));
        }
    }
}
```

Although you call the same method, *DoMath( )*, twice, the delegate points to a different method on each call so you get two different results, as shown in the following output:

```
9.8695877281
1.7724531023415
```

Adding Multiple Methods to a Delegate

Delegates come in two types, *single-cast* and *multi-cast*. According to the MSDN documentation, a multi-cast delegate must declare a method that does not return a value—a *void* type. A single-cast delegate, on the other hand, can return a value of any type.

▶ *NOTE*

Although the documentation says a multi-cast delegate cannot return a value, the current build of the compiler does not seem to make this distinction. You can assign multiple methods that return values to a delegate. This probably will be corrected by the time Microsoft releases Visual Studio .NET. For now, however, you should be careful not to assign multiple methods that return values to a delegate. The results could be unpredictable depending upon the order in which you assign the methods.

To assign multiple methods to a multi-cast delegate, you use the += operator. To remove a method, you use the −= operator. The following short program, *MultiDlg.cs*, first assigns only one method to the delegate and then calls the method. Then it adds a second method and calls again to show that both methods execute. Finally, it removes the first method from the delegate and executes once again.

```
// MultiDlg.cs -- Demonstrates adding multiple methods to a delegate.
//
//              Compile this program with the following command line.
//                    C:>csc MultiDlg.cs
using System;

namespace nsDelegates
```

```
{
    class clsMain
    {
        public delegate void MultiMethod ();

        static public void Main ()
        {
            MultiMethod dlg;
// Assign the first method to the delegate.
            dlg = new MultiMethod (FirstDelegate);
// Call it to show the first method is being called.
            dlg ();
// Add a second method to the delegate.
            dlg += new MultiMethod (SecondDelegate);
// Call it to show both methods execute.
            Console.WriteLine ();
            dlg ();
// Remove the first method from the delegate.
            dlg -= new MultiMethod (FirstDelegate);
// Call it to show that only the second method executes.
            Console.WriteLine ();
            dlg ();
        }
        static public void FirstDelegate()
        {
            Console.WriteLine ("First delegate called");
        }
        static public void SecondDelegate()
        {
            Console.WriteLine ("Second delegate called");
        }
    }
}
```

The output from *MultiDlg.cs* shows that the second call did execute both methods. The first call executed only the first method, and the third call executed only the second method:

```
First delegate called

First delegate called
Second delegate called

Second delegate called
```

Using Events Within C# Programs

Delegates are often used with *events*. An object can use an event to notify another object that something has occurred. Multiple objects can "subscribe" to the same event, and the object methods will be called in the order in which they subscribed.

Events are used extensively in Windows application programming. In the .NET Framework, a Windows message becomes an event, and the objects that have subscribed to the event will have a chance to respond to it.

In a Windows form application, for example, you might add a button the user can click to signal an action to be taken. The action may be to close the application or to get a new set of data from a database. To respond to the request, your application subscribes to the event. If you added an event handler for the button click event, you will see a line similar to the following in the *InitializeComponent()* method:

```
this.button2.Click += new System.EventHandler(this.button2_Click);
```

The statement adds a delegate to the system events list so that when the user clicks *button2*, Windows will call the *button2_Click()* event in your program.

USE IT   Delegates for system events are always multi-cast delegates. Thus, the method that you pass as an event handler must be of type *void*. The following program, *Subscrib.cs*, shows how multiple objects can subscribe to the same event:

```
// Subscrib.cs -- Shows how multiple objects may subscribe to the same
//                event.
//
//                Compile this program with the following command line:
//                     C:>csc Subscrib.cs
using System;

namespace nsEvents
{
    class clsDelegate
    {
// Declare a delegate for the event.
        public delegate void StringHandler (string str);
// A variable to hold the delegate
        public event StringHandler DoEvent;
// This method will trigger the event.
        public void FireEvent (string str)
        {
            if (DoEvent != null)
                DoEvent (str);
```

```
        }
    }

    class clsMain
    {
// Declare an instance of the clsDelegate class. The event variable
// is not static.
        static public clsDelegate dlg = new clsDelegate ();
        static public void Main ()
        {

// Add clsMain to the event list.
            dlg.DoEvent += new clsDelegate.StringHandler (ShowEvent);
// Create subscribers for the event.
            clsSubscriber sub = new clsSubscriber ();
            clsNextSubscriber sub2 = new clsNextSubscriber ();
// Fire the event.
            dlg.FireEvent ("Fired from Main()");
        }
        static public void ShowEvent (string str)
        {
            Console.WriteLine ("Main handled event: " + str);
        }
    }
    class clsSubscriber
    {
        public clsSubscriber ()
        {
            clsMain.dlg.DoEvent +=
                        new clsDelegate.StringHandler (SubscribeEvent);
        }
        public void SubscribeEvent (string str)
        {
            Console.WriteLine ("Subscriber handled event: " + str);
        }
    }
    class clsNextSubscriber
    {
        public clsNextSubscriber ()
        {
            clsMain.dlg.DoEvent +=
                        new clsDelegate.StringHandler (SubscribeEvent);
        }
        public void SubscribeEvent (string str)
        {
```

```
            Console.WriteLine ("Next Subscriber handled event: " + str);
        }
    }
}
```

The output from *Subscrib.cs* shows that each object got a chance to handle the event in the order in which it subscribed:

```
Main handled event: Fired from Main()
Subscriber handled event: Fired from Main()
Next Subscriber handled event: Fired from Main()
```

Writing an Event Handler

When you write handlers to respond to events, the form of the method must exactly match the form declared by the delegate. You cannot cast the return type or the arguments to a type other than that declared in the delegate.

If you must have a handler that uses different argument types, it is best to declare your delegate arguments using an *object* rather than specific data types. In the event handler, you can check the type of the argument and perform any necessary cast.

 The following program, *ObjEvent.cs*, defines an event handler that takes an object as an argument. It expects either an *int* or a *long* argument, and thus performs the necessary cast:

```
// ObjEvent.cs -- Demonstrates passing an object to an event handler and
//                performing the proper cast in the method.
//
//                Compile this program with the following command line:
//                    C:>csc ObjEvent.cs
using System;

namespace nsEvents
{
    class clsMain
    {
        public delegate void EventHandler (object obj);
        public event EventHandler EvInvoke;

        public void FireEvent (object obj)
        {
            if (obj != null)
                EvInvoke (obj);
        }
```

```
        static public void Main ()
        {
            clsMain main = new clsMain ();
            main.EvInvoke = new clsMain.EventHandler (ObjEvent);
            main.FireEvent (42);
            main.FireEvent (42.0);
        }
        static void ObjEvent (object obj)
        {
            if (obj is double)
            {
                Console.WriteLine ("Received a double object: " +
                                       (double) obj);
            }
            else if (obj is int)
            {
                Console.WriteLine ("Received an int object: " + (int) obj);
            }
        }
    }
}
```

For Windows forms applications, the events generated by controls pass two arguments to the event handler. The first is an argument of type *object* that identifies the sender. The second is an event object derived from *System.EventArgs*.

For Windows forms created using Visual Studio, writing an event handler is as simple as selecting the event from the Properties tool window, entering the name of the event handler method, and pressing ENTER. Visual Studio will create the method with the proper arguments.

To create "roll your own" forms, you can look in the MSDN documentation under the *EventArgs* class, where more than 90 classes listed are derived from *System.EventArgs*.

Many controls have a number of events, most of which you will not use normally. However, you can take advantage of these events to produce some pleasing effects in your applications. For example, the simple button control has 49 events, but normally you would use only the *Click* event to respond to a user mouse click.

USE IT   You've probably noticed that, when you move the mouse over a button, Visual Studio changes the color of the button as the mouse passes over. It's easy to add the same effect to your own projects.

1. Open the *AddControls* application from Chapter 13.

2. Select one of the buttons in the Forms Designer, and then select the Events button on the Properties tool window.

3. Scroll until you find the *MouseEnter* event and add an event handler named *Buttons_OnMouseEnter*.

4. Move to the *MouseLeave* event and add an event handler named *Buttons_OnMouseLeave*.

5. Select the second button and add the same event handlers to it. The code for the event handlers is simple and short, as shown in the following listing:

```
private void Buttons_OnMouseEnter(object sender, System.EventArgs e)
{
    Button btn = (Button) sender;
    btn.BackColor = Color.LightGray;
}

private void Buttons_OnMouseLeave(object sender, System.EventArgs e)
{
    Button btn = (Button) sender;
    btn.BackColor = SystemColors.Control;
}
```

6. Build and run the project.

7. Move the mouse over one of the buttons. As soon as the mouse cursor enters the button's control area, the color changes to a lighter shade of gray. When the mouse leaves, the color changes back to the original color.

Events such as this do not consume a lot of system resources, but they do give the user a feeling of action when using a form.

Sorting Objects Using a Delegate

Delegates are handy for sorting objects when the object field that will be used for the sort cannot be determined at compile time. The *Employee* class from Chapter 13 contains fields to hold an employee's name along with address information.

A user may want to sort employee information by name, ZIP code, or employee ID number. You could provide separate methods for each sort that you want to perform, but that would be a waste of code. A sort function works by determining the relative values of objects, whether one object is greater than or less than another. The *String.Compare()* method provides this comparison for *string* objects, and for numeric values you can use arithmetic operations.

USE IT   In the following program, *SortEmpl.cs*, the *clsEmployee* class is derived from the *System.ComponentModel.Component* class and also implements a *clsEmployeeContainer* class to store the employee records in a *Container* object.

The *clsEmployee* class defines the sort methods, but the *clsEmployeeContainer* class implements a delegate to hold the proper sort method. In this way, you need only provide a single sort routine to sort the records by different fields.

For brevity, the *clsEmployee* class has fields only for the employee name, ZIP code, and employee ID number. You could provide additional sort methods for other fields such as city or state.

```csharp
// SortEmpl.cs -- Demonstrates using a delegate with a container class
//                to sort a collection and return a sorted array using
//                different sort criteria.
//
//                Compile this program with the following command line:
//                    C:>csc SortEmpl.cs
using System;
using System.ComponentModel;

namespace nsDelegates
{
    public class clsEmployee : Component
    {
// Define an employee class to hold one employee's information.
        public clsEmployee (string First, string Last, string Zip, int ID)
        {
            FirstName = First;
            LastName = Last;
            EmployeeID = ID;
            ZipCode = Zip;
        }
        public string    FirstName;
        public string    LastName;
        public string    ZipCode;
        public int       EmployeeID;

// Define a method to sort by name.
        static public int CompareByName (object o1, object o2)
        {
            clsEmployee emp1 = (clsEmployee) o1;
            clsEmployee emp2 = (clsEmployee) o2;
            return (String.Compare (emp1.LastName, emp2.LastName));
        }

// Define a method to sort by ZIP code.
        static public int CompareByZip (object o1, object o2)
        {
            clsEmployee emp1 = (clsEmployee) o1;
            clsEmployee emp2 = (clsEmployee) o2;
            return (String.Compare (emp1.ZipCode, emp2.ZipCode));
        }
```

```
// Define a method to sort by employee ID number.
      static public int CompareByID (object o1, object o2)
      {
          clsEmployee emp1 = (clsEmployee) o1;
          clsEmployee emp2 = (clsEmployee) o2;
          return (emp1.EmployeeID - emp2.EmployeeID);
      }
// Override ToString() for diagnostic purposes.
      public override string ToString ()
      {
          return (FirstName + " " + LastName + ", ZIP "
                + ZipCode + ", ID "  + EmployeeID);
      }
   }


// Define a class to hold the clsEmployee objects.
   class clsEmployeeContainer : Container
   {
      private Container cont = new Container();
      public void Add (clsEmployee empl)
      {
          cont.Add (empl);
      }
// Declare an array to return to the caller.
      clsEmployee [] arrEmployee;

// Declare a delegate to compare one employee object to another.
      public delegate int CompareItems (object obj1, object obj2);


// Define a sort function that takes a delegate as a parameter. The Reverse
// parameter can be used to reverse the sort.
      public clsEmployee [] SortItems (CompareItems sort, bool Reverse)
      {
// Get the clsEmployee objects in the container.
          ComponentCollection employees = cont.Components;
// Create an array large enough to hold the references.
          arrEmployee = new clsEmployee[employees.Count];
// Copy the collection into the array. The Container class will not
// let us sort the collection itself.
          employees.CopyTo (arrEmployee, 0);

// Do a simple bubble sort. There are more efficient sorting algorithms,
// but a simple sort is all we need.
          while (true)
```

```
        {
            int sorts = 0;
            for (int x = 0; x < arrEmployee.Length - 1; ++x)
            {
                int result;
// Sort in the reverse order if the Reverse parameter equals true.
// The comparison calls the sort method in the delegate.
                if (Reverse == true)
                    result = sort (arrEmployee[x + 1], arrEmployee[x]);
                else
                    result = sort (arrEmployee[x], arrEmployee[x + 1]);
// Reverse the two elements if the result is greater than zero.
                if (result > 0)
                {
                    clsEmployee temp = arrEmployee[x];
                    arrEmployee[x] = arrEmployee[x+1];
                    arrEmployee[x+1] = temp;
                    ++sorts;
                }
            }
// If we did no sorts on this go around, the sort is complete.
            if (sorts == 0)
                break;
        }
// Return the sorted array to the caller.
        return (arrEmployee);
    }
// Return the collection to the caller.
    public ComponentCollection GetEmployees ()
    {
        return (cont.Components);
    }
}


class clsMain
{
// Declare an enum for the sort methods.
    enum SortBy {Name, ID, ZIP};
// Create a container to get the clsEmployee object collection.
    static public clsEmployeeContainer container =
                                        new clsEmployeeContainer ();
    static public void Main ()
    {
// Add some employee records in random order. These could just as easily
```

```
// be read from a data file or from a database.
            container.Add (new clsEmployee ("John", "Smith",
                                             "87678", 1234));
            container.Add (new clsEmployee ("Marty", "Thrush",
                                             "80123", 1212));
            container.Add (new clsEmployee ("Milton", "Aberdeen",
                                             "87644", 1243));
            container.Add (new clsEmployee ("Marion", "Douglas",
                                             "34567", 3454));
            container.Add (new clsEmployee ("John", "Winters",
                                             "53422", 3458));
            container.Add (new clsEmployee ("William", "Marmouth",
                                             "12964", 3658));
            container.Add (new clsEmployee ("Miles", "O'Brien",
                                             "63445", 6332));
            container.Add (new clsEmployee ("Benjamin", "Sisko",
                                             "57553", 9876));

// Show the unsorted employee list.
            Console.WriteLine ("Unsorted employee list:");
            ComponentCollection collectionList = container.GetEmployees();
            foreach (clsEmployee emp in collectionList)
            {
                Console.WriteLine ("\t" + emp);
            }

// Sort the employees by last name and show the list.
            Console.WriteLine ("\r\nSorted by last name:");
            clsEmployee [] arr = SortList (SortBy.Name);
            foreach (clsEmployee emp in arr)
            {
                Console.WriteLine ("\t" + emp);
            }

// Sort the employees by ID number and show the list.
            Console.WriteLine ("\r\nSorted by employee ID:");
            arr = SortList (SortBy.ID);
            foreach (clsEmployee emp in arr)
            {
                Console.WriteLine ("\t" + emp);
            }

// Sort the employees by ZIP code and show the list.
            Console.WriteLine ("\r\nSorted by ZIP code:");
```

```
            arr = SortList (SortBy.ZIP);
            foreach (clsEmployee emp in arr)
            {
                Console.WriteLine ("\t" + emp);
            }
        }
// Define a method that will create the proper delegate according to
// the sort that is needed.
        static clsEmployee [] SortList (SortBy iSort)
        {
            clsEmployeeContainer.CompareItems sort = null;
            switch (iSort)
            {
                case SortBy.Name:
                    sort = new clsEmployeeContainer.CompareItems(
                                        clsEmployee.CompareByName);
                    break;
                case SortBy.ID:
                    sort = new clsEmployeeContainer.CompareItems(
                                        clsEmployee.CompareByID);
                    break;
                case SortBy.ZIP:
                    sort = new clsEmployeeContainer.CompareItems(
                                        clsEmployee.CompareByZip);
                    break;
            }
// Do the sort and return the sorted array to the caller.
            return (container.SortItems (sort, false));
        }
    }
}
```

Instead of having to write three different sort routines to arrange the records by name, ZIP code, or employee ID, you "calculate" the sort method you want to use and then assign it to the delegate. Then you call a generic sort routine, which in turn calls the method in the delegate.

Running the program should show the following output:

```
Unsorted employee list:
    John Smith, ZIP 87678, ID 1234
    Marty Thrush, ZIP 80123, ID 1212
    Milton Aberdeen, ZIP 87644, ID 1243
    Marion Douglas, ZIP 34567, ID 3454
    John Winters, ZIP 53422, ID 3458
    William Marmouth, ZIP 12964, ID 3658
```

```
    Miles O'Brien, ZIP 63445, ID 6332
    Benjamin Sisko, ZIP 57553, ID 9876

Sorted by last name:
    Milton Aberdeen, ZIP 87644, ID 1243
    Marion Douglas, ZIP 34567, ID 3454
    William Marmouth, ZIP 12964, ID 3658
    Miles O'Brien, ZIP 63445, ID 6332
    Benjamin Sisko, ZIP 57553, ID 9876
    John Smith, ZIP 87678, ID 1234
    Marty Thrush, ZIP 80123, ID 1212
    John Winters, ZIP 53422, ID 3458

Sorted by employee ID:
    Marty Thrush, ZIP 80123, ID 1212
    John Smith, ZIP 87678, ID 1234
    Milton Aberdeen, ZIP 87644, ID 1243
    Marion Douglas, ZIP 34567, ID 3454
    John Winters, ZIP 53422, ID 3458
    William Marmouth, ZIP 12964, ID 3658
    Miles O'Brien, ZIP 63445, ID 6332
    Benjamin Sisko, ZIP 57553, ID 9876

Sorted by ZIP code:
    William Marmouth, ZIP 12964, ID 3658
    Marion Douglas, ZIP 34567, ID 3454
    John Winters, ZIP 53422, ID 3458
    Benjamin Sisko, ZIP 57553, ID 9876
    Miles O'Brien, ZIP 63445, ID 6332
    Marty Thrush, ZIP 80123, ID 1212
    Milton Aberdeen, ZIP 87644, ID 1243
    John Smith, ZIP 87678, ID 1234
```

The enumerated value *SortBy* provides the sort key. To expand to use other fields, add items to this enumeration and add the sort methods to the *clsEmployee* class.

Using a *static* Delegate

In many of the examples in this chapter, implementing a delegate means creating an instance of the class. In these cases, the delegate is an *instance* member of the class. The delegate does not exist until you instantiate the class object.

Delegates may also be *static*, in which case one delegate object is shared between instances of the class. In addition, a *static* delegate may be created and used before a class instance is created. A delegate may also invoke a *static* method.

USE IT In the following program, *StaticDl.cl,* the *Main()* method is *static*, and thus it would not be able to assign a delegate to the instance field. By declaring the delegate field, *DoString, static* as well, the *Main()* method is able to assign and invoke the delegate.

```csharp
// StaticDl.cs -- Demonstrates using a static delegate without declaring
//                an instance of the class.
//
//                Compile this program with the following command line:
//                     C:>csc StaticDl.cs
using System;

namespace nsDelegates
{
    class clsMain
    {
        public delegate void StringHandler (string str);
        static public StringHandler DoString;

        static public void Main ()
        {
// Create a delegate in this class.
            DoString = new StringHandler (ShowString);
            DoString ("Static delegate called");
//
// Show that the static delegate in another class is shared by instances.
            clsDelegate.DoMath = new clsDelegate.MathHandler (SquareRoot);
            clsDelegate dlg1 = new clsDelegate (49);
            clsDelegate dlg2 = new clsDelegate (3.14159);
        }
// The method used with the string delegate
        static private void ShowString (string str)
        {
            Console.WriteLine (str);
        }
// The method used with the double delegate
        static private double SquareRoot (double val)
        {
            double result = Math.Sqrt (val);
            Console.WriteLine ("The square root of " + val +
                               " is " + result);
            return (result);
```

```
        }
    }
    class clsDelegate
    {
        public delegate double MathHandler (double val);
        static public MathHandler DoMath;
// The constructor invokes the delegate if it is not null.
        public clsDelegate (double val)
        {
            value = val;
            if (DoMath != null)
                sqrt = DoMath (value);
        }
        double value;
        double sqrt = 0;
    }
}
```

You may notice with curiosity that the *DoMath()* method is private to *clsMain*, but the constructor in *clsDelegate* is able to invoke the method through the delegate. This is another advantage of using delegates. A class may give other objects access to its private members through delegates. To do this, a method in *clsMain* must assign the delegate in the foreign class. The *clsDelegate* class cannot assign a *private* method in another class to its delegate.

Viewing a Delegate's Invocation List

The *Delegate* class stores the name of the method that it will invoke when the delegate is called. You may use *reflection* to get the instance of the *MethodInfo* class that contains the name of the method.

In addition, a multi-cast delegate contains a collection of *Delegate* objects, each of which contains the name of the individual method that it will invoke. When you invoke a multi-cast delegate, each of the methods in the collection is invoked.

The method to invoke is contained in a member property called *Method*. This is a read-only property. The only way to assign a value to it is to create the delegate in your code.

USE IT   The following program, *InvkList.cs*, assigns three methods to the *DoList* delegate, and then retrieves the individual delegates from the collection. The value obtained from *GetInvocationList* is an array of type *Delegate*. The *MethodInfo* class is a member of the *System.Reflection* namespace, so be sure to include the *using* statement at the top:

```
// InvkList.cs -- Demonstrates getting and printing the invocation list
//                for a delegate.
//
//                Compile this program with the following command line:
```

```csharp
//                   C:>csc InvkList.cs
using System;
using System.Reflection;

namespace nsDelegates
{
    class clsMain
    {
        public delegate void ListHandler ();
        public ListHandler DoList;
        static public void Main ()
        {
            clsMain main = new clsMain ();
            main.DoList += new ListHandler (DelegateMethodOne);
            main.DoList += new ListHandler (DelegateMethodThree);
            main.DoList += new ListHandler (DelegateMethodTwo);
            Delegate [] dlgs = main.DoList.GetInvocationList ();
            foreach (Delegate dl in dlgs)
            {
                MethodInfo info = dl.Method;
                Console.WriteLine (info.Name);
            }
        }
        static void DelegateMethodOne ()
        {
            Console.WriteLine ("In delegate method one");
        }
        static void DelegateMethodTwo ()
        {
            Console.WriteLine ("In delegate method two");
        }
        static void DelegateMethodThree ()
        {
            Console.WriteLine ("In delegate method three");
        }
    }
}
```

Compiling and running *InvkList.cs* will show the names of each of the methods contained in the multi-cast delegate's invocation list:

```
DelegateMethodOne
DelegateMethodThree
DelegateMethodTwo
```

You may invoke any or all of the delegates directly from this list using the *Invoke( )* member method in the *MethodInfo* class. Change the *foreach* loop in the preceding sample to the following:

```
foreach (Delegate dl in dlgs)
{
    MethodInfo info = dl.Method;
    Console.WriteLine (info.Name);
    info.Invoke (main, null);
}
```

The loop now will list the name of the method and then invoke the method. The first argument to *MethodInfo.Invoke( )* is the class instance that created the method. If there is no class instance (for example, you created a *static* delegate in a *static* method using only *static* methods for the delegates), you may pass *null* for this argument. The second argument is an array of type *object* containing the parameters the method will need. If there are no arguments, as in this example, you may pass a null value.

Combining and Removing Delegate Methods

When you create a multi-cast delegate, you can add methods to the delegate by using the += operator and remove methods by using the −= operator. The previous examples of delegates have used these operators to build multi-cast delegates containing more than one method.

You may also add two delegates together to produce a new delegate containing the methods of both delegates you used in the operation. Or you may subtract one delegate from a multi-cast delegate to produce a new delegate.

USE IT   Manipulating delegates is useful when you want to perform more than one operation on a value. The following program, *DlgOps.cs*, creates three delegates, each containing a single method. Then it adds them to produce a new delegate containing all three of the single-method delegates. Finally, it creates a fifth delegate by subtracting one delegate.

```
// DlgOps.cs -- Demonstrates combining and removing delegates to create
//              new delegates.
//
//              Compile this program with the following command line:
//                  C:>csc DlgOps.cs
using System;

namespace nsDelegates
{
    class clsMain
    {
        public delegate void MathHandler (double val);
```

```
        static public void Main ()
        {
            clsMain main = new clsMain ();
            MathHandler dlg1, dlg2, dlg3;
            dlg1 = new MathHandler (main.TheSquareRoot);
            dlg2 = new MathHandler (main.TheSquare);
            dlg3 = new MathHandler (main.TheCube);
// Combine the delegates so you can execute all three at once on one value.
            MathHandler dlgCombo = dlg1 + dlg2 + dlg3;
            Console.WriteLine ("Executing the combined delegate");
            dlgCombo (42);
// Now remove the second delegate.
            MathHandler dlgMinus = dlgCombo - dlg2;
            Console.WriteLine
                    ("\r\nExecuting the delegate with the second removed");
            dlgMinus (42);
// Show that the individual delegates are still available.
// Execute the delegates one at a time using different values.
            Console.WriteLine ("\r\nExecute the delegates individually:");
            dlg1 (64);
            dlg2 (12);
            dlg3 (4);
        }
        public void TheSquareRoot (double val)
        {
            Console.WriteLine ("The square root of " + val + " is "
                            + Math.Sqrt (val));
        }
        public void TheSquare (double val)
        {
            Console.WriteLine ("The square of " + val + " is "
                            + val * val);
        }
        public void TheCube (double val)
        {
            Console.WriteLine ("The cube of " + val + " is "
                            + val * val * val);
        }
    }
}
```

Notice from the output that combining the three delegates did not affect the original variable. They still contain a single method:

```
Executing the combined delegate
The square root of 42 is 6.48074069840786
The square of 42 is 1764
The cube of 42 is 74088

Executing the delegate with the second removed
The square root of 42 is 6.48074069840786
The cube of 42 is 74088

Executing the delegates individually
The square root of 64 is 8
The square of 12 is 144
The cube of 4 is 64
```

Responding to Timer Events

Timers generate events at user-defined intervals and give the programmer an opportunity to provide background processing in the event-handling method.

The .NET Framework provides three *Timer* classes. The first *Timer* class is in the *System. Windows.Forms* namespace. This *Timer* class is optimized for forms and requires a Windows message pump. Thus, it should be used with forms or windows. This is the class used to implement the Timer control in the Visual Studio Forms Designer.

The second *Timer* class is *System.Threading.Timer*, which uses a *callback* method. This class will be covered in the next tip.

The third *Timer* class is the *System.Timers.Timer* class, which provides a general-purpose timer for multi-threaded environments. The *System.Timers* namespace contains only two classes other than *Timer*. One is *TimerEventArgs,* which contains information about the timer event. A usable member of *TimerEventArgs* is *SignalTime*, which contains a *DateTime* object indicating when the timeout occurred. The other class is an attribute class that you can use to label the object. The namespace also includes a delegate class to hold the method the timer will call when the preset time expires.

The *System.Timers.Timer* class contains two constructors. You can create a timer object without any arguments, or optionally you may pass it a *long* value to indicate the timer interval.

 USE IT   You can set the timer to generate a single event or to repeat the event at a predefined interval using the *AutoReset* property. When you set the timer object to repeat, each event runs in its own thread and succeeding events do not affect the interval.

To respond to the timer event, you must assign a method to the *Elapse* delegate member of the class.

The following program, *Timer.cs,* uses a *System.Timers.Timer* class to generate an event every second. At the end of 10 seconds, the program exits.

```
// Timer.cs -- Demonstrates using the System.Timers.Timer class.
//
//              Compile this program with the following command line:
//                    C:>csc Timer.cs
using System;
using System.Windows.Forms;
using System.Timers;


namespace nsDelegates
{
    class clsMain
    {
        static int countdown = 10;
        static System.Timers.Timer timer;
        static public void Main ()
        {
// Create the timer object.
            timer = new System.Timers.Timer (1000);
// Make it repeat. Setting this to false will cause just one event.
            timer.AutoReset = true;
// Assign the delegate method.
            timer.Elapsed += new ElapsedEventHandler(ProcessTimerEvent);
// Start the timer.
            timer.Start ();
// Just wait. You just wait.
            MessageBox.Show ("Waiting for countdown", "Text");
        }
// Method assigned to the timer delegate.
        private static void ProcessTimerEvent (Object obj, ElapsedEventArgs e)
        {
            --countdown;
// If countdown has reached 0, it's time to exit.
            if (countdown == 0)
            {
                timer.Close ();
                Environment.Exit (0);
            }
// Make a string for a new message box.
            string sigtime = e.SignalTime.ToString ();
```

```
        string str = "Signal time is "
                 + sigtime.Substring (sigtime.IndexOf (" ") + 1);
        str += "\r\nCountdown = " + countdown;
// Show a message box.
        MessageBox.Show (str, "Timer Thread");
    }
  }
}
```

When you compile and run *Timer.cs*, you will see the message box in the *Main()* method appear first. After about 1 second, you should see a second message box from the *ProcessTimerEvent()* method. About every second thereafter, a new message box will appear. At the end of 10 seconds, all the message boxes will disappear and the program will exit.

You need to be aware that the timer object will handle any exceptions that occur in the delegate method and perform no action. The delegate method, and the thread, will simply abort and you have no way to know that it happened. If it is possible that your code may throw an exception, place it within a *try ... catch* block within the delegate method itself.

Responding to *System.Threading.Timer* Events

The *System.Threading.Timer* class operates in its own thread, similar to the *Timer* in *System.Timers*, but it uses a *callback* method rather than an event when the timeout interval expires.

In addition, you may pass the timer an *object* in the constructor. The timer object then will pass a reference to the object as an argument to the callback method. If you do not need an object reference, you can use *null* for this argument.

The *System.Threading.Timer* class accepts two additional arguments: the time for the first timeout event and the interval to repeat. The general form for constructing a *Timer* object is shown in the following snippet:

```
System.Threading.Timer timer = new System.Threading.Timer (callback method,
                                        object, first time, interval time);
```

To create a single time event, pass a *0* as the interval argument. Passing 0 as the first time argument will cause the timeout event to occur immediately.

USE IT The *ThrdTime.cs* program shown in the following listing implements a thread object created from the *System.Threading.Timer* class. It operates much the same as the preceding example, showing a series of message boxes until the countdown reaches 0.

```
// ThrdTime.cs -- Demonstrates using the System.Threading.Timer object.
//
//              Compile this program with the following command line:
```

```csharp
//                        C:>csc ThrdTime.cs
using System;
using System.Windows.Forms;
using System.Threading;

namespace nsDelegates
{
    class clsMain
    {
        static int countdown = 10;
        static System.Threading.Timer timer;
        static public void Main ()
        {
// Create the timer callback delegate.
            System.Threading.TimerCallback cb =
                    new System.Threading.TimerCallback (ProcessTimerEvent);
// Create the object for the timer.
            clsTime time = new clsTime ();
// Create the timer. It is autostart, so creating the timer will start it.
            timer = new System.Threading.Timer (cb, time, 4000, 1000);
// Blessed are those who wait.
            MessageBox.Show ("Waiting for countdown", "Text");
        }
// Callback method for the timer. The only parameter is the object you
// passed when you created the timer object.
        private static void ProcessTimerEvent (object obj)
        {
            --countdown;
// If countdown is complete, exit the program.
            if (countdown == 0)
            {
                timer.Dispose ();
                Environment.Exit (0);
            }
            string str = "";
// Cast the obj argument to clsTime.
            if (obj is clsTime)
            {
                clsTime time = (clsTime) obj;
                str = time.GetTimeString ();
            }
            str += "\r\nCountdown = " + countdown;
            MessageBox.Show (str, "Timer Thread");
        }
```

```
        }
// Define a class to use as the object argument for the timer.
    class clsTime
    {
        public string GetTimeString ()
        {
            string str = DateTime.Now.ToString ();
            int index = str.IndexOf (" ");
            return (str.Substring (index + 1));
        }
    }
}
```

One difference you will note from the previous example is that the first timer message box does not appear right away. The first timeout value passed to the constructor is 4000, so the first timeout will not occur for 4 seconds. Thereafter, a message box should appear about every second.

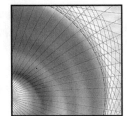

Index

INTERNATIONAL CONTACT INFORMATION

AUSTRALIA
McGraw-Hill Book Company Australia Pty. Ltd.
TEL +61-2-9417-9899
FAX +61-2-9417-5687
http://www.mcgraw-hill.com.au
books-it_sydney@mcgraw-hill.com

CANADA
McGraw-Hill Ryerson Ltd.
TEL +905-430-5000
FAX +905-430-5020
http://www.mcgrawhill.ca

**GREECE, MIDDLE EAST,
NORTHERN AFRICA**
McGraw-Hill Hellas
TEL +30-1-656-0990-3-4
FAX +30-1-654-5525

MEXICO (Also serving Latin America)
McGraw-Hill Interamericana Editores S.A. de C.V.
TEL +525-117-1583
FAX +525-117-1589
http://www.mcgraw-hill.com.mx
fernando_castellanos@mcgraw-hill.com

SINGAPORE (Serving Asia)
McGraw-Hill Book Company
TEL +65-863-1580
FAX +65-862-3354
http://www.mcgraw-hill.com.sg
mghasia@mcgraw-hill.com

SOUTH AFRICA
McGraw-Hill South Africa
TEL +27-11-622-7512
FAX +27-11-622-9045
robyn_swanepoel@mcgraw-hill.com

**UNITED KINGDOM & EUROPE
(Excluding Southern Europe)**
McGraw-Hill Education Europe
TEL +44-1-628-502500
FAX +44-1-628-770224
http://www.mcgraw-hill.co.uk
computing_neurope@mcgraw-hill.com

ALL OTHER INQUIRIES Contact:
Osborne/McGraw-Hill
TEL +1-510-549-6600
FAX +1-510-883-7600
http://www.osborne.com
omg_international@mcgraw-hill.com